THE ORDER OF MASS

A ROMAN MISSAL STUDY EDITION AND WORKBOOK

MICHAEL S. DRISCOLL

J. MICHAEL JONCAS

LTP

LITURGY
TRAINING
PUBLICATIONS

Nihil Obstat
Very Reverend Daniel A. Smilanic, JCD
Vicar of Canonical Services
Archdiocese of Chicago
July 29, 2011

Imprimatur
Reverend Monsignor John F. Canary, STL, DMIN
Vicar General
Archdiocese of Chicago
July 29, 2011

Musical setting of the Lord's Prayer by Robert Snow, 1964.

Abbot Marcel Rooney, OSB, provided the chant tips for the Prefaces.

THE ORDER OF MASS: A ROMAN MISSAL STUDY EDITION AND WORKBOOK © 2011, Archdiocese of Chicago: Liturgy Training Publications, 3949 South Racine Avenue, Chicago, IL 60609, 1-800-933-1800, fax; 1-800-933-7094; e-mail: orders@ltp.org. All rights reserved. See our website at www.LTP.org and www.RevisedRomanMissal.org.

Printed in the United States of America

ISBN 978-1-56854-989-7

OMSE

Contents

Introduction

Growing attention in recent years has been directed at the *ars celebrandi*. The Bishops' Synod on the Eucharist in 2005 called particular attention to how the liturgy is celebrated, especially from the perspective of the Priest Celebrant. Archbishop Wilton Gregory of Atlanta, a U.S. delegates to the Synod and a professional liturgist by formation, was particularly articulate on the matter: "The priest skilled in the *ars celebrandi* will offer the prayers from a heart so conformed to the heart of Christ that 'by the way he says the divine words he must convey to the faithful the living presence of Christ' "([*General Instruction of the Roman Missal,* 93] October 11, 2005).

"The *ars celebrandi* should foster a sense of the sacred," Pope Benedict XVI states in the papal exhortation *Sacramentum Caritatis,* in which he notes the importance of the harmony of the rite, the furnishings, the vestments and the sacred space. He underscores that a correct *ars celebrandi* requires "an attentiveness to the various kinds of language that the liturgy employs: words and music, gestures and silence, movement, the liturgical colors of the vestments. By its very nature the liturgy operates on different levels of communication which enable it to engage the whole human person," *Sacramentum Caritatis,* 40.

As both Archbishop Gregory and the Pope point out, the art of celebrating the liturgy well, goes beyond simply following rubrics. If good liturgy only required following rubrics, good liturgy would be everywhere. Rather, good liturgy requires mindful celebration in which action and words are executed in a deliberate and artful manner. The manner in which the words of the liturgy are prayed, the postures and gestures of the Priest Celebrant, combined with the other elements of good liturgy can influence faith. As the U.S. Bishops note in *Sing to the Lord: Music in Divine Worship* (STL), "Faith grows when it is well expressed in celebration. Good celebrations can foster and nourish faith. Poor celebrations may weaken it" (STL, 5). This volume is aimed primarily at helping Priests preside well at the celebration of the Eucharist.

The Order of Mass: A Roman Missal Study Edition and Workbook has been designed as a resource to be consulted weekly while preparing to celebrate the liturgy. The procla-mation and chant tips will aid the Priest Celebrant in praying the Mass confidently, and the pastoral commentaries will enrich the understanding of the prayers, helping the Priest to pray from the heart.

We were especially concerned to help readers identify and understand varying genres of liturgical texts: dialogues (e.g., greetings; the versicles and responses of the Penitential Act, Form B); acclamations (e.g., the Gospel Acclamation and Verse; the Sanctus; the Memorial Acclamations; the Amen concluding the Eucharistic Prayer); litanies (e.g., the Lord, have mercy / Kyrie, eleison [whether troped as in Penitential Act, Form C, or not]; the Universal Prayer; the Lamb of God / *Agnus Dei*); hymns (e.g., the Glory to God / *Gloria in excelsis*; sequences); minor euchology (e.g., the Collect; the Prayer over the Offerings; the Prayer after Communion; the Solemn Blessings; the Prayers over the People); or major euchology (e.g., Prefaces; Eucharistic Prayers; Blessing of Baptismal Water). We are convinced that a deeper understanding of the structure and purpose of these texts will help those who pray them to discover their theological and spiritual riches. It is also our hope that many more of the liturgical options supplied by the Missal will be exercised. Therefore, the reader should not be surprised to find repetition of ideas and of liturgical principles and structures in the hope that by reading these often, they will become a part of the liturgical psyche of the Priest Celebrant.

Singing the Liturgy

But this workbook is not exclusively for Priests. Our hope is that liturgical musicians will gain knowledge about the Order of the Mass that will help them in their ministry. If the goal of the liturgical reforms of the Second Vatican Council was to sing the liturgy and not simply sing at the liturgy, this workbook should be of great assistance. Liturgical musicians can be of special assistance to their pastors in encouraging them to learn and sing the parts of the Mass. Musicians also might teach their pastors how to sing the parts, particularly if Priests are self-conscious or reticent about singing. Prior to the Second Vatican Council, the singing presider was a *sine qua non*. In recent decades, it is the exception to the rule. Our hope is that the simplified methods for singing will inspire Priests with the help of their musicians to chant the Mass. Some Africans are fond of saying that if you can talk, then you can sing. One way to think of singing is as heightened speech or speaking on pitch. Our goal is to inspire Priests, Deacons, and seminarians to learn the various chants and to use them often. Finally, the workbook should prove helpful to parish liturgical commissions and anyone interested in the rich liturgical heritage that is ours.

Transmitting the Tradition

The workbook is designed like the medieval commentary and gloss. The liturgy (like the Bible and legal texts) has always attracted the attention of commentators. Mass commentaries abounded, especially in the Middle Ages. Comments, sometimes placed in the margins around the text being expounded upon, or even squeezed in between the lines, were called glosses. In Greek, *glossa* means "tongue" or "language." Originally, the word was used to denote an explanation of an unfamiliar word, but its scope gradually expanded to the more general sense of a commentary. The glossators used to write in the margins of the old texts (*glosa marginalis*) or between the lines (*glosa interlinearis*—interlinear glosses). Liturgical books, along with Bibles and law books, were especially targeted for this kind of writing. Later, glosses were gathered into large collections, first copied as separate books, but also quickly written in the margins of the texts. The scholars of the eleventh- and twelfth-century legal schools in Italy, France, and Germany are identified as glossators in a specific sense. The glossators conducted detailed text studies that resulted in collections of explanations. Finally, commentators started to take over from the glossators. In fact, the early medieval scholars wrote commentaries and lectures as well, but their main effort was, indeed, creating glosses. Theirs was a work of compilers, as they gathered information of all sorts to squeeze into the margins or between the lines. The compilations were not necessarily original, but they were interesting and essential for transmitting the tradition.

The current volume qualifies as both a commentary and a gloss. At the bottom of each page are three columns of commentary. Often, the commentary attempts to identify the biblical or Patristic sources of the prayers or parts of the Mass. Other times, the reflection is more along the lines of the homiletic tradition. Still other times, legal texts are cited—but not too often. You will see that the work of the commentator is to spin out columns of thought based upon scant lines of liturgical text. Our hope is that this book will serve to help the reader come to a deeper appreciation of the liturgical texts and pray them more intentionally. The glosses that are found in the margins are intended to give tips to Priest Celebrants on how to pray the translation of *The Roman Missal* (third edition) beautifully, intelligibly, and meaningfully. Special attention has been given to the musical elements while avoiding technical musical terminology. The simplest form of solfege (do-re-mi-fa-sol-la-ti-do) is offered to help the non-musician find the musical notes in the chants found in the Missal. More is said about this in the Appendices of this volume, where attention is given to various chants for the Order of Mass, such as the presidential prayers, the Penitential Act, chanting the readings, the Universal Prayer, and the Solemn Blessings.

Since music is an aural-oral tradition, it is difficult to write about the musical elements without a demonstration of them. Therefore, Liturgy Training Publications has produced other aids to help Priest Celebrants and Deacons learn the chants. A companion to this volume is the CD *Learning the Chants of the Missal, Part I: The Order of Mass,* on which Jan Michael Joncas has chanted the prayers of the Order of Mass. On a second CD, *Learning the Chants of the Missal, Part II: Essential Presidential Prayers and Texts,* Joncas has chanted the presidential prayers. That CD is a companion to *Essential Presidential Prayers and Texts: A Roman Missal Study Edition,* by Father Daniel Merz and Abbot Marcel Rooney, OSB.

Rev. Michael S. Driscoll
University of Notre Dame, Notre Dame, IN

Rev. Jan Michael Joncas
University of St. Thomas, St. Paul, MN

THE ORDER OF MASS

THE INTRODUCTORY RITES

1.   When the people are gathered, the Priest approaches the altar with the ministers while the Entrance Chant is sung.

When he has arrived at the altar, after making a profound bow with the ministers, the Priest venerates the altar with a kiss and, if appropriate, incenses the cross and the altar. Then, with the ministers, he goes to the chair.

When the Entrance Chant is concluded, the Priest and the faithful, standing, sign themselves with the Sign of the Cross, while the Priest, facing the people, says:

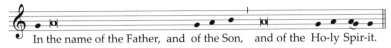
In the name of the Father, and of the Son, and of the Ho-ly Spir-it.

In the name of the Father, and of the Son, and of the Holy Spirit.

Emphasize **Father**, **Son**, and **Holy Spirit**.

The people reply:

A-men.

Amen.

Correlate the gestures with the text.

2.   Then the Priest, extending his hands, greets the people, saying:

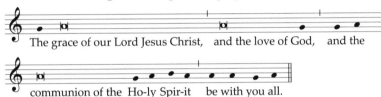
The grace of our Lord Jesus Christ, and the love of God, and the

communion of the Ho-ly Spir-it   be with you all.

**The grace of our Lord Jesus Christ,
and the love of God,
and the communion of the Holy Spirit
be with you all.**

Emphasize **grace of our Lord Jesus Christ**, **love of God**, and **communion of the Holy Spirit**.

1. The liturgy begins with a recognition of the Trinitarian dynamics of Catholic Christian worship. To say that the liturgy is prayed in the name of the Triune God is to say that it is under the power of, the protection of, the aegis of the Triune God. To begin the liturgy in the name of the Father, Son, and Holy Spirit also makes known that everything that occurs in the liturgy from this point on is in the name of the three persons of the Trinity. So it is significant. Appendix I (page 282) contains an alternative chant for the Trinitarian invocation.

Some priests have a custom of preceding the Sign of the Cross with introductory words. We do not want to do this. For two reasons, we should not say, "Now we begin." First, the ritual states that the liturgy starts with the singing of the Entrance Chant. Second, no rubric states that we begin with an introduction by the Priest.

We begin by invoking the Triune God. The Priest Celebrant wants to evoke from the people an "Amen." He is calling on the people to affirm the invocation that he has made.

2. The issue with the Greeting is which of the three forms to choose and why. Priest Celebrants should not fall into the habit of always using the same form of the Greeting—the first because of its placement or the third because of its brevity. You want to vary your use of the Greetings.

The focus in all three Greetings conjoined to the rubric is an address to the congregation as a whole. The response to each of the Greetings is "And with your spirit."

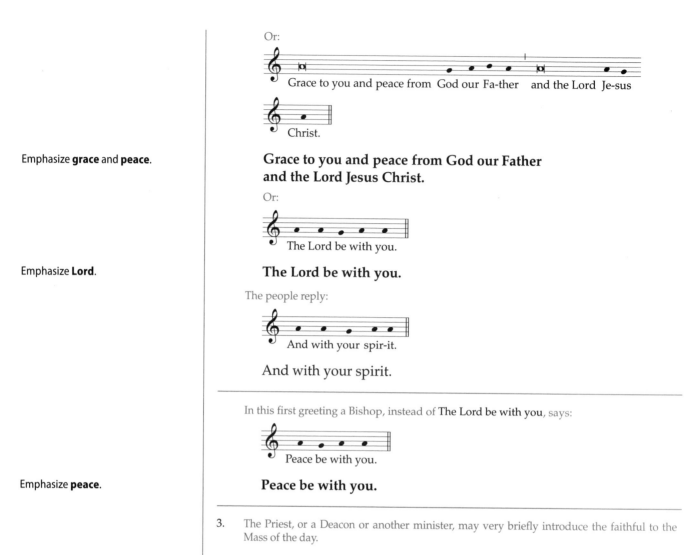

Or:

Grace to you and peace from God our Fa-ther   and the Lord Je-sus

Christ.

**Grace to you and peace from God our Father
and the Lord Jesus Christ.**

Or:

The Lord be with you.

The Lord be with you.

The people reply:

And with your spir-it.

And with your spirit.

In this first greeting a Bishop, instead of **The Lord be with you**, says:

Peace be with you.

Peace be with you.

3.   The Priest, or a Deacon or another minister, may very briefly introduce the faithful to the Mass of the day.

Emphasize **grace** and **peace**.

Emphasize **Lord**.

Emphasize **peace**.

The second form of the Greeting is a Pauline greeting and is interesting in that it is not Trinitarian. This form is a binary Greeting in which both grace and peace are viewed as gifts of the Father and the Lord Jesus. It is a very different rhetorical pattern.

The final Greeting, "The Lord be with you," is the one that most people know. This Greeting is a biblical form such as we find in Judges 6:12, Ruth 2:4, 2 Chronicles 15:2, and Luke 1:28. We also see a form of this Greeting coming from the mouth of Jesus in his promise in Matthew 28:20. This

biblical response is also found in the epistolary tradition in 2 Timothy 4:22, Galatians 6:18, Philippians 4:23, and Philemon 1:25.

Although these expressions are used in the opening Greeting, some of them have been adapted from the farewell greetings in Saint Paul's letters. (See Galatians 6:18; Philippians 4:23, Philemon 1:25, and 2 Timothy 4:22.)

The rubrical gesture of the Sign of the Cross invokes the Triune God's protection, whereas, the Greeting acknowledges the

presence of God, understood as the Triune presence of God.

3. The rubric allows freedom on the part of the Priest, Deacon, or another minister to provide a declaration. The statement is to be brief; it simply announces the Saint honored or where we are in liturgical time (for example, the First Sunday of Advent), or introduces the Mass. It is not an opportunity for mystagogy on the Introductory Rites or a mini-homily. The statement should not be more than one or two sentences.

Penitential Act*

4. Then follows the Penitential Act, to which the Priest invites the faithful, saying:

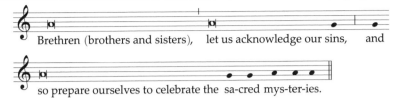

Brethren (brothers and sisters), let us acknowledge our sins, and

so prepare ourselves to celebrate the sa-cred mys-ter-ies.

Brethren (brothers and sisters), let us acknowledge our sins, and so prepare ourselves to celebrate the sacred mysteries.

A brief pause for silence follows. Then all recite together the formula of general confession:

I**confess to almighty God
and to you, my brothers and sisters,
that I have greatly sinned,
in my thoughts and in my words,
in what I have done and in what I have failed to do,**

And, striking their breast, they say:

**through my fault, through my fault,
through my most grievous fault;**

Then they continue:

**therefore I ask blessed Mary ever-Virgin,
all the Angels and Saints,
and you, my brothers and sisters,
to pray for me to the Lord our God.**

The absolution by the Priest follows:

May almighty God have mercy on us, forgive us our sins,

and bring us to ever - last-ing life.

**May almighty God have mercy on us,
forgive us our sins,
and bring us to everlasting life.**

---

* From time to time on Sundays, especially in Easter Time, instead of the customary Penitential Act, the blessing and sprinkling of water may take place (as in Appendix II, pp. 1453–1456) as a reminder of Baptism.

Sidebar notes:

Brothers and sisters is the normative address in the United States.

Begin on a tone in your mid-range. This is the reciting tone. Keep the tempo at a speaking pace. Move down from "re" to "do" on the word **sacred**, moving back to the reciting tone on **mysteries**.

Lead this in such a way that you establish the speed and flow of the text while not dominating it.

Correlate the gesture of breast beating with the threefold **fault**.

Begin on a tone in your mid-range. Move to the reciting tone on **almighty** and stay on it until **sins**. Lift after **us** and pause with a breath after **sins**. Then return to the original tone on **bring**. Try not to stop or slow down when you move from the reciting tone to the note below before moving to the new note. On the last word, slow the two notes down to create a natural ending cadence.

4–7. Notice this is the Penitential Act, not the Penitential Rite. This change in vocabulary may have occurred because we are trying to conserve the reference "Penitential Rite" to the sacrament of Penance.

All of the forms of the Penitential Act have the same structure. The Priest calls for the act, the act is done by the community, and the Priest offers a concluding absolution. The Priest concludes the Penitential Act by a request for God's mercy, to which the people reply, "Amen." Though the rubric states that this is an absolution, it is not the

same type of absolution as in the sacrament of Penance. During the sacrament of Penance, the absolution is a declaration. This absolution is a request. The form of the non-sacramental absolution is in the optative mode: "May almighty God have mercy on us . . ." rather than the declarative mode that we find in the Sacrament of Reconciliation, during which the Priest declares "I absolve you from your sins . . . ."

There are three choices for the Penitential Act. The first option uses the formula known as the *Confiteor*. Notice that

the *Confiteor* is in the first person singular, indicating its origins as a private sacerdotal apologia. If the liturgy is focusing on personal sinfulness, the *Confiteor* is a good option. If the focus is more on the collective idea of God's loving mercy (*hesed* in Hebrew), then the other options may be better suited, especially the last one.

Prior to the Missal of Pope Paul VI, the *Confiteor* and the Sign of the Cross were not in the Mass proper but were recited at the foot of the altar. The genre of prayer corresponds to the medieval dispositional

The people reply:

A-men.

Amen.

Or:

5. The Priest invites the faithful to make the Penitential Act:

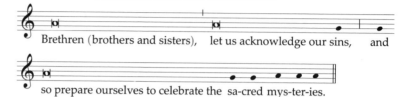

Brethren (brothers and sisters),   let us acknowledge our sins,   and

so prepare ourselves to celebrate the sa-cred mys-ter-ies.

Brethren (brothers and sisters), let us acknowledge our sins, and so prepare ourselves to celebrate the sacred mysteries.

A brief pause for silence follows.

The Priest then says:

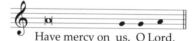

Have mercy on us, O Lord.

Have mercy on us, O Lord.

The people reply:

For we have sinned a-gainst you.

For we have sinned against you.

The Priest:

Show us, O Lord, your mer-cy.

Show us, O Lord, your mercy.

Brothers and sisters is the normative address in the United States.

Begin on the same tone in your mid-range. This is the reciting tone. Move one step down the distance from "re" to "do" on the words **us, O,** then finish on the reciting tone. Observe the normal pause for the comma.

Begin on the reciting tone and sing in regular speech speed, changing to the lower notes on the word **sinned** and the syllable **a-**, moving back on the syllable **-gainst**.

Do the same as above. Pause after **Lord**.

prayers that the Priest would say, beginning with vesting prayers in the sacristy. The tenor of these prayers is heavily penitential and is intended to help the Priest maintain his contrite demeanor. By the time of the Council of Trent, the Mass was overladen with this type of prayer. Several versions of prayers in the style of the *Confiteor* existed. But Trent mandated the removal of most of these prayers and regularized the form. The prayer, thus, survived and eventually was incorporated into the Mass itself after the Second Vatican Council.

Given the strongly devotional nature of the *Confiteor*, it is especially suited to penitential times and to daily Eucharistic Celebrations.

The second option of the Penitential Act has a dialogical nature in which the people finish the sentences begun by the Priest.

For all three options, musical notation is provided for the Invitation and the absolution. When the Greeting is sung, the sung Penitential Act flows nicely. It is necessary to remain in the same musical key, which is quite easy, since both the Greeting

and the Penitential Act vacillate between two pitches.

The *General Instruction of the Roman Missal* (GIRM) strongly advocates singing the liturgy, not simply singing at the liturgy: "Great importance should therefore be attached to the use of singing in the celebration of the Mass, with due consideration for the culture of peoples and abilities of each liturgical assembly. Although it is not always necessary (e.g., in weekday Masses) to sing all the texts that are in principle meant to be sung, every care should

The people:

And grant us your sal-va-tion.

And grant us your salvation.

The absolution by the Priest follows:

May almighty God have mercy on us, forgive us our sins,

and bring us to ever - last-ing life.

**May almighty God have mercy on us,
forgive us our sins,
and bring us to everlasting life.**

The people reply:

A-men.

Amen.

Or:

6. The Priest invites the faithful to make the Penitential Act:

Brethren (brothers and sisters), let us acknowledge our sins, and

so prepare ourselves to celebrate the sa-cred mys-ter-ies.

**Brethren (brothers and sisters), let us acknowledge our sins,
and so prepare ourselves to celebrate the sacred mysteries.**

A brief pause for silence follows.

Begin on a tone in your mid-range. Move to the reciting tone on **almighty** and stay on it until **sins**. Lift after **us** at the quarter bar and pause with a breath after **sins**. Return to the original reciting tone on **bring**. Try not to stop or slow down when you move from the reciting tone to the note below before moving to the new note. On the last word, slow the two notes down to create a natural ending cadence.

Brothers and sisters is the normative address in the United States.

Begin on a tone in your mid-range. This is the reciting tone. Keep the tempo at a speaking pace. Move down from "re" to "do" on the word **sacred**, moving back to the reciting tone on **mysteries**.

---

be taken that singing by the ministers and the people not be absent in celebrations that occur on Sundays and on Holydays of Obligation.

"However, in the choosing of the parts actually to be sung, preference is to be given to those that are of greater importance and especially to those which are to be sung by the Priest or the Deacon or a reader, with the people replying, or by the Priest and people together" (GIRM, 40).

The phenomenon of the non-singing Priest Celebrant is rather recent in the long history of the Church. Prior to the Second Vatican Council, singing the liturgy was a *sine qua non* and seminarians' classes included instruction on how to chant the prayers, especially the dialogues. But in the past fifty or so years, many priests have ceased to sing, convinced that they cannot carry a tune. The Africans have an expression that if you can talk, you can sing. Maybe one way to get over the mental block about singing is for Priests to simply think of it as speaking on pitch. In most cases, there are only two notes for which to

be concerned, so chanting the Mass should not be an insurmountable obstacle.

It is clear that many of the new translations may pose some initial difficulties for the assembly to learn. It will be difficult, for example, for some to move from "And also with you" to "And with your spirit." Chanting the dialogues will go a long way in retooling the assembly with new ways to respond to that which has become so familiar over time. Chanting the dialogues also will aid the ritual flow as Priest and Deacon respond back and forth with the people.

Think of a pitch in your mid-range. Now sing down "do," "ti," "la, "so." Your first three notes for **You were sent** are on the pitches "so" "ti" "do," with "do" as the reciting tone. These are the only three notes that you need for the troped version of the Lord, have mercy. If you use the Greek **Kyrie** and **Christe**, you begin on the note on which you finished the preceding phrase and move on the syllable "le." When you have two notes on one syllable, back off the second note.

Try to keep the trope phrases flowing at normal speech pace and flowing. Accent the normally accented syllables in English.

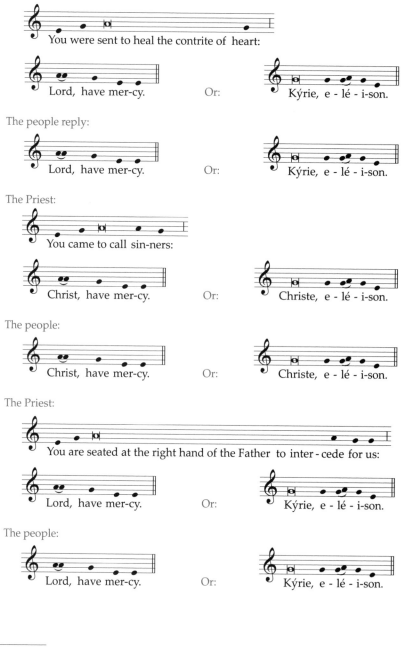

The Priest, or a Deacon or another minister, then says the following or other invocations with Kyrie, eleison (Lord, have mercy):

You were sent to heal the contrite of heart:

Lord, have mer-cy.   Or: Kýrie, e - lé - i-son.

The people reply:

Lord, have mer-cy.   Or: Kýrie, e - lé - i-son.

The Priest:

You came to call sin-ners:

Christ, have mer-cy.   Or: Christe, e - lé - i-son.

The people:

Christ, have mer-cy.   Or: Christe, e - lé - i-son.

The Priest:

You are seated at the right hand of the Father to inter - cede for us:

Lord, have mer-cy.   Or: Kýrie, e - lé - i-son.

The people:

Lord, have mer-cy.   Or: Kýrie, e - lé - i-son.

Sample invocations are found in Appendix VI, pp. **1474–1480**.

In the case of chanting the second option of the Penitential Act, the fact that it is through-composed will greatly help the ritual integrity of the piece.

We can see that the third option of the Penitential Act is the troped *Kyrie, eleison,* in which invocations are prefixed to the acclamation, "Lord, have mercy / Christ, have mercy." This form can be executed by Priest, Deacon, or another minister, most likely a cantor. The Missal shows a clear indication that the invocations, in addition to "Lord, have mercy / Christ, have mercy," be

chanted. It is interesting because it shows three ministers (the Priest, Deacon, or another minister) to say the invocations for the Penitential Act.

The rubric states that the following or other invocations are found in option three. One should go to Appendix VI to look at alternative invocations. Seven sample invocations are there, but we are not limited to those. Other invocations may be constructed. However, these invocations must be Christo-centric, insofar as they are titles or characteristics of Christ, as the sample invo-

cations demonstrate. They are not to be mini examinations of conscience in which the invocations focus on the assembly's misdeeds. (An example of such an invocation would be "We have been unjust. Lord, have mercy.") Also, we are not to follow the pattern of the medieval tropes, in which the first invocation was addressed to God the Father, the second to God the Son, and the third to God the Holy Spirit. Rather, in this form, we are proclaiming God's loving mercy in the person of Christ.

The absolution by the Priest follows:

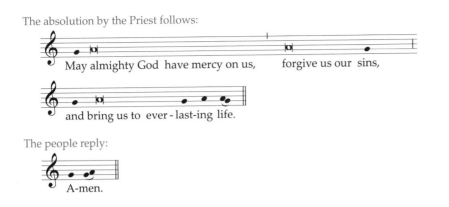

May almighty God have mercy on us,   forgive us our sins,

and bring us to ever-last-ing life.

The people reply:

A-men.

Begin on a tone in your mid-range. Move to the reciting tone on **almighty** and stay on it until **sins**. Lift after **us** and pause with a breath after **sins**. Then return to the original tone on **bring**. Try not to stop or slow down when you move from the reciting tone to the note below before moving to the new note. On the last word, slow the two notes down to create a naturally ending cadence.

The Priest, or a Deacon or another minister, then says the following or other invocations* with Kyrie, eleison (Lord, have mercy):

You were sent to heal the contrite of heart:
Lord, have mercy.   Or: **Kyrie, eleison.**

Emphasize **heal** and **contrite**.

The people reply:
Lord, have mercy.   Or: Kyrie, eleison.

The Priest:
You came to call sinners:
Christ, have mercy.   Or: **Christe, eleison.**

Emphasize **came** and **sinners**.

The people:
Christ, have mercy.   Or: Christe, eleison.

The Priest:
You are seated at the right hand of the Father to intercede for us:
Lord, have mercy.   Or: **Kyrie, eleison.**

Emphasize **seated**, **Father**, and **intercede**.

The people:
Lord, have mercy.   Or: Kyrie, eleison.

The absolution by the Priest follows:
May almighty God have mercy on us,
forgive us our sins,
and bring us to everlasting life.

Emphasize **God**, **mercy**, **forgive**, and **life**.

The people reply:
Amen.

---

*   Sample invocations are found in Appendix VI, pp. 1474–1480.

The tropes might be inspired by the readings, especially the Gospel, for the specific occasion. Central to the tropes is the idea of God's *hesed*, the Hebrew word for "kindness." The word *hesed* also is commonly translated as "loving-kindness," "merciful love," or "loving mercy." When we ask for God to be merciful, we also are proclaiming God's eternal and boundless love manifested in Christ.

Obviously, when option three is used, we do not repeat the *Kyrie, eleison*, since this would be redundant. A choice is given to use either English or Greek in the *Kyrie*. The liturgy of the early Church was in Greek before it was changed to Latin as the vernacular of that age. Since the *Kyrie* is one of the few vestiges of the early Church, it is desirable to use it, from time to time, and to preach on its theological meaning.

This *Kyrie, eleison* litany occurs after the Penitential Act, unless the third option is chosen. It's interesting that two chant settings for the *Kyrie, eleison* appear in the Missal. One setting is for option three of the Penitential Act, and the other setting is for when the *Kyrie* is sung on its own. The melodies for the "Lord, have mercy" should be musically related, whereas in the *Kyrie* litany, they can be freestanding.

The adaptation of the Gregorian Chant allows only a rote response when sung in English. But when sung in Greek, either the rote response or the historical ending may be sung. In the chant tradition, there are at least 18 settings of the Kyrie. The one appearing in the Missal is the simplest one—Masses for *ferias* throughout the year. The vernacular version borrows the

The melody in the English version is derived from the Greek **Kyrie** (below).

Lengthen the third note on **Lord** and back off the second note of **mercy**. The melody is simply "do -re-mi."

Christ begins on the "sol." Lengthen **Christ**.

7.   The Kyrie, eleison (Lord, have mercy) invocations follow, unless they have just occurred in a formula of the Penitential Act.

V. **Lord, have mercy.**   R. Lord, have mercy.
V. **Christ, have mercy.**   R. Christ, have mercy.
V. **Lord, have mercy.**   R. Lord, have mercy.

Or:

Treat this like the English version (above). Back off the second note on the **-ri** syllable and lengthen the last note over **-son** to create a natural cadence. Do this throughout.

V. **Kyrie, eleison.**   R. Kyrie, eleison.
V. **Christe, eleison.**   R. Christe, eleison.
V. **Kyrie, eleison.**   R. Kyrie, eleison.

melody from the Latin, adapting it to the English. In time, as congregations become more secure, more difficult versions may be attempted, but many of the Latin chants are so florid that the simple Penitential Act could easily take more time than merited.

An alternative to the Penitential Act is the Rite of Sprinkling found in Appendix II (page 319).

8. The Gloria. The *General Instruction of the Roman Missal*, 53, states, "The Gloria in excelsis (Glory to God in the highest) is a most ancient and venerable hymn by which the Church, gathered in the Holy Spirit, glorifies and entreats God the Father and the Lamb. The text of this hymn may not be replaced by any other. It is intoned by the Priest or, if appropriate, by a cantor or by the choir; but it is sung either by everyone together, or by the people alternately with the choir, or by the choir alone. If not sung, it is to be recited either by

everybody together or by two choirs responding one to the other.

"It is sung or said on Sundays outside Advent and Lent, and also on Solemnities and Feasts, and at particular celebrations of a more solemn character."

This text is a hymn of praise modeled after a New Testament canticle, and, as the term suggests, it is preferably sung and not recited. It was introduced into the Roman Mass in the sixth century in Frankish lands at the Christmas Mass of Bishops, since the text was appropriate to the Feast and to

8.   Then, when it is prescribed, this hymn is either sung or said:

Glo-ry to God in the high-est,

and on earth peace to peo-ple of good will.

We praise you,   we bless you,   we a-dore you,   we glo-ri-fy you,

we give you thanks for your great glo-ry,

Lord God, heav-en-ly King,   O God, al - might-y Fa-ther.

Lord Je-sus Christ, On-ly Be-got-ten Son,

Lord God, Lamb of God,   Son of the Fa-ther,

you take a-way the sins of the world,   have mer-cy on us;

you take a-way the sins of the world,   re-ceive our prayer;

you are seat-ed at the right hand of the Fa-ther,   have mer-cy on us.

For you a-lone are the Ho-ly One,   you a-lone are the Lord,

you a-lone are the Most High, Je-sus Christ,   with the Ho-ly Spir-it,

in the glo-ry of God the Fa - ther.   A - men.

The rubrics do not indicate that the Priest must intone the Gloria, but this is not forbidden and is a longstanding tradition. To sing it, choose a note in the mid-range of your voice, sing down "do-ti-la-sol." Then begin on "sol" and sing "ti-do," ascending to **God**, then descend on **the highest** to the note on which you began.

By the organization of the words on the page, the four-part division of this text can be immediately perceived. The first sentence is a joyful declaration of the glory of God, echoing the song of the Angels to the shepherds at Bethlehem. Immediately, we then move into a litanic series of ejaculations addressed to God in the highest. This culminates in the sentence **Lord, we give you thanks . . .** , echoing the idea of Eucharist as a thanksgiving. In the third section, we turn our attention to Christ and bid his mercy. Finally, in the fourth part, we conclude as we do so in many of our liturgical prayers with a Trinitarian conclusion. This is in the form of a doxological acclamation of the Trinity but addressed to Christ. If this text is recited, try to give some space among the four parts. Let the second part mount in excitement, and avoid letting it become sing-songy.

add to the Solemnity. Later usage was expanded to include Sundays and Masses for martyrs when the Bishop presided. Gradually, it was accorded to Priests. Following the principle of progressive solemnity, several versions in addition to the chant could be learned to distinguish the major feasts from Ordinary Time.

In the newly translated version, two lines that were omitted in the earlier translation have been reinserted, and the word "adore" replaces the word "worship." Thus, the opening has the feel of a litany, in

which we keep adding verbs onto the list of praise that culminates in the line "we give you thanks for your great glory." Remember that the word *Eucharist* means "to give thanks." In this hymn, we are already anticipating the great thanksgiving in the Preface and Eucharistic Prayer.

The second section of the Gloria focuses our attention on Christ and his role in salvation. The tone of this section resembles the Creed, with expressions such as "Only Begotten Son" and "you are seated at the right hand of the Father."

The third section culminates in a Trinitarian doxology with special Christic emphasis.

This multipart structure lends itself to special treatment musically, if the textual beauty is to be appreciated. The refrain versions that were so popular until recently will probably need to be rethought, since they do not accommodate easily. It is likely that through-composed texts will capture the words better.

The Gloria structurally has four parts: it begins with the song of the Angels to the shepherds, in Luke's account of the Gospel, praising God in the highest; it continues with five ejaculatory phrases that function like a litany addressed to God; the third part, beginning with **Lord Jesus Christ,** is in praise of Christ and bidding him for mercy; and the fourth part, beginning with **For you alone**, is a type of doxology addressed to the Trinity. Try to convey this four-part structure in the way you phrase the words. The second part might crescendo and climax on the line **we give you thanks . . .** , which is the translation of the Greek word *eucharistein*. Because this hymn is a *cento* of four texts, it is a challenge for proclaiming it well. As a New Testament canticle (from *cantare*, meaning "so sing"), it is best to sing it whenever possible.

Glory to God in the highest,
and on earth peace to people of good will.

We praise you,
we bless you,
we adore you,
we glorify you,
we give you thanks for your great glory,
Lord God, heavenly King,
O God, almighty Father.

Lord Jesus Christ, Only Begotten Son,
Lord God, Lamb of God, Son of the Father,
you take away the sins of the world,
   have mercy on us;
you take away the sins of the world,
   receive our prayer;
you are seated at the right hand of the Father,
   have mercy on us.

For you alone are the Holy One,
you alone are the Lord,
you alone are the Most High,
Jesus Christ,
with the Holy Spirit,
in the glory of God the Father.
Amen.

9.   When this hymn is concluded, the Priest, with hands joined, says:

Let us pray.

And all pray in silence with the Priest for a while.

Then the Priest, with hands extended, says the Collect prayer, at the end of which the people acclaim:

Amen.

The invitation to prayer should be taken literally. Therefore, after the invitation to prayer is extended, allow a significant amount of time for the assembly to enter into prayer. The Priest can model this personal quiet prayer by lowering his eyes and doing nothing with the book until he lifts his eyes. Then, singing or reciting the Collect, the Priest collects all the individual prayers into a corporate liturgical prayer.

9. The Priest, with hands joined, says, "Let us pray." The first element in this is a directive addressed to the assembly. The second element is silent prayer by Priest and people. (The presumption is that all will pray silently with the Priest at this time.) The third element is that the Priest, with hands extended in the orans position, prays the Collect aloud. The fourth element is the people's acclamation, "Amen."

Normally, the Collect, too, involves four elements. The first is a direct address to God (normally in the Roman Rite this is *Deus*, with modifying adjectives such as *almighty* and *ever-living*. This direct address will be expanded by a relative clause that will either delineate a characteristic of God or an act of God in history. The third element of the prayer is a petition, a request made on behalf of the praying community; sometimes the consequences of that request will be indicated in the prayer. (Send your grace into our hearts that we may do . . . .) The final element is the stereotypical conclusion. Most often, the prayer is addressed to God the Father, so the conclusion is "through the Son in the Holy Spirit." Traditionally, Roman Rite collects are brief, sparse, addressed to the mind rather than the heart, allude to rather than quote from the Bible, and revel in binary oppositions. (An example of a binary opposition is "May we look down upon the things of earth so that we may look up to the things of heaven.")

THE LITURGY OF THE WORD

10. Then the reader goes to the ambo and reads the First Reading, while all sit and listen.

To indicate the end of the reading, the reader acclaims:

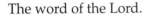

The word of the Lord.

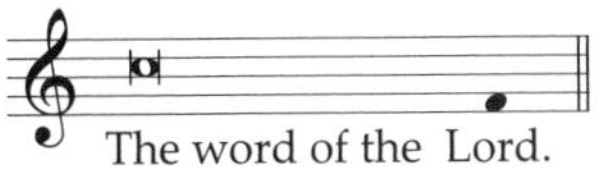

The word of the Lord.

All reply:

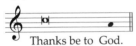
Thanks be to God.

Thanks be to God.

11. The psalmist or cantor sings or says the Psalm, with the people making the response.

12. After this, if there is to be a Second Reading, a reader reads it from the ambo, as above.

To indicate the end of the reading, the reader acclaims:

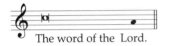
The word of the Lord.

The word of the Lord.

All reply:

Thanks be to God.

Thanks be to God.

13. There follows the **Alleluia** or another chant laid down by the rubrics, as the liturgical time requires.

14. Meanwhile, if incense is used, the Priest puts some into the thurible. After this, the Deacon who is to proclaim the Gospel, bowing profoundly before the Priest, asks for the blessing, saying in a low voice:
Your blessing, Father.

The Priest says in a low voice:
May the Lord be in your heart and on your lips,
that you may proclaim his Gospel worthily and well,
in the name of the Father, and of the Son, ✝ and of the Holy Spirit.

The Deacon signs himself with the Sign of the Cross and replies:
Amen.

Sidebar notes:

Find a pitch in the lower middle of your range. Sing "do-mi-sol." The "sol" is your first note as a reciting tone. Then move to the "do" on the word **Lord**.

The assembly imitates the same note sequence in the response.

Find a pitch in the lower middle of your range. Sing "do-mi-sol." The "sol" is your first note as a reciting tone. Then move to the "mi" on the word **Lord**.

The assembly imitates the same note sequence in the response.

This blessing is a private exchange between the Deacon and the Priest and is of a private dispositional nature. Thus, it should be prayed in a low voice over the Deacon.

Correlate the gestures with the text.

---

10. The reader is invited to chant the acclamation, "The word of the Lord," which concludes the First Reading. This chanting clearly distinguishes the reading from the acclamation.

12. The reader of the Second Reading also is invited to chant, "The word of the Lord." The chant melody is different, thus suggesting the difference in the two readings. The First Reading usually is taken from the Old Testament and the Second Reading

from the New Testament. Nothing in the rubrics states that the book is held up.

The GIRM makes it clear that there are many more options for the execution of the Psalm than are suggested in this rubric. In the United States, we are allowed the "Responsorial Gradual from the *Graduale Romanum*, or the Responsorial Psalm or the *Alleluia* Psalm from the *Graduale Simplex* . . . or an antiphon and Psalm from another collection of Psalms and antiphons, including Psalms arranged in metrical form, providing that they have been approved by

the Conference of Bishops or the Diocesan Bishop" (GIRM, 61). But the preference is clearly for the chanting of the Psalm.

There follows the "Alleluia" or another chant. In the present Roman Rite, there are two obligatory sequences for Easter and Pentecost and two optional ones for Corpus Christi and Our Lady of Sorrows.

14. A quiet interchange occurs around the blessing. The Deacon requests this in a low voice. It is meant to be a private exchange

In the absence of a Deacon, the Priest bows before the altar as the symbol of Christ and prays a private dispositional prayer quietly.

If, however, a Deacon is not present, the Priest, bowing before the altar, says quietly:

Cleanse my heart and my lips, almighty God, that I may worthily proclaim your holy Gospel.

If sung, the salutation, **The Lord be with you**, will ideally evoke the proper response from the assembly. Find a pitch in the lower middle of your range. Sing "do-mi-sol." The "sol" is your first note as a reciting tone. Then move to the "mi" on the word **be** and back to the reciting tone on **with you**.

15.   The Deacon, or the Priest, then proceeds to the ambo, accompanied, if appropriate, by ministers with incense and candles. There he says:

The Lord be with you.

The Lord be with you.

The people reply:

And with your spir-it.

The assembly imitates the same note sequence in the response.

And with your spirit.

The Deacon, or the Priest:

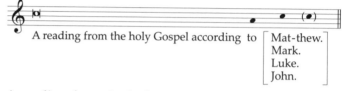
A reading from the holy Gospel according to ⎡Mat-thew.⎤
Mark.
Luke.
John.

Return to the reciting tone and sing **A reading from the holy Gospel according**, then sing the **to** on the "mi," returning to the reciting tone on the name of the evangelist.

A reading from the holy Gospel according to N.

and, at the same time, he makes the Sign of the Cross on the book and on his forehead, lips, and breast.

The people acclaim:

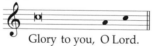
Glory to you, O Lord.

The assembly imitates the same note sequence in the response.

Glory to you, O Lord.

Then the Deacon, or the Priest, incenses the book, if incense is used, and proclaims the Gospel.

16.   At the end of the Gospel, the Deacon, or the Priest, acclaims:

Grab the reciting tone and sing **The Gospel of**, and on **the** go to the "mi," returning to the reciting tone on **Lord**.

The Gospel of the Lord.

The Gospel of the Lord.

---

between the Priest and Deacon that is not overheard by the worshippers. The Deacon says the "Amen." These both function like the apologia prayers in which God is asked to equip the minister for the ministry. Because these prayers are more private, they do not intrude on the public prayer of the liturgy.

15. Dialogue before the Gospel. The Priest or Deacon greets the assembly, saying, "The Lord be with you." The people respond,

"And with your spirit," the same response as during the Introductory Rites.

The Priest announces the Gospel and the people acclaim, "Glory, to you O, Lord." The rubric states that the Priest, at the time of announcing the Gospel, makes a Sign of the Cross with his thumb on the book itself and on his forehead, mouth, and breast, "which everyone else does as well," GIRM, 134.

At the conclusion of the Gospel, the Deacon or Priest calls for the people's

response, "Praise to you, Lord Jesus Christ." It is preferred that this is chanted.

The Deacon or Priest kisses the book, saying, "May our sins be wiped away." That also is meant to be inaudible to the community as a whole. Just as in the case of the readers, no rubric suggests a gesture of pointing to the book.

17. A Homily, which is understood as an address offered by Priest or Deacon, inspired by the scriptures proclaimed or

All reply:

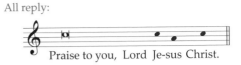

Praise to you, Lord Je-sus Christ.

Praise to you, Lord Jesus Christ.

Then he kisses the book, saying quietly:

**Through the words of the Gospel
may our sins be wiped away.**

17. Then follows the Homily, which is to be preached by a Priest or Deacon on all Sundays and Holydays of Obligation; on other days, it is recommended.

18. At the end of the Homily, the Symbol or Profession of Faith or Creed, when prescribed, is either sung or said:

I be-lieve in one God, the Fa-ther al-might-y, mak-er of heav-en

and earth, of all things vis-i-ble and in-vis-i-ble.

I be-lieve in one Lord Je-sus Christ, the Only Be-got-ten Son

of God, born of the Father be-fore all a-ges. God from God,

Light from Light, true God from true God, be-got-ten, not made,

con-sub-stan-tial with the Fa-ther; through him all things were

made. For us men and for our sal-va-tion he came down from

At the words that follow, up to and including **and became man**, all bow.

heav-en, and by the Ho-ly Spir-it was in-car-nate of the Vir-gin

Mar-y, and be-came man.

The assembly imitates the same note sequence in the response.

The Priest prays a sacerdotal apologia *quietly, kissing the book at the same time.*

The rubrics do not indicate that the Priest must intone the Creed, but this is not forbidden and is a long-standing tradition. To sing it, choose a note in the lower mid-range of your voice, and sing down "do-mi-sol." Then sing "sol-mi-fa-re-mi-sol-la" with the words, **I believe in one God**.

The double vertical lines signify logical places to alternate between choir/cantor and congregation. The single vertical lines indicate where breaths should be taken. These follow the sense line. The shorter half and quarter vertical lines indicate a lift but not necessarily a breath, since too many breaths will fragment the text. Generally, the vertical lines correspond with the punctuation marks within the texts. Try to keep the text at normal speaking rate, and try not to slow down when changing pitches. Any time two or more notes are over one syllable, back off the second (and third) note(s).

All bow at the line **and became man** *as a sign of respect for the Incarnation.*

the liturgical texts prayed, the liturgical time of year or Feast celebrated, and illuminating the life of the worshipping assembly, is then offered.

A word must be said about the need for moments of silence, especially during the Liturgy of the Word. The GIRM is clear on this matter: "The Liturgy of the Word is to be celebrated in such a way as to favor meditation, and so any kind of haste that hinders recollection is clearly to be avoided. In the course of it, brief periods of silence are also appropriate, accommo-

dated to the assembled congregation; by means of these, under the action of the Holy Spirit, the Word of God may be grasped by the heart and a response through prayer may be prepared. It may be appropriate to observe such periods of silence, for example, before the Liturgy of the Word itself begins, after the First and Second Reading, and lastly at the conclusion of the Homily" (GIRM, 56).

A case can be made that our first response to the readings is silence, from which flows the Responsorial Psalm and

Gospel Acclamation. But the silence needs to be intentional.

18–19. GIRM, 68, states that the Creed can be intoned by the Priest, another minster, or the faithful. It can be sung by everyone all the way through or alternating with choir and the congregation: "If it is sung, it is intoned by the Priest or, if appropriate, by a cantor or by the choir. It is then sung either by everybody together or by the people alternating with the choir."

If this text is sung with choir and cantor, consider alternating between choir and cantor with the assembly at each double-bar line. Singing the text will assist in relearning the Creed with the new translation and will facilitate its liturgical performance.

Since the Creed is organized around the three persons of the Trinity, a big breath between each part will help draw attention to this tripartite structure. The tendency to race through the text should be avoided at all cost. But singing or reciting it too slowly and lugubriously also should be avoided.

Although the text reads **I believe**, in singing it together, the liturgical and public nature of this confession of faith will be accentuated.

It is probably significant that we have two chant settings for the Creed. (The alternate setting is in Appendix I, page 305.) More important, however, is that the Apostles' Creed is now presented as the preferred Creed to be used during Lent and Easter Time. It is significant that the use of the Apostles' Creed, which had been reserved for Masses with children, has been expanded to be said during Lent and Easter.

The Apostles' Creed is the baptismal Creed associated with the Church of Rome. Initially, the use of the Creed was in the interrogatory form as a series of three questions posed to the catechumens before they were immersed in the waters of Baptism. Gradually, the form changed from interrogatory to a declaratory form as the catechumens received this in the *traditio symbolum*. It was introduced into the Eucharistic Liturgy at a much later date. In the East and in Spain, the Creed was recited immediately before reception of Communion as a declaration of orthodoxy. In the West, however, it was recited after the Liturgy of the Word as a response to what preceded it.

Also significant is that a chant is not provided for the Apostles' Creed. It should be noted that, over the past half century, in most places in the United States, the Creed has become more of a recited text than a sung one. Singing the text, however, will add greater solemnity to the liturgy and also will help the congregation learn the new textual changes. The new translation favors English words that are derived from the Latin *cognates*, such as *incarnate* and

An alternate musical setting of the Creed may be found in Appendix I, pp. 1439–1441.

I believe in one God,
the Father almighty,
maker of heaven and earth,
of all things visible and invisible.

I believe in one Lord Jesus Christ,
the Only Begotten Son of God,
born of the Father before all ages.
God from God, Light from Light,
true God from true God,
begotten, not made, consubstantial with the Father;
through him all things were made.
For us men and for our salvation
he came down from heaven,

At the words that follow, up to and including and became man, all bow.

and by the Holy Spirit was incarnate of the Virgin Mary,
and became man.

For our sake he was crucified under Pontius Pilate,
he suffered death and was buried,
and rose again on the third day
in accordance with the Scriptures.
He ascended into heaven
and is seated at the right hand of the Father.
He will come again in glory
to judge the living and the dead
and his kingdom will have no end.

I believe in the Holy Spirit, the Lord, the giver of life,
who proceeds from the Father and the Son,
who with the Father and the Son is adored and glorified,
who has spoken through the prophets.

I believe in one, holy, catholic and apostolic Church.
I confess one Baptism for the forgiveness of sins
and I look forward to the resurrection of the dead
and the life of the world to come. Amen.

If the Creed is recited, it is important that the text not be rushed and that a natural speaking pace establish itself. The Priest can aid this along by establishing the tempo and by regulating with his own voice the natural speaking pace. Observe all the punctuation marks. Since this is a text that is recited by all, it should therefore have a communal quality. The Priest should not speed up or slow down on various words or phrases that would give the perception that this is a sacerdotal text, rather than a text of all the baptized.

The gesture of bowing occurs on the words **and became man**, drawing attention to the mystery of the Incarnation.

---

consubstantial. (From time to time, during the Homily, the theological meaning of these words might be unpacked for the congregation.)

Consideration also might be given to singing this ancient creedal formula in Latin, alternating lines with the choir or cantor. Youth at World Youth Day, for example, have experienced this form with great delight, although those from the United States seem to be unfamiliar with this version. But the experience of singing this ancient formula of faith in a universal lan-guage is meaningful. Since the English translation follows the Latin so closely, intelligibility of the Latin will become less of an issue over time.

Finally, singing the Creed will under-score that this is a liturgical action of the entire congregation. Although the text has been translated literally from the Latin *Credo* as "I believe," singing will ensure that the Profession of Faith is not seen as simply a private, individual expression of faith, but the entire Church professing her faith. The purpose of the Creed in this position, according to GIRM, 67, is a response to the Liturgy of the Word and a confession of the mysteries of faith according to the rule of faith.

The Apostles' Creed, which originated as a baptismal creed in the interrogatory form, is the preferred form during Lent and Easter Time, given the strong baptismal character of the liturgical time, both in preparation for Easter initiation and the celebration at the Easter Vigil and the period of mystagogy that extends from Easter to Pentecost.

The Creed is in the first person singular, but to the extent that this is recited as a liturgical creed, it is important that all the baptized do so with synchronicity.

Again, the gesture is coordinated with the phrase **who was conceived by the Holy Spirit, born of the Virgin Mary**, to underscore the mystery of the Incarnation.

See Appendix V for suggestions for the Universal Prayer. Often a sung response addressed to Christ is suggested to bring out the litanic character of this prayer.

19. Instead of the Niceno-Constantinopolitan Creed, especially during Lent and Easter Time, the baptismal Symbol of the Roman Church, known as the Apostles' Creed, may be used.

**I believe in God,
the Father almighty,
Creator of heaven and earth,
and in Jesus Christ, his only Son, our Lord,**

At the words that follow, up to and including the Virgin Mary, all bow.

**who was conceived by the Holy Spirit,
born of the Virgin Mary,
suffered under Pontius Pilate,
was crucified, died and was buried;
he descended into hell;
on the third day he rose again from the dead;
he ascended into heaven,
and is seated at the right hand of God the Father almighty;
from there he will come to judge the living and the dead.**

**I believe in the Holy Spirit,
the holy catholic Church,
the communion of saints,
the forgiveness of sins,
the resurrection of the body,
and life everlasting. Amen.**

20. Then follows the Universal Prayer, that is, the Prayer of the Faithful or Bidding Prayers.

20. With the revised translation of the Missal, there is a new term for the Prayer of the Faithful. Now, it also is called the Universal Prayer or Bidding Prayer. GIRM, 69, provides the structure of the Universal Prayer, suggesting a certain number of items, in a specific order, that underscores the universal nature of this prayer: a) for the needs of the Church; b) for public authorities and the salvation of the whole world; c) for those burdened by any kind of difficulty; d) for the local community.

Nevertheless, in any particular celebration, such as a Confirmation, a Marriage, or at a funeral, the series of intentions may be concerned more closely with the particular occasion.

The Priest calls for the prayer. A minister other than the Priest offers the intercessions or petitions. The community as a whole makes a response to the intercessions. Then the Priest concludes the listing with an oration. It is for the Priest Celebrant to regulate this prayer from the chair.

The change of name is significant, since the term "Prayer of the Faithful" seemed to suggest that this was the people's prayer vis-à-vis the Priest's prayer. Actually, the term "faithful" is to be regarded in relation to catechumens who technically have not yet received the Creed. For this reason, the catechumens are dismissed prior to the Creed and the faithful, including the Priest (namely, all the baptized), are invited to stand and profess their faith and then are invited to bring petitions to God.

THE LITURGY OF THE EUCHARIST

21.　When all this has been done, the Offertory Chant begins. Meanwhile, the ministers place the corporal, the purificator, the chalice, the pall, and the Missal on the altar.

22.　It is desirable that the faithful express their participation by making an offering, bringing forward bread and wine for the celebration of the Eucharist and perhaps other gifts to relieve the needs of the Church and of the poor.

23.　The Priest, standing at the altar, takes the paten with the bread and holds it slightly raised above the altar with both hands, saying in a low voice:

> **Blessed are you, Lord God of all creation,**
> **for through your goodness we have received**
> **the bread we offer you:**
> **fruit of the earth and work of human hands,**
> **it will become for us the bread of life.**

Then he places the paten with the bread on the corporal.

If, however, the Offertory Chant is not sung, the Priest may speak these words aloud; at the end, the people may acclaim:

> Blessed be God for ever.

24.　The Deacon, or the Priest, pours wine and a little water into the chalice, saying quietly:

> **By the mystery of this water and wine**
> **may we come to share in the divinity of Christ**
> **who humbled himself to share in our humanity.**

25.　The Priest then takes the chalice and holds it slightly raised above the altar with both hands, saying in a low voice:

> **Blessed are you, Lord God of all creation,**
> **for through your goodness we have received**
> **the wine we offer you:**
> **fruit of the vine and work of human hands,**
> **it will become our spiritual drink.**

Then he places the chalice on the corporal.

If, however, the Offertory Chant is not sung, the Priest may speak these words aloud; at the end, the people may acclaim:

> Blessed be God for ever.

26.　After this, the Priest, bowing profoundly, says quietly:

> **With humble spirit and contrite heart**
> **may we be accepted by you, O Lord,**
> **and may our sacrifice in your sight this day**
> **be pleasing to you, Lord God.**

Here begins the transition from the Liturgy of the Word to the Liturgy of the Eucharist. Attention should be given to make this as smooth as possible.

The text, inspired by a Jewish blessing (*berakah*), elicits the Jewish roots of Christian Eucharist. If there is no music, the blessing is recited audibly; otherwise, the assembly will not be cued to respond. The bread is slightly raised above the altar.

The phrase **work of human hands** is in apposition to **the bread we offer you**. These last two lines cue the people's response.

The text and the action need to be correlated.

If there is no music, the blessing is recited audibly. Otherwise, the assembly will not be cued to respond. The chalice is raised slightly above the altar.

This dispositional prayer is said quietly, although it is meant not just for the Priest but for all, since it uses the first person plural **we**. The bow expresses the penitential mood of the prayer.

---

21. The Preparation of the Gifts requires several elements and signals a transition from the Liturgy of the Word to the Liturgy of the Eucharist. The altar is dressed while a collection is taken.

23–25. The prayer said holding the bread and wine is derived from Jewish blessing prayers. This prayer was not a part of the Tridentine Missal but was added after the Second Vatican Council to underscore the Jewish roots of Christian worship. When no music covers this action, the Priest lifts the

bread and says aloud the prayer, thus cuing the assembly to respond, "Blessed be God for ever." The same ocurs as the chalice is lifted. When there is music, the Priest says these prayers quietly and there is no response on the part of the people.

24. Between the bread and the wine, the chalice is prepared, as a small amount of water is placed in the chalice with the wine. Cutting wine with water was common in the ancient world, since wine was thicker and needed to be reconstituted.

But the action is accompanied by a prayer that opens up an allegorical interpretation of the commingling of the humanity and divinity in Christ. This exchange of properties, known as the *sacrum commercium*, has been fertile ground for theologians to explore the deeper meaning of the Incarnation in which divinity and humanity are commingled.

26. That the Priest says this prayer bowing profoundly and with quiet recitation suggests that it is an apologia.

27.   If appropriate, he also incenses the offerings, the cross, and the altar. A Deacon or other minister then incenses the Priest and the people.

28.   Then the Priest, standing at the side of the altar, washes his hands, saying quietly:

**Wash me, O Lord, from my iniquity
and cleanse me from my sin.**

The private sacerdotal apologia is prayed inaudibly while the Priest washes his hands. The prayer is for his ministry.

To sing the invitation, sing from "do" to "re." This will be the reciting tone. Keep the text moving at normal speech tempo and descend to the "do" on the syllables **might-y**, ascending back to the reciting tone on **Father**. Try not to slow down when changing notes.

Brothers and sisters would be the norm.

Emphasize **pray**, **acceptable**, and **God**.

If the Priest intones the invitation, the assembly should respond in the same modality, beginning with the reciting tone. Breathe after **name**.

29.   Standing at the middle of the altar, facing the people, extending and then joining his hands, he says:

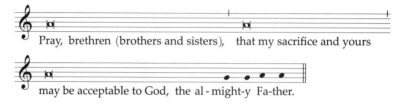

Pray, brethren (brothers and sisters),   that my sacrifice and yours

may be acceptable to God, the al-might-y Fa-ther.

**Pray, brethren (brothers and sisters),
that my sacrifice and yours
may be acceptable to God,
the almighty Father.**

The people rise and reply:

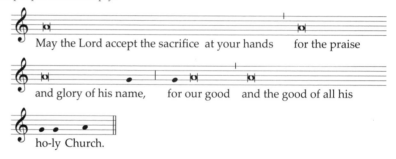

May the Lord accept the sacrifice at your hands   for the praise

and glory of his name,   for our good   and the good of all his

ho-ly Church.

May the Lord accept the sacrifice at your hands
for the praise and glory of his name,
for our good
and the good of all his holy Church.

30.   Then the Priest, with hands extended, says the Prayer over the Offerings, at the end of which the people acclaim:

Amen.

---

27. When incense is used, the gifts, the altar, and the cross are incensed to show the relationship of the offerings with the Passion of Christ and to draw attention to the fact that the altar, having been anointed with chrism (similar to chrismation or christening) in the Rite of Dedication, also is a symbol of Christ. It is because the altar is a symbol of Christ that the Priest greets it with a kiss at the beginning and the end of the liturgy.

28. The hand washing is accompanied by a private prayer that falls again under the category of sacerdotal apologiae. The fact that the prayer is said quietly, and in the first person singular, points to the private nature of the prayer.

29. The Priest invites the people to pray that his sacrifice and theirs be acceptable. Much debate has taken place over whether we are talking about multiple sacrifices or one. That the word is in the singular seems to suggest that we are talking about one

sacrifice. Thus, "my sacrifice and yours" means "our sacrifice." A change is noticed in the prayer, "Pray, brethren (brothers and sisters), that my sacrifice and yours may be . . . ." Previously, the translation was "our sacrifice." The current phrase probably indicates that the one sacrifice of Christ is being offered both by the ministerial priesthood and the baptismal priesthood.

The Priest then offers the Prayer over the Offerings in response to the dialogue. These prayers, which are variable according to the feast and time of the liturgical

THE EUCHARISTIC PRAYER

31.   Then the Priest begins the Eucharistic Prayer.

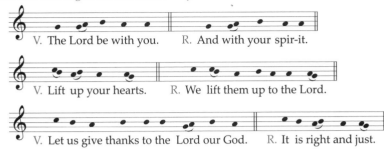

V. The Lord be with you.   R. And with your spir-it.

V. Lift up your hearts.   R. We lift them up to the Lord.

V. Let us give thanks to the Lord our God.   R. It is right and just.

Extending his hands, he says:
The Lord be with you.

The people reply:
And with your spirit.

The Priest, raising his hands, continues:
Lift up your hearts.

The people:
We lift them up to the Lord.

The Priest, with hands extended, adds:
Let us give thanks to the Lord our God.

The people:
It is right and just.

The Priest, with hands extended, continues the Preface.

The Preface dialogue is prayed back and forth in a series of versicles.

Find a note in the upper register of the voice. This is "do." Mentally sing down the scale "do-ti-la-sol." Begin the dialogue on "sol," rising "sol-la-ti-la." Line two begins on the upper "do" and descends "do-ti-la-ti-la la-sol."

The third versicle also begins on the upper "do," descending and rising in a step-like fashion.

When spoken, the Priest extends his hands toward the assembly, then lifts them high, correlative to the text **lift**.

For line three, leave hands elevated in the orans position.

Since these three versicles are intended dialogically, move seamlessly from one to the other without delay. One line leads into the next one and climaxes with the third line. Allow for voice modulation.

year, draw special attention to the liturgical year. On certain Saints' Feast days, the Prayer over the Offerings often helps us see how the Saints configured their lives to Christ. When there is no specific prayer, one is taken from the Commons, of which there are a dozen from Ordinary Time, but care should be taken to choose a prayer that fits the specific Saint as best as one is able.

31. We see here three sets of versicles and responses that are very ancient. In this

exchange between Priest and people, we understand the dialogical nature of liturgical prayer. It is as though the congregation completes the sentences of the Priest, responding to or acknowledging his words. In the second set of exchanges, "Lift up your hearts" is a command. The people's response ("We lift then up to the Lord") is legal terminology from the Roman Empire. The covenanted people of God are saying that this is precisely what should be done; it is the proper action. It is the appropriate response that the covenanted

people of God would make to what God has done.

"We lift them up to the Lord" is a pastoral paraphrase to the underlying Latin. The underlying Latin is a single declarative sentence that states, "We hold our hearts up to the Lord."

In the third set, the Priest invites the people to join in the Eucharist (a word that means thanksgiving) as he asks them to give thanks to God, to which they respond, "It is right and just."

See the next section for the sung Prefaces. When the Preface is sung, the Holy, Holy, Holy should flow from it in the same key and without break. Observe the punctuation. Note that the third **Holy** directly modifies **Lord God of Hosts** (*Sabbaoth*). Lengthen the note on **Lord**, **earth**, and **he**. On the syllables with two notes, back off the second note, so that the second note functions like a passing tone. As an acclamation, it is desirable that the Holy, Holy, Holy be sung.

If, however, the Holy, Holy, Holy is recited, observe the punctuation marks.

At the end of the Preface he joins his hands and concludes the Preface with the people, singing or saying aloud:

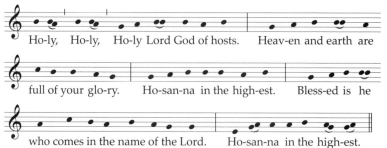

Holy, Holy, Holy Lord God of hosts.
Heaven and earth are full of your glory.
Hosanna in the highest.
Blessed is he who comes in the name of the Lord.
Hosanna in the highest.

Or:

The melody for the English version is derived from the Latin version. Note the short vertical lines after **Sanctus**, and again after the second **Sanctus**. Lift without breathing, putting a little space between the words. Breathe at the single vertical bar line after **tua** and again after **Dómini**.

Music for the Eucharistic Prayers is provided in the Appendix to the Order of Mass, beginning on page 185. When it is sung, it should flow from the Holy, Holy, Holy, which immediately preceded it to create a seamless musical piece.

32. In all Masses, the Priest celebrant is permitted to sing parts of the Eucharistic Prayer provided with musical notation below, pp. 693ff., especially the principal parts.

In Eucharistic Prayer I, the Roman Canon, the words included in brackets may be omitted.

We are now making a direct transition that the Priest is acknowledging the people in whose name he prays to God. Much of this dialogue is coming out of Roman culture, which was deeply law-bound. Over and over, we hear that we are to fulfill our *vota*. The invitation is for all those present to enter into the great prayer of thanksgiving together.

Every Preface culminates in the acclamation of the Holy, Holy, Holy comprised in two parts. The first part is from the book of Isaiah 6:3, describing the first vision before

the throne of God surrounded by six-winged, ministering seraphim. This text was used from ancient times by the Jewish people in the liturgy of the synagogue during the *kedasha*, a prayer said during the cantor's repetition of the 18 benedictions before the opening of the ark. The text of the second part, beginning with the word *Benedictus* (Latin for "Blessed"), is taken from the Gospel according to Matthew 21:9, describing Jesus' Palm Sunday entry into Jerusalem.

32. Singing the Eucharistic Prayer is permitted, in which case the sung prayer punctuated by the three acclamations ideally are in the same musical mode, or key, in order to create a cohesive whole and to avoid ritual fragmentation.

THE PREFACES

This section provides commentary, and proclamation and chant tips for the 49 Prefaces that are within the Order of Mass. Before exploring the commentaries, let us look at the composition of the Preface.

The structure of the Preface in the Roman Rite comprises three parts. The prayer begins with the protocol. This is the stereotypical transition from the final versicle and response of the dialogue into the prayer of praise and thanksgiving. The second part of the Preface, the body, provides the particular theology of the Preface and reasons for praising God. The third part of the Preface, the eschatocol, is the stereotypical conclusion to the prayer. The Angels and Saints are called upon, and our prayer joins theirs in praising God. While praying the Preface, pause briefly between each of the parts to emphasize the usual structure.

When preparing to sing the Preface, read it once aloud and mark the words that you would like to accentuate. Then find a note in the upper part of your range. This will be the reciting tone. Now sing down "do-ti-la" to find your first note. Move directly to the reciting tone. Lift after the word *just* in the protocol, observing the quarter vertical line, and take a breath after *salvation*, observing the half vertical line. In the usual structure of the Preface, the protocol may end in either of two ways, with the phrase *through*

Christ our Lord, followed by a full vertical line or with the phrase *eternal God*, followed by a half vertical line. Whether a full or half vertical line is encountered, breathe and pause a little before proceeding. This will indicate that the protocol is ending and you are moving into the body of the Preface. Pause after the vertical lines in the body of the Preface, especially after the line prior to the eschatocol. The pause at that line will indicate the movement to the conclusion.

As you sing the Preface, follow normal speech patterns, and at the end of a sentence, allow your speed to slow to show the natural cadence. It is particularly important that, while singing a number of words on the reciting tone, that the words are accentuated in a normal speaking manner. Try not to accent the weak syllables, as this will distort the text. Any time two notes are on one syllable, back off the second tone.

Respect the commas throughout the eschatocol but try to keep the section together without taking big breaths.

Chant tips are provided throughout this section; however, please keep in mind that interpretations of music vary. While listening to others sing this music on the Internet or CDs, you will notice differences.

PREFACE I OF ADVENT

The two comings of Christ

33.   The following Preface is said in Masses of Advent from the First Sunday of Advent to December 16 and in other Masses that are celebrated in Advent and have no proper Preface.

V. The Lord be with you.   R. And with your spir-it.

V. Lift up your hearts.   R. We lift them up to the Lord.

V. Let us give thanks to the Lord our God.   R. It is right and just.

Bring out the accent on **be** in **The Lord be with you**.

Make a strong accent on **Lift**, and slow both notes of **hearts**.

In the third dialogue, move to the word **thanks** before accenting, and hold that word slightly to give it emphasis. Broaden both notes of **Lord**, and hold **God**.

Emphasize **first coming** and **when he comes again** to parallel the two comings.

Emphasize **fulfilled** and **opened** to indicate the purpose of the first coming.

Emphasize **in glory and majesty** and **all . . . manifest** to indicate the future hope.

It is truly right and just, our duty and our salvation,
always and everywhere to give you thanks,
Lord, holy Father, almighty and eternal God,
through Christ our Lord.

For he assumed at his first coming
the lowliness of human flesh,
and so fulfilled the design you formed long ago,
and opened for us the way to eternal salvation,
that, when he comes again in glory and majesty
and all is at last made manifest,
we who watch for that day
may inherit the great promise
in which now we dare to hope.

And so, with Angels and Archangels,
with Thrones and Dominions,
and with all the hosts and Powers of heaven,
we sing the hymn of your glory,
as without end we acclaim:

Holy, Holy, Holy Lord God of hosts . . .

33. In **Preface I of Advent: The two comings of Christ**, the "first coming" has two consequences—fulfilling God's design and opening the way to eternal salvation. The Second Coming will have the consequences—everything will be made manifest and we will inherit the promise. The Latin *adventus* is the translation of the Greek word *parousia*, commonly used in reference to the Second Coming of Christ. For Christians, the time of Advent serves as a reminder of the original waiting that was done by the Hebrews for the birth of

their messiah as well as our waiting for Christ's return.

The idea of two comings is highlighted in 1 Corinthians 16:22, which includes the Aramaic word *Maranatha*. This word is found in the early second-century document the *Didache*, which provides the order for the early Church in Syria. It has been transliterated into Greek letters rather than translated. Depending on how the last syllables are divided, *Maranatha* can hold different meanings. The syllables divided as "Maran-atha" mean "The Lord

has come" (an indicative statement looking to the past—it becomes a credal declaration); divided as "Marana-tha" it means "Come, O Lord" (an imperative statement looking to the future—it is a prayer for the early return of Christ). The imperative interpretation is supported by what appears to be a Greek equivalent of this acclamation in Revelation 22:20: "Amen! Come, Lord Jesus!"

Singing the word without break would beg the question whether one is declaring a past event or imploring a future one. The intentional ambiguity

It is truly right and just, our duty and our sal-va-tion, al-ways and everywhere to give you thanks, Lord, holy Father, almighty and e-ter-nal God, through Christ our Lord. For he assumed at his first coming the lowliness of hu-man flesh, and so fulfilled the design you formed long a-go, and opened for us the way to e-ter-nal sal-va-tion, that, when he comes again in glo-ry and maj-es-ty and all is at last made man-i-fest, we who watch for that day may inherit the great promise in which now we dare to hope. And so, with Angels and Archangels, with Thrones and Do-min-ions, and with all the hosts and Pow-ers of heav-en, we sing the hymn of your glo-ry, as without end we ac-claim:

Holy, Holy, Holy Lord God of hosts . . .

Sing this proclamation cursively in a reciting tone. In **salvation**, do not hold **-va**; only broaden the two notes slightly. The last syllable, **-tion**, should be held. **Always** and **everywhere** require a slight broadening and clear enunciation. The accent of the phrase falls on **thanks**, which should be held briefly. In the next sentence, clearly make distinct phrases of the text, by respecting the commas.

Sing the first two phrases together, with a break at **coming**. Pause briefly at **flesh**, **ago**, **-tion** of **salvation**, taking a breath after salvation. Keep the next two phrases together, without a breath after **majesty**, but with a slight hold on **-ty**. Hold **-fest** of **manifest**. In the next phrase, slow **for that day** and place the accent on the last word there, but do not take a break, for the sense calls for going right on to **may inherit**. Broaden the last words **we dare to hope**.

In the concluding phrase, make a slight pause after **And so**. Respect the commas but try to keep this section together, without big breaks for breaths. Broaden the last phrase, especially on **glory**. Slow **we ac-**, and put emphasis on **-claim**, so as to evoke the response of **Holy, Holy, Holy** . . . .

makes this word so appropriate for the time of Advent, when we are recalling a double *adventus*—the coming of Jesus two thousand years ago and a future coming as he promised.

The phrase *Maranatha* may have been a greeting among early Christians, and it is possible that Saint Paul used the word in this way.

Two of the Memorial Acclamations pick up on this theme that Christ has come and will come again:

We proclaim your Death, O Lord, and profess your Resurrection until you come again.

When we eat this Bread and drink this Cup, we proclaim your Death, O Lord, until you come again.

The two comings of Jesus also suggest that, in the interim period between the first and final coming, Christ comes to us collectively and individually. For this reason, the focus of Advent is not simply on the nativity of Jesus in history but also on the many comings or advents, throughout history. The Church, therefore, is gathered in this eschatological advent between the two comings. This Preface, with its double focus, is equally divided.

Early Christians expected Jesus to return within a generation of his Death. When the Second Coming did not occur, the early Christian communities were thrown into turmoil and the Second Coming was reinterpreted to an indefinite future time.

PREFACE II OF ADVENT

The twofold expectation of Christ

34.   The following Preface is said in Masses of Advent from December 17 to December 24 and in other Masses that are celebrated in Advent and have no proper Preface.

V. The Lord be with you.   R. And with your spir-it.

V. Lift up your hearts.   R. We lift them up to the Lord.

V. Let us give thanks to the Lord our God.   R. It is right and just.

Bring out the accent on **be** in **The Lord be with you**.

It is truly right and just, our duty and our salvation,
always and everywhere to give you thanks,
Lord, holy Father, almighty and eternal God,
through Christ our Lord.

Make a strong accent on **Lift**, and slow both notes of **hearts**.

In the third dialogue, move to the word **thanks** before accenting, and hold that word slightly to give it emphasis. Broaden both notes of **Lord**, and hold **God**.

For all the oracles of the prophets foretold him,
the Virgin Mother longed for him
with love beyond all telling,
John the Baptist sang of his coming
and proclaimed his presence when he came.

Emphasize the four verbs **foretold**, **longed**, **sang**, and **proclaimed**.

It is by his gift that already we rejoice
at the mystery of his Nativity,
so that he may find us watchful in prayer
and exultant in his praise.

Emphasize what we are doing: **rejoicing, remaining watchful in prayer** and **exulting**.

And so, with Angels and Archangels,
with Thrones and Dominions,
and with all the hosts and Powers of heaven,
we sing the hymn of your glory,
as without end we acclaim:

Holy, Holy, Holy Lord God of hosts . . .

34. Preface II of Advent: The twofold expectation of Christ is prayed the last week of Advent, from December 17 to 24. This is the time that the O Antiphons make their appearance in the Liturgy of the Hours as the antiphon that accompanies the Magnificat at Evening Prayer. As with the O Antiphons, this Preface insists upon Jesus as the fulfillment of the prophets that culminated with John the Baptist.

Each day during this week a foretold title for Jesus becomes the focus of the Liturgy of the Hours. If one starts with the last title and takes the first letter of each one—*Emmanuel* (God-with-us), *Rex* (king), *Oriens* (dayspring), *Clavis* (key), *Radix* (root), *Adonai* (Lord), *Sapientia* (wisdom)—the Latin words *ero cras* are formed, meaning, "Tomorrow, I will come." Therefore, Jesus, whose coming Christians have prepared for in Advent and whom they have addressed in these seven messianic titles, now speaks to them: "Tomorrow, I will come." The O Antiphons, then, not only bring intensity to Advent preparation, but also bring it to a joyful conclusion.

The title of "O Come, O Come, Emmanuel," the Advent carol associated with these antiphons, is based upon the last of the O Antiphons. Technically, this hymn should be reserved for the last week of Advent, but it has become almost synonymous with the entire season. Each verse culminates with the line "Rejoice! Rejoice! Emmanuel shall come to you, O Israel." Thus, the attitude of those awaiting the Lord is one of rejoicing.

Advent has been punctuated by Gaudete or Rejoice Sunday (third Sunday),

It is truly right and just, our duty and our sal-va-tion, al-ways and everywhere to give you thanks, Lord, holy Father, almighty and e-ter-nal God, through Christ our Lord. For all the oracles of the proph-ets fore-told him, the Virgin Mother longed for him with love be-yond all tell-ing, John the Baptist sang of his com-ing and proclaimed his pres-ence when he came. It is by his gift that already we rejoice at the mystery of his Na-tiv-i-ty, so that he may find us watch-ful in prayer and ex-ult-ant in his praise. And so, with Angels and Archangels, with Thrones and Do-min-ions, and with all the hosts and Pow-ers of heav-en, we sing the hymn of your glo-ry, as without end we ac-claim:

Holy, Holy, Holy Lord God of hosts . . .

Sing this proclamation cursively in a reciting tone. In **salvation**, do not hold **-va**; only broaden the two notes slightly. The last syllable, **-tion**, should be held. **Always** and **everywhere** require a slight broadening and clear enunciation. The accent of the phrase falls on **thanks**, which should be held briefly. In the next sentence, clearly make distinct phrases of the text, by respecting the commas.

The body of the first sentence has three clauses, so even if **him** and **telling** are slightly lengthened, continue the movement until **came** (which should be held). In the next phrase, enunciate carefully **gift**. Briefly hold on **-ty** of **Nativity**, since the sentence calls for going on to **so that**. Hold **prayer** but do not take a breath or break. As always, broaden the last syllables, in this case, **-tant in his praise**.

In the concluding phrase, make a slight pause after **And so**. Respect the commas but try to keep this section together, without big breaks for breaths. Broaden the last phrase, especially on **glory**. Slow **we ac-**, and put emphasis on **-claim**, so as to evoke the response of **Holy, Holy, Holy** . . . .

due to the Second Reading in Years B and C and to the Introit that begins with *Gaudete in Domino semper* ("Rejoice in the Lord always"). Rose-colored vestments allowed on this day mark special joyfulness. Gaudete Sunday and the hymn "O Come, O Come Emmanuel" are reminders of why Advent is called a season of joyful expectation. It should not be regarded as a mini-Lent, even though violet is the liturgical color. Vestments are sometimes available in contrasting shades of blue violet and red violet to distinguish between Advent and

Lent that help avoid the confusion between these two liturgical times.

Our joy, though, is moderated and interiorized since it is not complete until Christmas. The *General Instruction of the Roman Missal* (GIRM) addresses this regarding use of the music and flowers: "In Advent the use of the organ and other musical instruments as well as flowers should be marked by a moderation suited to the character of this time of year, without expressing in anticipation the full joy

of the Nativity of the Lord" (See GIRM, 310 and 313).

Following the principle of progressive solemnity, we gauge our joy as we move steadily toward the Solemnity of the Nativity of the Lord. Using a musical term, we might say that Advent is a gradual crescendo leading to Christmas. The two liturgical periods should seem to be connected. The mood of the season is captured in the expressions: rejoice at the mystery, watchful in prayer, and exultant in his praise.

PREFACE I OF THE NATIVITY OF THE LORD

Christ the Light

35. The following Preface is said in Masses of the Nativity of the Lord and of its Octave Day, and within the Octave, even in Masses that otherwise might have a proper Preface, with the exception of Masses that have a proper Preface concerning the divine mysteries or divine Persons. It is also used on weekdays of Christmas Time.

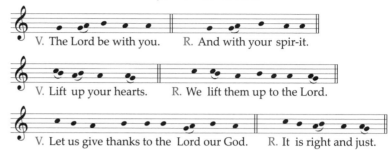

V. The Lord be with you.   R. And with your spir-it.

V. Lift up your hearts.   R. We lift them up to the Lord.

V. Let us give thanks to the Lord our God.   R. It is right and just.

Bring out the accent on **be** in **The Lord be with you**.

Make a strong accent on **Lift**, and slow both notes of **hearts**.

In the third dialogue, move to the word **thanks** before accenting, and hold that word slightly to give it emphasis. Broaden both notes of **Lord**, and hold **God**.

Emphasize **Word made flesh** and **new light of your glory**. Draw out the binary contrast between **God made visible** and **things invisible**.

It is truly right and just, our duty and our salvation,
always and everywhere to give you thanks,
Lord, holy Father, almighty and eternal God.

For in the mystery of the Word made flesh
a new light of your glory has shone upon the eyes of our mind,
so that, as we recognize in him God made visible,
we may be caught up through him in love of things invisible.

And so, with Angels and Archangels,
with Thrones and Dominions,
and with all the hosts and Powers of heaven,
we sing the hymn of your glory,
as without end we acclaim:

Holy, Holy, Holy Lord God of hosts . . .

When the Roman Canon is used, there is a proper **Communicantes**, p. 637. At the Vigil Mass and the Mass during the Night of the Nativity of the Lord: **Celebrating the most sacred night**, etc., is said, while **Celebrating the most sacred day**, etc., is then said throughout the Octave of the Nativity of the Lord.

35. Preface I of the Nativity of the Lord: Christ the Light is the first of three Prefaces for the Nativity of the Lord. All three Prefaces are intended for Christmas Eve and Day and the Octave of Christmas, unless there is a feast with its proper Preface, such as the Solemnity of Mary, the Holy Mother of God.

The Preface seeks to proclaim the Incarnation of God's Word with the central imagery of light or radiance. It is obvious here that radiance cannot be perceived by bodily eyes but only by eyes of faith.

Apparent, too, is that light, seeing, and perceiving lead to love. In other words, "seeing" evokes our love.

The key to the Preface is that "we recognize in him God made visible" the means by which "we may be caught up in love of things invisible." The binary contrasts (between "visible" and "invisible" and "in him" and "through him") are within the lines that contain the key words of the Preface. Prior to those lines, the phrase "upon the eyes of our mind" indicates the Roman character of this Preface.

The author of this ancient Preface is unknown, but it is thought that it may have been written by Pope Leo the Great. In Leo the Great's first Christmas homily, we hear of how we were brought into God's light: "Christian, acknowledge your dignity, and becoming a partner in the Divine nature, refuse to return to the old baseness by degenerate conduct. Remember the Head and the Body of which you are a member. Recollect that you were rescued from the power of darkness and brought out into

It is truly right and just, our duty and our sal-va-tion, al-ways and everywhere to give you thanks, Lord, holy Father, almighty and e-ter-nal God. For in the mystery of the Word made flesh a new light of your glory has shone upon the eyes of our mind, so that, as we recognize in him God made vis-i-ble, we may be caught up through him in love of things in-vis-i-ble. And so, with Angels and Archangels, with Thrones and Do-min-ions, and with all the hosts and Pow-ers of heav-en, we sing the hymn of your glo-ry, as without end we ac-claim:

Holy, Holy, Holy Lord God of hosts . . .

Sing this proclamation cursively in a reciting tone. In **salvation**, do not hold **-va**; only broaden the two notes slightly. The last syllable, **-tion**, should be held. **Always** and **everywhere** require a slight broadening and clear enunciation. The accent of the phrase falls on **thanks**, which should be held briefly. In the next sentence, clearly make distinct phrases of the text, by respecting the commas.

Broaden **Word made flesh**, as it is the core of the Mystery celebrated today. Do not pause or breathe at **glory**, but continue the sentence to **mind**, at which point one may hold slightly and take a breath. Pause after **so that**. Slight hold on -**ble** of **visible**, so that the sense is retained by continuing on to **we may**. Broaden **of things invisible**.

In the concluding phrase, make a slight pause after **And so**. Respect the commas but try to keep this section together, without big breaks for breaths. Broaden the last phrase, especially on **glory**. Slow **we ac-**, and put emphasis on -**claim**, so as to evoke the response of **Holy, Holy, Holy** . . . .

God's light and kingdom" (Sermon 21.3). For Leo, the Incarnation has completely changed human existence. Christian joy is profoundly rooted in this mystery when the Lord comes to free us from sin and set us free. From this we can deduce that Leo's attention is not on the birth of a child, but the deeper meaning of the Incarnation—the Word made flesh. The theme of the Word becoming flesh, so characteristic of the Prologue of John's account of the Gospel, was interpreted theologically for its deeper sense. Tertullian, for example, states that the flesh is the hinge of our salvation (*caro cardis salutis*).

Christmas, therefore, is when we encounter Christ, and this encounter transforms us. The encounter is a sacramental one through the Church and the sacraments. Through these, God is made visible.

The emphasis on light also reminds those in the northern hemisphere that this is the darkest time of the year. The winter solstice, however, has just occurred and gradually, almost imperceptibly, the days will now get longer. The light has broken the back of darkness. The new light, Christ, shines in the darkness to dispel it. Those things cloaked in darkness now are made visible and we see with new eyes—the eyes of our mind.

The Gospel acclamation at the Mass during the Day proclaims this beautifully: "Come, you nations, and adore the Lord. / For today a great light has come upon the earth."

PREFACE II OF THE NATIVITY OF THE LORD

The restoration of all things in the Incarnation

36. The following Preface is said in Masses of the Nativity of the Lord and of its Octave Day, and within the Octave, even in Masses that otherwise might have a proper Preface, with the exception of Masses that have a proper Preface concerning the divine mysteries or divine Persons. It is also used on weekdays of Christmas Time.

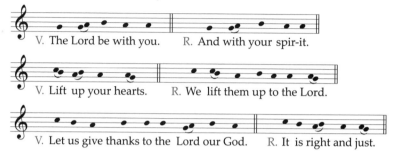

V. The Lord be with you.   R. And with your spir-it.

V. Lift up your hearts.   R. We lift them up to the Lord.

V. Let us give thanks to the Lord our God.   R. It is right and just.

It is truly right and just, our duty and our salvation,
always and everywhere to give you thanks,
Lord, holy Father, almighty and eternal God,
through Christ our Lord.

For on the feast of this awe-filled mystery,
though invisible in his own divine nature,
he has appeared visibly in ours;
and begotten before all ages,
he has begun to exist in time;
so that, raising up in himself all that was cast down,
he might restore unity to all creation
and call straying humanity back to the heavenly Kingdom.

And so, with all the Angels, we praise you,
as in joyful celebration we acclaim:

Holy, Holy, Holy Lord God of hosts . . .

When the Roman Canon is used, there is a proper **Communicantes**, p. 637. At the Vigil Mass and the Mass during the Night of the Nativity of the Lord: **Celebrating the most sacred night**, etc., is said, while **Celebrating the most sacred day**, etc., is then said throughout the Octave of the Nativity of the Lord.

Side notes (left margin):

Bring out the accent on **be** in **The Lord be with you**.

Make a strong accent on **Lift**, and slow both notes of **hearts**.

In the third dialogue, move to the word **thanks** before accenting, and hold that word slightly to give it emphasis. Broaden both notes of **Lord**, and hold **God**.

Emphasize **awe-filled mystery**.

Draw out the binary opposition between **invisible** and **visibly**.

The phrase **so that** introduces the result of restoring unity and calling back strayed humanity.

---

36. Preface II of the Nativity of the Lord: The restoration of all things in the Incarnation is the second of three Prefaces for Christmas. All three are intended for Christmas Eve and Day and the octave of Christmas, unless there is a feast with its proper Preface, such as the Solemnity of Mary, the Holy Mother of God.

This Preface, which follows classical prayer forms, was a new composition in the Missal of Paul VI. It was inspired by Leo the Great, Sermon 22.2: "In a new order, because being invisible in His own nature

He became visible in ours, and He whom nothing could contain, was content to be contained."

The key to the proclamation of Preface II of the Nativity of the Lord is to understand that God is being praised for the effect of the Incarnation in history.

The Preface revels in three binary oppositions. Lines two and thee indicate opposition between an invisible divine nature appearing visible in human nature. The second binary opposition is that the second person of the Trinity begins to exist

as the son of Mary. We see the third binary opposition between "raising up" and "all that was cast down, / he might restore unity to all creation." We see that Christ exalts humanity beyond its capabilities. The "cast down" refers to sin.

The phrase "in himself" shows that Christ restores humanity to their original innocence but also does so much more than that. Christ brings humanity into the interior life of the Trinity.

As Christ restores all things and calls back straying humanity, there is reconcilia-

It is truly right and just, our duty and our sal-va-tion, al-ways and everywhere to give you thanks, Lord, holy Father, almighty and e- -ter-nal God, through Christ our Lord. For on the feast of this awe- -filled mystery, though invisible in his own di-vine na-ture, he has appeared visi-bly in ours; and begotten be-fore all ag-es, he has begun to ex-ist in time; so that, raising up in himself all that was cast down, he might restore unity to all cre-a-tion and call stray-ing hu-man-i-ty back to the heav-en-ly King-dom. And so, with all the An-gels, we praise you, as in joyful cele- -bra-tion we ac-claim:

Holy, Holy, Holy Lord God of hosts . . .

Sing this proclamation cursively in a reciting tone. In **salvation**, do not hold **-va**; only broaden the two notes slightly. The last syllable, **-tion**, should be held. **Always** and **everywhere** require a slight broadening and clear enunciation. The accent of the phrase falls on **thanks**, which should be held briefly. In the next sentence, make distinct phrases of the text, by respecting the commas.

Articulate carefully **For** and **feast**. Similarly, articulate carefully **awe-filled mystery**, and pause slightly. Hold **-ture** of **nature** briefly, and continue with **he has**. A slight pause after **and**, in the next phrase, will help to communicate the meaning of the next two phrases, which contrast with one another. Any hold on **-es** of **ages** should be brief. Broaden **exist in time**. Pause after **so that**. The two phrases following **that** belong together, so hold **down** briefly. The last phrase belongs with the previous two, but is too long not to take a breath and break at **-tion** of **creation**. Make the break brief. Do not hold **-ty** of **humanity**. Broaden **heavenly Kingdom**.

In the concluding phrase, make a slight pause after **And so**. Respect the commas but try to keep this section together, without big breaks for breaths. Broaden the last phrase, especially on **praise**. Slow **we ac-**, and put emphasis on **-claim**, so as to evoke the response of **Holy, Holy, Holy . . . .**

tion with God, a major theme of the Preface. In Paul's letter to the Colossians, a rich theology of reconciliation as tied to the Incarnation is put forth: "For in him all the fullness was pleased to dwell, and through him to reconcile all things for him, making peace by the blood of his cross [through him], whether those on earth or those in heaven" (Colossians 1:19–20). Paul demonstrates that the ultimate meaning of the Incarnation, the Word becoming flesh, was to reconcile humanity who had strayed from God. This seems a bit odd for

the Solemnity of the Nativity, but it plumbs the theological depths of the meaning behind this salvific event.

This same theme about the reconciliatory dimension of Christmas is reflected in the two Eucharistic Prayers for Reconciliation: "and, though time and again we have broken your covenant, / you have bound the human family to yourself / through Jesus your Son, our Redeemer, / with a new love bond of love so tight / that it can never be undone" (Reconciliation I). Incarnation, therefore, is God bound to

humanity. And again, "He [Christ] himself is the Word that brings salvation, / the hand you extend to sinners, / the way by which your peace is offered to us. / When we ourselves had turned away from you / on account of our sins, / you brought us back to be reconciled, O Lord, / so that, converted at last to you, / we might love one another . . . . And now, celebrating the reconciliation / Christ has brought us . . . ." (Reconciliation II). This theme is rich and worthwhile to consider for preaching during Christmas Time.

PREFACE III OF THE NATIVITY OF THE LORD

The exchange in the Incarnation of the Word

37. The following Preface is said in Masses of the Nativity of the Lord and of its Octave Day, and within the Octave, even in Masses that otherwise might have a proper Preface, with the exception of Masses that have a proper Preface concerning the divine mysteries or divine Persons. It is also used on weekdays of Christmas Time.

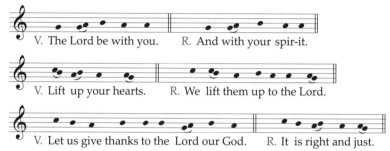

V. The Lord be with you.   R. And with your spir-it.

V. Lift up your hearts.   R. We lift them up to the Lord.

V. Let us give thanks to the Lord our God.   R. It is right and just.

Bring out the accent on **be** in **The Lord be with you**.

Make a strong accent on **Lift**, and slow both notes of **hearts**.

In the third dialogue, move to the word **thanks** before accenting, and hold that word slightly to give it emphasis. Broaden both notes of **Lord**, and hold **God**.

I t is truly right and just, our duty and our salvation,
always and everywhere to give you thanks,
Lord, holy Father, almighty and eternal God,
through Christ our Lord.

Emphasize **holy exchange**, **splendor**, and **wondrous union**.

For through him the holy exchange that restores our life
has shone forth today in splendor:
when our frailty is assumed by your Word

Play on the contrast of
not only . . . but.

not only does human mortality receive unending honor
but by this wondrous union we, too, are made eternal.

And so, in company with the choirs of Angels,
we praise you, and with joy we proclaim:

Holy, Holy, Holy Lord God of hosts . . .

When the Roman Canon is used, there is a proper **Communicantes**, p. 637. At the Vigil Mass and the Mass during the Night of the Nativity of the Lord: **Celebrating the most sacred night**, etc., is said, while **Celebrating the most sacred day**, etc., is then said throughout the Octave of the Nativity of the Lord.

---

37. Preface III of the Nativity of the Lord: The exchange in the Incarnation of the Word is the third of three Prefaces for Christmas. All three are intended for Christmas Eve and Day and the octave of Christmas, unless there is a feast with its proper Preface, such as the Solemnity of Mary, the Holy Mother of God, or the Feast of the Holy Family.

In this Preface, the central image is the *sacrum commercium*, the holy exchange. In the holy exchange of gifts, sinful humanity is granted restorative transformative divin-

ity. We offer our frailty, which is assumed by the Word of God. Now everything we are is transformed, illumined by the Word. Through this transformation and illumination, we are made eternal. This transformation goes far beyond restoring our humanity.

The mystery of the Incarnation is a wonderful exchange between divinity and humanity. The early Church explored this idea deeply in the notion of *sacrum commercium*. The antiphon for first vespers of the octave of Christmas picks up this theme beautifully: "O admirable exchange,"

we sing, "the Creator of the human race, taking upon Himself a body and a soul, has vouchsafed to be born of a Virgin, and, appearing here below as man, has made us partakers of His Divinity."

In the East this concept is called *theosis*, which in the West we simply call divinization. The idea might seem strange to us at first, that God became human so that humans might become gods. Saint Athanasius, in his sermon "On the Incarnation" 54:3, expressed this idea

It is truly right and just, our duty and our sal-va-tion, al-ways and everywhere to give you thanks, Lord, holy Father, almighty and e-ter-nal God, through Christ our Lord. For through him the holy exchange that re-stores our life has shone forth to-day in splen-dor: when our frailty is as-sumed by your Word not only does human mortality receive un-end-ing hon-or but by this won-drous un-ion we, too, are made e-ter-nal. And so, in company with the choirs of An-gels, we praise you, and with joy we pro-claim:

Holy, Holy, Holy Lord God of hosts . . .

Sing this proclamation cursively in a reciting tone. In **salvation**, do not hold **-va**; only broaden the two notes slightly. The last syllable, **-tion**, should be held. **Always** and **everywhere** require a slight broadening and clear enunciation. The accent of the phrase falls on **thanks**, which should be held briefly. In the next sentence, clearly make distinct phrases of the text, by respecting the commas.

Try to accent **him** in the first phrase, even if the music lends itself to accenting **through**. Articulate **life** carefully but do not hold it, but then continue to **has shone** to keep the sense line clear. Make a slight hold on **Word** in the next phrase. The next two long phrases are to be kept together as best one can, with only a slight hold on **-or** of **honor** and **-ion** of **union**. Broaden **are made eternal**.

In the concluding phrase, make a slight pause after **And so**. Respect the commas but try to keep this section together, without big breaks for breaths. Broaden the last phrase, especially on **praise**. Slow **we ac-**, and put emphasis on **-claim**, so as to evoke the response of **Holy, Holy, Holy . . . .**

clearly. The early Church had many battles with those who denied Jesus' divinity. Because they defended his divinity, they had the chance to meditate on what it means for the Logos to become flesh. One of the great riches that came from their meditations was the teaching that God became human so that humans could become divine. Of course, this process of divinization is not of our own doing. Rather, God takes the initiative and we simply respond by living lives that reflect the splendor of God.

We find the same idea expressed in the commingling of water with wine at the Preparation of the Gifts in reference to Christ, who humbled himself to share in our humanity so that we might share in his divinity.

Pope John Paul II expresses this idea in the encyclical *Veritatis Splendor,* in which he sees the splendor of truth that shines forth in all the works of the Creator and, in a special way, in humanity, created in the image and likeness of God. Truth enlightens human intelligence and shapes human freedom, leading humanity to know and love the Lord; hence, the psalmist prays: "LORD, show us the light of your face!" (Psalm 4:7). Human existence restored by this divine exchange achieves wondrous union with God. By the mystery of the Incarnation, we are made eternal, even in our frailty as mere mortals. This is the great mystery that we celebrate when the Word became flesh.

PREFACE OF THE EPIPHANY OF THE LORD

Christ the light of the nations

38. The following Preface is said in Masses of the Solemnity of the Epiphany. This Preface, or one of the Prefaces of the Nativity, may be said even on days after the Epiphany up to the Saturday that precedes the Feast of the Baptism of the Lord.

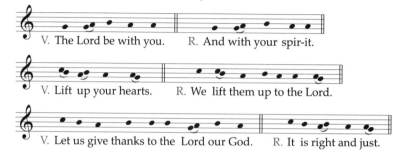

V. The Lord be with you.   R. And with your spir-it.

V. Lift up your hearts.   R. We lift them up to the Lord.

V. Let us give thanks to the Lord our God.   R. It is right and just.

Bring out the accent on **be** in **The Lord be with you.**

Make a strong accent on **Lift**, and slow both notes of **hearts.**

In the third dialogue, move to the word **thanks** before accenting, and hold that word slightly to give it emphasis. Broaden both notes of **Lord**, and hold **God.**

It is truly right and just, our duty and our salvation,
always and everywhere to give you thanks,
Lord, holy Father, almighty and eternal God.

For today you have revealed the mystery
of our salvation in Christ
as a light for the nations,
and, when he appeared in our mortal nature,
you made us new by the glory of his immortal nature.

And so, with Angels and Archangels,
with Thrones and Dominions,
and with all the hosts and Powers of heaven,
we sing the hymn of your glory,
as without end we acclaim:

Holy, Holy, Holy Lord God of hosts . . .

When the Roman Canon is used on the Solemnity of the Epiphany, there is a proper *Communicantes*, p. 637.

Emphasize **today**, **mystery**, and **light for the nations.**

Contrast the difference between **today** and **when he appeared** to emphasize the ongoing nature of Epiphany. Contrast **mortal** and **immortal.**

38. The key to the **Preface of the Epiphany of the Lord: Christ the light of the nations** is that Christ is revealed to the Gentiles. The implications of the light that was shining for the Jewish people in Preface I of the Nativity of the Lord is explicitly extended to the Gentiles.

Like many of the Collects and Antiphons, the Preface uses the word "today" (*hodie*), insisting upon the "eternal today" of the liturgy. Rather than thinking of this feast as a commemoration of a his-torical event, it is the celebration of God's continuous presence throughout history.

Our mortal and immortal natures are contrasted in the Preface. Christ appears in our mortal nature. That is irradiated by his immortal nature.

"Epiphany" means "manifestation" or "shining forth," and its significance is as real to us as it was to those who saw Jesus in the flesh. The epiphany of Christ takes place for us, not by a miraculous sight "out there" to be seen by those who happen to be present, but by an interior insight, which is possible for all but demands the willingness to see. Epiphany, like insight, is a kind of seeing in a new way. Thus, our lives are, in fact, full of epiphanies. The "star" that points to Christ shines in the minds and hearts of those who refuse to take life for granted but who wonder and marvel and seek love and meaning, and are willing to journey afar to find it.

In the history of the Church's liturgy, the Epiphany has referred to numerous

It is truly right and just, our duty and our sal-va-tion, al-ways and everywhere to give you thanks, Lord, holy Father, almighty and e-ter-nal God. For today you have revealed the mystery of our salva-tion in Christ as a light for the na-tions, and, when he appeared in our mor-tal na-ture, you made us new by the glory of his im-mor-tal na-ture. And so, with Angels and Archangels, with Thrones and Do-min-ions, and with all the hosts and Pow-ers of heav-en, we sing the hymn of your glo-ry, as without end we ac-claim:

Holy, Holy, Holy Lord God of hosts . . .

Sing this proclamation cursively in a reciting tone. In **salvation**, do not hold **-va**; only broaden the two notes slightly. The last syllable, **-tion**, should be held. **Always** and **everywhere** require a slight broadening and clear enunciation. The accent of the phrase falls on **thanks**, which should be held briefly. In the next sentence, clearly make distinct phrases of the text, by respecting the commas.

Articulate carefully **Christ**, but continue without a break to **as a light**, pausing and breathing only after **nations**. Take only a brief hold at **-ture** of **nature**, so as to continue the sense with **you made**. It would be good to extend slightly **new** for the sake of accenting it. Broaden the last two words **immortal nature**.

In the concluding phrase, make a slight pause after **And so**. Respect the commas but try to keep this section together, without big breaks for breaths. Broaden the last phrase, especially on **glory**. Slow **we ac-**, and put emphasis on **-claim**, so as to evoke the response of **Holy, Holy, Holy** . . . .

manifestations of God. The liturgy reflects three such in the threefold miracle (*Tribus Miraculis)*. An ancient antiphon that accompanied the Magnificat at Epiphany vespers speaks to multiple epiphanies in the New Testament. In the liturgical tradition, Epiphany celebrates the presentation to the Magi, the baptism of the Lord, and the wedding feast at Cana—all are sorts of epiphanies. It used to be that all three events were evoked on the one Feast of the Epiphany, but today we celebrate them

separately and in serial order. For this reason, it would be appropriate to think of the Sunday of the Baptism of the Lord as the Second Sunday of Epiphany and the Sunday when we hear the Gospel about the wedding feast of Cana as the Third Sunday of Epiphany.

Through these events, Epiphany is explored in all its fullness and not restricted to a single event in the life of Christ or the Church. These events, too, point to the fact that epiphanies happen all around us all

the time. To the degree that we have eyes, we have the possibility of seeing the manifestation of God around us.

Saint Augustine and the Venerable Bede add a fourth miracle (the multiplication of the loaves and fishes) to the Epiphany, and the Mozarabic Rite adds a fifth, a renewed commemoration of the Nativity of the Lord. In all cases, the miracles are considered manifestations of the divine saving power of Christ.

PREFACE I OF LENT

The spiritual meaning of Lent

39.   The following Preface is said in Masses of Lent, especially on Sundays when a more specific Preface is not prescribed.

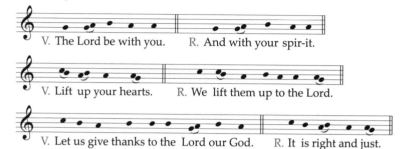

V. The Lord be with you.   R. And with your spir-it.

V. Lift up your hearts.   R. We lift them up to the Lord.

V. Let us give thanks to the Lord our God.   R. It is right and just.

Bring out the accent on **be** in **The Lord be with you**.

It is truly right and just, our duty and our salvation,
always and everywhere to give you thanks,
Lord, holy Father, almighty and eternal God,
through Christ our Lord.

Make a strong accent on **Lift**, and slow both notes of **hearts**.

In the third dialogue, move to the word **thanks** before accenting, and hold that word slightly to give it emphasis. Broaden both notes of **Lord**, and hold **God**.

For by your gracious gift each year
your faithful await the sacred paschal feasts
with the joy of minds made pure,
so that, more eagerly intent on prayer
and on the works of charity,
and participating in the mysteries
by which they have been reborn,
they may be led to the fullness of grace
that you bestow on your sons and daughters.

Emphasize **each year** and **sacred paschal feasts**. The expected result is increased prayer and works of charity. (Elsewhere, we will find the third member of the trilogy; namely, fasting.)

Emphasize **reborn** as a reference to Baptism.

And so, with Angels and Archangels,
with Thrones and Dominions,
and with all the hosts and Powers of heaven,
we sing the hymn of your glory,
as without end we acclaim:

Holy, Holy, Holy Lord God of hosts . . .

39. Preface I of Lent: The spiritual meaning of Lent is a statement of the 40 days of Lent as a preparation for the Paschal feast. This period of preparation is presented in the first line as a "gift." That Lent is both a gift and time of joy is a far different approach than many have for this period.

This powerful Preface makes it clear that during Lent the faithful prepare for the Paschal feast through works of charity and prayer that will become normative in their lives.

The principle ideas behind this Preface are announced in the Gospel for Ash Wednesday, which call us to pray, to fast, and to give alms, meaning to engage in acts of charity. The Preface references two of these three tasks assigned to all the baptized. But it also expresses the hope of Christians, that we do these things in order to be reborn and to be led to the fullness of grace.

The phrase "the mysteries / by which they have been reborn" points us toward those who are part of the Rite of Christian

Initiation of Adults and will come into the Church at the Easter Vigil.

Although the number 40 is not explicitly mentioned, the reference to God's gracious gift, which leads us to the Paschal feasts infers the period of 40 days.

According to the scriptures, 40 is the number of the waiting, the preparation, the test, or the punishment. The Bible often resorts to the number 40 when a new chapter of the history of salvation begins. Forty also would indicate the dura-

It is truly right and just, our duty and our sal-va-tion, al-ways and everywhere to give you thanks, Lord, holy Father, almighty and e- -ter-nal God, through Christ our Lord. For by your gracious gift each year your faithful await the sacred pas-chal feasts with the joy of minds made pure, so that, more eagerly in-tent on prayer and on the works of char-i-ty, and participating in the mysteries by which they have been re-born, they may be led to the full-ness of grace that you bestow on your sons and daugh-ters. And so, with Angels and Archangels, with Thrones and Do-min-ions, and with all the hosts and Pow-ers of heav-en, we sing the hymn of your glo-ry, as without end we ac-claim:

Holy, Holy, Holy Lord God of hosts . . .

Sing this proclamation cursively in a reciting tone. In **salvation**, do not hold -**va**; only broaden the two notes slightly. The last syllable, -**tion**, should be held. **Always** and **every-where** require a slight broadening and clear enunciation. The accent of the phrase falls on **thanks**, which should be held briefly. In the next sentence, clearly make distinct phrases of the text, by respecting the commas.

If possible, sing the phrases from the beginning, **For by your** through **made pure** with one breath. Make a slight hold on **year** and **feasts**, and, of course, on **pure** at the end of the sense line. Make a slight hold on **that**. Hold **prayer**, but do not breathe there. Hold -**ty** of **charity**, and there take a breath. Connect **mysteries** and **by which** without holding or pausing. Hold -**born** of **reborn** just slightly, and take a very quick breath. Then, without breaking the sense, continue with **they**. Hold **grace**, but do not breathe there; rather, continue with **that you**. Broaden and slow **your sons and daughters**.

In the concluding phrase, make a slight pause after **And so**. Respect the commas but try to keep this section together, without big breaks for breaths. Broaden the last phrase, especially on **glory**. Slow **we ac-**, and put emphasis on -**claim**, so as to evoke the response of **Holy, Holy, Holy . . . .**

tion of a generation or a long period, the exact length we ignore.

As a period of preparation, we find Christ in the desert for 40 days, a time in which he is preparing for his public ministry. Noah remains in the ark for 40 days in preparation for a new creation and a second chance after the fall. The Israelites wander in the desert with Moses for 40 years as they prepare to enter the Promised Land.

The number 40 is a recurring leitmotif in speaking about Moses: He was 40 years old when he was called by God; he kept the herd of Jethro for 40 years; he resided finally 40 days and 40 nights to the summit of Mount Sinai before receiving the Tables of the Law (Exodus 24:18). Elijah walked 40 days before reaching Mount Horeb. He fasted during 40 days before beginning his public ministry, and he remained 40 days on Mount Carmel (1 Kings 19:8). In all these cases, 40 is synonymous with a time of grace and a gift from God.

The 40 days of Lent give way to the 50 days of Easter. Fifty also is a highly symbolic number. In the Hebraic religion a jubilee has a duration of 50 years, during which a year had to be devoted to God and to rest. The feast of Pentecost was celebrated by the Jewish people 50 days after the Passover as a time of joy and feasting.

This Preface can be prayed on any Sunday during Lent not assigned a Preface.

PREFACE II OF LENT

Spiritual penance

40.   The following Preface is said in Masses of Lent, especially on Sundays when a more specific Preface is not prescribed.

V. The Lord be with you.   R. And with your spir-it.

V. Lift up your hearts.   R. We lift them up to the Lord.

V. Let us give thanks to the Lord our God.   R. It is right and just.

It is truly right and just, our duty and our salvation,
always and everywhere to give you thanks,
Lord, holy Father, almighty and eternal God.

For you have given your children a sacred time
for the renewing and purifying of their hearts,
that, freed from disordered affections,
they may so deal with the things of this passing world
as to hold rather to the things that eternally endure.

And so, with all the Angels and Saints,
we praise you, as without end we acclaim:

Holy, Holy, Holy Lord God of hosts . . .

Bring out the accent on **be** in **The Lord be with you**.

Make a strong accent on **Lift**, and slow both notes of **hearts**.

In the third dialogue, move to the word **thanks** before accenting, and hold that word slightly to give it emphasis. Broaden both notes of **Lord**, and hold **God**.

Emphasize **sacred time**, **renewing**, and **purifying**.

Contrast **passing world** with **things that eternally endure**.

40. Preface II of Lent: Spiritual penance is similar to Preface I of Lent but without the complexity. This Preface, though, does not mention almsgiving, prayer, or fasting. It speaks of this liturgical time as given to God's children "for the renewing and purifying of their hearts."

The binary opposition is seen in the phrases "the things of this passing world" and "the things that eternally endure." Notice that the prayer states to "deal with the things of this passing world." We are not asked to despise what is in this world; rather,

we are to deal with what is temporal. We are to deal with it with the perspective of "the things that eternally endure." As Christians, we know that the eternal is part of our lives. It is from that vantage point that we are to deal with "this passing world." Thus, we might say this in another way: Let us live in this changing world with our eyes fixed on a world that will never change.

Two themes emerge as central to this Preface: God gives us a sacred time, and this time is for the renewal of our hearts. Although the number 40 is not explicitly

mentioned, reference is made to sacred time as God's gift to us.

Continuing the reflection on sacred time from Preface I of Lent, we look to Saint Augustine's commentary on the Ten Commandments. He notes the number 40 holds the perfection of the Law, and the Law is not fulfilled except in the double commandment of love. As the whole world is composed of four parts, multiplying 10 by 4, yields 40. It is by the four accounts of the Gospel that the Law is accomplished.

It is truly right and just, our duty and our sal-va-tion, al-ways and everywhere to give you thanks, Lord, holy Father, almighty and e-ter-nal God. For you have given your children a sa-cred time for the renewing and puri-fy-ing of their hearts, that, freed from dis-or-dered af-fec-tions, they may so deal with the things of this pass-ing world as to hold rather to the things that e-ter-nal-ly en-dure. And so, with all the An-gels and Saints, we praise you, as without end we ac-claim:

Holy, Holy, Holy Lord God of hosts . . .

Sing this proclamation cursively in a reciting tone. In **salvation**, do not hold **-va**; only broaden the two notes slightly. The last syllable, **-tion**, should be held. **Always** and **everywhere** require a slight broadening and clear enunciation. The accent of the phrase falls on **thanks**, which should be held briefly. In the next sentence, clearly make distinct phrases of the text, by respecting the commas.

If at all possible, do not hold **time** or breathe there, at the end of the first phrase, but instead continue the sense by going right on to **for the**. Hold **hearts** and take a breath. Hold **-tions** of **affections**, and take a quick breath there, so that the sense of continuing with **they may** is clear. Hold **world**, but do not breathe (if possible), but rather continue with **as to**. Slow and broaden **eternally endure**.

In the concluding phrase, make a slight pause after **And so**. Respect the commas but try to keep this section together, without big breaks for breaths. Broaden the last phrase, especially on **praise**. Slow **we ac-**, and put emphasis on **-claim**, so as to evoke the response of **Holy, Holy, Holy . . . .**

Therefore, the period of 40 days of Lent is a time to renew and purify our hearts for the double commandment of love.

The theme of purification of hearts is central to one of the seven penitential Psalms; namely, number 50 (using the Septuagint numbering; or 51, using the Masoretic numbering)—known as the *Miserere*. Cassiodorus († ca. 580) is the first commentator to single out Psalms 6, 31, 37, 50, 101, 129, and 142 as being specifically penitential. In his concluding remarks on Psalm 50, he delineates the seven Psalms by number and extracts a line or two directly from each.

Psalm 50, however, is particularly important in Lent because it challenges us to pray to God to turn our hearts of stone into hearts of flesh. It is associated with Ash Wednesday as the Responsorial Psalm. In the Roman Catholic Church, a priest may assign this Psalm to a penitent as a penance after confession. Verse 7 of the Psalm is traditionally sung during the sprinkling rite outside of Easter Time, in what is known as the *"Asperges me,"* the first two words of the verse in Latin. It also is prayed during Morning Prayer every Friday in the Liturgy of the Hours.

Particularly relevant in the face of this Preface is Psalm 51:12: "A clean heart create for me, God; renew in me a steadfast spirit." The Preface reiterates this praying for the renewal and purification of hearts.

PREFACE III OF LENT

The fruits of abstinence

41.   The following Preface is said in Masses of the weekdays of Lent and on days of fasting.

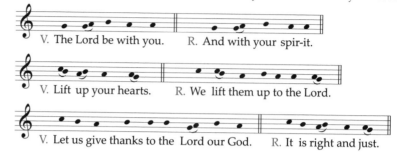

V. The Lord be with you.   R. And with your spir-it.

V. Lift up your hearts.   R. We lift them up to the Lord.

V. Let us give thanks to the Lord our God.   R. It is right and just.

It is truly right and just, our duty and our salvation,
always and everywhere to give you thanks,
Lord, holy Father, almighty and eternal God.

For you will that our self-denial should give you thanks,
humble our sinful pride,
contribute to the feeding of the poor,
and so help us imitate you in your kindness.

And so we glorify you with countless Angels,
as with one voice of praise we acclaim:

Holy, Holy, Holy Lord God of hosts . . .

Bring out the accent on **be** in **The Lord be with you.**

Make a strong accent on **Lift**, and slow both notes of **hearts.**

In the third dialogue, move to the word **thanks** before accenting, and hold that word slightly to give it emphasis. Broaden both notes of **Lord**, and hold **God.**

Emphasize three things willed by God: **that our self-denial should give [God] thanks, [should] humble our sinful pride,** and **[should] help us imitate [God] in [his] kindness.**

---

41. Preface III of Lent: The fruits of abstinence is stunning! The prayer is brief and concise and yet presents four reasons why we engage in self-denial and mortification. The first reason, for the practice of abstinence, is to give God thanks. Self-denial, we can see here, has little to do with us but everything to do with God. Second, self-denial helps us let go of things that we use to build ourselves up and helps us understand that we are not the source of our virtue. Self-denial makes us aware that everything that we have is pure gift and

can lead to acts of thanks. Third, self-denial can lead to the feeding of the poor. Instead of turning us inward, abstinence helps us to look outward to the needs of others. Finally, self-denial will helps us imitate God's kindness. If we are seeking to act as God does, we will perform our acts of kindness as God does, whose reign falls on the just and the unjust. We will not be concerned that our kindness is to the "deserving poor." We will be kind to the poor.

Self-denial does not consist in either doing or omitting anything from selfish

motives. It is impossible to deny self for selfish reasons. It is absurd to talk of denying self to promote self-interest; for this is not self-denial but is only denying self in one respect for the sake of gratifying self in another respect. In those instances, self is, after all, at the bottom. And self-interest is the grand reason of every change of this kind.

Self-denial implies the joyful giving up that opens us to giving for the sake of love, for the purpose of doing a greater good to others. For an example, let us con-

It is truly right and just, our duty and our sal-va-tion, al-ways and everywhere to give you thanks, Lord, holy Father, almighty and e-ter-nal God. For you will that our self-denial should give you thanks, hum-ble our sin-ful pride, contribute to the feeding of the poor, and so help us imitate you in your kind-ness. And so we glorify you with count-less An-gels, as with one voice of praise we ac-claim:

Holy, Holy, Holy Lord God of hosts . . .

Sing this proclamation cursively in a reciting tone. In **salvation**, do not hold **-va**; only broaden the two notes slightly. The last syllable, **-tion**, should be held. **Always** and **everywhere** require a slight broadening and clear enunciation. The accent of the phrase falls on **thanks**, which should be held briefly. In the next sentence, clearly make distinct phrases of the text, by respecting the commas.

By careful articulation, bring out **will** in the first phrase as a verb. Hold slightly **thanks**, and take a quick breath there. Do the same with **pride**. Hold **poor** slightly, but do not breathe there, but continue with **And so**. Accent slightly **help**. Slow and broaden the last four syllables, holding **-ness** of **kindness**.

In the concluding phrase, make a slight pause after **And so**. Respect the commas but try to keep this section together, without big breaks for breaths. Broaden the last phrase, especially on **praise**. Slow **we ac-**, and put emphasis on **-claim**, so as to evoke the response of **Holy, Holy, Holy . . . .**

sider a person who has been to the bakery and purchased a loaf of bread for supper. This person has labored hard, and really needs the bread. But in passing a miserable habitation of poverty, a little, pale, emaciated child stands at the door, and, stretching out little beggar hands, asks for bread. The person is induced to enter this abode of wretchedness, and finds a widowed mother, sick and famishing, surrounded with her starving babes. The person who bought the bread is hungry, but they are starving. The person with the bread has no more money, and if the bread is given, there will be no supper. Giving everything will afford but a scanty pittance to this starving family. However, the individual gives the bread instantly and joyfully, with tears of gratitude, that by self-denial a fatherless family is kept from absolute starvation. This is self-denial.

It was self-denial in God to send Christ to die for sinners, and self-denial in Christ to undertake and accomplish the great work of our salvation. "Since God had foreknowledge of the Fall and our human sinfulness, God was not obliged to empty God-self for us as though it were a debt to be paid and the Incarnation as an effect or consequence of human sin. Rather God showed the depth of God's love by the self-emptying of Christ." We celebrate this as we sing the St. Louis Jesuits' interpretation of Psalm 34: "The Lord hears the cry of the poor. Blessed be the Lord!" This also evokes the Gospel from Ash Wednesday when we are enjoined to pray, fast, and to give alms, which we should interpret to mean to do acts of charity.

PREFACE IV OF LENT

The fruits of fasting

42. The following Preface is said in Masses of the weekdays of Lent and on days of fasting.

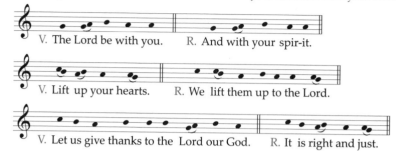

V. The Lord be with you.   R. And with your spir-it.

V. Lift up your hearts.   R. We lift them up to the Lord.

V. Let us give thanks to the Lord our God.   R. It is right and just.

Bring out the accent on **be** in **The Lord be with you.**

Make a strong accent on **Lift,** and slow both notes of **hearts.**

In the third dialogue, move to the word **thanks** before accenting, and hold that word slightly to give it emphasis. Broaden both notes of **Lord,** and hold **God.**

Emphasize **bodily fasting** and the double-intended result: to **raise up our minds and bestow both virtue and its rewards.**

It is truly right and just, our duty and our salvation,
always and everywhere to give you thanks,
Lord, holy Father, almighty and eternal God.

For through bodily fasting you restrain our faults,
raise up our minds,
and bestow both virtue and its rewards,
through Christ our Lord.

Through him the Angels praise your majesty,
Dominions adore and Powers tremble before you.
Heaven and the Virtues of heaven and the blessed Seraphim
worship together with exultation.
May our voices, we pray, join with theirs
in humble praise, as we acclaim:

Holy, Holy, Holy Lord God of hosts . . .

42. Preface IV of Lent: The fruits of fasting lists three things that fasting does. First, the physical act of fasting restrains faults; second, it raises our minds; and third, it bestows virtue. When we have fasted from food, we find that we are able also to discipline ourselves in other areas of our lives that call for restraint. The practice of fasting from food, then, can help us, for example, in keeping our anger in check. Fasting is a very powerful spiritual discipline in the Christian disciplines. Through fasting and prayer, we invite the Holy Spirit to transform our lives.

Fasting and prayer can also work on a much grander scale. According to scripture, when God's people fast with a proper motive (namely, to seek God's face with a broken, repentant, and contrite spirit), God will raise our minds and heal our lives, our churches, our communities, nation, and world. Fasting and prayer can bring about revival, a change in the direction of nation, the nations of earth, and the fulfillment of the Great Commission. We can see that in the practice of fasting during both the Old Testament and in the history of the Church. In Nehemiah 9, the people repent during a

collective fast. In Isaiah 58, it is obvious that fasting is part of the practice of prayer. However, the people are told that a just life and acts of justice must undergird fasting. Only when such is the case will God answer prayers. Pope Gregory the Great understood the effects of fasting when he asked for a collective fast and the praying of a litany as pestilence ravaged Rome.

The awesome power can be released through us as we fast through the enabling of the Holy Spirit. While fasting is one of the three practices encouraged during Lent, with prayer and almsgiving, or acts of

It is truly right and just, our duty and our sal-va-tion, al-ways and everywhere to give you thanks, Lord, holy Father, almighty and e--ter-nal God. For through bodily fasting you re-strain our faults, raise up our minds, and bestow both virtue and its rewards, through Christ our Lord. Through him the Angels praise your maj-es-ty, Do-min-ions a-dore and Powers trem-ble be-fore you. Heav-en and the Virtues of heaven and the bless-ed Ser-a-phim worship to-geth-er with ex-ul-ta-tion. May our voices, we pray, join with theirs in hum-ble praise, as we ac-claim:

Holy, Holy, Holy Lord God of hosts . . .

Sing this proclamation cursively in a reciting tone. In **salvation**, do not hold **-va**; only broaden the two notes slightly. The last syllable, **-tion**, should be held. **Always** and **everywhere** require a slight broadening and clear enunciation. The accent of the phrase falls on **thanks**, which should be held briefly. In the next sentence, clearly make distinct phrases of the text, by respecting the commas.

In the first phrases, hold **faults** and **minds** just slightly, but try not to breathe at those points, so as to keep the sense of the sentence together. Take just a very quick breath before **through Christ our Lord**, which words broaden and slow, breathing after **Lord**.

In the concluding phrase, make a slight pause after **And so**. Respect the commas but try to keep this section together, without big breaks for breaths. Broaden the last phrase, especially on **praise**. Slow **we ac-**, and put emphasis on **-claim**, so as to evoke the response of **Holy, Holy, Holy . . . .**

charity, it is one of the most neglected spiritual admonitions. In fact, it has been ignored for so long that it is difficult to find information on the "how-to's" of this life-changing experience.

However, Lisa-Marie Calderone-Stewart, EdD, explained in the March 2008 *Pastoral Liturgy* article "Slowing Down by Fasting" some of the benefits of this spiritual discipline. "We also slow down when we fast. With our hectic pace, we miss much in life. Fasting slows us down. It makes us humble. We realize how dependent we are on food, and we begin to remember all our blessings. Instead of feeling entitled to our wealth, we get a sense of our limitations. We experience a bit more solidarity with the poor, with those who have only a bowl of rice and a tiny swallow of water each day. We allow God to come into our lives in a deeper way and remind us of who we are. We feel less arrogant. Fasting has all these benefits. . . .Fasting also has some physical benefits. Cleaning out the system and getting rid of toxins is a good idea. But ridding ourselves of whatever can spoil our spiritual lives is even more important."

But if fasting is undertaken simply to drop a few pounds, the virtues and rewards promised in this Preface probably will be compromised because the motivation is wrong.

It is little wonder that fasting is practiced in so many religions of the world and highly esteemed for its spiritual value. The combination of fasting and praying is neither a fad nor a novelty approach to spiritual discipline. Fasting and praying are Bible-based disciplines that are appropriate for believers of all ages throughout all centuries in all parts of the world.

PREFACE I OF THE PASSION OF THE LORD

The power of the Cross

43.   The following Preface is said during the Fifth Week of Lent and in Masses of the mysteries of the Cross and Passion of the Lord.

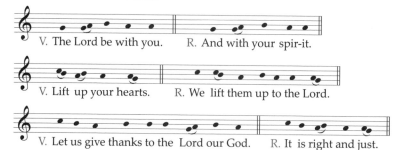

V. The Lord be with you.   R. And with your spir-it.

V. Lift up your hearts.   R. We lift them up to the Lord.

V. Let us give thanks to the Lord our God.   R. It is right and just.

It is truly right and just, our duty and our salvation,
always and everywhere to give you thanks,
Lord, holy Father, almighty and eternal God.

For through the saving Passion of your Son
the whole world has received a heart
to confess the infinite power of your majesty,
since by the wondrous power of the Cross
your judgment on the world is now revealed
and the authority of Christ crucified.

And so, Lord, with all the Angels and Saints,
we, too, give you thanks, as in exultation we acclaim:

Holy, Holy, Holy Lord God of hosts . . .

Bring out the accent on **be** in **The Lord be with you**.

Make a strong accent on **Lift**, and slow both notes of **hearts**.

In the third dialogue, move to the word **thanks** before accenting, and hold that word slightly to give it emphasis. Broaden both notes of **Lord**, and hold **God**.

Emphasize **saving Passion**.

Contrast **wondrous power of the Cross** with **judgment on the world** and **authority of Christ**.

43. The key to the entire body of **Preface I of the Passion of the Lord: The power of the Cross** is in the last two lines: "your judgment on the world is revealed / and the authority of Christ crucified."

We have said that the prayers in the liturgy of the Roman Rite allude to scripture rather than quote it directly. John the Baptist proclaimed a judgment of God that would come as fire and destruction; certain chosen people might be spared that judgment if they underwent a baptism of repentance. Jesus, too, portrays the judgment of God, but in contrast, that judgment is deeply connected with a person's relationship with Jesus himself. The judgment is mercy.

Another contrast of Jesus' proclamation is that the people come to John the Baptist, but Jesus goes to the people and, in fact, invites himself to meals. The contrast is clear. Jesus will even declare that salvation has come to that house when he himself has come to that house. The judgment is mercy. Thus, the Passion of Christ on the cross reveals God's judgment of mercy on the world because Jesus undergoes death rather than calling on all the power of all in heaven upon those who murdered him. The Passion and cross reveal his authority. Jesus has *exousia*—that authority that arises from his very being. Pilate's authority, on the other hand, comes from an ascribed office.

This Preface alludes to the power of the cross. On Good Friday we are invited to

It is truly right and just, our duty and our sal-va-tion, al-ways and everywhere to give you thanks, Lord, holy Father, almighty and e-ter-nal God. For through the saving Passion of your Son the whole world has re-ceived a heart to confess the infinite pow-er of your maj-es-ty, since by the wondrous power of the Cross your judgment on the world is now re-vealed and the authori-ty of Christ cru-ci-fied. And so, Lord, with all the An-gels and Saints, we, too, give you thanks, as in exul-ta-tion we ac-claim:

Holy, Holy, Holy Lord God of hosts . . .

Sing this proclamation cursively in a reciting tone. In **salvation**, do not hold -**va**; only broaden the two notes slightly. The last syllable, -**tion**, should be held. **Always** and **everywhere** require a slight broadening and clear enunciation. The accent of the phrase falls on **thanks**, which should be held briefly. In the next sentence, clearly make distinct phrases of the text, by respecting the commas.

Hold **Son**, **heart**, and -**ty** (in **majesty**), and try not to breathe after **Son** and particularly not after **heart** — if possible. Otherwise, take the breaths quickly. Tie together **Cross** and **your**, holding briefly -**vealed** of **revealed**, but without breathing, if possible, at the end of either. Slow and enunciate well **Christ crucified**, holding the last syllable.

In the concluding phrase, make a slight pause after **And so**. Respect the commas but try to keep this section together, without big breaks for breaths. Broaden the last phrase, especially on **thanks**. Slow **we ac-**, and put emphasis on -**claim**, so as to evoke the response of **Holy, Holy, Holy** . . . .

approach the Cross to recognize how its wood is the living wood that brings about our salvation. The liturgy betrays the reason: "Behold the wood of the Cross on which hung the salvation of the world."

Now we know that crosses come in all sizes, shapes, and material. Some are jeweled, others are intricately carved. Good Friday brings us back to the reality that it is about a wooden cross and, more importantly, about the one who died upon it.

When Egeria, a nun from Galicia in Spain, goes to Jerusalem in the fourth cen-tury, she encounters the rite of venerat-ing the cross at the Church of the Holy Sepulcher. She recounts that in the mid-dle of the city is the Church of the Holy Sepulcher built by Constantine. Egeria refers to it as the Anastasis. In front of that is the basilica, which Egeria calls the Martrium. The hill of Calvary, called "the Cross" by Egeria, stood in an open space between the two buildings.

Egeria visited the Holy Land only 60 years after Christianity had become legal and 54 years after the empress Helena had made a similar journey and, according to tradition, discovered the True Cross. The adoration of the True Cross, according to Egeria's diary, formed the high point of the Easter festival. The elaborate liturgy that Egeria describes clearly developed very rapidly once Christianity became legal and pilgrims started to visit the holy places.

PREFACE II OF THE PASSION OF THE LORD

The victory of the Passion

44.   The following Preface is said on Monday, Tuesday, and Wednesday of Holy Week.

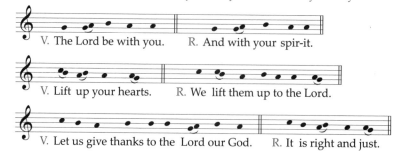

V. The Lord be with you.   R. And with your spir-it.

V. Lift up your hearts.   R. We lift them up to the Lord.

V. Let us give thanks to the Lord our God.   R. It is right and just.

Bring out the accent on **be** in **The Lord be with you.**

Make a strong accent on **Lift**, and slow both notes of **hearts**.

In the third dialogue, move to the word **thanks** before accenting, and hold that word slightly to give it emphasis. Broaden both notes of **Lord**, and hold **God**.

Emphasize **Passion** and **Resurrection**, holding together the full Paschal Mystery. Contrast **pride** and **mystery of our redemption**.

It is truly right and just, our duty and our salvation,
always and everywhere to give you thanks,
Lord, holy Father, almighty and eternal God,
through Christ our Lord.
For the days of his saving Passion
and glorious Resurrection are approaching,
by which the pride of the ancient foe is vanquished
and the mystery of our redemption in Christ is celebrated.

Through him the host of Angels adores your majesty
and rejoices in your presence for ever.
May our voices, we pray, join with theirs
in one chorus of exultant praise, as we acclaim:

Holy, Holy, Holy Lord God of hosts . . .

44. Preface II of the Passion of the Lord: The victory of the Passion is an anticipation of the Triduum and is intended for the first three days of Holy Week. The prime image here is Christ as victor in this combat. This is a combat between God's champion, who is Christ, and Satan, and that very primitive soteriology. The victory of the Passion is an anticipation of the Triduum and is intended for the first three days of Holy Week. It anticipates what we will sing in the Exsultet as we proclaim: "This is the night when Christ broke the prison-bars of death . . . ." Christ is victorious over sin and death and has vanquished the ancient foe.

Where death is vanquished by the Prince of Life (Easter Sequence), the Prince of Life, by dying, destroys death. The Easter Triduum, or Paschal Triduum, is the period of three days from Holy Thursday to Easter Day. It begins with the Mass of the Lord's Supper on Thursday of Holy Week and ends with Evening Prayer on Easter Sunday. It remembers the events as portrayed in the Gospel accounts. These are the highest holy days of the Christian calendar and everything culminates in these Three Days.

Since the 1955 reform by Pope Pius XII, the Easter Triduum, including as it does Easter Sunday, has been more clearly distinguished as a separate liturgical period. Previously, all these celebrations were advanced by more than twelve hours. The Mass of the Lord's Supper and the Easter Vigil were celebrated in the morning of Thursday and Saturday, respectively, and Holy Week and Lent were seen as ending only on the approach of Easter Sunday.

It is truly right and just, our duty and our sal-va-tion, al-ways and everywhere to give you thanks, Lord, holy Father, almighty and e-ter-nal God, through Christ our Lord. For the days of his saving Passion and glorious Resurrection are ap-proach-ing, by which the pride of the ancient foe is van-quished and the mystery of our re-demption in Christ is cel-e-brat-ed. Through him the host of An-gels a-dores your maj-es-ty and re-joic-es in your pres-ence for ev-er. May our voices, we pray, join with theirs in one chorus of ex-ult-ant praise, as we ac-claim:

Holy, Holy, Holy Lord God of hosts . . .

Sing this proclamation cursively in a reciting tone. In **salvation**, do not hold **-va**; only broaden the two notes slightly. The last syllable, **-tion**, should be held. **Always** and **everywhere** require a slight broadening and clear enunciation. The accent of the phrase falls on **thanks**, which should be held briefly. In the next sentence, clearly make distinct phrases of the text, by respecting the commas.

Hold **-ing** of **approaching** and take a short breath there. Hold **-quished** of **vanquished**, and try not to breathe but rather continue with **and the**. Slow and broaden **celebrated**.

In the concluding phrase, make a slight pause after **And so**. Respect the commas but try to keep this section together, without big breaks for breaths. Broaden the last phrase, especially on **praise**. Slow **we ac-**, and put emphasis on **-claim**, so as to evoke the response of **Holy, Holy, Holy** . . . .

Today the days are regarded as a single feast celebrated over three days. Attempts are made liturgically so that each day flows from the day before and leads to the following day.

On the Table of Liturgical Days, according to their order of preference, the Paschal Triduum of the Passion and the Resurrection of the Lord are assigned the number one place. In the *Universal Norms on the Liturgical Year and the General Roman Calendar*, we find a very clear statement about this matter: "Since Christ accomplished his work of human redemption and of the perfect glorification of God principally through his Paschal Mystery, in which by dying he has destroyed our death, and by rising restored our life, the sacred Paschal Triduum of the Passion and Resurrection of the Lord shines forth as the high point of the entire liturgical year. Therefore the preeminence that Sunday has in the week, the Solemnity of Easter has in the liturgical year" (18).

This Preface prepares us to anxiously await this three-day remembrance of the events that bring about our salvation. Since the prayer is reserved for Monday, Tuesday, and Wednesday of Holy Week, one can sense in the language of the prayer the pride of place given to this three-day feast when the pride of the ancient foe is vanquished. The prayer holds together linguistically what the Triduum celebrates liturgically; namely, the Death and Resurrection of the Lord. This is the most central dogma of the Christian faith, the Paschal Mystery—that Christ has died, that Christ is risen, and that Christ will come again in glory!

PREFACE I OF EASTER

The Paschal Mystery

45. The following Preface is said during Easter Time.

At the Easter Vigil, is said **on this night**; on Easter Sunday and throughout the Octave of Easter, is said **on this day**; on other days of Easter Time, is said **in this time**.

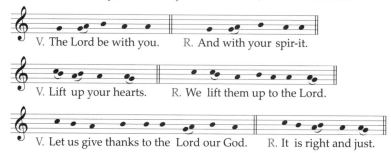

V. The Lord be with you.   R. And with your spir-it.

V. Lift up your hearts.   R. We lift them up to the Lord.

V. Let us give thanks to the Lord our God.   R. It is right and just.

Bring out the accent on **be** in **The Lord be with you**.

Make a strong accent on **Lift**, and slow both notes of **hearts**.

In the third dialogue, move to the word **thanks** before accenting, and hold that word slightly to give it emphasis. Broaden both notes of **Lord**, and hold **God**.

In the body, choose the appropriate temporal reference.

Emphasize **Christ our Passover**, **Lamb**, and **sins of the world**.

Contrast **dying** with **rising**.

It is truly right and just, our duty and our salvation,
at all times to acclaim you, O Lord,
but (on this night / on this day / in this time) above all
to laud you yet more gloriously,
when Christ our Passover has been sacrificed.

For he is the true Lamb
who has taken away the sins of the world;
by dying he has destroyed our death,
and by rising, restored our life.

Therefore, overcome with paschal joy,
every land, every people exults in your praise
and even the heavenly Powers, with the angelic hosts,
sing together the unending hymn of your glory,
as they acclaim:

Holy, Holy, Holy Lord God of hosts . . .

When the Roman Canon is used, there is a proper **Communicantes** and a proper Hanc igitur, as below, p. 637. In the **Communicantes** at the Easter Vigil, Celebrating the most sacred night, etc. is said.

---

45. Preface I of Easter: The Paschal Mystery is the first of five Prefaces for Easter, demonstrating liturgically the central importance of the Solemnity of Easter, the queen of all Feasts. The internal reference to "this night" or "this day" is a clear indicator that this is the preferred Preface for the Easter Vigil or Easter Sunday.

The Lamb of God is the central image in Preface I of Easter. We see the image first in the Pauline phrase in the last line of the first paragraph of the body. That phrase recalls 1 Corinthians 5:7, "For our paschal lamb, Christ, has been sacrificed."

In the next paragraph, the "true Lamb / who has taken away the sins of the world" is the Johannine Lamb of God that is present in the book of Revelation. The title Lamb of God (*Agnus Dei*) appears in the Gospel according to John, with the exclamation of John the Baptist: "Behold, the Lamb of God, who takes away the sin of the world" (John 1:29) when he sees Jesus.

Although in Christian teachings, Lamb of God refers to Jesus Christ in his role of the perfect sacrificial offering, specific Christological arguments disassociate it from the Old Testament concept of a "scapegoat" that is subjected to punishment for the sins of others, without knowing it or willing it. These teachings emphasize that Jesus chose to suffer at Calvary as a sign of his full obedience to the will of his Father, as an "agent and servant of God."

It is truly right and just, our duty and our sal-va-tion,   at all times to ac-claim you, O Lord,   but (on this night / on this day / in this time) above all to laud you yet more glo-rious-ly,   when Christ our Pass-o-ver has been sac-ri-ficed.   For he is the true Lamb   who has taken away the sins of the world;   by dying he has de-stroyed our death,   and by ris-ing, re-stored our life.   There-fore,   o-vercome with pas-chal joy,   every land, eve-ry peo-ple ex-ults in your praise   and even the heavenly Powers,   with the an-gel-ic hosts,   sing together the unending hymn of your glo-ry,   as they ac-claim:

Holy, Holy, Holy Lord God of hosts . . .

Sing this proclamation cursively in a reciting tone. In **salvation**, do not hold **-va**; only broaden the two notes slightly. The last syllable, **-tion**, should be held. In this Preface, the protocol moves into the body of the Preface without a break. The temporal reference changes according to the situation. The body is divided into two phrases, each ending with a vertical line. Pause especially after the second phrase to indicate movement from the body into the eschatocol.

As you sing, follow normal speech patterns and, when you come to the end of a sentence, allow your speed to slow a little to show the natural cadence.

It is important that, when you are singing a number of words on the reciting tone, the words are accentuated in a normal reciting tone. Try not to accent the weak syllables, as this will distort the text. At the word **glory**, hold onto the first note "la" for a little longer, then move up the scale to "ti-do," backing off the the two notes to arrive on the syllable **-ry**.

In the ancient world, the making of a pact or a covenant (*berith*) was done during a ceremony in which an animal was cut in half. There were two types of covenants in ancient times. One was a parity covenant made between two parties who were equal and bound themselves together in a contract. The other covenant was the suzerainty covenant made between a strong party and a weak party. Here the king walked through the bloody parts. He would say that his body parts should be separated if he breaks the covenant.

The sacrificial animal, which was either a lamb or a kid, was necessarily a one-year-old male without blemish. Each family or society offered one animal together. The animal was slain on the eve of Passover, on the afternoon of the 14th of Nisan, after the Tamid sacrifice had been killed (i.e., at three o'clock, or, in case the eve of the Passover fell on Friday, at two).

The term "Christ our Passover" refers to the "Paschal Lamb," which is the sacrifice that the Torah mandates to be brought on the eve of Passover, and eaten on the first night of the holiday with bitter herbs and matzo. According to the Torah, it was first offered on the night of the Israelites' Exodus from Egypt. Through Christ, the Paschal Lamb, the covenant (of the suzerainty type) with God takes place.

PREFACE II OF EASTER

New life in Christ

46.   The following Preface is said during Easter Time.

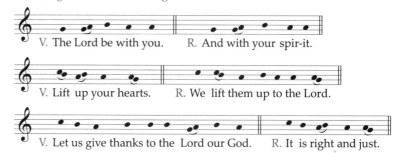

V. The Lord be with you.   R. And with your spir-it.

V. Lift up your hearts.   R. We lift them up to the Lord.

V. Let us give thanks to the Lord our God.   R. It is right and just.

It is truly right and just, our duty and our salvation,
at all times to acclaim you, O Lord,
but in this time above all to laud you yet more gloriously,
when Christ our Passover has been sacrificed.

Through him the children of light rise to eternal life
and the halls of the heavenly Kingdom
are thrown open to the faithful;
for his Death is our ransom from death,
and in his rising the life of all has risen.

Therefore, overcome with paschal joy,
every land, every people exults in your praise
and even the heavenly Powers, with the angelic hosts,
sing together the unending hymn of your glory,
as they acclaim:

Holy, Holy, Holy Lord God of hosts . . .

Bring out the accent on **be** in **The Lord be with you.**

Make a strong accent on **Lift**, and slow both notes of **hearts**.

In the third dialogue, move to the word **thanks** before accenting, and hold that word slightly to give it emphasis. Broaden both notes of **Lord**, and hold **God**.

Emphasize **children of light** and **faithful**, putting the focus on Baptism.

Contrast **Death** with **rising**.

46. Preface II of Easter: New life in Christ is the second of five Prefaces for Easter, demonstrating liturgically the central importance of the feast of Easter.

The imagery of the Lamb of God in Preface I gives way in Preface II of Easter to "the children of light" and their dwelling places. We see here that the "children of light rise to eternal life / and the halls of the heavenly Kingdom / are thrown open to the faithful." This alludes to the many dwelling places referred to in John 14:2: "In my Father's house there are many dwelling places."

In today's Preface, the many dwelling places of the heavenly people are "thrown open" to the faithful, because Christ himself has entered into this place. So "by dying he has destroyed our death, and by rising he has restored our life."

Children of light probably refers to 1 Thessalonians 5:5: "For all of you are children of the light and children of the day. We are not of the night or of darkness."

At the Easter Vigil, catechumens are baptized, confirmed, and brought to the Eucharistic table. Once washed in the waters of Baptism and anointed with the sacred chrism, they are presented with a candle. No longer are they called catechumens. Now they are the "*phosphatoi*" or the "enlightened ones." To be children of the light refers to all the baptized, but especially those who are the neophytes or the "newly born."

It is truly right and just, our duty and our sal-va-tion, at all times to ac-claim you, O Lord, but in this time above all to laud you yet more glo-rious-ly, when Christ our Pass-o-ver has been sac-ri-ficed. Through him the children of light rise to e-ter-nal life and the halls of the heav-en-ly King-dom are thrown o-pen to the faith-ful; for his Death is our ran-som from death, and in his ris-ing the life of all has ris-en. There-fore, o-vercome with pas-chal joy, every land, eve-ry peo-ple ex-ults in your praise and even the heavenly Powers, with the an-gel-ic hosts, sing to--gether the unending hymn of your glo-ry, as they ac-claim:

Holy, Holy, Holy Lord God of hosts . . .

Sing this proclamation cursively in a reciting tone. In **salvation**, do not hold **-va**; only broaden the two notes slightly. The last syllable, **-tion**, should be held. **Always** and **every-where** require a slight broadening and clear enunciation. The accent of the phrase falls on **thanks**, which should be held briefly. In the next sentence, clearly make distinct phrases of the text, by respecting the commas.

At the end of the first phrase, hold **life** and pause very briefly. In the next phrase, tie together **Kingdom** and **are thrown**. Hold **-ful** of **faithful** and pause. In the next phrase, articulate carefully **Death** and **death**, holding the second briefly. If necessary, take a very quick breath there. (Notice in this phrase the word **our**—which is sung and proclaimed as two syllables, **ow-were** rather than one syllable as in the verb **are**.) Slow and broaden from **rising** to **risen**. Hold the last syllable and take a good breath.

In the concluding phrase, make a slight pause after **And so**. Respect the commas but try to keep this section together, without big breaks for breaths. Broaden the last phrase, especially on **glory**. Slow **we ac-**, and put emphasis on **-claim**, so as to evoke the response of **Holy, Holy, Holy** . . . .

The reference to birth in the context of Baptism draws from John's account of the Gospel that speaks about Baptism as rebirth. Jesus answered, "Amen, amen, I say to you, no one can enter the kingdom of God without being born of water and Spirit" (John 3:5).

In a complementary way, Paul, in his letter to the Romans, uses more the image of Baptism as dying and rising with Christ: "[A]re you unaware that we who were baptized into Christ Jesus were baptized into his death? We were indeed buried with him through baptism into death, so that, just as Christ was raised from the dead by the glory of the Father, we too might live in newness of life" (Romans 6:3–4). For this reason, Baptism by immersion is preferred for the symbolism of being buried with Christ in order to rise with him.

In addition to Baptism being regarded as dying and rising with Christ (Romans 6), the early Church also focused on the idea of being reborn in Christ. For this reason, the shape of the font was fashioned both as a tomb and a womb. Sometimes the font incorporated features from both metaphors. Also, some fonts in the shape of pools for immersion have three steps descending into and ascending from the font to signify the three days of Christ in the tomb.

The Easter fire and especially the Paschal candle also are reference points, particularly as they received much attention at the Easter Vigil with the singing the Exsultet, celebrating Christ our

PREFACE III OF EASTER

Christ living and always interceding for us

47. The following Preface is said during Easter Time.

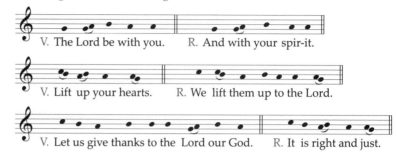

V. The Lord be with you.   R. And with your spir-it.

V. Lift up your hearts.   R. We lift them up to the Lord.

V. Let us give thanks to the Lord our God.   R. It is right and just.

It is truly right and just, our duty and our salvation,
at all times to acclaim you, O Lord,
but in this time above all to laud you yet more gloriously,
when Christ our Passover has been sacrificed.

He never ceases to offer himself for us
but defends us and ever pleads our cause before you:
he is the sacrificial Victim who dies no more,
the Lamb, once slain, who lives for ever.

Therefore, overcome with paschal joy,
every land, every people exults in your praise
and even the heavenly Powers, with the angelic hosts,
sing together the unending hymn of your glory,
as they acclaim:

Holy, Holy, Holy Lord God of hosts . . .

Bring out the accent on **be** in **The Lord be with you.**

Make a strong accent on **Lift**, and slow both notes of **hearts.**

In the third dialogue, move to the word **thanks** before accenting, and hold that word slightly to give it emphasis. Broaden both notes of **Lord**, and hold **God.**

The protocol makes specific reference to **this time above all.**

Contrast the binary opposition between **never ceases** (meaning always) and **defends** and **pleads.** Emphasize **sacrificial Victim.**

47. Preface III of Easter: Christ living and always interceding for us is the third of five Prefaces for Easter, demonstrating liturgically the central importance of Easter.

The key to Preface III of Easter is found in the first lines. We see Christ continuously offering himself, defending us, and pleading for us.

This image of Christ connects to the high priestly prayer Jesus offers in John 17:1–26. There, Jesus prays, "Consecrate them in the truth . . . . And I consecrate

myself for them, so that they also may be consecrated in truth" (v. 17–19).

Christ prays for all who have been given to him. "Father, they are your gift to me. I wish that where I am they also may be with me" (v. 24). Christ remains forever the intercessor mediator.

Christ continually offering himself and pleading our cause is a rich theme. The Gellone Sacramentary (Paris, Bibliotheque Nationale, Ms. Lat. 12048, ca. 750), a Gelasian-style Mass book from Gaul—probably from St. Guilhem le Desert

in the Hérault department in Languedoc-Roussillon in southern France—features an interesting Christ on the cross that corresponds to this Preface. In the canon of the Mass (the Eucharistic Prayer), we find an illuminated letter forming the "T" of "*Te igitur*," the prayer which asks for God's blessing of the bread and the wine of the Eucharist. The "T" is transformed into a cross with Christ affixed to it. These words are situated at the bottom of the page, at the level of Christ's knees. What is curious is that Christ is not

It is truly right and just, our duty and our sal-va-tion, at all times to ac-claim you, O Lord, but in this time above all to laud you yet more glo-rious-ly, when Christ our Pass-o-ver has been sac-ri-ficed. He never ceases to offer him-self for us but defends us and ever pleads our cause be-fore you: he is the sacrificial Vic--tim who dies no more, the Lamb, once slain, who lives for ev-er. There-fore, o-vercome with pas-chal joy, every land, eve-ry peo-ple ex-ults in your praise and even the heavenly Powers, with the an-gel-ic hosts, sing together the unending hymn of your glo-ry, as they ac-claim:

Holy, Holy, Holy Lord God of hosts . . .

Sing this proclamation cursively in a reciting tone. In **salvation**, do not hold **-va**; only broaden the two notes slightly. The last syllable, **-tion**, should be held. **Always** and **every-where** require a slight broadening and clear enunciation. The accent of the phrase falls on **thanks**, which should be held briefly. In the next sentence, clearly make distinct phrases of the text, by respecting the commas.

At the end of the first phrase, hold **us** slightly, but then continue without a breath with **but defends**. Hold **you** at the end of the phrase. In the next phrase, hold slightly **more**, and take a quick breath, before going on to **the Lamb**. Pause briefly at the two commas of that phrase; then slow and broaden the last four words.

In the concluding phrase, make a slight pause after **And so**. Respect the commas but try to keep this section together, without big breaks for breaths. Broaden the last phrase, especially on **glory**. Slow **we ac-**, and put emphasis on **-claim**, so as to evoke the response of **Holy, Holy, Holy** . . . .

suffering in this image, and he is flanked by two Angels. With eyes wide open, he looks up to the heavens and continually pleads to God on our behalf. This historiated initial belongs to both the *Sanctus* and *Te igitur* prayers, and visually transitions from the Preface to the Eucharist to the prayers of the Eucharist itself. The prayer of the *Sanctus* is the speech of the Angels, and Christ on the cross offers the ultimate ref-erent for the *Te igitur*.

The Johannine imagery of the slain Lamb continues in this Preface, but in com-parison with the preceding Preface, this is no longer a suffering sacrificial victim but one "who lives for ever." His is more the image of the lamb that we find in Revelation 5: "Then I saw standing in the midst of the throne . . . , a Lamb that seemed to have been slain," to whom the hymn is sung: "Worthy are you . . . , for you were slain and with your blood you purchased for God those from every tribe and tongue, people and nation. You made them a king-dom and priests for our God. . . . Worthy is the Lamb that was slain to receive power and riches, wisdom and strength, honor and glory and blessing. . . . and to the Lamb be blessing and honor, glory and might, forever and ever" (v. 6, 9, 10, 12, 13).

The idea of Christ continually offering himself in sacrifice stands in sharp contrast to the letter to the Hebrews that insists that he did it once for all (*ephapax*) when he offered up himself (Hebrews 7:27).

PREFACE IV OF EASTER

The restoration of the universe through the Paschal Mystery

48.   The following Preface is said during Easter Time.

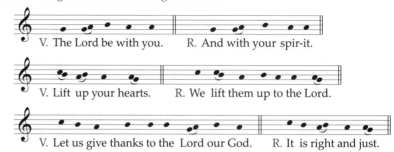

V. The Lord be with you.   R. And with your spir-it.

V. Lift up your hearts.   R. We lift them up to the Lord.

V. Let us give thanks to the Lord our God.   R. It is right and just.

It is truly right and just, our duty and our salvation,
at all times to acclaim you, O Lord,
but in this time above all to laud you yet more gloriously,
when Christ our Passover has been sacrificed.

For, with the old order destroyed,
a universe cast down is renewed,
and integrity of life is restored to us in Christ.

Therefore, overcome with paschal joy,
every land, every people exults in your praise
and even the heavenly Powers, with the angelic hosts,
sing together the unending hymn of your glory,
as they acclaim:

Holy, Holy, Holy Lord God of hosts . . .

Bring out the accent on **be** in **The Lord be with you**.

Make a strong accent on **Lift**, and slow both notes of **hearts**.

In the third dialogue, move to the word **thanks** before accenting, and hold that word slightly to give it emphasis. Broaden both notes of **Lord**, and hold **God**.

In the protocol emphasize **this time** and **Christ our Passover**.

In the body, contrast **the old order destroyed** with the **universe** being **renewed** and **restored**.

48. Preface IV of Easter: The restoration of the universe through the Paschal Mystery is the fourth of five Easter Prefaces, demonstrating liturgically the central importance of the feast of Easter.

Phrases in Preface IV of Easter probably allude to canticles in the Pauline writings. For example, in Romans 6:6, a text associated with Baptism, we read: "We know that our old self was crucified with him, so that our sinful body might be done away with, that we might no longer be in slavery to sin." This probably is the old order to which the Preface refers.

In Ephesians 1:13–14, we hear how those "who have heard the word of truth . . . were sealed with the promised holy Spirit, . . . the first installment . . . toward redemption." We have heard the truth in the text of this Preface: "integrity of life is restored to us in Christ."

Just as Christ is lauded in this Preface, he is in the Christological hymns cited in Paul's letters. In Colossians 1:15–20, it is proclaimed, "He is before all things, and in him all things hold together" (v. 17). This hymn proclaims that in Christ "all the fullness was pleased to dwell" (v. 19). It is in this fullness that "integrity of life is restored to us in Christ." The hymn in Colossians also proclaims that through Christ all things were reconciled to God. In that reconciliation, as we see in this Preface, "a universe cast down is renewed."

A second hymn found in the letter to the Philippians 2:6–11, and closely associated with Palm Sunday of the Passion of the Lord as the Second Reading, uses the

It is truly right and just, our duty and our sal-va-tion, at all times to ac-claim you, O Lord, but in this time above all to laud you yet more glo-rious-ly, when Christ our Pass-o-ver has been sac-ri-ficed. For, with the old order destroyed, a universe cast down is re-newed, and integrity of life is restored to us in Christ. There-fore, o-vercome with pas-chal joy, every land, eve-ry peo-ple ex-ults in your praise and even the heavenly Powers, with the an-gel-ic hosts, sing together the unending hymn of your glo-ry, as they ac-claim:

Holy, Holy, Holy Lord God of hosts . . .

Sing this proclamation cursively in a reciting tone. In **salvation**, do not hold **-va**; only broaden the two notes slightly. The last syllable, **-tion**, should be held. **Always** and **every-where** require a slight broadening and clear enunciation. The accent of the phrase falls on **thanks**, which should be held briefly. In the next sentence, clearly make distinct phrases of the text, by respecting the commas.

At the end of the first phrase, **destroyed**, respect the comma with an inflection of the voice, but do not hold it or pause here. Hold **-newed** of **renewed** at the end of the phrase. If a breath is absolutely needed, take a very quick one, so as not to break the sense, with the upcoming phrase beginning with **and**. Hold and articulate clearly **Christ**, taking a good breath at that point.

In the concluding phrase, make a slight pause after **And so**. Respect the commas but try to keep this section together, without big breaks for breaths. Broaden the last phrase, especially on **glory**. Slow **we ac-**, and put emphasis on **-claim**, so as to evoke the response of **Holy, Holy, Holy** . . . .

parallel idea of humbling and exalting. The hymn can be divided into six verses, followed by a sentence that recapitulates the entire hymn with a creedal formula that Jesus the Christ is the Lord. The first three verses emphasize God becoming human (Incarnation). The Greek word *kenosis* speaks of emptying oneself out to become fully human, taking on our human form and living a fully human life unto death, death on a cross. The second set of three verses speaks to God's response to Jesus' obedience by raising him up. To this end, all

of creation, whether above the earth, on the earth, or under the earth, sing to the praise and glory of God that Jesus is the Christ (the Messiah or Anointed One) and the Lord, the one who is definitively inaugurated as *Kyrios* at the Resurrection. The hymn forms a chiastic structure (A-B-C-C-B-A).

This hymn is the epitome of a balanced Christology, emphasizing equally the humanity and divinity of Christ. It also addresses the dual idea of hominization and divinization. The Preface picks up on this twofold movement as it underscores

how the Paschal Victim brought down has restored integrity of life. The world brought down is raised up and renewed. Life that was destroyed in death is now restored. The Preface presents these binary oppositions in an attempt to show that distance between death and resurrection, between the old and the new orders, between sin and redemption.

PREFACE V OF EASTER

Christ, Priest and Victim

49.   The following Preface is said during Easter Time.

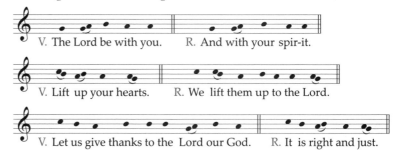

V. The Lord be with you.   R. And with your spir-it.

V. Lift up your hearts.   R. We lift them up to the Lord.

V. Let us give thanks to the Lord our God.   R. It is right and just.

Bring out the accent on **be** in **The Lord be with you**.

Make a strong accent on **Lift**, and slow both notes of **hearts**.

In the third dialogue, move to the word **thanks** before accenting, and hold that word slightly to give it emphasis. Broaden both notes of **Lord**, and hold **God**.

The protocol makes temporal reference to **this time above all**.

Emphasize **oblation** and **sacrifices**, as these are related.

Emphasize **Priest, the Altar, and the Lamb of sacrifice**, as these are also sacrificial terms.

It is truly right and just, our duty and our salvation,
at all times to acclaim you, O Lord,
but in this time above all to laud you yet more gloriously,
when Christ our Passover has been sacrificed.

By the oblation of his Body,
he brought the sacrifices of old to fulfillment
in the reality of the Cross
and, by commending himself to you for our salvation,
showed himself the Priest, the Altar, and the Lamb of sacrifice.

Therefore, overcome with paschal joy,
every land, every people exults in your praise
and even the heavenly Powers, with the angelic hosts,
sing together the unending hymn of your glory,
as they acclaim:

Holy, Holy, Holy Lord God of hosts . . .

49. Preface V of Easter: Christ, Priest and Victim is the last of five Prefaces for Easter, demonstrating liturgically the central importance of the feast of Easter.

The key to Preface V of Easter is that Christ is found in the three images "Priest," "Altar," and "Lamb of sacrifice."

The Preface should be read in the light of the letter to the Hebrews, chapters 3–10, on the interpretation of Christ's Passion, Death, and Resurrection in terms of the sacrificial worship of the Old Testament.

We read in these chapters the details of the sacrifice of the high priest, who once a year went into the inner tabernacle, "not without blood that he offers for himself and for the sins of the people" (Hebrews 9:7). However, Christ as high priest passed through a tabernacle not made by human hands: "Christ did not enter into a sanctuary made by hands, . . . but heaven itself, that he might now appear before God on our behalf" (Hebrews 9:24). Unlike the high priest who annually offered

a sacrifice "with blood that is not his own" (Hebrews 9:25), "[N]ow once for all he has appeared at the end of the ages to take away sin by his sacrifice" (Hebrews 9:26). The author of Hebrews continues to explain that Christ only needed to be sacrificed once. Hebrews 10:9 refers to Jesus' statement, "Behold, I come to do your will." Though the high priest offered the sacrifice each year, "By this 'will,' we have been consecrated through the offering of the body of Jesus Christ once for all" (Hebrews 10:10).

It is truly right and just, our duty and our sal-va-tion, at all times

to ac-claim you, O Lord, but in this time above all to laud you

yet more glo-rious-ly, when Christ our Pass-o-ver has been

sac-ri-ficed. By the oblation of his Body, he brought the sacrifices

of old to fulfillment in the reality of the Cross and, by commend-

-ing himself to you for our sal-va-tion, showed him-self the Priest,

the Altar, and the Lamb of sac-ri-fice. There-fore, o-vercome with

pas-chal joy, every land, eve-ry peo-ple ex-ults in your praise

and even the heavenly Powers, with the an-gel-ic hosts, sing to-

-gether the unending hymn of your glo-ry, as they ac-claim:

Holy, Holy, Holy Lord God of hosts . . .

Sing this proclamation cursively in a reciting tone. In **salvation**, do not hold **-va**; only broaden the two notes slightly. The last syllable, **-tion**, should be held. **Always** and **every-where** require a slight broadening and clear enunciation. The accent of the phrase falls on **thanks**, which should be held briefly. In the next sentence, clearly make distinct phrases of the text, by respecting the commas.

Use careful articulation to bring the meaning of all the important words in the first phrase, but if possible do not pause for breathing until after **Cross** (which should be held slightly). Notice the two notes on **our** in the next phrase make it easy to pro-nounce it correctly as two syllables. Hold **-tion** of **salvation**, but if possible do not break the text here, but finish the next phrase beginning with **showed himself**. Pause slightly at **Priest** and **Altar**. Broaden and slow the last three words, holding the last syllable and taking a breath.

In the concluding phrase, make a slight pause after **And so**. Respect the commas but try to keep this section together, without big breaks for breaths. Broaden the last phrase, especially on **glory**. Slow **we ac-**, and put emphasis on **-claim**, so as to evoke the response of **Holy, Holy, Holy** . . . .

The phrase "By commending himself to you for our salvation" is drawn from Jesus' prayer to the Father in John 17: "Father, the hour has come. Give glory to your son, so that your son may glorify you, . . . so that he may give eternal life to all you gave him" (1–2). Jesus is handing himself to the Father so that he may be sacrificed to give glory to the Father and eternal life to all who were given to him.

We find a similar interplay between Christ the Priest and the Victim in Preface I of the Most Holy Eucharist: "For he is the true and eternal Priest, / who instituted the pattern of an everlasting sacrifice / and was the first to offer himself as the saving Victim, / commanding us to make this offering as his memorial."

In addition, this prayer also refers to Christ as the altar upon which the sacrifice is offered. Since the altar was anointed with chrism in the Rite of Dedication of a Church and an Altar, it is a symbol of Christ, whose name means the "Anointed One." For this reason, the Priest reverences the altar with a kiss at the beginning and the

end of every Eucharist. This is especially poignant in the Maronite Rite at the final prayer, which is one of farewell to the altar: "Remain in Peace Holy Altar of God, I hope to return to you in peace . . . . I know not whether I will return to you again to offer sacrifice." It is also for this reason that when we pass in front of the altar, the symbol of Christ, during the liturgy we reverence it. Also, to show reverence to the altar, it should not be used as a plant stand or be cluttered.

PREFACE I OF THE ASCENSION OF THE LORD

The mystery of the Ascension

50.   The following Preface is said on the day of the Ascension of the Lord. It may be said on the days between the Ascension and Pentecost in all Masses that have no proper Preface.

V. The Lord be with you.   R. And with your spir-it.

V. Lift up your hearts.   R. We lift them up to the Lord.

V. Let us give thanks to the Lord our God.   R. It is right and just.

Bring out the accent on **be** in **The Lord be with you**.

Make a strong accent on **Lift**, and slow both notes of **hearts**.

In the third dialogue, move to the word **thanks** before accenting, and hold that word slightly to give it emphasis. Broaden both notes of **Lord**, and hold **God**.

The body has two parts: the first part acclaims Jesus as the King of glory who conquers and ascends. The second amplifies on Jesus as the God-Man, with an extended reflection on the meaning of the Ascension.

Contrast binary opposition **ascended, not to . . .** with **we might be confident**.

It is truly right and just, our duty and our salvation,
always and everywhere to give you thanks,
Lord, holy Father, almighty and eternal God.
For the Lord Jesus, the King of glory,
conqueror of sin and death,
ascended (today) to the highest heavens,
as the Angels gazed in wonder.

Mediator between God and man,
judge of the world and Lord of hosts,
he ascended, not to distance himself from our lowly state
but that we, his members, might be confident of following
where he, our Head and Founder, has gone before.

Therefore, overcome with paschal joy,
every land, every people exults in your praise
and even the heavenly Powers, with the angelic hosts,
sing together the unending hymn of your glory,
as they acclaim:

Holy, Holy, Holy Lord God of hosts . . .

When the Roman Canon is used on the Ascension, there is a proper Communicantes, p. 637.

50.   Preface I of the Ascension of the Lord: The mystery of the Ascension of the Lord is the first of two Prefaces for the Ascension. The key to Preface I of the Ascension is found in the binary opposition in the second paragraph. The prayer states that Christ "ascended, not to distance himself from our lowly state / but that we . . . might be confident of following / . . . where he . . . has gone before." We pray here, then, that Christ ascended not to abandon history but to give a purpose to history. That purpose is

so that we might follow to the place where he, our Head and Founder, has gone.

This Preface is grounded in the Lucan narrative in the Gospel account and the Acts of the Apostles. It alludes to the scene in Acts 1:6–11, in which the Apostles watched as Jesus "was lifted up, and a cloud took him from their sight" (v. 9). As the Apostles continued to look at the sky, two men dressed in white told them, "This Jesus who has been taken up from you into heaven will return" (v. 11). In Luke 24:52,

we read of the "joy" to which this prayer alludes. Luke recounts, "They did him homage and then returned to Jerusalem with great joy." The joy that was theirs should be ours today as we celebrate Christ's Ascension. In ascending to heaven, he has preceded us to the place where we eventually will dwell.

Key to this Preface is the notion of Christ as mediator. In that he descended to us from God, Christ mediates God's love for us (grace). To the degree that he ascends to God, he mediates our love for God (wor-

It is truly right and just, our duty and our sal-va-tion, al-ways and

everywhere to give you thanks, Lord, holy Father, almighty and e-

-ter-nal God. For the Lord Jesus, the King of glory, conqueror of

sin and death, ascended (today) to the high-est heav-ens, as the

An-gels gazed in won-der. Me-diator between God and man,

judge of the world and Lord of hosts, he ascended, not to distance

himself from our low-ly state but that we, his members, might be

confident of fol-low-ing where he, our Head and Founder, has gone

be-fore. There-fore, o-vercome with pas-chal joy, every land,

eve-ry peo-ple ex-ults in your praise and even the heavenly

Powers, with the an-gel-ic hosts, sing together the unending hymn

of your glo-ry, as they ac-claim:

Holy, Holy, Holy Lord God of hosts . . .

Sing this proclamation cursively in a reciting tone. In **salvation**, do not hold -va; only broaden the two notes slightly. The last syllable, **-tion**, should be held. **Always** and **everywhere** require a slight broadening and clear enunciation. The accent of the phrase falls on **thanks**, which should be held briefly. In the next sentence, clearly make distinct phrases of the text, by respecting the commas.

Hold **-ry** of **glory** to set off the next phrase which is in apposition to the first. Try not to break or breathe after **death**, but continue the sense by going on to **ascended**. Similarly, after **heavens**. Slow slightly **Angels gazed in wonder**. The next two phrases are very hard to articulate correctly with the melodies that are given. It is important not to accent **-di** in **Mediator** or **of** in **judge of the**. Some Priest Celebrants might find it easier to begin both phrases on the high "C" so as to accent the first syllable or word correctly. Hold **man** slightly, to set off the phrase. The next phrase is a musical parallel: hold **hosts**. In the next phrase, hold **state**. Merely broaden **following** rather than holding any note there. Slow **has gone before**, and hold the last syllable and breathe.

In the concluding phrase, pause after **And so**. Respect the commas but try to keep this section together, without big breaks for breaths. Broaden the last phrase, especially on **glory**. Slow **we ac-**, and put emphasis on **-claim**, so as to evoke the response of **Holy, Holy, Holy . . . .**

ship). The Council of Chalcedon in 451, in declaring that Jesus was both human and divine underscored his role as mediator. In the union of these two natures, the mediation moves in both directions.

But Jesus is also referred to as judge of the world and Lord of hosts. This corresponds with the old world three-story cosmology that viewed God as sitting high above the firmament, ruling and judging the world. Christ is in the highest realm in the company of the Angels who engage in eternal worship. But even in his absence,

he remains eternally present. As Head and Founder he beckons us to follow him.

"The Lord of hosts" comes from the Hebrew expression *"Yahweh Sabaoth"* and is used hundreds of times to refer to God: "The Lord of hosts is with us; our stronghold is the God of Jacob" (Psalm 46:8). The image this title brings to mind is of a mighty military commander, one who can at a mere word summon rank upon rank of protective power. In some Old Testament stories, the use of "Lord Sabaoth" is particularly apt. When David approached

Goliath, he responded to the warrior's taunts, saying, "You come against me with sword and spear and scimitar, but I come against you in the name of the LORD of hosts" (1 Samuel 17:45). This is the same Lord that we sing to in the Holy, Holy, Holy—the God of power and might.

PREFACE II OF THE ASCENSION OF THE LORD

The mystery of the Ascension

51.   The following Preface is said on the day of the Ascension of the Lord. It may be said on the days between the Ascension and Pentecost in all Masses that have no proper Preface.

V. The Lord be with you.   R. And with your spir-it.

V. Lift up your hearts.   R. We lift them up to the Lord.

V. Let us give thanks to the Lord our God.   R. It is right and just.

Bring out the accent on **be** in **The Lord be with you**.

Make a strong accent on **Lift**, and slow both notes of **hearts**.

In the third dialogue, move to the word **thanks** before accenting, and hold that word slightly to give it emphasis. Broaden both notes of **Lord**, and hold **God**.

It is truly right and just, our duty and our salvation,
always and everywhere to give you thanks,
Lord, holy Father, almighty and eternal God,
through Christ our Lord.

For after his Resurrection
he plainly appeared to all his disciples
and was taken up to heaven in their sight,
that he might make us sharers in his divinity.

Emphasize **appeared** and **taken up**.

The phrase **that he might** explains the meaning and result of the feast.

Therefore, overcome with paschal joy,
every land, every people exults in your praise
and even the heavenly Powers, with the angelic hosts,
sing together the unending hymn of your glory,
as they acclaim:

Holy, Holy, Holy Lord God of hosts . . .

When the Roman Canon is used on the Ascension, there is a proper **Communicantes**, p. 637.

51. Preface II of the Ascension of the Lord: The mystery of the Ascension alludes to Acts 1:6–11 and Luke 24:50–53, as does Preface I of the Ascension. Unlike Preface I, though, there is no binary opposition in the prayer.

An accounting of Christ's actions is seen in this prayer. We are told that Christ made himself known to his apostles. After rising from the dead, he plainly appeared to them while with the two disciples on the road to Emmaus, where he became known in the breaking of the bread (Luke 24:13–53). Second, he appeared to the disciples in Jerusalem (Luke 24:36–48). In that appearance, he said, "You are witnesses of these things." They will preach "repentance, for the forgiveness of sins . . . in his name to all the nations, beginning from Jerusalem" (v. 47–48).

Among the "things" the apostles witness, this Preface reminds us, is the Ascension. As Luke 24:50–51 recounts, "Then he led them [out] as far as Bethany, raised his hands, and blessed them. As he blessed them he parted from them and was taken up to heaven." He ascended, we pray, "that he might make us sharers in his divinity."

Acts 1:7–11 describes the scene thus: "He answered them: 'It is not for you to know the times or seasons that the Father has established by his own authority. But you will receive power when the holy Spirit comes upon you, and you will be my witnesses in Jerusalem, throughout Judea and Samaria, and to the ends of the earth.' When he had said this, as they were looking on, he was lifted up, and a cloud took

It is truly right and just, our duty and our sal-va-tion, al-ways and everywhere to give you thanks, Lord, holy Father, almighty and e-ter-nal God, through Christ our Lord. For after his Resurrection he plainly appeared to all his dis-ci-ples and was taken up to heaven in their sight, that he might make us shar-ers in his di-vin-i-ty. There-fore, o-vercome with pas-chal joy, every land, eve-ry peo-ple ex-ults in your praise and even the heavenly Powers, with the an-gel-ic hosts, sing together the unending hymn of your glo-ry, as they ac-claim:

Holy, Holy, Holy Lord God of hosts . . .

Sing this proclamation cursively in a reciting tone. In **salvation**, do not hold **-va**; only broaden the two notes slightly. The last syllable, **-tion**, should be held. **Always** and **everywhere** require a slight broadening and clear enunciation. The accent of the phrase falls on **thanks**, which should be held briefly. In the next sentence, clearly make distinct phrases of the text, by respecting the commas.

At the end of the first phrase, hold **-ples** of **disciples** and take a very quick breath there. In the next phrase, hold **sight** briefly, but without breathing, go on to **that he**. Articulate carefully every syllable from **make us** on.

In the concluding phrase, make a slight pause after **And so**. Respect the commas but try to keep this section together, without big breaks for breaths. Broaden the last phrase, especially on **glory**. Slow **we ac-**, and put emphasis on **-claim**, so as to evoke the response of **Holy, Holy, Holy** . . . .

him from their sight. While they were looking intently at the sky as he was going, suddenly two men dressed in white garments stood beside them. They said, 'Men of Galilee, why are you standing there looking at the sky? This Jesus, who has been taken up from you into heaven will return in the same way as you have seen him going into heaven.' "

The Preface, however, proffers the meaning and purpose behind the Ascension of Jesus when it states that he does this "that he might make us sharers in his divinity."

The idea might seem strange to us at first, that God became human so that humans might become divine. Saint Athanasius in his *On the Incarnation* 54:3 expressed this idea clearly.

This idea is also expressed in the mixing of water with the wine at the Preparation of the Gifts. A small amount of water is placed in the chalice with the wine. The action is accompanied by a prayer that opens up an allegorical meaning of the commingling of the humanity and divinity in Christ. This exchange of properties

known as the *sacrum commercium* has been fertile ground for theologians to explore the deeper meaning of the Incarnation, in which divinity and humanity are commingled. In the East, theologians speak of this as *theosis* or divinization, while in the West it is called sanctification.

PREFACE I OF THE SUNDAYS IN ORDINARY TIME

The Paschal Mystery and the People of God

52.   The following Preface is said on Sundays in Ordinary Time.

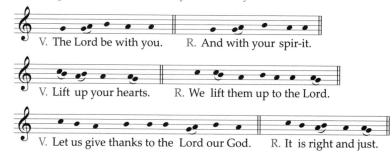

V. The Lord be with you.   R. And with your spir-it.

V. Lift up your hearts.   R. We lift them up to the Lord.

V. Let us give thanks to the Lord our God.   R. It is right and just.

It is truly right and just, our duty and our salvation,
always and everywhere to give you thanks,
Lord, holy Father, almighty and eternal God,
through Christ our Lord.

For through his Paschal Mystery,
he accomplished the marvelous deed,
by which he has freed us from the yoke of sin and death,
summoning us to the glory of being now called
a chosen race, a royal priesthood,
a holy nation, a people for your own possession,
to proclaim everywhere your mighty works,
for you have called us out of darkness
into your own wonderful light.

And so, with Angels and Archangels,
with Thrones and Dominions,
and with all the hosts and Powers of heaven,
we sing the hymn of your glory,
as without end we acclaim:

Holy, Holy, Holy Lord God of hosts . . .

Bring out the accent on **be** in **The Lord be with you**.

Make a strong accent on **Lift**, and slow both notes of **hearts**.

In the third dialogue, move to the word **thanks** before accenting, and hold that word slightly to give it emphasis. Broaden both notes of **Lord**, and hold **God**.

Pay attention to the comma after **Paschal Mystery**. Ignore the comma after **deed**.

The phrase **summoning us** is meant to be gerundive.

Set off **a chosen race, a royal priesthood, a holy nation, a people for your own possession**.

52. Preface I of the Sundays in Ordinary Time: The Paschal Mystery and the People of God comes from 1 Peter 2:9: "But you are 'a chosen race, a royal priesthood, a holy nation, a people of his own, so that you may announce the praises' of him who called you out of darkness into his wonderful light."

The first line of the body of Preface I of the Sundays in Ordinary Time sets up the particular reason for which we praise God. We praise God, because it is through the Paschal Mystery—Christ's Passion, Death,

and Resurrection—that the Church was established. We thank God, because it is through the Paschal Mystery that we have been allowed to be part of the worshipping community that finds itself grafted onto the life and promises given to the community that has existed for 21 centuries.

Through the Paschal Mystery, we are freed from the burdens of sin and death and we are summoned to glory. But we have not just had the "yoke of sin and death" taken from us. As stated in 1 Peter 2:9, what Christ has done for us through

the Paschal Mystery has set us apart. We are "a chosen race, a royal priesthood, a holy nation." But just a short time ago, we were none of those. As 1 Peter 2:10 states, "Once you were 'no people' but now you are God's people." Yes, we are "a people for your own possession." And what do we do as his people? 1 Peter 2:9 states, " 'announce the praises' " of him who called you out of darkness into his wonderful light." As today's Preface states, we "proclaim everywhere your mighty works, / for you have called us out of darkness,

It is truly right and just, our duty and our sal-va-tion, al-ways and

everywhere to give you thanks, Lord, holy Father, almighty and e-

-ter-nal God, through Christ our Lord. For through his Paschal

Mystery, he accomplished the mar-vel-ous deed, by which he has

freed us from the yoke of sin and death, sum-moning us to the glo-

-ry of be-ing now called a chosen race, a royal priesthood, a holy

nation, a people for your own pos-ses-sion, to proclaim every-

-where your might-y works, for you have called us out of dark-ness

into your own won-der-ful light. And so, with Angels and Arch-

-angels, with Thrones and Do-min-ions, and with all the hosts and

Pow-ers of heav-en, we sing the hymn of your glo-ry, as without

end we ac-claim:

Holy, Holy, Holy Lord God of hosts . . .

Sing this proclamation cursively in a reciting tone. In **salvation**, do not hold **-va**; only broaden the two notes slightly. The last syllable, **-tion**, should be held. **Always** and **everywhere** require a slight broadening and clear enunciation. The accent of the phrase falls on **thanks**, which should be held briefly. In the next sentence, clearly make distinct phrases of the text, by respecting the commas.

Do not hold or pause after **Mystery** in the first phrase, but continue on to **he accomplished**. Hold **deed** at the end of the phrase, however, and take a very short breath. At **death**, the end of the next phrase, hold the word and take a quick breath. Similarly, at **called** in the next phrase. Respect the commas of the next three short phrases, by holding the word before the comma. Hold **-sion** of **possession** and take a short breath there. At the end of the next phrase, hold **works**, but try to continue without a breath (or else after taking only a very short one) into the next phrase, **for you**. Do not hold or prolong **darkness**, but rather continue on with **into your**. Slow and broaden **wonderful light**, holding the last word and then taking a breath.

In the concluding phrase, make a slight pause after **And so**. Respect the commas but try to keep this section together, without big breaks for breaths. Broaden the last phrase, especially on **glory**. Slow **we ac-**, and put emphasis on **-claim**, so as to evoke the response of **Holy, Holy, Holy** . . . .

into your own wonderful light." We the Church have work to do. We are to proclaim God's mighty works. That was the work that the first disciples were to do, and it continues to be our task as "a chosen race" and a "holy people." We are, after all, possessed by God.

The "Paschal Mystery," as a phrase, can be separated and examined to more fully understand the concept it represents. "Paschal" can be broken down to the root word from the Aramaic *pasha*. This word means Passover. Melito of Sardis, a second-

century Bishop from Anatolia, expands upon the original sense to include suffering (*paschein*). The second word, "mystery," describes not an idea that must be unlocked or solved (like a mystery novel), but a truth not yet understood; a truth that is still unfolding, and the mystery about it is that we can never fully understand it. Putting these two words together, the phrase describes a truth not understood that is still unfolding about the passing over (the life, suffering, Death, and glorification) of Christ.

No wonder Saint Paul regarded Baptism as entrance into the Paschal Mystery: "We were indeed buried with him through baptism into death, so that, just as Christ was raised from the dead by the glory of the Father, we too might live in newness of life" (Romans 6:4).

PREFACE II OF THE SUNDAYS IN ORDINARY TIME

The mystery of salvation

53.   The following Preface is said on Sundays in Ordinary Time.

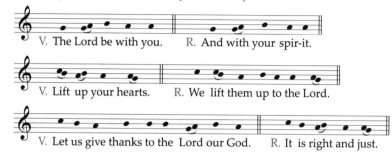

V. The Lord be with you.   R. And with your spir-it.

V. Lift up your hearts.   R. We lift them up to the Lord.

V. Let us give thanks to the Lord our God.   R. It is right and just.

Bring out the accent on **be** in **The Lord be with you.**

It is truly right and just, our duty and our salvation,
always and everywhere to give you thanks,
Lord, holy Father, almighty and eternal God,
through Christ our Lord.

Make a strong accent on **Lift**, and slow both notes of **hearts.**

For out of compassion for the waywardness that is ours,
he humbled himself and was born of the Virgin;
by the passion of the Cross he freed us from unending death,
and by rising from the dead he gave us life eternal.

In the third dialogue, move to the word **thanks** before accenting, and hold that word slightly to give it emphasis. Broaden both notes of **Lord**, and hold **God.**

And so, with Angels and Archangels,
with Thrones and Dominions,
and with all the hosts and Powers of heaven,
we sing the hymn of your glory,
as without end we acclaim:

In the body, treat each sense line separately.

Pay attention to all punctuation.

Holy, Holy, Holy Lord God of hosts . . .

53. In **Preface II of the Sundays in Ordinary Time: The mystery of salvation**, we have a repetition of the phrases of the Creed: "He . . . . was born of the Virgin." Two sets of words stand out as being yoked in the central part of the prayer. The word "compassion" in the first sentence is linked to "passion" in the third, and the idea of being "humbled," or brought low, stands in binary opposition to "rising."

Two words that stand out in this prayer that merit further discussion are "compassion" and "humbled." The English

noun "compassion," meaning "to suffer together with," comes from the Latin. Its prefix "com" is an archaic version of the Latin preposition and affix *cum*, meaning "with." The passion segment is derived from *passus*, past participle of the dependnent verb *patior, pati, passus sum*. "Compassion" is thus related in origin, form, and meaning to the English noun "patient" as one who suffers, from *patiens*, present participle of the same *patior*, and is akin to the Greek verb *paskhein*, to suffer and to its cognate noun *pathos*. "Compassion," therefore,

from Latin "co-suffering" is a virtue, one in which the emotional capacities of empathy and sympathy (for the suffering of others) are regarded as a part of love itself, and a cornerstone of greater social interconnectedness and humanism, foundational to the highest principles in philosophy, society, and personhood. More vigorous than empathy, the feeling commonly gives rise to an active desire to be present to another's suffering.

The word "humbling" poses some problems in English translation. Some

It is truly right and just, our duty and our sal-va-tion, al-ways and everywhere to give you thanks, Lord, holy Father, almighty and e--ter-nal God, through Christ our Lord. For out of compassion for the waywardness that is ours, he hum-bled him-self and was born of the Vir-gin; by the passion of the Cross he freed us from un-end-ing death, and by rising from the dead he gave us life e-ter-nal. And so, with Angels and Archangels, with Thrones and Do-min-ions, and with all the hosts and Pow-ers of heav-en, we sing the hymn of your glo-ry, as without end we ac-claim:

Holy, Holy, Holy Lord God of hosts . . .

Sing this proclamation cursively in a reciting tone. In **salvation**, do not hold **-va**; only broaden the two notes slightly. The last syllable, **-tion**, should be held. **Always** and **everywhere** require a slight broadening and clear enunciation. The accent of the phrase falls on **thanks**, which should be held briefly. In the next sentence, clearly make distinct phrases of the text, by respecting the commas.

In the first phrases, hold **ours**, **-self** of **himself** and **-gin** of **Virgin**. Slow slightly at **born** to the end of the phrase. Hold **Cross**, but do not breathe there. Hold **death** and take a breath there. In the next phrase, hold **dead**, but do not take a breath there. Rather, take the breath with a slight pause after **eternal**.

In the concluding phrase, make a slight pause after **And so**. Respect the commas but try to keep this section together, without big breaks for breaths. Broaden the last phrase, especially on **glory**. Slow **we ac-**, and put emphasis on **-claim**, so as to evoke the response of **Holy, Holy, Holy** . . . .

would speak about the humiliation of Christ, but this sounds like the psychological state of being embarrassed. The idea here is rather that of abasement and it is intimately bound to the idea of emptying out, or *kenosis*. The Greek word *tapeino* is a verb expressing the action of humbling rather than the condition of humility. In classical Greek, *tapeino* means "to make small" or "to weaken." In Luke 14:7–11, the word is used in contrast to those who will be exalted: "For everyone who exalts him-

self will be humbled, but the one who humbles himself will be exalted" (v. 11).

Related to humbling is the Greek word *kenosis*, which means "to empty" or "make empty." This theological term is found in the Christological hymn in Philippians 2:7, which says that Christ "emptied himself." (See the commentary for Easter IV, where the hymn is treated in greater depth, including a structural analysis.)

The pairing of "humbled" with "rising" is quite intentional, and this is a result of

both Christ's compassion (an expression of selfless love) and his Passion on the cross. To the extent that Jesus humbled himself, taking on our human condition even unto Death on a cross is the degree that he is exalted and given the name above every other name. He is both the Messiah or Anointed One and the Lord.

PREFACE III OF THE SUNDAYS IN ORDINARY TIME

The salvation of man by a man

54. The following Preface is said on Sundays in Ordinary Time.

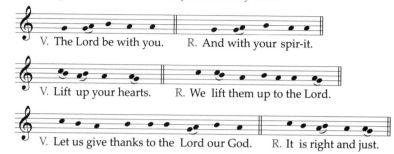

V. The Lord be with you.   R. And with your spir-it.

V. Lift up your hearts.   R. We lift them up to the Lord.

V. Let us give thanks to the Lord our God.   R. It is right and just.

Bring out the accent on **be** in **The Lord be with you**.

Make a strong accent on **Lift**, and slow both notes of **hearts**.

In the third dialogue, move to the word **thanks** before accenting, and hold that word slightly to give it emphasis. Broaden both notes of **Lord**, and hold **God**.

Emphasize the twofold action of coming (**came**) and fashioning (**fashioned**). Draw out the binary opposition between **divinity** and **mortality**.

It is truly right and just, our duty and our salvation,
always and everywhere to give you thanks,
Lord, holy Father, almighty and eternal God.

For we know it belongs to your boundless glory,
that you came to the aid of mortal beings with your divinity
and even fashioned for us a remedy out of mortality itself,
that the cause of our downfall
might become the means of our salvation,
through Christ our Lord.

Through him the host of Angels adores your majesty
and rejoices in your presence for ever.
May our voices, we pray, join with theirs
in one chorus of exultant praise, as we acclaim:

Holy, Holy, Holy Lord God of hosts . . .

54. The key to **Preface III of the Sundays in Ordinary Time: The salvation of man by a man** is in lines four and five: "that the cause of our downfall / might become the means of our salvation."

This is not a particularly easy prayer to pray aloud. The difficulty stems from the abstract wording. "[T]hat you came to the aid of mortal beings with your divinity" is another way of saying "by dying you destroyed our death."

A binary opposition is evident in lines two and three with the phrases "aid of mortal beings with your divinity" and "remedy out of mortality."

The Preface presents the mystery of the Incarnation as a remedy for sin. This medicinal metaphor was extended sacramentally in the early Church to include Baptism (see Ambrose of Milan, De Sacramentis, 2, 17). By the early Middle Ages, it was penance that was the normal remedy for sin (see Alcuin of York, Ad Pueros Sanctii Martini).

The classical theological position was that the Incarnation was necessitated by the Fall, since it provided the grace as a remedy for sin. This was certainly the opinion of Leo the Great: "For God the almighty and merciful, . . . as soon as the devil's malignity killed us by the poison of his hatred, foretold at the very beginning of the world the remedy His piety had prepared for the restoration of us mortals, . . . signifying no doubt that Christ would come in the flesh, God and man, Who . . . should . . . condemn the despoiler of the human stock" (Sermon 22.1).

It is truly right and just, our duty and our sal-va-tion, al-ways and everywhere to give you thanks, Lord, holy Father, almighty and e-ter-nal God. For we know it belongs to your bound-less glo-ry, that you came to the aid of mor-tal be-ings with your di-vin-i-ty and even fashioned for us a remedy out of mor-tal-i-ty it-self, that the cause of our down-fall might become the means of our sal-va-tion, through Christ our Lord. Through him the host of An-gels a-dores your maj-es-ty and re-joic-es in your pres-ence for ev-er. May our voices, we pray, join with theirs in one chorus of ex-ult-ant praise, as we ac-claim:

Holy, Holy, Holy Lord God of hosts . . .

Sing this proclamation cursively in a reciting tone. In **salvation**, do not hold **-va**; only broaden the two notes slightly. The last syllable, **-tion**, should be held. **Always** and **every-where** require a slight broadening and clear enunciation. The accent of the phrase falls on **thanks**, which should be held briefly. In the next sentence, clearly make distinct phrases of the text, by respecting the commas.

At the end of the first phrase, hold **-ry** of **glory**, but if at all possible do not take a breath or break there; rather continue with **that you came**. Tie together without holding or break **beings** and **with**. Hold the last syllable of the phrase and take a breath. In the next phrase, tie together **remedy** and **out of** without holding or pause. Similarly, tie together **downfall** and **might become**, without holding or pausing. If one needs a breath after **salvation**, it should be very short, so as to continue with **through**, holding **Lord** at the end and taking a breath there.

In the concluding phrase, make a slight pause after **And so**. Respect the commas but try to keep this section together, without big breaks for breaths. Broaden the last phrase, especially on **praise**. Slow **we ac-**, and put emphasis on **-claim**, so as to evoke the response of **Holy, Holy, Holy . . . .**

In the twelfth century, a debate was waged on the matter. Honorius of Autun argued against the idea of the Incarnation as a remedy for human sin. Rupert of Deutz argued in a similar vein that the Incarnation, rather than being a remedy for sin, was the perfection of creation.

It fell to Saint Thomas Aquinas to adjudicate the debate. Uneasy with the speculative nature of the debate, he argued that the coming of Christ was in response to the Fall, but added that there was little to be gained by considering alternatives. He wrote, "There are different opinions about this question. For some say that even if man had not sinned, the Son of Man would have become incarnate. Others assert the contrary, and seemingly our assent ought rather to be given to this opinion. For such things as spring from God's will, and beyond the creature's due, can be made known to us only through being revealed in the Sacred Scripture, in which the Divine Will is made known to us. Hence, since everywhere in the Sacred Scripture the sin of the first man is assigned as the reason of Incarnation, it is more in accordance with this to say that the work of Incarnation was ordained by God as a remedy for sin; so that, had sin not existed, Incarnation would not have been. And yet the power of God is not limited to this; even had sin not existed, God could have become incarnate" (Sum. Th, 3.1.3).

PREFACE IV OF THE SUNDAYS IN ORDINARY TIME

The history of salvation

55.   The following Preface is said on Sundays in Ordinary Time.

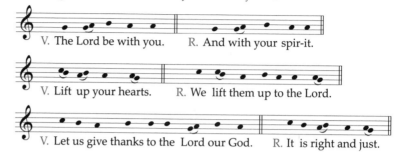

V. The Lord be with you.   R. And with your spir-it.

V. Lift up your hearts.   R. We lift them up to the Lord.

V. Let us give thanks to the Lord our God.   R. It is right and just.

It is truly right and just, our duty and our salvation,
always and everywhere to give you thanks,
Lord, holy Father, almighty and eternal God,
through Christ our Lord.

For by his birth he brought renewal
to humanity's fallen state,
and by his suffering, canceled out our sins;
by his rising from the dead
he has opened the way to eternal life,
and by ascending to you, O Father,
he has unlocked the gates of heaven.

And so, with the company of Angels and Saints,
we sing the hymn of your praise,
as without end we acclaim:

Holy, Holy, Holy Lord God of hosts . . .

Sidebar notes:

Bring out the accent on **be** in **The Lord be with you**.

Make a strong accent on **Lift**, and slow both notes of **hearts**.

In the third dialogue, move to the word **thanks** before accenting, and hold that word slightly to give it emphasis. Broaden both notes of **Lord**, and hold **God**.

Speech should ascend through the paragraph. Treat lines 1 and 2 as one line. Pause significantly after **state**. Treat line 3 as a single line with a long pause at the semicolon. Lower your pitch and sing slower than you did for lines 1 and 2. Treat lines 4 and 5 as one line. Pause at the comma. Read lines 6 and 7 as one line.

Continue through **we acclaim** at a higher pitch and faster rate.

---

55. Preface IV of the Sundays in Ordinary Time: The history of salvation is a spectacular Preface that calls upon the Priest Celebrant to pay attention to the speech pattern. Four parallel phrases are in ascending order in this prayer. The first three lines should be prayed in the same pitch, the next two lines should be higher, and the next two lines higher yet. The voice will be mirroring in pitch and volume the ascension that occurs in the prayer.

Although this prayer does not directly quote Philippians 2:6–11, it is drawn from that hymn. We see, in this Preface, the Christ who humbled himself by coming in human form and dying on the cross. The Philippians' hymn states that, at the name of Jesus, "every knee should bend, of those in heaven and on earth and under the earth" (v. 10). Jesus, who in Philippians was found "human in appearance," is the one who "brought renewal to humanity's fallen state." In the phrase "by his suffering, canceled out our sins" is the Philippians' Jesus who became "obedient to death, even death on a cross."

In the hymn, it is acclaimed that "God greatly exalted him and bestowed on him the name that is above every other name." In this Preface, it is acclaimed that "he has opened the way to eternal life" and "unlocked the gates of heaven."

Within this Preface, we see an ascension of events just as occurs in Philippians. In Christ's birth, we see the one who "did not regard equality with God . . . coming in human likeness" (v. 6–7). The one who rises from the dead correlates to the one

It is truly right and just, our duty and our sal-va-tion, al-ways and everywhere to give you thanks, Lord, holy Father, almighty and e-ter-nal God, through Christ our Lord. For by his birth he brought renewal to humanity's fall-en state, and by his suf-fer-ing, can-celled out our sins; by his rising from the dead he has opened the way to e-ter-nal life, and by ascending to you, O Fa-ther, he has unlocked the gates of heav-en. And so, with the company of An-gels and Saints, we sing the hymn of your praise, as without end we ac-claim:

Holy, Holy, Holy Lord God of hosts . . .

Sing this proclamation cursively in a reciting tone. In **salvation**, do not hold **-va**; only broaden the two notes slightly. The last syllable, **-tion**, should be held. **Always** and **every-where** require a slight broadening and clear enunciation. The accent of the phrase falls on **thanks**, which should be held briefly. In the next sentence, clearly make distinct phrases of the text, by respecting the commas.

In the first phrase, tie together without holding or pause **renewal** and **to**. Hold **state** briefly and take a short breath. Be careful in the next phrase not to accent **-celled** in **cancelled** — which is difficult not to do, as there are two notes on it. It would have been easier to sing with only one note on both **can-** (the "B" that is there) and **celled** (an "A" alone would have made it easier to sing with proper accenting). Hold **sins** and take a short breath there. Tie together **dead** and **he** in the next phrase. Hold **life** at the end of the phrase and take a short breath. It would be appropriate to inflect the voice slightly at the comma after **you**, in order to set off the **O Father** (hold the last syllable slightly but do not take a breath there). Slow slightly **the gates of heaven**.

In the concluding phrase, make a slight pause after **And so**. Respect the commas but try to keep this section together, without big breaks for breaths. Broaden the last phrase, especially on **praise**. Slow **we ac-**, and put emphasis on **-claim**, so as to evoke the response of **Holy, Holy, Holy . . . .**

whom "every tongue confess that Jesus Christ is Lord, to the glory of the Father."

Birth leads to renewal, suffering leads to forgiveness of sins, Resurrection to eternal life, and Ascension to heaven. The life of Christ is depicted as the history of salvation, as the title of the Preface suggests. The Incarnation in this instance is more than simply the nativity of Jesus. It is his entire existence from womb to tomb and beyond the grave. Notice that all four terms are presented as binary oppositions: "birth" against our "fallen state," "suffer-ing" against "sins," "rising" against "dead," and "ascending" against "locked gates." The four phases of Christ's life are antidotes to the fallen human condition.

Canceling sin is reminiscent of Anselm of Canterbury's making satisfaction for sin. His satisfaction theory teaches that Christ suffered as a substitute on behalf of humankind, satisfying the demands of God's honor by his infinite merit. Anselm speaks of human sin as defrauding God of the honor God is due. Christ's Death, the ultimate act of obedience, brings God great honor. As it was beyond the call of duty for Christ, it is more honor than he was obliged to give. Christ's surplus can, therefore, repay our deficit, and thus his suffering cancels our sins. Hence, Christ's Death is substitutionary; he pays the honor instead of us. The key for Anselm is satisfaction as an alternative to punishment. By Christ satisfying our debt of honor to God, we avoid punishment.

PREFACE V OF THE SUNDAYS IN ORDINARY TIME

Creation

56.   The following Preface is said on Sundays in Ordinary Time.

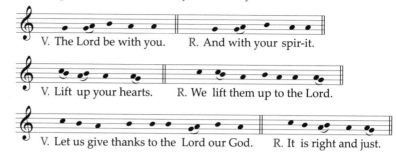

V. The Lord be with you.   R. And with your spir-it.

V. Lift up your hearts.   R. We lift them up to the Lord.

V. Let us give thanks to the Lord our God.   R. It is right and just.

It is truly right and just, our duty and our salvation,
always and everywhere to give you thanks,
Lord, holy Father, almighty and eternal God.

For you laid the foundations of the world
and have arranged the changing of times and seasons;
you formed man in your own image
and set humanity over the whole world in all its wonder,
to rule in your name over all you have made
and for ever praise you in your mighty works,
through Christ our Lord.

And so, with all the Angels, we praise you,
as in joyful celebration we acclaim:

Holy, Holy, Holy Lord God of hosts . . .

Bring out the accent on **be** in **The Lord be with you**.

Make a strong accent on **Lift**, and slow both notes of **hearts**.

In the third dialogue, move to the word **thanks** before accenting, and hold that word slightly to give it emphasis. Broaden both notes of **Lord**, and hold **God**.

Add a significant pause after **seasons**.

Contrast lines 1 and 2 from the rest of the paragraph.

---

56. Preface V of the Sundays in Ordinary Time: Creation alludes to the Yahwist creation narrative in Genesis 1–2:4a. In this short text can be seen the entire account of creation.

The Priest Celebrant should note that the first two lines contrast with the rest of the prayer. Those first lines tell of the creation of the world, and the next five of the formation of humanity, its dominion over creation, and how it will praise God's mighty works.

"For you laid the foundations of the world / and have arranged the changing of times and seasons." These two lines take us to the first lines of Genesis "In the beginning, when God created the heavens and the earth" (1:1) through to the end of the first chapter.

The line "you formed man in your own image" recalls, "Then God said: 'Let us make man in our image, after our likeness'" (v. 26).

The last of creation, humankind, is given "dominion over the fish of the sea,

the birds of the air, and the cattle, and over all the wild animals and all the creatures that crawl on the ground" (v. 26). The prayer makes this dominion evident as it states, God "set humanity over the whole world in all its wonder, / to rule in your name over all you have made."

We find this very positive theology of creation equally well but more succinctly articulated in Psalm 8: "When I consider your heavens, the work of your fingers, the moon and the stars, which you have set in place, what is mankind that you

It is truly right and just, our duty and our sal-va-tion, al-ways and everywhere to give you thanks, Lord, holy Father, almighty and e-ter-nal God. For you laid the foundations of the world and have arranged the chang-ing of times and sea-sons; you formed man in your own im-age and set humanity over the whole world in all its won-der, to rule in your name over all you have made and for ever praise you in your might-y works, through Christ our Lord. And so, as with all the An-gels, we praise you, as in joyful cele-bra-tion we ac-claim:

Holy, Holy, Holy Lord God of hosts . . .

Sing this proclamation cursively in a reciting tone. In **salvation**, do not hold **-va**; only broaden the two notes slightly. The last syllable, **-tion**, should be held. **Always** and **everywhere** require a slight broadening and clear enunciation. The accent of the phrase falls on **thanks**, which should be held briefly. In the next sentence, clearly make distinct phrases of the text, by respecting the commas.

In the first phrase, hold **world**, but do not break or breathe there; rather, continue with **and have**. Hold the second syllable of **seasons**. In the next phrase, hold **-age** of **image**, but continue without a breath (if possible) to **and set**. Hold slightly **-der** of **wonder** in the next phrase, and if necessary, take a quick breath, so as not to lose the sense, which should go on to **to rule**. A breath will probably be necessary also at **made** in that phrase. In the next phrase, hold **works**, but do not pause or breathe before going on to **through Christ our Lord**, which should be slowed and the last word held, and then a breath taken.

In the concluding phrase, make a slight pause after **And so**. Respect the commas but try to keep this section together, without big breaks for breaths. Broaden the last phrase, especially on **praise**. Slow **we ac-**, and put emphasis on **-claim**, so as to evoke the response of **Holy, Holy, Holy** . . . .

are mindful of them, human beings that you care for them? You have made them a little lower than the angels and crowned them with glory and honor. You made them rulers over the works of your hands; you put everything under their feet: all flocks and herds, and the animals of the wild, the birds in the sky, and the fish in the sea, all that swim the paths of the seas. LORD, our Lord, how majestic is your name in all the earth!" (New International Version [NIV]).

The theology of creation is also a theology of stewardship. Humanity is seen very positively as the pinnacle of creation. The creation of humanity on the sixth day also establishes the correlative expectation for humankind to protect and care for creation, first in naming all the creatures but also in being good stewards in the care of creation.

Shakespeare, in Hamlet's soliloquy, begins with the same optimistic view: "What a piece of work is a man, how noble in reason! how infinite in faculties! in form and moving how express and admirable! in action how like an angel! in apprehension how like a god! the beauty of the world! the paragon of animals!" (Act II, Scene 2). But then melancholy sets in and Hamlet concludes: "And yet, to me, what is this quintessence of dust? man delights not me: no, nor woman neither, though by your smiling you seem to say so."

The Preface resists Hamlet's melancholy and proposes that we rule over the world, praising God through Christ.

PREFACE VI OF THE SUNDAYS IN ORDINARY TIME

The pledge of the eternal Passover

57.   The following Preface is said on Sundays in Ordinary Time.

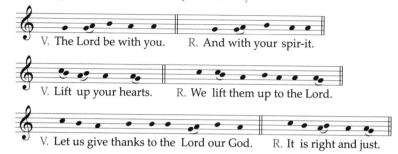

V. The Lord be with you.   R. And with your spir-it.

V. Lift up your hearts.   R. We lift them up to the Lord.

V. Let us give thanks to the Lord our God.   R. It is right and just.

Bring out the accent on **be** in **The Lord be with you**.

Make a strong accent on **Lift**, and slow both notes of **hearts**.

In the third dialogue, move to the word **thanks** before accenting, and hold that word slightly to give it emphasis. Broaden both notes of **Lord**, and hold **God**.

Say the first line slowly and reverently. Be mindful that we are being drawn from the here and now.

This paragraph capitalizes on the first paragraph. This last line is the climax of the Preface.

It is truly right and just, our duty and our salvation,
always and everywhere to give you thanks,
Lord, holy Father, almighty and eternal God.

For in you we live and move and have our being,
and while in this body
we not only experience the daily effects of your care,
but even now possess the pledge of life eternal.

For, having received the first fruits of the Spirit,
through whom you raised up Jesus from the dead,
we hope for an everlasting share in the Paschal Mystery.

And so, with all the Angels, we praise you,
as in joyful celebration we acclaim:

Holy, Holy, Holy Lord God of hosts . . .

57. Preface VI of the Sundays in Ordinary Time: The pledge of the eternal Passover alludes to Saint Paul's address before the Council of Areopagus. In his witness to the Athenians, Paul quotes the Greek poet Epimenides: "For 'In him we live and move and have our being,' as even some of your poets have said."

We see here that our Roman Rite not only uses the prayer texts of the Jewish people but quotes a pagan Greek poet.

The phrase "having received the first fruits of the Spirit" is Pauline. In Romans 8, Saint Paul says, "[B]ut we ourselves, who have the firstfruits of the Spirit, we also groan within ourselves as we wait for adoption, the redemption of our bodies" (v. 23). Here, Paul speaks of the groaning of all of creation as it longs for life eternal. It is apparent to Paul that the here and now is insufficient for humanity. Paul states, "For in hope we were saved" (v. 24). As our prayer states, "we hope for an everlasting share in the Paschal Mystery." This

climax of the prayer is the aim of our lives. We hold fast that we "even now possess the pledge of life eternal."

A word should be said about the expression "first fruits" in the context of an eternal Passover. First fruits are a religious offering of the first agricultural produce of the harvest. In classical Greek, Roman, Hebrew, and Christian religions, the first fruits were offered to the temple or church. First fruits were often a primary source of income to maintain the religious leaders and the facility.

It is truly right and just, our duty and our sal-va-tion, al-ways and everywhere to give you thanks, Lord, holy Father, almighty and e-ter-nal God. For in you we live and move and have our be-ing, and while in this body we not only experience the daily ef-fects of your care, but e-ven now possess the pledge of life e-ter-nal. For, having received the first fruits of the Spirit, through whom you raised up Jesus from the dead, we hope for an ever-last-ing share in the Pas-chal Mys-ter-y. And so, with all the An-gels, we praise you, as in joyful cele-bra-tion we ac-claim:

Holy, Holy, Holy Lord God of hosts . . .

Sing this proclamation cursively in a reciting tone. In **salvation**, do not hold -va; only broaden the two notes slightly. The last syllable, **-tion**, should be held. **Always** and **everywhere** require a slight broadening and clear enunciation. The accent of the phrase falls on **thanks**, which should be held briefly. In the next sentence, clearly make distinct phrases of the text, by respecting the commas.

At the end of the first phrase, hold **-ing** of **being** slightly. Tie together without hold or break **body** and **we**. Hold **care** briefly and pause briefly. Hold **now** slightly. Slow **eternal** at the end of the phrase. Respect the comma after **Spirit** by inflecting the voice slightly before going right on to **through whom**. Hold **dead** very briefly, but with only a quick breath, continue with **we hope**. Articulate the last words and syllables of the phrase (e.g., one might want to hold very briefly **share**). Be careful not to accent **the** just because it has two notes — it might have been better for accentuation if there had been only one note there (an "A") — the accent goes on **Paschal**. Hold the last syllable of **Mystery** and take a breath.

In the concluding phrase, make a slight pause after **And so**. Respect the commas but try to keep this section together, without big breaks for breaths. Broaden the last phrase, especially on **praise**. Slow **we ac-**, and put emphasis on **-claim**, so as to evoke the response of **Holy, Holy, Holy** . . . .

In ancient Israel, first fruits were a type of sacrificial gift brought up to the altar. The major obligation to bring first fruits to the Temple began at the Festival of Weeks (Shavuot) and continued until the Festival of Booths (Sukkot). This tithe was limited to the traditional seven agricultural products (wheat, barley, grapes in the form of wine, figs, pomegranates, olives in the form of oil, and dates) grown in Israel. (Thus, the first fruits of the Spirit may be a reference to the seven gifts.) By giving God the first fruits, Israel acknowledged that all good things come from God, and that everything belongs to God. Giving the first fruits was also a way of expressing trust in God's provision; just as God provided the first fruits, so God would provide everything that is needed.

Since Passover (Pesach) was the first of the three holidays, the first fruits were offered in connection with that holiday. The Passover lambs were sacrificed on the 14th day of the month of Nisan, the first day of Passover was the 15th, and the Feast of First Fruits fell on the 16th of Nisan.

In the Christian context, the first fruits are associated with a pledge for eternal life. Our hearts are always longing for God in whom we live and move and have our being. It is, as Saint Augustine said, "Because God has made us for himself, our hearts are restless until they rest in him" (*Confessions of St. Augustine*).

PREFACE VII OF THE SUNDAYS IN ORDINARY TIME

Salvation through the obedience of Christ

58.   The following Preface is said on Sundays in Ordinary Time.

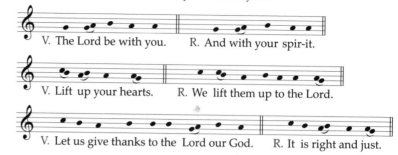

V. The Lord be with you.   R. And with your spir-it.

V. Lift up your hearts.   R. We lift them up to the Lord.

V. Let us give thanks to the Lord our God.   R. It is right and just.

Bring out the accent on **be** in **The Lord be with you.**

Make a strong accent on **Lift**, and slow both notes of **hearts.**

In the third dialogue, move to the word **thanks** before accenting, and hold that word slightly to give it emphasis. Broaden both notes of **Lord**, and hold **God.**

Treat lines 1 to 3 of the body as one line. Ignore the comma after **Redeemer.**

Insert a short pause after **Son.**

Treat these last two lines as one. Treat **by sinning** as parenthetical. Except for the parenthetical, read the line quickly.

It is truly right and just, our duty and our salvation,
always and everywhere to give you thanks,
Lord, holy Father, almighty and eternal God.

For you so loved the world
that in your mercy you sent us the Redeemer,
to live like us in all things but sin,
so that you might love in us what you loved in your Son,
by whose obedience we have been restored to those gifts of yours
that, by sinning, we had lost in disobedience.

And so, Lord, with all the Angels and Saints,
we, too, give you thanks, as in exultation we acclaim:

Holy, Holy, Holy Lord God of hosts . . .

---

58. Preface VII of the Sundays in Ordinary Time: Salvation through the obedience of Christ alludes, in the first two lines, to John 3:16: "For God so loved the world that he gave his only Son, so that everyone who believes in him might not perish but might have eternal life."

The line "that you might love in us what you loved in your Son," recalls the line in Christ's prayer in John 17: "And I have given them the glory you gave me, . . . so . . . that the world may know that you

sent me, and that you loved them even as you loved me" (v. 22–23).

And again in verse 26, Jesus speaks of the Father's love for him and for us. "I made known to them your name . . . , that the love with which you loved me may be in them and I in them."

The obedience of which this prayer speaks is evident in John 12:27, as Jesus prays: "I am troubled now. Yet what should I say? 'Father, save me from this hour'?"

The phrase "by whose obedience we have been restored to those gifts of yours"

recalls how Christ returned to us what originally had been ours. John the Baptist said, "From his fullness we have all received, grace in place of grace, because while the law was given through Moses, grace and truth came through Jesus Christ" (John 1:16–17). These are the gifts we lost in our disobedience.

In the Preface, God's love is associated with God's mercy. In the Hebrew language, this is captured in the word *hesed*, which also includes the idea of kindness. The word is used many times to describe one

It is truly right and just, our duty and our sal-va-tion, al-ways and everywhere to give you thanks, Lord, holy Father, almighty and e-ter-nal God. For you so loved the world that in your mer-cy you sent us the Re-deem-er, to live like us in all things but sin, so that you might love in us what you loved in your Son, by whose obedience we have been restored to those gifts of yours that, by sin-ning, we had lost in dis-o-be-di-ence. And so, Lord, with all the An-gels and Saints, we, too, give you thanks, as in exul-ta-tion we ac-claim:

Holy, Holy, Holy Lord God of hosts . . .

Sing this proclamation cursively in a reciting tone. In **salvation**, do not hold **-va**; only broaden the two notes slightly. The last syllable, **-tion**, should be held. **Always** and **everywhere** require a slight broadening and clear enunciation. The accent of the phrase falls on **thanks**, which should be held briefly. In the next sentence, clearly make distinct phrases of the text, by respecting the commas.

Briefly hold **world** and without pausing go on to **that**. Slightly broaden **mer-cy**, and without taking a breath, continue with **you sent**. Hold the last syllable of **Redeemer**. Carefully articulate **all things but sin**, holding the last word slightly. Hold **Son** after carefully articulating **loved in your Son**. If a breath is needed, take a quick one there. Tie together **restored** and **to**, holding **yours**. If a breath is needed, take a quick one. Briefly hold **-ning** of **sinning**. Try not to accent the **o** in **disobedience**.

In the concluding phrase, make a slight pause after **And so**. Respect the commas but try to keep this section together, without big breaks for breaths. Broaden the last phrase, especially on **thanks**. Slow **we ac-**, and put emphasis on **-claim**, so as to evoke the response of **Holy, Holy, Holy** . . . .

of God's favorite attributes. Micah 7:18 says, "Who is there like you, the God who removes guilt and pardons sin for the remnant of his inheritance; Who does not persist in anger forever, but delights rather in clemency." The NIV translates *hesed* as "mercy" while the New American Standard Bible translates it as "unchanging love." Notice that the Lord delights in mercy or unchanging love. Hence, God takes great pleasure in showing mercy. Parallelism can be seen vividly in the Preface and in the

passage from Micah. God pardons iniquity and passes by transgression. God does not retain anger but delights in mercy. Certainly, ours is a God of justice and judgment; but God is many times portrayed as rich in mercy.

Mercy, love, truth, and forgiveness are closely linked when describing God. The extent of God's love and mercy are indescribable and unfathomable to the human mind. Often in translation, we need to use a paraphrase to capture the richness of the

word *hesed*. So we might say God's merciful love or loving mercy. Or loving kindness would also approximate the deep meaning. To avoid redundancy, the Preface distinguishes between God's love and mercy, yet these are all manifestations of a God who is love as John is so found of saying in his letters. And Christ is the sign of God's merciful love who is like us in all things except sin.

PREFACE VIII OF THE SUNDAYS IN ORDINARY TIME

The Church united by the unity of the Trinity

59.   The following Preface is said on Sundays in Ordinary Time.

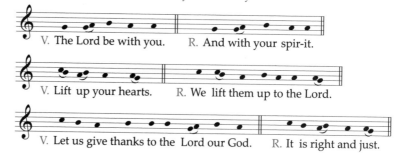

V. The Lord be with you.   R. And with your spir-it.

V. Lift up your hearts.   R. We lift them up to the Lord.

V. Let us give thanks to the Lord our God.   R. It is right and just.

It is truly right and just, our duty and our salvation,
always and everywhere to give you thanks,
Lord, holy Father, almighty and eternal God.

For, when your children were scattered afar by sin,
through the Blood of your Son and the power of the Spirit,
you gathered them again to yourself,
that a people, formed as one by the unity of the Trinity,
made the body of Christ and the temple of the Holy Spirit,
might, to the praise of your manifold wisdom,
be manifest as the Church.

And so, in company with the choirs of Angels,
we praise you, and with joy we proclaim:

Holy, Holy, Holy Lord God of hosts . . .

Bring out the accent on **be** in **The Lord be with you**.

Make a strong accent on **Lift**, and slow both notes of **hearts**.

In the third dialogue, move to the word **thanks** before accenting, and hold that word slightly to give it emphasis. Broaden both notes of **Lord**, and hold **God**.

Follow the sense lines throughout the prayer. Emphasize the parallel ideas of **scattering** and **gathering**.

Emphasize **body of Christ** and **the Church** as correlative.

---

59. Preface VIII of the Sundays in Ordinary Time: The Church united by the unity of the Trinity is dedicated to the work of the Trinity in uniting the Church. This Preface, however, is not the Preface for Trinity Sunday, which is found in the section of the Missal entitled "Solemnities of the Lord." This section additionally contains the Solemnities of the Most Holy Body and Blood of Christ (Corpus Christi), the Most Sacred Heart and Our Lord Jesus Christ, King of the Universe. Thus, the special Prefaces associated with these Feasts will not be found in the section on Prefaces but attached directly to the Solemnities found immediately following the Thirty-fourth Sunday in Ordinary Time.

The themes in Preface VIII in the Sundays of Ordinary Time would be especially appropriate for Masses of Reconciliation. The core of the body of the Preface is: "when your children were scattered afar by sin, / . . . / you gathered them again to yourself, / that a people . . . / . . . / might / be manifest as the Church." The other phrases are parenthetical expressions and should be treated as secondary.

The parenthetical portions of the prayer insist upon the work of the Trinity. The Father calls through the blood of the Son and the power of the Holy Spirit. In a parallel fashion, each person of the Trinity is attributed a specific aspect of this unity. The Father is responsible for the calling to unity. The Son gathers us as one Body, and the Holy Spirit forms us as a Temple. Let us take each of these actions in order.

It is truly right and just, our duty and our sal-va-tion, al-ways and everywhere to give you thanks, Lord, holy Father, almighty and e-ter-nal God. For, when your children were scattered a-far by sin, through the Blood of your Son and the power of the Spir-it, you gath-ered them a-gain to your-self, that a people, formed as one by the unity of the Trin-i-ty, made the body of Christ and the temple of the Ho-ly Spir-it, might, to the praise of your ma-ni-fold wis-dom, be mani-fest as the Church. And so, in company with the choirs of An-gels, we praise you, and with joy we pro-claim:

Holy, Holy, Holy Lord God of hosts . . .

Sing this proclamation cursively in a reciting tone. In **salvation**, do not hold **-va**; only broaden the two notes slightly. The last syllable, **-tion**, should be held. **Always** and **every-where** require a slight broadening and clear enunciation. The accent of the phrase falls on **thanks**, which should be held briefly. In the next sentence, clearly make distinct phrases of the text, by respecting the commas.

Hold **sin** briefly, and take a short breath, if needed. Hold **Son** without breaking or breathing to go on through **Spirit**, holding the last syllable. Take a short breath, if necessary. Tie everything together without holding or breaking until the last syllable of **Trinity**. Sing the next phrase through to the last syllable of **Trinity**. Broaden both syllables of **wisdom** and continue without a breath to **be**. Hold **Church** and take a good breath.

In the concluding phrase, make a slight pause after **And so**. Respect the commas but try to keep this section together, without big breaks for breaths. Broaden the last phrase, especially on **praise**. Slow **we ac-**, and put emphasis on **-claim**, so as to evoke the response of **Holy, Holy, Holy . . . .**

The Father calls all to unity. Just as the Trinity is a unity of persons, so too God's people share in the life of the Trinity. In the first letter of John, it is carefully stated that the initiative is always from the side of God: "In this way the love of God was revealed to us: God sent his only Son into the world so that we might have life through him. In this is love: not that we have loved God, but that he loved us and sent his Son as expiation for our sins" (1 John 4:9–10). Therefore the initiative is from God. But it is through the Blood of Christ that we are made the Body of Christ and the power of the Spirit, which forms us as a temple.

According to this doctrine, God exists as three persons but is one God, meaning that God the Son and God the Holy Spirit have exactly the same nature or being as God the Father in every way. Whatever attributes and power God the Father has, God the Son and God the Holy Spirit have as well. Thus, God the Son and God the Holy Spirit are also eternal, omnipresent, omnipotent, infinitely wise, infinitely holy, infinitely loving, and omniscient as the Father is.

Although each member of the Trinity is attributed a different aspect, this must not be regarded as modalism, which is the non-Trinitarian belief that the heavenly Father, resurrected Son, and Holy Spirit are different modes or aspects of one God, as perceived by the believer, rather than three distinct persons in God-self.

PREFACE I OF THE MOST HOLY EUCHARIST

The Sacrifice and the Sacrament of Christ

60.   The following Preface is said in the Mass of the Lord's Supper (text with music, p. 304). It may also be said on the Solemnity of the Most Holy Body and Blood of Christ (Corpus Christi) and in Votive Masses of the Most Holy Eucharist.

Bring out the accent on **be** in **The Lord be with you.**

> V. **The Lord be with you.**
> R. And with your spirit.

Make a strong accent on **Lift**, and slow both notes of **hearts.**

> V. **Lift up your hearts.**
> R. We lift them up to the Lord.

In the third dialogue, move to the word **thanks** before accenting, and hold that word slightly to give it emphasis. Broaden both notes of **Lord**, and hold **God**.

> V. **Let us give thanks to the Lord our God.**
> R. It is right and just.

It is truly right and just, our duty and our salvation,
always and everywhere to give you thanks,
Lord, holy Father, almighty and eternal God,
through Christ our Lord.

The body comprises two complete sentences. The first deals with Christ, and the second deals with us.

For he is the true and eternal Priest,
who instituted the pattern of an everlasting sacrifice
and was the first to offer himself as the saving Victim,
commanding us to make this offering as his memorial.
As we eat his flesh that was sacrificed for us,
we are made strong,
and, as we drink his Blood that was poured out for us,
we are washed clean.

Emphasize the parallel terms **flesh** and **Blood**, as well as **we are washed clean**, to bring out the Johannine language.

And so, with Angels and Archangels,
with Thrones and Dominions,
and with all the hosts and Powers of heaven,
we sing the hymn of your glory,
as without end we acclaim:

Holy, Holy, Holy Lord God of hosts . . .

When the Roman Canon is used in the Mass of the Lord's Supper, there is a proper Communicantes, Hanc igitur and Qui pridie. For ease of use, the entire Canon has been printed with these incorporated, pp. 635–643.

60. Preface I of the Most Holy Eucharist: The Sacrifice and the Sacrament of Christ, like Preface II of the Most Holy Eucharist, are modern compositions that follow the ancient patterns of liturgical prayer. The Missal from Trent had no special Preface for the Feast of Holy Thursday. Rather the Preface for the Holy Cross (*de sancta Cruce*) was used. This Preface, however, makes no mention of the Last Supper, and as you might expect, it anticipates Good Friday. Provision was made for the Chrism Mass that is found immediately before the Solemn Mass of the Supper of the Lord in the Missal with its own Preface that references the sacred oils to be blessed on that occasion. It is curious that the blessings of the three oils take place at different moments with the Mass: the oil for the sick is blessed before the Our Father, while Holy Chrism and the oil of catechumens are blessed after the clergy have received Holy Communion.

Following the reforms of the Second Vatican Council but also the liturgical reforms of Holy Week promulgated by Pope Pius XII beginning in 1951, a new preface was necessary to draw out the themes of the liturgy for Holy Thursday evening.

Preface I of the Most Holy Eucharist underscores two pairs of ideas: that Christ is the eternal Priest and the true Victim, and that we are to eat his sacrificial flesh and drink his Blood. The second pair is reflecting the command to eat and drink that we find in the Eucharistic prayers that reflect the Synoptic Gospel accounts and Paul's first letter to the community at Corinth.

V. The Lord be with you.   R. And with your spir-it.

V. Lift up your hearts.   R. We lift them up to the Lord.

V. Let us give thanks to the Lord our God.   R. It is right and just.

It is truly right and just, our duty and our sal-va-tion, al-ways and

everywhere to give you thanks, Lord, holy Father, almighty and e-

-ter-nal God, through Christ our Lord. For he is the true and eter-

-nal Priest, who instituted the pattern of an ever-last-ing sac-ri-fice

and was the first to offer himself as the sav-ing Vic-tim, command-

-ing us to make this of-fer-ing as his me-mo-ri-al. As we eat his

flesh that was sacrificed for us, we are made strong, and, as we

drink his Blood that was poured out for us, we are washed clean.

And so, with Angels and Archangels, with Thrones and Do-min-ions,

and with all the hosts and Pow-ers of heav-en, we sing the hymn

of your glo-ry, as without end we ac-claim:

Sing this proclamation cursively in a reciting tone. In **salvation**, do not hold **-va**; only broaden the two notes slightly. The last syllable, **-tion**, should be held. **Always** and **everywhere** require a slight broadening and clear enunciation. The accent of the phrase falls on **thanks**, which should be held briefly. In the next sentence, clearly make distinct phrases of the text, by respecting the commas.

In the very long sentence that begins the body of the text, the melodies on **-lasting sacrifice**, **saving Victim**, and **as his memorial** call for broadening and a hold (but not too long) at the ending syllable. Sing **As we eat** with careful articulation and pausing, bringing out the contrast between the eating and drinking and their consequences.

In the concluding phrase, make a slight pause after **And so**. Respect the commas but try to keep this section together, without big breaks for breaths. Broaden the last phrase, especially on **glory**. Slow **we ac-**, and put emphasis on **-claim**, so as to evoke the response of **Holy, Holy, Holy** . . . .

The first pair of images draws a line from the ancient Verona Sacramentary (Ver. 96) that mentions that Christ offers himself to God for us like the priest offers and the Holy Lamb demonstrates. But the new Preface goes on in both cases to amplify the meaning, so Christ is the true and eternal Priest who instituted the pattern of an everlasting sacrifice and Christ is the saving Victim who commands us to make this offering as a memorial.

If the first pair of images draws our attention to Christ, the second pair directs the attention to us who eat and drink, demonstrating the result of our reception of Holy Communion. Thus in eating of the flesh we are made strong and in drinking his Blood, we are washed clean.

This second pair is a blending of the Synoptic and Pauline tradition that focus on eating and drinking in the course of a meal, and the Johannine tradition that contains the Bread of Life Discourse (John 6:33) and the washing in the blood of the Lamb (Revelations 1:5).

But it is the *De Sacramentis* of St. Ambrose and Sermon 58 of Leo the Great that take these paired ideas of Priest and Victim, and eating and drinking, and place them within the paschal context: "But Jesus . . . fulfilled the New Testament and founded a new Passover" (Sermon 58,3).

PREFACE II OF THE MOST HOLY EUCHARIST

The fruits of the Most Holy Eucharist

61. The following Preface is said on the Solemnity of the Most Holy Body and Blood of Christ (Corpus Christi) and in Votive Masses of the Most Holy Eucharist (text with music, p. 500).

V. **The Lord be with you.**
R. And with your spirit.

V. **Lift up your hearts.**
R. We lift them up to the Lord.

V. **Let us give thanks to the Lord our God.**
R. It is right and just.

It is truly right and just, our duty and our salvation,
always and everywhere to give you thanks,
Lord, holy Father, almighty and eternal God,
through Christ our Lord.

For at the Last Supper with his Apostles,
establishing for the ages to come the saving memorial of the Cross,
he offered himself to you as the unblemished Lamb,
the acceptable gift of perfect praise.

Nourishing your faithful by this sacred mystery,
you make them holy, so that the human race,
bounded by one world,
may be enlightened by one faith
and united by one bond of charity.

And so, we approach the table of this wondrous Sacrament,
so that, bathed in the sweetness of your grace,
we may pass over to the heavenly realities here foreshadowed.

Therefore, all creatures of heaven and earth
sing a new song in adoration,
and we, with all the host of Angels,
cry out, and without end we acclaim:

Holy, Holy, Holy Lord God of hosts . . .

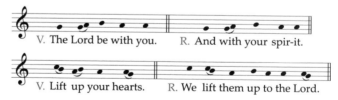

Margin notes:

Bring out the accent on **be** in **The Lord be with you**.

Make a strong accent on **Lift**, and slow both notes of **hearts**.

In the third dialogue, move to the word **thanks** before accenting, and hold that word slightly to give it emphasis. Broaden both notes of **Lord**, and hold **God**.

In the body, the first sentence establishes the context in the life of Christ.

Make a longer pause after **holy**. Treat **so that . . . charity** as one phrase, with **bounded by one world** a parenthetical. Emphasize **one** in both lines. Follow the commas for pauses.

Emphasize **bathed**.

Treat these last two lines as one.

61. Preface II of the Most Holy Eucharist: The fruits of the Most Holy Eucharist, like Preface I of the Most Holy Eucharist, is a modern composition that follows the ancient patterns of liturgical prayer. It has an extended body that expands the second part of the prayer into three distinct sentences, making this one of the longest Prefaces in the Missal. This Preface is intended for the Solemnity of the Body and Blood of Christ (Corpus Christi) and is also found in the section of the Missal containing the Solemnities of the Lord,

immediately following the Sundays in Ordinary Time.

The noticeable length of this Preface for the Most Holy Eucharist can be explained in that it is a modern composition. The Missal from Trent had no special Preface for the Solemnity of Corpus Christi. Rather, the Preface for Christmas (de Nativitate) was specified (which was the Preface used in Masses lacking a proper Preface).

The central idea that permeates all three sentences is that Eucharist is a meal. Beginning with the Last Supper, reference

is made to the Jewish Passover meal in which the unblemished Lamb is the precursor for the saving memorial of the cross. Christ is the *Agnus Dei* that constitutes the acceptable gift of perfect praise.

In the second sentence, the focus shifts from Christ to the faithful who are sanctified by receiving this food as nourishment, so that they are enlightened by faith and brought into unity or Holy Communion.

In the third sentence, again reference is made to the faithful who are invited to

V. Let us give thanks to the Lord our God.   R. It is right and just.

It is truly right and just, our duty and our sal-va-tion, al-ways and everywhere to give you thanks, Lord, holy Father, almighty and e-ter-nal God, through Christ our Lord. For at the Last Supper with his A-pos-tles, es-tablishing for the ages to come the saving memo-rial of the Cross, he offered himself to you as the un-blem-ished Lamb, the acceptable gift of per-fect praise. Nour-ishing your faithful by this sa-cred mys-ter-y, you make them holy, so that the human race, bounded by one world, may be enlightened by one faith and united by one bond of char-i-ty. And so, we approach the table of this won-drous Sac-ra-ment, so that, bathed in the sweetness of your grace, we may pass o-ver to the heavenly reali-ties here fore-shad-owed. There-fore, all creatures of heav-en and earth sing a new song in ad-o-ra-tion, and we, with all the host of An-gels, cry out, and without end we ac-claim:

Sing this proclamation cursively in a reciting tone. In **salvation**, do not hold -**va**; only broaden the two notes slightly. The last syllable, -**tion**, should be held. **Always** and **everywhere** require a slight broadening and clear enunciation. The accent of the phrase falls on **thanks**, which should be held briefly. In the next sentence, clearly make distinct phrases of the text, by respecting the commas.

From **For at the Last** to **praise** comprises one sentence and thought. Because of the melodic development on **Apostles**, it might be best to take a breath there. Do not hold **come** in the next phrase, but continue to **the saving**. Hold **Cross** and take a short breath. Hold **Lamb**, but do not pause for breath, but go on to **the acceptable**. Accent **Nour** in **Nourishing**, although this is difficult because of the rise in the melody that follows. Hold -**y** of **mystery**, and breathe quickly. Do not stop at or hold **race**, but continue on to **bounded**. Hold **world** slightly, but try not to breathe at that point, but continue the sense of **may be enlightened** . . . . Hold **faith** briefly, but try not to breathe, so as to tie this phrase to that which ends with **charity**. Hold **so** and pause briefly. Hold -**ment** in **Sacrament** and pause briefly. Hold **that** and pause briefly. If possible, do not breathe after **grace**, but continue on to **we may pass**. Do not hold -**ver** in **over** but connect it to **to the heavenly**. Broaden **here foreshadowed**.

In the concluding phrase, pause after **And so**. Respect the commas but try to keep this section together, without big breaks for breaths.

approach the table in order to be bathed in the sweetness of grace and to pass over from this world that changes to an unchanging world; namely, heaven.

It may strike a discordant note that the faithful have to be invited to approach the table, but when one considers the historical context when the Feast of Corpus Christi was established, this invitation is clear.

The appearance of Corpus Christi as a Feast in the Christian calendar was primarily due to the petitions of the thirteenth-century Augustinian nun Juliana of Liège.

From her early youth, she had a veneration for the Blessed Sacrament and always longed for a special feast in its honor. This desire is said to have been increased by a vision of the Church under the appearance of the full moon having one dark spot, which signified the absence of such a solemnity. In 1208, she reported her first vision of Christ in which she was instructed to plead for the institution of the Feast of Corpus Christi.

A new liturgy for the Feast was composed by Saint Thomas Aquinas. This

liturgy has come to be used not only on the Solemnity of Corpus Christi itself, but also throughout the liturgical year at events related to the Blessed Sacrament. He also composed the propers for the Mass of Corpus Christi, including the sequence *Lauda Sion Salvatorem*, but no special Preface.

PREFACE I OF THE BLESSED VIRGIN MARY

The Motherhood of the Blessed Virgin Mary

62. The following Preface is said in Masses of the Blessed Virgin Mary, with the mention at the appropriate place of the particular celebration, as indicated in the individual Masses.

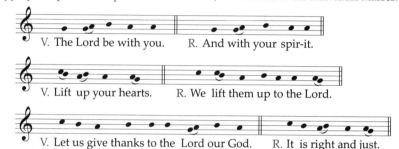

V. The Lord be with you.   R. And with your spir-it.

V. Lift up your hearts.   R. We lift them up to the Lord.

V. Let us give thanks to the Lord our God.   R. It is right and just.

Bring out the accent on **be** in **The Lord be with you**.

Make a strong accent on **Lift**, and slow both notes of **hearts**.

In the third dialogue, move to the word **thanks** before accenting, and hold that word slightly to give it emphasis. Broaden both notes of **Lord**, and hold **God**.

In the protocol there is a temporal reference to establish the Feast or Solemnity for which the Preface is being used.

Make a short pause after **For**. Emphasize **she conceived**. Make a short pause after **and**. Emphasize **brought forth**.

It is truly right and just, our duty and our salvation,
always and everywhere to give you thanks,
Lord, holy Father, almighty and eternal God,
and to praise, bless, and glorify your name
(on the Solemnity of the Motherhood /
on the feast day / on the Nativity / in veneration)
of the Blessed ever-Virgin Mary.

For by the overshadowing of the Holy Spirit
she conceived your Only Begotten Son,
and without losing the glory of virginity,
brought forth into the world the eternal Light,
Jesus Christ our Lord.

Through him the Angels praise your majesty,
Dominions adore and Powers tremble before you.
Heaven and the Virtues of heaven and the blessed Seraphim
worship together with exultation.
May our voices, we pray, join with theirs
in humble praise, as we acclaim:

Holy, Holy, Holy Lord God of hosts . . .

62. Preface I of the Blessed Virgin Mary: The Motherhood of the Blessed Virgin Mary is appropriate for the particular feasts of Mary's birth (September 8, nine months after her Immaculate Conception on December 8), and especially the Solemnity of Mary, the Holy Mother of God (January 1). The Preface is also suitable for optional memorials (votive masses) on Saturdays in Ordinary Time when no obligatory memorial occurs in honor of the Blessed Virgin Mary. The protocol of the prayer (first part) must be adjusted accordingly.

The Solemnity of Mary, the Holy Mother of God, is a liturgical Feast of the Blessed Virgin Mary, celebrated by the Roman Catholic Church on January, 1, the Octave Day of Christmas. The day is a holy day of obligation in the United States and many other countries.

This solemnity was celebrated in the East before it was in the West, but by the fifth century, it was celebrated in France and Spain on the Sunday before Christmas. In Rome, even before the seventh century, January 1 was used as a celebration of the

Maternity of the Blessed Virgin Mary. In the thirteenth and fourteenth centuries, the Feast of the Circumcision of Christ had come to replace the Marian feast on January 1. The celebration of the Feast of the Circumcision on January 1 was expanded to the entire Roman Catholic Church in 1570, when Pope Pius V promulgated *The Roman Missal*. In 1914, the Feast of the "Maternity of the Blessed Virgin Mary" was established in Portugal, occurring on October 11. In 1931, this feast was extended to the entire Roman Catholic

It is truly right and just, our duty and our sal-va-tion, al-ways and everywhere to give you thanks, Lord, holy Father, almighty and e-ter-nal God, and to praise, bless, and glori-fy your name

(on the Solemnity of the Motherhood)
on the feast day
on the Nativity
in veneration

of the Blessed ev-er-Vir-gin Mar-y. For by the overshadowing of the Holy Spirit she conceived your Only Be-got-ten Son, and without losing the glory of virginity, brought forth into the world the e-ter-nal Light, Je-sus Christ our Lord. Through him the Angels praise your maj-es-ty, Domin-ions a-dore and Powers trem-ble be-fore you. Heav-en and the Virtues of heaven and the bless-ed Ser-a-phim worship to-geth-er with ex-ul-ta-tion. May our voices, we pray, join with theirs in hum-ble praise, as we ac-claim:

Holy, Holy, Holy Lord God of hosts . . .

Sing this proclamation cursively in a reciting tone. In **salvation**, do not hold -va; only broaden the two notes slightly. The last syllable, **-tion**, should be held. **Always** and **everywhere** require a slight broadening and clear enunciation. The accent of the phrase falls on **thanks**, which should be held briefly. In the next sentence, clearly make distinct phrases of the text, by respecting the commas.

With the first phrase, **For by the overshadowing**, do not pause at the musical incise after **Spirit**, but rather continue on with **she conceived**. Broaden but do not really slow down -**gotten Son**, and then take a quick breath. Continue with **and without**, but not as if it is a totally new sentence. Articulate carefully **virginity** in the next phrase, but there should be no break before **brought forth**. Broaden -**ternal Light**, but keep the sense of the union of the two phrases, but taking only a very quick breath (if necessary) before **Jesus Christ our Lord** — the latter words of which should be broadened to emphasize their importance. Pause and take a good breath at **Lord**.

In the concluding phrase, make a slight pause after **And so**. Respect the commas but try to keep this section together, without big breaks for breaths. Broaden the last phrase, especially on **praise**. Slow **we ac-**, and put emphasis on -**claim**, so as to evoke the response of **Holy, Holy, Holy** . . . .

Church by Pope Pius XI and maintained on October 11. Following the Second Vatican Council in 1974, Pope Paul VI removed the Feast of the Circumcision of Christ from the liturgical calendar, and replaced it with the "Solemnity of Mary, Mother of God."

The Solemnity is a celebration of Mary's motherhood of Jesus. The title "Mother of God" is a western derivation from the Greek: *Theotokos*, the God-bearer. The term *Theotokos* was adopted at the Council of Ephesus as a way to assert the divinity of Christ, from which it follows that

what is predicated of Christ is predicated of God. So, if Mary is the mother of Jesus, she is the Mother of God. Therefore, the title "Mother of God" and the "Solemnity of Mary, the Holy Mother of God," which celebrates her under this title, are at once Mariological and Christological. Mary is the Mother of Jesus Christ.

This Preface emphasizes the work of the Holy Spirit when the angel Gabriel announces that Mary will bear a son. There is a special Preface intended for the Feast of the Annunciation (March 25) that resem-

bles this Preface but makes more specific reference to the angel's role. Although this prayer references Mary, it is in her relationship to Christ as his mother that she is venerated.

PREFACE II OF THE BLESSED VIRGIN MARY

The Church praises God with the words of Mary

63. The following Preface is said in Masses of the Blessed Virgin Mary.

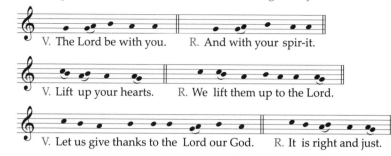

V. The Lord be with you.   R. And with your spir-it.

V. Lift up your hearts.   R. We lift them up to the Lord.

V. Let us give thanks to the Lord our God.   R. It is right and just.

It is truly right and just, our duty and our salvation,
to praise your mighty deeds in the exaltation of all the Saints,
and especially, as we celebrate the memory of the Blessed Virgin Mary,
to proclaim your kindness as we echo her thankful hymn of praise.

For truly even to earth's ends you have done great things
and extended your abundant mercy from age to age:
when you looked on the lowliness of your handmaid,
you gave us through her the author of our salvation,
your Son, Jesus Christ, our Lord.

Through him the host of Angels adores your majesty
and rejoices in your presence for ever.
May our voices, we pray, join with theirs
in one chorus of exultant praise, as we acclaim:

Holy, Holy, Holy Lord God of hosts . . .

Bring out the accent on **be** in **The Lord be with you**.

Make a strong accent on **Lift**, and slow both notes of **hearts**.

In the third dialogue, move to the word **thanks** before accenting, and hold that word slightly to give it emphasis. Broaden both notes of **Lord**, and hold **God**.

The protocol references the memory of Mary and her words in the Magnificat.

Emphasize **you have done great things** and **lowliness of your handmaid**, referencing the Magnificat.

---

63. Preface II of the Blessed Virgin Mary: The Church praises God with the words of Mary reflects Mary's words to her cousin Elizabeth that Luke records in his Gospel as a canticle (Magnificat) and the protocol in this prayer virtually supplies the footnote with the citation.

The Magnificat (Latin: My soul magnifies), also known as the Song of Mary, is a canticle frequently sung (as the term "canticle" denotes) liturgically in Christian liturgies. It is one of the eight most ancient Christian hymns and perhaps the earliest Marian hymn.

The text of the canticle is taken directly from the Gospel account of Luke (1:46–55), during which it is spoken by the Virgin Mary upon the occasion of her Visitation to her cousin Elizabeth. In the narrative, after Mary greets Elizabeth, who is pregnant with John the Baptist, the child moves within Elizabeth's womb. When Elizabeth praises Mary for her faith, in response, Mary sings what is now known as the Magnificat.

The canticle echoes several Old Testament biblical passages, but the most pronounced allusions are to the Song of Hannah, from the book of Samuel (1 Samuel 2:1–10). Along with the Benedictus, as well as several Old Testament canticles, the Magnificat is included in the Book of Odes, an ancient liturgical collection found in some manuscripts of the Septuagint.

Within Christianity, the Magnificat is most frequently recited within the Liturgy of the Hours. In Western Christianity, the Magnificat is most often sung or recited

It is truly right and just, our duty and our sal-va-tion, to praise

your mighty deeds in the exaltation of all the Saints, and especial-

-ly, as we celebrate the memory of the Blessed Vir-gin Mar-y, to pro-

-claim your kind-ness as we echo her thank-ful hymn of praise.

For truly even to earth's ends you have done great things and ex-

-tended your a-bun-dant mer-cy from age to age: when you looked

on the lowliness of your hand-maid, you gave us through her the

author of our sal-va-tion, your Son, Je-sus Christ, our Lord.

Through him the host of Angels a-dores your maj-es-ty and re-

-joic-es in your pres-ence for ev-er. May our voices, we pray, join

with theirs in one chorus of ex-ult-ant praise, as we ac-claim:

Holy, Holy, Holy Lord God of hosts . . .

Sing this proclamation cursively in a reciting tone. In **salvation**, do not hold **-va**; only broaden the two notes slightly. The last syllable, **-tion**, should be held. **Always** and **everywhere** require a slight broadening and clear enunciation. The accent of the phrase falls on **thanks**, which should be held briefly. In the next sentence, clearly make distinct phrases of the text, by respecting the commas.

Make a slight elongation of **truly** in the first phrase, as if it had a comma after it, but continue without break or breath. Broaden **have done great things**, to bring out the importance of the citation from the Magnificat. Take only a very short breath after **things** and only if necessary. Slow and broaden **abundant mercy from age to age**. After that, take a breath and a short pause. At the end of the next phrase, **of your handmaid**, make just the slightest elongation of **-maid**, but do not break before continuing with **you gave us**. Lengthen **-tion** of **salvation** just slightly, but try, without a breath, to continue the sense with **your Son**. Broaden **Jesus Christ our Lord**.

In the concluding phrase, make a slight pause after **And so**. Respect the commas but try to keep this section together, without big breaks for breaths. Broaden the last phrase, especially on **praise**. Slow **we ac-**, and put emphasis on **-claim**, so as to evoke the response of **Holy, Holy, Holy . . . .**

during the main evening prayer service called Vespers. In Eastern Christianity, the Magnificat is usually sung at Sunday Matins.

The Preface is more than a restatement of Mary's hymn. Rather, it reinterprets it for the Church at prayer. In the protocol of the Preface, reference is made to the Blessed Virgin Mary proclaiming the kindness of God. Luke's version, rather, has Mary magnifying the Lord, thus the word "Magnificat" picks up on this. This is sometimes translated as "my soul proclaims the

greatness of the Lord" or "my soul glorifies the Lord." The kindness of the Lord is God's *hesed* (which has been discussed in the commentary on the Penitential Act).

"Kindness" is synonymous with "mercy," "love," "truth," and "forgiveness," all of which are words used to describe God. The extent of God's love and mercy are indescribable and unfathomable to the human mind. Often in translation, we need to use a paraphrase to capture the richness of the word *hesed*. We might say God's merciful love or

loving mercy. Loving kindness also would approximate the deep meaning.

That God has done great things (*Mirabilia Dei*) and has extended mercy (*hesed*) to the ends of the earth is a proclamation that the Magnificat of Mary becomes the Magnificat of the Church, especially the Church at prayer.

PREFACE I OF APOSTLES

The Apostles, shepherds of God's people

64.   The following Preface is said in Masses of the Apostles, especially of Saints Peter and Paul.

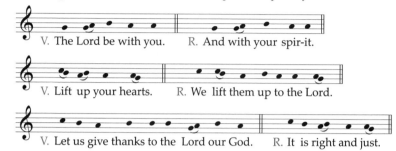

V. The Lord be with you.   R. And with your spir-it.

V. Lift up your hearts.   R. We lift them up to the Lord.

V. Let us give thanks to the Lord our God.   R. It is right and just.

It is truly right and just, our duty and our salvation,
always and everywhere to give you thanks,
Lord, holy Father, almighty and eternal God.

For you, eternal Shepherd, do not desert your flock,
but through the blessed Apostles
watch over it and protect it always,
so that it may be governed
by those you have appointed shepherds
to lead it in the name of your Son.

And so, with Angels and Archangels,
with Thrones and Dominions,
and with all the hosts and Powers of heaven,
we sing the hymn of your glory,
as without end we acclaim:

Holy, Holy, Holy Lord God of hosts . . .

Bring out the accent on **be** in **The Lord be with you**.

Make a strong accent on **Lift**, and slow both notes of **hearts**.

In the third dialogue, move to the word **thanks** before accenting, and hold that word slightly to give it emphasis. Broaden both notes of **Lord**, and hold **God**.

Emphasize **eternal Shepherd** and **flock** as correlated.

Emphasize **Apostles**, **watch**, and **protect**.

64. Preface I of Apostles: The Apostles, shepherds of God's people presents the pastoral image of shepherd. Like Christ the eternal Shepherd, the Apostles share in this pastoral ministry as overseers. The term "Apostle" is derived from the New Testament Greek word *apostolos*, meaning "one who is sent forth as a messenger," and should not be confused with a disciple (who is a follower or a student who learns from a "teacher"). Traditionally, Jesus is said to have had Twelve Apostles who spread the Gospel after his Resurrection.

Noor of Israel also claimed the title of Apostle to the Gentiles, even though other Apostles actively recruited Gentiles and Peter's role was never restricted to just Apostle to the Jews. Indeed, traditionally the first Gentile convert is considered to be Cornelius the Centurion, who was recruited by Peter. Paul claimed a special commission from the risen Jesus, separate from the Great Commission given to the Twelve. Paul's mentor, Barnabas, is also termed an Apostle. Paul did not restrict the term Apostle to the Twelve, either because he

didn't know it or resisted it. This restricted usage appears in Revelation. In modern usage, major missionaries are sometimes termed Apostles, as in Saint Patrick, Apostle of Ireland.

The period of early Christianity during the lifetimes of the Apostles is called the Apostolic Age. In the second century, association with the apostles was esteemed as evidence of authority and orthodoxy. Paul's epistles were accepted as scripture, and two of the four accounts of the Gospel were associated with Apostles, as were

It is truly right and just, our duty and our sal-va-tion, al-ways and everywhere to give you thanks, Lord, holy Father, almighty and e-ter-nal God. For you, eternal Shepherd, do not de-sert your flock, but through the blessed A-pos-tles watch over it and pro-tect it al-ways, so that it may be governed by those you have ap-point-ed shep-herds to lead it in the name of your Son. And so, with Angels and Archangels, with Thrones and Do-min-ions, and with all the hosts and Pow-ers of heav-en, we sing the hymn of your glo-ry, as without end we ac-claim:

Holy, Holy, Holy Lord God of hosts . . .

Sing this proclamation cursively in a reciting tone. In **salvation**, do not hold **-va**; only broaden the two notes slightly. The last syllable, **-tion**, should be held. **Always** and **everywhere** require a slight broadening and clear enunciation. The accent of the phrase falls on **thanks**, which should be held briefly. In the next sentence, clearly make distinct phrases of the text, by respecting the commas.

Treat the comma after the second word **you**, by lengthening it slightly, but then continue with **eternal Shepherd**, treating the last syllable again with a slight lengthening, to express the comma of the text. However, do not breathe before continuing with **do not**. Make a slight elongation of **flock**, and a short breath can be taken there. Simply articulate very carefully **Apostles** and that will slow the word sufficiently; continue without break with **watch over**. Broaden the end of the phrase, **protect it always**. Do not take a long breath there, because the sense demands moving on to **so that**, but a short breath is okay. No pause at **governed** but continue with **by those**. Lengthen **-perds** of **shepherds** slightly, but do not break or pause there, but rather continue the sense by going on to **to lead**. That last word should be broadened, as should the words **name of your Son**.

In the concluding phrase, make a slight pause after **And so**. Respect the commas but try to keep this section together, without big breaks for breaths. Broaden the last phrase, especially on **glory**. Slow **we ac-**, and put emphasis on **-claim**, so as to evoke the response of **Holy, Holy, Holy** . . . .

other New Testament works. Various Christian texts, such as the *Didache* and the Apostolic Constitutions, were attributed to the Twelve Apostles. Bishops traced their lines of succession back to individual Apostles, who were said to have established churches across great territories. Catholic bishops have traditionally claimed authority deriving, by apostolic succession, from the Twelve. Early Church Fathers came to be associated with Apostles, such as Pope Clement I with Peter the Apostle. The Apostles' Creed, popular in the West,

was said according to legend to have been composed by the apostles themselves.

The Apostles are associated as shepherds with Christ, who is the Good Shepherd. This image refers to a pericope found in John 10:1–21 in which Jesus is depicted as the Good Shepherd who lays down his life for the sheep. Similar imagery is used in Psalm 23. The Good Shepherd is revisited throughout the four Gospel accounts in references to Jesus' not letting himself lose any of his sheep. It is the most common of the symbolic representations of Christ

found in Early Christian art in the Catacombs of Rome, before Christian imagery could be made explicit. Images of the Good Shepherd often include a sheep on the shoulders, as in the Lucan version of the Parable of the Lost Sheep (Luke 15:3–7).

PREFACE II OF APOSTLES

The apostolic foundation and witness

65.   The following Preface is said in Masses of the Apostles and Evangelists.

V. The Lord be with you.   R. And with your spir-it.

V. Lift up your hearts.   R. We lift them up to the Lord.

V. Let us give thanks to the Lord our God.   R. It is right and just.

Bring out the accent on **be** in **The Lord be with you**.

Make a strong accent on **Lift**, and slow both notes of **hearts**.

In the third dialogue, move to the word **thanks** before accenting, and hold that word slightly to give it emphasis. Broaden both notes of **Lord**, and hold **God**.

Emphasize **firm** and **foundations**. Those words are the focus. Emphasize **holiness** and **teaching**.

It is truly right and just, our duty and our salvation,
always and everywhere to give you thanks,
Lord, holy Father, almighty and eternal God,
through Christ our Lord.

For you have built your Church
to stand firm on apostolic foundations,
to be a lasting sign of your holiness on earth
and offer all humanity your heavenly teaching.

Therefore, now and for ages unending,
with all the host of Angels,
we sing to you with all our hearts,
crying out as we acclaim:

Holy, Holy, Holy Lord God of hosts . . .

65. Preface II of the Apostles: The apostolic foundation and witness assigns to the Apostles three attributes: to stand firm as a foundation to a building, to be lasting signs of holiness, and to offer heavenly teachings to all people. These are not ordered in any particular manner.

Traditionally, the Twelve Apostles include Peter (whom some denominations consider the "Prince of the Apostles"), Andrew, James the Greater, James the Lesser, John, Philip, Bartholomew, Matthew, Thomas, Thaddeus, Simon, and Judas Iscariot. Judas had been one of the Twelve, but he betrayed Jesus and committed suicide. With Judas gone, Matthias became one of the Twelve (Acts 1:15–26). In the synoptic Gospel accounts, Mark names the Twelve, Matthew follows Mark, and Luke substitutes Jude for Mark's Thaddeus. John refers to the Twelve without naming them all, adds the name Nathanael, and uses the term "beloved disciple" (presumably for John). Jesus' inner circle of twelve disciples probably corresponds to the twelve tribes of Israel (Matthew 19:28; Luke 22:28–30).

In the synoptic accounts of the Gospel, Jesus selects Peter, James, and John to witness his divine Transfiguration and to be with him when he prays at Gethsemane. In Mark, the Twelve are obtuse, failing to understand the importance of Jesus' miracles and parables.

The Acts of the Apostles recounts the deeds of the Apostles in the years after Jesus' Crucifixion. This fifth book of the

It is truly right and just, our duty and our sal-va-tion, al-ways and everywhere to give you thanks, Lord, holy Father, almighty and e-ter-nal God, through Christ our Lord. For you have built your Church to stand firm on apos-tol-ic foun-da-tions, to be a lasting sign of your ho-li-ness on earth and offer all hu-man-i-ty your heav-en-ly teach-ing. There-fore, now and for ages unending, with all the host of An-gels, we sing to you with all our hearts, crying out as we ac-claim:

Holy, Holy, Holy Lord God of hosts . . .

Sing this proclamation cursively in a reciting tone. In **salvation**, do not hold **-va**; only broaden the two notes slightly. The last syllable, **-tion**, should be held. **Always** and **every-where** require a slight broadening and clear enunciation. The accent of the phrase falls on **thanks**, which should be held briefly. In the next sentence, clearly make distinct phrases of the text, by respecting the commas.

At **Church** do not lengthen or pause, but continue the sense with **to stand firm**. Lengthen slightly **-tions** of **foundations**. Take just a very short breath there, if necessary. Broaden the phrase **holiness on earth**, and take a very short breath there, if necessary. Tie together **humanity** and **your heavenly**. Articulate carefully **heavenly teaching** to emphasize this important role of the apostles.

In the concluding phrase, make a slight pause after **And so**. Respect the commas but try to keep this section together, without big breaks for breaths. Broaden the last phrase, especially on **hearts**. Slow **we ac-**, and put emphasis on **-claim**, so as to evoke the response of **Holy, Holy, Holy . . . .**

New Testament outlines the history of the Apostolic Age. The author is traditionally identified as Luke the Evangelist.

While the precise identity of the author is debated, the consensus is that this work was composed by a (*Koine*) Greek-speaking Gentile writing for an audience of Gentile Christians. The early Church Fathers wrote that Luke was a physician in Antioch and an adherent of the Apostle Paul. The author of the Gospel of Luke is believed to be the same as the author of the Acts of the Apostles. Tradition holds that the text was written by Luke, the companion of Paul (named in Colossians 4:14) and this traditional view of Lucan authorship is "widely held as the view which most satisfactorily explains all the data." The list of scholars maintaining authorship by Luke the physician is lengthy and represents scholars from a wide range of theological opinion.

The Preface attributes to the Apostles, those on whom the Church has been built: to stand firm, to be lasting signs of holiness, and to be teachers. This sometimes is called the threefold *munera* or office of teaching, governing, and sanctifying. All the baptized share in this ministry as they are anointed in Baptism with chrism as Christ himself was anointed priest, prophet, and king. Bishops are regarded as sharing intimately in this threefold office that is shared with Priests, Deacons, and all the faithful.

PREFACE I OF SAINTS

The glory of the Saints

66.   The following Preface is said in Masses of All Saints, of Patron Saints and of Saints who are Titulars of a church, and on Solemnities and Feasts of Saints, unless a proper Preface is to be said. This Preface may be said also on Memorials of Saints.

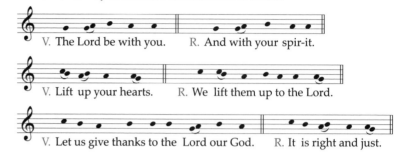

V. The Lord be with you.   R. And with your spir-it.

V. Lift up your hearts.   R. We lift them up to the Lord.

V. Let us give thanks to the Lord our God.   R. It is right and just.

I t is truly right and just, our duty and our salvation,
always and everywhere to give you thanks,
Lord, holy Father, almighty and eternal God.

For you are praised in the company of your Saints
and, in crowning their merits, you crown your own gifts.
By their way of life you offer us an example,
by communion with them you give us companionship,
by their intercession, sure support,
so that, encouraged by so great a cloud of witnesses,
we may run as victors in the race before us
and win with them the imperishable crown of glory,
through Christ our Lord.

And so, with the Angels and Archangels,
and with the great multitude of the Saints,
we sing the hymn of your praise,
as without end we acclaim:

Holy, Holy, Holy Lord God of hosts . . .

Bring out the accent on **be** in **The Lord be with you**.

Make a strong accent on **Lift**, and slow both notes of **hearts**.

In the third dialogue, move to the word **thanks** before accenting, and hold that word slightly to give it emphasis. Broaden both notes of **Lord**, and hold **God**.

Treat these first two lines as one.

Treat lines 3 and 5 as parallels.

Pause with the commas at the end of the lines.

[S]o that . . . we may run . . . and win provides the force. The rest is a parenthetical or elaboration.

---

66. Preface I of Saints: The glory of the Saints is multifunctional. It is prayed in Masses of All Saints, of Patron Saints, and of Saints who are titulars of a church, and on Solemnities and Feasts of Saints, unless a proper Preface is to be said. This Preface may be said also on Memorials of Saints.

The prayer is a rich compendium of attributes that mark the Saints individually and collectively. The Saints offer example, provide companionship, and intercede through prayer.

Reference is made to this "great cloud of witnesses." The persons who are linked in this communion include those who have died and whom Hebrews 12:1 pictures as a cloud of witnesses encompassing Christians on earth. In the same chapter, Hebrews 12:22–23 says Christians on earth "have approached Mount Zion and the city of the living God, the heavenly Jerusalem, and countless angels in festal gathering, and the assembly of the firstborn enrolled in heaven, and God the judge of all, and the spirits of the just made perfect."

In Catholic terminology, the Communion of Saints is thus said to comprise the Church militant (those alive on earth), the Church penitent (those undergoing purification in Purgatory in preparation for heaven), and the Church Triumphant (those already in heaven). The damned are not among the Communion of Saints. The Roman Catholic Church, the Eastern Orthodox Church, the Oriental Orthodox Church, Anglican Communion, and the Assyrian Church of the East point to this doctrine in support of their practice of ask-

It is truly right and just, our duty and our sal-va-tion, al-ways and everywhere to give you thanks, Lord, holy Father, almighty and e-ter-nal God. For you are praised in the company of your Saints and, in crown-ing their mer-its, you crown your own gifts. By their way of life you offer us an ex-am-ple, by communion with them you gave us com-pan-ion-ship, by their inter-ces-sion, sure sup-port, so that, encouraged by so great a cloud of wit-ness-es, we may run as victors in the race be-fore us and win with them the imperishable crown of glo-ry, through Christ our Lord. And so, with the Angels and Arch-an-gels, and with the great mul-ti-tude of the Saints, we sing the hymn of your praise, as without end we ac-claim:

Holy, Holy, Holy Lord God of hosts . . .

Sing this proclamation cursively in a reciting tone. In **salvation**, do not hold **-va**; only broaden the two notes slightly. The last syllable, **-tion**, should be held. **Always** and **everywhere** require a slight broadening and clear enunciation. The accent of the phrase falls on **thanks**, which should be held briefly. In the next sentence, clearly make distinct phrases of the text, by respecting the commas.

Slightly lengthen **Saints**, continue without a breath to **and, in crowning**, and do not break or breathe on **merits**. Articulate carefully and slow down on **crown your own gifts**. The three phrases beginning with **by** need to be sung to bring out the musical alliteration. Slightly lengthen **-ple** of **example**, **-ship** of **companionship**, and **-port** of **support**. Broaden **sure support**. After a short break, continue with **so that**. Try not to breathe after **witnesses** but go on to **we may run**. Broaden **before us** and, if necessary, take a breath. Continue with the conclusion **through Christ**.

In the concluding phrase, make a slight pause after **And so**. Respect the commas but try to keep this section together, without big breaks for breaths. Broaden the last phrase, especially on **praise**. Slow **we ac-**, and put emphasis on **-claim**, so as to evoke the response of **Holy, Holy, Holy . . . .**

ing the intercession of the Saints in heaven, whose prayers (see Revelation 5:8) are seen as helping their fellow Christians on earth. These same churches refer to this doctrine in support of the practice of praying for the dead (as seen in 2 Timothy 1:16–18).

Reference is also made to the Saints as wearing crowns and running races. Saint Paul, in his first letter to the Corinthians, uses the athletic metaphor: "Every athlete exercises discipline in every way. They do it to win a perishable crown, but we an imperishable one" (1 Corinthians 9:25). Crowning athletes may be a reference to the Olympic Games held for representatives of various city-states of Ancient Greece in honor of Zeus. The exact origins of the games are shrouded in myth and legend, but records indicate that they began in 776 BC in Olympia in Greece. They were celebrated until 393 AD when they were suppressed by Theodosius I as part of the campaign to impose Christianity as a state religion. The games were usually held every four years, or olympiad, as the unit of time came to be known. During a celebration of the games, an Olympic truce was enacted so that athletes could travel from their countries to the games in safety. The prizes for the victors were olive wreaths or crowns.

PREFACE II OF SAINTS

The action of the Saints

67. The following Preface is said in Masses of All Saints, of Patron Saints and of Saints who are Titulars of a church, and on Solemnities and Feasts of Saints, unless a proper Preface is to be said. This Preface may be said also on Memorials of Saints.

V. The Lord be with you.   R. And with your spir-it.

V. Lift up your hearts.   R. We lift them up to the Lord.

V. Let us give thanks to the Lord our God.   R. It is right and just.

Bring out the accent on **be** in **The Lord be with you.**

Make a strong accent on **Lift**, and slow both notes of **hearts**.

It is truly right and just, our duty and our salvation,
always and everywhere to give you thanks,
Lord, holy Father, almighty and eternal God,
through Christ our Lord.

In the third dialogue, move to the word **thanks** before accenting, and hold that word slightly to give it emphasis. Broaden both notes of **Lord**, and hold **God**.

For in the marvelous confession of your Saints,
you make your Church fruitful with strength ever new
and offer us sure signs of your love.
And that your saving mysteries may be fulfilled,
their great example lends us courage,
their fervent prayers sustain us in all we do.

Follow sense lines and punctuation.

Emphasize **strength** and **love**.

And so, Lord, with all the Angels and Saints,
we, too, give you thanks, as in exultation we acclaim:

Emphasize **example** and **prayers sustain**.

Holy, Holy, Holy Lord God of hosts . . .

67. Preface II of Saints: The action of the Saints is sparser than Preface I of the Saints. As with the previous Preface, Preface II is appropriate for Masses of All Saints, of Patron Saints, and of Saints who are Titulars of a church, and on Solemnities and Feasts of Saints, unless a proper Preface is to be prayed. This Preface may be said also on Memorials of Saints.

In comparison with Preface I of Saints, this prayer emphasizes in a sober way that the Saints are confessors who strengthen the Church and act as signs of God's love

and examples for the faithful to follow due to their courage and lives of prayer that still sustains us.

The Communion of Saints is the spiritual union of all members of the Christian Church, living and dead, those on earth, in heaven, and those also who are in that state of purification. They are all part of a single "mystical body," with Christ as the head, in which each member contributes to the good of all and shares in the welfare of all.

The earliest known use of this term to refer to the belief in a mystical bond unit-

ing both the living and the dead in a confirmed hope and love is by Saint Nicetas of Remesiana (ca. 335–414); the term has since then played a central role in formulations of the Christian creed.

The term is included in the Apostles' Creed, a major profession of the Christian faith whose current form was settled in the eighth century, but which originated not long after the year 100, as the basic statement of the Church's faith.

It is truly right and just, our duty and our sal-va-tion, al-ways and everywhere to give you thanks, Lord, holy Father, almighty and e-ter-nal God, through Christ our Lord. For in the marvelous con-fession of your Saints, you make your Church fruitful with strength ev-er new and offer us sure signs of your love. And that your saving mysteries may be ful-filled, their great example lends us cour-age, their fer-vent prayers sus-tain us in all we do. And so, Lord, with all the An-gels and Saints, we, too, give you thanks, as in exul - ta-tion we ac-claim:

Holy, Holy, Holy Lord God of hosts . . .

Sing this proclamation cursively in a reciting tone. In **salvation**, do not hold **-va**; only broaden the two notes slightly. The last syllable, **-tion**, should be held. **Always** and **everywhere** require a slight broadening and clear enunciation. The accent of the phrase falls on **thanks**, which should be held briefly. In the next sentence, clearly make distinct phrases of the text, by respecting the commas.

Articulate carefully **marvelous confession**. Lengthen **Saints**, but do not break or breathe there, but rather continue with **you make**. Hold slightly **new** at the end of the next phrase, but then continue without break with the following phrase, **and offer**, broadening the last four words, **signs of your love**. Take a breath there. Treat **And** as if it had a comma after it, so that the phrase seems to begin with **that your saving**. Hold slightly **-filled** of **fulfilled**, and because the next two phrases should be kept together, it may be necessary to take a quick breath there. Hold **-age** of **courage** just slightly, and try to continue with **their fervent**. Articulate carefully **sustain us**, which will probably mean slowing the two words slightly. Broaden the last four words, holding **do** and taking a breath there.

In the concluding phrase, make a slight pause after **And so**. Respect the commas but try to keep this section together, without big breaks for breaths. Broaden the last phrase, especially on **thanks**. Slow **we ac-**, and put emphasis on **-claim**, so as to evoke the response of **Holy, Holy, Holy** . . . .

The doctrine of the Communion of Saints is based on 1 Corinthians 12, in which Paul compares Christians to a single body. The words translated into English as "saints" can refer to Christians, who, whatever their personal sanctity as individuals, are called holy because they are consecrated to God and Christ. This usage of the word "saints" is found some fifty times in the New Testament. Paul addresses his letter to the saint (*hagioi*) of such and such a place, so the idea of sanctity included not only the dead, but the living as well.

Lumen Gentium, 50, evokes the role of the Saints when it declares: "Nor is it by the title of example only that we cherish the memory of those in heaven, but still more in order that the union of the whole Church may be strengthened in the Spirit by the practice of fraternal charity. For just as Christian communion among wayfarers brings us closer to Christ, so our companionship with the saints joins us to Christ, from Whom as from its Fountain and Head issues every grace and the very life of the people of God. . . . For every genuine testimony of love shown by us to those in heaven, by its very nature tends toward and terminates in Christ who is the 'crown of all saints,' and through Him, in God Who is wonderful in his saints and is magnified in them." Thus, the Saints always point beyond themselves to Christ, the supreme Saint.

PREFACE I OF HOLY MARTYRS

The sign and example of martyrdom

68.   The following Preface is said on the Solemnities and Feasts of Holy Martyrs. It may also be said on their Memorials.

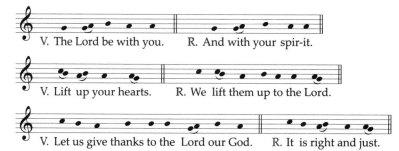

V. The Lord be with you.   R. And with your spir-it.

V. Lift up your hearts.   R. We lift them up to the Lord.

V. Let us give thanks to the Lord our God.   R. It is right and just.

Bring out the accent on **be** in **The Lord be with you.**

Make a strong accent on **Lift**, and slow both notes of **hearts.**

In the third dialogue, move to the word **thanks** before accenting, and hold that word slightly to give it emphasis. Broaden both notes of **Lord**, and hold **God.**

Emphasize **blood.**

Emphasize **poured out.**

Emphasize **shows forth.**

Emphasize **weakness, perfect, power, feeble, bestow,** and **strength.**

It is truly right and just, our duty and our salvation,
always and everywhere to give you thanks,
Lord, holy Father, almighty and eternal God.

For the blood of your blessed Martyr N.,
poured out like Christ's to glorify your name,
shows forth your marvelous works,
by which in our weakness you perfect your power
and on the feeble bestow strength to bear you witness,
through Christ our Lord.

And so, with the Powers of heaven,
we worship you constantly on earth,
and before your majesty
without end we acclaim:

Holy, Holy, Holy Lord God of hosts . . .

68. Preface I of Holy Martyrs: The sign and example of martyrdom, like Preface II of Holy Martyrs that follows, this Preface is intended for Solemnities and Feasts of Martyrs as well as Memorials. The main structure of the body insists that the blood of the Martyr pours out to glorify God's name and to bear witness. These are the main themes that need to be emphasized. The key is in lines four and five. God perfects God's power in our weakness and bestows strength on our fragility to bear

him witness. This prayer alludes to 2 Corinthians 4:7–12. In those verses, we read that Saint Paul states how we are afflicted in every way, perplexed, and persecuted. Though those trials are part of our lives, the surpassing power is from God. And finally, Paul states how our lives are to manifest what God does: "For we who live are constantly being given up to death for the sake of Jesus, so that the life of Jesus may be manifested in our mortal flesh" (v. 11).

In its original meaning, the word "Martyr," meaning "witness," was used in the secular sphere as well as in the New Testament of the Bible. During the early Christian centuries, the term acquired the extended meaning of a believer who is called to witness for their religious belief, and on account of this witness, endures suffering and/or death. The term, in this later sense, entered the English language as a loanword. The death of a Martyr, or the value attributed to it, is called martyrdom.

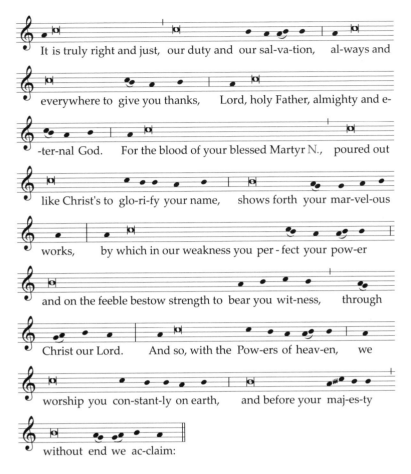

It is truly right and just, our duty and our sal-va-tion, al-ways and everywhere to give you thanks, Lord, holy Father, almighty and e- -ter-nal God. For the blood of your blessed Martyr N., poured out like Christ's to glo-ri-fy your name, shows forth your mar-vel-ous works, by which in our weakness you per-fect your pow-er and on the feeble bestow strength to bear you wit-ness, through Christ our Lord. And so, with the Pow-ers of heav-en, we worship you con-stant-ly on earth, and before your maj-es-ty without end we ac-claim:

Holy, Holy, Holy Lord God of hosts . . .

Sing this proclamation cursively in a reciting tone. In **salvation**, do not hold **-va**; only broaden the two notes slightly. The last syllable, **-tion**, should be held. **Always** and **everywhere** require a slight broadening and clear enunciation. The accent of the phrase falls on **thanks**, which should be held briefly. In the next sentence, clearly make distinct phrases of the text, by respecting the commas.

Articulate the name of the martyr (if it is the feast day), but do not pause after the name, but rather continue singing **poured out** so as to keep the sense. **Like** and **Christ's** have difficult syllables, so it may be well to slow those words slightly, perhaps setting them off a little as if they were surrounded by commas in the text. Lengthen **name** just slightly, but if possible continue with **shows forth** without a break or a breath. Broaden **marvelous works**. At the end of the next phrase, lengthen slightly **-er** of **power**, and it may be necessary to take a very quick breath so as to complete the next phrase properly. Articulate carefully **bestow strength** as well as **bear you witness**. But do not break or breathe there, rather continuing with the conclusion, **through Christ our Lord**.

In the concluding phrase, make a slight pause after **And so**. Respect the commas but try to keep this section together, without big breaks for breaths. Broaden the last phrase, especially on **majesty**. Slow **we ac-**, and put emphasis on **-claim**, so as to evoke the response of **Holy, Holy, Holy** . . . .

The early Christians who first began to use the term "Martyr" in its new sense saw Jesus as the first and greatest Martyr, on account of his Crucifixion. The early Christians appear to have seen Jesus as the archetypal Martyr.

The early Church, however, referred to degrees of martyrdom that could be distinguished by colors. Pope Gregory I, in his *Homilia in Evangelia*, explains three modes of martyrdom, designated by the colors red, blue (or green), and white. This triad is unique but draws on earlier distinc-tions between "red" and "white" martyr-dom. "Red" martyrdom, involved violent death as a result of religious persecution. Saint Jerome had used the term "white martyrdom" for those such as desert her-mits who aspired to the condition of mar-tyrdom through strict asceticism. The distinction is made by Gregory between inward and outward martyrdom. Blue (or green) martyrdom involves the denial of desires, as through fasting and penitent labors, without necessarily implying a jour-ney or complete withdrawal from life; while red martyrdom requires torture or death.

Ultimately, the notion of red martyr-dom won out over white and blue (green). The hymn *Decora lux* captures the sense of red martyrdom: "*O Roma felix quae duorum principum es consacrata glorioso sanguine*" ("O happy Rome! Who in thy martyr princes' blood, A twofold stream, art washed and doubly sanctified"). This hymn is sung to Peter and Paul, the two princes of Rome, on their June 29 feast day.

PREFACE II OF HOLY MARTYRS

The wonders of God in the victory of the Martyrs

69.   The following Preface is said on the Solemnities and Feasts of Holy Martyrs. It may also be said on their Memorials.

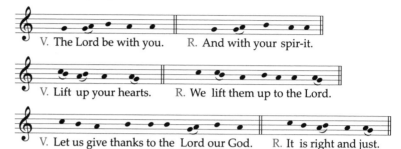

V. The Lord be with you.   R. And with your spir-it.

V. Lift up your hearts.   R. We lift them up to the Lord.

V. Let us give thanks to the Lord our God.   R. It is right and just.

It is truly right and just, our duty and our salvation,
always and everywhere to give you thanks,
Lord, holy Father, almighty and eternal God.

For you are glorified when your Saints are praised;
their very sufferings are but wonders of your might:
in your mercy you give ardor to their faith,
to their endurance you grant firm resolve,
and in their struggle the victory is yours,
through Christ our Lord.

Therefore, all creatures of heaven and earth
sing a new song in adoration,
and we, with all the host of Angels,
cry out, and without end we acclaim:

Holy, Holy, Holy Lord God of hosts . . .

Bring out the accent on **be** in **The Lord be with you.**

Make a strong accent on **Lift**, and slow both notes of **hearts**.

In the third dialogue, move to the word **thanks** before accenting, and hold that word slightly to give it emphasis. Broaden both notes of **Lord**, and hold **God**.

The first two lines establish the reason for our praise and thanksgiving. **Glorified** and **praise** are strong words. Emphasize **mercy**, **ardor**, and **faith**. Emphasize **endurance**, **grant**, and **resolve**.

---

69. Preface II of Holy Martyrs: The wonders of God in the victory of the Martyrs is new to the third edition of *The Roman Missal* and it speaks to how the Saints reflect the wonders of God (*Mirabilia Dei*). God is glorified as the Martyrs are praised. Lines one and two establish the reason for our praise and thanksgiving. The parallel rhetoric in the next three lines is beautiful. Mercy gives ardor to faith, so mercy gives feeling. What is important, then, is endurance. Endurance is granted.

The climax is that the Martyrs persevere to the grace operating in their lives.

The early Church cherished those who had witnessed to the faith in the ultimate act of dying for it. "The Acts of the Martyrs," accounts of the suffering and death of a Christian martyr or group of martyrs, gives testimony to their veneration. These accounts were collected and used in church liturgies from early times, as attested by Saint Augustine.

These accounts vary in authenticity. The most reliable follow accounts from tri-

als. Very few of these have survived. Perhaps the most perfect of these is the account of Saint Cyprian. The account of Scillitan Martyrs is also based on trial records, though it has been embellished with miraculous and apocryphal material.

A second category, the "*Passiones*," are based on eyewitness accounts. These include the martyrdoms of Saint Ignatius of Antioch, Saint Polycarp, the Martyrs of Lyons, the famous Acts of Perpetua and Felicitias, and the Passion of Saint Irenaeus. In these accounts, miraculous elements are

It is truly right and just, our duty and our sal-va-tion, al-ways and everywhere to give you thanks, Lord, holy Father, almighty and e-ter-nal God. For you are glorified when your Saints are praised; their ver-y suf-fer-ings are but won-ders of your might: in your mercy you give ardor to their faith, to their endurance you grant firm re-solve, and in their strug-gle the victory is yours, through Christ our Lord. There-fore, all creatures of heaven and earth sing a new song in ad-o-ra-tion, and we, with all the host of An-gels, cry out, and without end we ac-claim:

Holy, Holy, Holy Lord God of hosts . . .

Sing this proclamation cursively in a reciting tone. In **salvation**, do not hold **-va**; only broaden the two notes slightly. The last syllable, **-tion**, should be held. **Always** and **everywhere** require a slight broadening and clear enunciation. The accent of the phrase falls on **thanks**, which should be held briefly. In the next sentence, clearly make distinct phrases of the text, by respecting the commas.

Lengthen slightly **praised**, and take a very brief breath there. Broaden **sufferings** but do not hold the last syllable, but rather continue with **are but**. Articulate **your** carefully to place the emphasis on God's power being the real grace that sustains the martyr. Also hold **might** and take a breath there. Treat **mercy** in the next phrase as if the text had a comma, with a renewed accent then on **you**. There are three phrases here which belong together in sense. So one lengthens **faith** at the end of the first phrase, and may make a slight break in the voice. Broaden **firm resolve**; there again, one may make a slight break in the voice. Slow and articulate the text clearly, **and in their struggle**, but put it together with **the victory**. Broaden **yours**, but do not break or breathe there before the conclusion **through Christ our Lord**.

In the concluding phrase, make a slight pause after **And so**. Respect the commas but try to keep this section together, without big breaks for breaths. Broaden the last phrase, especially on **adoration**. Slow **we ac-**, and put emphasis on **-claim**, so as to evoke the response of **Holy, Holy, Holy** . . . .

restricted, a feature that proved unpopular. These accounts were often later embellished with legendary material.

Eusebius of Caesarea was likely the first Christian author to produce a collection of acts of the Martyrs. The attribute of Martyrs is that they all wear the crown of victory. Probably the most famous is Stephen, the protomartyr of Christianity. Stephen's name is derived from the Greek "*Stephanos*," meaning "crown." He is often depicted in art with three stones and the

Martyrs' palm. In Eastern Christian iconography, he is shown as a young beardless man with a tonsure, wearing a Deacon's vestments, and often holding a miniature church building or a censer.

According to The Acts of the Apostles, Stephen was tried by the Sanhedrin for blasphemy against Moses and God (Acts 6:11) and speaking against the Temple and the Law (Acts 6:13–14). While on trial, he experienced a theophany in which he saw both God the Father and God the Son:

"Behold, I see the heavens opened and the Son of Man standing at the right hand of God" (Acts 7:56). Acts 6–7 describe his trial. He was stoned to death (ca. AD 34–35) by an infuriated mob encouraged by Saul of Tarsus. He is the very example of being strong in faith, firm in resolve, and victorious in struggle.

PREFACE OF HOLY PASTORS

The presence of holy Pastors in the Church

70. The following Preface is said on the Solemnities and Feasts of Holy Pastors. It may also be said on their Memorials.

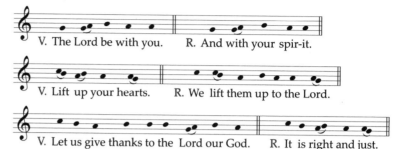

V. The Lord be with you.   R. And with your spir-it.

V. Lift up your hearts.   R. We lift them up to the Lord.

V. Let us give thanks to the Lord our God.   R. It is right and just.

It is truly right and just, our duty and our salvation,
always and everywhere to give you thanks,
Lord, holy Father, almighty and eternal God,
through Christ our Lord.

For, as on the festival of Saint N. you bid your Church rejoice,
so, too, you strengthen her by the example of his holy life,
teach her by his words of preaching,
and keep her safe in answer to his prayers.

And so, with the company of Angels and Saints,
we sing the hymn of your praise,
as without end we acclaim:

Holy, Holy, Holy Lord God of hosts . . .

Sidebar notes:

Bring out the accent on **be** in **The Lord be with you**.

Make a strong accent on **Lift**, and slow both notes of **hearts**.

In the third dialogue, move to the word **thanks** before accenting, and hold that word slightly to give it emphasis. Broaden both notes of **Lord**, and hold **God**.

Emphasize **festival**.
Emphasize **strengthen** and **example**.
Emphasize **teach** and **preaching**.
Emphasize **safe** and **prayers**.

---

70. The body of the **Preface of Holy Pastors: The presence of holy Pastors in the Church** suggests that there are three effects to keeping the liturgical Feast of a Holy Pastor. The Church is strengthened by the model life of the Saint. The Church is taught by his preaching and teaching, and the Church is protected by his intercession.

The Common for pastors includes several groups of people. One begins with the Bishop of Rome, then moves to Bishops, then pastors, then for founders of churches, and finally for missionaries. Therefore, pas-tors in all these categories are called to prolong the presence of Christ, the one high priest, embodying his way of life and making him visible in the midst of the flock entrusted to their care. The first letter of Peter states this clearly: "So I exhort the presbyters among you, as a fellow presby-ter and witness to the sufferings of Christ and one who has a share in the glory to be revealed. Tend the flock of God in your midst, [overseeing] not by constraint but willingly, as God would have it, not for shameful profit but eagerly. Do not lord it over those assigned to you, but be exam-ples to the flock." (1 Peter 5:1–3).

Following the Synod of Bishops in 1990, John Paul II issued a post-synodal exhortation entitled *"Pastores dabo vobis"* in which he addresses the theme of pas-tors specifically in rapport with Priests: "In the Church and on behalf of the Church, priests are a sacramental representation of Jesus Christ—the head and shepherd—authoritatively proclaiming his word, repeat-ing his acts of forgiveness and his offer of

It is truly right and just, our duty and our sal-va-tion,   al-ways and everywhere to give you thanks,   Lord, holy Father, almighty and e--ter-nal God,   through Christ our Lord.   For, as on the festival of Saint N. you bid your Church re-joice,   so, too, you strengthen her by the example of his ho-ly life,   teach her by his words of preach-ing,   and keep her safe in an-swer to his prayers.   And so, with the company of An-gels and Saints,   we sing the hymn of your praise,   as without end we ac-claim:

Holy, Holy, Holy Lord God of hosts . . .

Sing this proclamation cursively in a reciting tone. In **salvation**, do not hold **-va**; only broaden the two notes slightly. The last syllable, **-tion**, should be held. **Always** and **everywhere** require a slight broadening and clear enunciation. The accent of the phrase falls on **thanks**, which should be held briefly. In the next sentence, clearly make distinct phrases of the text, by respecting the commas.

Articulate the name of the Saint well, which may necessitate slowing slightly. But do not break or breathe before continuing with **you bid**. A slight pause and breath is appropriate at the end of the phrase, **rejoice**. Understand that the next three phrases go together as descriptive of the graced benefits of celebrating a holy Pastor. Lengthen slightly **too**, the second word, but continue then with **you**. Hold **life** at the end of the phrase, and make a slight break in the voice to indicate that the sense must continue. Do not rush the second phrase. Some may also find it helpful to begin the singing of the phrase, **teach** by placing it on "doh" along with **her** — it may bring out the sense better. Hold slightly **-ing** of **preaching**, and again make a slight break in the voice to bring out the sense. In the third phrase, it may be well to set off the opening word **and**, by treating it musically as if the text had a comma after it. Hold slightly **safe** in the middle of the phrase, but do not break or breathe there; rather, conclude the phrase by continuing with **in answer**, holding **prayers** at the end, and taking a breath there.

salvation—particularly in baptism, penance and the Eucharist, showing his loving concern to the point of a total gift of self for the flock, which they gather into unity and lead to the Father through Christ and in the Spirit. In a word, priests exist and act in order to proclaim the Gospel to the world and to build up the Church in the name and person of Christ the head and shepherd" (#15).

He draws on the scriptural allusion in John 10:11 and 14. "I am the good shepherd. A good shepherd lays down his life for the sheep. . . . I am the good shepherd, and I know mine and mine know me." This Preface underscores how the "pastors," or those who have been appointed shepherds, carry out the work of Christ, continuing to lead and shepherd the flock. The body of the prayer highlights the three things that pastors are to do for the Church. They are to lead by example, preach the Gospel, and intercede for the Church in prayer.

Pastors are called on to intercede in prayer, due to their proximity to God, because of their holiness, and their accessibility to humans beings. If those living here on earth can intercede on behalf of each other, then those already glorified in heaven, and even closer "in Christ," are made holy as "one" unified through him.

PREFACE OF HOLY VIRGINS AND RELIGIOUS

The sign of a life consecrated to God

71. The following Preface is said on the Solemnities and Feasts of Holy Virgins and Religious. It may also be said on their Memorials.

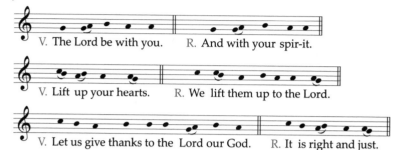

V. The Lord be with you.   R. And with your spir-it.

V. Lift up your hearts.   R. We lift them up to the Lord.

V. Let us give thanks to the Lord our God.   R. It is right and just.

It is truly right and just, our duty and our salvation,
always and everywhere to give you thanks,
Lord, holy Father, almighty and eternal God.

For in the Saints who consecrated themselves to Christ
for the sake of the Kingdom of Heaven,
it is right to celebrate the wonders of your providence,
by which you call human nature back to its original holiness
and bring it to experience on this earth
the gifts you promise in the new world to come.

And so, with all the Angels and Saints,
we praise you, as without end we acclaim:

Holy, Holy, Holy Lord God of hosts . . .

Bring out the accent on **be** in **The Lord be with you**.

Make a strong accent on **Lift**, and slow both notes of **hearts**.

In the third dialogue, move to the word **thanks** before accenting, and hold that word slightly to give it emphasis. Broaden both notes of **Lord**, and hold **God**.

Emphasize **consecrated**, **Kingdom of Heaven**, **wonders**, and **original holiness**. Bring out parallel movement of calling back and bringing to.

71. The key to **Preface of Holy Virgins and Religious: The sign of a life consecrated to God** is in the third line of the body: "It is right to celebrate the wonders of your providence." The first two lines show how their wonders are manifested. They have consecrated themselves to Christ for the sake of the Kingdom of Heaven. First, what the holy virgins have done is restorative; their actions restore men and women to the life prior to the Fall. This call of human nature back to its original holiness recalls the Edenic experience.

The last lines of the body, "and bring it to experience on this earth / the gifts you promise in the new world to come" show the end-times experience is being lived now.

Holy Virgins here are synonymous with consecrated virgins. These are women who have dedicated themselves to a life of perpetual virginity in the service of God and the Church in a form that is recognized by the Church. A life of virginity for the sake of Christ and his Church is an ancient form of Christian religious living already mentioned in the New Testament.

It preceded the foundation of religious orders. Hence, traditionally a Christian virgin was not a member of a religious community. For a while after the Middle Ages, the rite fell out of practice, but it was restored by Pope Paul VI in 1970. This Sacramental can be bestowed both on women living in the world and on those in some religious orders. Thus, it is fitting to group Holy Virgins with Religious.

There are also individual religious sisters, that is to say, members of religious

It is truly right and just, our duty and our sal-va-tion, al-ways and everywhere to give you thanks, Lord, holy Father, almighty and e-ter-nal God. For in the Saints who consecrated themselves to Christ for the sake of the King-dom of Heav-en, it is right to celebrate the wonders of your prov-i-dence, by which you call human nature back to its o-rig-i-nal ho-li-ness and bring it to experience on this earth the gifts you promise in the new world to come. And so, with all the An-gels and Saints, we praise you, as without end we ac-claim:

Holy, Holy, Holy Lord God of hosts . . .

Sing this proclamation cursively in a reciting tone. In **salvation**, do not hold **-va**; only broaden the two notes slightly. The last syllable, **-tion**, should be held. **Always** and **everywhere** require a slight broadening and clear enunciation. The accent of the phrase falls on **thanks**, which should be held briefly. In the next sentence, clearly make distinct phrases of the text, by respecting the commas.

In the middle of the first phrase, do not pause at **Christ** but rather continue the sense by going right on to **for the sake**. Lengthen slightly **-en** of **Heaven** and make a short break there, taking a very short breath also. At the end of the next phrase, hold **-dence** of **providence**, and take a very short breath there. The next two phrases really belong together. Broaden **original holiness**, holding the last syllable slightly. Do not make a real break there, but just a break in the voice (perhaps a quick breath, if necessary), so as to continue with **and bring**. Slow and broaden **on this earth** in the last phrase, holding **earth** just slightly, before going right on with **the gifts**. Slow and articulate carefully **new world to come**.

In the concluding phrase, make a slight pause after **And so**. Respect the commas but try to keep this section together, without big breaks for breaths. Broaden the last phrase, especially on **praise**. Slow **we ac-**, and put emphasis on **-claim**, so as to evoke the response of **Holy, Holy, Holy . . . .**

communities, who have taken a vow of virginity in addition to the religious vows they already have taken like all the other sisters of their order. The approved liturgical rite, whereby the respective diocesan Bishop consecrates the candidate, is the solemn rite of *Consecratio Virginum*.

Since the Second Vatican Council, canon 604 of the 1983 Code of Canon Law is normative for those who feel a vocation to consecrate their virginity to God and to do so in a form recognized by the Church, but without feeling called to join a reli-

gious community. Canon 604: §1 states: "Similar to these forms of consecrated life is the order of virgins, who, committed to the holy plan of following Christ more closely, are consecrated to God by the diocesan bishop according to the approved liturgical rite, are betrothed mystically to Christ, the Son of God, and are dedicated to the service of the Church, §2. In order to observe their commitment more faithfully and to perform by mutual support service to the Church which is in harmony with

their state, these virgins can form themselves into associations."

What is important is that Virgins forego the pleasures of this world not because they despise the flesh but as witnesses for the sake of the Kingdom of Heaven (along with hermits, anchorites, and consecrated widows and widowers, but they should not be confused with them).

COMMON PREFACE I

The renewal of all things in Christ

72.   The following Preface is said in Masses that have no proper Preface, and for which a Preface related to a specific liturgical time is not indicated.

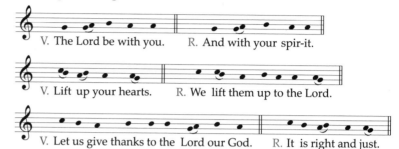

V. The Lord be with you.   R. And with your spir-it.

V. Lift up your hearts.   R. We lift them up to the Lord.

V. Let us give thanks to the Lord our God.   R. It is right and just.

Bring out the accent on **be** in **The Lord be with you**.

Make a strong accent on **Lift**, and slow both notes of **hearts**.

In the third dialogue, move to the word **thanks** before accenting, and hold that word slightly to give it emphasis. Broaden both notes of **Lord**, and hold **God**.

It is truly right and just, our duty and our salvation,
always and everywhere to give you thanks,
Lord, holy Father, almighty and eternal God,
through Christ our Lord.

In him you have been pleased to renew all things,
giving us all a share in his fullness.
For though he was in the form of God, he emptied himself
and by the blood of his Cross brought peace to all creation.
Therefore he has been exalted above all things,
and to all who obey him,
has become the source of eternal salvation.

Emphasize **renew** and **fullness**.

Accentuate the binary opposition of **emptied** and **exalted**.

Emphasize **eternal salvation**.

And so, with Angels and Archangels,
with Thrones and Dominions,
and with all the hosts and Powers of heaven,
we sing the hymn of your glory,
as without end we acclaim:

Holy, Holy, Holy Lord God of hosts . . .

---

72. Common Preface I: The renewal of all things in Christ was a new Preface in the *Missale Romanum* 1970. This Preface alludes to Philippians 2; however, phrases also are from other epistles.

The first line, which speaks of how God has renewed all things in Christ, refers to Ephesians 1:10. There, Paul tells of "a plan for the fullness of times, to sum up all things in Christ, in heaven and on earth." In the second line is a reference to John 1:16, "From his fullness we have all received, grace in place of grace." The third and

fourth lines recall Philippians 2:6–9, in which the early Christian hymn tells of how Christ "did not regard equality with God something to be grasped" (v. 6) and "humbled himself . . . to . . . death on a cross" (v. 8). The last two lines in the body: "to all who obey him, has become the source of eternal salvation" reference Hebrews 5:9 "and when he was made perfect, he became the source of eternal salvation for all who obey him."

In Sermon 24,2 of Leo the Great on the Feast of the Nativity, we find a similar

attestation: "Let the righteous then rejoice in the Lord, and let the hearts of believers turn to God's praise, and the sons of men confess His wondrous acts; since in this work of God especially our humble estate realizes how highly its Maker values it: in that, after His great gift to humanity in making us after His image, He contributed far more largely to our restoration when the Lord Himself took on Him 'the form of a slave.' For though all that the Creator expends upon His creature is part of one

It is truly right and just, our duty and our sal-va-tion, al-ways and everywhere to give you thanks, Lord, holy Father, almighty and e-ter-nal God, through Christ our Lord. In him you have been pleased to re-new all things, giving us all a share in his full-ness. For though he was in the form of God, he emp-tied him-self and by the blood of his Cross brought peace to all cre-a-tion. There-fore he has been exalted a-bove all things, and to all who o-bey him, has become the source of e-ter-nal sal-va-tion. And so, with Angels and Archangels, with Thrones and Do-min-ions, and with all the hosts and Pow-ers of heav-en, we sing the hymn of your glo-ry, as without end we ac-claim:

Holy, Holy, Holy Lord God of hosts . . .

Sing this proclamation cursively in a reciting tone. In **salvation**, do not hold **-va**; only broaden the two notes slightly. The last syllable, **-tion**, should be held. **Always** and **everywhere** require a slight broadening and clear enunciation. The accent of the phrase falls on **thanks**, which should be held briefly. In the next sentence, clearly make distinct phrases of the text, by respecting the commas.

Slightly lengthen **him**, treating it as if the text had a comma. Lengthen slightly **things**, but do not breathe, if possible, rather continuing with **giving us all**. Broaden the last four words, **share in his fullness**. In the next phrase, hold briefly **God** to respect the comma in the text. Slow and broaden **emptied himself**, holding the last syllable just slightly. If necessary, take a very quick breath there, but not so as to lose the sense of continuing with the **and** beginning the next phrase. Slow and broaden **of his Cross**, but do not break or breathe there; rather, continue with **brought peace**. Broaden the last four words. One might find it easier to sing **There-** on "doh", along with **-fore**, so as not to sound as though accenting the second syllable when the voice moves to "doh." Hold **things** briefly and, if possible, continue without a breath to **and to all**. Do not hold or breathe at **him**, but rather continue the sense by going on directly to **has become**. Broaden the last five syllables with their strong musical elaboration.

and the same Fatherly love, yet it is less wonderful that man should advance to divine things than that God should descend to humanity."

Leo is referencing the *sacrum commercium* of God becoming human so that humans might become divine. But he comments that it is far greater that God can take on human form, referencing the mystery of the Incarnation in Christ, than for humans to become divinized.

The mystery of the Incarnation is a wonderful exchange between divinity and humanity that renews all things. In the East this concept is called *theosis*, which in the West we simply call divinization. The idea that God became human so that humans might become divine might seem strange to us at first, and Saint Athanasius in his *On the Incarnation* 54:3 expresses this idea clearly. The early Church had many battles with those who denied Jesus' divinity. Because they defended his divinity, they had the chance to meditate on what it means for the Logos to become flesh. One of the great riches that came from their meditations was the teaching that God became human so that humans could become divine. Of course, this process of divinization is not of our own doing. Rather, God takes the initiative and we simply respond by living lives that reflect the splendor of God.

COMMON PREFACE II

Salvation through Christ

73. The following Preface is said in Masses that have no proper Preface, and for which a Preface related to a specific liturgical time is not indicated.

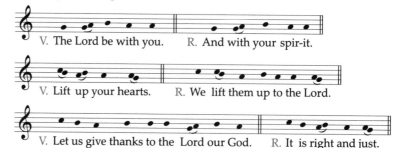

V. The Lord be with you.　　R. And with your spir-it.

V. Lift up your hearts.　　R. We lift them up to the Lord.

V. Let us give thanks to the Lord our God.　　R. It is right and just.

It is truly right and just, our duty and our salvation,
always and everywhere to give you thanks,
Lord, holy Father, almighty and eternal God.

For in goodness you created man
and, when he was justly condemned,
in mercy you redeemed him,
through Christ our Lord.

Through him the Angels praise your majesty,
Dominions adore and Powers tremble before you.
Heaven and the Virtues of heaven and the blessed Seraphim
worship together with exultation.
May our voices, we pray, join with theirs
in humble praise, as we acclaim:

Holy, Holy, Holy Lord God of hosts . . .

Bring out the accent on **be** in **The Lord be with you.**

Make a strong accent on **Lift**, and slow both notes of **hearts.**

In the third dialogue, move to the word **thanks** before accenting, and hold that word slightly to give it emphasis. Broaden both notes of **Lord**, and hold **God.**

Emphasize **In mercy you redeemed him.** It is in binary opposition to **when he was justly condemned.**

73. The first lines of **Common Preface II: Salvation through Christ** allude to Genesis 1:31, in which "God looked at everything he had made, and found it very good."

Lines two and three are from Ephesians 2:4–6: "But God, who is rich in mercy, because of the great love he had for us, even when we were dead in our transgressions, brought us to life with Christ (by grace you have been saved), raised us up with him, and seated us with him in the heavens in Christ Jesus."

If God creates us in his own image, then we are created good. Theologians have examined the difference between the concepts of the "image of God" and the "likeness of God" in human nature. Origen viewed the image of God as something given at creation, while the likeness of God as something bestowed upon a person at a later time. The theologian Irenaeus made a distinction between God's image and his likeness by pointing to Adam's supernatural endowment bestowed upon him by the Spirit. As Irenaeus's view progressed, what

eventually arose was: "The image was the human's natural resemblance to God, the power of reason and will. The likeness was a *donum superadditum*—a divine gift added to basic human nature. This likeness consisted of the moral qualities of God, whereas, the image involved the natural attributes of God. When Adam fell, he lost the likeness, but the image remained fully intact. Humanity as humanity was still complete, but the good and holy being was spoiled." The image of God and the

It is truly right and just, our duty and our sal-va-tion, al-ways and everywhere to give you thanks, Lord, holy Father, almighty and e-ter-nal God. For in goodness you cre-at-ed man and, when he was just-ly con-demned, in mercy you re-deemed him, through Christ our Lord. Through him the Angels praise your maj-es-ty, Domin-ions a-dore and Powers trem-ble be-fore you. Heav-en and the Virtues of heaven and the bless-ed Ser-a-phim worship to-geth-er with ex-ul-ta-tion. May our voices, we pray, join with theirs in hum-ble praise, as we ac-claim:

Holy, Holy, Holy Lord God of hosts . . .

Sing this proclamation cursively in a reciting tone. In **salvation**, do not hold **-va**; only broaden the two notes slightly. The last syllable, **-tion**, should be held. **Always** and **everywhere** require a slight broadening and clear enunciation. The accent of the phrase falls on **thanks**, which should be held briefly. In the next sentence, clearly make distinct phrases of the text, by respecting the commas.

The body of this Preface is divided into two phrases, stressing that God **created** and then **redeemed** humanity. Pause especially after the second phrase to indicate movement from the body into the eschatocol.

In the concluding phrase, make a slight pause after **And so**. Respect the commas but try to keep this section together, without big breaks for breaths. Broaden the last phrase, especially on **praise**. Slow **we ac-**, and put emphasis on **-claim**, so as to evoke the response of **Holy, Holy, Holy** . . . .

likeness are similar, but at the same time they are different. The image is just that; mankind is made in the image of God, whereas the likeness is a spiritual attribute of the moral qualities of God. Medieval theologians made a distinction between the image and likeness of God. The former referred to a natural, innate resemblance to God, and the latter referred to the moral attributes (God's attributes) that were lost in the Fall.

Redeemed in God's mercy seems to stand in binary opposition to having been created in God's goodness. This opposition is resolved, however, in the central idea of God's *hesed*, the Hebrew word for "kindness." It is also commonly translated as "loving-kindness," "merciful love," or "loving mercy." When we ask for God to be merciful, we also are proclaiming God's eternal and boundless love manifested in Christ. Therefore, referencing God's goodness and mercy is richly contained in the Hebrew *hesed*. The word is used many times to describe one of God's favorite attributes. The NIV translates *hesed* as

"mercy" while the New American Standard Bible (NASB) translates it as "unchanging love." Notice that the Lord delights in mercy or unchanging love. Hence, God takes great pleasure in showing mercy. God does not retain anger and delights in mercy. Certainly, ours is a God of justice and judgment; but God is many times portrayed as full of goodness and rich in mercy without any conflict.

COMMON PREFACE III

Praise to God for the creation and restoration of the human race

74. The following Preface is said in Masses that have no proper Preface, and for which a Preface related to a specific liturgical time is not indicated.

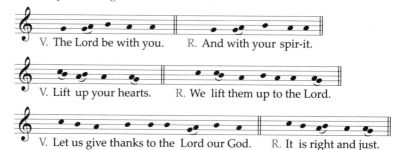

V. The Lord be with you.   R. And with your spir-it.

V. Lift up your hearts.   R. We lift them up to the Lord.

V. Let us give thanks to the Lord our God.   R. It is right and just.

It is truly right and just, our duty and our salvation,
always and everywhere to give you thanks,
Lord, holy Father, almighty and eternal God.

For just as through your beloved Son
you created the human race,
so also through him
with great goodness you formed it anew.

And so, it is right that all your creatures serve you,
all the redeemed praise you,
and all your Saints with one heart bless you.
Therefore, we, too, extol you with all the Angels,
as in joyful celebration we acclaim:

Holy, Holy, Holy Lord God of hosts . . .

Bring out the accent on **be** in **The Lord be with you**.

Make a strong accent on **Lift**, and slow both notes of **hearts**.

In the third dialogue, move to the word **thanks** before accenting, and hold that word slightly to give it emphasis. Broaden both notes of **Lord**, and hold **God**.

Emphasize **created** and **formed it anew**. Emphasize **through** in both cases to bring out the parallel structure.

74. The phrase "created the human race" in **Common Preface III: Praise to God for the creation and restoration of the human race** is from Genesis 1:1, 14, 27–28, but the prayer is emphatic about the role of Christ in creation.

The nature of Jesus Christ as the Son of God, one and equal with the Father and the Holy Spirit, is a primary doctrine of Christianity. Thus, Jesus Christ was also the co-Creator of the universe, a prime participant in the entire process of creation. John paralleled this idea with the opening verses of Genesis: "In the beginning was the Word, and the Word was with God, and the Word was God. He was in the beginning with God. All things came to be through him, and without him nothing came to be" (John 1:1–3).

Paul picks up on this theme when he states: "For in him were created all things in heaven and on earth, the visible and the invisible, whether thrones or dominions or principalities or powers; all things were created through him and for him" (Colossians 1:16).

The doctrine of the Trinity states that in the unity of the Godhead there are three eternal and co-equal Persons: Father, Son, and Holy Spirit, the same in essence but distinct in role—three Persons and one Being. The different senses of one-ness and three-ness mean that the doctrine is not contradictory.

The phrase "you formed it anew" is from Philippians 3:20–21. There, Paul states that "our citizenship is in heaven, and from it we also await a savior, the Lord Jesus Christ. He will change our lowly body

It is truly right and just, our duty and our sal-va-tion, al-ways and everywhere to give you thanks, Lord, holy Father, almighty and e-ter-nal God. For just as through your beloved Son you created the hu-man race, so al-so through him with great goodness you formed it a-new. And so, it is right that all your crea-tures serve you, all the re-deemed praise you, and all your Saints with one heart bless you. There-fore, we, too, extol you with all the An-gels, as in joyful cele-bra-tion we ac-claim:

Holy, Holy, Holy Lord God of hosts . . .

Sing this proclamation cursively in a reciting tone. In **salvation**, do not hold **-va**; only broaden the two notes slightly. The last syllable, **-tion**, should be held. **Always** and **everywhere** require a slight broadening and clear enunciation. The accent of the phrase falls on **thanks**, which should be held briefly. In the next sentence, clearly make distinct phrases of the text, by respecting the commas.

The body comprises two sentences emphasizing that God **created humanity in Christ** and that God has **formed humanity anew in Christ**. Pause especially after the second phrase to indicate movement from the body to the eschatocol.

In the concluding phrase, make a slight pause after **And so**. Respect the commas but try to keep this section together, without big breaks for breaths. Broaden the last phrase, especially on **extol**. Slow **we ac-**, and put emphasis on **-claim**, so as to evoke the response of **Holy, Holy, Holy** . . . .

to conform with his glorified body by the power that enables him also to bring all things into subjection to himself."

Christ as making all things new is a reference to him as the new Adam. Since the first creation (that God created "good") was spoiled due to the fall of the first Adam, Christ is seen as a new Adam, making all things new in a new creation. Paul is insistent on this point in his letter to the Romans: "Therefore, just as through one person sin entered the world, and through sin, death, and thus death came to all, inas-much as all sinned—for up to the time of the law, sin was in the world, though sin is not accounted when there is no law. But death reigned from Adam to Moses, even over those who did not sin after the pattern of the trespass of Adam, who is the type of the one who was to come" (Romans 5:12–14).

Paul continues with his rich theology of Baptism in chapter 6: "[A]re you unaware that we who were baptized into Christ Jesus were baptized into his death? We were indeed buried with him through baptism into death, so that, just as Christ was raised from the dead by the glory of the Father, we too might live in newness of life" (v. 3–4). So by entering into Christ's Death and Resurrection at Baptism, we become a new creation. We are re-created or created anew.

The Preface, therefore, emphasizes equally Christ as Co-Creator and Re-Creator. As the New Adam, he represents redeemed humanity.

COMMON PREFACE IV

Praise, the gift of God

75. The following Preface is said in Masses that have no proper Preface, and for which a Preface related to a specific liturgical time is not indicated.

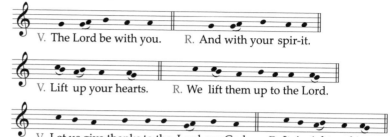

V. The Lord be with you.   R. And with your spir-it.

V. Lift up your hearts.   R. We lift them up to the Lord.

V. Let us give thanks to the Lord our God.   R. It is right and just.

It is truly right and just, our duty and our salvation,
always and everywhere to give you thanks,
Lord, holy Father, almighty and eternal God.

For, although you have no need of our praise,
yet our thanksgiving is itself your gift,
since our praises add nothing to your greatness
but profit us for salvation,
through Christ our Lord.

And so, in company with the choirs of Angels,
we praise you, and with joy we proclaim:

Holy, Holy, Holy Lord God of hosts . . .

Bring out the accent on **be** in **The Lord be with you.**

Make a strong accent on **Lift**, and slow both notes of **hearts.**

In the third dialogue, move to the word **thanks** before accenting, and hold that word slightly to give it emphasis. Broaden both notes of **Lord**, and hold **God.**

Two sets of oppositions appear. Emphasize **praise** and **thanksgiving.** Emphasize **no need** and **add nothing.**

---

75. Common Preface IV: Praise, the gift of God is a stunning Preface that touches upon the very nature of the Eucharist. The body strongly emphasizes a paradox at the heart of Christian prayer. That paradox is that we pray because we need to pray. We do not pray because God needs our prayers.

Two binary oppositions are present in this Preface. The first binary opposition is apparent in the phrases "although you have no need of our praise" and "our thanksgiving is itself your gift." The other binary opposition is found in the phrases

"since our praises add nothing to your greatness" and "but profit us for salvation."

"Eucharist," from Greek *eucharistia*, means "thanksgiving." The verb form was the usual word for "to thank" in the Septuagint and the New Testament and is found in the major texts concerning the Lord's Supper, including the earliest reference in Paul's first letter to the Corinthians: "For I received from the Lord what I also handed on to you, that the Lord Jesus, on the night he was handed over, took bread, and, after he had given thanks,

broke it and said, 'This is my body that is for you. Do this in remembrance of me' " (1 Corinthians 11:23–24).

In the Preface, Eucharist is connected to praise. In common parlance, praise is the act of using words to celebrate good things and can be used as part of worship to glorify God, or given to other people in recognition of a job well done. In modern Christianity, praise is a key part of most services, along with intercession, confession, Bible readings, thanksgiving, and Communion. In the

It is truly right and just, our duty and our sal-va-tion, al-ways and everywhere to give you thanks, Lord, holy Father, almighty and e-ter-nal God. For, although you have no need of our praise, yet our thanks-giv-ing is it-self your gift, since our praises add nothing to your great-ness, but profit us for sal-va-tion, through Christ our Lord. And so, in company with the choirs of An-gels, we praise you, and with joy we pro-claim:

Holy, Holy, Holy Lord God of hosts . . .

Sing this proclamation cursively in a reciting tone. In **salvation**, do not hold **-va**; only broaden the two notes slightly. The last syllable, **-tion**, should be held. **Always** and **everywhere** require a slight broadening and clear enunciation. The accent of the phrase falls on **thanks**, which should be held briefly. In the next sentence, clearly make distinct phrases of the text, by respecting the commas.

The body of this Preface is divided into two sets of binary oppositions, each ending with a full vertical line, Pause at those lines, especially after the second binary opposition, to indicate movement from the body into the eschatocol.

In the concluding phrase, make a slight pause after **And so**. Respect the commas but try to keep this section together, without big breaks for breaths. Broaden the last phrase, especially on **praise**. Slow **we ac-**, and put emphasis on **-claim**, so as to evoke the response of **Holy, Holy, Holy** . . . .

scriptures, many of the Psalms are hymns of praise, while Jesus includes praise in the Lord's Prayer that he teaches to his disciples (captured in the phrase "hallowed be thy name").

In the English language, these ideas get linked together in the unique word "worship." The word is derived from the Old English *worthscipe*, meaning "worthiness" or "worth-ship"—to give, at its simplest, "worth to something"; for example, Christian worship. But in the context of liturgical prayer, it has many resonances

that pick up on thanksgiving, praise, and blessing.

Evelyn Underhill, a writer on religion and mysticism, defines worship this way: "The absolute acknowledgment of all that lies beyond us—the glory that fills heaven and earth. It is the response that conscious beings make to their Creator, to the Eternal Reality from which they came forth; to God, however they may think of Him or recognize Him, and whether He be realized through religion, through nature, through history, through science, art, or human life

and character" (*Education and the Spirit of Worship*, London, 1946, p. 193).

The beauty of this Preface is that we come to prayer with our hands wide open. We ask for nothing but simply are moved out of gratitude and praise. So in worship we come to give praise and thanksgiving, rather than asking to receive anything.

COMMON PREFACE V

The proclamation of the mystery of Christ

76. The following Preface is said in Masses that have no proper Preface, and for which a Preface related to a specific liturgical time is not indicated.

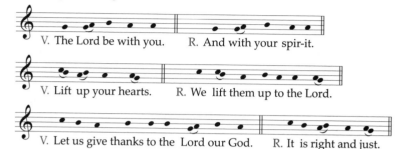

Bring out the accent on **be** in **The Lord be with you**.

Make a strong accent on **Lift**, and slow both notes of **hearts**.

In the third dialogue, move to the word **thanks** before accenting, and hold that word slightly to give it emphasis. Broaden both notes of **Lord**, and hold **God**.

It is truly right and just, our duty and our salvation,
always and everywhere to give you thanks,
Lord, holy Father, almighty and eternal God,
through Christ our Lord.

His Death we celebrate in love,
his Resurrection we confess with living faith,
and his Coming in glory we await with unwavering hope.

And so, with all the Angels and Saints,
we praise you, as without end we acclaim:

Holy, Holy, Holy Lord God of hosts . . .

Emphasize **Death**, **Resurrection**, and **Coming**, which echo the Mystery of Faith. In proclaiming this text, parallel the rhetoric of death with that of love, resurrection, coming glory, and await.

76. Common Preface V: The proclamation of the mystery of Christ is a fairly new Preface, first becoming part of the Missal with the 1970 *Missale Romanum*. It evokes Memorial Acclamation I:

We proclaim your Death, O Lord,
and profess your Resurrection
until you come again.

This Preface alludes to Titus 2:13–14: "as we await the blessed hope, the appearance of the glory of the great God and of our savior Jesus Christ, who gave himself for us to deliver us from all lawlessness and to cleanse for himself a people as his own, eager to do what is good."

The trinary structure of Death, Resurrection, and future Coming is the central mystery of Christ. The Preface holds together linguistically what the liturgy celebrates annually; namely the life, Death, Resurrection, and future Coming of the Lord. This is the most central dogma of the Christian faith—the Paschal Mystery, that Christ has died, that Christ is risen, and that Christ will come again in glory!

Looking at the tenses of the verbs of this declaration of faith, we note past, present, and future. It is important to notice especially that the Resurrection of Christ is regarded as a present event and is not relegated simply to the past. Christ *is* risen. These three statements can be correlated to the three theological virtues of faith, hope, and love.

Faith is oriented to the past. As Saint Paul said, if Christ truly did not live, die and rise from the dead, "then empty [too] is our preaching; empty, too, your faith" (1 Corinthians 15:14). But if faith looks toward the past, hope tends toward the future. Much as we would not say "I hope

It is truly right and just, our duty and our sal-va-tion, al-ways and everywhere to give you thanks, Lord, holy Father, almighty and e-ter-nal God, through Christ our Lord. His Death we cel-e-brate in love, his Resurrection we confess with liv-ing faith, and his Coming in glo-ry we await with un-wa-ver-ing hope. And so, with all the An-gels and Saints, we praise you, as without end we ac-claim:

Holy, Holy, Holy Lord God of hosts . . .

Sing this proclamation cursively in a reciting tone. In **salvation**, do not hold **-va**; only broaden the two notes slightly. The last syllable, **-tion**, should be held. **Always** and **everywhere** require a slight broadening and clear enunciation. The accent of the phrase falls on **thanks**, which should be held briefly. In the next sentence, clearly make distinct phrases of the text, by respecting the commas.

The body of this Preface is divided into three phrases focusing on the words **Death**, **Resurrection**, and **Coming**. Pause especially after the third phrases to indicate the movement from the body into the eschatocol.

In the concluding phrase, make a slight pause after **And so**. Respect the commas but try to keep this section together, without big breaks for breaths. Broaden the last phrase, especially on **praise**. Slow **we ac-**, and put emphasis on **-claim**, so as to evoke the response of **Holy, Holy, Holy . . . .**

the weather will be nice yesterday," so, too, we look to the future coming of Christ in hope. We stand then in tension between past and future, in a sort of eschatological tension. But as Saint Paul also said, "So faith, hope, love remain, these three; but the greatest of these is love" (1 Corinthians 13:13). Therefore, the present moment is the time of Resurrection and this period between the two comings of Christ is marked by love. The present moment of Resurrection is marked by our willingness to love and experience the Risen Lord in Christian charity.

Two of the Memorial Acclamations pick up on this theme as well:

We proclaim your Death, O Lord, and profess your Resurrection until you come again,

When we eat this Bread and drink this Cup, we proclaim your Death, O Lord, until you come again.

The two Comings of Jesus also suggest that in the interim period between the first and final coming, Christ comes to us collectively and individually. For this reason, the focus is not simply on past events in history, but on the present moment in which the Church gathers as she looks to the future coming of Christ. In this eschatological tension between the two comings of Christ, we live in the present moment of Resurrection.

COMMON PREFACE VI

The mystery of salvation in Christ

77.   The following Preface is said in Masses that have no proper Preface, and for which a Preface related to a specific liturgical time is not indicated.

V. The Lord be with you.   R. And with your spir-it.

V. Lift up your hearts.   R. We lift them up to the Lord.

V. Let us give thanks to the Lord our God.   R. It is right and just.

Bring out the accent on **be** in **The Lord be with you.**

Make a strong accent on **Lift**, and slow both notes of **hearts.**

In the third dialogue, move to the word **thanks** before accenting, and hold that word slightly to give it emphasis. Broaden both notes of **Lord**, and hold **God.**

The body of this Preface starts with the words **your Word.** This is an adjustment to a different pattern in the prayer.

In the second paragraph, follow the sense lines.

It is truly right and just, our duty and our salvation,
always and everywhere to give you thanks, Father most holy,
through your beloved Son, Jesus Christ,
your Word through whom you made all things,
whom you sent as our Savior and Redeemer,
incarnate by the Holy Spirit and born of the Virgin.

Fulfilling your will and gaining for you a holy people,
he stretched out his hands as he endured his Passion,
so as to break the bonds of death and manifest the resurrection.

And so, with the Angels and all the Saints,
we declare your glory,
as with one voice we acclaim:

Holy, Holy, Holy Lord God of hosts . . .

77. Common Preface VI: The mystery of salvation in Christ is taken from the Apostolic Tradition and is the prescribed Preface for Eucharistic Prayer II. The text is part of a Eucharistic Prayer that a Bishop prays on his ordination.

This Preface looks at Christ's Incarnation and the redemption; in other words, at the beginning and end of Christ's life. Not found in the prayer is Christ's public ministry—his work as healer, sage, teller of parables. It is, we might say, the bookends of Jesus' life that are emphasized here.

The Priest Celebrant will find that, because the beginning of the body meshes with the protocol, this is a difficult prayer to pray. If the prayer is thought of as a litany, especially with the first paragraph, the proclamation will be easier. You can see how the prayer is like a litany in that, phrase after phrase, it describes Jesus and what he has done.

The prayer resembles a creedal formula with its use of direct declaratory phrases and no hint of a subordinate clause anywhere, much like the Apostles' Creed.

As in the Nicene Creed, a distinction is made between becoming incarnate by the Holy Spirit and being born of the Virgin Mary. The use of the Latin cognate "incarnate" provides an opportunity to preach about the mystery of the Incarnation.

The image of Jesus stretching out his hands evokes a similar image found in the Eucharistic Prayer for Reconciliation I: "But before his arms were outstretched between heaven and earth, to become the lasting sign of your covenant."

It is truly right and just, our duty and our sal-va-tion, al-ways and everywhere to give you thanks, Fa-ther most ho-ly, through your be--loved Son, Je-sus Christ, your Word through whom you made all things, whom you sent as our Savior and Re-deem-er, incarnate by the Ho-ly Spir-it and born of the Vir-gin. Ful-filling your will and gaining for you a ho-ly peo-ple, he stretched out his hands as he en-dured his Pas-sion, so as to break the bonds of death and manifest the res-ur-rec-tion. And so, with the Angels and all the Saints, we declare your glo-ry, as with one voice we ac-claim:

Holy, Holy, Holy Lord God of hosts . . .

Sing this proclamation cursively in a reciting tone. In **salvation**, do not hold **-va**; only broaden the two notes slightly. The last syllable, **-tion**, should be held. **Always** and **everywhere** require a slight broadening and clear enunciation. The accent of the phrase falls on **thanks**, which should be held briefly. In the next sentence, clearly make distinct phrases of the text, by respecting the commas.

The body of this Preface is unusual in that it is anticipated within the protocol. At a full vertical line, breathe and pause a little before proceeding. The body, beginning with **your Word**, is subdivided into three phrases, each ending with a full vertical line. Pause, especially after the second phrase, to indicate movement from the body into the eschatocol.

In the concluding phrase, make a slight pause after **And so**. Respect the commas but try to keep this section together, without big breaks for breaths. Broaden the last phrase, especially on **glory**. Slow **we ac-**, and put emphasis on **-claim**, so as to evoke the response of **Holy, Holy, Holy . . . .**

The document, usually called by scholars the "Apostolic Tradition," is one of the most enigmatic sources of early Christian literature. For a while, consensus seemed to have been reached regarding its date (early third century), provenance (Rome), and authorship (Hippolytus of Rome). During the last few years, however, scholars have questioned practically all of the commonly accepted ideas about the origin of this source. At the moment, very little is left of the old consensus. An increasing number of scholars are abandoning the very idea that the source under consideration would be the work of a single author or redactor. The document is viewed rather as an anonymous composite work invested with apostolic authority and containing community rules from disparate traditions which, moreover, continued being updated for a long period in Eastern and Western churches (a process that accounts for the differences between the numerous translations and versions).

Nevertheless, this Church Order has been indispensable for gauging what early Christian worship looked like, and it has served ecumenically in the liturgical reforms of all the liturgically minded churches.

PREFACE I FOR THE DEAD

The hope of resurrection in Christ

78.   The following Preface is said in Masses for the Dead.

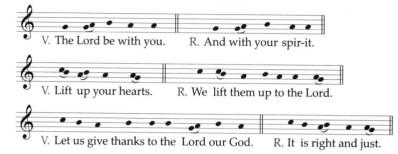

V. The Lord be with you.   R. And with your spir-it.

V. Lift up your hearts.   R. We lift them up to the Lord.

V. Let us give thanks to the Lord our God.   R. It is right and just.

Bring out the accent on **be** in **The Lord be with you**.

Make a strong accent on **Lift**, and slow both notes of **hearts**.

In the third dialogue, move to the word **thanks** before accenting, and hold that word slightly to give it emphasis. Broaden both notes of **Lord**, and hold **God**.

It is truly right and just, our duty and our salvation,
always and everywhere to give you thanks,
Lord, holy Father, almighty and eternal God,
through Christ our Lord.

Emphasize **In him the hope of blessed resurrection has dawned**. This important sentence should be spoken slowly. The implications of that line are in the next two lines, but those lines are not as important as the first sentence.

In him the hope of blessed resurrection has dawned,
that those saddened by the certainty of dying
might be consoled by the promise of immortality to come.
Indeed for your faithful, Lord,
life is changed not ended,
and, when this earthly dwelling turns to dust,
an eternal dwelling is made ready for them in heaven.

And so, with Angels and Archangels,
with Thrones and Dominions,
and with all the hosts and Powers of heaven,
we sing the hymn of your glory,
as without end we acclaim:

Holy, Holy, Holy Lord God of hosts . . .

78. The central contrast for the body of **Preface I for the Dead: The hope of resurrection in Christ** is the contrast between an earthly dwelling turning to dust and the eternal dwelling having permanence. This is easily seen in lines six and seven of the body, "and, when this earthly dwelling turns to dust, / an eternal dwelling is made ready for them in heaven."

This Preface alludes to 2 Corinthians 5:1–7, which tells of the eternal dwelling that has been made for us in heaven: "For we know that if our earthly dwelling . . .

should be destroyed, we have a building from God, a dwelling not made with hands, eternal in heaven" (v. 1). As does scripture, the Preface contrasts our earthly habitation with the heavenly dwelling.

The first sentence of the body, "In him the hope of blessed resurrection has dawned," is an important sentence. The implications of that line are in the next two lines. Those lines, however, are not as important as the first sentence.

The focus of this prayer is in the next two lines, "Indeed for your faithful, Lord, /

life is changed not ended." The phrase "life is changed not ended" should stand out in the proclamation of the prayer. This thesis sentence is parallel to the thesis sentence at the beginning of the prayer.

The body of the prayer ends with a binary opposition; however, that binary opposition is not as important as "life is changed not ended."

The death of someone we know is always a painful time. Death arouses in us distressing feelings: shock, grief, anger, loneliness, fear. A person may be feeling

It is truly right and just, our duty and our sal-va-tion, al-ways and everywhere to give you thanks, Lord, holy Father, almighty and e--ter-nal God, through Christ our Lord. In him the hope of blessed resur-rec-tion has dawned, that those saddened by the certain-ty of dy-ing might be consoled by the prom-ise of immor-tal-i-ty to come. In-deed for your faithful, Lord, life is changed not end-ed, and, when this earthly dwelling turns to dust, an e-ter-nal dwell-ing is made ready for them in heav-en. And so, with Angels and Archangels, with Thrones and Do-min-ions, and with all the hosts and Pow-ers of heav-en, we sing the hymn of your glo-ry, as without end we ac-claim:

Holy, Holy, Holy Lord God of hosts . . .

Sing this proclamation cursively in a reciting tone. In **salvation**, do not hold **-va**; only broaden the two notes slightly. The last syllable, **-tion**, should be held. **Always** and **everywhere** require a slight broadening and clear enunciation. The accent of the phrase falls on **thanks**, which should be held briefly. In the next sentence, clearly make distinct phrases of the text, by respecting the commas.

Make a slight hold on **dawned** and, because of the length of the next phrases, it might be well to steal a quick breath at that point. The next two phrases should be joined together: after holding slightly the syllable **-ing** of dying, continue without breath to **might be consoled**. A slight pause for emphasis after **Indeed** would be appropriate. Also, hold **Lord** slightly. A pause in the next phrase, after **and** will help bring out the sense. Hold **dust**, but do not take a breath, but rather continue with **an eternal**, slowing the words **for them in heaven**, holding the last syllable and taking a good breath there.

In the concluding phrase, make a slight pause after **And so**. Respect the commas but try to keep this section together, without big breaks for breaths. Broaden the last phrase, especially on **glory**. Slow **we ac-**, and put emphasis on **-claim**, so as to evoke the response of **Holy, Holy, Holy . . . .**

some of these emotions during such a time and may face many questions about life and death. Someone else's death may remind us of our own mortality: today it is this person; tomorrow another; one day it will be me.

What happened to Jesus Christ gives us hope. He lived a life of trust in God, whom he calls "Father." Though Christ died a cruel death at the hands of humanity, the Father raised him to new life in glory.

Christians believe that Jesus is alive today. He invites us to share in his victory over sin and death by putting our trust in him. But belief in Christ does not mask the tragedy of death. The death of someone close may come as a shock. We may feel angry, too. It is a time of regret. One may feel helpless, lost, and fearful. Often, it is also a time of loneliness. However, even though the death of someone dear to us is painful, with God there is hope, peace, and joy.

The Preface does not attempt to hide the horror of death or gloss over the normal feelings that we have in the face of the death of a loved one. Rather, the Catholic Church gathers with the family and friends of the deceased because they share the belief that "life is changed not ended," and that heaven is our ultimate destiny.

PREFACE II FOR THE DEAD

Christ died so that we might live

79.   The following Preface is said in Masses for the Dead.

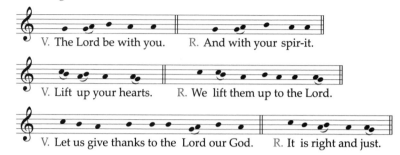

V. The Lord be with you.   R. And with your spir-it.

V. Lift up your hearts.   R. We lift them up to the Lord.

V. Let us give thanks to the Lord our God.   R. It is right and just.

It is truly right and just, our duty and our salvation,
always and everywhere to give you thanks,
Lord, holy Father, almighty and eternal God,
through Christ our Lord.

For as one alone he accepted death,
so that we might all escape from dying;
as one man he chose to die,
so that in your sight we all might live for ever.

And so, in company with the choirs of Angels,
we praise you, and with joy we proclaim:

Holy, Holy, Holy Lord God of hosts . . .

Bring out the accent on **be** in **The Lord be with you**.

Make a strong accent on **Lift**, and slow both notes of **hearts**.

In the third dialogue, move to the word **thanks** before accenting, and hold that word slightly to give it emphasis. Broaden both notes of **Lord**, and hold **God**.

Emphasize **alone accepted death** and **all escape dying**.

Emphasize **as one**, **choose**, **dies**, and **all might live**. Binary oppositions are apparent in the first two lines and then in the last two lines of the body of the prayer.

79. A strong scriptural foundation from 2 Corinthians 5:14 underlies **Preface II for the Dead: Christ died so that we might live**. In that verse, Saint Paul tells the people of Corinth: "For the love of Christ impels us, once we have come to the conviction that one died for all; therefore, all have died."

That one might die for the many, and that through the death of one person all might have life is a rich theme in Patristic writings. Often the question was posed in the form of death as a debt paid by one for the many. Much debate was in response to the vexed problem of Romans 2:6 in which Paul says that God "will repay everyone according to his works." Why, then, would an innocent person be chosen to pay the debt for the sins of all? The following are a *cento* of Patristic texts that try to answer this question.

Leo the Great, in his letter to Flavian, makes the point that only Christ as the innocent one could pay the price for sin: "To pay the debt of our condition, inviola-ble nature was joined to passable nature" (Ephesians 28).

Others said the following:

• Athanasius, On the Incarnation of the Divine Word 9: "For the Word, knowing that only by dying was it possible for the corruption of people to be removed, since the Word, being immortal, could not die . . . took to Himself a body that could die. . . . The Word of God . . . paid the debt in death."

It is truly right and just, our duty and our sal-va-tion, al-ways and everywhere to give you thanks, Lord, holy Father, almighty and e-ter-nal God, through Christ our Lord. For as one alone he accept-ed death, so that we might all es-cape from dy-ing; as one man he chose to die, so that in your sight we all might live for ev-er. And so, in company with the choirs of An-gels, we praise you, and with joy we pro-claim:

Holy, Holy, Holy Lord God of hosts . . .

Sing this proclamation cursively in a reciting tone. In **salvation**, do not hold **-va**; only broaden the two notes slightly. The last syllable, **-tion**, should be held. **Always** and **everywhere** require a slight broadening and clear enunciation. The accent of the phrase falls on **thanks**, which should be held briefly. In the next sentence, clearly make distinct phrases of the text, by respecting the commas.

It would be appropriate to treat **one** and **alone** as if commas were after them. Connect **death** and **so that**, but try not to breathe there. In the next phrase, a slight pause after **man** would be appropriate. Hold **die** at the end of the phrase, but do not breathe but rather continue with **so that**. Hold **sight** briefly. Broaden the final words **live forever**.

In the concluding phrase, make a slight pause after **And so**. Respect the commas but try to keep this section together, without big breaks for breaths. Broaden the last phrase, especially on **praise**. Slow **we ac-**, and put emphasis on **-claim**, so as to evoke the response of **Holy, Holy, Holy . . . .**

• Origen, On Matthew 20:28: "Now to whom did He give His life as a price of redemption for the many? For it was not to God. Was it then to the Evil One? For he had us in his power, until the life of Jesus was given to him as a ransom for us—to him who was deceived, as though he could hold that life."

• Ambrose, Epistle 72: "Without doubt he [Satan] demanded a price to set free from slavery those whom he held bound. Now the price of our liberty was the blood of Jesus, which necessarily had to be paid to him to whom we had been sold by our sins."

• Augustine, Sermon 329: "For on the cross He carried out a great exchange. There the sack of our price was paid, when his side was opened by the lance of the one who struck it, from there flowed out the price for the whole world."

• Gregory of Nazianzus, Oration 45, on Easter 22: "Now if the ransom goes to none other than the captor: I ask, to whom was it brought and why? If to the Evil One—what a mockery! If that robber receives not just something from God, but God Himself. . . . But if it was paid to the Father—first of all, how? For we were not held captive by Him. Secondly, why would the blood of His only begotten please the Father. . . . Or is it not clear instead that the Father did receive the offering, even though He did not ask for it or need it, but He received it as a result of His divine plan and because it was right that humanity should be sanctified by the humanity of God."

PREFACE III FOR THE DEAD

Christ, the salvation and the life

80.   The following Preface is said in Masses for the Dead.

V. The Lord be with you.   R. And with your spir-it.

V. Lift up your hearts.   R. We lift them up to the Lord.

V. Let us give thanks to the Lord our God.   R. It is right and just.

Bring out the accent on **be** in **The Lord be with you**.

Make a strong accent on **Lift**, and slow both notes of **hearts**.

In the third dialogue, move to the word **thanks** before accenting, and hold that word slightly to give it emphasis. Broaden both notes of **Lord**, and hold **God**.

Pray lines 1 through 3 with an ascending pitch and volume.

It is truly right and just, our duty and our salvation,
always and everywhere to give you thanks,
Lord, holy Father, almighty and eternal God,
through Christ our Lord.

For he is the salvation of the world,
the life of the human race,
the resurrection of the dead.

Through him the host of Angels adores your majesty
and rejoices in your presence for ever.
May our voices, we pray, join with theirs
in one chorus of exultant praise, as we acclaim:

Holy, Holy, Holy Lord God of hosts . . .

---

80. Johannine references are apparent in **Preface III for the Dead: Christ, the salvation and the life** in the phrases "salvation of the world," "life of the human race," and "resurrection of the dead." Let us examine each of these in succession.

Christ reveals himself throughout his earthly life as the Savior sent by the Father for the salvation of the world. In John 4:42 we read: "[T]hey said to the woman, 'We no longer believe because of your word; for we have heard for ourselves, and we know that this is truly the savior of the world." The name "Jesus" expresses this mission. It means: "God saves." It is a name given as a result of heavenly instruction: both Mary (Luke 1:31) and Joseph (Matthew 1:21) receive the order to call him by this name. The message to Joseph explains: "[Y]ou are to name him Jesus, because he will save his people from their sins."

In saying that Jesus came to give his life as a ransom for many, Jesus is referring to the prophecy of the Suffering Servant who "gives his life as an offering for sin" (Isaiah 53:10). It is a life given "as a ransom for many"; that is, for the immense multitude of humanity.

The expression "Life of the human race" also evokes the words from John's account of the Gospel: "Jesus said to him, 'I am the way and the truth and the life. No one comes to the Father except through me.'" (John 14:6). Life, in this sense, is in all its richness. "The glory of God is a human being 'fully alive,'" said Saint Irenaeus, a second-century Bishop and writer, almost two thousand years ago. God made each

It is truly right and just, our duty and our sal-va-tion, al-ways and everywhere to give you thanks, Lord, holy Father, almighty and e-ter-nal God, through Christ our Lord. For he is the salvation of the world, the life of the hu-man race, the resur-rec-tion of the dead. Through him the host of Angels a-dores your maj-es-ty and re-joic-es in your pres-ence for ev-er. May our voices, we pray, join with theirs in one chorus of ex-ult-ant praise, as we ac-claim:

Holy, Holy, Holy Lord God of hosts . . .

Sing this proclamation cursively in a reciting tone. In **salvation**, do not hold **-va**; only broaden the two notes slightly. The last syllable, **-tion**, should be held. **Always** and **everywhere** require a slight broadening and clear enunciation. The accent of the phrase falls on **thanks**, which should be held briefly. In the next sentence, clearly make distinct phrases of the text, by respecting the commas.

Try to tie together the entire first sentence of three phrases without breathing — although a slight lengthening should be made on **world**, **race**, and **dead**.

In the concluding phrase, make a slight pause after **And so**. Respect the commas but try to keep this section together, without big breaks for breaths. Broaden the last phrase, especially on **praise**. Slow **we ac-**, and put emphasis on **-claim**, so as to evoke the response of **Holy, Holy, Holy . . . .**

of us with purpose that only we can fulfill with God's grace. This special purpose lies dormant in us until we are awakened by a burning desire. When we make a decision to choose life and truly be who we are meant to be, no matter the cost, we become like the snowcapped mountain, the towering oak, the eagle, or the ant. We join those who choose to submit to what they truly are. We become, as Irenaeus said, "a human being who is fully alive!"

The third expression, "Resurrection of the dead," also recalls John: "I am the res-urrection and the life; whoever believes in me, even if he dies, will live" (John 11:25). The Resurrection of Jesus is one of the central doctrines in Christianity. It is codified in the Apostles' Creed, which is the fundamental creed of Christian baptismal faith. According to Paul, the entire Christian faith hinges upon the centrality of the Resurrection of Jesus and the hope for a life after death. Paul wrote in his first letter to the Corinthians: "If for this life only we have hoped in Christ, we are the most pitiable people of all. But now Christ has been raised from the dead, the firstfruits of those who have fallen asleep" (15:19–20).

These three expressions "salvation of the world," "life of the human race," and "resurrection of the dead," taken together form a fundamental creedal statement about Christ and the basis for our belief in the Resurrection.

PREFACE IV FOR THE DEAD

From earthly life to heavenly glory

81. The following Preface is said in Masses for the Dead.

V. The Lord be with you.   R. And with your spir-it.

V. Lift up your hearts.   R. We lift them up to the Lord.

V. Let us give thanks to the Lord our God.   R. It is right and just.

It is truly right and just, our duty and our salvation,
always and everywhere to give you thanks,
Lord, holy Father, almighty and eternal God.

For it is at your summons that we come to birth,
by your will that we are governed,
and at your command that we return,
on account of sin,
to that earth from which we came.

And when you give the sign,
we who have been redeemed by the Death of your Son,
shall be raised up to the glory of his Resurrection.

And so, with the company of Angels and Saints,
we sing the hymn of your praise,
as without end we acclaim:

Holy, Holy, Holy Lord God of hosts . . .

Bring out the accent on **be** in **The Lord be with you**.

Make a strong accent on **Lift**, and slow both notes of **hearts**.

In the third dialogue, move to the word **thanks** before accenting, and hold that word slightly to give it emphasis. Broaden both notes of **Lord**, and hold **God**.

The three rhetorical lines in the first paragraph should be represented. These are the **summons that we come to birth**, the **will that we are governed**, and the **command that we return**. Contrasting these three rhetorical statements, in the second paragraph, are **when you give the sign**, **we who have been redeemed**, and **shall be raised up to the glory**.

---

81. The strongest biblical material underlying **Preface IV for the Dead: From earthly life to heavenly glory** is 1 Corinthians 15:55–56. Those verses provide a question and answer about death. "Where, O death, is your victory? Where, O death, is your sting?" The sting of death is sin, and the power of sin is the law."

The first paragraph of the body is a series of declarations. It is by God's summons that we come to birth, will that we are governed, and command that we return to the earth.

The two paragraphs in the body discuss two kinds of experience. The first paragraph tells of what we can know in this space and time. We know that God's will brings us to birth, oversees us in this world of space and time, and witnesses our death.

Paragraph two is a profound act of faith and hope. What we do not see, but what we hope, is that we who are redeemed will be given a sign and will be raised in glory. We do not know this. We have not seen it, but we believe this.

In Genesis we are told that God warned Adam that if he eats from the tree of the knowledge of good and evil, he will surely die. This was communicated also to Eve. The serpent, however, being deceptive, promised Eve that she and Adam would not die from eating it. So she ate the fruit, and also gave it to her husband. As a result of eating the fruit, Adam and Eve realized for the first time that they were naked, so they covered themselves with fig leaves. When they heard the sound of God

It is truly right and just, our duty and our sal-va-tion, al-ways and everywhere to give you thanks, Lord, holy Father, almighty and e-ter-nal God. For it is at your summons that we come to birth, by your will that we are gov-erned, and at your command that we return, on ac-count of sin, to that earth from which we came. And when you give the sign, we who have been redeemed by the Death of your Son, shall be raised up to the glo-ry of his Res-ur-rec-tion. And so, with the company of An-gels and Saints, we sing the hymn of your praise, as without end we ac-claim:

Holy, Holy, Holy Lord God of hosts . . .

Sing this proclamation cursively in a reciting tone. In **salvation**, do not hold **-va**; only broaden the two notes slightly. The last syllable, **-tion**, should be held. **Always** and **everywhere** require a slight broadening and clear enunciation. The accent of the phrase falls on **thanks**, which should be held briefly. In the next sentence, clearly make distinct phrases of the text, by respecting the commas.

The ideal would be to connect the entire first sentence together without a breath, from **For it is at** through **which we came**. But that may be too much for most. If so, take a very short breath at **governed**, before the **and**. Similarly, the ideal would be to tie together from **And** to **Resurrection**. Hold briefly **sign** and **Son** — and if necessary take a very short breath after **Son**. Slow and broaden **glory** and enunciate the word very clearly.

In the concluding phrase, make a slight pause after **And so**. Respect the commas but try to keep this section together, without big breaks for breaths. Broaden the last phrase, especially on **praise**. Slow **we ac-**, and put emphasis on **-claim**, so as to evoke the response of **Holy, Holy, Holy** . . . .

walking in the garden in the cool of the day, they hid from him among the trees. He called out to them, asking where they were and whether they had eaten from the forbidden tree. Adam blamed Eve, and Eve blamed the serpent. God then cursed all three of them. One of the punishments was death.

Often, this has been misunderstood to mean that physical death is a consequence for sin. But the biblical scholars explain otherwise; that "death" here means separation from God, the giver of "life."

The reason for the second explanation is the obvious fact that in the story Adam did not die. When God spoke of Adam's eventual death, He mentioned it not as a consequence of sin, but as a natural outcome of Adam's having been created from dust, and to dust he must return.

When Paul says, "For the wages of sin is death, but the gift of God is eternal life through Christ Jesus our Lord" (Romans 6:23), he is referring to being cut off from God, and Christ redeems humanity by

restoring the relationship with God that was ruptured by sin.

The Preface is nicely balanced, comparing death as a result of sin with Resurrection as a result of the Death of Christ who was raised up and restored to God.

PREFACE V FOR THE DEAD

Our resurrection through the victory of Christ

82.   The following Preface is said in Masses for the Dead.

V. The Lord be with you.   R. And with your spir-it.

V. Lift up your hearts.   R. We lift them up to the Lord.

V. Let us give thanks to the Lord our God.   R. It is right and just.

Bring out the accent on **be** in **The Lord be with you**.

It is truly right and just, our duty and our salvation,
always and everywhere to give you thanks,
Lord, holy Father, almighty and eternal God.

Make a strong accent on **Lift**, and slow both notes of **hearts**.

For even though by our own fault we perish,
yet by your compassion and your grace,
when seized by death according to our sins,
we are redeemed through Christ's great victory,
and with him called back into life.

In the third dialogue, move to the word **thanks** before accenting, and hold that word slightly to give it emphasis. Broaden both notes of **Lord**, and hold **God**.

And so, with the Powers of heaven,
we worship you constantly on earth,
and before your majesty
without end we acclaim:

Emphasize the first line.

Holy, Holy, Holy Lord God of hosts . . .

Treat lines 4 and 5 as a single line. This will be difficult because of the length of the lines. Lines 4 and 5 are parallel with line 1. The middle lines are parenthetical.

82. Preface V for the Dead: Our resurrection through the victory of Christ is rooted in Romans 5:12, 15, and 17. In these verses, Paul explains, "For if, by the transgression of one person, death came to reign through that one, how much more will those who receive the abundance of grace and the gift of justification come to reign in life through the one person Jesus Christ" (v. 17).

Attention can be drawn to the word "fault." In this Preface, we recognize that we perish as result of our own faults. But

these faults are reversed in Christ. This gives rise to the beautiful theology of the *felix culpa*" a Latin phrase that means "happy," "lucky," or "blessed," modifying the word "fault" or "fall." In the tradition, it is most often translated "happy fault."

The Latin expression *felix culpa* derives from Saint Augustine's famous allusion to one unfortunate event, the Fall of Man, Adam and Eve's Fall and the loss of the Garden of Eden, known theologically as the source of original sin. The phrase is sung annually in the Exsultet of the Easter

Vigil: "O happy fault that earned so great, so glorious a Redeemer." The medieval theologian Thomas Aquinas cited this line when he explained how the principle that "God allows evils to happen in order to bring a greater good therefrom" underlies the causal relation between original sin and the Divine Redeemer's Incarnation, thus concluding that a higher state is not inhibited by sin. Ambrose also speaks of the fortunate ruin of Adam in the Garden of Eden, in that his sin brought more good

It is truly right and just, our duty and our sal-va-tion, al-ways and everywhere to give you thanks, Lord, holy Father, almighty and e-ter-nal God. For even though by our own fault we per-ish, yet by your compassion and your grace, when seized by death according to our sins, we are redeemed through Christ's great vic-to-ry, and with him called back in-to life. And so, with the Pow-ers of heav-en, we worship you con-stant-ly on earth, and before your maj-es-ty without end we ac-claim:

Holy, Holy, Holy Lord God of hosts . . .

Sing this proclamation cursively in a reciting tone. In **salvation**, do not hold **-va**; only broaden the two notes slightly. The last syllable, **-tion**, should be held. **Always** and **everywhere** require a slight broadening and clear enunciation. The accent of the phrase falls on **thanks**, which should be held briefly. In the next sentence, clearly make distinct phrases of the text, by respecting the commas.

A slight pause after **For** would set off the text of the phrase very nicely. Similarly, in the next phrase, a slight pause after **yet** would do the same. A short breath should be taken after holding briefly **grace** and **sins**. Tie togehter **victory** and **and with him**. Broaden the last words **back into life**.

In the concluding phrase, make a slight pause after **And so**. Respect the commas but try to keep this section together, without big breaks for breaths. Broaden the last phrase, especially on **majesty**. Slow **we ac-**, and put emphasis on **-claim**, so as to evoke the response of **Holy, Holy, Holy . . . .**

to humanity than if he had stayed perfectly innocent.

In a literary context, the term *felix culpa* can describe how a series of miserable events will eventually lead to a happier outcome.

The concept also comes up in Hebrew tradition in the Exodus of the Israelites from Egypt, and is associated with God's judgment. Although it is not a fall, the thinking goes that, without their exile in the desert, the Israelites would not have had the joy of finding the Promised Land. With their suf-

fering came the hope of victory and their life restored. For this they sing, that even if all these bad things had not befallen them (which provided God the opportunity to intervene on their behalf), then *dayenu*, "it would have been enough."

Paul understands the deeper mystery of Christ's life, Death, and Resurrection in relation to redeeming sinful humanity almost as an antidote. Thus, flesh redeems flesh. "When this which is corruptible clothes itself with incorruptibility and this which is mortal clothes itself with immor-

tality, then the word that is written shall come about: 'Death is swallowed up in victory. Where, O death, is your victory? Where, O death, is your sting?' The sting of death is sin, and the power of sin is the law. But thanks be to God who gives us the victory through our Lord Jesus Christ" (1 Corinthians 15: 54–57).

THE EUCHARISTIC PRAYERS

EUCHARISTIC PRAYER I
(THE ROMAN CANON)

83.   V. **The Lord be with you**.
      R. And with your spirit.

      V. **Lift up your hearts.**
      R. We lift them up to the Lord.

      V. **Let us give thanks to the Lord our God.**
      R. It is right and just.

Then follows the Preface to be used in accord with the rubrics, which concludes:

Holy, Holy, Holy Lord God of hosts.
Heaven and earth are full of your glory.
Hosanna in the highest.
Blessed is he who comes in the name of the Lord.
Hosanna in the highest.

84.   The Priest, with hands extended, says:

To you, therefore, most merciful Father,
we make humble prayer and petition
through Jesus Christ, your Son, our Lord:

Celebrant alone

He joins his hands and says:

that you accept

He makes the Sign of the Cross once over the bread and chalice together, saying:

and bless ✠ these gifts, these offerings,
these holy and unblemished sacrifices,

With hands extended, he continues:

which we offer you firstly
for your holy catholic Church.
Be pleased to grant her peace,
to guard, unite and govern her
throughout the whole world,
together with your servant N. **our Pope**
and N. **our Bishop,**[*]
and all those who, holding to the truth,
hand on the catholic and apostolic faith.

---

[*]   Mention may be made here of the Coadjutor Bishop, or Auxiliary Bishops, as noted in the *General Instruction of the Roman Missal*, no. 149.

Side margin notes:

The greeting is addressed to the assembly. The Priest stands with hands extended.

While he says, **Lift up your hearts**, the Priest lifts up his hands.

He returns to the first position of addressing the assembly with hands extended.

The Priest joins his hands for the singing or the recitation of the Holy, Holy, Holy, which he sings along with the assembly.

Te igitur:
Emphasize **Father** as the addressee of the prayer. Emphasize **prayer and petition**.

Emphasize **bless** and correlate the word with the gesture of blessing. Revel in the appositive phrases **these gifts, these offerings, these . . . sacrifices**.

Emphasize **which we offer** and **for your . . . Church**.

---

83. It is a little surprising that the rubrics for the opening dialogue of the Eucharistic Prayer are not reprinted as they are found in #31. GIRM, 148, states: "As he begins the Eucharistic Prayer, the Priest extends his hands and sings or says, 'The Lord be with you.' The people reply, 'And with your spirit.' As he continues, saying, 'Lift up your hearts,' he raises his hands. The people reply, 'We lift them up to the Lord.' Then the Priest, with hands extended, adds, 'Let us give thanks to the Lord our God,' and the people reply, 'It is right and just.' After this, the Priest, with hands extended, continues the Preface. At its conclusion, he joins his hands and, together with all those present, sings or says aloud the *Sanctus* (Holy, Holy, Holy) (cf. no. 79 b)." It is very important to correlate the gestures with the Preface dialogue and Preface.

Although the text does not say that the Holy, Holy, Holy should be sung or spoken, it appears in the GIRM that the preference is for it to be sung. Singing is listed first in the GIRM, which seems to indicate a preference.

84. Notice that Eucharistic Prayer I is structured as a series of discreet paragraphs (indicated in the margins in Latin by the first words in each paragraph). These paragraphs are organized according to a principle, or chiasm, so that the central part of the text is seen as the most important, with parallel elements appearing on either side of this central segment. Thus, for the Roman Canon, the Institution narrative and Consecration appear in the center of the text, where a memorial of the living appears prior to it and a memorial of the

Memento, Domine:
The Priest may wish to name living persons for whom he is offering this Mass, but he is not bound to do so.

Pause after **For them**. Make a longer pause after **this sacrifice of praise**. Treat **or they offer . . . dear to them** as one line.

Communicantes:
Yoke **In communion with those whose memory we venerate . . . we ask . . .**, even though many names may be mentioned between the first and second phrases.

A Priest may wish to choose Eucharistic Prayer I for feasts of those Saints mentioned in this list. He would emphasize that name while reciting the list.

Each of the constitutive parts of the Roman Canon ends with the phrase **Through Christ our Lord. Amen**. The phrase is in parentheses to indicate that it is optional. If you think that it makes the prayer seem fragmented, simply omit it throughout.

85.   Commemoration of the Living.

> **Remember, Lord, your servants N. and N.**   Celebrant or one concelebrant

The Priest joins his hands and prays briefly for those for whom he intends to pray.

Then, with hands extended, he continues:

> **and all gathered here,**
> **whose faith and devotion are known to you.**
> **For them, we offer you this sacrifice of praise**
> **or they offer it for themselves**
> **and all who are dear to them:**
> **for the redemption of their souls,**
> **in hope of health and well-being,**
> **and paying their homage to you,**
> **the eternal God, living and true.**

86.   Within the Action.

> **In communion with those whose memory we venerate,**   Celebrant or one concelebrant
> **especially the glorious ever-Virgin Mary,**
> **Mother of our God and Lord, Jesus Christ,**
> † **and blessed Joseph, her Spouse,**
> **your blessed Apostles and Martyrs,**
> **Peter and Paul, Andrew,**
> > **(James, John,**
> > **Thomas, James, Philip,**
> > **Bartholomew, Matthew,**
> > **Simon and Jude;**
> > **Linus, Cletus, Clement, Sixtus,**
> > **Cornelius, Cyprian,**
> > **Lawrence, Chrysogonus,**
> > **John and Paul,**
> > **Cosmas and Damian)**
> **and all your Saints;**
> **we ask that through their merits and prayers,**
> **in all things we may be defended**
> **by your protecting help.**
> **(Through Christ our Lord. Amen.)**

dead after it, just as a prayer of union with Apostles and Saints appears before it and another prayer of union with Saints appears after it. It is difficult to make that structure clear simply by the way one prays the text, but treating each of the paragraphs as a unity may help.

Although the Eucharistic Prayer, as its name indicates, is a prayer of thanksgiving, the Roman Canon, as we presently have it, is primarily a prayer of petition, beginning with article 84, in which we pray that God

accepts the gifts of bread and wine to be offered for the Church and her leadership.

85. Continuing our prayers of petition, we pray on behalf of the living. The Priest may name those for whom the Mass is offered.

Following these petitions for the living, we pray in communion for those who have gone before us in faith (*communicantes*). Twenty-four Saints are named in two groups of 12: 12 Apostles and 12 Martyrs. The list is preceded by a commemoration of the Virgin Mary, who has a special place

separate from the others. Pope John XXIII introduced the name of Joseph into the Canon after Mary's name. Then appear the 12 Apostles (Peter, Paul, Andrew, James, John, Thomas, James, Philip, Bartholomew, Matthew, Simon, and Jude). Interestingly, Paul is mentioned along with Peter at the start of the list of the Apostles, even though Paul never knew the historical Jesus. Peter and Paul are first in the list because they are considered the foundational Apostles for the Church of Rome.

PROPER FORMS OF THE *COMMUNICANTES*

On the Nativity of the Lord and throughout the Octave

Celebrating the most sacred night (day)
on which blessed Mary the immaculate Virgin
brought forth the Savior for this world,
and in communion with those whose memory we venerate,
especially the glorious ever-Virgin Mary,
Mother of our God and Lord, Jesus Christ, †

On the Epiphany of the Lord

Celebrating the most sacred day
on which your Only Begotten Son,
eternal with you in your glory,
appeared in a human body, truly sharing our flesh,
and in communion with those whose memory we venerate,
especially the glorious ever-Virgin Mary,
Mother of our God and Lord, Jesus Christ, †

From the Mass of the Easter Vigil until the Second Sunday of Easter

Celebrating the most sacred night (day)
of the Resurrection of our Lord Jesus Christ in the flesh,
and in communion with those whose memory we venerate,
especially the glorious ever-Virgin Mary,
Mother of our God and Lord, Jesus Christ, †

On the Ascension of the Lord

Celebrating the most sacred day
on which your Only Begotten Son, our Lord,
placed at the right hand of your glory
our weak human nature,
which he had united to himself,
and in communion with those whose memory we venerate,
especially the glorious ever-Virgin Mary,
Mother of our God and Lord, Jesus Christ, †

On Pentecost Sunday

Celebrating the most sacred day of Pentecost,
on which the Holy Spirit
appeared to the Apostles in tongues of fire,
and in communion with those whose memory we venerate,
especially the glorious ever-Virgin Mary,
Mother of our God and Lord, Jesus Christ, †

Variable prayers exist for certain special feasts and liturgical times of the year: to be used on the Nativity of the Lord and throughout the Octave of Christmas; on the Epiphany of the Lord, from the Mass of the Easter Vigil until the Second Sunday of Easter; the Ascension of the Lord; and on Pentecost Sunday. Each must be adapted if the liturgy is celebrated during the day or at night, on the feast itself or during the octave. Since this is one of the few variable parts within the Roman Canon proper, make a point to emphasize this part in terms of modulation of the voice.

Then 12 Martyrs follow. First, some early Roman Bishops are named: Linus, Cletus, Clement, Sixtus, Cornelius, and Cyprian. Included among them is the North African Bishop (because North Africa, like Rome, by this era used Latin in its liturgical prayer). Deacon Lawrence of Rome; Chrysogonus, an Eastern Saint; John and Paul, western Martyrs whose house church was located in Rome; and then Cosmas and Damian, Eastern Saints whose relics were located at a shrine in Rome. It should be clear that this list of Saints is carefully organized and related to the unique set of Saints associated with the city and province of Rome.

In the revision of the Canon after the Second Vatican Council, the number of names that had to be mentioned was reduced, lest the long list be a hindrance to the vernacular proclamation of the text. For this reason, the names that are within parentheses are optional.

Notice that a special form of this prayer of communion (*communicantes*) is to be used on the Nativity of the Lord and throughout the octave of Christmas, on the Epiphany of the Lord, from the Mass of the Easter Vigil until the Second Sunday of Easter, the Ascension of the Lord, and on Pentecost Sunday. The *communicantes* helps focus the prayer for specific liturgical feasts or times of the liturgical year.

Hanc igitur:
Emphasize **we pray** and **accept**.

Revel in the rhetorical parallels of **order our days**, **command that we be delivered** and **counted among the flock**.

This is the only other part of Eucharistic Prayer I that is variable. The fact that it is prayed from Easter Time through its octave demonstrates the supreme importance of the Paschal Feast.

Quam oblationem:
Deliberately extend hands over the offerings and keep them in place throughout the prayer.

Emphasize **bless, acknowledge**, and **spiritual and acceptable**.

Emphasize **Body and Blood**.

Speak slowly and deliberately, following the commas and sense lines.

87. With hands extended, the Priest continues:

> **Therefore, Lord, we pray:**
> **graciously accept this oblation of our service,**
> **that of your whole family;**
> **order our days in your peace,**
> **and command that we be delivered from eternal damnation**
> **and counted among the flock of those you have chosen.**

Celebrant alone

He joins his hands.

> **(Through Christ our Lord. Amen.)**

From the Mass of the Easter Vigil until the Second Sunday of Easter

> **Therefore, Lord, we pray:**
> **graciously accept this oblation of our service,**
> **that of your whole family,**
> **which we make to you**
> **also for those to whom you have been pleased to give**
> **the new birth of water and the Holy Spirit,**
> **granting them forgiveness of all their sins;**
> **order our days in your peace,**
> **and command that we be delivered from eternal damnation**
> **and counted among the flock of those you have chosen.**

He joins his hands.

> **(Through Christ our Lord. Amen.)**

------

88. Holding his hands extended over the offerings, he says:

> **Be pleased, O God, we pray,**
> **to bless, acknowledge,**
> **and approve this offering in every respect;**
> **make it spiritual and acceptable,**
> **so that it may become for us**
> **the Body and Blood of your most beloved Son,**
> **our Lord Jesus Christ.**

Celebrant with concelebrants

He joins his hands.

87. Having prayed in union with Saints, especially those associated with Rome, we return to a prayer of petition, asking God to accept our offering and to grant us the fruits that flow from it. Notice that a special form of this prayer is used in the Masses from the Easter Vigil until the Second Sunday of Easter.

88. During this paragraph of petition, the Priest extends his hands over the offerings, simply praying that they be transformed into the Body and Blood of Christ. This normally would be called an epiclesis, in which we pray to God to send the Holy Spirit upon the gifts to transform them. The prayer is accompanied by hand-laying. In this prayer, there is hand-laying and a request for transformation but no reference to the Holy Spirit. Some might argue that the Holy Spirit is implicit in the hand-laying gesture. But this is unclear. The absence of a typical epiclesis in the Roman Canon has led some scholars to assume that the *Quam oblationem* ("We pray you, God") is the first epiclesis. This assumption especially is made by those who force somewhat the interpretation of the words "to make this offering wholly blessed," so as to read into them a clear allusion to the Holy Spirit. However, the corresponding prayer in the Ambrosian and Mozarabic Eucharistic Prayers is not a consecratory epiclesis in the modern sense of the term, and so this view is called into question. Other scholars would look at #94 (page 133) as the vestiges of an epiclesis.

89.   In the formulas that follow, the words of the Lord should be pronounced clearly and distinctly, as the nature of these words requires.

On the day before he was to suffer,

He takes the bread and, holding it slightly raised above the altar, continues:

he took bread in his holy and venerable hands,

He raises his eyes.

**and with eyes raised to heaven
to you, O God, his almighty Father,
giving you thanks, he said the blessing,
broke the bread
and gave it to his disciples, saying:**

He bows slightly.

**TAKE THIS, ALL OF YOU, AND EAT OF IT,
FOR THIS IS MY BODY,
WHICH WILL BE GIVEN UP FOR YOU.**

He shows the consecrated host to the people, places it again on the paten, and genuflects in adoration.

90.   After this, the Priest continues:

In a similar way, when supper was ended,

He takes the chalice and, holding it slightly raised above the altar, continues:

**he took this precious chalice
in his holy and venerable hands,
and once more giving you thanks, he said the blessing
and gave the chalice to his disciples, saying:**

He bows slightly.

**TAKE THIS, ALL OF YOU, AND DRINK FROM IT,
FOR THIS IS THE CHALICE OF MY BLOOD,
THE BLOOD OF THE NEW AND ETERNAL COVENANT,
WHICH WILL BE POURED OUT FOR YOU AND FOR MANY
FOR THE FORGIVENESS OF SINS.**

DO THIS IN MEMORY OF ME.

He shows the chalice to the people, places it on the corporal, and genuflects in adoration.

Qui pridie:

The rubric states, "He takes the bread and, holding it slightly raised above the altar . . . ." This may seem to suggest that the Priest is impersonating Christ; in fact, the Priest continues to address God the Father. Nor is the Priest to appear as though addressing the bread.

Notice that the rubric before the text "Take this, all of you, and eat of it" does not call for the Priest Celebrant to break the host; the rubric simply calls for him to bow slightly.

The Priest shows the consecrated host. The rubric does not say "elevate." The Priest Celebrant genuflects in adoration.

The rubric reads, "He takes the chalice and, holding it slightly raised above the altar . . . ." Again, the Priest continues to address God the Father.

Notice that the rubric before the text "Take this, all of you, and drink from it," does not call for the Priest to speak into the cup. The rubric calls for the Priest to bow slightly.

The Priest shows the chalice. The rubric does not say "elevate." The Priest Celebrant genuflects in adoration.

89–90. The coordination of texts and gestures for the Institution narrative is very important. The Priest must remember that he is continuing to recount the great deeds of God now focused in Christ Jesus on the night before he died. He should be sure that his gestures and posture do not make it appear that he is addressing these texts to the bread and wine. The Priest's posture should reflect that this prayer continues to be part of a Eucharistic Prayer addressed to the Father.

Although rubrics such as "He takes the bread and, holding it slightly raised above the altar . . ." suggest that the Priest is impersonating Christ; in fact, the Priest continues to address God the Father, here, recounting one of the great deeds of God In history, the Institution narrative. Notice that the rubric before the text "Take this, all of you, and eat of it" does not call for the Priest Celebrant to break the host; it simply calls for him to bow slightly.

Similarly, after speaking the text, the Priest shows the consecrated host. The rubric does not say "elevates." The Priest Celebrant genuflects in adoration.

The command "Do this in memory of me" is in reference to the entire action and should not seem to reference the chalice only. In 1 Corinthians 11:24–25, we find the memorial command after both the bread and the wine. A pause inserted before the memorial command may help to clarify this phrase.

Mysterium fidei:

The Priest may sing **The mystery of faith**, which will serve as a prompt for the assembly to sing one of the three acclamations.

That there are two formulas of introduction and three musical settings for the acclamation suggests that this is inherently a musical prayer. If the Priest sings, it should match what is to follow. Therefore, the assembly begins on whatever note the Priest finishes on for the first formula. For the second acclamation, the assembly imitates the Priest's line, using the first of the two formulas. The second formula of introduction might be reserved for the third acclamation, since the melodic contours resemble one another. Further, the musical melody will serve as a cue to signal which acclamation will be sung. If another modern composition is used, the Priest should verify whether a lead-in was composed. It makes no sense to sing a modal lead-in when a tonal acclamation will follow. This only necessitates the organist's having to intervene with an introduction to establish the key for the acclamation of faith.

91.   Then he says:

The mystery of faith.

Celebrant alone

And the people continue, acclaiming:

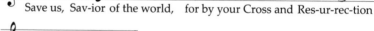

We proclaim your Death, O Lord,
and profess your Resurrection
until you come again.

Or:

When we eat this Bread and drink this Cup,
we proclaim your Death, O Lord,
until you come again.

Or:

Save us, Savior of the world,
for by your Cross and Resurrection
you have set us free.

91. The Priest's text "The mystery of faith" functions as a cue for the people to sing the Memorial Acclamation. It is helpful to understand that the Priest's words are actually an exclamation, not a declaration.

Notice that the Missal prints two possible chants for this exclamation by the Priest. The first is slightly simpler than the second, suggesting that the first might be used for *ferial* occasions, and the second for more festive occasions. These correlate to the Memorial Acclamation chants of the Missal; but there may be other musical set-

tings of the Mystery of Faith correlated to other musical settings of the congregation's Memorial Acclamations that the Priest should then learn. What the Priest sings and what the people sing should be congruent. In other words, if the Memorial Acclamation the people sing is from a contemporary composer, the melody the Priest sings for "The mystery of faith" should also come from that composer.

The three acclamations of faith are all addressed directly to Christ. It is interesting that the Priest addresses God the Father

throughout the Eucharistic Prayer; except, during the Institution narrative, he speaks about the Last Supper event in a historical mode. But when the assembly is asked to pray, they address their acclamation to Christ, whom they believe is really present in the Eucharistic species.

92. Liturgical scholars call this section of the prayer the "anamnesis-offering." The Priest expands upon the acclamation articulated by the congregation, calling to mind

92. *Then the Priest, with hands extended, says:*

> Therefore, O Lord,
> as we celebrate the memorial of the blessed Passion,
> the Resurrection from the dead,
> and the glorious Ascension into heaven
> of Christ, your Son, our Lord,
> we, your servants and your holy people,
> offer to your glorious majesty
> from the gifts that you have given us,
> this pure victim,
> this holy victim,
> this spotless victim,
> the holy Bread of eternal life
> and the Chalice of everlasting salvation.

Celebrant with concelebrants

93.
> Be pleased to look upon these offerings
> with a serene and kindly countenance,
> and to accept them,
> as once you were pleased to accept
> the gifts of your servant Abel the just,
> the sacrifice of Abraham, our father in faith,
> and the offering of your high priest Melchizedek,
> a holy sacrifice, a spotless victim.

94. *Bowing, with hands joined, he continues:*

> In humble prayer we ask you, almighty God:
> command that these gifts be borne
> by the hands of your holy Angel
> to your altar on high
> in the sight of your divine majesty,
> so that all of us, who through this participation at the altar
> receive the most holy Body and Blood of your Son,

He stands upright again and signs himself with the Sign of the Cross, saying:

> may be filled with every grace and heavenly blessing.

He joins his hands.

> (Through Christ our Lord. Amen.)

Unde et memores:
Make **we celebrate the memorial** parallel to **we offer . . . to your glorious majesty**.

Emphasize **Passion, Resurrection, Ascension**.

Revel in the parallels **pure victim**, **holy victim**, **spotless victim**, **Bread of eternal life**, and **Chalice of everlasting salvation**.

Supra quae:
Make **Be pleased to look** parallel to **accept . . . the gifts of**.

Revel in the three names **Abel the just**; **Abraham, our father in faith**; **Melchizedek**.

Supplices te:
Concentrate on the phrase **command . . . altar on high**.

---

the Paschal Mystery and offers the Sacrament of the Paschal Mystery, the transformed bread and wine.

93. The anamnesis-offering is followed by a prayer for acceptance of the sacrifice. We return to prayers of petition, asking God to accept the consecrated elements as God was pleased to accept some typological Old Testament offerings: the sacrifices of Abel, Abraham, and Melchizedek. These three serve as exemplars of classical

instances of sacrifice acceptable to God and, therefore, models of what our sacrifice should be.

94. Throughout this next paragraph of petitionary prayer, the Priest is asked to bow. Some liturgical scholars see in this prayer a "reverse epiclesis," rather than asking the Father to send the Holy Spirit upon the gifts from this altar to the heavenly altar. These same scholars think that the original reference for God's Angel was

to Christ, since he is the messenger (*angelos*) between God the Father and humanity. The purpose of the angelic mediation is to give our celebration the fruitfulness described in 1 Corinthians 10:18. Those who eat of the victim become participants in the altar. We participate in the heavenly altar because we eat at the earthly table.

Memento etiam:
Emphasize **Remember** and
your servants.

Emphasize **them** and **all**.

Emphasize **refreshment** and **light**
and peace.

Nobis quoque peccatoribus:
Correlate the gesture of striking the
breast with **us** or **sinners**.

Emphasize **admit us . . . into their**
company.

95.   Commemoration of the Dead.

With hands extended, the Priest says:

> **Remember also, Lord, your servants N. and N.,**
> **who have gone before us with the sign of faith**
> **and rest in the sleep of peace.**

Celebrant or
one concelebrant

He joins his hands and prays briefly for those who have died and for whom he intends
to pray.

Then, with hands extended, he continues:

> **Grant them, O Lord, we pray,**
> **and all who sleep in Christ,**
> **a place of refreshment, light and peace.**

He joins his hands.

> **(Through Christ our Lord. Amen.)**

96.   He strikes his breast with his right hand, saying:

> **To us, also, your servants, who, though sinners,**

Celebrant or
one concelebrant

And, with hands extended, he continues:

> **hope in your abundant mercies,**
> **graciously grant some share**
> **and fellowship with your holy Apostles and Martyrs:**
> **with John the Baptist, Stephen,**
> **Matthias, Barnabas,**
> **(Ignatius, Alexander,**
> **Marcellinus, Peter,**
> **Felicity, Perpetua,**
> **Agatha, Lucy,**
> **Agnes, Cecilia, Anastasia)**
> **and all your Saints;**
> **admit us, we beseech you,**
> **into their company,**
> **not weighing our merits,**
> **but granting us your pardon,**

He joins his hands.

> **through Christ our Lord.**

95. Parallel to the earlier prayers of intercession for the living is this paragraph of prayer for the dead. Once again, the Priest may mention the names for whom Mass is being celebrated. The naming of living and deceased people within the Eucharistic Prayer corresponds to the liturgical use of diptychs, which were a focus of dispute, particularly in the East. The diptychs were two-leafed folders containing the list of names for public and official recognition. The inclusion of a person's name was somewhat of a recognition of the person's orthodoxy and solidarity with the communion of the Church. The persons for whom the Priest prays are called "servants" (*famuli*), a title which, in the first instance, connotes family.

96. Parallel to our prayer of communion with Apostles and Saints is this prayer of communion with further Saints. Once again, connection with the Roman Church is emphasized. Notice the places of honor given to the seven female Martyr Saints. Again, only the first four names are obligatory, lest the prayer become too ponderous. But the names of the other prominent Roman Martyrs can be added easily.

This section begins with a prayer for ourselves, also considered "servants." But to this, we add the designation "sinners." In ancient Roman practice, it was common for people to sign documents, adding the word "sinner" (*peccator*) to their signature.

97.   And he continues:

Through whom   Celebrant alone
you continue to make all these good things, O Lord;
you sanctify them, fill them with life,
bless them, and bestow them upon us.

Per quem:
Emphasize **sanctify**, **fill**,
bless, and **bestow**.

98.   He takes the chalice and the paten with the host and, raising both, he says:

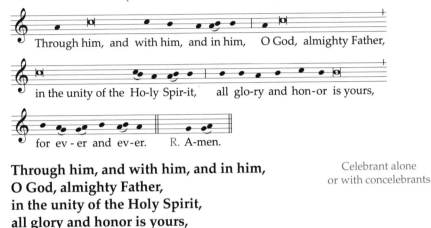

Through him, and with him, and in him,   O God, almighty Father,

in the unity of the Ho-ly Spir-it,   all glo-ry and hon-or is yours,

for ev - er and ev-er.   R. A-men.

For singing purposes, find a note in
your upper-range. This is "do." Now
sing down "do-ti-la" to find your
opening note. Return immediately to
"do." The traditional melody revolves
around these three notes.

Through him, and with him, and in him,   Celebrant alone
O God, almighty Father,   or with concelebrants
in the unity of the Holy Spirit,
all glory and honor is yours,
for ever and ever.

The people acclaim:

Amen.

Then follows the Communion Rite, p. 663.

Doxology:
Pause at the commas and the
sense lines, and continue to
increase in volume, so as to cue
the congregation's **Amen**.

97. This paragraph may seem to be ungrammatical. In fact, it is an extension of the conclusion of the last paragraph, lauding Christ as the means by which God the Father continues to bless humanity. In this paragraph, we commemorate the goodness of God, who is described as the one who creates all good things, sanctifies them, endows them with life, blesses them, and bestows them on us. The paragraph, which is one sentence, summarizes God's great generosity and helps us to reach the conclusion of the prayer.

98. The Canon ends with the doxology that sums up all the themes of the Eucharistic Prayer in a proclamation of the Divine Name. Everything belongs to God, and all honor and glory ascend to him in a Christological movement denoted by three prepositions: "through," "with," and "in." The Holy Name is great throughout the entire world and put on the lips of the faithful who proclaim God's glory.

The conclusion of the Eucharistic Prayer calls for the Priest to lift the paten with host, and the Deacon (or in his absence, the Priest) chants or recites the doxology. The Missal provides chant setting of this doxology that leads to the community's chanted "Amen"; however, there may be other musical settings of the doxology correlated to the congregation's "Amen." The Priest's doxology and the people's "Amen" should be musically congruent, to form a seamless garment.

EUCHARISTIC PRAYER II

99.   Although it is provided with its own Preface (text with music, p. **721**), this Eucharistic Prayer may also be used with other Prefaces, especially those that present an overall view of the mystery of salvation, such as the Common Prefaces.

V. **The Lord be with you.**
R. And with your spirit.

V. **Lift up your hearts.**
R. We lift them up to the Lord.

V. **Let us give thanks to the Lord our God.**
R. It is right and just.

It is truly right and just, our duty and our salvation,
always and everywhere to give you thanks, Father most holy,
through your beloved Son, Jesus Christ,
your Word through whom you made all things,
whom you sent as our Savior and Redeemer,
incarnate by the Holy Spirit and born of the Virgin.

Fulfilling your will and gaining for you a holy people,
he stretched out his hands as he endured his Passion,
so as to break the bonds of death and manifest the resurrection.

And so, with the Angels and all the Saints
we declare your glory,
as with one voice we acclaim:

Holy, Holy, Holy Lord God of hosts.
Heaven and earth are full of your glory.
Hosanna in the highest.
Blessed is he who comes in the name of the Lord.
Hosanna in the highest.

The opening exchange establishes the dialogical nature of liturgical prayer. Thus, the Priest's lines are intended to elicit the response of the assembly. Vocal intonation and eye contact will help in this regard. The gestures should be correlated to the words.

Emphasize **truly, always, everywhere,** and **thanks.** Think of the following as an invocation in the litany: **your beloved Son, your Word, our Savior and Redeemer, incarnate, born, Fulfilling, gaining, stretched out, endured, break,** and **manifest.** The emphasis evokes the memory of Jesus under many titles and activities. Emphasize **declare** and **acclaim,** cuing the congregation's **Holy, Holy, Holy . . . .**

---

99. When Eucharistic Prayer II was introduced into the euchology of the Roman Rite, scholars believed that the so-called Apostolic Tradition was the work of Hippolytus of Rome and that the Eucharistic Prayer found in the Apostolic Tradition was, therefore, an ancient Roman Anaphora. Contemporary liturgical scholarship no longer holds that the document in which this Eucharistic Prayer is found is the product of Hippolytus of Rome, nor should it be called the Apostolic Tradition, but rather

Diataxeis tôn hagiôn apostolôn (The Statutes of the Twelve Apostles).

Consensus seems to be that the Eucharistic Prayer of the *Diataxeis* is connected to West Syrian euchological tradition. Nevertheless, the liturgists who constructed Eucharistic Prayer II did not simply reproduce the prayer from Apostolic Tradition (*Diataxeis*) but modified it to fit their understanding of a Eucharistic Prayer. ("The Anaphora of the So-Called 'Apostolic Tradition' and the Roman Eucharistic Prayer,"

Matthieu Smyth, in *Issues in Eucharistic Praying in East and West: Essays in Liturgical and Theological Analysis*, ed. Maxwell E. Johnson, Liturgical Press, 2010).

The proper Preface for Eucharistic Prayer II also appears as Common Preface VI. In this Preface, the protocol and body of the Preface structure are meshed. The text looks at Christ's Incarnation and Redemption, the beginning and end of Christ's life. Not found in the prayer, and not part of the memorials, is Christ's public

Emphasize **indeed** and **all**.

Extend the hands, indicating the summoning of the Holy Spirit. Emphasize **Make holy**. Treat **we pray** as though it were in parentheses. Emphasize **by sending down your Spirit.**

Correlate the gesture of signing the cross over the gifts with the words.

The rubric states, "He takes the bread and, holding it slightly raised above the altar . . . ." This may suggest that the Priest is impersonating Christ; in fact, the Priest continues to address God the Father. Nor is the Priest to appear to be addressing the bread. Notice that the rubric before the text "Take this, all of you, and eat of it" does not call for the Priest Celebrant to break the host; it calls for him to bow slightly.

The Priest shows the consecrated host. The rubric does not say "elevate." The Priest Celebrant genuflects in adoration.

---

100. The Priest, with hands extended, says:

You are indeed Holy, O Lord,
the fount of all holiness.

Celebrant alone

101. He joins his hands and, holding them extended over the offerings, says:

Make holy, therefore, these gifts, we pray,
by sending down your Spirit upon them like the dewfall,

Celebrant with concelebrants

He joins his hands
and makes the Sign of the Cross once over the bread and the chalice together, saying:

so that they may become for us
the Body and ✠ Blood of our Lord Jesus Christ.

He joins his hands.

102. In the formulas that follow, the words of the Lord should be pronounced clearly and distinctly, as the nature of these words requires.

At the time he was betrayed
and entered willingly into his Passion,

He takes the bread and, holding it slightly raised above the altar, continues:

he took bread and, giving thanks, broke it,
and gave it to his disciples, saying:

He bows slightly.

TAKE THIS, ALL OF YOU, AND EAT OF IT,
FOR THIS IS MY BODY,
WHICH WILL BE GIVEN UP FOR YOU.

He shows the consecrated host to the people, places it again on the paten, and genuflects in adoration.

---

ministry—his work as healer, sage, teller of parables. We might say that the bookends of Jesus' life are emphasized here. The Priest Celebrant will find that, because the protocol meshes with the body of the prayer, it is a difficult prayer to proclaim just in terms of length. The opening sentence alone comprises six long sense lines. Proclamation will be easier, especially in the first paragraph, if the prayer is thought of as a litany, with phrase after phrase, describing Jesus and what he has done.

100. This short paragraph makes a transition from the acclamation to the invocation of the Spirit. Just as the protocol of the Preface made a transition by adding "truly" to "right and just," so this paragraph makes a transition by adding "indeed" to "Holy." Notice that the Priest should pray this paragraph with hands extended (orans).

101. This paragraph represents the epiclesis over the gifts, an invocation of God the

Father to send the Holy Spirit to transform the gifts of bread and wine. The Priest should extend his hands over the gifts throughout the paragraph, making a single Sign of the Cross over the bread and chalice while reciting the words "Body and Blood."

102–103. The coordination of texts and gestures for the Institution narrative is very important. The Priest must remember that he is continuing to recount the

103. After this, he continues:

In a similar way, when supper was ended,

He takes the chalice and, holding it slightly raised above the altar, continues:

**he took the chalice
and, once more giving thanks,
he gave it to his disciples, saying:**

He bows slightly.

**TAKE THIS, ALL OF YOU, AND DRINK FROM IT,
FOR THIS IS THE CHALICE OF MY BLOOD,
THE BLOOD OF THE NEW AND ETERNAL COVENANT,
WHICH WILL BE POURED OUT FOR YOU AND FOR MANY
FOR THE FORGIVENESS OF SINS.**

DO THIS IN MEMORY OF ME.

He shows the chalice to the people, places it on the corporal, and genuflects in adoration.

104. Then he says:

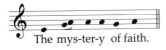

The mys-ter-y of faith.

The mystery of faith. Celebrant alone

And the people continue, acclaiming:

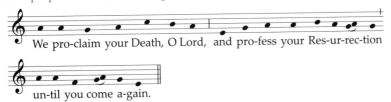

We pro-claim your Death, O Lord, and pro-fess your Res-ur-rec-tion

un-til you come a-gain.

We proclaim your Death, O Lord,
and profess your Resurrection
until you come again.

Or:

The rubric reads, "He takes the chalice and, holding it slightly raised above the altar . . . ." Again, the Priest continues to address God the Father, and not the chalice. Notice that the rubric before the text "Take this, all of you, and drink from it," does not call for him to speak into the cup; it simply calls for him to bow slightly.

The Priest then shows the chalice. The rubric does not say "elevate." The Priest Celebrant genuflects in adoration.

The Priest may sing **The mystery of faith**, which will serve as a prompt for the assembly to sing one of the three acclamations.

The formula of introduction and three musical settings for the acclamation suggest that this is inherently a musical item. If the Priest sings, it should be congruent with what follows. Therefore, the assembly begins on whatever note the Priest finishes. For the second acclamation, the assembly imitates the Priest's line. The musical melody also will serve as a cue to signal which acclamation will be sung. If another modern composition is used, the Priest should verify whether a lead-in was composed. It makes no sense to sing a modal lead-in when a tonal acclamation will be sung. This only necessitates the organist's having to intervene with an introduction to establish the key for the Memorial Acclamation.

---

great deeds of God now focused on Christ Jesus on the night before he died, but the Priest should not appear to be addressing these texts to the bread and wine. The prayer continues to be part of a Eucharistic Prayer addressed to the Father. Although rubrics such as "He takes the bread and, holding it slightly raised above the altar . . ." suggest that the Priest is impersonating Christ; in fact, the Priest continues to address God the Father, here, recounting one of the great

deeds of God in history, the Institution Narrative. Notice that the rubric before the text "Take this all of you and eat it" does not call for the Priest to speak to the host; it simply calls for him to bow slightly.

Similarly, after speaking the text, the Priest shows the consecrated host. The rubric does not say "elevate." The Priest then genuflects in adoration.

104. The Priest's text "The mystery of faith" functions as a cue, although it is an exclamation. The Priest's chant correlates to the Memorial Acclamation Chants of the Missal, but there may be other musical settings of the Mystery of Faith correlated to musical settings of the congregation's Memorial Acclamations that the Priest should learn. What the Priest sings and what the people sing should be congruent.

When we eat this Bread and drink this Cup, we proclaim your

Death, O Lord, until you come again.

When we eat this Bread and drink this Cup,
we proclaim your Death, O Lord,
until you come again.

Or:

Save us, Savior of the world, for by your Cross and Resurrection

you have set us free.

Save us, Savior of the world,
for by your Cross and Resurrection
you have set us free.

The Priest resumes the orans position to emphasize the Eucharistic Prayer is addressed to God, whereas the Memorial Acclamation is addressed to Christ. In both cases, the designation "Lord" is used, but the context and internal references make the designation known.

Emphasize **we celebrate**.

Emphasize **we offer**.

Emphasize **we pray**.

Emphasize **fullness of charity** to show the four major elements of this section. The greeting is addressed to the assembly.

105.   Then the Priest, with hands extended, says:

Therefore, as we celebrate
the memorial of his Death and Resurrection,
we offer you, Lord,
the Bread of life and the Chalice of salvation,
giving thanks that you have held us worthy
to be in your presence and minister to you.

Celebrant
with concelebrants

Humbly we pray
that, partaking of the Body and Blood of Christ,
we may be gathered into one by the Holy Spirit.

Remember, Lord, your Church,
spread throughout the world,
and bring her to the fullness of charity,
together with N. our Pope and N. our Bishop*
and all the clergy.

Celebrant or
one concelebrant

---

* Mention may be made here of the Coadjutor Bishop, or Auxiliary Bishops, as noted in the *General Instruction of the Roman Missal*, no. 149.

105. This paragraph enacts a number of liturgical functions. First, along with the Memorial Acclamation just sung or recited, it recalls the great deeds of salvation, the anamnesis of Christ's Death and Resurrection. Second, it is the means by which the community offers the transformed bread and wine, now the bread of life and the chalice of salvation. Third, it enacts the epiclesis over the assembly, asking that those who partake in the Body and Blood of Christ may be made one by the Holy Spirit. Fourth, it prays for the Church and her members—the clerical leadership, the dead, and the Saints—that all may be brought to unity by the Holy Spirit.

The double or split epiclesis, asking that we may become the Body of Christ, is congruent with the understanding that Saint Paul proffers in 1 Corinthians 12:12–14: "As a body is one though it has many parts, and all the parts of the body, though many, are one body, so also Christ. For in one Spirit we were all baptized into one body, whether Jews or Greeks, slaves or free persons, and we were all given to drink of one Spirit. Now the body is not a single part, but many." The point may be made that Eucharist is both what is on the table and who is at the table. As Saint Augustine said, we are to become what we celebrate. We are to become bread broken and wine poured out for the world.

The intercessions, or remembrances, are in three distinct sections. First, we remember the Church spread throughout the world, insisting upon the unity of the Church, rather than churches. In the sec-

In Masses for the Dead, the following may be added:

Remember your servant N.,
whom you have called (today)
from this world to yourself.
Grant that he (she) who was united with your Son in a death like his,
may also be one with him in his Resurrection.

Remember also our brothers and sisters
who have fallen asleep in the hope of the resurrection,
and all who have died in your mercy:
welcome them into the light of your face.
Have mercy on us all, we pray,
that with the Blessed Virgin Mary, Mother of God,
with the blessed Apostles,
and all the Saints who have pleased you throughout the ages,
we may merit to be coheirs to eternal life,
and may praise and glorify you

He joins his hands.

through your Son, Jesus Christ.

106. He takes the chalice and the paten with the host and, raising both, he says:

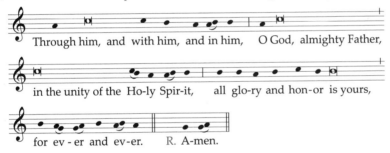

Through him, and with him, and in him, O God, almighty Father,

in the unity of the Ho-ly Spir-it, all glo-ry and hon-or is yours,

for ev - er and ev-er. R. A-men.

Through him, and with him, and in him,
O God, almighty Father,
in the unity of the Holy Spirit,
all glory and honor is yours,
for ever and ever.

Celebrant
with concelebrants

The people acclaim:

Amen.

Then follows the Communion Rite, p. 663.

For singing purposes, find a note in your upper-range. This is "do." Now sing down "do-ti-la" to find your opening note. Return immediately to "do." The traditional melody revolves around these three notes.

The doxology is the third and final of the Eucharistic Acclamations (along with the Holy, Holy, Holy and Memorial Acclamation). The fact that music is supplied in the Missal strongly suggests that this is an inherently musical item. Pause at the commas and the sense lines, and continue to increase in volume, cuing the congregation's **Amen.**

ond section, we pray for the dead. In Masses for the Dead, provision is made to mention the deceased by name. The third section terminates the intercessions with prayers for the living. At this point, we commemorate Mary, the Apostles and the Saints, as among the living.

106. The Eucharistic Prayer ends with the great final doxology, which sums up all the themes of the Eucharistic Prayer in a proclamation of the Divine Name. Everything belongs to God, and all honor

and glory ascend to him in a Christological movement denoted by three prepositions: through, with, and in. The Holy Name is great throughout the entire world and put on the lips of the faithful who proclaim God's glory.

The conclusion of the Prayer calls for the Priest to lift the paten with host and the Deacon (or in his absence, the Priest) chants or recites the doxology.

The Missal provides the chant setting of this doxology that leads to the community's chanted "Amen"; however, there may

be other musical settings of the doxology correlated to the congregation's "Amen." The Priest's doxology and the people's "Amen" should be musically congruent, to form a seamless garment.

EUCHARISTIC PRAYER III

The greeting is addressed to the assembly. The Priest stands with hands extended.

As he says, **Lift up your hearts**, the Priest lifts up his hands.

107. V. **The Lord be with you**.
      R. And with your spirit.

      V. **Lift up your hearts.**
      R. We lift them up to the Lord.

      V. **Let us give thanks to the Lord our God.**
      R. It is right and just.

Then follows the Preface to be used in accord with the rubrics, which concludes:

Holy, Holy, Holy Lord God of hosts.
Heaven and earth are full of your glory.
Hosanna in the highest.
Blessed is he who comes in the name of the Lord.
Hosanna in the highest.

The Priest returns to the first position of addressing the assembly with hands extended. He joins his hands for the singing or the recitation of the Holy, Holy, Holy, which the Priest sings along with the assembly.

Emphasize **indeed**, **all**, and **praise**.

108. The Priest, with hands extended, says:

You are indeed Holy, O Lord,   *Celebrant alone*
      and all you have created
rightly gives you praise,
for through your Son our Lord Jesus Christ,
by the power and working of the Holy Spirit,
you give life to all things and make them holy,
and you never cease to gather a people to yourself,
so that from the rising of the sun to its setting
a pure sacrifice may be offered to your name.

Make a parallel between **through your Son** and **by the power . . . of the Holy Spirit**.

Emphasize **life**, **make them holy**, and **gather a people**. Revel in the scriptural phrase **from the rising of the sun to its setting**, which has both temporal and geographic connotations. Emphasize **sacrifice may be offered.**

The first sense line is an introduction to the entire petition. Emphasize **make holy these gifts.**

109. He joins his hands and, holding them extended over the offerings, says:

Therefore, O Lord, we humbly implore you: *Celebrant*
by the same Spirit graciously make holy   *with concelebrants*
these gifts we have brought to you for consecration,

He joins his hands
and makes the Sign of the Cross once over the bread and chalice together, saying:

that they may become the Body and ✚ Blood
of your Son our Lord Jesus Christ,

He joins his hands.

at whose command we celebrate these mysteries.

Though it is parenthetical, do not lose the force of the phrase **at whose command we celebrate these mysteries**.

---

107. It is surprising that the rubrics for the opening dialogue of the Eucharistic Prayer are not printed in place but are found in #31 and GIRM, 148.

     As with Eucharistic Prayer I, Eucharistic Prayer III lacks a proper Preface and can be used with all the Prefaces in the Missal. It is intended for use on Feast days and Sundays of the year as an alternative to Eucharistic Prayer I. Unlike Eucharistic Prayer I, II, and IV, there is no single ancient anaphora that serves as a model for this prayer. Rather, it combines structures of

Antiochene and Alexandrian anaphoras. In its present form, It is clearly related to some proposals that Cyprian Vagaggini offered in 1966 for the reform of the canon of the Mass.

108. Like the protocol of the Preface, which makes a transition by adding "truly" to "right and just," this paragraph makes a transition from the Holy, Holy, Holy to the epiclesis by adding "indeed" to the "Holy." The Priest should notice four things about the text. First, the act of creation is explic-

itly Trinitarian. Second, creation includes giving life and holiness. Third, the creation and maintenance of the Church is part of God's activity; and fourth, part of the Church's activity is the ongoing praise of God, as exemplified by the typological reading of Malachi 1:11: "For from the rising of the sun, even to its setting, my name is great among the nations."

109. This paragraph comprises the epiclesis over the gifts. Note that the Priest should extend his hands over the offerings

110. In the formulas that follow, the words of the Lord should be pronounced clearly and distinctly, as the nature of these words requires.

For on the night he was betrayed

He takes the bread and, holding it slightly raised above the altar, continues:

he himself took bread,
and, giving you thanks, he said the blessing,
broke the bread and gave it to his disciples, saying:

He bows slightly.

TAKE THIS, ALL OF YOU, AND EAT OF IT,
FOR THIS IS MY BODY,
WHICH WILL BE GIVEN UP FOR YOU.

He shows the consecrated host to the people, places it again on the paten, and genuflects in adoration.

111. After this, he continues:

In a similar way, when supper was ended,

He takes the chalice and, holding it slightly raised above the altar, continues:

he took the chalice,
and, giving you thanks, he said the blessing,
and gave the chalice to his disciples, saying:

He bows slightly.

TAKE THIS, ALL OF YOU, AND DRINK FROM IT,
FOR THIS IS THE CHALICE OF MY BLOOD,
THE BLOOD OF THE NEW AND ETERNAL COVENANT,
WHICH WILL BE POURED OUT FOR YOU AND FOR MANY
FOR THE FORGIVENESS OF SINS.

DO THIS IN MEMORY OF ME.

He shows the chalice to the people, places it on the corporal, and genuflects in adoration.

112. Then he says:

The mys-ter-y of faith.

The mystery of faith.   Celebrant alone

The rubric reads, "He takes the bread and, holding it slightly raised above the altar . . . ." This may seem to suggest that the Priest is impersonating Christ; in fact, the Priest continues to address God the Father. Nor should the Priest appear to be addressing the bread. Notice that the rubric before the text "Take this, all of you, and eat of it" does not call for the Priest Celebrant to break the host; it simply calls for him to bow slightly.

The Priest shows the consecrated host. The rubric does not say "elevate." The Priest Celebrant genuflects in adoration.

The rubric states, "He takes the chalice and, holding it slightly raised above the altar . . . ." Again, the Priest continues to address God the Father, and not the chalice. Notice that the rubric before the text "Take this, all of you, and drink from it" does not call for him to speak into the cup; it simply calls for him to bow slightly.

The Priest shows the chalice. The rubric does not say "elevate." The Priest Celebrant genuflects in adoration.

The Priest may sing **The mystery of faith**, which will serve as a prompt for the assembly to sing one of the three acclamations.

---

and keep them extended throughout the recitation of the text, except when he makes a single Sign of the Cross over the bread and chalice while reciting the text "Body and Blood."

110–111. The coordination of texts and gestures for the Institution narrative is very important. The Priest must remember that he is continuing to recount the great deeds of God now focused in Christ Jesus on the night before he died. The Priest should be sure that his gestures and posture do not

make it appear that he is addressing these texts to the bread and wine. The Priest's posture should reflect that this prayer continues to be part of a Eucharistic Prayer addressed to the Father.

Although rubrics such as "He takes the bread and, holding it slightly raised above the altar . . ." suggest that the Priest is impersonating Christ; in fact, the Priest continues to address God the Father, here, recounting one of the great deeds of God in history, the Institution narrative. Notice that the rubric before the text "Take this, all

of you, and eat of it" does not call for the Priest to speak to the host; it simply calls for him to bow slightly.

Similarly, after speaking the text, the Priest shows the consecrated host. The rubric does not say "elevate." The Priest Celebrant genuflects in adoration.

112. The Priest's text "The mystery of faith" functions as a cue, although it is an exclamation. The music accompanying the Priest's text correlates to the Memorial Acclamation chants, but there may be

That there is a musical setting for the introduction and three musical settings for the acclamation suggests that this is inherently a musical item. If the Priest sings, it should match what is to follow. Therefore, the assembly begins on whatever note the Priest finishes. The musical melody will serve as a cue to signal which acclamation will be sung. If another modern composition is used for the Memorial Acclamation, the Priest should verify whether a lead-in was composed. It makes no sense to sing a modal lead-in when a tonal acclamation will be sung.

And the people continue, acclaiming:

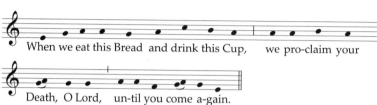

We proclaim your Death, O Lord,
and profess your Resurrection
until you come again.

Or:

When we eat this Bread and drink this Cup,
we proclaim your Death, O Lord,
until you come again.

Or:

Save us, Savior of the world,
for by your Cross and Resurrection
you have set us free.

other musical settings of the Mystery of Faith correlated to other musical settings of the congregation's Memorial Acclamations that the Priest should learn. What the Priest sings and what the people sing should be congruent.

This is the second set of three acclamations (along with the Holy, Holy, Holy and doxology) that punctuates the Eucharistic Prayer. That music is supplied in the Missal more than suggests that this is a

sung element. For this reason, it is desirable that all three acclamations match somehow musically, to create a coherent whole. In musical terms, this would be the second great crescendo, which will culminate in the doxology and "Amen."

Notice that all three Memorial Acclamations are addressed to Christ, whereas, the Eucharistic Prayer is addressed to the Father.

113. Then the Priest, with hands extended, says:

Therefore, O Lord, as we celebrate the memorial — Celebrant with concelebrants
of the saving Passion of your Son,
his wondrous Resurrection
and Ascension into heaven,
and as we look forward to his second coming,
we offer you in thanksgiving
this holy and living sacrifice.

Look, we pray, upon the oblation of your Church
and, recognizing the sacrificial Victim by whose death
you willed to reconcile us to yourself,
grant that we, who are nourished
by the Body and Blood of your Son
and filled with his Holy Spirit,
may become one body, one spirit in Christ.

May he make of us — Celebrant or one concelebrant
an eternal offering to you,
so that we may obtain an inheritance with your elect,
especially with the most Blessed Virgin Mary, Mother of God,
with your blessed Apostles and glorious Martyrs
(with Saint N.: the Saint of the day or Patron Saint)
and with all the Saints,
on whose constant intercession in your presence
we rely for unfailing help.

The Priest resumes the **orans** position to emphasize that the entire Eucharistic Prayer is addressed to God, whereas the Memorial Acclamation is addressed to Christ. In both cases, we use the designation "Lord," but the context and internal references make the designation known.

Though subordinate, emphasize: **Passion, Resurrection, Ascension, second coming**, to emphasize even more **we offer you . . . this holy and living sacrifice**.

Parallel the phrases **Look . . . upon the oblation of your Church** and **grant that we . . . may become one body, one Spirit in Christ**, recognizing that **to yourself . . . who are nourished . . . and filled with his Holy Spirit** are parenthetical expressions and should be treated as such.

Emphasize **eternal offering**.

---

113. The texts in this article have multiple functions. Paragraph one comprises the anamnesis-offering. We recall the Paschal Mystery, and in that light offer to God the "holy and living sacrifice." The second paragraph is an epiclesis over the community, asking that those who are nourished by partaking in Holy Communion may become "one body, one spirit in Christ" by the Holy Spirit. In paragraphs three, four, and five, we add the intercessions for the living and the dead. We further pray that the gift of Eucharistic union unites us with

the Saints, other human beings, and with the living members of the Church. We especially pray that God would grant mercy to all the dead—Christians and non-Christians.

The double or split epiclesis, asking that we may become the Body of Christ, is congruent with the understanding that Saint Paul proffers in 1 Corinthians 12:12–14: "As a body is one though it has many parts, and all the parts of the body, though many, are one body, so also Christ. For in one Spirit we were all baptized into one body,

whether Jews or Greeks, slaves or free persons, and we were all given to drink of one Spirit. Now the body is not a single part, but many." The point can be made that Eucharist is both what is on the table and who is at the table. As Saint Augustine said, we are to become what we celebrate. We are to become bread broken and wine poured out for the world.

Emphasize **peace, salvation, all**.

Emphasize **confirm in faith and charity** and **your pilgrim Church on earth**.

Celebrant or one concelebrant

May this Sacrifice of our reconciliation,
we pray, O Lord,
advance the peace and salvation of all the world.
Be pleased to confirm in faith and charity
your pilgrim Church on earth,
with your servant N. our Pope and N. our Bishop,*
the Order of Bishops, all the clergy,
and the entire people you have gained for your own.

Listen graciously to the prayers of this family,
whom you have summoned before you:
in your compassion, O merciful Father,
gather to yourself all your children
scattered throughout the world.

Emphasize **gather to yourself all your children**.

Celebrant or one concelebrant

† To our departed brothers and sisters
and to all who were pleasing to you
at their passing from this life,
give kind admittance to your kingdom.
There we hope to enjoy for ever the fullness of your glory

He joins his hands.

through Christ our Lord,
through whom you bestow on the world all that is good. †

114.   He takes the chalice and the paten with the host and, raising both, he says:

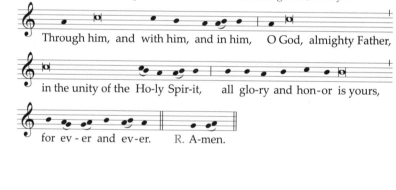

Through him, and with him, and in him,   O God, almighty Father,

in the unity of the Ho-ly Spir-it,   all glo-ry and hon-or is yours,

for ev-er and ev-er.   R. A-men.

For singing purposes, find a note in your upper-range. This is "do." Now sing down "do-ti-la" to find your opening note. Return immediately to "do." The traditional melody revolves around these three notes.

The doxology is the third and final of the eucharistic acclamations (along with the Holy, Holy, Holy and Memorial Acclamation). The fact that music is supplied in the Missal strongly suggests that this is an inherently musical item. Pause at the commas and the sense lines and continue to increase in volume, so as to cue the congregation's **Amen**.

The intercessions are insistent on the reconciliatory dimension of Eucharist that binds all Christians together in Holy Communion. This prayer is reminiscent of the table thanksgiving found in the *Didache* 9,4 that prays for the unity of the Church using the imagery of grain scattered: "As this broken bread was scattered over the mountains, and when brought together became one, so let your Church be brought together from the ends of the earth into your kingdom."(Aaron Milavec,

The Didache: Text, Translation, Analysis, and Commentary (Liturgical Press, 2003).

114. The Eucharistic Prayer ends with the doxology that sums up all the themes of the Eucharistic Prayer in a proclamation of the Divine Name. Everything belongs to God, and all honor and glory ascend to him in a Christological movement denoted by three prepositions: through, with, and in. The Holy Name is great throughout the entire world and put on the lips of the faithful who proclaim God's glory.

The Missal provides chant settings of this doxology that lead to the community's chanted "Amen"; however, there may be other musical settings of the doxology correlated to the congregation's "Amen." The doxology that the Priest sings and the "Amen" the people sing should be musically congruent, to form a seamless garment. The doxology is the ultimate crescendo of the Eucharistic Prayer, culminating in praise of God.

Through him, and with him, and in him,

O God, almighty Father,

in the unity of the Holy Spirit,

all glory and honor is yours,

for ever and ever.

Celebrant alone or with concelebrants

The people acclaim:

Amen.

Then follows the Communion Rite, p. 663.

---

115. *When this Eucharistic Prayer is used in Masses for the Dead, the following may be said:*

† **Remember your servant N.**

whom you have called (today)

from this world to yourself.

Grant that he (she) who was united with your Son in a death like his,

may also be one with him in his Resurrection,

when from the earth

he will raise up in the flesh those who have died,

and transform our lowly body

after the pattern of his own glorious body.

To our departed brothers and sisters, too,

and to all who were pleasing to you

at their passing from this life,

give kind admittance to your kingdom.

There we hope to enjoy for ever the fullness of your glory,

when you will wipe away every tear from our eyes.

For seeing you, our God, as you are,

we shall be like you for all the ages

and praise you without end,

He joins his hands.

through Christ our Lord,

through whom you bestow on the world all that is good. †

The emphasis should be on the first full sentence and the speaking of the person's name.

Play up the contrast between **death** and **Resurrection,** **earth** and **raise up,** and **lowly body** and **glorious body.** Contrast **our departed** (i.e., Christians) and **all who were pleasing to you.**

Emphasize **you will wipe away every tear from our eyes . . . seeing you . . . as you are.**

---

115. This embolism is used only for funeral Masses or a Mass on the day of death itself. Notice that the embolism is structured in three categories: first, for the named deceased person; second, for all the dead; and third, for ourselves, the members of the praying assembly. Appropriate pauses during each of these categories will help to make the structure of the categories clear to the listeners.

This prayer alludes to Jesus' words in John 11:25–26: "I am the resurrection and the life; whoever believes in me, even if he dies, will live, and everyone who lives and believes in me will never die." It also alludes to 2 Corinthians 5:1–7, which tells of the eternal dwelling that has been made for us in heaven: "For we know that if our earthly dwelling . . . should be destroyed, we have a building from God, a dwelling not made with hands, eternal in heaven." As does scripture, the prayer contrasts our passage from this life to our heavenly dwelling.

The focus of this prayer is found in the idea of transformation. Binary opposition contrasts uniting to Christ in death and then to his Resurrection. Also, the lowly body is asked to be transformed into a glorious body.

The prayer does not attempt to hide the sadness of death nor gloss over the normal feelings that we have in the face of the death of a loved one. Rather, we pray for the time when we are in God's glory, and every tear is wiped away.

The opening exchange establishes the dialogical nature of liturgical prayer. The Priest's lines are intended to elicit the response of the assembly. Vocal intonation and eye contact will help in this regard.

Parallel **truly**, **give thanks**, **truly**, **give glory**, emphasizing **Father most holy**, as the addressee of the prayer and paralleling God's characteristics: **one**, **living**, **true**, **existing**, **dwelling**. Make a contrast with **yet you . . . have made all that is**. Parallel **so that you might fill** with **and bring joy**.

Emphasize **countless**, **Angels**, **day**, **night**, **gazing**, **glory**, **glorify**, **ceasing**. Those words should evoke a sense of wonder in prayer.

Emphasize **we**, **too**, **confess**, **giving voice**, and **acclaim**.

EUCHARISTIC PRAYER IV

116. It is not permitted to change the Preface of this Eucharistic Prayer because of the structure of the Prayer itself, which presents a summary of the history of salvation (text with music, p. 736).

V. **The Lord be with you.**
R. And with your spirit.

V. **Lift up your hearts.**
R. We lift them up to the Lord.

V. **Let us give thanks to the Lord our God.**
R. It is right and just.

It is truly right to give you thanks,
truly just to give you glory, Father most holy,
for you are the one God living and true,
existing before all ages and abiding for all eternity,
dwelling in unapproachable light;
yet you, who alone are good, the source of life,
have made all that is,
so that you might fill your creatures with blessings
and bring joy to many of them by the glory of your light.

And so, in your presence are countless hosts of Angels,
who serve you day and night
and, gazing upon the glory of your face,
glorify you without ceasing.

With them we, too, confess your name in exultation,
giving voice to every creature under heaven,
as we acclaim:

Holy, Holy, Holy Lord God of hosts.
Heaven and earth are full of your glory.
Hosanna in the highest.
Blessed is he who comes in the name of the Lord.
Hosanna in the highest.

116. The rubrics for the opening dialogue of the Eucharistic Prayer are not printed in place but are found at #31 and in GIRM, 148. Although the text does not say that the "Holy, Holy, Holy" should be sung or spoken, it appears in the GIRM that the preference is for it to be sung. Singing is the first option in the GIRM, which seems to indicate a preference. Eucharistic Prayer IV has a proper Preface and, therefore, it should not be used when other proper Prefaces are assigned for a particular feast; for example, this Eucharistic Prayer would not be used on the First Sunday of Lent. Eucharistic Prayer IV draws its inspiration from Eastern anaphoras, especially the Syro-Antiochene model. The protocol of the Preface makes a transition from the last phrase of the dialogue, adding "truly" to "right and just," addressing God as Father most holy, an echo of John 17:11. The body of the Preface begins by lauding God simply as God is—living, true, existing, abiding, and dwelling in unapproachable light. Only then does the prayer praise God for creating all that is and blessing it. The eschatocol of the prayer emphasizes the Angels' role in constantly praising this creator God. In a powerful phrase, the praying assembly recognizes its role as the poets of creation by giving voice (language) to the praise that is offered by every other creature simply by existing. The Holy, Holy, Holy, thus, becomes the song of Angels, human beings, and the cosmos adoring the God who brought them into being.

117. The Priest, with hands extended, says:

Celebrant alone

We give you praise, Father most holy,
     for you are great
and you have fashioned all your works
in wisdom and in love.
You formed man in your own image
and entrusted the whole world to his care,
so that in serving you alone, the Creator,
he might have dominion over all creatures.
And when through disobedience he had lost your friendship,
you did not abandon him to the domain of death.
For you came in mercy to the aid of all,
so that those who seek might find you.
Time and again you offered them covenants
and through the prophets
taught them to look forward to salvation.

And you so loved the world, Father most holy,
that in the fullness of time
you sent your Only Begotten Son to be our Savior.
Made incarnate by the Holy Spirit
and born of the Virgin Mary,
he shared our human nature
in all things but sin.
To the poor he proclaimed the good news of salvation,
to prisoners, freedom,
and to the sorrowful of heart, joy.
To accomplish your plan,
he gave himself up to death,
and, rising from the dead,
he destroyed death and restored life.

And that we might live no longer for ourselves
but for him who died and rose again for us,
he sent the Holy Spirit from you, Father,
as the first fruits for those who believe,
so that, bringing to perfection his work in the world,
he might sanctify creation to the full.

The opening sentence sets the theme for the entire article. Emphasize **Father most holy** (the title from the Preface John 17:11).

Emphasize **fashioned all your works in wisdom and love**. Parallel this sentence to the first sentence of the article with the emphasis on **Father most holy**.

Follow the sense lines and commas to announce the individual examples almost like a litany of how God has fashioned all his works in **wisdom and love**.

Follow the sense lines and the commas to articulate the life and ministry of Jesus, but notice that the phrases are conspicuously shorter than the ones in the earlier paragraph and, therefore, can be spoken differently.

Emphasize the first three lines **And that . . .** with an acknowledgment of the addressee, **Father**.

---

117. This lengthy prayer praises God for his activity in history. It may be helpful if the Priest thinks of the article in three sections: the first, comprising the creation of humanity up to the coming of Christ; the second, a recounting of the Incarnation and the saving activity of Christ; and the third, human history since the coming of Christ marked by the gifts of this Spirit. The task for the one proclaiming the prayer is to make each of the elements remembered like a family heirloom.

The line "you formed man in your own image" recalls the first creation account in Genesis 1:26: "Then God said: 'Let us make man in our image after our likeness.'" The prayer goes on to the notion of stewardship for creation, stating that God has entrusted the whole world to his care. We find here a very positive theology of creation similar to what is articulated in Psalm 8: "You have given them rule over the works of your hands, / put all things at their feet: / All sheep and oxen, even the

beasts of the field, / the birds of the air, the fish of the sea, / and whatever swims the paths of the seas" (v. 7–9).

The metaphor of friendship is used to describe the need for reconciliation after humanity had strayed. Covenants are made and prophets are sent to bring humanity back. Ultimately, Christ, who shares in our human nature, comes to proclaim good news to the poor, freedom to prisoners, and joy to the sorrowful by living, dying, and being raised from the dead.

Emphasize **same, Spirit, graciously, sanctify,** and **offerings**.

Be aware of these final three sense lines, which though parenthetical, are still important.

The rubric reads, He takes the bread and, holding it slightly raised above the altar. This may seem to suggest that the Priest is impersonating Christ; in fact, the Priest continues to address God the Father. The Priest should not appear to be addressing the bread. Notice that the rubric before the text, "Take this all of you, and eat of it," does not call for the Priest Celebrant to break the host; it calls for him to bow slightly.

The Priest shows the consecrated host. The rubric does not say "elevate." The Priest Celebrant genuflects in adoration.

118.   He joins his hands and, holding them extended over the offerings, says:

Celebrant with concelebrants

Therefore, O Lord, we pray:
may this same Holy Spirit
graciously sanctify these offerings,

He joins his hands and makes the Sign of the Cross once over the bread and chalice together, saying:

that they may become
the Body and ✠ Blood of our Lord Jesus Christ

He joins his hands.

for the celebration of this great mystery,
which he himself left us
as an eternal covenant.

119.   In the formulas that follow, the words of the Lord should be pronounced clearly and distinctly, as the nature of these words requires.

For when the hour had come
for him to be glorified by you, Father most holy,
having loved his own who were in the world,
he loved them to the end:
and while they were at supper,

He takes the bread and, holding it slightly raised above the altar, continues:

he took bread, blessed and broke it,
and gave it to his disciples, saying:

He bows slightly.

TAKE THIS, ALL OF YOU, AND EAT OF IT,
FOR THIS IS MY BODY,
WHICH WILL BE GIVEN UP FOR YOU.

He shows the consecrated host to the people, places it again on the paten, and genuflects in adoration.

118. This article is the epiclesis over the gifts invoking the Holy Spirit for the transformation over the offering that Christ has left us for the celebration of this great mystery, which is Christ himself as an eternal covenant. The Priest should extend his hands over the offerings before he begins to recite the text, and he should keep them extended until he makes the Sign of the Cross once, over the bread and chalice together, while saying the words "Body and Blood."

119. The coordination of texts and gestures for the Institution narrative is very important. The Priest must remember that he is continuing to recount the great deeds of God now focused in Christ Jesus on the night before he died. This continues to be a part of a Eucharistic Prayer addressed to the Father. The Priest should not appear to be addressing the prayer to the bread and wine. Although rubrics such as "He takes the bread and, holding it slightly raised above the altar . . ." suggest that the Priest is impersonating Christ; in fact, the Priest continues to address God the Father, here, recounting one of the great deeds of God in history, the Institution narrative. Notice that the rubric before the text "Take this all of you and eat of it" does not call for him to bow slightly. Similarly, after speaking the text, the Priest shows the consecrated host. The rubric does not say "elevate." The Priest then genuflects in adoration.

120. *After this, he continues:*

In a similar way,

He takes the chalice and, holding it slightly raised above the altar, continues:

taking the chalice filled with the fruit of the vine,
he gave thanks,
and gave the chalice to his disciples, saying:

He bows slightly.

TAKE THIS, ALL OF YOU, AND DRINK FROM IT,
FOR THIS IS THE CHALICE OF MY BLOOD,
THE BLOOD OF THE NEW AND ETERNAL COVENANT,
WHICH WILL BE POURED OUT FOR YOU AND FOR MANY
FOR THE FORGIVENESS OF SINS.

DO THIS IN MEMORY OF ME.

He shows the chalice to the people, places it on the corporal, and genuflects in adoration.

121. *Then he says:*

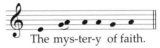

The mys-ter-y of faith.

The mystery of faith.   Celebrant alone

And the people continue, acclaiming:

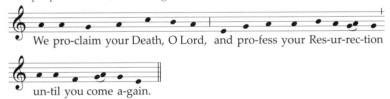

We pro-claim your Death, O Lord,   and pro-fess your Res-ur-rec-tion
un-til you come a-gain.

We proclaim your Death, O Lord,
and profess your Resurrection
until you come again.
Or:

The rubric reads "He takes the chalice and, holding it slightly raised above the altar." Again, the Priest continues to address God the Father, and not the chalice. Notice that the rubric before the text "Take this all of you, and drink from it," does not call for him to speak into the cup; it simply calls for him to bow slightly.

The Priest then shows the chalice. The rubric does not say "elevate." The Priest Celebrant genuflects in adoration.

The Priest may sing **The mystery of faith**, which will serve as a prompt for the assembly to sing one of the three acclamations.

The presence of a musical formula of introduction, plus three musical settings for the acclamation, suggest that this is inherently a musical item. If the Priest sings, it should match what is to follow. Therefore, the assembly begins on the note on which the Priest finishes.

In Eucharistic Prayer IV, the leading metaphor is that of covenant. It is noteworthy that passing mention is made to the Last Supper in the Institution narrative, while the prayer uses Johannine language: "when the hour had come for him to be glorified . . . having loved his own in the world."

121. The Priest's text "The mystery of faith" functions as a cue, although it is an exclamation. Originally, the phrase *mysterium fidei* was part of the consecratory text,

but Paul VI, on his authority, removed them from the consecratory words and made them this exclamation. The Latin text does not say, "Let us proclaim the mystery of faith"; nor does it provide a full sentence. Rather, the phrase could best be interpreted as "Oh, the mystery of faith!" a moment of contemplative awe and surrender that serves as a cue to the congregation's response.

The Priest's chant is correlated to the Memorial Acclamation chants of the Missal; but there may be other musical settings of

the Mystery of Faith correlated to other musical settings of the congregation's Memorial Acclamations that the Priest should learn. What the Priest sings and what the people sing should be congruent.

This is the second set of three acclamations that punctuate the Eucharistic Prayer (along with the Holy, Holy, Holy, the doxology, and Amen). That music is supplied in the Missal strongly suggests that this is a sung element. For this reason, it is desirable that all three acclamations match somehow musically, to create a coherent

For the second acclamation, the assembly imitates the Priest's line. The melody will serve as a cue to signal which acclamation will be sung. If another modern composition is used, the Priest should verify whether a lead-in was composed for it. It makes no sense to sing a modal lead-in when a tonal acclamation will be sung.

When we eat this Bread and drink this Cup,
we proclaim your Death, O Lord,
until you come again.

Or:

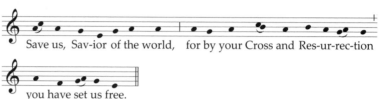

Save us, Savior of the world,
for by your Cross and Resurrection
you have set us free.

The Priest resumes the orans position to emphasize that the entire Eucharistic Prayer is addressed to God, whereas, the Memorial Acclamations are addressed to Christ. In both cases, we use the designation Lord, but the context and internal references make the designation known.

122. Then, with hands extended, the Priest says:

Celebrant
with concelebrants

**Therefore, O Lord,
as we now celebrate the memorial of our redemption,
we remember Christ's Death
and his descent to the realm of the dead,
we proclaim his Resurrection
and his Ascension to your right hand,
and, as we await his coming in glory,
we offer you his Body and Blood,
the sacrifice acceptable to you
which brings salvation to the whole world.**

**Look, O Lord, upon the Sacrifice
which you yourself have provided for your Church,
and grant in your loving kindness
to all who partake of this one Bread and one Chalice
that, gathered into one body by the Holy Spirit,
they may truly become a living sacrifice in Christ
to the praise of your glory.**

whole. In musical terms, this would be the second great crescendo, which will culminate in the doxology and Amen.

Notice that all three acclamations for the Mystery of Faith are addressed to Christ. After the Memorial Acclamation, the Eucharistic Prayer returns immediately to addressing the Father.

122. Many liturgical functions occur here. The first paragraph is an anamnesis-offering in which the community makes memory of the Paschal Mystery and offers to God the Father the sacrifice of the Cross. The second paragraph is an epiclesis on the community itself, praying that those who receive Holy Communion be united by the Holy Spirit. The double, or split, epiclesis, asking that we may become the

Body of Christ, is congruent with the understanding that Saint Paul proffers in 1 Corinthians 12:12–14. The point can be made that Eucharist is both what is on the table and who is at the table. As Saint Augustine said, we are to become what we celebrate. We are to become bread broken and wine poured out for the world. Third, that prayer for unity is specified as a prayer for the Church's leadership and her

Therefore, Lord, remember now
all for whom we offer this sacrifice:
especially your servant N. our Pope,
N. our Bishop,* and the whole Order of Bishops,
all the clergy,
those who take part in this offering,
those gathered here before you,
your entire people,
and all who seek you with a sincere heart.

Remember also
those who have died in the peace of your Christ
and all the dead,
whose faith you alone have known.

To all of us, your children,
grant, O merciful Father,
that we may enter into a heavenly inheritance
with the Blessed Virgin Mary, Mother of God,
and with your Apostles and Saints in your kingdom.
There, with the whole of creation,
freed from the corruption of sin and death,
may we glorify you through Christ our Lord,

He joins his hands.

through whom you bestow on the world all that is good.

Celebrant or one concelebrant

Emphasize **all** those present, those who lead the Church and the **entire people**.

There is no indication to insert the name(s) of the deceased, but a pause after this paragraph may be in order.

Celebrant or one concelebrant

Emphasize **O merciful Father**—hearkening back to most holy Father—**that we may enter into a heavenly inheritance**.

Emphasize each word: **whole, freed, glorify, all that is good**. The voice should become louder and possibly higher in pitch, giving progressive emphasis.

---

* Mention may be made here of the Coadjutor Bishop, or Auxiliary Bishops, as noted in the *General Instruction of the Roman Missal*, no. 149.

---

people—all who seek God with a sincere heart. As in all the Eucharistic Prayers, the names of the Pope and local Bishop, along with coadjutor or auxiliary Bishops, are inserted, demonstrating the rapport between the local Church and the universal Church. We, then, remember all those who have died—both Christian and others whose faith is known only to God. Finally, we pray for ourselves, that we may enter into the Communion of Saints. Only the name of the Blessed Virgin Mary is men

tioned specifically along with Apostles and Saints who remain unnamed. There is no provision in this Eucharistic Prayer to add specific names of Saints.

The prayer terminates with the same idea with which it began; namely, creation. But, as the first creation, which was good, experienced the Fall due to the sin of Adam, we recognize that the whole of creation has been redeemed through Christ, in whose name we glorify God who has bestowed all that is good to us.

In this theology of creation, human beings understand themselves to be in solidarity with God and the created order. Separated by sin, nevertheless, humanity is redeemed by Christ, thus supplying the created world with a voice that has again been restored through the redemptive work of Christ. Humanity has the task of becoming one again with nature and the cosmos and to continually sing to God hymns of praise.

For singing purposes, find a note in your upper-range. This is "do." Now sing down "do-ti-la" to find your opening note. Return immediately to do. The traditional melody revolves around these three notes.

The doxology is the third and final of the eucharistic acclamations (along with the Holy, Holy, Holy and Memorial Acclamation). The fact that music is supplied in the Missal strongly suggests that this is an inherently musical item. Pause at the commas and the sense lines and continue to increase in volume so as to cue the congregation's **Amen.**

123.　He takes the chalice and the paten with the host and, raising both, he says:

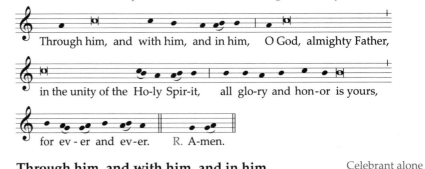

**Through him, and with him, and in him,
O God, almighty Father,
in the unity of the Holy Spirit,
all glory and honor is yours,
for ever and ever.**

Celebrant alone
or with concelebrants

The people acclaim:
　Amen.

Then follows the Communion Rite, p. 663.

123. The Eucharistic Prayer ends with the great final doxology, which sums up the themes of the Eucharistic Prayer in a proclamation of the Divine Name. Everything belongs to God and all honor and glory ascend to him in a Christological movement denoted by three prepositions: through, with, and in. The Holy Name is great throughout the entire world and put on the lips of the faithful who proclaim God's glory.

The conclusion of the prayer calls for the Priest to lift the paten with host and the Deacon (or in his absence, the Priest) chants or recites the doxology.

The Missal provides a chant setting of this doxology that leads to the community's chanted "Amen," however, there may be other musical settings of the doxology correlated to the congregation's "Amen." The Priest's doxology and the people's "Amen" should be musically congruent to form a seamless garment. The doxology is the ultimate crescendo of the Eucharistic Prayer, culminating in praise of God.

Not only is the doxology the high point of the Eucharistic Prayer, insofar as the latter is a proclamation and profession of faith, it also climaxes the sanctificatory movement of the prayer, since the Divine Name is formally proclaimed in its fullest and most explicit form. This draws from the Old Testament idea that the Divine Name has the power to sanctify. We find this clearly in Exodus 20:24: "In whatever place I choose for the remembrance of my name I will come to you and bless you."

THE COMMUNION RITE

124. After the chalice and paten have been set down, the Priest, with hands joined, says:

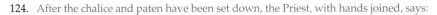
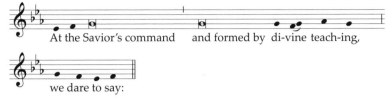

At the Savior's command
and formed by divine teaching,
we dare to say:

He extends his hands and, together with the people, continues:

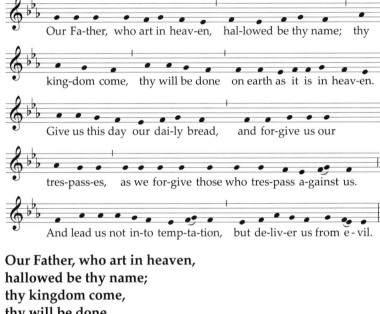

**Our Father, who art in heaven,
hallowed be thy name;
thy kingdom come,
thy will be done
on earth as it is in heaven.
Give us this day our daily bread,
and forgive us our trespasses,
as we forgive those who trespass against us;
and lead us not into temptation,
but deliver us from evil.**

Or:

Emphasize **Savior's command, formed, teaching, we dare to say.** Pause after **command.** Pause after **teaching.**

This is a cue, not a declarative sentence. The voice should come to a full stop, inviting the community's prayer.

If the Priest is able, he should intone the Our Father. Be careful to pitch it high enough so that it does not bog down.

---

124. The structure of the Lord's Prayer at a Roman Rite Eucharist consists of four elements. The first is a call to the prayer chanted by the Priest. The second is the chanting or recitation of the body of the prayer along with the Priest. The third is an expansion, technically called an embolism, expanding on the final petition of the Lord's Prayer, said or chanted by the Priest. Fourth, a doxology is said or chanted by the community along with the Priest. It is important that the four elements be expe-rienced as a unit. If the invitation is chanted, then the Priest's embolism also should be chanted. If the body of the prayer is chanted, the doxology of the prayer is chanted, too. The gestures also support the structure of the prayer. The first part is an invitation to prayer; thus, the Priest joins his hands and addresses the assembly. In the body of the prayer, the Priest assumes the orans position, which he continues to maintain through the embolism, demonstrating that the embolism is simply an amplifica-tion of the last line, "deliver us from evil." The doxology, "For the kingdom, the power and the glory," flows logically from the embolism, to conclude the prayer on a high note of praise. Due to the liturgical inser-tion of the embolism, it is easy to think that the prayer ends with the words "deliver us from evil." But the doxological conclusion is the logical termination of such a prayer, in much the same way we end the Psalms or Psalm sections at the Liturgy of the Hours, with doxologies.

The traditional musical version of the *Pater Noster* is here, although only the body of the prayer is provided in Latin. The doxology in Latin *(quia tuum est regnum et posestas et gloria in saecula)* might also be learned by the assembly since this is found in the *editio typica* of the *Missale Romanum*, 124, and it is the completion of the prayer. If the Priest is able, he might learn the invitation *(Praeceptis salutaribus moniti . . .)* and the embolism *(Libera nos, quaesumus, Domine . . .)* in Latin, so that the entire prayer holds together as one ritual unit. The *editio typica*, in addition to the traditional melody here, provides two other plainchant tones in Appendix I.

Pa-ter nos-ter, qui es in cae-lis: san-cti-fi-cé-tur no-men tu-um; ad-vé-ni-at reg-num tu-um; fi-at vo-lún-tas tu-a, si-cut in cae-lo, et in ter-ra. Pa-nem nos-trum co-ti-di-á-num da no-bis hó-di-e; et di-mít-te no-bis dé-bi-ta nos-tra, si-cut et nos di-mít-ti-mus de-bi-tó-ri-bus nos-tris; et ne nos in-dú-cas in ten-ta-ti-ó-nem; sed lí-be-ra nos a ma-lo.

Alternate musical settings of the Lord's Prayer may be found in Appendix I, pp. **1443–1444**.

125.   With hands extended, the Priest alone continues, saying:

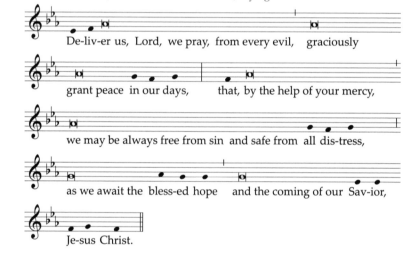

De-liv-er us, Lord, we pray, from every evil, graciously grant peace in our days, that, by the help of your mercy, we may be always free from sin and safe from all dis-tress, as we await the bless-ed hope and the coming of our Sav-ior, Je-sus Christ.

Provision is made to sing the *Pater Noster,* using the traditional chant melody. What is curious, however, is that the invitation, the embolism, and doxology are not provided in Latin. This may have the undesirable effect of isolating the Latin text from the entire prayer, resulting in fragmentation. It was probably determined that people would only know the prayer proper in Latin. Consideration might be given to singing the entire prayer in its four constitutive parts in Latin, or at least the prayer proper and the doxology *(quia tuum est regnum et potestas et gloria in saecula)*, since they are intimately connected. The Lord's Prayer concludes with "deliver us from evil" in Matthew, and with "lead us not into temptation" in Luke. The liturgical form is Matthean. Some Christians, particularly Protestants, conclude the prayer with a doxology, an addendum appearing in some manuscripts of Matthew. The justification for this is seen in the parallel practice of Christians praying the Psalms in the Liturgy of the Hours, during which (at the end of each Psalm or Psalm part) a doxology is interpolated in order to orientate the prayer in a Christian fashion. It is also argued that early Christians would have automatically added the doxology, since ending a prayer with the word "evil" or "temptation" would be unseemly.

Deliver us, Lord, we pray, from every evil,
graciously grant peace in our days,
that, by the help of your mercy,
we may be always free from sin
and safe from all distress,
as we await the blessed hope
and the coming of our Savior, Jesus Christ.

He joins his hands.

The people conclude the prayer, acclaiming:

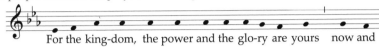

For the king-dom, the power and the glo-ry are yours now and
for ev-er.

For the kingdom,
the power and the glory are yours
now and for ever.

Deliver us is a request. Voice drops with we pray. Full stop at the end of evil. In effect, start a new sentence with graciously. Emphasize peace. Pause after peace in our days. Voice lowers for by the help of your mercy.

Lines 5 and 6 should be read as one. The consequences of free(dom) from sin and safe(ty) from distress are then one.
Present blessed hope and coming as one thing that we await.

If the Our Father is sung, the doxology should be sung, and in the same mode or tone, so as to create one ritual unit. Ideally, the Priest should sing the invitation and the embolism, for fuller ritual cohesion.

125. This text that separates the prayer proper from the doxology is called an "embolism." The word literally means a "patch," as it patches the two elements together. The embolism picks up on the words "deliver us from evil" and amplifies their meaning, reorienting the prayer in an eschatological sense.

Ideally, if the Our Father is sung, the Priest should sing the invitation and embolism. Singing the invitation will cue the assembly that the prayer itself is to be sung and will establish the musical key in which it will be sung. Singing the embolism will bridge the prayer to the doxology and impress upon those praying that this is a single prayer unit. But if singing the prayer in its entirety is not possible, at least the doxology should be sung in a congruent manner to the prayer proper, so the prayer does not appear fragmented.

The lead-in to the Rite of Peace flows from the doxology. Music is provided and will ensure ritual flow in bridging the Our Father and the Sign of Peace.

Correlate gestures with the words.

The title **Jesus Christ** is the climax of the embolism.

126. Then the Priest, with hands extended, says aloud:

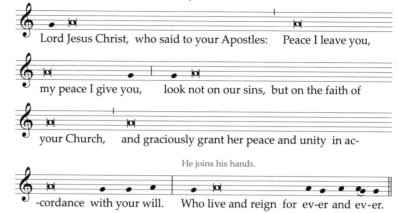

Lord Jesus Christ,
who said to your Apostles:
Peace I leave you, my peace I give you,
look not on our sins,
but on the faith of your Church,
and graciously grant her peace and unity
in accordance with your will.

He joins his hands.
Who live and reign for ever and ever.

The people reply:

Amen.

Set off the address, **Lord Jesus Christ,** with a pause. A slight pause after **Apostles** makes it clear that a quote follows. Emphasize **peace** both times. Read lines 4 and 5 as one. Emphasize **sins** and **faith.** From **graciously grant** should be taken as one phrase. Emphasize **peace, unity,** and **will.**

An **Amen** is sung after the lead-in to the Rite of Peace. Do not tag an **Amen** to the doxology.

127. The Priest, turned towards the people, extending and then joining his hands, adds:

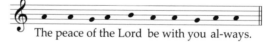

The peace of the Lord be with you always.

The people reply:

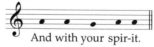

And with your spirit.

Notice that the congregation's response to **The peace of the Lord be with you always** is **And with your spirit** just as in the Introductory Rites.

Correlate the words with the rubrical gesture.

Singing the **peace** greeting will help the assembly to sing the proper response.

126. After the Our Father is the prayer leading into the Sign of Peace. Unlike the other prayers of the Roman Rite, this prayer is addressed to Christ. In it, the Priest, praying on behalf of the congregation, asks for a fruit of Holy Communion—peace in the assembly. (The only other time within the Eucharistic Prayer that a text is addressed to Christ is the Memorial Acclamation. Each of the three forms is a direct address to Christ by the people, but the Priest immediately returns the prayer addressed to God.)

Each time Christ encountered his Apostles after the Resurrection, he greeted them with the expression "Peace be with you" (John 20:20). The text here is a paraphrase of the story about Thomas, in which Jesus greets the Apostles, breathes his Spirit on them, and tells them that the sins that they forgive are forgiven, and the sins that they bind are bound.

127. Notice that the congregation's response to "The peace of the Lord be with you always" is "And with your spirit," just as in the Introductory Rites and elsewhere. In light of the Johannine context for this greeting, in which Christ breathes out his Spirit on the Apostles, the response "And with your Spirit" seems quite fitting. Musical notation is included that may be beneficial in helping congregations learn the new response.

128. Sign of Peace: The Rite of Peace is the sign by which the Church entreats peace and unity for herself and for the whole human family, and the faithful express to

128. Then, if appropriate, the Deacon, or the Priest, adds:

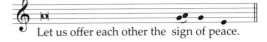

Let us offer each other the sign of peace.

Let us offer each other the sign of peace.

And all offer one another a sign, in keeping with local customs, that expresses peace, communion, and charity. The Priest gives the sign of peace to a Deacon or minister.

129. Then he takes the host, breaks it over the paten, and places a small piece in the chalice, saying quietly:

May this mingling of the Body and Blood
of our Lord Jesus Christ
bring eternal life to us who receive it.

130. Meanwhile the following is sung or said:

Lamb of God, * you take a-way the sins of the world,

have mer-cy on us.

Lamb of God, * you take a-way the sins of the world,

have mer-cy on us.

Lamb of God, * you take a-way the sins of the world,

grant us peace.

Lamb of God, you take away the sins of the world,
have mercy on us.
Lamb of God, you take away the sins of the world,
have mercy on us.
Lamb of God, you take away the sins of the world,
grant us peace.

Or:

This is a quiet ritual text, said in an inaudible voice. It is a wish, a velleity. It is a prayer seeking that the individual minister be equipped to seek his ministry. It is a prayer for the fruits of Communion on behalf of the Priest.

The Lamb of God is intended as a litany to cover the action of the Fraction of the Bread. If large hosts are to be broken, the litany might extend beyond the usual threefold use. If only one host is to be broken, the threefold form will suffice.

each other their ecclesial communion and mutual charity before communicating in the Sacrament.

As for the Sign of Peace to be given, the manner is to be established by the Conferences of Bishops, in accordance with the culture and customs of the peoples. However, it is appropriate that each person, in a sober manner, offer the sign of peace only to those who are nearest. It is clear from the rubric that the Priest is not intended to give the sign of peace to everyone in the congregation, lest this sign become clericalized.

129. Fraction and commingling rite: In the fraction and commingling rite, the large host is broken and a small portion of the consecrated host is placed into the chalice. The Priest quietly recites the prayer that accompanies this gesture. This particular rite has lent itself to much allegorical interpretation of reuniting body and soul, or reuniting body and blood. This interpretation should be avoided. Rather, the rite should be seen alongside the rite of the mixing of water with wine at the Preparation of the Gifts, and the meaning is more along the lines of the *sacrum commercium*—by our coming into contact with the Body and Blood of Christ, we pray for eternal life in Christ.

130. The threefold Lamb of God was initially a litany to cover the action of the "breaking of the bread." When unleavened

The *Agnus Dei* is from the Mass **Deus Genitor alme**. It is one of dozens of plainchant versions intended for weekdays of Advent and Lent. There is a version for Masses for the Dead with the appropriate endings. Due to its simplicity with syllabic notation, it lends itself for easy accessibility and singability.

A-gnus De - i, * qui tol-lis pec-cá-ta mun-di: mi-se-ré-re no-bis.

A-gnus De - i, * qui tol-lis pec-cá-ta mun-di: mi-se-ré-re no-bis.

A-gnus De - i, * qui tol-lis pec-cá-ta mun-di: do-na no-bis pa-cem.

The invocation may even be repeated several times if the fraction is prolonged. Only the final time, however, is **grant us peace** said.

131.   Then the Priest, with hands joined, says quietly:

The sacerdotal apologia is a private prayer and thus should be prayed inaudibly.

> **Lord Jesus Christ, Son of the living God,**
> **who, by the will of the Father**
> **and the work of the Holy Spirit,**
> **through your Death gave life to the world,**
> **free me by this, your most holy Body and Blood,**
> **from all my sins and from every evil;**
> **keep me always faithful to your commandments,**
> **and never let me be parted from you.**

Or:

This alternative apologia is said inaudibly. It is a private prayer in which the minister asks to be equipped for ministry.

> **May the receiving of your Body and Blood,**
> **Lord Jesus Christ,**
> **not bring me to judgment and condemnation,**
> **but through your loving mercy**
> **be for me protection in mind and body**
> **and a healing remedy.**

bread was introduced into the Latin Rite in the ninth century, the fraction rite gradually became reduced to breaking less and less bread. Ultimately, it was reduced to breaking only the Priest's host. Nevertheless, the term "breaking of the bread" is employed in almost a technical sense, as it is used in the Acts of the Apostles 2 and the Emmaus story in Luke 26.

The Fraction of the Bread corresponds to one of the four verbs used in the syn-optic account of the Last Supper: "take," "bless," "break," "give." Therefore, attention to the rite is important if people are to understand the fourfold action. Care can be taken that the singing or recitation of the Lamb of God coincides with the breaking of the bread. Large and clear gestures also can draw attention to this important gesture. The Fraction Rite should, at all cost, not be obfuscated by the Rite of Peace.

131. A choice of two private prayers is said inaudibly by the Priest. These prayers fit in the genre of private dispositional prayers or sacerdotal apologiae, and for this reason, reference the Priest in the first person singular. The first prayer has a strong penitential tone, while the second prayer uses medicinal imagery, asking for protection in mind and body.

132. The Priest genuflects, takes the host and, holding it slightly raised above the paten or above
the chalice, while facing the people, says aloud:

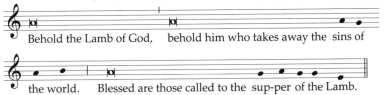

Behold the Lamb of God,   behold him who takes away the sins of

the world.   Blessed are those called to the sup-per of the Lamb.

**Behold the Lamb of God,
behold him who takes away the sins of the world.
Blessed are those called to the supper of the Lamb.**

And together with the people he adds once:

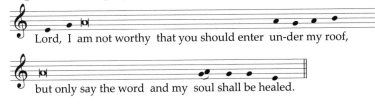

Lord, I am not worthy that you should enter un-der my roof,

but only say the word and my soul shall be healed.

**Lord, I am not worthy
that you should enter under my roof,
but only say the word
and my soul shall be healed.**

133. The Priest, facing the altar, says quietly:

**May the Body of Christ
keep me safe for eternal life.**

And he reverently consumes the Body of Christ.

Then he takes the chalice and says quietly:

**May the Blood of Christ
keep me safe for eternal life.**

And he reverently consumes the Blood of Christ.

134. After this, he takes the paten or ciborium and approaches the communicants. The Priest
raises a host slightly and shows it to each of the communicants, saying:

The Body of Christ.

The communicant replies:

Amen.

And receives Holy Communion.

If a Deacon also distributes Holy Communion, he does so in the same manner.

---

*Emphasize **Behold** both times.
Correlate the gestures with the words.*

*If the assembly will sing the response,
the Priest's chant introduction would
serve as an excellent cue.*

*This is a quiet ritual text, said in an
inaudible voice.*

*It is a wish, a velleity. It is a prayer
seeking protection for the individual
minister. It is a prayer for the fruits of
communion on behalf of the Priest.*

*Note that the declaration **Body of
Christ** is made without the demonstrative **This is**. This functions in
much the same way as the Gospel
acclamation **The Gospel of the Lord**,
so as to not limit the meaning.*

---

132. In this translation, the use of the word "Behold" calls attention to a disclosure. "Blessed are those called to the supper of the Lamb" is a liturgical beatitude. One can consider the sentence in light of "Blessed are the poor in Spirit" or "Blessed are the meek." Those who are called to the Supper of the Lamb also are blessed.

The congregation's response to the call to Holy Communion is to take upon its lips the text that the centurion addresses to Jesus when inviting him to cure his servant. In Luke 7:6–7, the centurion says, "I am not worthy to have you enter under my roof . . . but say the word and let my servant be healed."

Catechesis may be necessary to make it clear that the reference is to the "roof" of the centurion's house and not to the "roof" of the communicant's mouth. The new translation accurately Indicates that my "soul" (*animam*) will be healed from the encounter with Jesus' word, but the biblical understanding of the human person as a psychosomatic unity should not limit the effects of the encounter with Jesus simply to "spiritual" healing.

133. Again, we note the private nature of this prayer said quietly and use the first person singular.

134. The statement is terse ("The Body of Christ"), recognizing the Real Presence in the Eucharistic species, in the person receiving and in the ecclesial body.

135. If any are present who are to receive Holy Communion under both kinds, the rite described in the proper place is to be followed.

136. While the Priest is receiving the Body of Christ, the Communion Chant begins.

137. When the distribution of Communion is over, the Priest or a Deacon or an acolyte purifies the paten over the chalice and also the chalice itself.

While he carries out the purification, the Priest says quietly:

What has passed our lips as food, O Lord,
may we possess in purity of heart,
that what has been given to us in time
may be our healing for eternity.

138. Then the Priest may return to the chair. If appropriate, a sacred silence may be observed for a while, or a psalm or other canticle of praise or a hymn may be sung.

139. Then, standing at the altar or at the chair and facing the people, with hands joined, the Priest says:

Let us pray.

All pray in silence with the Priest for a while, unless silence has just been observed. Then the Priest, with hands extended, says the Prayer after Communion, at the end of which the people acclaim:

Amen.

This is a quiet ritual text, said in an inaudible voice.

It is a wish, a velleity. However, it is a prayer for all those who have received Communion. It is a prayer for the fruits of Communion on behalf of all.

The invitation to prayer is extended, followed by a period of sacred silence, so that the assembly may heed the call. After a brief period of silence, the Priest continues with the Prayer after Communion. During the period of sacred silence, try to pray yourself and do not tend to the Missal. Your prayer models prayer for others.

---

135. Holy Communion under both kinds: Taking Christ's words at face value, he commanded us to eat and to drink. Provision is made for this in the USCCB document "This Holy and Living Sacrifice." The directory is based on the 1975 edition of the *General Instruction of the Roman Missal.* The Bishops' Committee on the Liturgy (now known as the Bishops' Committee on Divine Worship) compiled it in order to assist Bishops in the implementation of an indult received from the Holy See permitting a wider use of Holy Communion under both species. The provisions for distribution of Holy Communion under both kinds found in the *Institutio Generalis* should be followed.

136. Communion Chant: Notice that the Communion Chant begins immediately. The music functions ritually to cover the action of Communion and to reflect upon what is happening.

137. Private dispositional prayer: This type of prayer, which is said silently, punctuates the entire liturgy and is meant as a dispositional prayer or sacerdotal apologiae. It is interesting that this prayer is in the first person plural.

138. Sacred silence: It is important that a sufficient period of silence be observed, so that all present may appropriate the Eucharistic Mystery to themselves.

139. The invitation to prayer is followed by a moment of silence.

THE CONCLUDING RITES

140. If they are necessary, any brief announcements to the people follow here.

141. Then the dismissal takes place. The Priest, facing the people and extending his hands, says:

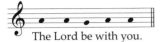
The Lord be with you.

The Lord be with you.

The people reply:

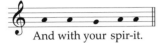
And with your spir-it.

And with your spirit.

The Priest blesses the people, saying:

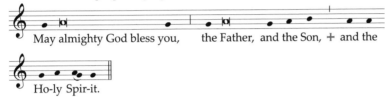
May almighty God bless you,   the Father, and the Son, ✛ and the

Ho-ly Spir-it.

**May almighty God bless you,
the Father, and the Son, ✛ and the Holy Spirit.**

The people reply:

A-men.

Amen.

142. On certain days or occasions, this formula of blessing is preceded, in accordance with the rubrics, by another more solemn formula of blessing or by a prayer over the people (cf. pp. **674ff.**).

The Concluding Rites are one ritual unit. The challenge is to keep the ritual flow moving, so as to eliminate ritual fragmentation.

Singing **The Lord be with you** cues the assembly to sing the correct response.

If there is no Solemn Blessing or Prayer over the People, the Priest sings the blessing, accompanied by the proper gesture. The assembly sings **Amen**.

140–142. The Concluding Rites: One is struck by the terse nature of the closing rites. Brief announcements are made at this point and can be a pastoral way to announce how this community is living the Eucharistic faith collectively and individually.

141. The interchange "The Lord be with you / And with your Spirit" that marks other major units of the Eucharistic Liturgy (e.g., The Introductory Rites, the proclamation of the Gospel, the beginning of the

Eucharistic Prayer) also marks the beginning of the final unit of the Eucharistic Liturgy, the Concluding Rites. The coordination of the gesture and the text is the same as at the beginning of Mass; namely, that this is addressed to the assembly. The Priest Celebrant follows this with a Trinitarian blessing, which may be in a simple or more extended form: (a Prayer over the People or a Solemn Blessing)

The gesture of blessing should coordinate with the text in such a way that the

Priest's right hand reaches a vertical high point on the word "Father," a vertical low point on "Son" and the Priest's horizontal left "Holy," and the Priest's horizontal right on "Spirit."

Note that the Missal offers chants for both of these, suggesting that this is the preferred form that these dialogues would be executed. Since the Solemn Blessing evokes an "Amen" from the assembly, music would help cue their response.

At a Pontifical Mass at which a Bishop is presiding (or simply giving the Final Blessing), the following dialogue is used. The first versicle is the usual melody.

143. In a Pontifical Mass, the celebrant receives the miter and, extending his hands, says:

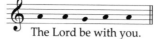
The Lord be with you.

The Lord be with you.

All reply:

And with your spir-it.

And with your spirit.

The celebrant says:

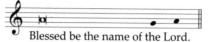
Blessed be the name of the Lord.

Blessed be the name of the Lord.

The second versicle uses the same melodic shape as the first versicle.

All reply:

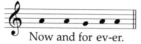
Now and for ev-er.

Now and for ever.

The assembly, thus cued by the music, responds singing.

The celebrant says:

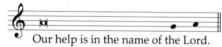
Our help is in the name of the Lord.

Our help is in the name of the Lord.

The final versicle is also sung using the two-note motive.

All reply:

Who made heav-en and earth.

Who made heaven and earth.

The assembly responds in kind.

Then the celebrant receives the pastoral staff, if he uses it, and says:

May almighty God bless you,

May almighty God bless you,

The usual Trinitarian Blessing is sung, with the appropriate gestures correlated.

---

143. In a Pontifical Mass presided over by the Bishop, a special form of the blessing is provided. It is dialogical in form, consisting of two sets of versicles and followed by the typical Trinitarian Blessing. A Bishop blesses the people with the appropriate formula, making the Sign of the Cross three times over the people. This macro-unit begins with the usual interchange "The Lord be with you / And with your Spirit." The text of the first versicle is derived from Psalm 113:2: "Blessed be the name of the Lord." The second versicle is from the Salzburg Missal, and the text is derived from Psalm 124:8: "Our help is in the name of the Lord." William Durandus, in his *Rationale Divinorum Officiorum* 4:59, 7, mentions that this form of the blessing is reserved to Bishops alone. Since there is a general unfamiliarity with this form as it is reserved to liturgies at which a Bishop presides, it may be necessary to rehearse this prior to the liturgy.

Musical notation in the Missal is an indication that this dialogical form of blessing functions best when sung. When the blessing is sung, the Dismissal should ideally be sung as well by a Deacon in order that the micro-unit hold together well. Other musical compositions may appear, but it is important for musical and ritual congruity that they be in the same modality or tonality.

making the Sign of the Cross over the people three times, he adds:

the Father, ✝ and the Son, ✝ and the Ho-ly ✝ Spir-it.

the Father, ✝ and the Son, ✝ and the Holy ✝ Spirit.

All:

A-men.

Amen.

The assembly responds with the normal two-note **Amen.**

144. Then the Deacon, or the Priest himself, with hands joined and facing the people, says:

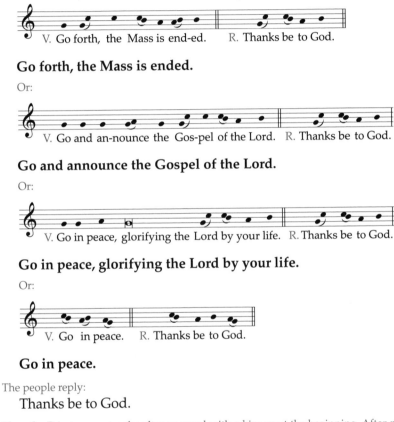

V. Go forth, the Mass is end-ed.   R. Thanks be to God.

Go forth, the Mass is ended.

Or:

V. Go and an-nounce the Gos-pel of the Lord.   R. Thanks be to God.

Go and announce the Gospel of the Lord.

Or:

V. Go in peace, glorifying the Lord by your life.   R. Thanks be to God.

Go in peace, glorifying the Lord by your life.

Or:

V. Go in peace.   R. Thanks be to God.

Go in peace.

The people reply:

Thanks be to God.

The Deacon (or Priest, in the absence of a Deacon) sings the Dismissal. Note that there are three formulas that can be chosen according to the feast or time of the liturgical year.

145. Then the Priest venerates the altar as usual with a kiss, as at the beginning. After making a profound bow with the ministers, he withdraws.

146. If any liturgical action follows immediately, the rites of dismissal are omitted.

144. The Deacon (or, in his absence, the Priest) dismisses the Eucharistic assembly. In the 2008 edition of the *Missale Romanum*, three new Dismissal formulas appeared. Their English translations now grace the Missal. These blessings appear with chant notation, again suggesting that the preferred way of executing these dialogues is through singing. The melodies are new; however, the earlier Dismissal, "Go in peace," remains with the more familiar chant melody.

145. The Priest exits the liturgy in approximately the opposite way as he entered into the liturgy. Both the beginning and end include a Sign of the Cross and a veneration of the altar. This gesture of kissing the altar stems from the Rite of Dedication of a Church and Altar in which the altar is consecrated with Holy Chrism. The title "Christ" comes from the Latin *Christos*, meaning the "Anointed One." Since the altar is a symbol of Christ, during the liturgy it is reverenced at numerous points.

Notice that no mention is made of a closing or recessional chant. Although singing at the recessional has become the custom in the United States, the conclusion to the Mass is the Dismissal (*Ite missa est*), from which the term "Mass" is derived.

146. In the case in which another liturgical action follows, such as the Rite of Commendation in the Rite of Funerals, the Dismissal Rite is omitted.

The Missal supplies 20 Solemn Blessings to be used in accordance with the liturgical year and the quality of the celebration. To the extent that the blessings are called "solemn," this suggests that the blessings should be used according to the principle of progressive solemnity. The usual form of the Solemn Blessings is threefold, although there are some notable exceptions (Nos. 10 and 14). Although the form is tripartite, they are not Trinitarian in address. Rather they are all addressed to God. But each Solemn Blessing terminates by invoking **almighty God** in the name of the Trinity.

The usual form is for the Deacon or Priest, after the liturgical greeting **The Lord be with you**, to invite the assembly to bow their heads for the blessing. The Priest, with outstretched hands, palms down, extended over the people, pronounces each part of the blessing, to which the people respond, **Amen**.

A pastoral difficulty presents itself in cuing the assembly for the **Amen**. Several strategies may be employed. A musical strategy would be to sing each petition recto-tono and drop down at the end of each petition to cue the assembly. Congruent musical settings for the **Amen** are suggested. Or, if the blessing is to be recited, end each petition by raising the voice, so that the inflection bids the response.

BLESSINGS AT THE END OF MASS AND PRAYERS OVER THE PEOPLE

SOLEMN BLESSINGS

The following blessings may be used, at the discretion of the Priest, at the end of the celebration of Mass, or of a Liturgy of the Word, or of the Office, or of the Sacraments.

The Deacon or, in his absence, the Priest himself, says the invitation: **Bow down for the blessing**. Then the Priest, with hands extended over the people, says the blessing, with all responding: **Amen**.

I. For Celebrations in the Different Liturgical Times

1. Advent

   May the almighty and merciful God,
   by whose grace you have placed your faith
   in the First Coming of his Only Begotten Son
   and yearn for his coming again,
   sanctify you by the radiance of Christ's Advent
   and enrich you with his blessing.
   R. Amen.

   As you run the race of this present life,
   may he make you firm in faith,
   joyful in hope and active in charity.
   R. Amen.

   So that, rejoicing now with devotion
   at the Redeemer's coming in the flesh,
   you may be endowed with the rich reward of eternal life
   when he comes again in majesty.
   R. Amen.

   And may the blessing of almighty God,
   the Father, and the Son, ✝ and the Holy Spirit,
   come down on you and remain with you for ever.
   R. Amen.

2. The Nativity of the Lord

   May the God of infinite goodness,
   who by the Incarnation of his Son has driven darkness from the world
   and by that glorious Birth has illumined this most holy night (day),
   drive far from you the darkness of vice
   and illumine your hearts with the light of virtue.
   R. Amen.

On certain days and occasions, the Final Blessings may be expanded and expressed by a more solemn formula. The 20 Solemn Blessings in the Missal are intended for specific Feasts and times of the liturgical year. They are mostly tripartite, and each part concludes with the assembly's responding "Amen."

1. Advent: This Solemn Blessing addresses the many advents of Christ. The first part emphasizes the "First Coming" fulfilling

God's design and opening the way to eternal salvation. The third part emphasizes the Second Coming, when everything will be made manifest and we will inherit the promise. The middle part emphasizes the present moment while we are still running the race, a reference drawn from Galatians 2:2 and 5:7. For Christians, the time of Advent serves as a reminder both of the original waiting done by the Hebrews for the birth of their messiah, as well as the waiting of Christians for Christ's return.

2. The Nativity of the Lord: The blessing evokes three themes associated with Christmas: light dispersing the darkness, the announcement of good news to the shepherds, and the mystery of the Incarnation. The emphasis on light also reminds us that in the northern hemisphere we are in the darkest time of the year. The winter solstice, however, has just occurred, and gradually, almost imperceptibly, the days get longer. The light has broken the back of darkness. The new light (Christ) shines in the darkness to dispel it.

May God, who willed that the great joy
of his Son's saving Birth
be announced to shepherds by the Angel,
fill your minds with the gladness he gives
and make you heralds of his Gospel.
R. Amen.

And may God, who by the Incarnation
brought together the earthly and heavenly realm,
fill you with the gift of his peace and favor
and make you sharers with the Church in heaven.
R. Amen.

And may the blessing of almighty God,
the Father, and the Son, ✝ and the Holy Spirit,
come down on you and remain with you for ever.
R. Amen.

3.   The Beginning of the Year

May God, the source and origin of all blessing,
grant you grace,
pour out his blessing in abundance,
and keep you safe from harm throughout the year.
R. Amen.

May he give you integrity in the faith,
endurance in hope,
and perseverance in charity
with holy patience to the end.
R. Amen.

May he order your days and your deeds in his peace,
grant your prayers in this and in every place,
and lead you happily to eternal life.
R. Amen.

And may the blessing of almighty God,
the Father, and the Son, ✝ and the Holy Spirit,
come down on you and remain with you for ever.
R. Amen.

The Solemn Blessings and Prayers over the People enrich the Eucharistic Celebration and can deepen the understanding of the liturgical year, as they are specified to the different feasts and times of the year. Additionally, use of the Solemn Blessings would be an occasion to single out various ministries, both liturgical and non-liturgical, so that those exercising these ministries may be commissioned and sent forth with a blessing. For example, extraordinary ministers of the Eucharist who bring Communion to the sick and homebound are within the assembly, but this ministry tends to be invisible, since ministers discreetly ask that their pyxes be filled during the Communion procession. What would happen if those bringing Communion to the sick and homebound came forward just before the blessing, at which time the consecrated bread would be placed in the pyx? If the assembly prayed over them that they be worthy ministers and commission them by sending them forward to represent the community to those who are not able to be present, the blessing formula would become more meaningful and a means of commissioning.

The shepherds were the first to receive the Good News of the divine birth that we have received ourselves today. Mention of the mystery of the Incarnation draws us into the deeper meaning of the Incarnation—the Word made flesh. The theme of the Word becoming flesh, characteristic of the Prologue of the Gospel according to John, is interpreted theologically for its deeper sense. Tertullian, for example, states that the flesh is the hinge of our salvation (*caro cardis salutis*).

3. The Beginning of the Year: In the first part we pray for grace in abundance; in the second, the three theological virtues are sought; and in the third part, we pray that our days be ordered and our deeds be peaceful. It is typical in New Year's greetings to wish people abundant blessings and prosperity, but this blessing need not be limited to January 1. To use the blessing at other times, simply omit the reference "throughout this year." Reference to God as the source and origin may strike the ear as somewhat redundant, but this is a direct translation of *fons et origo*, and there is a certain poetic quality to the phrase. The second part of the blessing is particularly beautiful, as we pray for the integrity of faith, endurance of hope, and perseverance in charity, adding that we also be given the gift of patience to the end. This idea gets picked up again in the third part, during which we ask that our present deeds be peaceful and that our days terminate with eternal life.

The Roman Missal supplies 20 Solemn Blessings to be used in accordance with the liturgical year and the quality of the celebration. To the extent that the blessings are called "solemn," suggests that they should be used according to the principle of Progressive Solemnity. The usual form of the Solemn Blessings is threefold, although there are notable exceptions (Nos. 10 and 14). Though the form of the blessing is tripartite, they are not Trinitarian in address; rather, they are addressed to God. But each Solemn Blessing terminates by invoking almighty God in the name of the Trinity.

The usual form is for the Deacon or Priest, after the liturgical greeting **The Lord be with you**, to invite the assembly to bow their heads for the blessing. The Priest, with outstretched hands, palms down, extended over the people, pronounces each part of the blessing, to which the people respond, **Amen**.

A pastoral difficulty presents itself in cuing the assembly for the **Amen**. Several strategies may be employed. A musical strategy would be to sing each petition recto-tono and drop down at the end of each petition to cue the assembly. Congruent musical settings for the **Amen** are suggested. If the blessing is to be recited, end each petition by raising the voice, so that the inflection bids the response.

4.   The Epiphany of the Lord

> **May God, who has called you**
> **out of darkness into his wonderful light,**
> **pour out in kindness his blessing upon you**
> **and make your hearts firm**
> **in faith, hope and charity.**
> R. Amen.

> **And since in all confidence you follow Christ,**
> **who today appeared in the world**
> **as a light shining in darkness,**
> **may God make you, too,**
> **a light for your brothers and sisters.**
> R. Amen.

> **And so when your pilgrimage is ended,**
> **may you come to him**
> **whom the Magi sought as they followed the star**
> **and whom they found with great joy, the Light from Light,**
> **who is Christ the Lord.**
> R. Amen.

> **And may the blessing of almighty God,**
> **the Father, and the Son, ✠ and the Holy Spirit,**
> **come down on you and remain with you for ever.**
> R. Amen.

5.   The Passion of the Lord

> **May God, the Father of mercies,**
> **who has given you an example of love**
> **in the Passion of his Only Begotten Son,**
> **grant that, by serving God and your neighbor,**
> **you may lay hold of the wondrous gift of his blessing.**
> R. Amen.

> **So that you may receive the reward of everlasting life from him,**
> **through whose earthly Death**
> **you believe that you escape eternal death.**
> R. Amen.

> **And by following the example of his self-abasement,**
> **may you possess a share in his Resurrection.**
> R. Amen.

4. The Epiphany of the Lord: What is unique to the Epiphany in the West is that Christ is the "light for the nations." That Christ is revealed to the Gentiles means that he is revealing himself to us. The light that was shining for the Jews is explicitly extended to the Gentiles, which means us. "Epiphany" means "manifestation" or "shining forth," and its significance is as real to us as it was to those who saw Jesus in the flesh. The epiphany of Christ takes place for us not by a miraculous sight "out there" to be seen by those who happen to be present, but demands eyes that are willing to see. Epiphany, like insight, is a kind of seeing in a new way. Thus, our lives are, in fact, full of epiphanies. The "star" that points to Christ shines in the minds and hearts of those who refuse to take life for granted but who wonder and marvel and seek love and meaning, and are willing to journey afar to find it.

5. The Passion of the Lord: The Cross of Christ, rather than an instrument of torture, is depicted as a sign or an example of love that calls for Christians to live their lives in imitation of it. The Cross is translated into acts of service toward God and neighbor. Just as Christ lived a full human life in obedience to God "to death, even death on a cross" (Philippians 2:8), so, too, we are called to follow his example of self-abasement in order that we might share in his Resurrection. In the Paschal Mystery, the two are never separated, so that even on the feast of Christ's Passion we anticipate already his Resurrection.

And may the blessing of almighty God,
the Father, and the Son, ✝ and the Holy Spirit,
come down on you and remain with you for ever.
R. Amen.

6.   *Easter Time*

May God, who by the Resurrection of his Only Begotten Son
was pleased to confer on you
the gift of redemption and of adoption,
give you gladness by his blessing.
R. Amen.

May he, by whose redeeming work
you have received the gift of everlasting freedom,
make you heirs to an eternal inheritance.
R. Amen.

And may you, who have already risen with Christ
in Baptism through faith,
by living in a right manner on this earth,
be united with him in the homeland of heaven.
R. Amen.

And may the blessing of almighty God,
the Father, and the Son, ✝ and the Holy Spirit,
come down on you and remain with you for ever.
R. Amen.

The Solemn Blessings and Prayers over the People enrich the Eucharistic Celebration and can deepen the understanding of the liturgical year, as they are specified to the different feasts and times of the liturgical year. Additionally, use of the Solemn Blessings would be an occasion to single out various ministries, both liturgical and non-liturgical, so that those exercising these ministries may be commissioned and sent forth with a blessing. Take, for example, those people involved in social ministries in the parish. Would this not be a good time to commission ministers on specified occasions throughout the liturgical year and send them forth to their mission, first having been nourished by the Word and the Eucharist? It would be fitting for the gathered assembly to commission with a special blessing those who work with the homeless, in soup kitchens, refugees, and so on. The *General Instruction of the Roman Missal* states: "On certain days and occasions this blessing . . . is expanded and expressed by a prayer over the People or another more solemn formula" (GIRM, 167).

6. Easter Time: "O day of days! O joyous feast of Easter! Thou queen of all the days of seasons bring. Today we raise joyful Alleluias. Today we greet our risen Lord and king" (from the "Risen Lord," by Adele Clere Ogden). "Hallowed, chosen dawn of praise, Easter, queen of all our days"(from "Christ the Lord Is Risen Today;" text ascribed to Wipo of Burgundy, tune *Gaudeamus Pariter*). So we sing that Easter is queen of all the days of the Christian year. Given the centrality of this festive event, this Solemn Blessing would be appropriate throughout all 50 days of Easter Time, marking with progressive solemnity its absolute importance.

At the Easter Vigil, catechumens are baptized, confirmed, and brought to the Eucharistic table. They are made children by adoption. The first part of the blessing, then, references that all the baptized are endowed with the gift of redemption and adoption. The third part evokes the baptismal theme again. Christians are to live in this changing world with their eyes fixed on a world that is unchangeable. Christians are "aliens" in this world. Thus, while we live on this earth, we are already praying to be united with God in our "homeland of heaven." The second part reiterates this idea of everlasting freedom and eternal inheritance, brought about by the redemption in Christ. The eternal effect of Christ's Death and Resurrection reminds all the baptized of the magnitude of God's love.

The Missal supplies 20 Solemn Blessings to be used in accordance with the liturgical year and the quality of the celebration. To the extent that the blessings are called solemn, this suggests that they should be used according to the principle of Progressive Solemnity. The usual form of the Solemn Blessings is threefold, although there are notable exceptions (Nos. 10 and 14). Although the form is tripartite, they are not Trinitarian in address. Rather, they are all addressed to God. But each Solemn Blessing terminates by invoking almighty God in the name of the Trinity.

The usual form is for the Deacon or Priest, after the liturgical greeting **The Lord be with you**, to invite the assembly to bow their heads for the blessing. Then the Priest with outstretched hands, palms down, extended over the people, pronounces each part of the blessing, to which the people respond **Amen**.

A pastoral difficulty presents itself in cuing the assembly for the **Amen** response. Several strategies may be employed. A musical strategy would simply be to sing each petition recto-tono and drop down at the end of each petition in order to cue the assembly. Congruent musical settings for the **Amen** are suggested. Or, if the blessing is to be recited, end each petition by raising the voice so that the inflection bids the response.

7.   The Ascension of the Lord

May almighty God bless you,
for on this very day his Only Begotten Son
pierced the heights of heaven
and unlocked for you the way
to ascend to where he is.
R. Amen.

May he grant that,
as Christ after his Resurrection
was seen plainly by his disciples,
so when he comes as Judge
he may show himself merciful to you for all eternity.
R. Amen.

And may you, who believe he is seated
with the Father in his majesty,
know with joy the fulfillment of his promise
to stay with you until the end of time.
R. Amen.

And may the blessing of almighty God,
the Father, and the Son, ✜ and the Holy Spirit,
come down on you and remain with you for ever.
R. Amen.

8.   The Holy Spirit

May God, the Father of lights,
who was pleased to enlighten the disciples' minds
by the outpouring of the Spirit, the Paraclete,
grant you gladness by his blessing
and make you always abound with the gifts of the same Spirit.
R. Amen.

May the wondrous flame that appeared above the disciples,
powerfully cleanse your hearts from every evil
and pervade them with its purifying light.
R. Amen.

And may God, who has been pleased to unite many tongues
in the profession of one faith,
give you perseverance in that same faith
and, by believing, may you journey from hope to clear vision.
R. Amen.

7. The Ascension of the Lord: This Solemn Blessing is grounded in the Lucan narrative in the Gospel account and the Acts of the Apostles. It alludes to the scene in Acts 1:6–11, in which the Apostles watched as Jesus "was lifted up, and a cloud took him from their sight." As the Apostles continued to look at the sky, two men dressed in white told them, "This Jesus who has been taken up from you into heaven will return." In the Gospel account, Luke recounts, "They did him homage and then returned to Jerusalem with great joy"

(24:52). The joy that was theirs should be ours today as we celebrate Christ's Ascension. Key to this blessing is that Christ ascends to unlock the heights of heaven for us and to sit in majesty with God as judge.

8. The Holy Spirit: This Solemn Blessing is suitable for Pentecost, but the content of the blessing does not limit its use only to this Solemnity. The Spirit is summoned to enlighten the minds and to bring gladness. The image of the flame or tongues of fire characterize the Pentecost account in Acts

2:3: "Then there appeared to them tongues as of fire, which parted and came to rest on each one of them." These same tongues led to the glossolalia event. We pray that we, too, may receive the flames that will enflame our hearts and that we may receive tongues, not so much to speak in foreign languages, but to profess our common faith that leads to our hope for a clear vision of God.

**And may the blessing of almighty God,
the Father, and the Son, ✝ and the Holy Spirit,
come down on you and remain with you for ever.**
R. Amen.

9.   Ordinary Time I

May the Lord bless you and keep you.
R. Amen.

**May he let his face shine upon you
and show you his mercy.**
R. Amen.

**May he turn his countenance towards you
and give you his peace.**
R. Amen.

**And may the blessing of almighty God,
the Father, and the Son, ✝ and the Holy Spirit,
come down on you and remain with you for ever.**
R. Amen.

10.   Ordinary Time II

**May the peace of God,
which surpasses all understanding,
keep your hearts and minds
in the knowledge and love of God,
and of his Son, our Lord Jesus Christ.**
R. Amen.

**And may the blessing of almighty God,
the Father, and the Son, ✝ and the Holy Spirit,
come down on you and remain with you for ever.**
R. Amen.

The Solemn Blessings and Prayers over the People enrich the Eucharistic celebration and can deepen the understanding of the liturgical year, as they are specified to the different feasts and times of the year. Additionally, use of the Solemn Blessings would be an occasion to single out various ministries, both liturgical and non-liturgical, so that people exercising these ministries may be commissioned and sent forth with a blessing. For example, we know that extraordinary ministers of the Eucharist who bring Holy Communion to the sick and homebound are within the assembly, but this ministry tends to be quite invisible. What would happen if those bringing Communion to the sick and homebound came forward just before the blessing when they would place the consecrated bread in the pix? The assembly could pray over them that they be worthy ministers and commission them by sending them forward to represent the community to those who are not able to be present. The blessing formula would then become more meaningful and the commissioning aspect would be more evident.

9. Ordinary Time I: This text is called the priestly blessing of Aaron (Numbers 6:24). The priests of the Old Testament were solemnly to bless the people in the name of the Lord. To be under the almighty protection of God our Savior; to enjoy his favor as the smile of a loving Father, or as the gleaming beams of the sun; while he mercifully forgives our sins, supplies our wants, consoles the heart, and prepares us by his grace for eternal glory — these things form the substance of this blessing and the sum total of all blessings. In so rich a list of mercies, worldly joys are not worthy to be mentioned. In the original, God's name is repeated three times.

10. Ordinary Time II: This Solemn Blessing is unusual, in that the form is not tripartite, but rather a simple statement derived from Philippians 4:7: "Then the peace of God that surpasses all understanding will guard your hearts and minds in Christ Jesus." We find an Old Testament parallel in Isaiah 26:3: "A nation of firm purpose you keep in peace; / in peace, for its trust in you." The epistles are replete with this kind of blessing. In Colossians 3:15, we read: "And let the peace of Christ control your hearts, the peace into which you were also called in one body. And be thankful." Also, the resurrected Christ greeted his disciples in the upper room with "Peace be with you" (John 20:19). We find a longer reflection on this theme of peace in John 14:27.

The *Roman Missal* supplies 20 Solemn Blessings to be used in accordance with the Church year and the quality of the celebration. To the extent that the blessings are called solemn, this suggests that they should be used according to the principle of Progressive Solemnity. The usual form of the Solemn Blessings is threefold, although there are some notable exceptions (Nos. 10 and 14). Although the form is tripartite, they are not Trinitarian in address. Rather, they are all addressed to God. But each Solemn Blessing terminates by invoking almighty God in the name of the Trinity.

The usual form is for the Deacon or Priest, after the liturgical greeting **The Lord be with you** to invite the assembly to bow their heads for the blessing. The Priest, with out-stretched hands, palms down, extended over the people, pro-nounces each part of the blessing, to which the people respond **Amen**.

A pastoral difficulty presents itself in cuing the assembly for the response of **Amen**. Several strategies may be employed. A musical strategy would be to sing each petition recto-tono and drop down at the end of each petition in order to cue the assembly. Congruent musical settings for the **Amen** are suggested. Or, if the blessing is to be recited, end each petition by raising the voice so that the inflection bids the response.

11.   Ordinary Time III

**May almighty God bless you in his kindness
and pour out saving wisdom upon you.**
R. Amen.

**May he nourish you always with the teachings of the faith
and make you persevere in holy deeds.**
R. Amen.

**May he turn your steps towards himself
and show you the path of charity and peace.**
R. Amen.

**And may the blessing of almighty God,
the Father, and the Son, ✛ and the Holy Spirit,
come down on you and remain with you for ever.**
R. Amen.

12.   Ordinary Time IV

**May the God of all consolation order your days in his peace
and grant you the gifts of his blessing.**
R. Amen.

**May he free you always from every distress
and confirm your hearts in his love.**
R. Amen.

**So that on this life's journey
you may be effective in good works,
rich in the gifts of hope, faith and charity,
and may come happily to eternal life.**
R. Amen.

**And may the blessing of almighty God,
the Father, and the Son, ✛ and the Holy Spirit,
come down on you and remain with you for ever.**
R. Amen.

11. Ordinary Time III: This Solemn Blessing turns on three sets of double requests: that God may bless with kindness and pour out wisdom, that God may nour-ish with faith and preserve our deeds, and that God may turn steps toward him and show us the path of charity and peace. Kindness here evokes the Hebrew word hesed, which means "love," "kindness," and "mercy." Wisdom can mean sophia, as is the term in the Septuagint for Hebrew chokhmah. In Judaism, chokhmah appears alongside the shekhinah, "the Glory of God," as an expression of the feminine aspect of God.

12. Ordinary Time IV: This Solemn Blessing also turns on three sets of double wishes: may God order days toward peace and grant blessing; may God free us from distress and confirm our hearts in love; and may God effect good works and the three theological virtues and bring us to a happy end. The expression "God of all consola-tion" seems to reflect 2 Corinthians 1:3: "Blessed be the God and Father of our Lord Jesus Christ, the Father of compassion and God of all encouragement."

13. Ordinary Time V: Again, this Solemn Blessing consists of three wishes, but only the first and the third are organized in paired sets. The second wish is unusual, in that it expresses a purpose or result in the subordinate clause—that our hearts may be filled with everlasting gladness. The second wish flows into the third, which has

13.   Ordinary Time V

> May almighty God always keep every adversity far from you
> and in his kindness pour out upon you the gifts of his blessing.
> R. Amen.
>
> May God keep your hearts attentive to his words,
> that they may be filled with everlasting gladness.
> R. Amen.
>
> And so, may you always understand what is good and right,
> and be found ever hastening along
> in the path of God's commands,
> made coheirs with the citizens of heaven.
> R. Amen.
>
> And may the blessing of almighty God,
> the Father, and the Son, ✝ and the Holy Spirit,
> come down on you and remain with you for ever.
> R. Amen.

14.   Ordinary Time VI

> May God bless you with every heavenly blessing,
> make you always holy and pure in his sight,
> pour out in abundance upon you the riches of his glory,
> and teach you with the words of truth;
> may he instruct you in the Gospel of salvation,
> and ever endow you with fraternal charity.
> Through Christ our Lord.
> R. Amen.
>
> And may the blessing of almighty God,
> the Father, and the Son, ✝ and the Holy Spirit,
> come down on you and remain with you for ever.
> R. Amen.

The Solemn Blessings and Prayers over the People enrich the Eucharistic celebration and can deepen the understanding of the liturgical year as they are specified to the different feasts and times of the year. Additionally, use of the Solemn Blessings would be an occasion to single out various ministries, both liturgical and non-liturgical, so that those exercising these ministries may be commissioned and sent forth with a blessing. Those involved in social ministries in the parish are an example. Would this not be a good time to commission ministers on specified occasions throughout the liturgical year and send them forth to their mission, first having been nourished by the Word and the Eucharist? It would be fitting for the gathered assembly to commission with a special blessing those who work with the homeless, in soup kitchens, refugees, and so on. The *General Instruction of the Roman Missal* states: "On certain days and occasions this blessing . . . is expanded and expressed by a prayer over the People or another more solemn formula" (GIRM, 167).

an eschatological hope—as we hasten to become coheirs with the citizens of heaven. This last line evokes Philippians 3:20–21: "But our citizenship is in heaven, and from it we also await a savior, the Lord Jesus Christ. He will change our lowly body to conform with his glorified body by the power that enables him also to bring all things into subjection to himself."

14. Ordinary Time VI: This Solemn Blessing is unusual, in that we have six wishes, but they are not arranged in three sets of couplets. Rather, we pray as in a litany for a number of things: that God may bless, sanctify, enrich, teach, instruct, endow. Rather than pairing ideas, like teaching and instructing, the blessing is organized more like a chain of wishes. Thus, blessing leads to sanctification, which in turn enriches us with the glory of God. Teaching the words of truth automatically leads to the instruction in the Gospel of salvation that is translated into fraternal charity.

Contrast may be made between earthly and heavenly blessing. For example, in

Ephesians 1:3 we read: "Blessed be the God and Father of our Lord Jesus Christ, who has blessed us in Christ with every spiritual blessing in the heavens." Again, we find the distinction between human love and God's love in Psalm 103:11 "As the heavens tower over the earth, / so God's love towers over the faithful."

The *Roman Missal* supplies 20 Solemn Blessings to be used in accordance with the liturgical year and the quality of the celebration. To the extent that the blessings are called "solemn," this suggests that they should be used according to the principle of Progressive Solemnity. The usual form of the Solemn Blessings is threefold, although there are some notable exceptions (Nos. 10 and 14). Although the form is tripartite, they are not Trinitarian in address. Rather, they are all addressed to God. But each Solemn Blessing terminates by invoking almighty God in the name of the Trinity.

The usual form is for the Deacon or Priest, after the liturgical greeting **The Lord be with you**, to invite the assembly to bow their heads for the blessing. The Priest, with outstretched hands, palms down, extended over the people, pronounces each part of the blessing, to which the people respond **Amen**.

A pastoral difficulty presents itself in cuing the assembly for the **Amen** response. Several strategies may be employed. A musical strategy would simply be to sing each petition recto-tono and drop down at the end of each petition in order to cue the assembly. Congruent musical settings for the Amen are suggested. If the blessing is to be recited, end each petition by raising the voice so that the inflection bids the response.

II. For Celebrations of the Saints

15. The Blessed Virgin Mary

May God, who through the childbearing of the Blessed Virgin Mary
willed in his great kindness to redeem the human race,
be pleased to enrich you with his blessing.
R. Amen.

May you know always and everywhere the protection of her,
through whom you have been found worthy to receive the author of life.
R. Amen.

May you, who have devoutly gathered on this day,
carry away with you the gifts of spiritual joys and heavenly rewards.
R. Amen.

And may the blessing of almighty God,
the Father, and the Son, ✚ and the Holy Spirit,
come down on you and remain with you for ever.
R. Amen.

16. Saints Peter and Paul, Apostles

May almighty God bless you,
for he has made you steadfast in Saint Peter's saving confession
and through it has set you on the solid rock of the Church's faith.
R. Amen.

And having instructed you
by the tireless preaching of Saint Paul,
may God teach you constantly by his example
to win brothers and sisters for Christ.
R. Amen.

So that by the keys of St Peter and the words of St Paul,
and by the support of their intercession,
God may bring us happily to that homeland
that Peter attained on a cross
and Paul by the blade of a sword.
R. Amen.

And may the blessing of almighty God,
the Father, and the Son, ✚ and the Holy Spirit,
come down on you and remain with you for ever.
R. Amen.

15. The Blessed Virgin Mary: The Solemn Blessing of the Blessed Virgin Mary in the usual tripartite form refers to Mary as the Theotokos, the protector, and the example of Christian life. It alludes to the account of the Annunciation in Luke 1:26–35. There we read, "The holy Spirit will come upon you, and the power of the Most High will overshadow you. Therefore the child to be born will be called holy, the Son of God" (v. 35). The first part of the blessing focuses on the motherhood of Mary, and as such, may be appropriate for the particu- lar Feasts of her birth (September 8, nine months after her Immaculate Conception on December 8) and especially the Solemnity of Mary, the Holy Mother of God (January 1). The blessing is also suitable for Optional Memorials (votive Masses) on Saturdays in Ordinary Time when no Obligatory Memorial occurs in honor of the Blessed Virgin Mary.

16. Saints Peter and Paul, Apostles: In spite of the famous "incident at Antioch"—the early Christian dispute between the Apostles Paul and Peter that occurred in the city of Antioch around the middle of the first century regarding whether Christian converts had to observe the Mosaic Law (see Galatians 2:11–14), Peter and Paul were paired together as the two Apostles to Rome since they both died there. The hymn *Decora lux* captures the importance of these two Apostles among the others. "*O Roma felix quae duorum principum es consacrata glorioso sanguine*" ("O happy Rome! Who in thy martyr princes' blood, A twofold stream, art washed and

17. The Apostles

> May God, who has granted you
> to stand firm on apostolic foundations,
> graciously bless you through the glorious merits
> of the holy Apostles N. and N. (the holy Apostle N.).
> R. Amen.
>
> And may he, who endowed you
> with the teaching and example of the Apostles,
> make you, under their protection,
> witnesses to the truth before all.
> R. Amen.
>
> So that through the intercession of the Apostles,
> you may inherit the eternal homeland,
> for by their teaching you possess firmness of faith.
> R. Amen.
>
> And may the blessing of almighty God,
> the Father, and the Son, ✠ and the Holy Spirit,
> come down on you and remain with you for ever.
> R. Amen.

18. All Saints

> May God, the glory and joy of the Saints,
> who has caused you to be strengthened
> by means of their outstanding prayers,
> bless you with unending blessings.
> R. Amen.
>
> Freed through their intercession from present ills
> and formed by the example of their holy way of life,
> may you be ever devoted
> to serving God and your neighbor.
> R. Amen.
>
> So that, together with all,
> you may possess the joys of the homeland,
> where Holy Church rejoices
> that her children are admitted in perpetual peace
> to the company of the citizens of heaven.
> R. Amen.
>
> And may the blessing of almighty God,
> the Father, and the Son, ✠ and the Holy Spirit,
> come down on you and remain with you for ever.
> R. Amen.

The Solemn Blessings and Prayers over the People enrich the Eucharistic Celebration and can deepen the understanding of the liturgical year, as they are specified to the different feasts and liturgical times of the year. Additionally, use of the Solemn Blessings would be an occasion to single out various ministries, both liturgical and non-liturgical, so that those exercising these ministries may be commissioned and sent forth with a blessing. For example, extraordinary ministers of the Eucharist who bring Holy Communion to the sick and homebound tend to be quite invisible in the assembly. What would happen if those bringing Communion to the sick and homebound came forward just before the blessing, at which time the consecrated bread would be placed in the pyx? The entire assembly could pray over the ministers, that they be worthy ministers, and commission them by sending them forward to represent the community to those who are not able to be present. The blessing formula, then, would become more meaningful and a means of commissioning.

doubly sanctified"). This hymn is sung to Peter and Paul, the two princes of Rome, on the Solemnity of Peter and Paul, Apostles, on June 29.

17. The Apostles: The Solemn Blessing of the Apostles draws on the scriptural allusion in John 10:11 and 14. "I am the good shepherd. A good shepherd lays down his life for the sheep. . . . I am the good shepherd, and I know mine and mine know me." This Blessing underscores how the "Apostles," or "those you have appointed

shepherds" carry out the work of Christ, continuing to govern and shepherd the flock. The blessing highlights three things that Apostles as pastors are to do for the Church; they are foundations, teachers, and intercessors.

18. All Saints: Taken together, the three parts of the Blessing for Saints constitute a statement about how God relates to the Saints. All three petitions are made to God but grant blessing due to the prayers of the Saints. In the second part, God helps us fol-

low the Saints' example, and in the third, we petition to enter into the Saints' company as citizens of heaven. The Saints model for us a way of life; they are comrades; and they intercede for us. They are not to be mistaken as mediators. Mediation is the role of Christ.

The Missal supplies 20 Solemn Blessings to be used in accordance with the Church year and the quality of the celebration. To the extent that the blessings are called "solemn," this suggests that they should be used according to the principle of progressive solemnity. The usual form of the Solemn Blessings is threefold, although there are notable exceptions (Nos. 10 and 14). Though the form is tripartite, they are not Trinitarian in address. Rather, they are all addressed to God. But each Solemn Blessing terminates by invoking almighty God in the name of the Trinity.

The usual form is for the Deacon or Priest, after the liturgical greeting **The Lord be with you** to invite the assembly to bow their heads for the blessing. The Priest, with outstretched hands, palms down, extended over the people, pronounces each part of the blessing, to which the people respond **Amen**.

A pastoral difficulty presents itself in cuing the assembly for the **Amen** response. Several strategies may be employed. A musical strategy would be to sing each petition recto-tono and drop down at the end of each petition in order to cue the assembly. Congruent musical settings for the **Amen** are suggested. If the blessing is to be recited, end each petition by raising the voice, so that the inflection bids the response.

III. Other Blessings

19.   For the Dedication of a Church

May God, the Lord of heaven and earth,
who has gathered you today for the dedication of this church,
make you abound in heavenly blessings.
R. Amen.

And may he, who has willed that all his scattered children
should be gathered together in his Son,
grant that you may become his temple
and the dwelling place of the Holy Spirit.
R. Amen.

And so, when you are thoroughly cleansed,
may God dwell within you
and grant you to possess with all the Saints
the inheritance of eternal happiness.
R. Amen.

And may the blessing of almighty God,
the Father, ✝ and the Son, ✝ and the Holy ✝ Spirit,
come down on you and remain with you for ever.
R. Amen.

20.   In Celebrations for the Dead

May the God of all consolation bless you,
for in his unfathomable goodness he created the human race,
and in the Resurrection of his Only Begotten Son
he has given believers the hope of rising again.
R. Amen.

To us who are alive, may God grant pardon for our sins,
and to all the dead, a place of light and peace.
R. Amen.

So may we all live happily for ever with Christ,
whom we believe truly rose from the dead.
R. Amen.

And may the blessing of almighty God,
the Father, and the Son, ✝ and the Holy Spirit,
come down on you and remain with you for ever.
R. Amen.

19. For the Dedication of a Church: In the strict sense, the Rite of Dedication of a Church denotes the building, but in the more primary sense, the Church is the People of God who are the living stones. Just as the term "Church" refers to the living temple, God's People, the term "church" also has been used to describe the building in which the Christian community gathers to hear the word of God, to pray together, to receive the Sacraments, and celebrate the Eucharist. Dedication means setting the building apart for something special or to commit or devote that building to the work of God. The dedication of a church building takes place soon after the building has been completed. A special liturgy occurs during which prayers are said to request that God bless the building, and to pray for all those who will worship in that building in the future.

20. In Celebrations for the Dead: The strongest biblical material underlying the theology of death is 1 Corinthians 15:55–56. Those verses provide a question and answer about death: " 'Where, O death, is your victory? / Where, O death, is your sting?' / The sting of death is sin, and the power of sin is the law." In this blessing, we first pray to the God of consolation to bless us with hope.

In the second part, we pray for the living (for forgiveness) and the dead (that they may find a place of light and peace). The third petition, for all, capitulates in the Christian belief in the Resurrection of Christ.

PRAYERS OVER THE PEOPLE

The following prayers may be used, at the discretion of the Priest, at the end of the celebration of Mass, or of a Liturgy of the Word, or of the Office, or of the Sacraments.

The Deacon or, in his absence, the Priest himself, says the invitation: Bow down for the blessing. Then the Priest, with hands outstretched over the people, says the prayer, with all responding: Amen.

After the prayer, the Priest always adds: And may the blessing of almighty God, the Father, and the Son, ✠ and the Holy Spirit, come down on you and remain with you for ever. R. Amen.

1. **Be gracious to your people, O Lord,**
   and do not withhold consolation on earth
   from those you call to strive for heaven.
   Through Christ our Lord.

2. **Grant, O Lord, we pray,**
   that the Christian people
   may understand the truths they profess
   and love the heavenly liturgy
   in which they participate.
   Through Christ our Lord.

3. **May your people receive your holy blessing,**
   O Lord, we pray,
   and, by that gift,
   spurn all that would harm them
   and obtain what they desire.
   Through Christ our Lord.

4. **Turn your people to you with all their heart,**
   O Lord, we pray,
   for you protect even those who go astray,
   but when they serve you with undivided heart,
   you sustain them with still greater care.
   Through Christ our Lord.

5. **Graciously enlighten your family, O Lord, we pray,**
   that by holding fast to what is pleasing to you,
   they may be worthy to accomplish all that is good.
   Through Christ our Lord.

In addition to the 20 Solemn Blessings, the Missal supplies 28 Prayers over the People to be used in accordance with the liturgical year and the quality of the celebration. Since these are not designated as solemn, they can be used whenever it is deemed appropriate. The usual form of the Prayers over the People is simple—four to seven lines addressed to God as Lord and concluded with the formula **Through Christ our Lord** to which the assembly responds **Amen**.

As with the Solemn Blessings, the usual form is for the Deacon or Priest, after the liturgical greeting **The Lord be with you**, to invite the assembly to bow their heads for the blessing. The Priest, with outstretched hands, palms down, extended over the people, pronounces the prayer, to which the people respond **Amen**.

A pastoral difficulty presents itself in cuing the assembly for the response **Amen**. Several strategies may be employed. A musical strategy would be to sing each petition recto-tono and drop down at the end of each petition in order to cue the assembly. However, the formula **Through Christ our Lord**, should facilitate the response. Congruent musical settings for the **Amen** is suggested with the Trinitarian blessing also sung. If the blessing is to be recited, end each petition by raising the voice so that the inflection bids the response.

On certain days and occasions the Final Blessing, in accordance with the rubrics, may be expanded and expressed by a Prayer over the People.

1. Mention is made to the God of consolation, making this prayer appropriate for Masses for the Dead, anniversary Masses for the Dead and other occasions where God's consolation is sought.

2. In this prayer we ask that we may understand the truths of the Gospel and love the liturgy that allows participation in these truths. This seems appropriate for any occasion.

3. This particular prayer could be used when there is perceived danger or harm present or when we are praying that God's will be done, so that our desires might correspond to God's will.

4. This prayer would be particularly appropriate when the theme of reconciliation is apparent.

5. As we pray for enlightenment, this might be used in academic settings or in times when the way seems obscured.

6. This prayer, which is penitential in tone, bids God for pardon and peace. It is derived from the event in John's account of the Gospel, during which Jesus appears to the Apostles in the absence of Thomas. Jesus greets the Apostles with "Peace be with you," then gives them the power to remit and retain sins.

In addition to the 20 Solemn Blessings, the Missal supplies 28 Prayers over the People to be used in accordance with the Church year and the quality of the celebration. Since these are not designated as solemn, they can be used whenever it is deemed appropriate. The usual form of the Prayers over the People is simple—four to seven lines addressed to God as Lord and concluded with the formula **Through Christ our Lord**, to which the assembly responds, **Amen**.

As with the Solemn Blessings, the usual form is for the Deacon or Priest, after the liturgical greeting **The Lord be with you**, to invite the assembly to bow their heads for the blessing. The Priest with outstretched hands, palms down, extended over the people pronounces the prayer, to which the people respond, **Amen**.

A pastoral difficulty presents itself in cuing the assembly for the response, **Amen**. Several strategies may be employed. A musical strategy would simply be to sing each petition recto-tono and drop down at the end of each petition in order to cue the assembly. However, the formula **Through Christ our Lord**, should facilitate the response. Congruent musical settings for the **Amen** is suggested with the Trinitarian blessing also sung. Or, if the blessing is to be recited, end each petition by raising the voice, so that the inflection bids the response.

6. **Bestow pardon and peace, O Lord, we pray,**
upon your faithful,
that they may be cleansed from every offense
and serve you with untroubled hearts.
Through Christ our Lord.

7. **May your heavenly favor, O Lord, we pray,**
increase in number the people subject to you
and make them always obedient to your commands.
Through Christ our Lord.

8. **Be propitious to your people, O God,**
that, freed from every evil,
they may serve you with all their heart
and ever stand firm under your protection.
Through Christ our Lord.

9. **May your family always rejoice together, O God,**
over the mysteries of redemption they have celebrated,
and grant its members the perseverance
to attain the effects that flow from them.
Through Christ our Lord.

10. **Lord God, from the abundance of your mercies**
provide for your servants and ensure their safety,
so that, strengthened by your blessings,
they may at all times abound in thanksgiving
and bless you with unending exultation.
Through Christ our Lord.

11. **Keep your family, we pray, O Lord,**
in your constant care,
so that, under your protection,
they may be free from all troubles
and by good works show dedication to your name.
Through Christ our Lord.

12. **Purify your faithful, both in body and in mind,**
O Lord, we pray,
so that, feeling the compunction you inspire,
they may be able to avoid harmful pleasures
and ever feed upon your delights.
Through Christ our Lord.

7. This prayer asks God to multiply the number of believers and make them obedient. The thrust is that we not only want more believers, but believers who really believe.

8. This is a penitential prayer asking for God's propitious, or forgiving, mercy.

9. This is a joyful prayer remembering Christ's work in redemption. Perseverance in the Christian life flows from the fact that God has taken the initiative to redeem us in Christ.

10. This prayer bids God for safety and strength so that, with God's blessing, we may bless God in thanksgiving and joy.

11. This is a prayer of care and protection. In asking that God keep us free from troubles, the prayer lends itself to all kinds of situations. But this protection will be translated into our good works dedicated to the name of God.

12. This prayer asks for purification in both mind and body. The word "compunction," meaning the "piercing of the heart," evokes the penitential notion of metanoia, a change of heart. Thus, the prayer bids God to protect us from harmful pleasures.

13. In this prayer, we implore God's sacred blessing to prepare the spiritual sustenance of the minds of all Christians. The desired result is that, with the strength of God's love, this will translate into works of charity.

13. **May the effects of your sacred blessing, O Lord,**
make themselves felt among your faithful,
to prepare with spiritual sustenance the minds of all,
that they may be strengthened by the power of your love
to carry out works of charity.
Through Christ our Lord.

14. **The hearts of your faithful submitted to your name,**
entreat your help, O Lord,
and since without you they can do nothing that is just,
grant by your abundant mercy
that they may both know what is right
and receive all that they need for their good.
Through Christ our Lord.

15. **Hasten to the aid of your faithful people**
who call upon you, O Lord, we pray,
and graciously give strength in their human weakness,
so that, being dedicated to you in complete sincerity,
they may find gladness in your remedies
both now and in the life to come.
Through Christ our Lord.

16. **Look with favor on your family, O Lord,**
and bestow your endless mercy on those who seek it:
and just as without your mercy,
they can do nothing truly worthy of you,
so through it,
may they merit to obey your saving commands.
Through Christ our Lord.

17. **Bestow increase of heavenly grace**
on your faithful, O Lord;
may they praise you with their lips,
with their souls, with their lives;
and since it is by your gift that we exist,
may our whole lives be yours.
Through Christ our Lord.

It is interesting that among the 28 special blessings, not one is for sending forth extraordinary ministers who will bring Holy Communion to the sick and homebound. The prayers in the Missal, however, while not covering every possible situation, provide a model for extemporized prayers. For example, #13 might be adapted to read: "May the effects of your sacred blessing, O Lord, make themselves felt among your faithful, especially those who are unable to be with us today due to sickness or infirmity. May these extraordinary ministers of Holy Communion, who will bring Holy Communion to those who are not with us be strengthened by the power of your love, carry out the works of charity and assure those who are ill and infirm of our love and support and of God's abundant blessing. Through Christ our Lord."

14. This prayer is another penitential prayer that entreats God from the hearts of people that God will grant divine mercy (*hesed*). Mercy, love, truth, and forgiveness are closely linked while describing God. The extent of God's love and mercy are indescribable and unfathomable to the human mind. Often in translation, we need to use a paraphrase to capture the richness of the word *hesed*. So we might say God's merciful love or loving mercy. Loving kindness also would approximate the profound meaning.

15. This prayer asks for help and strength in order to dedicate with complete sincerity. Asking for God's remedies may be a reference to penance, which in medical terminology is the antidote to sin. Reference to "in the life to come" may refer to purgatory.

16. This prayer begs for God's loving mercy (*hesed*). When we ask for God to be merciful, we are also proclaiming God's eternal and boundless love manifested in Christ.

17. In bidding God for an increase of grace, we ask that we may praise God with our lips, with our souls, and with our lives. This emphasizes the aspect of the whole human person.

18. This prayer is penitential in tone. Ultimately, it requests God's loving mercy. The prayer is confident that God's loving mercy will outweigh God's anger.

In addition to the 20 Solemn Blessings, the Missal supplies 28 Prayers over the People to be used in accordance with the liturgical year and the quality of the celebration. Since these are not designated as solemn, they can be used whenever it is deemed appropriate. The usual form of the Prayers over the People is simple—four to seven lines addressed to God as Lord and concluded with the formula **Through Christ our Lord**, to which the assembly responds, **Amen.**

As with the Solemn Blessings, the usual form is for the Deacon or Priest, after the liturgical greeting **The Lord be with you**, to invite the assembly to bow their heads for the blessing. The priest with outstretched hands, palms down, extended over the people, pronounces the prayer, to which the people respond, **Amen.**

A pastoral difficulty presents itself in cuing the assembly for the response, **Amen.** Several strategies may be employed. A musical strategy would simply be to sing each petition recto-tono and drop down at the end of each petition in order to cue the assembly. However, the formula, **Through Christ our Lord**, should facilitate the response. Congruent musical settings for the **Amen** are suggested, with the Trinitarian blessing also sung. Or, if the blessing is to be recited, end each petition by raising the voice so that the inflection bids the response.

18. **Direct your people, O Lord, we pray,**
     with heavenly instruction,
     that by avoiding every evil
     and pursuing all that is good,
     they may earn not your anger
     but your unending mercy.
     Through Christ our Lord.

19. **Be near to those who call on you, O Lord,**
     and graciously grant your protection
     to all who place their hope in your mercy,
     that they may remain faithful in holiness of life
     and, having enough for their needs in this world,
     they may be made full heirs of your promise for eternity.
     Through Christ our Lord.

20. **Bestow the grace of your kindness**
     upon your supplicant people, O Lord,
     that, formed by you, their creator,
     and restored by you, their sustainer,
     through your constant action they may be saved.
     Through Christ our Lord.

21. **May your faithful people, O Lord, we pray,**
     always respond to the promptings of your love
     and, moved by wholesome compunction,
     may they do gladly what you command,
     so as to receive the things you promise.
     Through Christ our Lord.

22. **May the weakness of your devoted people**
     stir your compassion, O Lord, we pray,
     and let their faithful pleading win your mercy,
     that what they do not presume upon by their merits
     they may receive by your generous pardon.
     Through Christ our Lord.

23. **In defense of your children, O Lord, we pray,**
     stretch forth the right hand of your majesty,
     so that, obeying your fatherly will,
     they may have the unfailing protection
     of your fatherly care.
     Through Christ our Lord.

19. This is a prayer asking for God's protection both in this world and the next. It asks for God's providence, due to God's loving mercy. It confidently bids God to grant us the grace to remain faithful in the holiness of life. The prayer is suitable for almost any occasion.

20. This prayer of supplication addresses God as Creator, Sustainer, and Savior. Addressed to God as Lord, the prayer avoids assigning these titles as different modes of the persons of the Trinity. But since the prayer is made through Christ our Lord, we can assume that the prayer is not addressed to Christ.

21. This is a penitential prayer requesting compunction of heart. It asks that the heart be pierced by God's love.

22. This is a prayer of supplication from those who are weak due to sin, but who are seeking God's loving mercy. The prayer expresses confidence in God's generous pardon.

23. This is a prayer of protection. We implore God's defense as a father would protect his children. God's stretching the right hand of majesty is a reference to God as a just judge.

24. This blessing is particularly suited for those in times of struggle who ask for God's perpetual succor. Rather than simply asking for deliverance, we pray that God will help them persevere in confessing God's name even in the face of adversity.

24. **Look, O Lord, on the prayers of your family,**
    and grant them the assistance they humbly implore,
    so that, strengthened by the help they need,
    they may persevere in confessing your name.
    Through Christ our Lord.

25. **Keep your family safe, O Lord, we pray,**
    and grant them the abundance of your mercies,
    that they may find growth
    through the teachings and the gifts of heaven.
    Through Christ our Lord.

26. **May your faithful people rejoice, we pray, O Lord,**
    to be upheld by your right hand,
    and, progressing in the Christian life,
    may they delight in good things
    both now and in the time to come.
    Through Christ our Lord.

On Feasts of Saints

27. **May the Christian people exult, O Lord,**
    at the glorification of the illustrious members of your Son's Body,
    and may they gain a share in the eternal lot
    of the Saints on whose feast day
    they reaffirm their devotion to you,
    rejoicing with them for ever in your glory.
    Through Christ our Lord.

28. **Turn the hearts of your people**
    always to you, O Lord, we pray,
    and, as you give them the help of such great patrons as these,
    grant also the unfailing help of your protection.
    Through Christ our Lord.

This repertory of prayers, which is by no means exhaustive, might also be selected on the basis of the readings in the Liturgy of the Word or on the basis of the feast or liturgical time of the year. Many of the prayers are particularly suited for penitential times.

During the course of the liturgical year, there may be times when special blessings are devised to send forth those involved in special ministries, both liturgical and extra-liturgical. These 28 prayers may serve as a helpful repertory for just such occasions. For example, #26 could be adapted for most ministries by inserting a mention of the particular ministry after the line "both now and in the time to come." Along these lines, one might add: "and especially we ask your blessing on these your servants who serve your people as lectors, readers, greeters, etc." If an existing prayer does not suit the particular occasion or ministry, extemporized prayers following the model of these prayers might be composed. But it is important that the prayers not become too prolix.

25. This blessing is a prayer for safety and imploring God's loving mercy. The NIV translates *hesed* as "mercy" while the NASB translates it as "unchanging love." Notice that the Lord delights in mercy or unchanging love. Hence, God takes great pleasure in showing mercy. God does not retain anger and delights in mercy. The desired blessing is to grow through the teachings and gifts of heaven. Might this be used for blessing students of all ages?

26. This blessing could serve a number of occasions due to its joyful and upbeat mood. This could be used for those who are progressing in faith and who "delight in good things both now and in the time to come," indicating a very positive opinion of God's creation.

27. As we exult in the Saint(s) being celebrated, we reaffirm our devotion to God. This blessing is somewhat generic, but instead of simply saying, "the Saints," the name(s) of the Saint(s) might be inserted.

28. We pray that, by the example of the Saint(s) whose feast is celebrated, our hearts may turn to God. In order to specify this prayer for the particular Saint's day, mention of the Saint's name might be inserted after the word "patrons."

CHANTS FOR THE EUCHARISTIC PRAYER

EUCHARISTIC PRAYER I
or THE ROMAN CANON

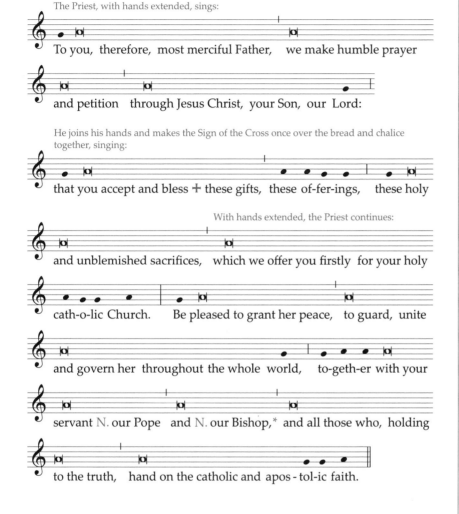

The Priest, with hands extended, sings:

To you, therefore, most merciful Father,   we make humble prayer

and petition   through Jesus Christ, your Son, our Lord:

He joins his hands and makes the Sign of the Cross once over the bread and chalice together, singing:

that you accept and bless ✠ these gifts, these of-fer-ings,   these holy

With hands extended, the Priest continues:

and unblemished sacrifices,   which we offer you firstly for your holy

cath-o-lic Church.   Be pleased to grant her peace, to guard, unite

and govern her throughout the whole world,   to-geth-er with your

servant N. our Pope   and N. our Bishop,* and all those who, holding

to the truth,   hand on the catholic and apos - tol-ic faith.

* Mention may be made here of the Coadjutor Bishop, or Auxiliary Bishops, as noted in the *General Instruction of the Roman Missal*, no. 149.

Find a pitch in your mid-range, then sing from "do" to "re." This will be your reciting tone, and occasionally you will descend to "do."

Te igitur:
Emphasize **Father** as the addressee of the prayer. Emphasize **prayer and petition**.

Emphasize **bless,** and correlate the word with the gesture of blessing. Revel in the appositive phrases **these gifts**, **these offerings**, **these sacrifices.**

Emphasize **which we offer** and **for your Church.**

Notice that Eucharistic Prayer I is structured as a series of discreet paragraphs or parts, each terminating with "Through Christ our Lord. Amen." These parts are identified in the margins by their Latin names, which are derived from the first couple of words in the paragraph. These elements are organized according to a principle, or chiasm, so that the central part of the text is seen as the most important, with parallel elements appearing on either side of this central segment. Thus, for the Roman Canon, the Institution narra-

tive and Consecration appear in the center of the text, where a memorial of the living appears prior to it and a memorial of the dead appears after it, just as a prayer of union with Apostles and Saints appears before it and another prayer of union with Saints appears after it. It is difficult to make that structure clear simply by how the text is proclaimed, but treating each of the paragraphs as a unity may help.

Although the Eucharistic Prayer, as its name indicates, is a prayer of thanksgiving, the Roman Canon, as we presently have it,

is primarily a prayer of petition, beginning with *Te igitur*, in which we pray that God accepts the gifts of bread and wine to be offered with the Church and the Church's leadership. This prayer is not, strictly speaking, a prayer for the Pope and the Bishop. It uses the words "together with" not "for," expressing unity with the Church.

Memento, Domine:
The Priest may wish to name the living individuals, for whom he is offering this Mass, but he is not bound to do so.

Pause after **for them.** Longer pause after **this sacrifice of praise.**

Treat **or they offer . . . dear to them** as one line.

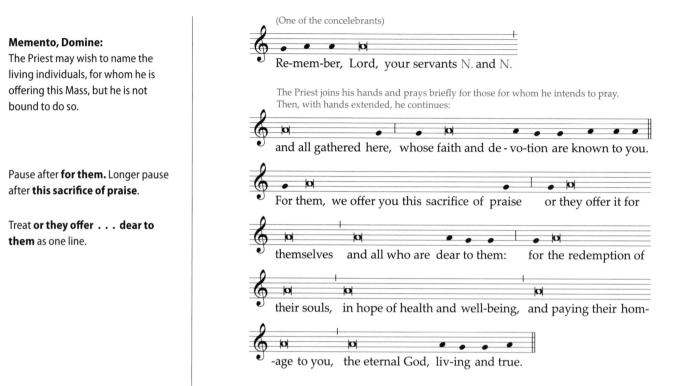

(One of the concelebrants)

Re-mem-ber, Lord, your servants N. and N.

The Priest joins his hands and prays briefly for those for whom he intends to pray. Then, with hands extended, he continues:

and all gathered here, whose faith and de - vo-tion are known to you.

For them, we offer you this sacrifice of praise   or they offer it for

themselves   and all who are dear to them: for the redemption of

their souls,   in hope of health and well-being,   and paying their hom-

-age to you,   the eternal God, liv-ing and true.

Continuing our prayers of petition, we pray on behalf of the living. The Priest may name those for whom the Mass is offered.

Following these petitions for the living, we pray in communion for those who have gone before us in faith (*communicantes*). Twenty-four Saints are named in two groups of 12: 12 Apostles and 12 Martyrs. The list is preceded by a commemoration of the Virgin Mary, who has a special place separate from all the others. Pope John XXIII introduced the name of Joseph into the Canon after Mary's name. Then appear

the 12 Apostles (Peter, Paul, Andrew, James, John, Thomas, James, Philip, Bartholomew, Matthew, Simon, and Jude). Interestingly, Paul is mentioned, along with Peter, at the start of the list of the Apostles, even though Paul never knew the historical Jesus. Peter and Paul are first in the list, because they are considered the foundational Apostles for the Church of Rome.

Then 12 Martyrs follow: first named are early Roman Bishops: Linus, Cletus, Clement, Sixtus, Cornelius, and Cyprian.

Included among them is the North African Bishop (because North Africa, like Rome, by this era used Latin in its liturgical prayer). The Deacon Lawrence of Rome, Chrysogonus, an Eastern Saint, John and Paul, Western Martyrs whose house church was located in Rome, and then Cosmas and Damian, Eastern Saints whose relics were located at a shrine in Rome. It should be clear that this list of Saints is carefully organized and related to the unique set of Saints associated with the city and province of Rome.

(Another of the concelebrants)   (proper formulas, pp. 704-709)

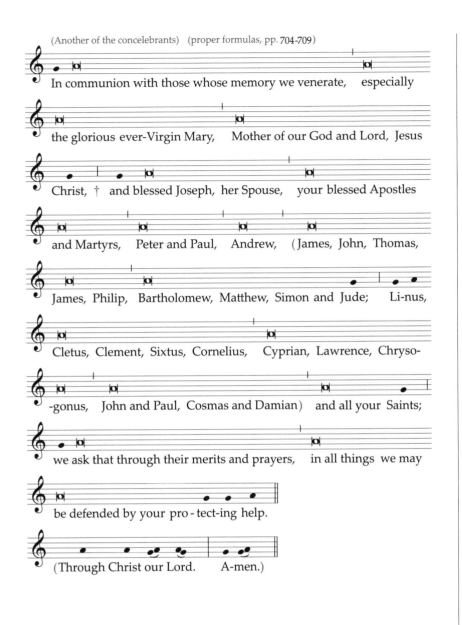

In communion with those whose memory we venerate,   especially

the glorious ever-Virgin Mary,   Mother of our God and Lord, Jesus

Christ, † and blessed Joseph, her Spouse,   your blessed Apostles

and Martyrs,   Peter and Paul,   Andrew,   (James, John, Thomas,

James, Philip,   Bartholomew, Matthew, Simon and Jude;   Li-nus,

Cletus, Clement, Sixtus, Cornelius,   Cyprian, Lawrence, Chryso-

-gonus,   John and Paul, Cosmas and Damian)   and all your Saints;

we ask that through their merits and prayers,   in all things we may

be defended by your pro - tect-ing help.

(Through Christ our Lord.   A-men.)

Communicantes:
Yoke **in communion with those whose memory we venerate . . . we ask . . .**, even though many names may be mentioned between the first phrase and the second.

A Priest may wish to choose Eucharistic Prayer I for Feasts of those Saints mentioned in this list. He would then emphasize that name when reciting the list.

Each of the constitutive parts of the Roman Canon ends with the phrase **Through Christ our Lord. Amen.** This phrase is in parentheses to indicate that it is optional. If you think that the phrase makes the prayer seem fragmented, simply omit it throughout.

In the revision of the Canon after the Second Vatican Council, the number of names that had to be mentioned was reduced, lest the long list be a hindrance to the vernacular proclamation of the text. For this reason, the names that are within parentheses are optional.

Notice that a special form of this prayer of communion (*communicantes*) is to be used on the Nativity of the Lord, throughout the Octave of Christmas, on the Epiphany of the Lord, from the Mass of the Easter Vigil until the Second Sunday of Easter, the Ascension of the Lord, and on Pentecost Sunday. This insertion, called the *infra actionem* (literally within the canon), helps focus the prayer for specific liturgical feasts or times of the year. The rubric *Infra actionem* was originally a heading over variations of this prayer. It resembles the Antiochene Liturgy of Saint James and the Byzantine Anaphora of Saint Basil. Its presence within the Roman Canon probably reflects times when the reading of the diptychs was in use in the East. The diptych, as the term suggests, was a two-leafed folder with names of the living faithful and the dead who were mentioned by name during Mass. Mention of living persons was a strong endorsement of their orthodoxy.

Hanc igitur:
Emphasize **we pray** and **accept**.

Revel in the rhetorical parallels of **order our days**, **command that we be delivered** and **counted among the flock.**

Quam oblationem:
Deliberately extend hands over the offerings and keep hands in place throughout the prayer.

Emphasize **bless**, **acknowledge, spiritual and acceptable Body, Blood.**

Follow the sense lines.

Sing slowly, deliberately, following the commas and sense lines.

With hands extended, the principal celebrant continues (proper formulas, pp. **704-709**):

There-fore, Lord, we pray: graciously accept this oblation of our service, that of your whole fa-mi-ly;   or-der our days in your peace, and command that we be delivered from eternal damnation   and counted among the flock of those you have cho-sen.

(He joins his hands.)

(Through Christ our Lord.   A-men.)

Holding his hands extended over the offerings, he sings (together with the concelebrants):

Be pleased, O God, we pray,   to bless, acknowledge, and approve this offering in every re - spect;   make it spiritual and acceptable, so that it may become for us   the Body and Blood of your most be--loved Son, our Lord Je-sus Christ.

He joins his hands.

Having prayed in union with Saints, especially those associated with Rome, we return to a prayer of petition, asking God to accept our offering, and to grant us the fruits that flow from it. Notice that a special form of this prayer is used in the Masses from the Easter Vigil until the Second Sunday of Easter.

During this further paragraph of petition, the Priest extends his hands over the offerings, praying that they be transformed into the Body and Blood of Christ. This normally would be called an epiclesis, in which we pray to God to send the Holy Spirit upon the gifts to transform them. The prayer is accompanied by hand laying. We find the hand laying in this prayer and the request for transformation. However, there is no reference made to the Holy Spirit. Some might argue that the Holy Spirit is implicit in the hand-laying gesture. But this is unclear.

The absence of a typical epiclesis in the Roman Canon has led some scholars to assume that the *Quam oblationem* ("We pray you, God") is the first epiclesis, especially by those who force somewhat the interpretation of the words "to make this offering wholly blessed," so as to read into them a clear allusion to the Holy Spirit. But the corresponding prayer in the Ambrosian and Mozarabic Eucharistic Prayers is not a consecratory epiclesis in the modern sense of the term which calls this argument into question. Other scholars regard the *Supplices te* (see page 193) as the vestiges of an epiclesis.

On the day before he was to suf-fer,

The Priest takes the bread, and, holding it slightly raised above the altar, continues:

he took bread in his holy and venerable hands,

He raises his eyes.

and with eyes raised to heaven to you, O God, his almighty Fa-ther,

giv-ing you thanks, he said the blessing, broke the bread and gave it

to his disciples, say-ing:

He bows slightly.

TAKE THIS, ALL OF YOU, AND EAT OF IT,   FOR THIS IS MY BOD-Y,

WHICH WILL BE GIV-EN UP FOR YOU.

He shows the consecrated host to the people, places it again on the paten, and genuflects in adoration.

Qui pridie:

The rubric reads "He takes the bread and, holding it slightly raised above the altar." This may seem to suggest that the Priest is impersonating Christ; in fact, the Priest continues to address God the Father. Nor is the Priest to seem to be addressing the bread.

Notice that the rubric before the text "Take this all of you, and eat of it," does not call for the Priest Celebrant to break the host; it simply calls for him to bow slightly.

Until this point, the melody of the words of Institution has been in a two-note pattern. This is introduced with the word **saying**, which rises to the next door note and back to the reciting tone. The words of Institution then begin on the lower "mi" and move above and below "la" to give special emphasis to these words.

The Priest shows the consecrated host. (The rubric does not say "elevate.") The Priest Celebrant genuflects in adoration.

The coordination of texts and gestures for the Institution narrative is very important. The Priest must remember that he is continuing to recount the great deeds of God now focused in Christ Jesus on the night before he died. He should be sure that his gestures and posture do not make it appear that he is addressing these texts to the bread and wine. The Priest's posture should reflect that this prayer continues to be part of a Eucharistic Prayer addressed to the Father.

Although rubrics, such as, "He takes the bread and, holding it slightly raised above the altar," may seem to suggest that the Priest is impersonating Christ; in fact, the Priest continues to address God the Father, here, recounting one of the great deeds of God In history, the Institution narrative. Notice that the rubric before the text, "Take this all of you, and eat of it," does not call for the Priest Celebrant to break the host; it simply calls for him to bow slightly.

Similarly, after speaking the text, the Priest shows the consecrated host. (The rubric does not say "elevate.") The Priest Celebrant genuflects in adoration. Before, as well as after 1970, the rubric in the Missal has the phrase "shows it (the consecrated host) to the people" (in Latin, ostendit populo) not, as some think, "elevates it." If the people are behind the Priest, the traditional way of showing the consecrated host is by raising it above the level of the Priest's head. This showing of the host was introduced in France in the twelfth century and

The rubric reads, "He takes the chalice and, holding it slightly raised above the altar." Again, the Priest continues to address God the Father, and not the chalice. Notice that the rubric before the text, "Take this all of you, and drink from it," does not call for him to speak into the cup; it simply calls for him to bow slightly.

Again, the melody of the words of Institution change from the two-note pattern that has been sung until this point. This is introduced with the word, "saying," which rises to the next door note. The intervals are "la-ti-do-re-do" and the cadence descends back to the "la."

The Priest then shows the chalice. The rubric does not say "elevate." The Priest Celebrant genuflects in adoration.

After this, he continues:

In a similar way, when supper was end-ed,

He takes the chalice and, holding it slightly raised above the altar, continues:

he took this precious chalice   in his holy and venerable hands,

and once more giving you thanks,   he said the blessing   and gave the

chalice to his disciples, say-ing:

He bows slightly.

TAKE THIS, ALL OF YOU, AND DRINK FROM IT,   FOR THIS IS THE CHALICE

OF MY BLOOD,   THE BLOOD OF THE NEW AND E-TER-NAL COV-E-NANT,

WHICH WILL BE POURED OUT FOR YOU AND FOR MANY   FOR THE FOR-

-GIVE-NESS OF SINS.   DO THIS IN MEM-O-RY OF ME.

The Priest shows the chalice to the people, places it on the corporal, and genuflects in adoration.

became general in the Roman Rite in the thirteenth. However, earlier texts speak of a gesture of adoration at the Consecration itself. The genuflection, in place of the previous bow of the head, was introduced only in the fourteenth century.

The actions and words attributed to Jesus in the prayer are not exactly the same as in any of the Gospel accounts of the Last Supper. The raising of Jesus's eyes to heaven is not mentioned in any of the Gospel narratives, though this action (without "to you, God, his almighty Father") is mentioned in the first of the two accounts of the multiplication of the loaves. The words of the Consecration of the wine come mainly from Matthew 26:16; "chalice of my Blood" is adapted from Luke and 1 Corinthians; "for you" comes from Luke, and "for many" from Matthew 26:27–28. The phrase "and eternal," modifying covenant, is found in no New Testament passage.

The command, "Do this in memory of me," is in reference to the entire action and should not seem to reference the chalice only. In 1 Corinthians 11:24–25, we find the memorial command after both the bread and the wine. A pause inserted before the memorial command may help to clarify this phrase.

The Priest's text, "The mystery of faith," functions as a cue for the people to sing the Memorial Acclamation. It is helpful to understand that the Priest's words are an exclamation, not a declaration.

For Eucharistic Prayer I, there are two possible chants for "The mystery of faith." The first is slightly simpler than the second,

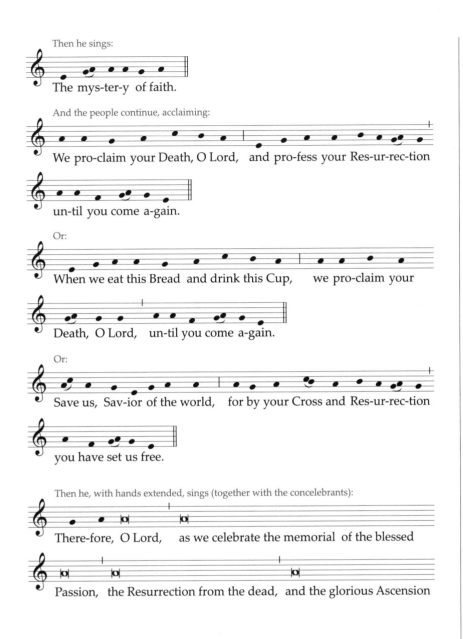

Then he sings:

The mys-ter-y of faith.

And the people continue, acclaiming:

We pro-claim your Death, O Lord,   and pro-fess your Res-ur-rec-tion

un-til you come a-gain.

Or:

When we eat this Bread and drink this Cup,   we pro-claim your

Death, O Lord,   un-til you come a-gain.

Or:

Save us, Sav-ior of the world,   for by your Cross and Res-ur-rec-tion

you have set us free.

Then he, with hands extended, sings (together with the concelebrants):

There-fore, O Lord,   as we celebrate the memorial of the blessed

Passion,   the Resurrection from the dead,   and the glorious Ascension

Mysterium fidei:
The Priest may sing **The mystery of faith,** which will serve as a prompt for the assembly to sing one of the three acclamations.

That there are two formulas of introduction (the other formula is found in the text section of the Missal) and three musical settings for the acclamation suggests that this is inherently a musical item. If the Priest sings, it should be congruent with what is to follow. Therefore, the assembly begins on whatever note the Priest finishes on for the first formula. For the second acclamation, the assembly imitates the Priest's line using the first of the two formulas. The second formula of introduction might be reserved for the third acclamation, since the melodic contours resemble one another. Further, the musical melody also will serve as a cue to signal which acclamation will be sung. If another modern composition is sung, the Priest should verify whether a lead-in was composed for it. It makes no sense to sing a modal lead-in when a tonal acclamation will be sung.

Unde et memores:
Make **we celebrate the memorial** parallel to **we offer to your glorious majesty.** Emphasize **Passion, Resurrection, Ascension.**

suggesting that the first might be used for ferial occasions and the second for more festive occasions. These are correlated to the Memorial Acclamation chants of *The Roman Missal*; but there may be other musical settings of the Mystery of Faith correlated to other musical settings of the congregation's Memorial Acclamations that the Priest should learn. What the Priest sings and what the people sing should be congruent. In other words, if the Memorial Acclamations the people sing are from a contemporary composer, the melody the Priest sings for "The mystery of faith" should also come from that composer.

All three Memorial Acclamations are addressed directly to Christ. It is interesting that the Priest prays in the first person plural, addressing God the Father throughout the Eucharistic Prayer, except during the Institution narrative, during which he speaks in the third person about the Last Supper event in a historical mode. But when the assembly is asked to pray, they address their acclamation to Christ whom they confess to be really present in the Eucharistic species.

In the Eucharistic Prayer, the words of Institution, concluding with, "Do this in memory of me," are followed by a solemn recalling of Christ's Death and Resurrection. "Anamnesis" is the term used to refer to this recalling. The anamnesis then turns seamlessly into a prayer of offering. Liturgical scholars call this section of the prayer the "anamnesis-offering." The Priest expands upon the acclamation articulated by the congregation, calling to mind the

Revel in the parallels **pure victim, holy victim, spotless victim, Bread of eternal life**, and **Chalice of everlasting salvation**.

Supra quae:
Make **Be pleased to look** parallel to **accept. . . .**

Revel in the three names **Abel the just, Abraham our father in faith, Melchizedek**.

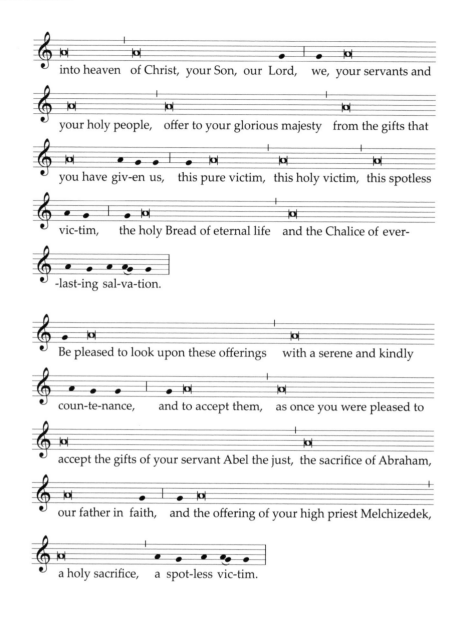

into heaven of Christ, your Son, our Lord, we, your servants and

your holy people, offer to your glorious majesty from the gifts that

you have giv-en us, this pure victim, this holy victim, this spotless

vic-tim, the holy Bread of eternal life and the Chalice of ever-

-last-ing sal-va-tion.

Be pleased to look upon these offerings with a serene and kindly

coun-te-nance, and to accept them, as once you were pleased to

accept the gifts of your servant Abel the just, the sacrifice of Abraham,

our father in faith, and the offering of your high priest Melchizedek,

a holy sacrifice, a spot-less vic-tim.

Paschal Mystery and offers the sacrament of the Paschal Mystery, the transformed bread and wine.

In the original Latin, there is a beautiful poetic play on the word *hostia,* meaning "victim" but also referring to the "host." The word is used three times in quick succession: *hostiam puram, hostiam sanctam, hostiam immaculatam,* translated as "this pure victim, this holy victim, this spotless victim" to capture the sense of the original.

The anamnesis-offering is followed by a prayer for acceptance of the sacrifice. We return to prayers of petition, asking God to accept the consecrated elements as God was pleased to accept some typological Old Testament offerings: the sacrifices of Abel, Abraham, and Melchizedek. These three Old Testament figures serve as exemplars of classical instances of sacrifice acceptable to God and, therefore, models of what our sacrifice should be. In other words, it asks that the oblation of the Church may be like theirs.

Throughout this next paragraph of petitionary prayer, the rubrics instruct the Priest to bow. Some liturgical scholars see in this prayer a "reverse epiclesis," rather than asking the Father to send the Holy Spirit upon the gifts from this altar to the heavenly altar. These same scholars think that the original reference for God's Angel was to Christ, since he is the messenger (*angelos*) between God the Father and humanity. This prayer was believed to once have been a regular epiclesis, in which the Holy Spirit was invoked upon those who are to receive the Body and Blood of Christ so as to sanctify them. It still ends with a

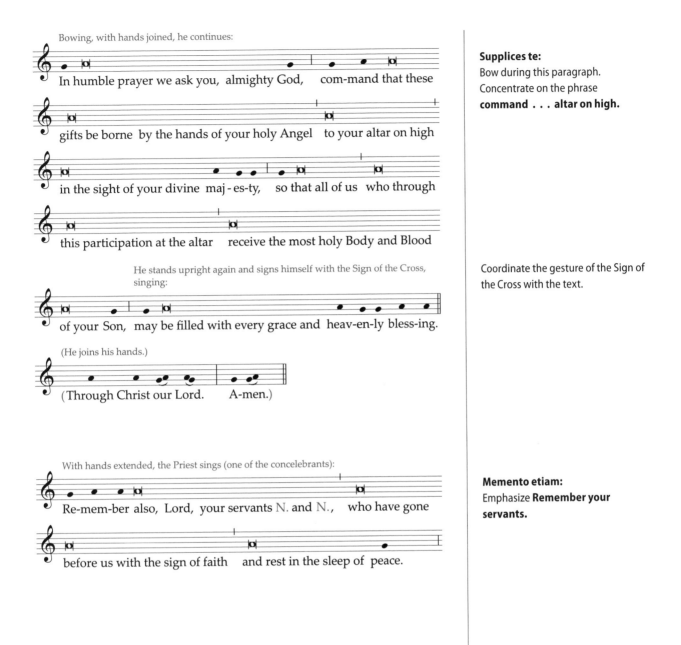

Bowing, with hands joined, he continues:

In humble prayer we ask you, almighty God,   com-mand that these gifts be borne by the hands of your holy Angel   to your altar on high in the sight of your divine maj - es-ty,   so that all of us who through this participation at the altar   receive the most holy Body and Blood

He stands upright again and signs himself with the Sign of the Cross, singing:

of your Son, may be filled with every grace and heav-en-ly bless-ing.

(He joins his hands.)

(Through Christ our Lord.   A-men.)

With hands extended, the Priest sings (one of the concelebrants):

Re-mem-ber also, Lord, your servants N. and N.,   who have gone before us with the sign of faith   and rest in the sleep of peace.

Supplices te:
Bow during this paragraph.
Concentrate on the phrase
command . . . altar on high.

Coordinate the gesture of the Sign of the Cross with the text.

Memento etiam:
Emphasize **Remember your servants.**

prayer that all who will receive the sacred Body and Blood of Christ will be filled with every heavenly blessing and grace. A phrase of Pope Gelasius I (492–496) has been interpreted as indicating that in his time the Roman Canon still had an express mention of the Holy Spirit, such as there is in all other ancient liturgies. He wrote: "How shall the Heavenly Spirit, when he is invoked to consecrate the divine mystery, come, if the Priest [and he] who prays him to come is guilty of bad actions?" (Ep., vii; Thiel, Ep. Rom. Pont., I, 486)—"and he"

corresponds here to the single word *et* in Latin, which may be a scribal error. It also has been suggested that the Angel mentioned here is the Holy Ghost—an attempt to bring the prayer more into line with the proper form of an epiclesis, but the evidence rather is against this interpretation.

Parallel to the earlier prayers of intercession for the living is this paragraph of prayer for the dead. Once again, the Priest may mention the names for whom Mass is being celebrated. The naming of living and deceased people within the Eucharistic

Prayer corresponds to the liturgical use of diptychs, which were a focus of dispute particularly in the East. The diptychs were two-leafed folders containing the list of names for public and official recognition. The inclusion of a person's name was somewhat of a recognition of the individual's orthodoxy and solidarity with the communion of the Church. The persons for whom the Priest prays are called "servants" (*famuli*), a title that, in the first instance, connotes family.

Emphasize **them** and **all.**

Emphasize **refreshment**, **light**, and **peace.**

Nobis quoque peccatoribus:
You are now back to your reciting tone with the two-note pattern. Correlate the gesture of striking the breast with **sinners**.

Emphasize **admit us . . . into their company**.

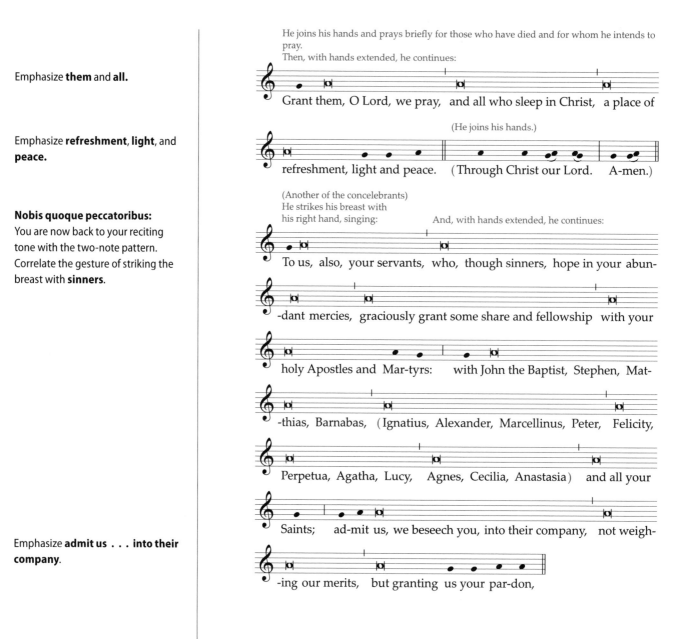

He joins his hands and prays briefly for those who have died and for whom he intends to pray.
Then, with hands extended, he continues:

Grant them, O Lord, we pray, and all who sleep in Christ, a place of

(He joins his hands.)

refreshment, light and peace. (Through Christ our Lord. A-men.)

(Another of the concelebrants)
He strikes his breast with his right hand, singing: And, with hands extended, he continues:

To us, also, your servants, who, though sinners, hope in your abun-

-dant mercies, graciously grant some share and fellowship with your

holy Apostles and Mar-tyrs: with John the Baptist, Stephen, Mat-

-thias, Barnabas, (Ignatius, Alexander, Marcellinus, Peter, Felicity,

Perpetua, Agatha, Lucy, Agnes, Cecilia, Anastasia) and all your

Saints;   ad-mit us, we beseech you, into their company, not weigh-

-ing our merits, but granting us your par-don,

Parallel to the pre-consecratory prayer of communion with Apostles and Saints is this prayer of communion with further Saints. Once again, connection with the Roman Church is emphasized. Notice the seven female Martyr Saints given places of honor in this list. Again, only the first four names are obligatory, lest the prayer become too ponderous. But one can easily add the names of the other prominent Roman Martyrs.

We pray also for ourselves, who are considered "servants." But to this, we add the designation "sinners." In ancient Roman practice, it was common for people to sign documents adding the word "sinner" (*peccator*) to the signature.

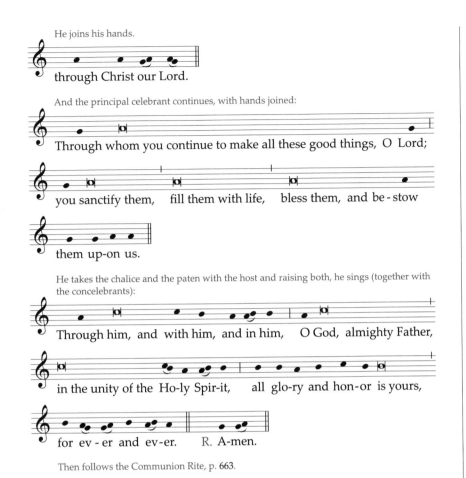

He joins his hands.

through Christ our Lord.

And the principal celebrant continues, with hands joined:

Through whom you continue to make all these good things, O Lord;

you sanctify them,   fill them with life,   bless them, and be-stow

them up-on us.

He takes the chalice and the paten with the host and raising both, he sings (together with the concelebrants):

Through him, and with him, and in him,   O God, almighty Father,

in the unity of the Ho-ly Spir-it,   all glo-ry and hon-or is yours,

for ev-er and ev-er.   R. A-men.

Then follows the Communion Rite, p. 663.

Emphasize **sanctify**, **fill**, **bless**, **bestow**.

For singing purposes, start where you have just ended on your reciting tone and move immediately up a minor third (the distance from "Lulla-bye"). Return immediately to "do." The traditional melody revolves around three notes.

Doxology:
Pause at the commas and the sense lines and continue to increase in volume, so as to cue the congregation's **Amen**.

The paragraph beginning with "Through whom you continue . . ." may seem to be ungrammatical. In fact, it is an extension of the conclusion of the last paragraph lauding Christ as the means by which God the Father continues to bless humanity. In this paragraph, we commemorate the goodness of God, who is described as the one who creates all good things, sanctifies them, endows them with life, blesses them, and bestows them on us. This sentence summarizes God's great gen-

erosity and helps us reach the conclusion of the prayer.

The Canon ends with the great doxology that sums up all the themes of the Eucharistic Prayer in a proclamation of the Divine Name. Everything belongs to God and all honor and glory ascend to him in a Christological movement denoted by three prepositions: through, with, and in. The Holy Name is great throughout the world and put on the lips of the faithful who proclaim God's glory.

The conclusion of the Eucharistic Prayer calls for the Priest to lift the paten with host and the Deacon (or, in his absence, the Priest) chants or recites the doxology. The Missal provides chant setting of this doxology that leads to the community's chanted "Amen"; however, other musical settings of the doxology may be correlated to the congregation's "Amen." The Priest's doxology and the people's "Amen" should be musically congruent, so as to form a seamless garment.

Communicantes:

Variable prayers exist for certain special Feasts and times of the year: to be used on the Nativity of the Lord and throughout the Octave of Christmas; on the Epiphany, from the Mass of the Easter Vigil until the Second Sunday of Easter; the Ascension of the Lord; and on Pentecost Sunday. Each must be adapted if the liturgy is celebrated in the day or at night, on the Feast itself or during the octave. Since this is one of the few variable parts within the Roman Canon proper, make a special point to emphasize this part in terms of modulation of the voice.

PROPER FORMS OF THE *COMMUNICANTES AND HANC IGITUR*

On the Nativity of the Lord and throughout the Octave

Cel-ebrating the most sacred night/day on which blessed Mary the im-maculate Virgin brought forth the Savior for this world, and in com-munion with those whose memory we ven-er-ate, es-pecially the glorious ever-Virgin Mary, Mother of our God and Lord, Jesus Christ, †

On the Epiphany of the Lord

Cel-ebrating the most sacred day on which your Only Begotten Son, eternal with you in your glory, appeared in a human body, truly sharing our flesh, and in communion with those whose memory we ven-er-ate, es-pecially the glorious ever-Virgin Mary, Mother of our God and Lord, Jesus Christ, †

Notice that there are five special forms of this prayer of first intercession *(communicantes)* to be used: (1) on the Nativity of the Lord and throughout the Octave of Christmas, (2) on the Epiphany, (3) from the Mass of the Easter Vigil until the Second Sunday of Easter, (4) on the Ascension of the Lord, and (5) on Pentecost Sunday. This insertion is called the *Infra actionem* (literally within the canon) and it helps focus the prayer for specific liturgical feasts or seasons. It resembles the Antiochene Liturgy of St. James and the Byzantine

Anaphora of St. Basil. Its presence within the Roman Canon probably reflects a time when the reading of the diptychs was in usage in the East. The diptych was a two-leafed folder with names of the living faithful and the dead who were mentioned by name during Mass. Mention of living persons was a strong endorsement of their orthodoxy.

Communicantes for the Nativity of the Lord: This prayer is inserted into the Roman Canon from Christmas Eve throughout the entire Octave of Christmas.

The prayer helps focus on the mystery of the Nativity of Christ and the Incarnation. Special place is accorded to the Blessed Virgin Mary.

Communicantes for the Epiphany of the Lord: The prayer insertion, rather than limiting the feast to the Magi, makes a broad sweep and addresses the appearance of Christ in a human body, emphasizing the Incarnation.

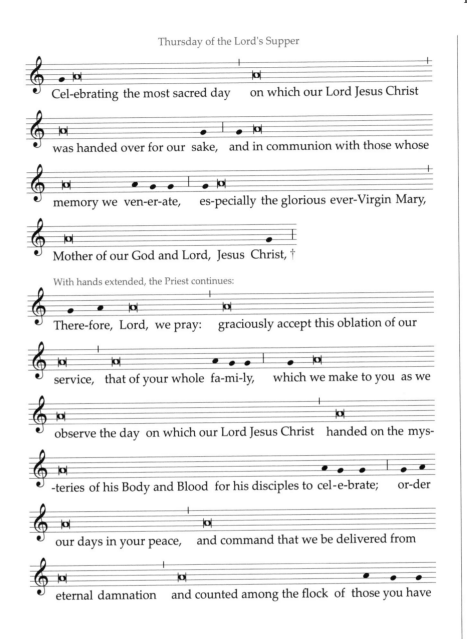

Thursday of the Lord's Supper

Cel-ebrating the most sacred day   on which our Lord Jesus Christ

was handed over for our sake,   and in communion with those whose

memory we ven-er-ate,   es-pecially the glorious ever-Virgin Mary,

Mother of our God and Lord, Jesus Christ, †

With hands extended, the Priest continues:

There-fore, Lord, we pray: graciously accept this oblation of our

service,   that of your whole fa-mi-ly,   which we make to you as we

observe the day on which our Lord Jesus Christ   handed on the mys-

-teries of his Body and Blood for his disciples to cel-e-brate;   or-der

our days in your peace,   and command that we be delivered from

eternal damnation   and counted among the flock of those you have

Communicantes:
On Holy Thursday, given the Eucharistic nature of the Feast, a series of variable prayers exist. Since several parts of the Eucharistic Prayer must be adapted for this special feast. Thus, the *Communicantes* through the words of Institution (for the bread) are reproduced in two places: within the Proper of Time for Holy Thursday and in the section of chants for the Eucharistic Prayer.

Hanc igitur:
Holy Thursday is unique because, in addition to the *Communicantes*, the *Hanc igitur* is adapted to take into consideration the special nature of this Feast when Jesus instituted the Eucharist.

Communicantes and Hanc Igitur for Holy Thursday: The *Missale Romanum* has a special *communicantes* and *hanc igitur* for Holy Thursday, but rather than placing it with the five other special insertions (Christmas, Epiphany, Easter, Ascension, and Pentecost) within the pages of the Roman Canon, we find a full Eucharistic prayer text in the Mass for Holy Thursday in the Proper of Time.

The prayer insertion historicizes the feast of Holy Thursday as the day when Christ establishes the Eucharist and was handed over. In the *Hanc igitur* the next part of the Roman Canon, the prayer is again adapted to make known that it was on this day the "Lord Jesus Christ handed on the mysteries of his Body and Blood . . . ." The text interprets theologically the meaning of this event as delivering us from eternal damnation and counting us among the flock of the chosen. The rich ecclesiology takes into consideration that we are a Eucharistic communion. In other words, we can say that the Eucharist makes the Church and the Church makes the Eucharist. These are correlative realities.

It is interesting liturgically that on the Feast of the Eucharist, the Gospel from John is used that does not reference the meal, per se, but what happens after the meal, namely, the washing of the feet. In a sense, the synoptic version is re-enacted in the celebration itself, which stands in complementarity to the feet washing. For this reason, Holy Thursday is often referred to as Maundy Thursday. Most scholars agree that the English word "Maundy" is derived

The variable parts for Holy Thursday continue with the *Quam oblationem* (Be pleased . . .) and the *Qui pridie* (On the day . . .), although this seems redundant.

In the case of the words of Institution, the phrase **that is, today** is added to adapt the prayer for this occasion. After the Consecration of the bread, one returns to the Order of Mass for the chalice. To eliminate awkward page turns, mark the page in advance.

(He joins his hands.)

cho-sen.   (Through Christ our Lord.   A-men.)

Holding his hands extended over the offerings, he sings (together with the concelebrants):

Be pleased, O God, we pray,   to bless, acknowledge, and approve this offering in every re - spect;   make it spiritual and acceptable, so that it may become for us   the Body and Blood of your most be- -loved Son, our Lord Je-sus Christ.

He joins his hands.

On the day before he was to suffer   for our salvation and the salva- -tion of all,   that is, to-day,

He takes the bread and, holding it slightly raised above the altar, continues:

he took bread in his holy and venerable hands,

He raises his eyes.

and with eyes raised to heaven   to you, O God, his almighty Fa-ther,

through Middle English and Old French *mandé*, from the Latin *mandatum*, the first word of the phrase *Mandatum novum do vobis ut diligatis invicem sicut dilexi vos* ("I give you a new commandment; that you love one another as I have loved you."), Jesus' statement in the Gospel according to John (13:34) by which he explained to the Apostles the significance of his washing their feet. The phrase is used as the antiphon sung during the "Mandatum" ceremony of the washing of the feet.

Others theorize that the English name "Maundy Thursday" arose from "maundsor baskets" or "maundy purses" of alms that the king of England distributed to certain poor at Whitehall before attending Mass on that day. Thus, "maund" is connected to the Latin *mendicare*, and French *mendier*, to beg.

Clearly, the feast's double focus emphasizes the Passover meal in which the Eucharist was instituted and the action of washing feet, showing that Eucharist leads to service. In this liturgy we have two commands: "Do this in memory of me" and "As I have done (wash your feet), so should you do." The title Maundy Thursday is doubly important as Jesus demonstrates how to put his words into action.

giv-ing you thanks, he said the blessing, broke the bread and gave it

to his disciples, say-ing:

He bows slightly.

TAKE THIS, ALL OF YOU, AND EAT OF IT,   FOR THIS IS MY BOD-Y,

WHICH WILL BE GIV-EN UP FOR YOU.

He shows the consecrated host to the people, places it again on the paten, and genuflects in adoration.

From the Mass of the Easter Vigil until the Second Sunday of Easter

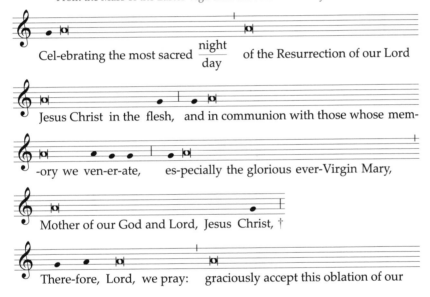

Cel-ebrating the most sacred $\frac{night}{day}$ of the Resurrection of our Lord

Jesus Christ in the flesh,   and in communion with those whose mem-

-ory we ven-er-ate,   es-pecially the glorious ever-Virgin Mary,

Mother of our God and Lord, Jesus Christ, †

There-fore, Lord, we pray: graciously accept this oblation of our

Communicantes:
Variable prayers exist for certain special Feasts and times of the year: to be used on the Nativity of the Lord and throughout the Octave of Christmas; on the Epiphany, from the Mass of the Easter Vigil until the Second Sunday of Easter; the Ascension of the Lord; and on Pentecost Sunday. Each must be adapted if the liturgy is celebrated in the day or at night, on the Feast itself or during the octave. Since this is one of the few variable parts within the Roman Canon proper, make a special point to emphasize this part in terms of modulation of the voice.

Communicantes for the Easter Vigil to Easter II: Given the centrality and supreme importance of the Paschal Mystery within the Christian faith, Easter is given special importance. The special or proper *communicantes* is used, therefore, from the Easter Vigil though the Octave to the Second Sunday of Easter. The text needs to be adapted for the specific time of day when the Eucharist is celebrated. The focus of the *communicantes* is clearly Easter Baptism.

Since Baptism is a rebirth to new life, a spiritual resurrection, it was most fitting that the Paschal Vigil be chosen for the administration of solemn Baptism. This is the reason that, during the Easter octave, the liturgy alludes so often to Baptism to remind the newly baptized, but also all of us, of what Baptism is and of what it demands.

We are encouraged to use the sprinkling rite during the Eastertide but especially during the octave to bring out the baptismal imagery of this time of the litur-

gical year. The text *Vidi aquam* is particularly appropriate to interpret the meaning of the rite: "I saw water coming out from the right side of the temple, alleluia! And all those, whom this water reached, were saved and will say: Alleluia, alleluia!" Then followed a verse from Psalm 118: "Give thanks to the LORD, who is good, whose love endures forever" (v. 1) It contained a twofold allusion to Ezekiel and to Saint John and applied their texts to Baptism.

This water, coming out from the right side of the Temple, naturally suggested the

service,   that of your whole fa-mi-ly,   which we make to you also

for those to whom you have been pleased to give   the new birth of

water and the Holy Spirit, granting them forgiveness of all their sins;

or-der our days in your peace,   and command that we be delivered

from eternal damnation   and counted among the flock of those you

(He joins his hands.)

have cho-sen.   (Through Christ our Lord.   A-men.)

On the Ascension of the Lord

Cel-ebrating the most sacred day   on which your Only Begotten Son,

our Lord,   placed at the right hand of your glory   our weak human

na-ture,   which he had united to him - self,   and in communion with

those whose memory we ven-er-ate,   es-pecially the glorious ever-

Communicantes:

Variable prayers exist for certain special Feasts and times of the liturgical year: to be used on the Nativity of the Lord and throughout the Octave of Christmas; on the Epiphany, from the Mass of the Easter Vigil until the Second Sunday of Easter; the Ascension of the Lord; and on Pentecost Sunday. Each must be adapted if the liturgy is celebrated in the day or at night, on the Feast itself or during the Octave. Since this is one of the few variable parts within the Roman Canon proper, make a special point to emphasize this part in terms of modulation of the voice.

water coming out from the right side of Jesus, who said of his body: "Destroy this temple and in three days I will raise it up" (John 2:19). This water from the side of Jesus was, for many of the Fathers, a symbol of Baptism, figured also by the curative and life-giving water described by Ezekiel, since it purifies from sin and bestows grace, that we may bear abundant fruit (John 15: 8).

Communicantes for the Ascension of the Lord: The Christian teaching about the Ascension of Jesus is found in the New

Testament. The Acts of the Apostles 1:9–11 tells of the Apostles watching as Jesus was taken up to heaven 40 days after the Resurrection. Jesus ascended to his Father and his heavenly throne, and now sits at the right hand of God the Father in heaven. An Angel told the watching disciples that Jesus' Second Coming would take place in the same manner as his Ascension, that is, he would descend in bodily form. This is also described in other biblical passages. Interestingly, this prayer insert focuses on the theological meaning, namely, that

Jesus lifts weak human nature up with him and leads us into communion with God. Jesus prepares a place for us at the right hand of God amidst all the saved. God's right hand is the privileged place for those who have escaped harsh judgment.

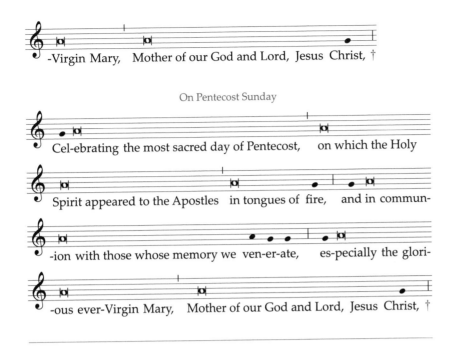

On Pentecost Sunday

-Virgin Mary, Mother of our God and Lord, Jesus Christ, †

Cel-ebrating the most sacred day of Pentecost, on which the Holy

Spirit appeared to the Apostles in tongues of fire, and in commun-

-ion with those whose memory we ven-er-ate, es-pecially the glori-

-ous ever-Virgin Mary, Mother of our God and Lord, Jesus Christ, †

Communicantes:
Variable prayers exist for certain special Feasts and times of the year: to be used on the Nativity of the Lord and throughout the Octave of Christmas; on the Epiphany, from the Mass of the Easter Vigil until the Second Sunday of Easter; the Ascension of the Lord; and on Pentecost Sunday. Each must be adapted if the liturgy is celebrated in the day or at night, on the feast itself or during the octave. Since this is one of the few variable parts within the Roman Canon proper, make a special point to emphasize this part in terms of modulation of the voice.

Communicantes for Pentecost:
Pentecost, from the Greek for 50, is one of the prominent Feasts commemorating the descent of the Holy Spirit upon the disciples of Christ after the Resurrection. The feast is also called Whitsunday, especially in the United Kingdom. Pentecost is celebrated seven weeks (50 days) after Easter Sunday, hence its name. This corresponds to the Lucan version of the giving of the Holy Spirit, whereas, in John's Gospel account, the Holy Spirit is bestowed on Easter, the day of his Resurrection.

Pentecost is historically and symbolically related to the Jewish harvest festival of Shavuot, which commemorates God's giving the Ten Commandments at Mount Sinai, 50 days after the Exodus. Among Christians, Pentecost commemorates the descent of the Holy Spirit upon the Apostles and other followers of Jesus in the form of a mighty wind and tongues of fire as described in the New Testament (Acts of the Apostles 2:1–31). For this reason, Pentecost is sometimes described as the "Birthday of the Church".

Notice the special place accorded to Mary in all these prayer inversions. She is acclaimed as glorious ever Virgin and Mother of Jesus. The † indicates that she is at the head of a long list of Saints who also have configured their lives to the life of Christ. The list can be abbreviated according to need and desire.

In addition to the ordinary tone, the Missal provides a solemn tone to mark degrees of solemnity. Find a pitch in your mid-range, then sing from "do" to "re." This will be your reciting tone, and occasionally you will descend to "do."

Te igitur:
Emphasize **Father** as the addressee of the prayer. Emphasize **prayer** and **petition**.

Emphasize **bless**, and correlate the word with the gesture of blessing. Revel in the appositive phrases **these gifts**, **these offerings**, **these sacrifices**.

Emphasize **which we offer** and **for your Church**.

EUCHARISTIC PRAYER I
or THE ROMAN CANON
(Solemn Tone)

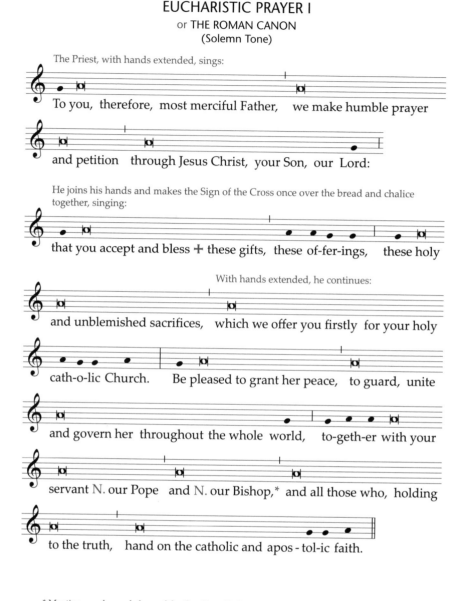

The Priest, with hands extended, sings:

To you, therefore, most merciful Father, we make humble prayer and petition through Jesus Christ, your Son, our Lord:

He joins his hands and makes the Sign of the Cross once over the bread and chalice together, singing:

that you accept and bless ✝ these gifts, these of-fer-ings, these holy

With hands extended, he continues:

and unblemished sacrifices, which we offer you firstly for your holy cath-o-lic Church. Be pleased to grant her peace, to guard, unite and govern her throughout the whole world, to-geth-er with your servant N. our Pope and N. our Bishop,* and all those who, holding to the truth, hand on the catholic and apos-tol-ic faith.

* Mention may be made here of the Coadjutor Bishop, or Auxiliary Bishops, as noted in the *General Instruction of the Roman Missal*, no. 149.

Notice that Eucharistic Prayer I is structured as a series of discreet paragraphs (indicated in the margins in bold print). The Latin names are derived from the first couple of words for each of these paragraphs and many of the paragraphs conclude with the formula "Through Christ our Lord," eliciting an "Amen." This formula, however, is placed within parentheses, indicating that it is optional. It may be omitted if you feel its inclusion causes fragmentation. These paragraphs are organized according to a principle, or chiasm, so that the central part of the text is seen as the most important with parallel elements appearing on either side of this central segment. Thus, for the Roman Canon, the Institution narrative and Consecration appear in the center of the text, with a memorial of the living appearing prior to the narrative and a memorial of the dead after the narrative, just as a prayer of union with Apostles and Saints appears before it and another prayer of union with Saints appears after it. It is difficult to make that structure clear simply by the way one proclaims the text, but treating each of the paragraphs as a unity may help.

Although the Eucharistic Prayer, as its name indicates, is a prayer of thanksgiving, the Roman Canon, as we presently have it, is primarily a prayer of petition, beginning with article 84, in which we pray that God accepts the gifts of bread and wine to be offered for the Church and the Church's leadership.

Continuing our prayers of petition, we pray on behalf of the living. The Priest may name those for whom the Mass is offered.

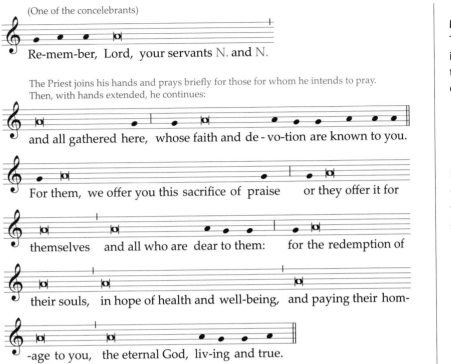

(One of the concelebrants)

Re-mem-ber, Lord, your servants N. and N.

The Priest joins his hands and prays briefly for those for whom he intends to pray.
Then, with hands extended, he continues:

and all gathered here, whose faith and de - vo-tion are known to you.

For them, we offer you this sacrifice of praise   or they offer it for

themselves   and all who are dear to them: for the redemption of

their souls,   in hope of health and well-being,   and paying their hom-

-age to you,   the eternal God, liv-ing and true.

Memento, Domine:
The Priest may wish to name living individuals, for whom he is offering this Mass, but he is not bound to do so.

Pause after **For them**. Longer pause after **this sacrifice of praise**.

Treat **or they offer . . . dear to them** as one line.

Praying for the living may reflect the early Christian use of diptychs in the liturgy. In early Christianity, it was customary to write on diptychs (meaning two panels, pages, or leaves) the names of those, living or dead, who were considered as members of the Church a signal evidence of the doctrine of the Communion of Saints; hence, the terms "diptychs of the living" and "diptychs of the dead." Such liturgical diptychs varied in shape and dimension. Their use (*sacrae tabulae, matriculae, libri vivorum et mortuorum*) is attested in the writings of Saint Cyprian (third century) and by the history of Saint John Chrysostom (fourth century). They did not disappear from the churches until the twelfth century in the West and the fourteenth century in the East. In the ecclesiastical life of antiquity, these liturgical diptychs served various purposes. It is probable that the names of the baptized were written on diptychs, which were thus a kind of baptismal register. The "diptychs of the living" would include the names of the Pope, Bishops, and illustrious persons, both lay and ecclesiastical, of the benefactors of a Church, and of those who offered the Holy Sacrifice.

Communicantes:
Yoke **In communion with those whose memory we venerate . . . we ask . . .** , even though many names may be mentioned between the first phrase and the second.

A Priest may wish to choose Eucharistic Prayer I for Feasts of those Saints mentioned in this list. He would then emphasize that name while reciting the list.

Each of the constitutive parts of the Roman Canon ends with the phrase **Through Christ our Lord. Amen.** This phrase is in parentheses to indicate that it is optional. If you think that it makes the prayer feel fragmented, simply omit it.

(Another of the concelebrants)   (proper formulas, pp. **704-709**)

In communion with those whose memory we venerate,   especially the glorious ever-Virgin Mary,   Mother of our God and Lord, Jesus Christ, † and blessed Joseph, her Spouse,   your blessed Apostles and Martyrs,   Peter and Paul,   Andrew,   (James, John, Thomas, James, Philip,   Bartholomew, Matthew, Simon and Jude;   Li-nus, Cletus, Clement, Sixtus, Cornelius,   Cyprian, Lawrence, Chryso--gonus,   John and Paul, Cosmas and Damian)   and all your Saints; we ask that through their merits and prayers,   in all things we may be defended by your pro - tect-ing help.

(Through Christ our Lord.   A-men.)

Following these petitions for the living, we pray in communion for those who have gone before us in faith (*communicantes*). Twenty-four Saints are named in two groups of 12: 12 Apostles and 12 Martyrs. The list is preceded by a commemoration of the Virgin Mary, who has a special place separate from the others. Pope John XXIII introduced the name of Joseph into the Canon following Mary's name. Then appear the 12 Apostles (Peter, Paul, Andrew, James, John, Thomas, James, Philip, Bartholomew, Matthew, Simon, and

Jude). Interestingly, Paul is mentioned along with Peter at the start of the list of the Apostles, even though Paul never knew the historical Jesus. Peter and Paul are first in the list because they are considered the foundational Apostles for the Church of Rome.

Then 12 Martyrs follow: first named are early Roman Bishops: Linus, Cletus, Clement, Sixtus, Cornelius, and Cyprian. Included among them is the North African bishop (because North Africa, like Rome, by this era used Latin in Its liturgical

prayer). Named after the Bishops are: Deacon Lawrence of Rome; Chrysogonus, an Eastern Saint; John and Paul, Western Martyrs whose house church was located in Rome; and then Cosmas and Damian, Eastern Saints, whose relics were located at a shrine in Rome. It should be clear that this list of Saints is carefully organized and related to the unique set of Saints associated with the city and province of Rome.

In the revision of the Canon after the Second Vatican Council, the number of names that had to be mentioned was

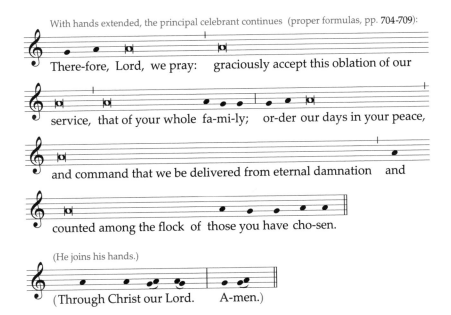

With hands extended, the principal celebrant continues (proper formulas, pp. 704-709):

There-fore, Lord, we pray: graciously accept this oblation of our service, that of your whole fa-mi-ly; or-der our days in your peace, and command that we be delivered from eternal damnation and counted among the flock of those you have cho-sen.

(He joins his hands.)

(Through Christ our Lord.   A-men.)

Hanc igitur:
Emphasize **we pray** and **accept**.

Revel in the rhetorical parallels of **order our days**, **command that we be delivered**, and **counted among the flock**.

reduced, lest the long list be a hindrance to the vernacular proclamation of the text. For this reason, the names within parentheses are optional.

Notice that there is a special form of this prayer of communion (*communicantes*) to be used on the Nativity of the Lord and throughout the Octave of Christmas, on the Epiphany, from the Mass of the Easter Vigil until the Second Sunday of Easter, the Ascension of the Lord, and on Pentecost Sunday. This helps focus the prayer for specific liturgical feasts or times of the year.

Having prayed in union with Saints, especially those associated with Rome, we return to a prayer of petition, asking God to accept our offering, and to grant us the fruits that flow from it. Notice that a special form of this prayer (*Hanc igitur*) is used in the Masses from the Easter Vigil until the Second Sunday of Easter.

In general, the Roman Canon is invariable. Only the *communicantes* changes on five occasions, but the alteration of the *Hanc Igitur* during the Easter Octave points to the supreme importance of the Paschal

Feast. Additionally, a more extensive adaptation of the Eucharistic Prayer is made on Holy Thursday, the feast of the institution of the Eucharist.

During this further paragraph of petition, the Priest extends his hands over the offerings, praying that they be transformed into the Body and Blood of Christ. This normally would be called an epiclesis, in which we pray to God to send the Holy Spirit upon the gifts to transform them. The prayer is accompanied by hand laying. We find the hand laying in this prayer and the

The melodic line becomes more complex here to reflect the solemn nature of this tone. Often two notes are used per syllable.

Quam oblationem:
Deliberately extend hands over the offerings and keep them in place throughout the prayer.

Emphasize **bless, acknowledge, spiritual,** and **acceptable body, blood.**

Follow the sense lines.

Sing slowly, deliberately, following the commas and sense lines.

Qui pridie:
The rubric reads "He takes the bread and, holding it slightly raised above the altar." This may seem to suggest that the Priest is impersonating Christ; in fact, the Priest continues to address God the Father. Notice that the rubric before the text "Take this all of you, and eat of it," does not call for the Priest Celebrant to break the host; it simply calls for him to bow slightly.

Holding his hands extended over the offerings, he sings (together with the concelebrants):

Be pleased, O God, we pray,   to bless, acknowledge, and approve this offering in ev'-ry re-spect;   make it spiritual and ac-cept-a-ble, so that it may become for us   the Body and Blood of your most belov--ed Son, our Lord Je-sus Christ.

He joins his hands.

On the day before he was to suf-fer,

He takes the bread and, holding it slightly raised above the altar, continues:

he took bread in his holy and vener - a-ble hands,

He raises his eyes.

and with eyes raised to hea-ven   to you, O God, his al - might-y Fa-ther,   giv-ing you thanks, he said the blessing,   broke the bread and gave it to his disciples, say-ing:

request for transformation. However, there is no reference made to the Holy Spirit. Some might argue that the Holy Spirit is implicit in the hand-laying gesture. But this is unclear.

The absence of a typical epiclesis in the Roman Canon has led some scholars to assume that the *Quam oblationem* ("We pray you, God") is the first epiclesis, especially by those who force somewhat the interpretation of the words "to make this offering wholly blessed," so as to read into them a clear allusion to the Holy Spirit. But the corresponding prayer in the Ambrosian and Mozarabic Eucharistic Prayers is not a consecratory epiclesis in the modern sense of the term, so this thought is called into question. Other scholars regard the article beginning "In humble prayer, we ask you . . . ." as the vestiges of an epiclesis. In the fourteenth century, the epiclesis became an issue in the polemics between Greeks and Latins, because all Eastern Eucharistic Prayers included an invocation of the Holy Spirit, while the Roman canon of the Mass did not.

He bows slightly.

TAKE THIS, ALL OF YOU, AND EAT OF IT,   FOR THIS IS MY BOD-Y,

WHICH WILL BE GIV-EN UP FOR YOU.

He shows the consecrated host to the people, places it again on the paten, and genuflects in adoration.

After this, he continues:

In a sim-i-lar way, when supper was end-ed,

He takes the chalice and, holding it slightly raised above the altar, continues:

he took this precious chalice   in his holy and vener - a-ble hands,

and once more giving you thanks, he said the blessing   and gave the

chalice to his disciples, say-ing:

He bows slightly.

TAKE THIS, ALL OF YOU, AND DRINK FROM IT,   FOR THIS IS THE CHALICE

OF MY BLOOD,   THE BLOOD OF THE NEW AND E - TER-NAL COV-E-NANT,

WHICH WILL BE POURED OUT FOR YOU AND FOR MAN-Y   FOR THE

The melody of the words of Institution, like the paragraphs immediately before it, change from the two-note pattern to a more complex pattern of notes. Rather than describing this pattern, it is suggested to listen to J. Michael Joncas sing them on the CD *Learning the Chants of the Missal, Part I: The Order of Mass*, published by Liturgy Training Publications. Other audio aids also are available.

The Priest shows the consecrated host. The rubric does not say "elevate." The Priest Celebrant genuflects in adoration.

The rubric reads "He takes the chalice and, holding it slightly raised above the altar." Again, the Priest continues to address God the Father. He should not appear to be addressing the chalice. Notice that the rubric before the text "Take this all of you, and drink from it," does not call for him to speak into the cup; it simply calls for him to bow slightly.

Again, the melody of the words of Institution, as with the paragraphs immediately before it, change from the two-note pattern to a more complex pattern of notes. It is suggested to listen to one of the audio aids to learn the solemn tone.

The Priest then shows the chalice. The rubric does not say "elevate." The Priest celebrant genuflects in adoration.

The coordination of texts and gestures for the Institution narrative is very important. The Priest must remember that he is continuing to recount the great deeds of God now focused in Christ Jesus on the night before he died. He should be sure that his gestures and posture do not make it appear that he is addressing these texts to the bread and wine. The Priest's posture should reflect that this prayer continues to be part of a Eucharistic Prayer addressed to the Father.

Although rubrics such as "He takes the bread and, holding it slightly raised above the altar" suggest that the Priest is impersonating Christ; in fact, the Priest continues to address God the Father, here, recounting one of the great deeds of God In history, the institution narrative. Notice that the rubric before the text "Take this all of you, and eat of it," does not call for the Priest Celebrant to break the host; it simply calls for him to bow slightly.

Similarly, after speaking the text, the Priest show the consecrated host. The

rubric does not say "elevate." The Priest celebrant genuflects in adoration.

The command "Do this in memory of me" is in reference to the entire action and should not seem to reference the chalice only. In 1 Corinthians 11: 24–25, we find the memorial command after both the bread and the wine. A pause inserted before the memorial command may help to clarify this phrase.

The Priest's text, "The mystery of faith," functions as a cue for the people to sing the Memorial Acclamation. It is helpful

Mysterium fidei:

The Priest may sing **The mystery of faith**, which will serve as a prompt for the assembly to sing one of the three acclamations.

That there are two formulas of introduction and three musical settings for the acclamation suggests that this is inherently a musical item. If the Priest sings, it should be congruent with what is to follow. Therefore, the assembly begins on whatever note the Priest finishes on for the first formula. For the second acclamation, the assembly imitates the Priest's line, using the first of the two formulas. The second formula of introduction might be reserved for the third acclamation, since the melodic contours resemble one another. Further, the musical melody also will serve as a cue to signal which acclamation will be sung. If another modern composition is being sung, the Priest should verify whether a lead-in was composed. It makes no sense to sing a modal lead-in when a tonal acclamation will be sung.

FOR-GIVE-NESS OF SINS.   DO THIS IN MEM-O-RY OF ME.

The Priest shows the chalice to the people, places it on the corporal, and genuflects in adoration.

Then he sings:

The mys-ter-y of faith.

Or:

The mys-ter-y of faith.

And the people continue, acclaiming:

We pro-claim your Death, O Lord, and pro-fess your Res-ur-rec-tion un-til you come a-gain.

Or:

When we eat this Bread and drink this Cup, we pro-claim your Death, O Lord, un-til you come a-gain.

Or:

Save us, Sav-ior of the world, for by your Cross and Res-ur-rec-tion you have set us free.

to understand that the Priest's words are actually an exclamation, not a declaration.

The chant for the Priest's text is correlated to the Memorial Acclamation chants of the Missal; but there may be other musical settings of the Mystery of Faith correlated to other musical settings of the congregation's Memorial Acclamation that the Priest should learn. What the Priest sings and what the people sing should be congruent. In other words, if the Memorial Acclamations the people sing is from a contemporary composer, the melody the

Priest sings for "The mystery of faith" should also come from that composer.

The three acclamation of faith are addressed directly to Christ. It is interesting that the Priest addresses God the Father throughout the Eucharistic Prayer, except during the Institution narrative, during which he speaks of the Last Supper event in a historical mode. When the assembly is asked to pray, their acclamation is addressed to Christ.

Liturgical scholars call this section of the prayer the "anamnesis-offering." The

Priest expands upon the acclamation articulated by the congregation, calling to mind the Paschal Mystery and offers the Sacrament of the Paschal Mystery, the transformed bread and wine.

The anamnesis-offering is followed by a prayer for acceptance of the sacrifice. We return to prayers of petition, asking God to accept the consecrated elements as God was pleased to accept some typological Old Testament offerings: the sacrifices of Abel, Abraham, and Melchizedek. These three serve as exemplars of classical

Then he, with hands extended, sings (together with the concelebrants):

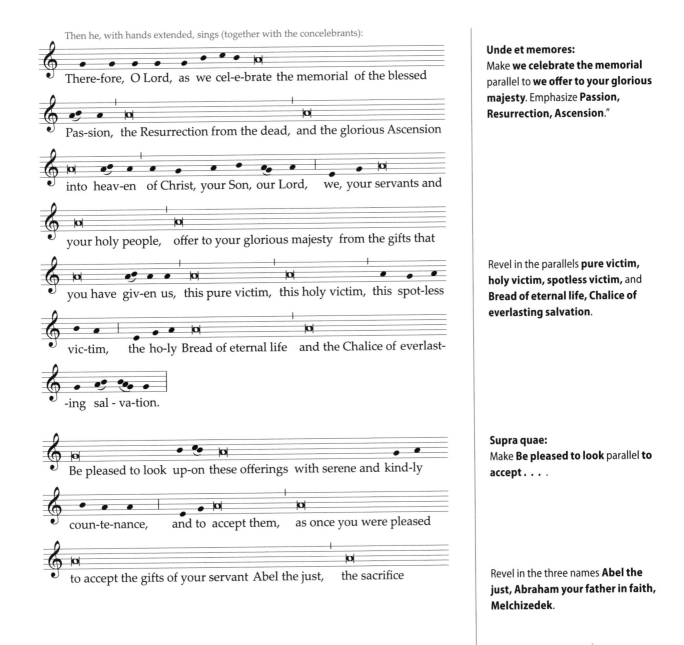

There-fore, O Lord, as we cel-e-brate the memorial of the blessed

Pas-sion, the Resurrection from the dead, and the glorious Ascension

into heav-en of Christ, your Son, our Lord,   we, your servants and

your holy people,   offer to your glorious majesty from the gifts that

you have giv-en us, this pure victim, this holy victim, this spot-less

vic-tim,   the ho-ly Bread of eternal life and the Chalice of everlast-

-ing sal - va-tion.

Be pleased to look up-on these offerings with serene and kind-ly

coun-te-nance,   and to accept them,   as once you were pleased

to accept the gifts of your servant Abel the just,   the sacrifice

Unde et memores:
Make **we celebrate the memorial** parallel to **we offer to your glorious majesty.** Emphasize **Passion, Resurrection, Ascension.**"

Revel in the parallels **pure victim, holy victim, spotless victim,** and **Bread of eternal life, Chalice of everlasting salvation.**

Supra quae:
Make **Be pleased to look** parallel **to accept . . . .**

Revel in the three names **Abel the just, Abraham your father in faith, Melchizedek.**

instances of sacrifice acceptable to God and, therefore, models of what our sacrifice should be.

This refers to Genesis 14:17–20, which says: "When Abram returned from his victory over Chedorlaomer and the kings who were allied with him, the king of Sodom went out to greet him in the Valley of Shaveh, (that is, the King's Valley). Melchizedek, king of Salem, brought out bread and wine, and being a priest of God Most High, he blessed Abram with these words:

Blessed be Abram by God Most High,
   the creator of heaven and earth;
And blessed be God Most High,
   who delivered your foes
      into your hand.'

As a "priest of God Most High," Melchizedek "brought out bread and wine." This is regarded as a foretelling of Jesus' sacrifice also in bread and wine.

of Abra - ham, our fa-ther in faith,   and the offering of your high

priest Mel - chiz-e-dek,   a holy sacrifice, a spot-less vic-tim.

Bowing, with hands joined, he continues:

In hum-ble prayer we ask you, almighty God: command that these

gifts be borne by the hands of your holy An-gel   to your altar on high

in the sight of your di-vine maj-es-ty,   so that all of us, who through

this participation at the al-tar receive the most holy Bo-dy and Blood

He stands upright again and signs himself with the Sign of the Cross, singing:

of your Son, may be filled with every grace and heav-en-ly bless-ing.

(He joins his hands.)

(Through Christ our Lord.   A-men.)

Supplices te:
Bow during this paragraph.
Concentrate on the phrase
command . . . altar on high.

Coordinate the gesture of the Sign of the Cross with the text.

Throughout this next paragraph of petitionary prayer, the Priest is asked to bow. Some liturgical scholars see in this prayer a "reverse epiclesis," rather than an asking of the Father to send the Holy Spirit upon the gifts from this altar to the heavenly altar. These same scholars think that the original reference for God's Angel was to Christ, since he is the messenger *(angelos)* between God the Father and humanity. The purpose of the angelic mediation is to give our celebration the fruitfulness described in 1 Corinthians 10:18. Those who eat of the victims become participants in the altar. We participate in the heavenly altar because we eat at the earthly table.

In the fourteenth century, the epiclesis became an issue in the polemics between Greeks and Latins, because all Eastern Eucharistic Prayers included an invocation of the Holy Spirit while the Roman canon of the Mass did not. Most modern scholars agree that there had been an epiclesis, in the original Eucharist of the early Church of Rome. Medieval Latin theology, however, allowed for the disappearance of the epiclesis, since it was believed that the Consecration of bread and wine and their transubstantiation into the Body and Blood of Christ took place when the Priest pronounced the words of institution. The question of the epiclesis was debated at the Council of Ferrara-Florence (1438–1445), but no formal definition was made until the Second Vatican Council, which reintroduced an epiclesis in the canon of the Mass.

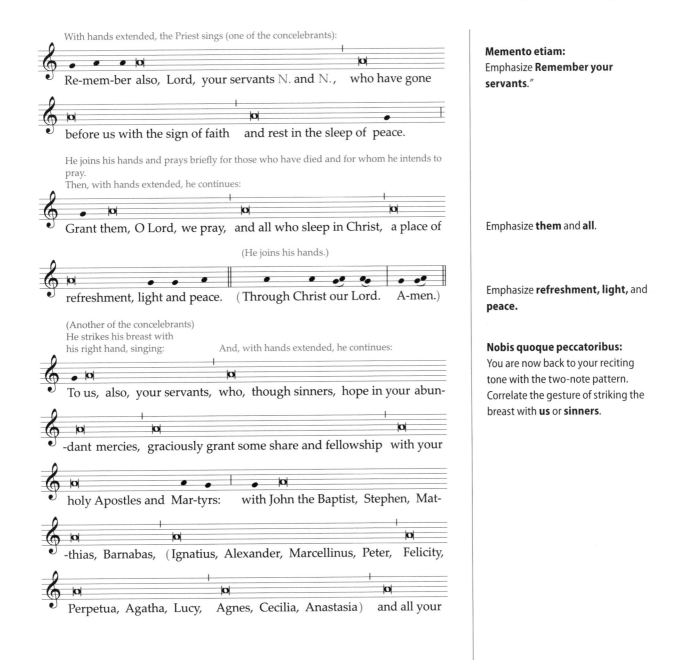

With hands extended, the Priest sings (one of the concelebrants):

Re-mem-ber also, Lord, your servants N. and N., who have gone before us with the sign of faith and rest in the sleep of peace.

He joins his hands and prays briefly for those who have died and for whom he intends to pray.
Then, with hands extended, he continues:

Grant them, O Lord, we pray, and all who sleep in Christ, a place of refreshment, light and peace. (Through Christ our Lord. A-men.)

(He joins his hands.)

(Another of the concelebrants)
He strikes his breast with his right hand, singing: And, with hands extended, he continues:

To us, also, your servants, who, though sinners, hope in your abun-dant mercies, graciously grant some share and fellowship with your holy Apostles and Mar-tyrs: with John the Baptist, Stephen, Mat-thias, Barnabas, (Ignatius, Alexander, Marcellinus, Peter, Felicity, Perpetua, Agatha, Lucy, Agnes, Cecilia, Anastasia) and all your

Memento etiam:
Emphasize **Remember your servants**."

Emphasize **them** and **all**.

Emphasize **refreshment, light,** and **peace**.

Nobis quoque peccatoribus:
You are now back to your reciting tone with the two-note pattern. Correlate the gesture of striking the breast with **us** or **sinners**.

Parallel to the earlier prayers of Intercession for the living is this paragraph of prayer for the dead. Once again, the Priest may mention the names for whom Mass is being celebrated. The naming of those living and deceased within the Eucharistic Prayer corresponds to the liturgical use of diptychs, which were a focus of dispute particularly in the East. The diptychs were two-leafed folders containing the list of names for public and official recognition. The inclusion of a person's name was somewhat of a recognition of the per-

son's orthodoxy and solidarity with the communion of the Church. The persons for whom the Priest prays are called "servants" (*famuli*), a title which in the first instance connotes family.

Parallel to our prayer of communion with Apostles and Saints is this prayer of communion with further Saints. Once again, connection with the Roman Church is emphasized. Notice the seven female Martyr Saints given places of honor in this list. Again, only the first four names are obligatory, lest the prayer become too

ponderous. But one can easily add the names of the other prominent Roman Martyrs.

We begin the next section with a prayer for ourselves who also are considered "servants." But to this we add the designation "sinners." In ancient Roman practice, it was common for people to sign documents adding the word "sinner" (*peccator*) to one's signature.

This paragraph may seem to be ungrammatical; in fact, it is an extension of the conclusion of the last paragraph lauding

Emphasize **admit us . . . into their company**.

Saints;   ad-mit us, we beseech you, into their company,   not weigh-

-ing our merits,   but granting us your par-don,

He joins his hands.

through Christ our Lord.

And the principal celebrant continues, with hands joined:

Through whom you continue to make all these good things, O Lord;

Emphasize **sanctify, fill, bless, bestow**.

you sanctify them,   fill them with life,   bless them, and be-stow

them up-on us.

He takes the chalice and the paten with the host and raising both, he sings (together with the concelebrants):

For singing purposes, start on the reciting tone on which you have just ended, moving immediately up a minor third (the distance from "Lulla-bye"). Return immediately to "do." The traditional melody revolves around three notes.

Through him, and with him, and in him,   O God, almighty Father,

Doxology:
Pause at the commas and the sense lines and continue to increase in volume, so as to cue the congregation's **Amen.**

in the unity of the Ho-ly Spir-it,   all glo-ry and hon-or is yours,

for ev-er and ev-er.   R. A-men.

Then follows the Communion Rite, p. 663.

Christ as the means by which God the Father continues to bless humanity. In this paragraph we commemorate the goodness of God who is described as the one who creates all good things, sanctifies them, endows them with life, blesses them, and bestows them on us. This sentence summarizes God's great generosity and helps us reach the conclusion of the prayer.

The Canon ends with the great final doxology that sums up the theme of the Eucharistic Prayer in a proclamation of the Divine Name. Everything belongs to God

and all honor and glory ascend to him in a Christological movement denoted by three prepositions: through, with, and in. The Holy Name is great throughout the world and put on the lips of the faithful who proclaim God's glory.

The conclusion of the Eucharistic Prayer calls for the Priest to lift the paten with host and the deacon (or in his absence, the Priest) chants or recites the doxology. The Missal provides a chant setting of this doxology that leads to the community's chanted "Amen"; however, there

may be other musical settings of the doxology correlated to the congregation's "Amen." The Priest's doxology and the people's "Amen" should be musically congruent, so as to form a seamless garment.

EUCHARISTIC PRAYER II

Although it is provided with its own Preface, this Eucharistic Prayer may also be used with other Prefaces, especially those that present an overall view of the mystery of salvation, such as the Common Prefaces.

V. The Lord be with you.   R. And with your spir-it.

V. Lift up your hearts.   R. We lift them up to the Lord.

V. Let us give thanks to the Lord our God.   R. It is right and just.

It is truly right and just, our duty and our sal-va-tion, al-ways and

everywhere to give you thanks, Fa-ther most ho-ly, through your

beloved Son, Je-sus Christ, your Word through whom you made all

things, whom you sent as our Savior and Re-deem-er, incarnate

by the Ho-ly Spir-it and born of the Vir-gin. Ful-filling your will

and gaining for you a ho-ly peo-ple, he stretched out his hands as

he en-dured his Pas-sion, so as to break the bonds of death

The opening exchange establishes the dialogical nature of liturgical prayer. Thus, the Priest's lines are intended to elicit the response of the assembly. Vocal intonation and eye contact will help in this regard. The gestures should be correlated to the words.

Emphasize **truly, always, everywhere, thanks.**

Think of the following as invocations in the litany: **your beloved Son, your Word, our Savior and Redeemer, incarnate, born, fulfilling, gaining, stretched out, endured, break, manifest.** By emphasizing these words, we evoke the memory of Jesus under many titles and activities.

When Eucharistic Prayer II was introduced into the euchology of the Roman Rite, scholars believed that the so-called Apostolic Tradition was the work of Hippolytus of Rome and that the Eucharistic Prayer found in the Apostolic Tradition was therefore an ancient Roman anaphora. Contemporary liturgical scholarship no longer holds that the document in which this Eucharistic Prayer is found is the product of Hippolytus of Rome, nor should it be called the Apostolic Tradition but

rather *Diataxeis tôn hagiôn apostolôn (The Statutes of the Twelve Apostles).*

Consensus seems to be that the Eucharistic Prayer of the *Diataxeis* is connected to West Syrian euchological tradition. Nevertheless, the liturgists who constructed Eucharistic Prayer II did not simply reproduce the prayer in Apostolic Tradition *(Diataxeis)* but modified it to fit their understanding of a Eucharistic Prayer. ("The Anaphora of the So-Called 'Apostolic Tradition' and the Roman Eucharistic Prayer," Matthieu Smyth, in *Issues in*

Eucharistic Praying in East and West: Essays in Liturgical and Theological Analysis, edited by Maxwell E. Johnson, Liturgical Press, 2010).

The proper Preface for Eucharistic Prayer II also appears as Common Preface VI. In it, the protocol and body of the Preface structure are meshed. The text looks at Christ's Incarnation and the Redemption, the beginning and end of Christ's life. Not found in the prayer is Christ's public ministry—his work as healer, sage, and teller of parables. We

Emphasize **declare** and **acclaim**, cuing the congregation's Holy, Holy, Holy.

and manifest the res-ur-rec-tion. And so, with the Angels and all the Saints we declare your glo-ry, as with one voice we ac-claim:

At the end of the Preface he joins his hands and concludes the Preface with the people, singing aloud:

Ho-ly, Ho-ly, Ho-ly Lord God of hosts. Heav-en and earth are full of your glo-ry. Ho-san-na in the high-est. Bless-ed is he who comes in the name of the Lord. Ho-san-na in the high-est.

The principal celebrant, with hands extended, sings:

Emphasize **indeed** and **all**. Hands are extended, indicating the summoning of the Holy Spirit.

You are indeed Holy, O Lord, the fount of all ho-li-ness.

He joins his hands and, holding them extended over the offerings, sings (together with the concelebrants):

Emphasize **make holy**. Treat **we pray** as though it were in parentheses. Emphasize **by sending down your Spirit**.

Make holy, therefore, these gifts, we pray, by sending down your Spirit upon them like the dew-fall,

He joins his hands and makes the Sign of the Cross once over the bread and the chalice together, singing:

Correlate the gesture of the Sign of the Cross with the words.

so that they may become for us the Body and ✠ Blood of our Lord

might say that the bookends of Jesus' life are emphasized here. The Priest Celebrant will find here that, because the protocol meshes with the body of the prayer, it is a difficult prayer to proclaim just in terms of length. The opening sentence alone comprises six long sense lines. If the prayer is thought of as a litany (with phrase after phrase describing what Jesus has done), however, the proclamation will be easier.

The short paragraph beginning with "You are indeed, Holy, O Lord" makes a transition from the acclamation to the

invocation of the Spirit. Just as the protocol of the Preface made a transition by adding "truly" to "right and just," so this paragraph makes a transition by adding "indeed" to "Holy." Notice that the Priest should pray this paragraph with hands extended (orans).

The paragraph beginning with "Make holy" represents the epiclesis over the gifts, an invocation to God the Father to send the Holy Spirit to transform the gifts of bread and wine. The Priest should extend his hands over the gifts throughout

the paragraph, making a single Sign of the Cross over the bread and chalice while reciting the text "Body and Blood."

In the paragraph beginning "At the time he was betrayed," the coordination of texts and gestures for the Institution narrative is very important. The Priest must remember that he is continuing to recount the great deeds of God now focused on Christ Jesus on the night before he died, but he should not appear to be addressing these texts to the bread and wine. It continues to be part of a Eucharistic Prayer

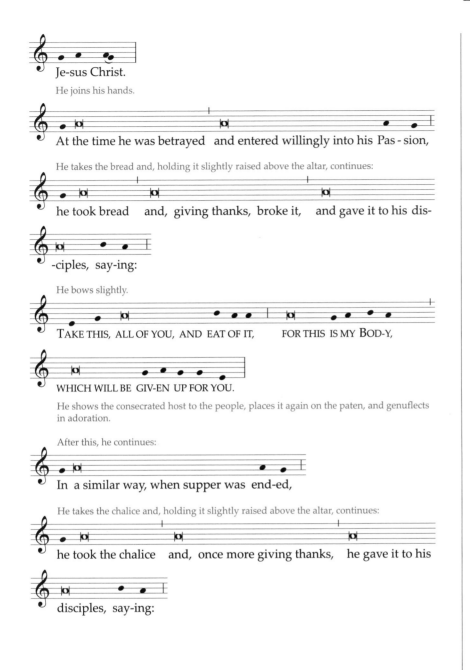

Je-sus Christ.

He joins his hands.

At the time he was betrayed   and entered willingly into his Pas - sion,

He takes the bread and, holding it slightly raised above the altar, continues:

he took bread   and, giving thanks, broke it,   and gave it to his dis-

-ciples, say-ing:

He bows slightly.

TAKE THIS, ALL OF YOU, AND EAT OF IT,   FOR THIS IS MY BOD-Y,

WHICH WILL BE GIV-EN UP FOR YOU.

He shows the consecrated host to the people, places it again on the paten, and genuflects in adoration.

After this, he continues:

In a similar way, when supper was end-ed,

He takes the chalice and, holding it slightly raised above the altar, continues:

he took the chalice   and, once more giving thanks,   he gave it to his

disciples, say-ing:

The rubric reads "He takes the bread and, holding it slightly raised above the altar." This may seem to suggest that the Priest is impersonating Christ; in fact, the Priest continues to address God the Father. Nor should the Priest seem to be addressing the bread. Notice that the rubric before the text "Take this all of you, and eat of it," does not call for the Priest Celebrant to break the host; it simply calls for him to bow slightly.

The Priest shows the consecrated host. The rubric does not say "elevate." The Priest Celebrant genuflects in adoration.

The rubric reads "He takes the chalice and, holding it slightly raised above the altar." Again, the Priest continues to address God the Father, and should not appear to be addressing the chalice. Notice that the rubric before the text "Take this all of you, and drink from it," does not call for him to speak into the cup, it simply calls for him to bow slightly.

addressed to the Father. Although rubrics such as "He takes the Bread and holding it slightly raised above the altar" may seem to suggest that the Priest is impersonating Christ; in fact, the Priest continues to address God the Father, here, recounting one of the great deeds of God in history, the institution narrative. Notice that the rubric before the text "Take this all of you, and eat of it" does not call for him to speak to the host; it simply calls for him to bow slightly.

Similarly, after speaking the text, the Priest shows the consecrated host. (The rubric does not say "elevate.") He then genuflects in adoration. He does the same with the chalice of wine. The rubrics read the same as with the bread. In the music a full stop separates the Consecration of the wine from the Memorial Command. In 1 Corinthians this command follows both the bread and the wine, leading us to understand that the command deals with the entire action, and not simply the wine. A

pause before the memorial command would help in this regard.

The Priest's text, "The mystery of faith," functions as a cue for the people to sing the Memorial Acclamation. It is helpful to understand that the Priest's words are an exclamation, not a declaration.

That chants are provided for the Priest's text and the Memorial Acclamation indicates that the preference is for these texts to be sung. The music for "The mystery of faith and the Memorial Acclamation

The Priest shows the chalice. The rubric does not say "elevate." The Priest Celebrant genuflects in adoration.

The Priest may sing **The mystery of faith**, which will serve as a prompt for the assembly to sing one of the three acclamations.

That there is a musical setting for the introduction and three musical settings for the acclamation suggests that this is inherently a musical item. If the Priest sings, it should be congruent with what follows. The assembly begins on whatever note the Priest finishes on for the first formula. For the second acclamation, the assembly imitates the Priest's line. If another modern composition is sung, the Priest should verify whether a lead-in also was composed. It makes no sense to sing a modal lead-in when a tonal acclamation will be sung. This only necessitates the organist having to intervene with an introduction to establish the key for the acclamation of faith.

chants of the Missal are correlated. There may be other musical settings of the Mystery of Faith correlated to other musical settings of the congregation's Memorial Acclamations that the Priest should learn. What the Priest sings and what the people sing should be congruent. In other words, if the Memorial Acclamations the people sing are from a contemporary composer, the melody the Priest sings for "The mystery of faith" should also come from that composer.

The three acclamations of faith are addressed directly to Christ. It is interesting that the Priest addresses God the Father throughout the Eucharistic Prayer, except during the Institution narrative, during which he speaks of the Last Supper in a historical mode. But when the congregation is asked to pray, the acclamation is addressed to Christ, whom we believe is really present in the Eucharistic species.

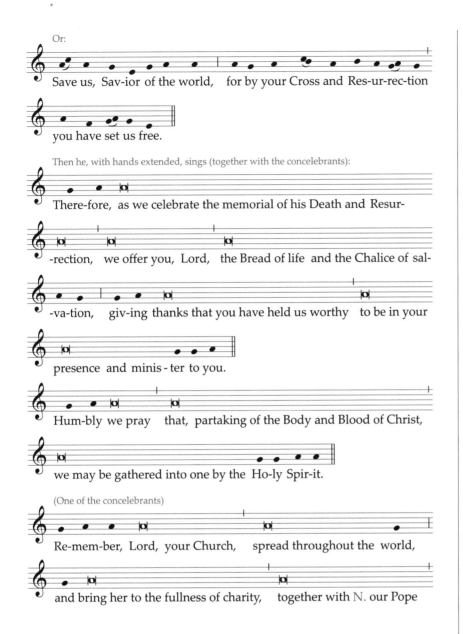

Or:

Save us, Sav-ior of the world,   for by your Cross and Res-ur-rec-tion you have set us free.

Then he, with hands extended, sings (together with the concelebrants):

There-fore, as we celebrate the memorial of his Death and Resur-rection,   we offer you, Lord,   the Bread of life and the Chalice of sal-va-tion,   giv-ing thanks that you have held us worthy   to be in your presence and minis-ter to you.

Hum-bly we pray   that, partaking of the Body and Blood of Christ, we may be gathered into one by the Ho-ly Spir-it.

(One of the concelebrants)

Re-mem-ber, Lord, your Church,   spread throughout the world, and bring her to the fullness of charity,   together with N. our Pope

The Priest resumes the orans position to emphasize that the entire Eucharistic Prayer is addressed to God, whereas, the acclamations of faith are addressed to Christ. In both cases, we use the designation "Lord," but the context and internal references make the designation known.

Emphasize **we celebrate**, **we offer**, **we pray**, **and have mercy** to show the four major elements of this paragraph. The greeting is addressed to the assembly. The Priest Celebrant stands with hands extended.

The paragraph, beginning with "Therefore, as we celebrate" enacts a number of liturgical functions. First, along with the Memorial Acclamation just sung or recited, it recalls the great deeds of salvation, the anamnesis of Christ's Death and Resurrection. Second, it is the means by which the community offers the transformed bread and wine now the Bread of life and the Chalice of salvation. Third, it enacts the epiclesis over the assembly, asking that those who partake in the Body and Blood of Christ may be made one by the Holy Spirit. Fourth, it prays for the Church and her members—the clerical leadership, the dead, the Saints—that all may be brought to unity by the Holy Spirit.

The double or split epiclesis asking that we may become the body of Christ is congruent with the understanding that Saint Paul proffers in 1 Corinthians 12:12–14: "As a body is one though it has many parts, and all the parts of the body, though many, are one body, so also Christ. For in one Spirit we were all baptized into one body, whether Jews or Greeks, slaves or free persons, and we were all given to drink of one Spirit. Now the body is not a single part, but many." This might be a good point to make that Eucharist is both what is on the table and who is at the table. As Saint Augustine said, we are to become what we celebrate. We are to become bread broken and wine poured out for the world.

The intercessions, or remembrances, are in three distinct sections. First we remember the Church spread throughout the world, insisting upon the unity of the

The passage uses the normal two-note pattern with "la" as the reciting tone. Follow the normal punctuation points that correspond in general with the vertical bar lines, to take your breaths. When there is a quarter vertical line, this does not mean breathe but rather lift, putting a little space in the text. This will help for the intelligibility of the text.

Emphasize **hope of the resurrection**, **died in your mercy**, **light of your face**.

Connect **Blessed Virgin Mary, Mother of God**.

and N. our Bishop * and all the cler-gy.

(Another of the concelebrants)
In Masses for the Dead, the proper form of the remembrance of the dead (**Remember your servant N.**) is sung (p. **727**); and, after it has been sung, the prayer **Have mercy on us all** immediately follows.

Re-mem-ber also our brothers and sisters   who have fallen asleep in

the hope of the resurrection,   and all who have died in your mer-cy:

wel-come them into the light of your face.

Have mercy on us all, we pray,   that with the Blessed Virgin Mary,

Mother of God,   with the blessed Apostles,   and all the Saints who

have pleased you throughout the ag-es,   we may merit to be

coheirs to eternal life,   and may praise and glorify you

He joins his hands.

through your Son, Je-sus Christ.

* Mention may be made here of the Coadjutor Bishop, or Auxiliary Bishops, as noted in the *General Instruction of the Roman Missal,* no. 149.

Church rather than churches. In the second section, we pray for the dead. In Masses for the Dead, provision is made to mention the deceased by name. The third section terminates the intercessions with prayers for the living. At this point we commemorate Mary, the Apostles, and the Saints, as among the living.

Within the prayer for the Church, we remember the Bishop of Rome by name as well as the name of the local bishop. *Lumen Gentium,* 26, reminds us that the Bishops are the guarantors of unity among

Christians: "A bishop marked with the fullness of the sacrament of Orders, is 'the steward of the grace of the supreme priesthood,' especially in the Eucharist, which he offers or causes to be offered, and by which the church continually lives and grows. This church of Christ is truly present in all legitimate local congregations of the faithful which, united with their pastors, are themselves called churches in the New Testament. For in their locality these are the new People called by God, in the Holy Spirit and in much fullness. In them the

faithful are gathered together by the preaching of the Gospel of Christ, and the mystery of the Lord's Supper is celebrated, that by the food and blood of the Lord's body the whole brotherhood may be joined together. In any community of the altar, under the sacred ministry of the bishop, there is exhibited a symbol of that charity and 'unity of the mystical Body, without which there can be no salvation.' In these communities, though frequently small and poor, or living in the Diaspora, Christ is present, and in virtue of His pres-

He takes the chalice and paten with the host and raising both, he sings (together with the concelebrants):

Through him, and with him, and in him,   O God, almighty Father,

in the unity of the Ho-ly Spir-it,   all glo-ry and hon-or is yours,

for ev - er and ev-er.   R. A-men.

Then follows the Communion Rite, p. 663.

In Masses for the Dead, the following may be sung:

Re-mem-ber your servant N.,   whom you have called (today) from

this world to your - self.   Grant that $\frac{he}{she}$ who was united with

your Son in a death like his,   may also be one with him in his

Res-ur-rec-tion.

For singing purposes, find a note in your upper-range. This is "do." Now sing down "do-ti-la" to find your opening note. Return immediately to "do." The traditional melody revolves around these three notes.

The doxology is the third and final of the Eucharistic acclamations (along with the Holy, Holy, Holy and Memorial Acclamation). The fact that music is supplied in the Missal strongly suggests that this is inherently a musical item. Pause at the commas and the sense lines and continue to increase the voice in volume, so as to cue the congregation's **Amen**.

ence there is brought together one, holy, catholic and apostolic Church. For 'the partaking of the body and blood of Christ does nothing other than make us be transformed into that which we consume'".

The Eucharistic Prayer ends with the great final doxology, which sums up all the themes of the Eucharistic Prayer in a proclamation of the Divine Name. Everything belongs to God and all honor and glory ascend to Him in a Christological movement denoted by three prepositions: through, with, and in. The Holy Name is

great throughout the entire world and put on the lips of the faithful who proclaim God's glory.

The conclusion of the Prayer calls for the Priest to lift the paten with host and the deacon (or in his absence, the Priest) chants or recites the doxology.

The Missal provides the chant setting of this doxology that leads to the community's chanted "Amen," however, there may be other musical settings of the doxology correlated to the congregation's "Amen." The Priest's doxology and the people's

"Amen" should be musically congruent so as to form a seamless garment.

EUCHARISTIC PRAYER III

The principal celebrant, with hands extended, sings:

You are indeed Holy, O Lord, and all you have created rightly gives you praise, for through your Son our Lord Jesus Christ, by the power and working of the Holy Spirit, you give life to all things and make them ho-ly, and you never cease to gather a people to yourself, so that from the rising of the sun to its setting a pure sacrifice may be offered to your name.

He joins his hands and, holding them extended over the offerings, sings (together with the concelebrants):

There-fore, O Lord, we humbly implore you: by the same Spirit graciously make holy these gifts we have brought to you for conse-

He joins his hands and makes the Sign of the Cross once over the bread and chalice together, singing:

-cra-tion, that they may become the Body and ✠ Blood of your Son

Emphasize **indeed, all** and **praise**. Make a parallel between **through your Son** and **by the power of the Holy Spirit**.

Emphasize **life, make them holy,** and **gather a people**.

Emphasize **sacrifice may be offered**. Revel in the scriptural phrase **from the rising of the sun to its setting,** which has both temporal and geographic connotations.

The first sense line is an introduction to the entire petition. Emphasize **make holy these gifts**.

It is a little surprising that the rubrics for the opening dialogue of the Eucharistic Prayer are not reprinted but are found in #31 (see GIRM, 148).

As with Eucharistic Prayer I, Eucharistic Prayer III lacks a proper Preface and can be used with all the Prefaces in the Missal. It is intended for use on Feast days and Sundays of the year as an alternative to Eucharistic Prayer I. Unlike Eucharistic Prayer I, II, and IV, there is no single ancient anaphora that serves as a model for this prayer. Rather, it combines structures of Antiochene and Alexandrian anaphoras. In its present form, It is clearly related to some proposals that Cyprian Vagaggini offered in 1966 for the reform of the canon of the Mass.

In the paragraph beginning "You are indeed Holy, O Lord," as with the protocol of the Preface, which makes a transition by adding "truly" to "right and just," this paragraph makes a transition from the Holy, Holy, Holy to the epiclesis by adding "indeed" to the "Holy, O Lord." The Priest should notice four things about the text.

First, the act of creation is explicitly Trinitarian. Second, creation includes giving life and holiness. Third, the creation and maintenance of the Church is part of God's activity, and fourth, part of the Church's activity is the ongoing praise of God, as exemplified by the typological reading of Malachi 1:11. "For from the rising of the sun, even to its setting, my name is great among the nations."

He joins his hands.

our Lord Jesus Christ,   at whose command we cele - brate these

mys-ter-ies.

For on the night he was be - trayed

He takes the bread and, holding it slightly raised above the altar, continues:

he himself took bread,   and, giving you thanks, he said the blessing,

broke the bread   and gave it to his disciples, say-ing:

He bows slightly.

TAKE THIS, ALL OF YOU, AND EAT OF IT,   FOR THIS IS MY BOD-Y,

WHICH WILL BE GIV-EN UP FOR YOU.

He shows the consecrated host to the people, places it again on the paten, and genuflects in adoration.

After this, he continues:

In a similar way, when supper was end-ed,

He takes the chalice and, holding it slightly raised above the altar, continues:

he took the chalice,   and, giving you thanks, he said the blessing,

Although it is parenthetical, be sure not to lose the force of the phrase "at whose command we celebrate these mysteries."

The rubric reads "He takes the bread and, holding it slightly raised above the altar." This may seem to suggest that the Priest is impersonating Christ; in fact, the Priest continues to address God the Father. Nor is the Priest to appear to be addressing the bread. Notice that the rubric before the text "Take this all of you, and eat of it," does not call for the Priest Celebrant to break the host; it simply calls for him to bow slightly.

The Priest then shows the consecrated host. The rubric does not say "elevate." The Priest Celebrant genuflects in adoration.

The rubric reads "He takes the chalice and, holding it slightly raised above the altar." Again, the Priest continues to address God the Father, and not the chalice. Notice that the rubric before the text "Take this all of you, and drink from it," does not call for him to speak into the cup; it simply calls for him to bow slightly.

The paragraph beginning "Therefore, O Lord, we humbly implore you" comprises the epiclesis over the gifts. Note that the Priest should extend his hands over the offerings and keep them extended throughout the recitation of the text, except when he makes a single Sign of the Cross over the bread and chalice while reciting the text "Body and Blood."

In the Institution narrative, the coordination of texts and gestures is very important. The Priest must remember that he is continuing to recount the great deeds of God now focused in Christ Jesus on the night before he died. He should be sure that his gestures and posture do not make it appear that he is addressing these texts to the bread and wine. The Priest's posture should reflect that this prayer continues to be part of a Eucharistic Prayer addressed to the Father.

Although rubrics, such as "He takes the bread and, holding it slightly raised above the altar," may seem to suggest that the Priest is impersonating Christ; in fact, the Priest continues to address God the Father, here, recounting one of the great deeds of God in history, the Institution narrative. Notice that the rubric before the text, "Take this all of you, and eat of it," does not call for him to speak to the host. The rubric calls for the Priest to bow slightly.

Similarly, after speaking the text, the Priest shows the consecrated host. The rubric does not say "elevate." The Priest Celebrant genuflects in adoration.

and gave the chalice to his disciples, say-ing:

He bows slightly.

TAKE THIS, ALL OF YOU, AND DRINK FROM IT,   FOR THIS IS THE CHALICE

OF MY BLOOD,   THE BLOOD OF THE NEW AND E - TER-NAL COV-E-NANT,

WHICH WILL BE POURED OUT FOR YOU AND FOR MANY   FOR THE FOR-

-GIVE-NESS OF SINS.   DO THIS IN MEM-O-RY OF ME.

He shows the chalice to the people, places it on the corporal, and genuflects in adoration.

Then he sings:

The mys-ter-y of faith.

And the people continue, acclaiming:

We pro-claim your Death, O Lord,   and pro-fess your Res-ur-rec-tion

un-til you come a-gain.

Or:

When we eat this Bread and drink this Cup,   we pro-claim your

The Priest then shows the chalice. The rubric does not say "elevate." The Priest Celebrant genuflects in adoration.

The Priest may sing the line **The mystery of faith**, which will serve as a prompt for the assembly to sing one of the three acclamations.

That there is music for both the introduction and the Memorial Acclamation indicates that the pieces are inherently musical. The congregation begins on whatever note the Priest finishes on for the first formula. For the second acclamation, the assembly imitates the Priest's line. If a modern composition is sung, the Priest should verify that the composer did not also compose the lead-in to create a seamless fit. It makes no sense to sing a modal lead-in when a tonal acclamation will be sung. This only necessitates the organist's having to intervene with an introduction to establish the key for the acclamation of faith.

The Priest's text "The mystery of faith" functions as a cue. Although many might think of it as a declaration, it is an exclamation. The Missal's chant for this text is correlated to the Memorial Acclamation chants. There may be other musical settings of the Mystery of Faith correlated to other musical settings of the congregation's Memorial Acclamations that the Priest should learn. What the Priest sings and what the people sing should be congruent.

This is the second set of three acclamations (along with the Holy, Holy, Holy and doxology) that punctuates the Eucharistic Prayer. That music is supplied in the Missal for both parts more than suggests that this is a sung element. For this reason, it is desirable that all three acclamations match somehow musically, so as to create a coherent unit. In musical terms, this would be the second great crescendo that will culminate in the doxology and the Amen.

Notice that all three acclamations for the Memorial Acclamation are addressed to Christ, while the Eucharistic Prayer is addressed to the Father.

Death, O Lord,   un-til you come a-gain.

Or:

Save us, Sav-ior of the world,   for by your Cross and Res-ur-rec-tion

you have set us free.

Then he, with hands extended, sings (together with the concelebrants):

There-fore, O Lord,   as we celebrate the memorial   of the saving Pas-

-sion of your Son,   his wondrous Resurrection and Ascension into

heaven,   and as we look forward to his second com-ing,   we offer

you in thanksgiving   this holy and liv-ing sac-ri-fice.

Look, we pray, upon the oblation of your Church   and, recognizing

the sacrificial Victim   by whose death you willed to reconcile us

to your-self,   grant that we,   who are nourished by the Body and

The Priest resumes the orans position to emphasize that the entire Eucharistic Prayer is addressed to the Father. The people's Memorial Acclamation is addressed to Christ.

Though subordinate, emphasize these words **Passion, Resurrection, Ascension, second coming,** so as even more to emphasize **we offer you this holy and living sacrifice.**

Parallel the phrases **Look . . . upon the oblation of your Church** and **grant that we . . . may become one body, one spirit in Christ,** recognizing that **to yourself . . . who are nourished . . . and filled with his Holy Spirit** are parenthetical expressions and should be treated as such.

The texts beginning "Therefore, O Lord, as we celebrate," have multiple functions. Paragraph one comprises the anamnesis-offering. We recall the Paschal Mystery, and in that light, offer to God the "holy and living sacrifice." The second paragraph is an epiclesis over the community asking that those who are nourished by partaking in Holy Communion may become "one body, one spirit in Christ" by the Holy Spirit. In paragraphs three, four and five, we add the intercessions for the living and the dead. We further pray that

the gift of Eucharistic union unites us with the Saints, other human beings, and with the living members of the Church. We especially pray that God would grant mercy to all the dead—Christian and non-Christian.

The double, or split epiclesis, asking that we may become the body of Christ is congruent with that understanding that Saint Paul proffers in 1 Corinthians 12:12–14: "As a body is one though it has many parts, and all the parts of the body, though many, are one body, so also Christ.

For in one Spirit we were all baptized into one body, whether Jews or Greeks, slaves or free persons, and we were all given to drink of one Spirit. Now the body is not a single part, but many." The point can be made that Eucharist is both what is on the table and who is at the table. As Saint Augustine said, we are to become what we celebrate. We are to become bread broken and wine poured out for the world.

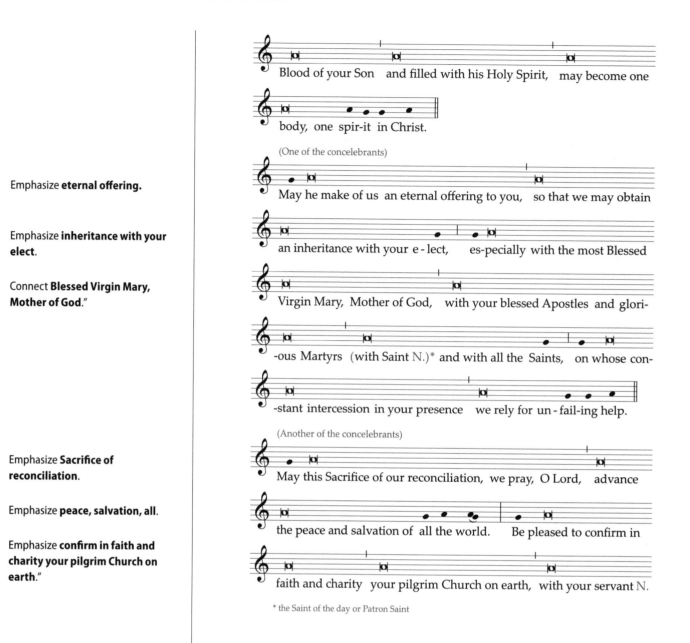

Blood of your Son   and filled with his Holy Spirit,   may become one body, one spir-it in Christ.

(One of the concelebrants)

May he make of us an eternal offering to you,   so that we may obtain an inheritance with your e-lect,   es-pecially with the most Blessed Virgin Mary, Mother of God,   with your blessed Apostles and glori--ous Martyrs   (with Saint N.)* and with all the Saints,   on whose con--stant intercession in your presence   we rely for un-fail-ing help.

(Another of the concelebrants)

May this Sacrifice of our reconciliation, we pray, O Lord,   advance the peace and salvation of all the world.   Be pleased to confirm in faith and charity   your pilgrim Church on earth,   with your servant N.

Emphasize **eternal offering.**

Emphasize **inheritance with your elect.**

Connect **Blessed Virgin Mary, Mother of God.**"

Emphasize **Sacrifice of reconciliation.**

Emphasize **peace, salvation, all.**

Emphasize **confirm in faith and charity your pilgrim Church on earth.**"

* the Saint of the day or Patron Saint

The intercessions are insistent on the reconciliatory dimension of Eucharist that binds all Christians together in Holy Communion. This prayer is reminiscent of the table thanksgiving found in *Didache,* 9, that prays for the unity of the Church using the imagery of grain scattered: "As this broken bread was scattered over the mountains, and when brought together became one, so let your Church be brought together from the ends of the earth into your kingdom."

It is important to remember that the fundamental mission of Christ is that of reconciliation. John wrote, "For this is the message you have heard from the beginning: we should love one another" (1 John 4:11). Reconciling with each other becomes nothing less than a necessary part of our calling.

Paul referred to reconciliation as our ministry or service. We serve as representatives of the kingdom of God. "And all this is from God, who has reconciled us to himself through Christ and given us the ministry of

reconciliation, namely, God was reconciling the world to himself in Christ, not counting their trespasses against them and entrusting to us the message of reconciliation. So we are ambassadors for Christ, as if God were appealing through Christ. We implore you on behalf of Christ, be reconciled to God" (2 Corinthians 5:18–20). We should not forget that Eucharist has a strong reconciliatory dimension.

An aspect of reconciliation is unity of all Christians. *Lumen Gentium,* 8, reminds us of this dimension: "This is the one

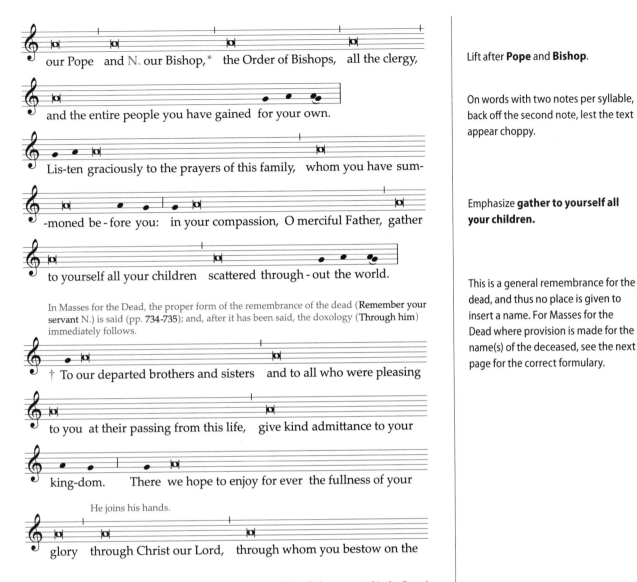

our Pope   and N. our Bishop,*   the Order of Bishops,   all the clergy,

and the entire people you have gained for your own.

Lis-ten graciously to the prayers of this family,   whom you have sum-

-moned be-fore you: in your compassion, O merciful Father,   gather

to yourself all your children   scattered through-out the world.

In Masses for the Dead, the proper form of the remembrance of the dead (**Remember your servant N.**) is said (pp. **734-735**); and, after it has been said, the doxology (**Through him**) immediately follows.

† To our departed brothers and sisters   and to all who were pleasing

to you at their passing from this life,   give kind admittance to your

king-dom.   There we hope to enjoy for ever the fullness of your

He joins his hands.

glory   through Christ our Lord,   through whom you bestow on the

* Mention may be made here of the Coadjutor Bishop, or Auxiliary Bishops, as noted in the *General Instruction of the Roman Missal*, no. 149.

Lift after **Pope** and **Bishop**.

On words with two notes per syllable, back off the second note, lest the text appear choppy.

Emphasize **gather to yourself all your children.**

This is a general remembrance for the dead, and thus no place is given to insert a name. For Masses for the Dead where provision is made for the name(s) of the deceased, see the next page for the correct formulary.

Church of Christ which in the Creed is professed as one, holy, catholic and apostolic, which our Saviour, after His Resurrection, commissioned Peter to shepherd, and him and the other Apostles to extend and direct with authority, which He erected for all ages as "the pillar and mainstay of the truth." This Church constituted and organized in the world as a society, subsists in the Catholic Church, which is governed by the successor of Peter and by the Bishops in communion with him, although many elements of sanctification and of truth are found outside of its visible structure. These elements, as gifts belonging to the Church of Christ, are forces impelling toward catholic unity." Thus the names of the reigning Bishop of Rome and the local ordinary are mentioned as the guarantor of the unity of the universal and local church. Again *Lumen Gentium,* 22, states: "Just as in the Gospel, the Lord so disposing, St. Peter and the other Apostles constitute one apostolic college, so in a similar way the Roman Pontiff, the successor of Peter, and the bishops, the successors of the Apostles, are joined together. Indeed, the very ancient practice whereby bishops duly established in all parts of the world were in communion with one another and with the Bishop of Rome in a bond of unity, charity and peace."

For singing purposes, find a note in your upper-range. This is "do." Now sing down "do-ti-la" to find your opening note. Return immediately to "do." The traditional melody revolves around these three notes.

The doxology is the third and final of the Eucharistic acclamations (along with the Holy, Holy, Holy and Acclamation of Faith). The fact that music is supplied in the Missal strongly suggests that this is an inherently musical item. Pause at the commas and the sense lines and continue to increase in volume so as to cue the congregation's **Amen**.

Then follows the Communion Rite, p. 663.

The Eucharistic Prayer ends with the great doxology that sums up all the themes of the Eucharistic Prayer in a proclamation of the Divine Name. Everything belongs to God and all honor and glory ascend to Him in a Christological movement denoted by three prepositions: through, with, and in. The Holy Name is great throughout the entire world and put on the lips of the faithful who proclaim God's glory.

The conclusion of the Prayer calls for the Priest to lift the paten with host and the deacon (or in his absence, the Priest) chants or recites the doxology.

The Missal provides a chant setting of this doxology that leads to the community's chanted "Amen," however, there may be other musical settings of the doxology correlated to the congregation's "Amen." The Priest's doxology and the people's "Amen" should be musically congruent so as to form a seamless garment. It is the ultimate crescendo of the Eucharistic Prayer culminating in praise of God.

The embolism beginning with the words "Remember your servant" is used only for funeral Masses or a Mass on the day of death itself. Notice that the embolism is structured in three categories: first, for the named deceased person; second, for all the dead; and third, for ourselves, the members of the praying assembly. Appropriate pauses during each of these categories will help to make the structure of the categories clearer to the listeners.

This prayer alludes to Romans 6:2–4: "How can we who died to sin yet live in it?

his own glo-ri-ous bod-y.   To our departed brothers and sisters, too,

and to all who were pleasing to you at their passing from this life,

give kind admittance to your king-dom.   There we hope to enjoy for

ever the fullness of your glory,   when you will wipe away every tear

from our eyes.   For seeing you, our God, as you are,   we shall be

He joins his hands.

like you for all the ages   and praise you without end,   through Christ

our Lord,   through whom you bestow on the world all that is good. †

Body is the only word in this paragraph where a syllable has two notes assigned to it. Back off the second note.

Emphasize **wipe away every tear**.

Emphasize **seeing you, our God, as you are**.

Or are you unaware that we who were baptized into Christ Jesus were baptized into his death? We were indeed buried with him through baptism into death, so that, just as Christ was raised from the dead by the glory of the Father, we too might live in newness of life." Allusion is also made to John 11:25–26: "I am the resurrection and the life; whoever believes in me, even if he dies, will live, and everyone who lives and believes in me will never die." This prayer also alludes to 2 Corinthians 5:1–7, which tells of the eternal dwelling that has been made for us in heaven. "For we know that if our earthly dwelling . . . should be destroyed, we have a building from God, a dwelling not made with hands, eternal in heaven." As does scripture, the prayer contrasts our passage from this life to our heavenly dwelling.

The focus of this prayer is found in the idea of transformation. Binary opposition contrasts uniting to Christ in death and then to his Resurrection. Also the lowly body is asked to be transformed into a glorious body.

The prayer does not attempt to hide the sadness of death nor gloss over the normal feelings that we have in the face of the death of a loved one. Rather, we pray that God will wipe away every tear from our eyes so that we can see God clearly.

EUCHARISTIC PRAYER IV

It is not permitted to change the Preface of this Eucharistic Prayer because of the structure of the Prayer itself, which presents a summary of the history of salvation.

V. The Lord be with you.   R. And with your spir-it.

V. Lift up your hearts.   R. We lift them up to the Lord.

V. Let us give thanks to the Lord our God.   R. It is right and just.

It is truly right to give you thanks,   tru-ly just to give you glory,

Fa-ther most ho-ly,   for you are the one God liv-ing and true, ex-

-isting before all ages and abiding for all e-ter-ni-ty,   dwelling in

un-ap-proach-a-ble light;   yet you, who alone are good,   the source

of life,   have made all that is,   so that you might fill your crea-tures

with bless-ings   and bring joy to many of them by the glo-ry of your

light.   And so, in your presence are countless hosts of An-gels,

Parallel **truly give thanks** with **truly give glory**, emphasizing **Father most holy**, as the addressee of the prayer and paralleling God's characteristics: **one, living, true, existing, dwelling**.

Make a contrast with **yet you . . .** and **have made all that is**. Parallel **so that you might fill** with **and bring joy**.

Emphasize **countless, Angels, day, night, gazing, glory, glorify, ceasing**: these words should evoke a sense of wonder in prayer.

What is a little surprising is that the rubrics for the opening dialogue of the Eucharistic Prayer are not reprinted, as they are found in #31 (see GIRM, 148). Although the text does not say that the Holy, Holy, Holy should be sung or spoken, it appears in the GIRM that the preference is for it to be sung. Singing is first in the GIRM, which seems to indicate a preference. Eucharistic Prayer IV has a proper Preface and, therefore, it should not be used when other proper Prefaces are assigned for a particular feast, for example,

one would not used Eucharistic Prayer IV on the first Sunday of Lent. It draws its inspiration from Eastern anaphoras, especially the Syro-Antiochene model. The protocol of the Preface makes a transition from the last phrase of the dialogue adding "truly" to both "right" and "just," addressing God as "Father most holy," an echo of John 17:11. The body of the Preface begins by lauding God simply as God is—living, true, existing, abiding, dwelling in unapproachable light. Only then, does the prayer praise God for creating all that is

and blessing it. The eschatocol of the prayer emphasizes the Angels' role in constantly praising this creator God. In a powerful phrase, the praying assembly recognizes its role as the poets of creation by giving voice (language) to the praise that is offered by every other creature simply by existing. The Holy, Holy, Holy, thus, becomes the song of Angels, humans, and the cosmos adoring the God who brought them into being.

This lengthy prayer, beginning with the words "We give you praise," lauds God

who serve you day and night   and, gazing upon the glory of your

face,   glorify you with-out ceas-ing.   With them we, too, confess

your name in ex-ul-ta-tion,   giving voice to every creature under

heaven, as we ac-claim:

At the end of the Preface he joins his hands and concludes the Preface with the people, singing aloud:

Ho-ly,   Ho-ly,   Ho-ly Lord God of hosts.   Heav-en and earth are

full of your glo-ry.   Ho-san-na in the high-est.   Bless-ed is he

who comes in the name of the Lord.   Ho-san-na in the high-est.

The principal celebrant, with hands extended, sings:

We give you praise, Father most holy, for you are great and you have

fashioned all your works in wisdom and in love.   You formed man

in your own image,   and entrusted the whole world to his care,

The melodic contours of these lines resemble the Preface dialogue and are intended to finish the Preface much like it began. When two notes are on a syllable, back off the second note, lest the text become too choppy.

Emphasize **we, too, confess, giving voice,** and **acclaim**.

The opening sentence sets the theme for this part of the prayer. Emphasize **Father most holy** (the title from the Preface and John 17:11). Emphasize **fashioned all your works in wisdom and in love**. Parallel this sentence to the first sentence of the prayer with the emphasis on **Father, most holy**.

Follow the sense lines and commas to announce the individual examples almost like a litany of how God has fashioned all his works in **wisdom and in love**.

for his activity in history. It may be helpful if the Priest thinks of the prayer in three sections; the first, comprising the creation of humanity up to the coming of Christ, the second, a recounting of the Incarnation and the saving activity of Christ, and the third, human history since the coming of Christ marked by the gifts of this Spirit. The task for the one proclaiming the prayer is to make each of the elements remembered like a family heirloom.

The line "you formed man in your own image" recalls the first creation account in

Genesis, "Then God said, 'Let us make man in our image, after our likeness.'" The prayer continues the notion of stewardship for creation as it states that God has entrusted the whole world to our care. We find here a very positive theology of creation similar to what is articulated in Psalm 8: "You have given them rule over the works of your hands, / put all things at their feet: / All sheep and oxen, even the beasts of the field, / The birds of the air, the fish of the sea, and whatever swims the paths of the seas" (v. 7–9).

The metaphor of friendship is used to describe the need for reconciliation after humanity had strayed. Covenants are made and prophets are sent to bring humanity back. Ultimately Christ, who shared in our human nature, comes to proclaim good news to the poor, freedom to prisoners and joy to the sorrowful by living, dying, and being raised from the dead. Allusion is made to Isaiah 61:1, a text that Jesus comments upon in the synagogue in Nazareth on the Sabbath: "The Spirit of the Lord GOD is upon me, / because the LORD

Follow the sense lines and the commas to articulate the life and ministry of Jesus, but notice that the phrases are conspicuously shorter than the ones in the earlier paragraph and, therefore, can be spoken differently.

so that in serving you alone, the Creator,   he might have dominion over all crea-tures.   And when through disobedience he had lost your friendship,   you did not abandon him to the domain of death.

For you came in mercy to the aid of all, so that those who seek might find you.   Time and again you offered them covenants and through the prophets   taught them to look forward to sal-va-tion.   And you so loved the world, Father most holy,   that in the fullness of time you sent your Only Begotten Son to be our Sav-ior.   Made incarnate by the Holy Spirit   and born of the Virgin Mary,   he shared our hu--man nature in all things but sin.   To the poor he proclaimed the good news of salvation,   to prisoners, freedom,   and to the sorrow-

has anointed me; He has sent me to bring glad tidings to the lowly, / to heal the bro-kenhearted, / To proclaim liberty to the captives and release to the prisoners."

In Eucharistic Prayer IV, the leading metaphor is that of covenant. It is note-worthy that passing mention is made to the Last Supper in the Institution narrative, while the prayer uses Johannine language: "when the hour had come for him to be glorified . . . having loved his own in the world."

In the ancient world, the making of a pact or a covenant (berith) was done dur-ing a ceremony in which an animal was slain and cut in half. There were two types of covenants in ancient times. One was a parity covenant made between two equal parties who bound themselves together in a contract. The other covenant was the suzerainty covenant made between a strong party and a weak party. Here, the king walked through the bloody parts. He would say that he should be dismembered if he breaks the covenant. The animal was

slain on the eve of the Passover, on the afternoon of the 14th of Nisan, after the Tamid sacrifice had been killed, i.e., at three o'clock, or, in case the eve of the Passover fell on Friday, at two.

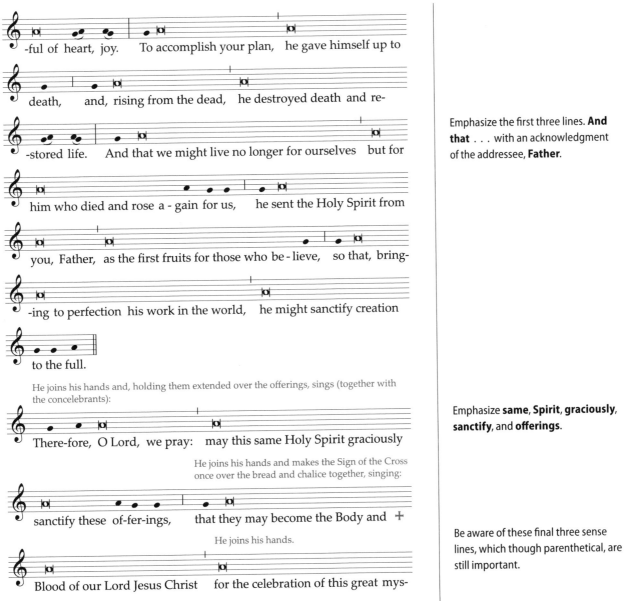

-ful of heart, joy.   To accomplish your plan,   he gave himself up to death,   and, rising from the dead,   he destroyed death and re-stored life.   And that we might live no longer for ourselves   but for him who died and rose a - gain for us,   he sent the Holy Spirit from you, Father,   as the first fruits for those who be - lieve,   so that, bring-ing to perfection his work in the world,   he might sanctify creation to the full.

He joins his hands and, holding them extended over the offerings, sings (together with the concelebrants):

There-fore, O Lord, we pray: may this same Holy Spirit graciously

He joins his hands and makes the Sign of the Cross once over the bread and chalice together, singing:

sanctify these of-fer-ings,   that they may become the Body and ✛

He joins his hands.

Blood of our Lord Jesus Christ   for the celebration of this great mys-

Emphasize the first three lines. **And that** . . . with an acknowledgment of the addressee, **Father**.

Emphasize **same**, **Spirit**, **graciously**, **sanctify**, and **offerings**.

Be aware of these final three sense lines, which though parenthetical, are still important.

The article beginning with the words "Therefore, O Lord, we pray" is the epiclesis over the gifts invoking the Holy Spirit for the transformation over the offering that Christ has left us for the celebration of this great mystery, which is Christ himself as an eternal covenant. The Priest should extend his hands over the offerings before he begins to recite the text, and he should keep them extended until he makes the Sign of the Cross once over the bread and chalice together while saying the words "Body and Blood."

In the fourteenth century, the epiclesis became an issue in the polemics between Greeks and Latins, because all Eastern Eucharistic Prayers included an invocation of the Holy Spirit, while the Roman canon of the Mass did not. Most modern scholars agree that there had been an epiclesis, in the original Eucharist of the early Church of Rome, in addition to the other Latin Eucharistic Prayers. Medieval Latin theology, however, allowed for the disappearance of the epiclesis since it was believed that the consecration of bread and wine

and their transubstantiation into the Body and Blood of Christ took place when the Priest pronounced the words of institution. The question of the epiclesis was debated at the Council of Ferrara-Florence (1438–45), but no formal definition was made. The medieval Latin view was then endorsed by the Council of Trent (1545–63), but the liturgical reforms adopted in Roman Catholicism after the Second Vatican Council (1962–65) have included the introduction of an epiclesis in the canon of the Mass. This epiclesis, however,

-tery,   which he himself left us as an e - ter-nal cov-e-nant.

For when the hour had come   for him to be glorified by you, Father

most holy,   having loved his own who were in the world,   he loved

them to the end: and while they were at supper,

He takes the bread and, holding it slightly raised above the altar, continues:

he took bread,   blessed and broke it,   and gave it to his disciples,

say-ing:

He bows slightly.

TAKE THIS, ALL OF YOU, AND EAT OF IT,   FOR THIS IS MY BOD-Y,

WHICH WILL BE GIV-EN UP FOR YOU.

He shows the consecrated host to the people, places it again on the paten, and genuflects in adoration.

After this, he continues: He takes the chalice and, holding it slightly raised above the altar, continues:

In a similar way,   taking the chalice filled with the fruit of the vine,

The rubric reads "He takes the bread and, holding it slightly raised above the altar." This may seem to suggest that the Priest is impersonating Christ; in fact, the Priest continues to address God the Father. Nor should the Priest seems to be addressing the bread. Notice that the rubric before the text "Take this all of you, and eat of it," does not call for the Priest Celebrant to break the host; it simply calls for him to bow slightly.

The Priest then shows the consecrated host. The rubric does not say "elevate." The Priest Celebrant genuflects in adoration.

The rubric reads "He takes the chalice and, holding it slightly raised above the altar." Again, the Priest continues to address God the Father, and should not appear to be addressing the chalice. Notice that the rubric before the text "Take this all of you, and drink from it," does not call for him to speak into the cup; it simply calls for him to bow slightly.

is placed before the words of Institution, so that the consecratory function of the latter can still be maintained.

For the Institution narrative the coordination of texts and gestures is very important. The Priest must remember that he is continuing to recount the great deeds of God now focused in Christ Jesus on the night before he died, but he is not addressing these texts to the bread and wine. It continues to be part of a Eucharistic Prayer addressed to the Father. Although rubrics such as "He takes the bread and, holding it

slightly raised above the altar" may seem to suggest that the Priest is impersonating Christ; in fact, the Priest continues to address God the Father; here, recounting one of the great deeds of God in history, the Institution narrative. Notice that the rubric before the text, "Take this all of you and eat of it," calls for him to bow slightly. After speaking the text, the Priest shows the consecrated host. (The rubric does not say "elevate.") The Priest then genuflects in adoration.

In Eucharistic Prayer IV, the leading metaphor is that of covenant. It is noteworthy that passing mention is made to the Last Supper in the Institution narrative, while the prayer uses Johannine language: "when the hour had come for him to be glorified . . . having loved his own in the world."

The Priest's text, "The mystery of faith" functions as a cue, although it is an exclamation. Originally, the phrase *mysterium fidei* was part of the consecratory text, but Pope Paul VI, on his authority, removed

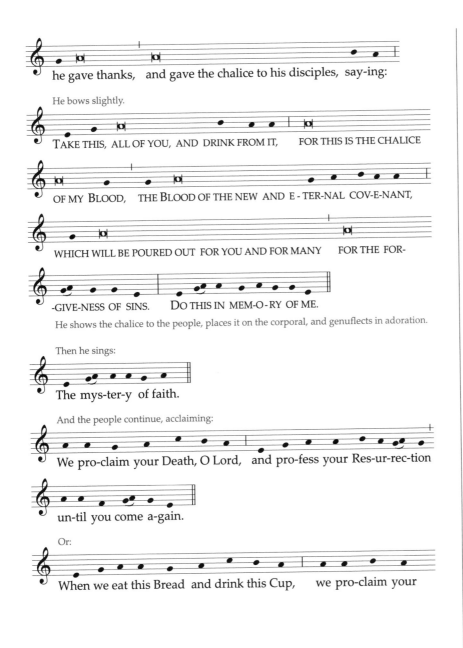

he gave thanks, and gave the chalice to his disciples, say-ing:

He bows slightly.

TAKE THIS, ALL OF YOU, AND DRINK FROM IT, FOR THIS IS THE CHALICE

OF MY BLOOD, THE BLOOD OF THE NEW AND E-TER-NAL COV-E-NANT,

WHICH WILL BE POURED OUT FOR YOU AND FOR MANY FOR THE FOR-

-GIVE-NESS OF SINS. DO THIS IN MEM-O-RY OF ME.

He shows the chalice to the people, places it on the corporal, and genuflects in adoration.

Then he sings:

The mys-ter-y of faith.

And the people continue, acclaiming:

We pro-claim your Death, O Lord, and pro-fess your Res-ur-rec-tion

un-til you come a-gain.

Or:

When we eat this Bread and drink this Cup, we pro-claim your

The Priest shows the chalice. The rubric does not say "elevate." The Priest Celebrant genuflects in adoration.

The Priest may sing **The mystery of faith**, which will serve as a prompt for the assembly to sing one of the three acclamations.

That there is a musical setting for the introduction and musical settings for the three acclamations suggests that this is inherently a musical item. If the Priest sings, it should match what is to follow. The assembly begins on whatever note the Priest finishes.

them from the consecratory words and made them this exclamation. The Latin text does not say, "Let us proclaim the mystery of faith," nor does it provide a full sentence. Rather, the phrase could best be interpreted as "Oh, the mystery of faith!" a moment of contemplative awe and surrender that serves as a cue to the congregation's response.

Notice that the Missal chant for this text is correlated to the Memorial Acclamation chants, but there may be other musical settings of the Mystery of Faith correlated to other musical settings of the congregation's Memorial Acclamations that the Priest should learn. What the Priest sings and what the people sing should be congruent.

This is the second set of three acclamations that punctuates the Eucharistic Prayer (along with the Holy, Holy, Holy, doxology, and "Amen"). That music is supplied in the Missal more than suggests that this is a sung element. For this reason, it is desirable that all three acclamations match somehow musically so as to create a coher-

ent whole. In musical terms, this would be the second great crescendo, which will culminate in the doxology and "Amen."

Notice that all three acclamations for the Mystery of Faith are addressed to Christ. After the Memorial Acclamation, the Eucharistic Prayer returns immediately to addressing the Father.

This part of the prayer, beginning with the words "Therefore, O Lord" has many liturgical functions. Its first paragraph is an anamnesis-offering in which the community makes memory of the Paschal Mystery

Death, O Lord,   un-til you come a-gain.

Or:

Save us, Sav-ior of the world,   for by your Cross and Res-ur-rec-tion

you have set us free.

Then he, with hands extended, sings (together with the concelebrants):

There-fore, O Lord,   as we now celebrate the memorial of our re-

-demption, we remember Christ's Death and his descent to the realm

of the dead,   we proclaim his Resurrection   and his Ascension

to your right hand,   and, as we await his coming in glory, we offer

you his Body and Blood, the sacrifice acceptable to you   which brings

salvation to the whole world.

Look, O Lord, upon the Sacrifice   which you yourself have provided

Resume the chant on the note below the reciting tone, moving directly to the reciting tone. Observe the quarter vertical bars to lift but not necessarily to breathe (unless you need a breath), which will help with the intelligibility of the text. Emphasize the four verbs: **celebrate, remember, proclaim,** and **await**, pausing after each of the four phrases.

and offers to God the Father the sacrifice of the cross. The second paragraph is an epiclesis on the community itself, praying that those who receive Holy Communion be united by the Holy Spirit. The double, or split epiclesis, asking that we may become the body of Christ is congruent with the understanding that Saint Paul proffers in 1 Corinthians 12:12–14. The point can be made that Eucharist is both what is on the table and who is at the table. As Saint Augustine said, we are to become what we

celebrate. We are to become bread broken and wine poured out for the world.

Thirdly, the prayer for unity is specified as a prayer for the Church's leadership and her people—all who seek God with a sincere heart. As in all the Eucharistic Prayers, the names of the Pope and local Bishop, along with coadjutor or auxiliary Bishops, are inserted, demonstrating the rapport between the local Church and the universal Church. We remember all those who have died—both Christian and other whose faith is known only to God. Finally,

we pray for ourselves that we may enter into the Communion of Saints. Only the name of the Blessed Virgin Mary is mentioned specifically along with Apostles and Saints who remain unnamed. There is no provision in this Eucharistic Prayer to add specific names of Saints.

The prayer terminates with the same idea with which it began, namely creation. But as the first creation, which was good, experienced the Fall due to the sin of Adam, we recognize that the whole of creation has been redeemed through Christ in

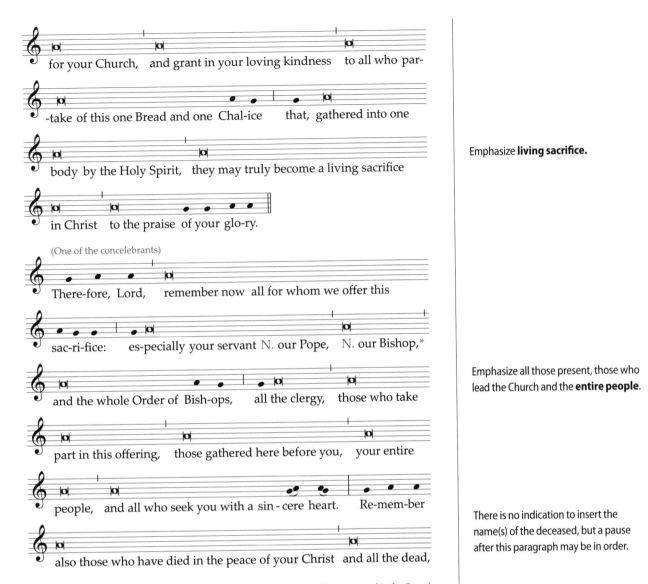

for your Church,   and grant in your loving kindness   to all who par-

-take of this one Bread and one Chal-ice   that, gathered into one

body by the Holy Spirit,   they may truly become a living sacrifice

in Christ   to the praise of your glo-ry.

(One of the concelebrants)

There-fore, Lord,   remember now all for whom we offer this

sac-ri-fice: es-pecially your servant N. our Pope,   N. our Bishop,*

and the whole Order of Bish-ops,   all the clergy,   those who take

part in this offering,   those gathered here before you,   your entire

people,   and all who seek you with a sin - cere heart.   Re-mem-ber

also those who have died in the peace of your Christ and all the dead,

Emphasize **living sacrifice.**

Emphasize all those present, those who lead the Church and the **entire people**.

There is no indication to insert the name(s) of the deceased, but a pause after this paragraph may be in order.

* Mention may be made here of the Coadjutor Bishop, or Auxiliary Bishops, as noted in the *General Instruction of the Roman Missal*, no. 149.

whose name we glorify God who has bestowed all that is good to us.

In this theology of creation, human beings understand themselves to be in solidarity with God and the created order. Separated by sin, nevertheless, humanity is redeemed by Christ, thus supplying the created world with a voice that has again been restored through the redemptive work of Christ. Humanity has the task of becoming one again with nature and the cosmos and to continually sing to God in praise.

Emphasize **O merciful Father**–hearkening back to most holy Father– **that we may enter into a heavenly inheritance**.

Emphasize each word: **whole, freed, glorify, all that is good**. Voice should be getting louder and possibly higher in pitch, giving progressive emphasis.

For singing purposes, find a note in your upper-range. This is "do." Now sing down "do-ti-la" to find your opening note. Return immediately to "do." The traditional melody revolves around these three notes.

The doxology is the third and final of the Eucharistic acclamations (along with the Holy, Holy, Holy and Memorial Acclamation). The fact that music is supplied in the Missal strongly suggests that this is inherently a musical item. Pause at the commas and the sense lines and continue to increase in volume so as to cue the congregation's **Amen**.

whose faith you a-lone have known.   To all of us, your children, grant, O merciful Father,   that we may enter into a heavenly inher-itance   with the Blessed Virgin Mary, Mother of God,   and with your Apostles and Saints in your king-dom.   There, with the whole of creation,   freed from the corruption of sin and death,   may we glorify

He joins his hands.

you through Christ our Lord,   through whom you bestow on the world all that is good.

He takes the chalice and the paten with the host and raising both, he sings (together with the concelebrants):

Through him, and with him, and in him,   O God, almighty Father, in the unity of the Ho-ly Spir-it,   all glo-ry and hon-or is yours, for ev-er and ev-er.   R. A-men.

Then follows the Communion Rite, p. 663.

The Eucharistic Prayer ends with the final doxology, which sums up all the themes of the Eucharistic Prayer in a proclamation of the Divine Name. Everything belongs to God and all honor and glory ascend to Him in a Christological movement denoted by three prepositions: through, with, and in. The Holy Name is great throughout the world and put on the lips of the faithful who proclaim God's glory.

The conclusion of the prayer calls for the Priest to lift the paten with host and the Deacon (or in his absence, the Priest) chants or recites the doxology.

The Missal provides a chant setting of this doxology that leads to the community's chanted "Amen"; however, there may be other musical settings of the doxology correlated to the congregation's "Amen." The Priest's doxology and the people's "Amen" should be musically congruent so as to form a seamless garment. It is the ultimate crescendo of the Eucharistic Prayer, culminating in praise of God.

Not only is the doxology the high point of the Eucharistic Prayer, insofar as the latter is a proclamation and profession of faith, it also climaxes the sanctificatory movement of the prayer, since the Divine Name is formally proclaimed in its fullest and most explicit form. This draws from the Old Testament idea that the Divine Name has the power to sanctify. We find this clearly in Exodus 20:24: "In whatever place I choose for the remembrance of my name I will come to you and bless you."

Appendix
to the Order of Mass

Eucharistic Prayer for Reconciliation I
in a concelebration

The Preface and **You are indeed Holy, O Lord** to just as **you yourself are holy** inclusive are said by the principal celebrant alone, with hands extended.

From **Look, we pray** to **we, too, are your sons and daughters** inclusive is said together by all the concelebrants, with hands extended toward the offerings.

From **But before** to **who heals every division** inclusive, all the concelebrants together speak in this manner:

a) The part **But before**, with hands joined.

b) While speaking the words of the Lord, each extends his right hand toward the bread and toward the chalice, if this seems appropriate; as the host and the chalice are elevated at the Consecration, however, the concelebrants look toward them and then bow profoundly.

c) The parts **Therefore, as we celebrate the memorial** and **Look kindly, most compassionate Father**, with hands extended.

It is appropriate that the intercession **Be pleased to keep us always in communion of mind and heart** be assigned to one or other of the concelebrants, who pronounces this prayer alone, with hands extended.

The following parts especially may be sung: **But before**; **As he ate with them**; **In a similar way**; **Therefore, as we celebrate the memorial**; **Look kindly, most compassionate Father**, as well as the concluding doxology.

The concluding doxology of the Eucharistic Prayer is pronounced by the principal celebrant alone, or by all the concelebrants together with the principal celebrant.

Concelebration is the practice by which "several priests, in virtue of Christ's own Priesthood and in the person of the High Priest, act together with one voice and one will; so also do they confect and offer a single sacrifice by a single sacramental act and likewise partake of the same" (*Guidelines for Concelebration of the Eucharist*, USCCB, 2003, #1).

The Fathers of the Second Vatican Council recommended concelebration as an expression of "the unity of the priesthood" and chose to extend permission for the practice to a number of particular instances, granting the Bishop of each diocese the authority to decide when concelebration was opportune at other times. The Council further directed that "a new rite for concelebration . . . be drawn up and inserted into the Pontifical and into the Roman Missal" (ibid. #2).

Concelebration should be understood as an appropriate way for priests to participate in the celebration of the Eucharist, expressive of their unique relationship with Christ the High Priest and of the unity of the Priesthood. From the earliest days of the Church, concelebration, while taking a variety of forms, has been celebrated for "much more than merely practical considerations" (ibid, #3). For such concelebration at Mass is expressive of the one sacrifice of the cross, the priesthood, and the action of the entire People of God, "ordered and acting hierarchically" (ibid, #4). Provision is made for concelebration in the Eucharistic Prayers for Reconciliation.

EUCHARISTIC PRAYERS
FOR RECONCILIATION

The Eucharistic Prayers for Reconciliation may be used in Masses in which the mystery of reconciliation is conveyed to the faithful in a special way, as, for example, in the Masses for Promoting Harmony, For Reconciliation, For the Preservation of Peace and Justice, In Time of War or Civil Disturbance, For the Forgiveness of Sins, For Charity, of the Mystery of the Holy Cross, of the Most Holy Eucharist, of the Most Precious Blood of our Lord Jesus Christ, as well as in Masses during Lent. Although these Eucharistic Prayers have been provided with a proper Preface, they may also be used with other Prefaces that refer to penance and conversion, as, for example, the Prefaces of Lent.

I

The opening exchange establishes the dialogical nature of liturgical prayer. Thus, the Priest's lines are intended to elicit the response of the assembly. Vocal intonation and eye contact will help in this regard.

Emphasize **Father, almighty and eternal God**, as the addressee of the prayer and paralleling God's characteristics: life giving, rich in mercy, forgiving. Parallel **rich in mercy** with **offer pardon**. Make a contrast with **sinners** and **forgiveness**.

There are two Eucharistic Prayers for Reconciliation. The inclusion of the Eucharistic Prayers for Reconciliation, along with those for Various Needs, in the new Latin Missal means that these Eucharistic Prayers now form a stable part of the Church's treasury of liturgical prayer.

Previously, these prayers were technically approved by various ad hoc or experimental measures, although usually with no established time limit. They already had been included in some official translations of the full Roman Missal, such as the Spanish and Italian translations.

Regarding the use of the Eucharistic Prayers for Reconciliation, the rubric notes the following: "The Eucharistic Prayers for Reconciliation may be used in Masses in which the mystery of reconciliation is conveyed to the faithful in a special way, as for example, in the Masses for Promoting Harmony, For Reconciliation, For the Preservation of Peace and Justice, In Time of War or Civil Disturbance, For the Forgiveness of Sins, For Charity, of the Mystery of the Holy Cross, of the Most Holy Eucharist, of the Most Precious Blood of Our Lord Jesus Christ, as well as in Masses during Lent."

Although these Eucharistic Prayers each have a proper Preface, it is permissible to use them with another Preface that refers in some way to the themes of penance and conversion, for example, with the Prefaces of Lent.

have bound the human family to yourself   through Jesus your Son,

our Re-deem-er, with a new bond of love so tight that it can nev-er

be un-done.   E-ven now you set before your people   a time of grace

and recon - ci - li - a -tion,   and, as they turn back to you in spirit,

you grant them hope in Christ Je-sus   and a desire to be of ser-vice

to all,   while they entrust them - selves more ful-ly to the Ho-ly

Spir-it.   And so, filled with wonder,   we extol the power of your

love,   and, proclaiming our joy   at the salvation that comes from

you,   we join in the heavenly hymn of count-less hosts, as without

end we ac-claim:

Holy, Holy, Holy Lord God of hosts . . .

Emphasize **Jesus your Son** and **bond of love**.

Emphasize **Even now** and **time of grace and reconciliation**.

Emphasize **wonder, power of your love, proclaiming our joy**. These words should evoke a sense of wonder in prayer.

Additionally, although they may be used during Lent, the rubrics make no distinction between weekdays and Sundays, and so there is no reason why their use would be restricted to the Lord's Day, provided that one respects the proper Prefaces that must be used on certain Lenten Sundays.

As well as the Masses suggested in the rubrics, these Eucharistic Prayers often prove useful during retreats and spiritual exercises when the time comes to seek reconciliation with God and rediscover his loving mercy.

The Preface is typical in structure. Several themes related to reconciliation are evident. God who is rich in mercy calls us to abundant life; thus, we are confident in God's constant pardoning of our sins. Sin is regarded as a turning away from God and reconciliation is the turning toward God. This theme is characteristic of the word "metanoia" as a change of heart or mind and a turning around. Reconciliation with God results in service towards others.

Central to the Preface is God's *hesed*, the Hebrew word for "kindness." It is also commonly translated as "loving," "merciful love," or "loving mercy." When we ask for God to be merciful, we also are proclaiming God's eternal and boundless love manifested in Christ. This is fulfilled when we entrust ourselves more fully to God in the Holy Spirit. The Trinitarian focus of this Preface is noteworthy.

Text without music:

1.

V. **The Lord be with you.**
R. And with your spirit.

V. **Lift up your hearts.**
R. We lift them up to the Lord.

V. **Let us give thanks to the Lord our God.**
R. It is right and just.

I**t is truly right and just
that we should always give you thanks,**
Lord, holy Father, almighty and eternal God.

**For you do not cease to spur us on
to possess a more abundant life
and, being rich in mercy,
you constantly offer pardon
and call on sinners
to trust in your forgiveness alone.**

**Never did you turn away from us,
and, though time and again we have broken your covenant,
you have bound the human family to yourself
through Jesus your Son, our Redeemer,
with a new bond of love so tight
that it can never be undone.**

**Even now you set before your people
a time of grace and reconciliation,
and, as they turn back to you in spirit,
you grant them hope in Christ Jesus
and a desire to be of service to all,
while they entrust themselves
more fully to the Holy Spirit.**

**And so, filled with wonder,
we extol the power of your love,
and, proclaiming our joy
at the salvation that comes from you,
we join in the heavenly hymn of countless hosts,
as without end we acclaim:**

Emphasize **Father, almighty and eternal God**, as the addressee of the prayer and paralleling God's characteristics: life giving, rich in mercy, forgiving. Parallel **rich in mercy** with **offer pardon**. Make a contrast with **sinners** and **forgiveness**.

Emphasize **covenant** and **human family**, **Jesus your Son** and **bond of love**.

Emphasize **Even now** and **time of grace and reconciliation**.

Emphasize **wonder**, **power of your love**, **proclaiming our joy**: these words should evoke a sense of wonder in prayer.

---

1. Three interrelated theological ideas underlie Preface I for Reconciliation: covenant, reconciliation, and change of heart.

In theology and biblical studies, the word "covenant" principally refers to any of a number of solemn agreements made between God and the children of Israel in the Old Testament, as well as to the New Covenant, which some Christians consider to be the replacement or final fulfilment of these.

Reconciliation is a theological term, meaning an element of salvation that refers to the results of atonement. Reconciliation as a theological concept describes the end of the estrangement, caused by sin, between God and humanity. It is part of the message of salvation that brings us back together with God. God is the author, Christ is the agent, and we are the ambassadors of reconciliation (see 2 Corinthians 5). Although used only five times in the Pauline corpus (Romans 5:10–11, 11:15,

2 Corinthians 5:18–20, Ephesians 2:14–17, and Colossians 1:19–22), reconciliation is an essential term, describing the substance of the Gospel and salvation.

Finally, there is a change of heart or repentance. In theology, metanoia refers to the change of mind that is brought about in repentance. Repentance is necessary and valuable because it brings about change of mind or metanoia. The two terms (repentance and metanoia) are often used interchangeably.

Holy, Holy, Holy Lord God of hosts.
Heaven and earth are full of your glory.
Hosanna in the highest.
Blessed is he who comes in the name of the Lord.
Hosanna in the highest.

The Priest joins his hands for the singing or recitation of the Holy, Holy, Holy, which he sings along with the assembly.

2.   The Priest, with hands extended, says:

You are indeed Holy, O Lord,
and from the world's beginning
are ceaselessly at work,
so that the human race may become holy,
just as you yourself are holy.

Celebrant alone

Emphasize **from the world's beginning**.

Make a parallel between **human race may become holy** and **just as you yourself are holy.**

3.   He joins his hands and, holding them extended over the offerings, says:

Look, we pray, upon your people's offerings
and pour out on them the power of your Spirit,

Celebrant with concelebrants

Correlate the hand-laying gesture with the words.

He joins his hands and makes the Sign of the Cross once over the bread and chalice together, saying:

that they may become the Body and ✠ Blood

He joins his hands.

of your beloved Son, Jesus Christ,
in whom we, too, are your sons and daughters.

Emphasize **your sons and daughters,** paralleling the phrase to **your beloved Son.**

Indeed, though we once were lost
and could not approach you,
you loved us with the greatest love:
for your Son, who alone is just,
handed himself over to death,
and did not disdain to be nailed for our sake
to the wood of the Cross.

Revel in the phrase **we once were lost and could not approach you**.

But before his arms were outstretched between heaven and earth,
to become the lasting sign of your covenant,
he desired to celebrate the Passover with his disciples.

Emphasize **arms outstretched between heaven and earth** as a rich allusion to the Crucifixion, as well as a gesture of gathering people in.

2. Exiting the Holy, Holy, Holy, the Priest, with hands extended in an orans position, continues to sing the praises of God, amplifying the theme of holiness of the Seraphic hymn.

3. During this further paragraph of petition, the Priest extends his hands over the offerings, simply praying that they be transformed into the Body and Blood of Christ. This is the epiclesis, in which we pray to God to send the Holy Spirit upon the gifts to transform them. The prayer is accompanied by hand-laying. In a post-epicletic prayer, the Priest expresses the need for reconciliation as coming from our side, since we were lost to God. It is we who have strayed, and it is Christ who was sent to bring us back to God by being nailed to the wood of the cross. The expression "wood of the Cross" hearkens to the Good Friday liturgy when the Cross is presented and three times we hear, "Behold the wood of the Cross on which was hung our salvation," to which all respond, "Come, let us adore." The prayer references the gesture of Christ stretching out his arms between heaven and earth, the gesture of the Crucifixion of Jesus seen as the lasting sign of God's covenant. The Passover context is recalled, establishing the first Eucharist and evoking a theme that Jesus is the Paschal lamb who will be slain.

The rubric reads, "He takes the bread and, holding it slightly raised above the altar." This may suggest that the Priest is impersonating Christ; in fact, the Priest continues to address God the Father. Nor is the Priest addressing the bread. Notice that the rubric before the text "Take this all of you, and eat of it," does not call for the Priest Celebrant to break the host; it simply calls for him to bow slightly.

The Priest then shows the consecrated host. The rubric does not say "elevate." The Priest Celebrant genuflects in adoration.

The rubric reads, "He takes the chalice and, holding it slightly raised above the altar." Again, the Priest continues to address God the Father, and not the chalice. Notice that the rubric before the text "Take this all of you, and drink from it," does not call for him to speak into the cup; it simply calls for him to bow slightly.

The Priest then shows the chalice. The rubric does not say "elevate." The Priest Celebrant genuflects in adoration.

4.   In the formulas that follow, the words of the Lord should be pronounced clearly and distinctly, as the nature of these words requires.

As he ate with them,

He takes the bread and, holding it slightly raised above the altar, continues:

**he took bread
and, giving you thanks, he said the blessing,
broke the bread and gave it to them, saying:**

He bows slightly.

**Take this, all of you, and eat of it,
for this is my Body,
which will be given up for you.**

He shows the consecrated host to the people, places it again on the paten, and genuflects in adoration.

5.   After this, he continues:

**In a similar way, when supper was ended,
knowing that he was about to reconcile all things in himself
through his Blood to be shed on the Cross,**

He takes the chalice and, holding it slightly raised above the altar, continues:

**he took the chalice, filled with the fruit of the vine,
and once more giving you thanks,
handed the chalice to his disciples, saying:**

He bows slightly.

**Take this, all of you, and drink from it,
for this is the chalice of my Blood,
the Blood of the new and eternal covenant,
which will be poured out for you and for many
for the forgiveness of sins.**

Do this in memory of me.

He shows the chalice to the people, places it on the corporal, and genuflects in adoration.

4–5. The words of Institution, or the historical narrative is now established, as in all the Eucharistic Prayers, in the course of a meal. Without exception, all the Eucharistic Prayers mention that Christ took the wine "when Supper was ended."

The coordination of texts and gestures for the Institution narrative is important. The Priest must remember that he is continuing to recount the great deeds of God now focused in Christ Jesus on the night before he died. He should be sure

that his gestures and posture do not make it appear that he is addressing these texts to the bread and wine. The Priest's posture should reflect that this prayer continues to be part of a Eucharistic Prayer addressed to the Father.

Although rubrics such as "He takes the bread and, holding it slightly raised above the altar" suggest that the Priest is impersonating Christ; in fact, the Priest continues to address God the Father, here, recounting one of the great deeds of God In

history, the Institution narrative. Notice that the rubric before the text "Take this all of you, and eat of it," does not call for the Priest Celebrant to break the host; it simply calls for him to bow slightly.

Similarly, after speaking the text, the Priest shows the consecrated host. (The rubric does not say "elevate.") The Priest Celebrant genuflects in adoration. The command "Do this in memory of me" is in reference to the entire action, not just the chalice.

6.   Then he says:

The mystery of faith.   *Celebrant alone*

And the people continue, acclaiming:

We proclaim your Death, O Lord,
and profess your Resurrection
until you come again.

Or:

When we eat this Bread and drink this Cup,
we proclaim your Death, O Lord,
until you come again.

Or:

Save us, Savior of the world,
for by your Cross and Resurrection
you have set us free.

7.   Then the Priest, with hands extended, says:

Therefore, as we celebrate   *Celebrant*
the memorial of your Son Jesus Christ,   *with concelebrants*
who is our Passover and our surest peace,
we celebrate his Death and Resurrection from the dead,
and looking forward to his blessed Coming,
we offer you, who are our faithful and merciful God,
this sacrificial Victim
who reconciles to you the human race.

Look kindly, most compassionate Father,
on those you unite to yourself
by the Sacrifice of your Son,
and grant that, by the power of the Holy Spirit,
as they partake of this one Bread and one Chalice,
they may be gathered into one Body in Christ,
who heals every division.

The Priest may sing **The mystery of faith**, which will serve as a prompt for the assembly to sing one of the three acclamations.

That musical settings are provided for the introduction and the Memorial Acclamations suggest that this is inherently a musical item.

The Priest resumes the orans position to emphasize that the entire Eucharistic Prayer is addressed to God, whereas, the Memorial Acclamations are addressed to Christ. In both cases, the designation is **Lord**, but the context and internal references make the designation known.

Emphasize **Passover, Death and Resurrection**, as we look forward to **blessed Coming**, so as even more to emphasize **sacrificial Victim who reconciles to you the human race**.

Parallel the phrases **Look . . . on those you unite** and **heals every division**.

---

6. The Priest's text "The mystery of faith" functions as a cue, although it is an exclamation.

7. The texts in this article have multiple functions. The first paragraph comprises the anamnesis-offering. We recall the Paschal Mystery, and in that light, offer to God the "holy and living sacrifice." The second paragraph is an epiclesis over the community, asking that those who are nourished by partaking in Holy Communion may be gathered into "one Body in Christ" by the Holy Spirit and adds, in harmony to the theme of reconciliation, that they also may be gathered by the one "who heals of every division." We further pray that the gift of Eucharistic union unites us with the living members of the Church, in particular, the Pope and the local Bishop, and with the Saints in heaven. We especially pray that God would grant mercy to our deceased brothers and sisters and free us from the wound of corruption.

Emphasize **communion of mind and heart**.

Be pleased to keep us always
in communion of mind and heart,
together with N. our Pope and N. our Bishop.*
Help us to work together
for the coming of your Kingdom,
until the hour when we stand before you,
Saints among the Saints in the halls of heaven,
with the Blessed Virgin Mary, Mother of God,
the blessed Apostles and all the Saints,
and with our deceased brothers and sisters,
whom we humbly commend to your mercy.

Celebrant or
one concelebrant

Emphasize **wound of corruption, new creation**, and **sing to you with gladness**.

Then, freed at last from the wound of corruption
and made fully into a new creation,
we shall sing to you with gladness

He joins his hands.

the thanksgiving of Christ,
who lives for all eternity.

The doxology is the third and final of the Eucharistic acclamations (along with the Holy, Holy, Holy and Memorial Acclamation). The fact that music is supplied in the Missal strongly suggests that this is an inherently musical item. Pause at the commas and the sense lines and continue to increase in volume so as to cue the congregation's **Amen.**

8.   He takes the chalice and the paten with the host and, raising both, he says:

**Through him, and with him, and in him,
O God, almighty Father,
in the unity of the Holy Spirit,
all glory and honor is yours,
for ever and ever.**

Celebrant alone
or with
concelebrants

The people acclaim:

Amen.

Then follows the Communion Rite, p. 663.

---

*   Mention may be made here of the Coadjutor Bishop, or Auxiliary Bishops, as noted in the *General Instruction of the Roman Missal*, no. 149.

8. The conclusion of the Eucharistic Prayer calls for the Priest to lift the paten with host and the Deacon (or in his absence, the Priest) chants or recites the doxology. A doxology is a short hymn of praise to God in Christian worship, and is often added to the end of canticles, Psalms, and hymns. The tradition derives from a similar practice in the Jewish synagogue, in which some version of the Kaddish serves to terminate each section of the service. Among Christian traditions, a doxology is typically a sung expression of praise to the Holy Trinity, the Father, the Son, and the Holy Spirit. It is common in high hymns for the final verse to take the form of a doxology.

The Missal provides chant settings of this doxology that leads to the community's chanted "Amen"; however, other musical settings of the doxology may be correlated to the congregation's "Amen." The Priest's doxology and the people's "Amen" should be musically congruent. The prayer reaches its climax with the doxology and "Amen." This is the last of three acclamations that punctuate the Eucharistic Prayer and ritually is the pinnacle of the prayer as we give honor and glory to God though Christ with the Holy Spirit.

Eucharistic Prayer for Reconciliation II
in a concelebration

The Preface and **You, therefore, almighty Father** to **handed over to death** inclusive are said by the principal celebrant alone, with hands extended.

From **And now, celebrating the reconciliation** to **when we celebrate these mysteries** inclusive is spoken together by all the concelebrants, with hands extended toward the offerings.

From **For when about to give his life** to **the Sacrifice of perfect reconciliation** inclusive, all the concelebrants together speak in this manner:

a) The part **For when about to give his life**, with hands joined.

b) While speaking the words of the Lord, each extends his right hand toward the bread and toward the chalice, if this seems appropriate; as the host and the chalice are elevated at the Consecration, however, the concelebrants look toward them and then bow profoundly.

c) The part **Celebrating therefore the memorial**, with hands extended.

It is appropriate that the intercessions **May he make your Church** and **Just as you have gathered us now** be assigned to one or other of the concelebrants, who pronounces this prayer alone, with hands extended.

The following parts especially may be sung: **And now, celebrating the reconciliation**; **For when about to give his life**; **In a similar way on that same evening**; **Celebrating therefore the memorial**, as well as the concluding doxology.

The concluding doxology of the Eucharistic Prayer is pronounced by the principal celebrant alone, or by all the concelebrants together with the principal celebrant.

Concelebration is the practice by which "several priests, in virtue of Christ's own Priesthood and in the person of the High Priest, act together with one voice and one will; so also do they confect and offer a single sacrifice by a single sacramental act and likewise partake of the same" (*Guidelines for Concelebration of the Eucharist*, USCCB, 2003, #1).

The Fathers of the Second Vatican Council recommended concelebration as an expression of "the unity of the priesthood" and chose to extend permission for the practice to a number of particular instances, granting the Bishop of each diocese the authority to decide when concelebration was opportune at other times. The Council further directed that "a new rite for concelebration . . . be drawn up and inserted into the Pontifical and into the Roman Missal" (ibid. #2).

Concelebration should be understood as an appropriate way for priests to participate in the celebration of the Eucharist, expressive of their unique relationship with Christ the High Priest and of the unity of the Priesthood. From the earliest days of the Church, concelebration, while taking a variety of forms, has been celebrated for "much more than merely practical considerations" (ibid, #3). For such concelebration at Mass is expressive of the one sacrifice of the cross, the priesthood, and the action of the entire People of God, "ordered and acting hierarchically" (ibid, #4). Provision is made for concelebration in the Eucharistic Prayers for Reconciliation.

For singing purposes, first speak the text aloud and mark in pencil the natural word accents.

After the sung dialogue, remember that the highest note of this dialogue is your reciting tone. The first tone is the note above where the assembly finished **just** or the first note of the two-notes on **just**. Grab that tone and move directly to the reciting tone. The note pattern over **almighty Father** is the same as over **Lift up your hearts**. The note pattern over **Lord, Jesus Christ** repeats at **to meet together**. Words that have two notes per syllable are marked this way, due to their relative importance. Come off the second note to avoid choppiness.

EUCHARISTIC PRAYER FOR RECONCILIATION

II

There are two Eucharistic Prayers for Reconciliation. The inclusion of the Eucharistic Prayers for Reconciliation, along with those for Various Needs, in the *Missale Romanum* means that these Eucharistic Prayers now form a stable part of the Church's treasury of liturgical prayer.

Previously, these prayers were technically approved by various ad hoc or experimental measures, although usually with no established time limit. They already had been included in some official translations of the full Roman Missal, such as the Spanish and Italian translations.

Regarding the use of the Eucharistic Prayers for Reconciliation, the rubric notes the following: "The Eucharistic Prayers for Reconciliation may be used in Masses in which the mystery of reconciliation is conveyed to the faithful in a special way, as for example, in the Masses for Promoting Harmony, For Reconciliation, For the Preservation of Peace and Justice, In Time of War or Civil Disturbance, For the Forgiveness of Sins, For Charity, of the Mystery of the Holy Cross, of the Most Holy Eucharist, of the Most Precious Blood of Our Lord Jesus Christ, as well as in Masses during Lent."

Although each of these Eucharistic Prayers has a proper Preface, it is permissible to use them with another Preface that refers in some way to the themes of penance and conversion, for example, with the Prefaces of Lent.

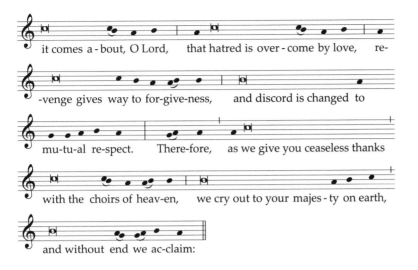

it comes a-bout, O Lord, that hatred is over-come by love, re-venge gives way to for-give-ness, and discord is changed to mu-tu-al re-spect. There-fore, as we give you ceaseless thanks with the choirs of heav-en, we cry out to your majes-ty on earth, and without end we ac-claim:

Holy, Holy, Holy Lord God of hosts . . .

Text without music:

1. V. **The Lord be with you.**
    R. And with your spirit.

    V. **Lift up your hearts.**
    R. We lift them up to the Lord.

    V. **Let us give thanks to the Lord our God.**
    R. It is right and just.

    **It is truly right and just
    that we should give you thanks and praise,
    O God, almighty Father,
    for all you do in this world,
    through our Lord Jesus Christ.**

    **For though the human race
    is divided by dissension and discord,
    yet we know that by testing us
    you change our hearts
    to prepare them for reconciliation.**

The opening exchange establishes the dialogical nature of liturgical prayer. Thus, the Priest's lines are intended to elicit the response of the assembly. Vocal intonation and eye contact will help in this regard.

Emphasize **O God**, **Father**, **almighty**, as the addressee of the prayer.

Make a contrast with **dissension and discord** and **change of hearts**.

Additionally, although they may be used during Lent, the rubrics make no distinction between weekdays and Sundays, and so there is no reason why their use would be restricted on the Lord's Day, provided that one respects the proper Prefaces that must be used on certain Lenten Sundays.

As well as the Masses suggested in the rubrics, these Eucharistic Prayers often prove useful during retreats and spiritual exercises when the time comes to bring about reconciliation with God and discover his mercy.

1. In the Preface for Reconciliation I, a binary opposition is created between the human race that is divided by dissension and discord and God who tests our hearts and effects reconciliation.

In a second paragraph, the work of changing people's hearts is the work of the Holy Spirit. Metanoia is the result of the Breath of God that moves hearts to overcome enmity. A lovely image is presented of enemies joining hands and people seeking to meet together for collaboration.

Three more binary oppositions are introduced in which hatred gives way to love, revenge is overcome by forgiveness, and discord transformed into mutual respect. Opposites are transformed, due to a change of heart and, mind, a metanoia.

In the context of theological discussion, where it is used often, metanoia is usually interpreted to mean repentance. However, some argue that the word should

Emphasize the binary tensions: **enemies may speak, adversaries join hands, peoples seek to meet together**.

Draw out the binary opposition between **hatred** and **love**, between **revenge** and **forgiveness**, and between **discord and mutual respect**.

Even more, by your Spirit you move human hearts
that enemies may speak to each other again,
adversaries join hands,
and peoples seek to meet together.

By the working of your power
it comes about, O Lord,
that hatred is overcome by love,
revenge gives way to forgiveness,
and discord is changed to mutual respect.

Therefore, as we give you ceaseless thanks
with the choirs of heaven,
we cry out to your majesty on earth,
and without end we acclaim:

Holy, Holy, Holy Lord God of hosts.
Heaven and earth are full of your glory.
Hosanna in the highest.
Blessed is he who comes in the name of the Lord.
Hosanna in the highest.

The Priest assumes the orans position, indicating that the prayer is addressed to God **almighty Father**.

Again we see the lovely metaphor of hands, this time the hand extended to sinners offering peace.

Emphasize **turned away** and **brought back**.

Emphasize **reconciled** and **converted**.

2.   The Priest, with hands extended, says:

You, therefore, almighty Father,   Celebrant alone
we bless through Jesus Christ your Son,
who comes in your name.
He himself is the Word that brings salvation,
the hand you extend to sinners,
the way by which your peace is offered to us.
When we ourselves had turned away from you
on account of our sins,
you brought us back to be reconciled, O Lord,
so that, converted at last to you,
we might love one another
through your Son,
whom for our sake you handed over to death.

The extension of hands over the gifts, the gesture, indicating the epiclesis when the Spirit is summoned to sanctify the gifts, is referenced for the celebration of reconciliation. It is a Spirit of peace and harmony.

Correlate the gesture with the words.

3.   He joins his hands and, holding them extended over the offerings, says:

And now, celebrating the reconciliation   Celebrant
Christ has brought us,   with concelebrants
we entreat you:
sanctify these gifts by the outpouring of your Spirit,

be interpreted more literally to denote changing one's mind, in the sense of embracing thoughts beyond its present limitations or thought patterns. This interpretation is compatible with the denotative meaning of repentance but replaces its negative connotation with a positive one, focusing on the superior state of being approached rather than the inferior prior state being departed from.

It is curious that the Preface references the role of the Father and Spirit in

bringing about a metanoia, but Christ is not mentioned.

2–3. Immediately after the Holy, Holy, Holy, our attention is drawn to Christ and his work of reconciliation. In typically Eucharistic fashion, we are blessing the Father for the work of Christ who comes in God's name. Christ is seen as the mediator between God and us who extends a hand from God to us to reconcile us back to God. In the expression "you brought us back," it

is clear that through sin it is we who have moved—not God. We are, therefore, prompted to move back into loving unity with God. The Death of Christ is God's sure sign of this desire to bring us back.

The Eucharist is then cast in this context of reconciliation. The prayer does not reference the historic occasion when the Eucharist was established, but instead addresses why Christ gave it to us—in order to celebrate reconciliation.

He joins his hands and makes the Sign of the Cross once over the bread and chalice together, saying:

that they may become the Body and ✚ Blood of your Son,
whose command we fulfill when we celebrate these mysteries.

He joins his hands.

4.   In the formulas that follow, the words of the Lord should be pronounced clearly and distinctly, as the nature of these words requires.

For when about to give his life to set us free,
as he reclined at supper,

He takes the bread and, holding it slightly raised above the altar, continues:

he himself took bread into his hands,
and, giving you thanks, he said the blessing,
broke the bread and gave it to his disciples, saying:

He bows slightly.

TAKE THIS, ALL OF YOU, AND EAT OF IT,
FOR THIS IS MY BODY,
WHICH WILL BE GIVEN UP FOR YOU.

He shows the consecrated host to the people, places it again on the paten, and genuflects in adoration.

5.   After this, he continues:

In a similar way, on that same evening,

He takes the chalice and, holding it slightly raised above the altar, continues:

he took the chalice of blessing in his hands,
confessing your mercy,
and gave the chalice to his disciples, saying:

He bows slightly.

TAKE THIS, ALL OF YOU, AND DRINK FROM IT,
FOR THIS IS THE CHALICE OF MY BLOOD,
THE BLOOD OF THE NEW AND ETERNAL COVENANT,
WHICH WILL BE POURED OUT FOR YOU AND FOR MANY
FOR THE FORGIVENESS OF SINS.

DO THIS IN MEMORY OF ME.

He shows the chalice to the people, places it on the corporal, and genuflects in adoration.

Notice the contextual reference made to the Last Supper when Jesus "reclined at supper."

The rubric reads "He takes the bread and, holding it slightly raised above the altar." This may suggest that the Priest is impersonating Christ; in fact, the Priest continues to address God the Father. Nor is the Priest addressing the bread. Notice that the rubric before the text "Take this all of you, and eat of it," does not call for the Priest Celebrant to break the host; it simply calls for him to bow slightly.

The Priest shows the consecrated host. The rubric does not say "elevate." The Priest genuflects in adoration.

The rubric reads, "He takes the chalice and, holding it slightly raised above the altar." Again, the Priest continues to address God the Father, and should not appear to be speaking into the chalice. Notice that the rubric before the text "Take this, all of you, and drink from it," calls for him to bow slightly.

Notice the space between "the forgiveness of sins" and "Do this in memory of me." This is subtle, but it signifies that the memorial command refers to the whole action and not simply the chalice.

The Priest shows the chalice. The rubric does not say "elevate." The Priest Celebrant genuflects in adoration.

4–5. The words of Institution, or the historical narrative is now established, as in all the Eucharistic Prayers, in the course of a meal. Without exception, all the Eucharistic Prayers mention that "after the Supper" Christ took the wine. But this prayer is somewhat unique in that it sets the stage with Christ reclining at table with his disciples "to give his life to set us free."

The coordination of texts and gestures for the Institution narrative is very important. The Priest must remember that he is continuing to recount the great deeds of God now focused in Christ Jesus on the night before he died. He should be sure that his gestures and posture do not make it appear that he is addressing these texts to the bread and wine. The Priest's posture should reflect that this prayer continues to be part of a Eucharistic Prayer addressed to the Father.

Although rubrics, such as, "He takes the bread and, holding it slightly raised above the altar," suggest that the Priest is impersonating Christ; in fact, the Priest continues to address God the Father, here, recounting one of the great deeds of God In history, the Institution narrative. Notice that the rubric before the text "Take this, all of you, and eat of it," does not call for the Priest Celebrant to break the host; it simply calls for him to bow slightly.

Similarly, after speaking the text, the Priest shows the consecrated host. The rubric does not say "elevate." The Priest Celebrant genuflects in adoration.

The Priest may sing **The mystery of faith**, which will serve as a prompt for the assembly to sing one of the three acclamations.

If the Priest sings, it should be musically congruent with what is to follow. If a modern composition is used, the Priest should verify that there is a lead-in in order to create a seamless piece. It makes no sense to sing one lead-in that is modal when a tonal acclamation is going to be sung. This only necessitates the organist's having to intervene with an introduction to establish the key for the Memorial Acclamation.

The Priest resumes the orans position to emphasize that the entire Eucharistic Prayer is addressed to God, whereas, the Memorial Acclamations are addressed to Christ. In both cases, we use the designation **Lord**, but the context and internal references make the designation known.

Though subordinate, emphasize **Death** and **Resurrection**, so as even more to emphasize **we offer you . . . the Sacrifice of perfect reconciliation**.

Parallel the phrases **sign of unity** and **instrument of peace**.

6.   Then he says:

> **The mystery of faith.**
>
> Celebrant alone

And the people continue, acclaiming:

> We proclaim your Death, O Lord,
> and profess your Resurrection
> until you come again.

Or:

> When we eat this Bread and drink this Cup,
> we proclaim your Death, O Lord,
> until you come again.

Or:

> Save us, Savior of the world,
> for by your Cross and Resurrection
> you have set us free.

7.   Then the Priest, with hands extended, says:

> **Celebrating, therefore, the memorial**
> **of the Death and Resurrection of your Son,**
> **who left us this pledge of his love,**
> **we offer you what you have bestowed on us,**
> **the Sacrifice of perfect reconciliation.**
>
> Celebrant with concelebrants
>
> **Holy Father, we humbly beseech you**
> **to accept us also, together with your Son,**
> **and in this saving banquet**
> **graciously to endow us with his very Spirit,**
> **who takes away everything**
> **that estranges us from one another.**
>
> **May he make your Church a sign of unity**
> **and an instrument of your peace among all people**
> **and may he keep us in communion**
> **with N. our Pope and N. our Bishop***
> **and all the Bishops**
> **and your entire people.**
>
> Celebrant or one concelebrant

---

*   Mention may be made here of the Coadjutor Bishop, or Auxiliary Bishops, as noted in the *General Instruction of the Roman Missal*, no. 149.

The command "Do this in memory of me" is in reference to the entire action and should not seem to reference the chalice only. In 1 Corinthians 11:24–25, we find the memorial command after both the bread and the wine. A pause inserted before the memorial command may help to clarify this phrase.

6. The Priest's text, "The mystery of faith," functions as a cue for the people to sing the Memorial Acclamation. It is helpful to understand that the Priest's words are an exclamation, not a declaration.

All three Memorial Acclamations are addressed directly to Christ. It is interesting that the Priest addresses God the Father throughout the Eucharistic Prayer, except during the Institution narrative, during which he speaks about the Last Supper event in a historical mode. But when the assembly is asked to pray, they address their acclamation to Christ, whom they believe is really present in the Eucharistic species.

7. Liturgical scholars call this section of the prayer the anamnesis-offering. The Priest expands upon the acclamation articulated by the congregation, calling to mind the Paschal Mystery and offers the "Sacrifice of perfect reconciliation," the transformed bread and wine. This paragraph enacts a number of liturgical functions. First, along

Just as you have gathered us now
    at the table of your Son,
so also bring us together,
with the glorious Virgin Mary, Mother of God,
with your blessed Apostles and all the Saints,
with our brothers and sisters
and those of every race and tongue
who have died in your friendship.
Bring us to share with them the unending banquet of unity
in a new heaven and a new earth,
where the fullness of your peace will shine forth

Celebrant or
one
concelebrant

Emphasize **you have gathered us now at the table of your Son**.

Emphasize **unending banquet of unity**.

He joins his hands.

in Christ Jesus our Lord.

8.   He takes the chalice and the paten with the host and, raising both, he says:

**Through him, and with him, and in him,
O God, almighty Father,
in the unity of the Holy Spirit,
all glory and honor is yours,
for ever and ever.**

Celebrant alone
or with
concelebrants

The doxology is the third and final of the Eucharistic acclamations (along with the Holy, Holy, Holy and Memorial Acclamation). It is strongly suggested that it be sung. Pause at the commas and the sense lines and continue to increase in volume, so as to cue the congregation's **Amen.**

The people acclaim:

Amen.

Then follows the Communion Rite, p. 663.

with the Memorial Acclamation just sung or recited, it recalls the great deeds of salvation, the anamnesis of Christ's Death and Resurrection. Second, it is the means by which the community offers the transformed bread and wine, now the bread of life and the chalice of salvation. Third, it enacts the epiclesis over the assembly, asking that God endow us with the Holy Spirit, "who takes away everything that estranges us from one another." Fourth, it prays for the Church and all her members—the clerical leadership, the dead, the Saints—that all may be a sign of unity and an instrument of peace. The image of gathering around a banquet table is the leading metaphor in speaking of reconciliation.

8. The conclusion of the Eucharistic Prayer calls for the Priest to lift the paten with host and the Deacon (or in his absence, the Priest) to chant or recite the doxology. Elsewhere, the Missal provides a chant setting of this doxology that leads to the community's chanted "Amen"; however, other musical settings of the doxology may be correlated to the congregation's "Amen." The Priest's doxology and the people's "Amen" should be musically congruent. The doxology is the climax of the Eucharistic Prayer. It is the last of three acclamations that punctuate the Eucharistic Prayer. In musical terms, this would be the final great crescendo.

Eucharistic Prayer for Various Needs
in a concelebration

The Preface and **You are indeed Holy** to **and breaks the bread** inclusive are said by the principal celebrant alone, with hands extended.

From **Therefore, Father most merciful** to **of our Lord Jesus Christ** inclusive is spoken together by all the concelebrants, with hands extended toward the offerings.

From **On the day before he was to suffer** to **in whose Body and Blood we have communion** inclusive, all the concelebrants together speak in this manner:

a) The part **On the day before he was to suffer**, with hands joined.

b) While speaking the words of the Lord, each extends his right hand toward the bread and toward the chalice, if this seems appropriate; as the host and the chalice are elevated at the Consecration, however, the concelebrants look toward them and then bow profoundly.

c) The parts **Therefore, holy Father** and **Look with favor on the oblation of your Church**, with hands extended.

It is appropriate that the intercessions **Lord, renew your Church**; or **And so, having called us to your table**; or **By our partaking**; or **Bring your Church, O Lord**; as well as **Remember our brothers and sisters**; be assigned to one or other of the concelebrants, who pronounces these prayers alone, with hands extended.

The following parts especially may be sung: **On the day before he was to suffer**; **In a similar way**; **Therefore, holy Father**; **Look with favor on the oblation of your Church**, as well as the concluding doxology.

The concluding doxology of the Eucharistic Prayer is pronounced by the principal celebrant alone, or by all the concelebrants along with the principal celebrant.

Concelebration is the practice by which "several priests, in virtue of Christ's own Priesthood and in the person of the High Priest, act together with one voice and one will; so also do they confect and offer a single sacrifice by a single sacramental act and likewise partake of the same" (*Guidelines for Concelebration of the Eucharist*, USCCB, 2003, #1).

The Fathers of the Second Vatican Council recommended concelebration as an expression of "the unity of the priesthood" and chose to extend permission for the practice to a number of particular instances, granting the Bishop of each diocese the authority to decide when concelebration was opportune at other times. The Council further directed that "a new rite for concelebration . . . be drawn up and inserted into the Pontifical and into the Roman Missal" (ibid. #2).

Concelebration should be understood as an appropriate way for priests to participate in the celebration of the Eucharist, expressive of their unique relationship with Christ the High Priest and of the unity of the Priesthood. From the earliest days of the Church, concelebration, while taking a variety of forms, has been celebrated for "much more than merely practical considerations" (ibid, #3). For such concelebration at Mass is expressive of the one sacrifice of the cross, the priesthood, and the action of the entire People of God, "ordered and acting hierarchically." (ibid, #4). Provision is made for concelebration in the Eucharistic Prayers for Reconciliation.

EUCHARISTIC PRAYER FOR USE IN MASSES FOR VARIOUS NEEDS

I

The Church on the Path of Unity

For singing purposes, first speak the text aloud and mark in pencil the natural word accents.

1. The following form of this Eucharistic Prayer is appropriately used with Mass formularies such as, For the Church, For the Pope, For the Bishop, For the Election of a Pope or a Bishop, For a Council or Synod, For Priests, For the Priest Himself, For Ministers of the Church, and For a Spiritual or Pastoral Gathering.

After the sung dialogue, remember that the highest note of this dialogue is your reciting tone. The first tone is the note above where the assembly finished **just** or the first note of the two notes on **just**. Grab that tone and move directly to the reciting tone. Several of the melodic motives in the Preface dialogue are repeated throughout the Preface. Words that have two notes per syllable are marked this way, due to their relative importance. Come off the second note to avoid choppiness.

The Eucharistic Prayer for Use in Masses for Various Needs is sometimes called the Swiss Synod Eucharistic Prayer. It was approved by the members of the National Conference of Catholic Bishops for use in the United States, as was its provisional (interim) English translation. This Eucharistic Prayer originally was prepared on the occasion of the Swiss Synod (1972–1975) and approved by the Sacred Congregation for Divine Worship in August 1974. The prayer was composed in German and then translated into French and Italian, since these are the languages used in Switzerland. By 1987, the prayer had been translated into 12 languages and was in use throughout the world. The Swiss Synod Eucharistic Prayer was included in the common Spanish translation of the Order of Mass and the Eucharistic Prayers (*Ordinario del la Misa*), which was published in this country in 1989. However, the prayer was not available for use in English in the United States.

In 1991, the Congregation for Divine Worship and the Discipline of the Sacraments published a revised Latin version of the Swiss Synod Eucharistic Prayer under the title "Eucharistic Prayer for Masses for Various Needs and Occasions." The Congregation noted that, "Since from the very beginning different editions of the text of this eucharistic prayer have been available in German, French, and Italian, it seems necessary to issue a Latin text of this prayer to serve as the *editio typica* for all languages." The Congregation also indicated that previously approved versions of this prayer must conform to the new typi-

the blessed hope of your King-dom   and shines bright as the sign

of your faith-ful-ness,   which in Christ Je-sus our Lord   you prom-

-ised would last for e-ter-ni-ty.   And so, with all the Powers of

heaven, we worship you con-stant-ly on earth,   while, with all the

Church,   as one voice we ac-claim:

Holy, Holy, Holy Lord God of hosts . . .

Text without music:

V. **The Lord be with you.**
R. And with your spirit.

V. **Lift up your hearts.**
R. We lift them up to the Lord.

V. **Let us give thanks to the Lord our God.**
R. It is right and just.

**It is truly right and just to give you thanks
and raise to you a hymn of glory and praise,
O Lord, Father of infinite goodness.**

**For by the word of your Son's Gospel
you have brought together one Church
from every people, tongue, and nation,
and, having filled her with life by the power of your Spirit,
you never cease through her
to gather the whole human race into one.**

The opening exchange establishes the dialogical nature of liturgical prayer. Thus, the Priest's lines are intended to elicit the response of the assembly. Vocal intonation and eye contact will help in this regard.

Emphasize **O Lord**, **Father of infinite goodness**, as the addressee of the prayer.

Emphasize **every people, tongue, and nation,** and **to gather the whole human race into one**.

cal edition when new editions of the Missal are published.

The new Eucharistic Prayer has corresponding sets of Prefaces and intercessions based on four themes: "The Church on the Path of Unity," "God Guides His Church along the Way of Salvation," "Jesus, the Way to the Father," and "Jesus, Who Went About Doing Good." Although printed as one Eucharistic Prayer, the new Eucharistic Prayer is, in reality, four prayers, each with its own theme. As its title indicates, the prayer is intended for use at Masses for

Various Needs. Because the Prefaces are integral to the prayer, the prayer may not be used with the variable Prefaces or on occasions when there is a proper Preface. The introductory notes printed with the Eucharistic Prayer indicate which theme is appropriate to each of the Masses for Various Needs in the Missal.

Since no mention of substituting the Preface is made in the Latin rubrics, these four prayers may not be separated from their Prefaces. For this reason, using these prayers is limited to occasions when a Mass

for Various Needs may be celebrated. Consequently, they are used, above all, during Ordinary Time as the celebration of these Masses is more or less restricted during the major liturgical seasons.

We are not referring to four Eucharistic Prayers, but to four versions of a single prayer that accentuate different themes. This accentuation is done, above all, during the Preface of each version and in a section of the intercessions following the Consecration. Thus, separating these prayers from their Preface would under-

Manifesting the covenant of your love,
she dispenses without ceasing
the blessed hope of your Kingdom
and shines bright as the sign of your faithfulness,
which in Christ Jesus our Lord
you promised would last for eternity.

And so, with all the Powers of heaven,
we worship you constantly on earth,
while, with all the Church,
as one voice we acclaim:

Holy, Holy, Holy Lord God of hosts.
Heaven and earth are full of your glory.
Hosanna in the highest.
Blessed is he who comes in the name of the Lord.
Hosanna in the highest.

The Priest assumes the orans position, indicating that the prayer is addressed to God.

We see the lovely metaphor of God walking **with us on the journey of life**. Emphasize **your Son, present in our midst** and **gathered by his love**.

2.   The Priest, with hands extended, says:

You are indeed Holy and to be glorified, O God,   *Celebrant alone*
who love the human race
and who always walk with us on the journey of life.
Blessed indeed is your Son,
present in our midst
when we are gathered by his love,
and when, as once for the disciples, so now for us,
he opens the Scriptures and breaks the bread.

mine the particular theme that the prayer seeks to stress.

The first version—"The Church on the Path to Unity"—is especially apt for Masses for the Pope, for the Bishop, for the election of a Pope, for a council or synod, for Priests, for the celebrating Priest, for the ministers of the Church, and on the occasion of a spiritual or ecclesial assembly.

This partial review of the Masses for Various Needs also affords us the opportunity of unearthing the treasury of the

Church's intercessory prayer, so often left concealed and confined in the Missal.

1. The Preface for the first formulary follows the classical euchological shape. In the body we pray for the one Church brought together from "every people, tongue, and nation" signaling her universality. Reference is made to the Holy Spirit who holds the entire human race in unity. The theme of covenant is evoked to indicate that the relationship of love was first

initiated by God and that both God and we are held to this relationship. This covenant was, therefore, ratified in Christ and the promise of its fulfillment is eternal. The Preface succinctly and beautifully sets the tone for this Mass dedicated to unity of all peoples.

2. This beautiful prayer depicts God as walking with us on the journey of life and Christ as in our midst in the scriptures and the breaking of the bread.

3.   He joins his hands and, holding them extended over the offerings, says:

Therefore, Father most merciful,
we ask that you send forth your Holy Spirit
to sanctify these gifts of bread and wine,

Celebrant
with concelebrants

He joins his hands and makes the Sign of the Cross once over the bread and chalice together, saying:

that they may become for us
the Body and ✠ Blood

He joins his hands.

of our Lord Jesus Christ.

4.   In the formulas that follow, the words of the Lord should be pronounced clearly and distinctly, as the nature of these words requires.

On the day before he was to suffer,
on the night of the Last Supper,

He takes the bread and, holding it slightly raised above the altar, continues:

he took bread and said the blessing,
broke the bread and gave it to his disciples, saying:

He bows slightly.

Take this, all of you, and eat of it,
for this is my Body,
which will be given up for you.

He shows the consecrated host to the people, places it again on the paten, and genuflects in adoration.

5.   After this, he continues:

In a similar way, when supper was ended,

He takes the chalice and, holding it slightly raised above the altar, continues:

he took the chalice, gave you thanks
and gave the chalice to his disciples, saying:

He bows slightly.

Take this, all of you, and drink from it,
for this is the chalice of my Blood,
the Blood of the new and eternal covenant,
which will be poured out for you and for many
for the forgiveness of sins.

Do this in memory of me.

He shows the chalice to the people, places it on the corporal, and genuflects in adoration.

The rubric reads "He takes the bread and, holding it slightly raised above the altar." This may seem to suggest that the Priest is impersonating Christ; in fact, the Priest continues to address God the Father. Nor is the Priest addressing the bread. Notice that the rubric before the text "Take this all of you, and eat of it," does not call for the Priest Celebrant to break the host; it simply calls for him to bow slightly.

The Priest then shows the consecrated host. The rubric does not say "elevate." The Priest Celebrant genuflects in adoration.

The rubric reads "He takes the chalice and, holding it slightly raised above the altar." Again, the Priest continues to address God the Father. Notice that the rubric before the text "Take this all of you, and drink from it," calls for the Priest to bow slightly.

Notice the space between "the forgiveness of sins" and "Do this in memory of me." This is subtle, but it signifies that the memorial command refers to the whole action and not simply the chalice.

The Priest shows the chalice. The rubric does not say "elevate." The Priest Celebrant genuflects in adoration.

---

3. This article is the epiclesis over the gifts invoking the Holy Spirit for the transformation of the offering.

4–5. The words of institution recounting the Last Supper are found in the usual position following the epiclesis and preceding the anamnesis. The final command "Do this in memory of me" is in reference to the entire meal and not simply to the chalice. In 1 Corinthians 11:24–25, we find the memorial command after both the bread and the wine.

The Priest may sing **The mystery of faith**, which will serve as a prompt for the assembly to sing one of the three Memorial Acclamations.

If the Priest sings, it should be musically congruent with what is to follow. If a modern composition is used, the Priest should verify whether a lead-in was composed, so that there will be a seamless fit to the piece. It makes no sense to sing one lead-in that is modal when a tonal acclamation is going to be sung. This necessitates the organist's having to intervene with an introduction to establish the key for the Memorial Acclamation.

The priest resumes the orans position to emphasize that the entire Eucharistic Prayer is addressed to God, whereas, the Memorial Acclamations are addressed to Christ. Though subordinate, emphasize **Passion and Death on the Cross** to **the glory of the Resurrection**, so as even more to emphasize **we offer you the Bread of life and the Chalice of blessing**.

Bring out the connection between **oblation** and **Sacrifice**.

6. Then he says:

The mystery of faith.

Celebrant alone

And the people continue, acclaiming:

We proclaim your Death, O Lord,
and profess your Resurrection
until you come again.

Or:

When we eat this Bread and drink this Cup,
we proclaim your Death, O Lord,
until you come again.

Or:

Save us, Savior of the world,
for by your Cross and Resurrection
you have set us free.

7. Then the Priest, with hands extended, says:

Celebrant with concelebrants

**Therefore, holy Father,
as we celebrate the memorial of Christ your Son, our Savior,
whom you led through his Passion and Death on the Cross
to the glory of the Resurrection,
and whom you have seated at your right hand,
we proclaim the work of your love until he comes again
and we offer you the Bread of life
and the Chalice of blessing.**

**Look with favor on the oblation of your Church,
in which we show forth
the paschal Sacrifice of Christ that has been handed on to us,
and grant that, by the power of the Spirit of your love,
we may be counted now and until the day of eternity
among the members of your Son,
in whose Body and Blood we have communion.**

6. The Priest's text, "The mystery of faith" functions as a cue, although it is an exclamation. Originally, the phrase *mysterium fidei* was part of the consecratory text, but Pope Paul VI, on his authority, removed them from the consecratory words and made them this exclamation. The Latin text does not say, "Let us proclaim the mystery of faith," nor does it provide a full sentence. The phrase could best be interpreted as "Oh, the mystery of faith!"

a moment of contemplative awe and surrender that serves as a cue to the congregations' response.

The Priest's chant of these words is correlated to the Missal's Memorial Acclamation chants, but there may be musical settings of the Mystery of Faith correlated to other musical settings of the congregation's Memorial Acclamations that the Priest Celebrant should learn.

7. Liturgical scholars call this section of the prayer the anamnesis-offering. The Priest expands upon the acclamation articulated by the congregation calling to mind the Paschal Mystery and offers the Sacrament of the Paschal Mystery, the transformed bread and wine.

In the Masses for Various Needs, this section along with the Preface are adapted to the themes celebrated in the four versions. This article does many liturgical

Lord, renew your Church (which is in N.)
by the light of the Gospel.
Strengthen the bond of unity
between the faithful and the pastors of your people,
together with N. our Pope, N. our Bishop, *
and the whole Order of Bishops,
that in a world torn by strife
your people may shine forth
as a prophetic sign of unity and concord.

*Celebrant or
one concelebrant*

Remember our brothers and sisters (N. and N.),
who have fallen asleep in the peace of your Christ,
and all the dead, whose faith you alone have known.
Admit them to rejoice in the light of your face,
and in the resurrection give them the fullness of life.

*Celebrant alone
or with
concelebrants*

Grant also to us,
when our earthly pilgrimage is done,
that we may come to an eternal dwelling place
and live with you for ever;
there, in communion with the Blessed Virgin Mary, Mother of God,
with the Apostles and Martyrs,
(with Saint N.: the Saint of the day or Patron)
and with all the Saints,
we shall praise and exalt you

He joins his hands.

through Jesus Christ, your Son.

8.   He takes the chalice and the paten with the host and, raising both, he says:

Through him, and with him, and in him,
O God, almighty Father,
in the unity of the Holy Spirit,
all glory and honor is yours,
for ever and ever.

*Celebrant alone
or with
concelebrants*

The people acclaim:

Amen.

Then follows the Communion Rite, p. 663.

---

*   Mention may be made here of the Coadjutor Bishop, or Auxiliary Bishops, as noted in the *General Instruction of the Roman Missal*, no. 149.

This part of the prayer differs in the four versions to bring out the theme that each prayer emphasizes. As the first Eucharistic Prayer for Masses for Various Needs prays for the Church on the Path of Unity, we pray here that the bond of unity be strengthened between the faithful and those who pastor God's people. In this context, we then pray for the Pope and local Ordinary with all the Bishops so that **in a world torn by strife your people may shine forth as a prophetic sign of unity and concord.**

Contrast **earthly pilgrimage** with **eternal dwelling place**.

The doxology is the third and final of the Eucharistic acclamations (along with the Holy, Holy, Holy and Memorial Acclamations). It is strongly suggested that it be sung. Pause at the commas and the sense lines and continue to increase in volume, so as to cue the congregation's **Amen.**

---

functions. Its first paragraph is an anamnesis-offering in which the community makes memory of the Paschal Mystery and offers to God the Father the Sacrifice of the Cross. The second paragraph is an epiclesis on the community itself, praying that those who receive Holy Communion be united by the Holy Spirit. In the third paragraph, we pray for renewal of the Church by the light of the Gospel and unity between the people and their pastors. In addition to the specific references of the Pope and the local Bishop, we pray for the whole Order of Bishops. In the fourth paragraph, we pray for those who have fallen asleep in the peace of Christ, with the opportunity to name them. We conclude with a prayer for the entire Church on pilgrimage. We ask that when our earthy pilgrimage is finished, we may come to an eternal dwelling and join those who have gone before us. Space is allowed for the mention of specific Saints. These words echo the theme already announced in the Preface "The Church on the Path of Unity."

8. The prayer reaches its climax with the doxology and the "Amen." This is the last of three acclamations that punctuate the Eucharistic Prayer and ritually is the pinnacle of the prayer, as we give honor and glory to God though Christ with the Holy Spirit.

II

God Guides His Church along the Way of Salvation

1. The following form of this Eucharistic Prayer is appropriately used with Mass formularies such as, For the Church, For Vocations to Holy Orders, For the Laity, For the Family, For Religious, For Vocations to Religious Life, For Charity, For Relatives and Friends, and For Giving Thanks to God.

For singing purposes, first speak the text aloud and mark in pencil the natural word accents.

V. The Lord be with you.   R. And with your spir-it.

V. Lift up your hearts.   R. We lift them up to the Lord.

V. Let us give thanks to the Lord our God.   R. It is right and just.

It is truly right and just, our duty and our sal-va-tion, al-ways and

everywhere to give you thanks, Lord, holy Father, creator of the

world and source of all life. For you never forsake the works of

your wis-dom, but by your prov-i-dence are even now at work in

our midst. With mighty hand and out-stretched arm you led your

peo-ple Is-ra-el through the de-sert. Now, as your Church makes

her pilgrim journey in the world, you always accompany her by the

power of the Ho-ly Spir-it and lead her along the paths of time

After the sung dialogue, remember that the highest note of this dialogue is your reciting tone. The first tone is the note above where the assembly finished **just** or the first note of the two notes on **just**. Grab that tone and move directly to the reciting tone. Several of the melodic motives in the Preface dialogue are repeated throughout the Preface. Words that have two notes per syllable are marked this way, due to their relative importance. Come off the second note to avoid choppiness.

The Eucharistic Prayer for Use in Masses for Various Needs is sometimes called the Swiss Synod Eucharistic Prayer. This Eucharistic Prayer was approved by the members of the National Conference of Catholic Bishops for use in the United States, as was its provisional (interim) English translation. Originally prepared on the occasion of the Swiss Synod (1972–1975), it was approved by the Sacred Congregation for Divine Worship in August 1974. The prayer was composed in German and then translated into French and Italian, since these are the languages used in Switzerland. By 1987, the prayer had been translated into 12 languages and was in use throughout the world. The Swiss Synod Eucharistic Prayer was included in the common Spanish translation of the Order of Mass and the Eucharistic Prayers (*Ordinario del la Misa*), published in this country in 1989. However, the prayer was not available for use in English in the United States.

The new Eucharistic Prayer has corresponding sets of Prefaces and intercessions based on four themes: "The Church on the Path of Unity," "God Guides His Church along the Way of Salvation," "Jesus, the Way to the Father," and "Jesus, Who Went about Doing Good." Although printed as one Eucharistic Prayer, the new Eucharistic Prayer is, in reality, four prayers, each with its own theme. As its title indicates, the prayer is intended for use at Masses for Various Needs.

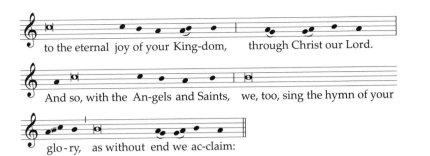

to the eternal joy of your King-dom,   through Christ our Lord.

And so, with the An-gels and Saints,   we, too, sing the hymn of your

glo-ry,   as without end we ac-claim:

Holy, Holy, Holy Lord God of hosts . . .

Text without music:

V. **The Lord be with you.**
R. And with your spirit.

V. **Lift up your hearts.**
R. We lift them up to the Lord.

V. **Let us give thanks to the Lord our God.**
R. It is right and just.

It is truly right and just, our duty and our salvation,
always and everywhere to give you thanks,
Lord, holy Father,
creator of the world and source of all life.

For you never forsake the works of your wisdom,
but by your providence are even now at work in our midst.
With mighty hand and outstretched arm
you led your people Israel through the desert.
Now, as your Church makes her pilgrim journey in the world,
you always accompany her
by the power of the Holy Spirit
and lead her along the paths of time
to the eternal joy of your Kingdom,
through Christ our Lord.

And so, with the Angels and Saints,
we, too, sing the hymn of your glory,
as without end we acclaim:

The opening exchange establishes the dialogical nature of liturgical prayer. Thus, the Priest's lines are intended to elicit the response of the assembly. Vocal intonation and eye contact will help in this regard.

Emphasize **Lord, holy Father**, as the addressee of the prayer.

Emphasize the parallels: **works of wisdom** and **work in our midst**. Emphasize **mighty hand and outstretched arm**.

These Eucharistic Prayers are four versions of a single prayer that accentuate different themes. This accentuation is done, above all, during the Preface of each version and in a section of the intercessions following the Consecration. Thus, separating these prayers from their Preface would also undermine the particular theme that the prayer seeks to stress.

This partial review of the Masses for Various Needs also affords us the opportunity of unearthing the treasury of the Church's intercessory prayer, so often left concealed and confined in the Missal.

1. The second variation—"God Guides His Church along the Way of Salvation"—is recommended for Masses for the Church, for vocations, for the laity, for the family, for religious, for postulating charity, for relatives and friends, and Masses in thanksgiving.

The Preface signals this theme using the Exodus theme, in which, as did Moses, Jesus stretches out his arm and leads us through the desert. The exodus of the ancient Israelites is a foreshadowing of the pilgrim journey that Christians are called to make. Ultimately, the pilgrimage leads along the paths of time to the eternal joy of heaven. The comparison of Christ to Moses, and the Church to ancient Israel demonstrates that God's providence is eternal.

Holy, Holy, Holy Lord God of hosts.
Heaven and earth are full of your glory.
Hosanna in the highest.
Blessed is he who comes in the name of the Lord.
Hosanna in the highest.

The Priest assumes the orans position, indicating that the prayer is addressed to God.

We see the lovely metaphor of God walking **with us on the journey of life**. Emphasize **your Son, present in our midst** and **gathered by his love**.

2.   The Priest, with hands extended, says:

You are indeed Holy and to be glorified, O God,   Celebrant alone
who love the human race
and who always walk with us on the journey of life.
Blessed indeed is your Son,
present in our midst
when we are gathered by his love
and when, as once for the disciples, so now for us,
he opens the Scriptures and breaks the bread.

The extension of hands over the gifts, the gesture indicating the epiclesis when the Spirit is summoned to sanctify the gifts is referenced for the celebration of reconciliation.

Correlate the gesture with the words.

3.   He joins his hands and, holding them extended over the offerings, says:

Therefore, Father most merciful,   Celebrant
we ask that you send forth your Holy Spirit   with concelebrants
to sanctify these gifts of bread and wine,

He joins his hands and makes the Sign of the Cross once over the bread and chalice together, saying:

that they may become for us
the Body and ✚ Blood

He joins his hands.

of our Lord Jesus Christ.

4.   In the formulas that follow, the words of the Lord should be pronounced clearly and distinctly, as the nature of these words requires.

On the day before he was to suffer,
on the night of the Last Supper,

He takes the bread and, holding it slightly raised above the altar, continues:

he took bread and said the blessing,
broke the bread and gave it to his disciples, saying:

He bows slightly.

Take this, all of you, and eat of it,
for this is my Body,
which will be given up for you.

The rubric reads "He takes the bread and, holding it slightly raised above the altar." This may seem to suggest that the Priest is impersonating Christ; in fact, the Priest continues to address God the Father. The Priest should not appear to be addressing the bread. Notice that the rubric before the text, "Take this all of you, and eat of it," does not call for the Priest Celebrant to break the host; it simply calls for him to bow slightly.

He shows the consecrated host to the people, places it again on the paten, and genuflects in adoration.

2. This beautiful prayer depicts God as walking with us on the journey of life and Christ as in our midst in the Sacred Scriptures and the breaking of bread.

3. This article is the epiclesis over the gifts invoking the Holy Spirit for the transformation over the offering. The Priest should extend his hands over the offerings before he begins to recite the text, and he should keep them extended until he makes the Sign of the Cross, once over the bread and

chalice together while saying the words, "Body and Blood."

4–5. The coordination of texts and gestures for the Institution narrative is very important. The Priest must remember that he is continuing to recount the great deeds of God now focused in Christ Jesus on the night before he died and should not appear to be addressing these texts to the bread and wine. It continues to be part of a

Eucharistic Prayer addressed to the Father. Although rubrics, such as "He takes the bread and, holding it slightly raised above the altar," suggest that the Priest is impersonating Christ; in fact, the Priest continues to address God the Father; here, recounting one of the great deeds of God in history, the Institution narrative. Notice that the rubric before the text, "Take this all of you and eat of it," calls for him to bow slightly. Similarly, after speaking the text, the Priest shows the consecrated host.

5. After this, he continues:

In a similar way, when supper was ended,

He takes the chalice and, holding it slightly raised above the altar, continues:

**he took the chalice, gave you thanks
and gave the chalice to his disciples, saying:**

He bows slightly.

**TAKE THIS, ALL OF YOU, AND DRINK FROM IT,
FOR THIS IS THE CHALICE OF MY BLOOD,
THE BLOOD OF THE NEW AND ETERNAL COVENANT,
WHICH WILL BE POURED OUT FOR YOU AND FOR MANY
FOR THE FORGIVENESS OF SINS.**

DO THIS IN MEMORY OF ME.

He shows the chalice to the people, places it on the corporal, and genuflects in adoration.

6. Then he says:

The mystery of faith.   Celebrant alone

And the people continue, acclaiming:

We proclaim your Death, O Lord,
and profess your Resurrection
until you come again.

Or:

When we eat this Bread and drink this Cup,
we proclaim your Death, O Lord,
until you come again.

Or:

Save us, Savior of the world,
for by your Cross and Resurrection
you have set us free.

The Priest shows the consecrated host. The rubric does not say "elevate." The Priest celebrant genuflects in adoration.

The rubric reads "He takes the chalice and, holding it slightly raised above the altar." Again, the Priest continues to address God the Father. Notice that the rubric before the text "Take this all of you, and drink from it," calls for him to bow slightly.

The Priest shows the chalice. The rubric does not say "elevate." The Priest Celebrant genuflects in adoration.

The Priest may sing **The mystery of faith**, which will serve as a prompt for the assembly to sing one of the three acclamations.

If the Priest sings, it should be musically congruent with what is to follow. If the assembly is to sing another modern composition of the Memorial Acclamation, the Priest should verify whether there is a lead-in in for his piece. It makes no sense to sing a modal lead-in when a tonal acclamation will be sung.

(The rubric does not say "elevate.") The Priest genuflects in adoration.

The command "Do this in memory of me" is in reference to the entire action and should not seem to reference the chalice only. In 1 Corinthians 11:24–25, we find the memorial command after both the bread and the wine. A pause inserted before the memorial command may help to clarify this phrase.

6. The Priest's text, "The mystery of faith" functions as a cue, although it is an exclamation. Originally, the phrase *mysterium fidei* was part of the consecratory text, but Pope Paul VI, on his authority, removed them from the consecratory words and made them this exclamation. The Latin text does not say, "Let us proclaim the mystery of faith," nor does it provide a full sentence. Rather, the phrase could best be interpreted as "Oh, the mystery of faith!" a moment of contemplative awe and surrender that serves as a cue to the congregations' response.

The Priest's text is correlated to the Memorial Acclamation chants of the Missal, but there may be other musical settings of the Mystery of Faith correlated to other musical settings of the congregation's Memorial Acclamation that the Priest should learn.

7. Liturgical scholars call this section of the prayer the anamnesis-offering. The Priest expands upon the acclamation articulated by the congregation, calling to

The Priest resumes the orans position to emphasize that the entire Eucharistic Prayer is addressed to God, whereas, the Memorial Acclamations are addressed to Christ. Though subordinate, emphasize **Passion and Death on the Cross to the glory of the Resurrection**, so as even more to emphasize **we offer you the Bread of life and the Chalice of blessing**.

Bring out the connection between **oblation** and **Sacrifice**.

7.   Then the Priest, with hands extended, says:

Celebrant with concelebrants

Therefore, holy Father,
as we celebrate the memorial
    of Christ your Son, our Savior,
whom you led through his Passion and Death on the Cross
to the glory of the Resurrection,
and whom you have seated at your right hand,
we proclaim the work of your love until he comes again
and we offer you the Bread of life
and the Chalice of blessing.

Look with favor on the oblation of your Church,
in which we show forth
the paschal Sacrifice of Christ that has been handed on to us,
and grant that, by the power of the Spirit of your love,
we may be counted now and until the day of eternity
among the members of your Son,
in whose Body and Blood we have communion.

This part of the prayer differs in the four variations to bring out the theme that each of the four prayers emphasizes. As the second Eucharistic Prayer for Masses for Various Needs prays to God as he guides his Church along the Way of Salvation, we pray here that the Table of the Lord may be a confirmation of communion together with those who pastor God's people. In this context, we pray for the Pope and local Ordinary with all the Bishops, Priests, and deacons, and the entire people that **as we walk your ways with faith and hope, / we may strive to bring joy and trust into the world**.

And so, having called us to your table, Lord,
confirm us in unity,
so that, together with N. our Pope and N. our Bishop,[*]
with all Bishops, Priests and Deacons,
and your entire people,
as we walk your ways with faith and hope,
we may strive to bring joy and trust into the world.

Celebrant or one concelebrant

Remember our brothers and sisters (N. and N.),
who have fallen asleep in the peace of your Christ,
and all the dead, whose faith you alone have known.
Admit them to rejoice in the light of your face,
and in the resurrection give them the fullness of life.

Celebrant or one concelebrant

---

*   Mention may be made here of the Coadjutor Bishop, or Auxiliary Bishops, as noted in the *General Instruction of the Roman Missal*, no. 149.

mind the Paschal Mystery and offers the Sacrament of the Paschal Mystery, the transformed bread and wine.

In the Masses for Various Needs, this section along with the Preface, are adapted to the themes celebrated in the four versions. This article has many liturgical functions. Its first paragraph is an anamnesis-offering in which the community makes memory of the Paschal Mystery and offers to God the Father the sacrifice of

the cross. The second paragraph is an epiclesis on the community itself, praying that those who receive Holy Communion be united by the Holy Spirit. In the third paragraph, we pray for unity of all who are called to share at the Table of the Lord confirmed by the Church's leadership. Inclusion is made of Priests and Deacons, along with bishops, with whom we strive to bring joy and trust into the world. In the fourth paragraph, we pray for those who

have fallen asleep in the peace of Christ with the opportunity to name them and all those who have died whose faith is known only to God. We conclude with a prayer for the entire Church on pilgrimage. We ask that, when our earthly pilgrimage is finished, we may come to an eternal dwelling and join those who have gone before us. These words echo the theme already

Grant also to us,
when our earthly pilgrimage is done,
that we may come to an eternal dwelling place
and live with you for ever;
there, in communion with the Blessed Virgin Mary, Mother of God,
with the Apostles and Martyrs,
(with Saint N.: the Saint of the day or Patron)
and with all the Saints,
we shall praise and exalt you

He joins his hands.

through Jesus Christ, your Son.

Contrast **earthly pilgrimage** with **eternal dwelling place**.

8.   *He takes the chalice and the paten with the host and, raising both, he says:*

Through him, and with him, and in him,
O God, almighty Father,
in the unity of the Holy Spirit,
all glory and honor is yours,
for ever and ever.

Celebrant alone or with concelebrants

The people acclaim:

Amen.

Then follows the Communion Rite, p. 663.

The doxology is the third and final of the Eucharistic acclamations (along with the Holy, Holy, Holy and Memorial Acclamation). It is strongly suggested that it be sung. Pause at the commas and the sense lines and continue to increase in volume so as to cue the congregation's **Amen**.

A word must be said about the oblation language that we find in the Eucharistic Prayers. Oblation is an offering (late Latin *oblatio*, from *offerre, oblatum*, to offer). It is a term, particularly in ecclesiastical usage, for a solemn offering or presentation to God. It is thus applied to certain parts of the Eucharistic service. In English, "oblation," "offering," "gift," and "sacrifice" are used indiscriminately for anything presented to God in worship, or for the service of the Temple or Priest.

In the Roman Rite, there are two oblations: the lesser oblation, previously known as the Offertory and now called the Preparation of the Gifts, in which the bread and wine yet unconsecrated are presented, and the greater oblation, the oblation proper, forming the latter part of the prayer of Consecration, during which the Body and Blood are ritually presented.

8. The conclusion of the Eucharistic Prayer calls for the Priest to lift the paten with

host and the Deacon (or in his absence, the Priest) chants or recites the doxology. The Missal provides a chant setting of this doxology that leads to the community's chanted "Amen"; however, there may be other musical settings of the doxology correlated to the congregation's "Amen." The Priest's doxology and the people's "Amen" should be musically congruent.

III

Jesus, the Way to the Father

1. The following form of this Eucharistic Prayer is appropriately used with Mass formularies such as, For the Evangelization of Peoples, For Persecuted Christians, For the Nation or State, For Those in Public Office, For a Governing Assembly, At the Beginning of the Civil Year, and For the Progress of Peoples.

For singing purposes, first speak the text aloud and mark in pencil the natural word accents.

After the sung dialogue, remember that the highest note of this dialogue is your reciting tone. The first tone is the note above which the assembly finished **just** or the first note of the two notes on **just**. Grab that tone and move directly to the reciting tone. Several of the melodic motives in the Preface dialogue are repeated throughout the Preface. Words that have two notes per syllable are marked this way, due to their relative importance. Come off the second note to avoid choppiness.

The Eucharistic Prayer for Use in Masses for Various Needs is sometimes called the Swiss Synod Eucharistic Prayer. This new Eucharistic Prayer was approved by the members of the National Conference of Catholic Bishops for use in the United States, as was its provisional (interim) English translation. Originally prepared on the occasion of the Swiss Synod (1972–1975), it was approved by the Sacred Congregation for Divine Worship in August 1974. The prayer was composed in German and then translated into French and Italian,

since these are the languages used in Switzerland. By 1987, the prayer had been translated into 12 languages and was in use throughout the world. The Swiss Synod Eucharistic Prayer was included in the common Spanish translation of the Order of Mass and the Eucharistic Prayers (*Ordinario de la Misa*), published in this country in 1989. However, the prayer was not available for use in English in the United States.

The new Eucharistic Prayer has corresponding sets of Prefaces and intercessions based on four themes: "The Church on the

Path of Unity," "God Guides His Church along the Way of Salvation," "Jesus, Way to the Father," and "Jesus, Who Went About Doing Good." Although printed as one Eucharistic Prayer, the new Eucharistic Prayer is, in reality, four prayers, each with its own theme. As its title indicates, the prayer is intended for use at Masses for Various Needs.

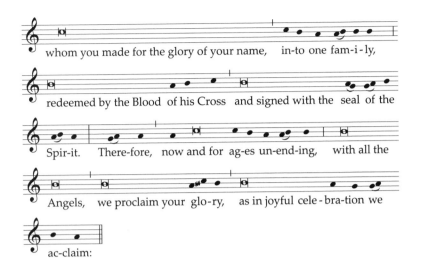

whom you made for the glory of your name,   in-to one fam-i-ly,

redeemed by the Blood of his Cross and signed with the seal of the

Spir-it.   There-fore, now and for ag-es un-end-ing,   with all the

Angels,   we proclaim your glo-ry,   as in joyful cele-bra-tion we

ac-claim:

Holy, Holy, Holy Lord God of hosts . . .

Text without music:

V. **The Lord be with you.**
R. And with your spirit.

V. **Lift up your hearts.**
R. We lift them up to the Lord.

V. **Let us give thanks to the Lord our God.**
R. It is right and just.

It is truly right and just, our duty and our salvation,
always and everywhere to give you thanks,
holy Father, Lord of heaven and earth,
through Christ our Lord.

For by your Word you created the world
and you govern all things in harmony.
You gave us the same Word made flesh as Mediator,
and he has spoken your words to us
and called us to follow him.
He is the way that leads us to you,
the truth that sets us free,
the life that fills us with gladness.

The opening exchange establishes the dialogical nature of liturgical prayer. Thus, the Priest's lines are intended to elicit the response of the assembly. Vocal intonation and eye contact will help in this regard.

Emphasize **Father, Lord of heaven and earth**, as the addressee of the prayer.

Emphasize the parallels: **created** and **govern**.

Draw out distinction between the **Word you created** and **Word made flesh**.

Emphasize the Johannine text **the way**, **the truth** and **the life**.

Actually, we are not referring to four Eucharistic Prayers, but of four versions of a single prayer, each of which accentuates a different theme. This accentuation is done, above all, during the Preface of each version and in a section of the intercessions after the Consecration. Thus, separating these prayers from their Preface would undermine the particular theme that the prayer seeks to stress.

This partial review of the Masses for Various Needs also affords us the opportunity of unearthing the treasury of the Church's intercessory prayer, so often left concealed and confined in the Missal.

1. The third variation—"Jesus the Way to the Father"—is particularly suitable for Masses for the evangelization of peoples, for persecuted Christians, for the country or the city, for the head of state or government, for the parliament, at the beginning of the civil year, and for the progress of peoples. Departing from the Prologue of John, in which Jesus is identified as the Word of God, the Preface references the presence of the Word from the creation of the world through the Incarnation. Jesus as the God-man is the mediator that speaks God's word to us and calls us to follow him. Again, paraphrasing John 14:6, Jesus is the way, the truth, and the life that leads to God and fills our lives with gladness. He gathers people in his name, and through his Cross, he redeems the world.

Through your Son
you gather men and women,
whom you made for the glory of your name,
into one family,
redeemed by the Blood of his Cross
and signed with the seal of the Spirit.

Therefore, now and for ages unending,
with all the Angels,
we proclaim your glory,
as in joyful celebration we acclaim:

Holy, Holy, Holy Lord God of hosts.
Heaven and earth are full of your glory.
Hosanna in the highest.
Blessed is he who comes in the name of the Lord.
Hosanna in the highest.

The Priest assumes the orans position, indicating that the prayer is addressed to God.

We see the lovely metaphor of God walking "with us on the journey of life." Emphasize **your Son, present in our midst** and **gathered by his love**.

The extension of hands over the gifts, the gesture indicating the epiclesis, when the Spirit is summoned to sanctify the gifts, is referenced for the celebration of reconciliation.

Correlate the gesture with the words.

2.   The Priest, with hands extended, says:

You are indeed Holy and to be glorified, O God,   Celebrant alone
who love the human race
and who always walk with us on the journey of life.
Blessed indeed is your Son,
present in our midst
when we are gathered by his love
and when, as once for the disciples, so now for us,
he opens the Scriptures and breaks the bread.

3.   He joins his hands and, holding them extended over the offerings, says:

Therefore, Father most merciful,   Celebrant
we ask that you send forth your Holy Spirit   with concelebrants
to sanctify these gifts of bread and wine,

He joins his hands and makes the Sign of the Cross once over the bread and chalice together, saying:

that they may become for us
the Body and ✠ Blood

He joins his hands.

of our Lord Jesus Christ.

2. This beautiful prayer depicts God as walking with us on the journey of life and Christ as in our midst in the Sacred Scriptures and the breaking of bread.

3. This article is the epiclesis over the gifts invoking the Holy Spirit for the transformation of the offering. The Priest should extend his hands over the offerings before he begins to recite the text, and he should keep his hands extended until he makes the Sign of the Cross once, over the bread and chalice together while saying the words, "Body and Blood."

4–5. The coordination of texts and gestures for the Institution narrative is very important. The Priest must remember that he is continuing to recount the great deeds of God now focused in Christ Jesus on the night before he died, but he should not appear to be addressing these texts to the bread and wine. It continues to be part of a Eucharistic Prayer addressed to the Father. Although rubrics, such as, "He takes the bread and, holding it slightly raised above the altar," suggest that the Priest is impersonating Christ; in fact, the Priest continues

to address God the Father; here, recounting one of the great deeds of God in history, the Institution narrative. Notice that the rubric before the text, "Take this all of you and eat of it," does not call for him to bow slightly. Similarly, after speaking the text, the Priest shows the consecrated host. (The rubric does not say "elevate.") The Priest then genuflects in adoration.

The command "Do this in memory of me" is in reference to the entire action and should not seem to reference the chalice only. In 1 Corinthians 11: 24–25, we find the

4.   In the formulas that follow, the words of the Lord should be pronounced clearly and distinctly, as the nature of these words requires.

On the day before he was to suffer,
on the night of the Last Supper,

He takes the bread and, holding it slightly raised above the altar, continues:

he took bread and said the blessing,
broke the bread and gave it to his disciples, saying:

He bows slightly.

TAKE THIS, ALL OF YOU, AND EAT OF IT,
FOR THIS IS MY BODY,
WHICH WILL BE GIVEN UP FOR YOU.

He shows the consecrated host to the people, places it again on the paten, and genuflects in adoration.

5.   After this, he continues:

In a similar way, when supper was ended,

He takes the chalice and, holding it slightly raised above the altar, continues:

he took the chalice, gave you thanks
and gave the chalice to his disciples, saying:

He bows slightly.

TAKE THIS, ALL OF YOU, AND DRINK FROM IT,
FOR THIS IS THE CHALICE OF MY BLOOD,
THE BLOOD OF THE NEW AND ETERNAL COVENANT,
WHICH WILL BE POURED OUT FOR YOU AND FOR MANY
FOR THE FORGIVENESS OF SINS.

DO THIS IN MEMORY OF ME.

He shows the chalice to the people, places it on the corporal, and genuflects in adoration.

6.   Then he says:

The mystery of faith.   Celebrant alone

And the people continue, acclaiming:

We proclaim your Death, O Lord,
and profess your Resurrection
until you come again.

Or:

When we eat this Bread and drink this Cup,
we proclaim your Death, O Lord,
until you come again.

The rubric reads "He takes the bread and, holding it slightly raised above the altar, ..." This may seem to suggest that the Priest is impersonating Christ; in fact, the Priest continues to address God the Father. Nor is the Priest to appear to be addressing the bread. Notice that the rubric before the text "Take this all of you, and eat of it," does not call for the Priest Celebrant to break the host; it simply calls for him to bow slightly.

The Priest then shows the consecrated host. The rubric does not say "elevate." The Priest Celebrant genuflects in adoration.

The rubric reads "He takes the chalice and, holding it slightly raised above the altar." Again, the Priest continues to address God the Father. Notice that the rubric before the text "Take this all of you, and drink from it," calls for him to bow slightly.

The Priest shows the chalice. The rubric does not say "elevate." The Priest Celebrant genuflects in adoration.

The Priest may sing **The mystery of faith**, which will serve as a prompt for the assembly to sing the Memorial Acclamation.

If the Priest sings, it should be musically congruent with what is to follow. If a modern composition is sung, the Priest should verify whether there is a lead-in to create a seamless fit. It makes no sense to sing a modal lead-in when a tonal acclamation is to be sung.

---

memorial command after both the bread and the wine. A pause inserted before the memorial command may help to clarify this phrase.

6. The Priest's text, "The mystery of faith," functions as a cue, although it is an exclamation. Originally, the phrase *mysterium fidei* was part of the consecratory text, but Pope Paul VI on his authority, removed them from the consecratory words and made them this exclamation. The Latin text does not say, "Let us proclaim the

mystery of faith," nor does it provide a full sentence. Rather, the phrase could best be interpreted as "Oh, the mystery of faith!" a moment of contemplative awe and surrender that serves as a cue to the congregations' response.

The Priest's text is correlated to the Memorial Acclamation chants of the Missal, but there may be other musical settings of the Mystery of Faith correlated to other musical settings of the congregation's Memorial Acclamations that the Priests should learn.

The Priest resumes the orans position to emphasize that the entire Eucharistic Prayer is addressed to God, whereas, the Memorial Acclamations are addressed to Christ. Though subordinate, emphasize **Passion and Death on the Cross to the glory of the Resurrection**, so as even more to emphasize **we offer you the Bread of life and the Chalice of blessing**.

Connect **oblation** with **Sacrifice**.

Or:

Save us, Savior of the world,
for by your Cross and Resurrection
you have set us free.

7.   Then the Priest, with hands extended, says: Celebrant
with concelebrants

Therefore, holy Father,
as we celebrate the memorial of Christ your Son, our Savior,
whom you led through his Passion and Death on the Cross
to the glory of the Resurrection,
and whom you have seated at your right hand,
we proclaim the work of your love until he comes again
and we offer you the Bread of life
and the Chalice of blessing.

Look with favor on the oblation of your Church,
in which we show forth
the paschal Sacrifice of Christ that has been handed on to us,
and grant that, by the power of the Spirit of your love,
we may be counted now and until the day of eternity
among the members of your Son,
in whose Body and Blood we have communion.

This part of the prayer differs in the four variations to bring out the theme that each of the four prayers emphasizes. As the third Eucharistic Prayer for Masses for Various Needs prays to Jesus as the way to the Father, we pray here to partake in the mystery of Christ that gives life through the Holy Spirit. We ask to be transformed into the image of Christ and confirmed in the bond of communion with the Holy Father, the local Ordinary, then all Bishops, Priests, Deacons, and the entire people of God.

By our partaking of this mystery, almighty Father,   Celebrant or
give us life through your Spirit,   one concelebrant
grant that we may be conformed to the image of your Son,
and confirm us in the bond of communion,
together with N. our Pope and N. our Bishop,[*]
with all other Bishops,
with Priests and Deacons,
and with your entire people.

Grant that all the faithful of the Church,
looking into the signs of the times by the light of faith,
may constantly devote themselves
to the service of the Gospel.

_____

[*]   Mention may be made here of the Coadjutor Bishop, or Auxiliary Bishops, as noted in the *General Instruction of the Roman Missal*, no. 149.

7. Liturgical scholars call this section of the prayer the anamnesis-offering. The Priest expands upon the acclamation articulated by the congregation, calling to mind the Paschal Mystery and offers the Sacrament of the Paschal Mystery, the transformed bread and wine.

In the Masses for Various Needs, this section and the Preface are adapted to the themes celebrated in the four versions. This article does many liturgical functions. Its first paragraph is an anamnesis-offering in which the community makes memory of

the Paschal Mystery and offers to God the Father the Sacrifice of the Cross. The second paragraph is an epiclesis on the community itself, praying that those who receive Holy Communion be united by the Holy Spirit. In the third paragraph, we pray that we may be conformed to the image of Christ and for unity as specified for the Church's leadership and all her people. Inclusion is made of Priests and Deacons along with Bishops. In the fourth paragraph, we pray for all the faithful who are "looking into the signs of the times by the

light of faith." We conclude this paragraph with a prayer that we may constantly devote ourselves to the service of the Gospel. These words echo the theme already announced in the Preface, "Jesus, the Way to the Father." In a fourth paragraph, we find a prayer for the entire Church who is on pilgrimage. We ask that when our earthy pilgrimage is finished, we may come to an eternal dwelling and join those who have gone before us.

Keep us attentive to the needs of all
that, sharing their grief and pain,
their joy and hope,
we may faithfully bring them the good news of salvation
and go forward with them
along the way of your Kingdom.

Celebrant or
one concelebrant

Remember our brothers and sisters (N. and N.),
who have fallen asleep in the peace of your Christ,
and all the dead, whose faith you alone have known.
Admit them to rejoice in the light of your face,
and in the resurrection give them the fullness of life.

Grant also to us,
when our earthly pilgrimage is done,
that we may come to an eternal dwelling place
and live with you for ever;
there, in communion with the Blessed Virgin Mary, Mother of God,
with the Apostles and Martyrs,
(with Saint N.: the Saint of the day or Patron)
and with all the Saints,
we shall praise and exalt you

He joins his hands.
through Jesus Christ, your Son.

8.   *He takes the chalice and the paten with the host and, raising both, he says:*
Through him, and with him, and in him,
O God, almighty Father,
in the unity of the Holy Spirit,
all glory and honor is yours,
for ever and ever.

Celebrant alone
or with
concelebrants

The people acclaim:
Amen.

Then follows the Communion Rite, p. 663.

The prayer, in keeping with the overall theme of this version, prays that we may be attentive to the needs of all, sharing grief and pain, as well as joy and hope. In this we imitate Christ who is the Way to the Father.

Contrast **earthly pilgrimage** with **eternal dwelling place**.

The doxology is the third and final of the Eucharistic acclamations (along with the Holy, Holy, Holy and Memorial Acclamations). It is strongly suggested that it be sung. Pause at the commas and the sense lines and continue to increase in volume, so as to cue the congregation's **Amen**.

---

8. The conclusion of the Eucharistic Prayer calls for the Priest to lift the paten with host and the Deacon (or in his absence, the Priest) chants or recites the doxology. A doxology is a short hymn of praise to God in Christian worship that is often added to the end of canticles, Psalms, and hymns. The tradition derives from a similar practice in the Jewish synagogue, in which some version of the Kaddish serves to terminate each section of the service. Among Christian traditions, a doxology is typically a sung expression of praise to the Holy Trinity, the Father, the Son, and the Holy Spirit. It is common in high hymns for the final verse to take the form of a doxology.

The Missal provides a chant setting of this doxology that leads to the community's chanted "Amen"; however, there may be other musical settings of the doxology correlated to the congregation's "Amen." The Priest's doxology and the people's "Amen" should be musically congruent. The prayer reaches its climax with the doxology and the "Amen." This is the last of three acclamations that punctuate the Eucharistic Prayer and ritually is the pinnacle of the prayer as we give honor and glory to God though Christ with the Holy Spirit.

IV

Jesus, Who Went About Doing Good

1. The following form of this Eucharistic Prayer is appropriately used with Mass formularies such as, For Refugees and Exiles, In Time of Famine or For Those Suffering Hunger, For Our Oppressors, For Those Held in Captivity, For Those in Prison, For the Sick, For the Dying, For the Grace of a Happy Death, and In Any Need.

For singing purposes, first speak the text aloud and mark in pencil the natural word accents.

After the sung dialogue, remember that the highest note of this dialogue is your reciting tone. The first tone is the note above which the assembly finished **just** or the first note of the two notes on **just**. Grab that tone and move directly to the reciting tone. Several of the melodic motives in the Preface Dialogue are repeated throughout the Preface. Words that have two notes per syllable are marked this way, due to their relative importance. Come off the second note to avoid choppiness.

The Eucharistic Prayer for Use in Masses for Various Needs is sometimes called the Swiss Synod Eucharistic prayer. This new Eucharistic Prayer was approved by the members of the National Conference of Catholic Bishops for use in the United States, as was its provisional (interim) English translation. Originally prepared on the occasion of the Swiss Synod (1972–1975) it was approved by the Sacred Congregation for Divine Worship in August 1974. The prayer was composed in German and then translated into French and Italian, since these are the languages used in Switzerland. By 1987, the prayer had been translated into 12 languages and was in use throughout the world. The Swiss Synod Eucharistic Prayer was included in the common Spanish translation of the Order of Mass and the Eucharistic Prayers (*Ordinario de la Misa*), published in this country in 1989. However, the prayer was not available for use in English in the United States.

The new Eucharistic Prayer has corresponding sets of Prefaces and intercessions based on four themes: "The Church on the Path of Unity," "God Guides His Church along the Way of Salvation," "Jesus, the Way to the Father," and "Jesus, Who Went About Doing Good." Although printed as one Eucharistic Prayer, the new Eucharistic Prayer is, in reality, four prayers, each with its own theme. As its title indicates, the prayer is intended for use at Masses for Various Needs.

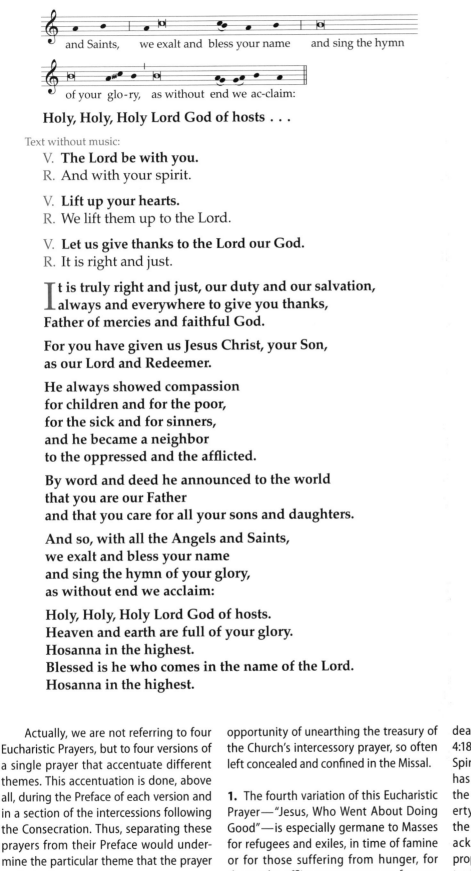

and Saints,   we exalt and bless your name   and sing the hymn

of your glo-ry,   as without end we ac-claim:

Holy, Holy, Holy Lord God of hosts . . .

Text without music:

V. **The Lord be with you.**
R. And with your spirit.

V. **Lift up your hearts.**
R. We lift them up to the Lord.

V. **Let us give thanks to the Lord our God.**
R. It is right and just.

It is truly right and just, our duty and our salvation,
always and everywhere to give you thanks,
Father of mercies and faithful God.

For you have given us Jesus Christ, your Son,
as our Lord and Redeemer.

He always showed compassion
for children and for the poor,
for the sick and for sinners,
and he became a neighbor
to the oppressed and the afflicted.

By word and deed he announced to the world
that you are our Father
and that you care for all your sons and daughters.

And so, with all the Angels and Saints,
we exalt and bless your name
and sing the hymn of your glory,
as without end we acclaim:

Holy, Holy, Holy Lord God of hosts.
Heaven and earth are full of your glory.
Hosanna in the highest.
Blessed is he who comes in the name of the Lord.
Hosanna in the highest.

The opening exchange establishes the dialogical nature of liturgical prayer. Thus, the Priest's lines are intended to elicit the response of the assembly. Vocal intonation and eye contact will help in this regard.

Emphasize **Father of mercies and faithful God**, as the addressee of the prayer. This is the same God through whose mercy sent Jesus as Redeemer.

Emphasize the binary tensions: **compassion** with **children and the poor** and **sick and sinners**. Contrast **neighbor** with **oppressed and afflicted**.

Emphasize **word** and **deed**.

Actually, we are not referring to four Eucharistic Prayers, but to four versions of a single prayer that accentuate different themes. This accentuation is done, above all, during the Preface of each version and in a section of the intercessions following the Consecration. Thus, separating these prayers from their Preface would undermine the particular theme that the prayer seeks to stress.

This partial review of the Masses for Various Needs also affords us the opportunity of unearthing the treasury of the Church's intercessory prayer, so often left concealed and confined in the Missal.

1. The fourth variation of this Eucharistic Prayer—"Jesus, Who Went About Doing Good"—is especially germane to Masses for refugees and exiles, in time of famine or for those suffering from hunger, for those who afflict or persecute us, for captives or those in prison, for the sick, for the dying, for imploring the grace of a good death, for any need. Drawing from Luke 4:18, in which Jesus quotes Isaiah 61:1: "The Spirit of the Lord is upon me, because he has anointed me to bring glad tidings to the poor. He has sent me to proclaim liberty to captives and recovery of sight to the blind, to release the oppressed," we acknowledge how Jesus fulfilled this prophecy by his life and words. He bids us to do the same in imitation of him and to demonstrate God's boundless love.

The Priest assumes the orans position, indicating that the prayer is addressed to God.

We see the lovely metaphor of God walking "with us on the journey of life." Emphasize **your Son, present in our midst** and **gathered by his love**.

The extension of hands over the gifts, the gesture indicating the epiclesis, when the Spirit is summoned to sanctify the gifts, is referenced for the celebration of reconciliation. Correlate the gesture with the words.

The rubric reads "He takes the bread and, holding it slightly raised above the altar." This may seem to suggest that the Priest is impersonating Christ; in fact, the Priest continues to address God the Father. Nor is the Priest to seem to be addressing the bread. Notice that the rubric before the text "Take this all of you, and eat of it," does not call for the Priest Celebrant to break the host; it simply calls for him to bow slightly.

The Priest then shows the consecrated host. The rubric does not say "elevate." The Priest Celebrant genuflects in adoration.

2. The Priest, with hands extended, says:

You are indeed Holy and to be glorified, O God,
who love the human race
and who always walk with us on the journey of life.
Blessed indeed is your Son,
present in our midst
when we are gathered by his love
and when, as once for the disciples, so now for us,
he opens the Scriptures and breaks the bread.

Celebrant alone

3. He joins his hands and, holding them extended over the offerings, says:

Therefore, Father most merciful,
we ask that you send forth your Holy Spirit
to sanctify these gifts of bread and wine,

Celebrant
with concelebrants

He joins his hands and makes the Sign of the Cross once over the bread and chalice together, saying:

that they may become for us
the Body and ✠ Blood

He joins his hands.

of our Lord Jesus Christ.

4. In the formulas that follow, the words of the Lord should be pronounced clearly and distinctly, as the nature of these words requires.

On the day before he was to suffer,
on the night of the Last Supper,

He takes the bread and, holding it slightly raised above the altar, continues:

he took bread and said the blessing,
broke the bread and gave it to his disciples, saying:

He bows slightly.

Take this, all of you, and eat of it,
for this is my Body,
which will be given up for you.

He shows the consecrated host to the people, places it again on the paten, and genuflects in adoration.

2. This beautiful prayer depicts God as walking with us on the journey of life and Christ as in our midst in the Sacred Scriptures and the breaking of bread.

3. This article is the epiclesis over the gifts invoking the Holy Spirit for the transformation over the offering. The Priest should extend his hands over the offerings before he begins to recite the text, and he should keep his hands extended until he makes the Sign of the Cross, once over the bread and chalice together while saying the words, "Body and Blood."

4–5. The coordination of texts and gestures for the Institution narrative is very important. The Priest must remember that he is continuing to recount the great deeds of God now focused in Christ Jesus on the night before he died. (He is not to appear to be addressing these texts to the bread and wine.) The prayer continues to be part of a Eucharistic Prayer addressed to the Father. Although rubrics, such as, "He takes the bread and, holding it slightly raised above the altar" suggest that the Priest is impersonating Christ; in fact, the Priest continues to address God the Father; here, recounting one of the great deeds of God in history, the Institution narrative. Notice that the rubric before the text, "Take this all of you and eat of it, does not call for him to bow slightly. Similarly, after speaking the text, the Priest shows the consecrated host. (The rubric does not say "elevate.") The priest then genuflects in adoration.

5.   After this, he continues:

In a similar way, when supper was ended,

He takes the chalice and, holding it slightly raised above the altar, continues:

**he took the chalice, gave you thanks
and gave the chalice to his disciples, saying:**

He bows slightly.

**TAKE THIS, ALL OF YOU, AND DRINK FROM IT,
FOR THIS IS THE CHALICE OF MY BLOOD,
THE BLOOD OF THE NEW AND ETERNAL COVENANT,
WHICH WILL BE POURED OUT FOR YOU AND FOR MANY
FOR THE FORGIVENESS OF SINS.**

DO THIS IN MEMORY OF ME.

He shows the chalice to the people, places it on the corporal, and genuflects in adoration.

6.   Then he says:

The mystery of faith.   Celebrant alone

And the people continue, acclaiming:

We proclaim your Death, O Lord,
and profess your Resurrection
until you come again.

Or:

When we eat this Bread and drink this Cup,
we proclaim your Death, O Lord,
until you come again.

Or:

Save us, Savior of the world,
for by your Cross and Resurrection
you have set us free.

The rubric states, "He takes the chalice and, holding it slightly raised above the altar." Again, the Priest continues to address God the Father, and not the chalice. Notice that the rubric before the text "Take this all of you, and drink from it," does not call for him to speak into the cup; it simply calls for him to bow slightly.

The Priest then shows the chalice. The rubric does not say "elevate." The Priest Celebrant genuflects in adoration.

The Priest may sing **The mystery of faith**, which will serve as a prompt for the assembly to sing one of the three acclamations.

If the Priest sings, it should be musically congruent with what is to follow. If a modern composition is being used, the Priest should verify whether there is a lead-in to create a seamless fit. It makes no sense to sing one lead-in that is modal when a tonal acclamation is going to be sung. This only necessitates the organist's having to intervene with an introduction to establish the key for the Memorial Acclamation.

The command "Do this in memory of me" is in reference to the entire action and should not seem to reference the chalice only. In 1 Corinthians 11:24–25, we find the memorial command after both the bread and the wine. A pause inserted before the memorial command may help to clarify this phrase.

6. The priest's text, "The mystery of faith" functions as a cue, although it is an exclamation. Originally, the phrase *mysterium fidei* was part of the consecratory text, but

Paul VI on his authority, removed them from the consecratory words and made them this exclamation. The Latin text does not say, "Let us proclaim the mystery of faith," nor does it provide a full sentence. Rather, the phrase could best be interpreted as "Oh, the mystery of faith!" a moment of contemplative awe and surrender that serves as a cue to the congregation's response.

The Priest's text is correlated to the Memorial Acclamation chants of the Missal, but there may be other musical settings of

the Mystery of Faith correlated to other musical settings of the congregation's Memorial Acclamations that the Priest should learn. What the Priest sings and what the people sing should be congruent.

The Priest resumes the orans position to emphasize that the entire Eucharistic Prayer is addressed to God, whereas, the Memorial Acclamation is addressed to Christ. Though subordinate, emphasize **Passion and Death on the Cross** to **the glory of the Resurrection**, so as even more to emphasize we offer you the Bread of life and the Chalice of blessing.

Connect **oblation** with **Sacrifice**.

7.   Then the Priest, with hands extended, says:

Celebrant
with concelebrants

Therefore, holy Father,
as we celebrate the memorial of Christ your Son, our Savior,
whom you led through his Passion and Death on the Cross
to the glory of the Resurrection,
and whom you have seated at your right hand,
we proclaim the work of your love until he comes again
and we offer you the Bread of life
and the Chalice of blessing.

Look with favor on the oblation of your Church,
in which we show forth
the paschal Sacrifice of Christ that has been handed on to us,
and grant that, by the power of the Spirit of your love,
we may be counted now and until the day of eternity
among the members of your Son,
in whose Body and Blood we have communion.

Celebrant or
one concelebrant

Bring your Church, O Lord,
to perfect faith and charity,
together with N. our Pope and N. our Bishop,*
with all Bishops, Priests and Deacons,
and the entire people you have made your own.

Open our eyes
to the needs of our brothers and sisters;
inspire in us words and actions
to comfort those who labor and are burdened.
Make us serve them truly,
after the example of Christ and at his command.
And may your Church stand as a living witness
to truth and freedom,
to peace and justice,
that all people may be raised up to a new hope.

This part of the prayer differs in the four variations to bring out the theme that each of the four prayers emphasizes. In the fourth Eucharistic Prayer for Use in Masses for Various Needs, we pray that our eyes may be opened to the needs of people and that the Eucharist may inspire us in words and actions to comfort those who are burdened. Following the example of Christ, we pray that we may be of service and stand as living witnesses **to truth and freedom**, **to peace and justice**. Emphasize these word pairings.

---

*   Mention may be made here of the Coadjutor Bishop, or Auxiliary Bishops, as noted in the *General Instruction of the Roman Missal*, no. 149.

7. Liturgical scholars call this section of the prayer the anamnesis-offering. The Priest expands upon the acclamation articulated by the congregation, calling to mind the Paschal Mystery and offers the Sacrament of the Paschal Mystery, the transformed bread and wine.

In the Masses for Various Needs, this section and the Preface are adapted to the themes celebrated in the four versions. Many liturgical functions are within this article. Its first paragraph is an anamnesis-offering in which the community makes memory of the Paschal Mystery and offers to God the Father the sacrifice of the Cross. The second paragraph is an epiclesis on the community itself, praying that those who receive Holy Communion be united by the Holy Spirit. In the third paragraph, we pray for unity as specified for the Church's leadership and her people—all who seek God with a sincere heart. In the fourth paragraph, we pray for the poor and downtrodden and for ourselves that we might serve them in the example of Christ. We conclude this paragraph with a prayer for the entire Church that she may stand "as a living witness to truth and freedom, to peace and justice and that all people may be raised to new hope." These words echo the theme already announced in the Preface "Jesus, Who Went About Doing Good." In the fourth paragraph, we conclude with a prayer for the entire Church on pilgrimage. We ask that, when our earthly pilgrimage is finished, we may come to an eternal dwelling and join those who have gone before us.

Remember our brothers and sisters (N. and N.),
who have fallen asleep in the peace of your Christ,
and all the dead, whose faith you alone have known.
Admit them to rejoice in the light of your face,
and in the resurrection give them the fullness of life.
Grant also to us,
when our earthly pilgrimage is done,
that we may come to an eternal dwelling place
and live with you for ever;
there, in communion with the Blessed Virgin Mary, Mother of God,
with the Apostles and Martyrs,
(with Saint N.: the Saint of the day or Patron)
and with all the Saints,
we shall praise and exalt you

Celebrant or one concelebrant

*Contrast **earthly pilgrimage** with **eternal dwelling place**.*

He joins his hands.

through Jesus Christ, your Son.

8. He takes the chalice and the paten with the host and, raising both, he says:

**Through him, and with him, and in him,
O God, almighty Father,
in the unity of the Holy Spirit,
all glory and honor is yours,
for ever and ever.**

Celebrant alone or with concelebrants

The people acclaim:

Amen.

Then follows the Communion Rite, p. 663.

The doxology is the third and final of the Eucharistic acclamations (along with the Holy, Holy, Holy and Memorial Acclamation). It is strongly suggested that it be sung. Pause at the commas and the sense lines and continue to increase in volume so as to cue the congregation's **Amen**.

8. The conclusion of the Eucharistic Prayer calls for the Priest to lift the paten with host, and the Deacon (or in his absence, the Priest) chants or recites the doxology. A doxology is a short hymn of praise to God in Christian worship, often added to the end of canticles, Psalms, and hymns. The tradition derives from a similar practice in the Jewish synagogue, where some version of the Kaddish serves to terminate each section of the service. Among Christian traditions, a doxology is typically a sung expression of praise to the Holy Trinity, the Father, the Son, and the Holy Spirit. It is common in high hymns for the final verse to take the form of a doxology.

The Missal provides a chant setting of this doxology that leads to the community's chanted "Amen"; however, there may be other musical settings of the doxology correlated to the congregation's "Amen." The Priest's doxology and the people's "Amen" should be musically congruent. The prayer reaches its climax with the doxology and the "Amen." This is the last of three acclamations that punctuate the Eucharistic Prayer and ritually is the pinnacle of the prayer as we give honor and glory to God though Christ with the Holy Spirit.

APPENDICES

From the outset, it must be said that the comments in these pages are aimed at the amateur singer. Lest a willing Priest Celebrant be scared away from trying the chants, technical musical language has been avoided, unless the terminology, such as flex, mediant, and full stop, appears in the Missal. For those interested in more serious chant studies, there are two currents of thought:

For the traditional Solesmes method, see the following:

Gregory Suñol, OSB, *Text Book of Gregorian Chant according to the Solesmes Method*, transl. from the 6th French ed. by G. M. Durnford (Tournai: Desclée, 1930; repr. Whitefish, Montana: Kessinger Publishing, 2003).

Theodore Marier, *A Gregorian Chant Master Class* (Bethlehem, Connecticut: Abbey of Regina Laudis, 2002).

For the newer semiological method, see the following:

Eugène Cardine, OSB, *Beginning Studies in Gregorian Chant*, transl. William Tortolano (Chicago: GIA Publications, 1988).

Robert M. Fowells, *Chant Made Simple*, 2nd ed. (Brewster, Massachusetts: Paraclete Press, 2007).
For a musicological and historical approach, see the following:

Richard L. Crocker, *An Introduction to Gregorian Chant* (New Haven: Yale University Press, 2000).

David Hiley, *Gregorian Chant*, Cambridge Introductions to Music (Cambridge: Cambridge University Press, 2009).

APPENDIX I
VARIOUS CHANTS FOR THE ORDER OF MASS

In choosing the simple or solemn tone (in place in the Order of Mass), it is desirable that the same tone for all parts of the Ordinary be used, in order to preserve the unity of the musical genre.

The Introductory Rites
Greeting

Greeting: The liturgy begins with a recognition of the Trinitarian dynamics of Catholic Christian worship. To say that the liturgy is prayed in the name of the Triune God is to say that it is under the power of, the protection of, the aegis of the Triune God. To begin the liturgy in the name of the Father, Son, and Holy Spirit also makes known that everything that happens in the liturgy from this point on is done in the name of the three Persons of the Trinity.

There are three forms of the Greeting. The issue is which form to choose and why. Priest Celebrants should not fall into always using one Greeting—the first one because of its placement or the third because it is the shortest. You want to vary your use of the forms of the Greeting.

The second form of the Greeting is a Pauline greeting. This form is interesting in that it is not Trinitarian. It is a binary Greeting in which both grace and peace are viewed as gifts of the Father and the Lord Jesus. It is a very different rhetorical pattern.

The final Greeting, "The Lord be with you," is the form that most people know. Each of the Greetings is addressed to the assembly as a whole. The response to each Greeting is "And with your spirit."

The rubrical gesture of the Sign of the Cross invokes the Triune God's protection, whereas, the Greeting acknowledges the presence of God, presumably the Triune presence of God.

Penitential Act

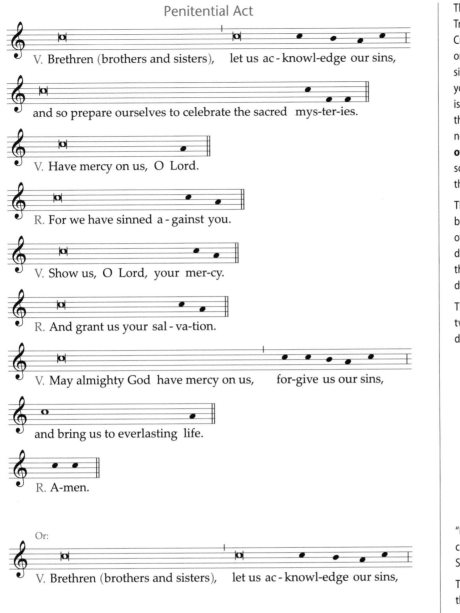

V. Brethren (brothers and sisters),   let us ac-knowl-edge our sins,

and so prepare ourselves to celebrate the sacred mys-ter-ies.

V. Have mercy on us, O Lord.

R. For we have sinned a-gainst you.

V. Show us, O Lord, your mer-cy.

R. And grant us your sal-va-tion.

V. May almighty God have mercy on us,   for-give us our sins,

and bring us to everlasting life.

R. A-men.

Or:

V. Brethren (brothers and sisters),   let us ac-knowl-edge our sins,

The alternative chant for the Trinitarian invocation (Sign of the Cross) and each form of the Greeting is on the previous page. For purposes of singing, grab a note in the top part of your vocal range. This will be "do" and is the reciting tone. Now sing down the scale "do-ti-la." These are the only notes you will need for the Greeting. **of the Son** moves stepwise down the scale "do-ti-la." **Spirit** jumps down the third, skipping the middle note.

The Penitential Act follows the same basic three-note pattern until the end of the line when the singer jumps down a fifth. To find this, sing down the scale "do-ti-la-sol-fa." Now jump directly from "do" to "fa."

The versicles revolve around a two-note pattern moving from "do" down to "la."

"Brothers and sisters" is the customary address in the United States.

This is the same melodic formula as that above.

The Penitential Act: Notice that we now refer to this as the Penitential Act, not the Penitential Rite. This change in vocabulary may have occurred because we are trying to conserve the reference "Penitential Rite" to the Sacrament of Penance.

All of the forms of the Penitential Act have the same structure. The Priest calls for the act, the act is done by the community, and the Priest offers a concluding absolution. The Priest concludes the Penitential Act by a request for God's mercy, to which the people reply, "Amen." Though the rubric states that this is an absolution, it is not the same type of absolution as in the Sacrament of Penance. During the Sacrament of Penance, the absolution is a declaration. This absolution is a request.

The form of the Penitential Act that we have here is dialogical in nature, in which the people finish the sentences begun by the Priest.

For each of the forms, musical notation is provided for the invitation and the absolution. If the Greeting is sung, the sung Penitential Act will flow nicely, but it is necessary to remain in the same musical key, which is quite easy, since both the Greeting and the Penitential Act vacillate between two pitches.

Since the *General Instruction of the Roman Missal* strongly advocates singing the liturgy, not simply singing at the liturgy, we can see the importance of singing the

For the tropes, move from "do" stepwise (do-ti-la), then back to "do." For the **Lord, have mercy**, jump from "do" to "la."

This pattern can be used with the suggested tropes found in the Appendix and with any composed tropes in the Penitential Act.

Penitential Act as well as other parts of the Mass.

We see here the third form of the Penitential Act, which is the troped Kyrie, eleison, in which invocations are prefixed to the acclamation, "Lord, have mercy / Christ, have mercy." This form is interesting in that it shows three ministers for the Penitential Act. It can be executed by Priest, Deacon, or another minister, most likely a cantor. The Missal shows a clear indication that both the invocations and

the "Lord, have mercy / Christ, have mercy" be chanted.

Alternative invocations are in Appendix VI, but we are not limited to those seven sample invocations. We may construct further invocations. However, our invocations must be Christo-centric, insofar as they are titles or characteristics of Christ, as the sample invocations demonstrate. They are not to be mini examinations of conscience, in which the invocations focus on the assembly's misdeeds. Secondly, we are not to fol-

low the pattern of the medieval tropes, in which the first invocation was addressed to God the Father, the second to God the Son, and the third to God the Holy Spirit. Rather, in this form, we are proclaiming God's loving mercy in the person of Christ.

The community may pray the invocation "Lord, have mercy / Christ have mercy" in either the vernacular or Greek.

The Concluding Rites
Blessing

V. The Lord be with you.   R. And with your spir-it.

V. May al-might-y God bless you,   the Father, and the Son, +

and the Holy Spir-it.   R. A-men.

Episcopal Blessing

V. The Lord be with you.   R. And with your spir-it.

V. Blessed be the name of the Lord.   R. Now and for ev-er.

V. Our help is in the name of the Lord.   R. Who made heaven and

earth.

V. May al-might-y God bless you,   the Father, + and the Son, +

and the Holy + Spir-it.   R. A-men.

This descending melodic pattern is the same as that of the Greeting in the Introductory Rites and is used each time we sing this greeting and response.

For the blessing, move stepwise down the scale and return to the reciting tone. Repeat for **the Son**. For **the Holy Spirit**, descend without using the passing tone.

The gesture of blessing should coordinate with the text in such a way that the Priest's right hand reaches a vertical high point on the word **Father**, a vertical low point on **Son,** the Priest's horizontal left on **Holy** and the Priest's horizontal right on **Spirit**.

The Concluding Rites: The terse nature of the closing rites is striking. The interchange of "The Lord be with you / And with your Spirit" that marks other major units of the Eucharistic Liturgy, e.g., the Introductory Rites, the proclamation of the Gospel, and the beginning of the Eucharistic Prayer, also marks the Concluding Rites. The coordination of the gesture and the text is the same as at the beginning of Mass, namely, that the words are addressed

to the congregation. The Priest Celebrant follows this with a Trinitarian blessing, which may be in a simple or more extended (a Prayer over the People or a Solemn Blessing) form.

In a Pontifical Mass presided over by the Bishop, a special form of the blessing is provided. It is dialogical in form, consisting of two sets of versicles and followed by the typical Trinitarian blessing. A Bishop blesses the people with the appropriate

formula, making the Sign of the Cross three times over the people. This macrounit begins with the usual interchange "The Lord be with you / And with your Spirit." The text of the first versicle is derived from Psalm 113:2: "Blessed be the name of the Lord." The second versicle is from the Salzburg Missal and the text is derived from Psalm 124:8: "Our help is in the name of the Lord." William Durandus, in his *Rationale Divinorum Officiorum* 4:59, 7,

Four versions of the Dismissal are provided in the Missal. The melodic contours of each is different one from the other, but the response of the assembly remains the same, in spite of the differences. Each Dismissal focuses on a different aspect of our mission. The first form of the Dismissal is literally from the Dismissal in Latin *Ite missa est*, whence comes the term "Mass." The second dismisses the assembly to announce the Gospel, while the third and fourth focus on peace.

For singing purposes, think of a pitch in the upper part of your range. This will be "do." Now sing down "do-ti-la-sol." "Sol" is your starting point for the first three formulas. All four end with the patterns of starting on high "do" and moving "ti-la-ti-la-sol," to which the assembly imitates the pattern. Several words have two notes per syllable, an indicator of the importance of these words. Back off the second of the two-note motives in each instance to ensure the flow of the chant, lest it become too choppy.

Dismissal

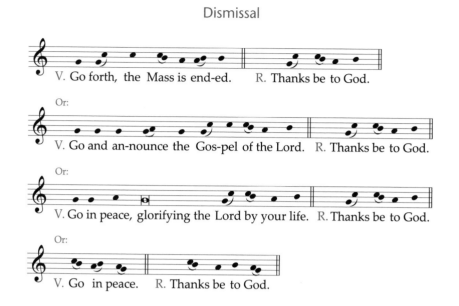

V. Go forth, the Mass is end-ed.   R. Thanks be to God.

Or:

V. Go and an-nounce the Gos-pel of the Lord.   R. Thanks be to God.

Or:

V. Go in peace, glorifying the Lord by your life.   R. Thanks be to God.

Or:

V. Go in peace.   R. Thanks be to God.

states that this form of the blessing is reserved to Bishops alone. Since it is unfamiliar, rehearsing it may be necessary.

Musical notation in the Missal is an indication that this dialogical form of blessing functions best when sung. Ideally, it should be sung by a Deacon, in order that the micro-unit hold together well. Other musical compositions may appear, but it is important for musical and ritual congruity that they be in the same modality or tonality.

The Deacon (or in his absence, the Priest) dismisses the Eucharistic assembly. In the 2008 edition of the *Missale Romanum*, three new Dismissal formulas appeared. Their English translations now grace *The Roman Missal*. These new formulas are accompanied by chant notation, again suggesting that the preferred way of executing these dialogues is in song. The melodies are new; however, the earlier Dismissal, "Go In peace," remains with the more familiar chant melody.

Since the term "Mass" is derived from the Latin Dismissal *Ite missa est*, the name tells us something about the importance of this rite. This is the same word from which is derived the term "mission," thus the Eucharist is the pulsating heart of mission for the Church. Ideally, the words of Dismissal should be the last words that people hear before they depart and to which they respond, "Thanks be to God."

Tones for the Presidential Prayers

Solemn Tone

All the presidential prayers in the Missal (Collects, Prayers over the Offerings, Prayers after Communion) may be pointed for use with the solemn tone according to the following formula. The reciting tone is preceded by one "G" (before ascending to "A"), including after the Flex. At every cadence, whether a Flex or a Full Stop, the grave (\) indicates where to descend to "G," and the acute (╱) indicates where to ascend back to "A." The grave at the Flex may or may not fall on the the text accent, depending on the textual accent pattern. The grave at the Full Stop is always applied to the second to last syllable before the final accent, without respect to the accentuation of that syllable. When the Eucharistic Prayer is sung according to the tone in the Missal, the Prayer over the Offerings must be sung according to the solemn tone.

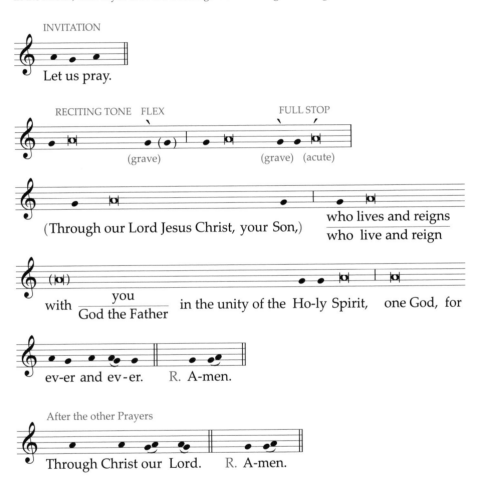

Pointing a text eliminates the need for providing musical notation. It also ensures that the speech quality of the text is given priority. The text is delivered, for the most part, on a reciting tone and only two notes are used. Begin on the note below the reciting tone and move immediately to the reciting tone. At a logical point halfway though the sentence, a pause, or flex, is added. This is marked by a backward slash, indicating a return to the lower note. Immediately using that note, resume the text. At the end of the sentence, use a backward (grave) and forward (acute) slash, indicating descent and return to the reciting tone. The slashes may be regarded as pointing to the direction of the melody. The conclusion is formulaic and intended to cue the assembly to sing their "Amen." Note that there are a couple of variations for the close. In the first form of the Trinitarian formula, we anticipate the verb's being addressed directly to God. In the second case, we speak about God in the third person plural, since we are talking about three persons. This formulation seems strange at first glance, but with study and practice, will flow easily.

The simpler conclusion makes the prayer "Through Christ our Lord."

These pages are offered as a way for Priest Celebrants to chant any or all of the presidential prayers using certain chant formulas. The musical rules for this application are not difficult, and once the formulaic tones are learned, anything can be sung. But a few words about chant, in general, are appropriate here.

Chant is a simple form of sung speech. Originally, chant was used for projecting the voice in a large space during worship.

Without microphones, the scriptures and prayers were chanted for the sound to carry more effectively. (Song carries better than speech.) This practice continued through Jesus' day and even to today in synagogues and churches. The Jewish method of chant was adopted by the early Church; many of whom were Jewish Christians. Later, chant became appreciated for its beauty and was further developed as another way to sing and praise God.

The difficulty today is that many people claim that they are non-singers. The Africans are fond of saying that if you can speak, you can sing. So singing shouldn't be a deal breaker if you are able to talk.

Here, then, are some thoughts about chant to provide you with confidence. Historically, the word "chant" is derived from the French chant (singing; song), but has become, in English, a polysemous catch-all that depends greatly on the context of its use for precise meaning and nuance.

Note the final words receive a special cadence, signaling that one has come to the end of the prayer and cuing the assembly to respond with "Amen."

In this Collect, one full sentence and a Trinitarian formula close the prayer. Note the two vertical bar lines separating the sentence from the Trinitarian formula and another between the closing formula and the "Amen." These full vertical lines signify full stops. In the full sentence, a number of commas are in the text, but they are not all treated in the same manner. In the first line, the commas set off the addressee, and thus are not observed, per se. After the word **coming**, however, the main clause is complete and a breath should be taken before moving to the purpose clause marked by the words **so that**. **Kingdom** marks the end of the full sentence, so take a big breath here before moving to the Trinitarian close.

The Epiphany text is pointed in such a manner that a pause, or flex, is taken after the word **Church**, since this completes the thought in the first phrase but is not the end of the sentence. The second line amplifies on **Church**, with **Jesus Christ** marking the full stop. The conclusion flows from the sentence and terminates in the usual manner.

In modern music, only two modes or scales are in general use: the Major scale (very upbeat) and the Minor scale (more subdued); whereas in chant, eight modes (according to the Medieval theory) allow for greater nuance. In this respect, the resourcefulness and variety of Plainsong chant outstrip modern music in terms of nuance.

A notion of what music should sound like is the great enemy of chant. Stylings heard on the radio or even in classical music need to be disregarded. To begin to understand chant, therefore:

- forget vibrato,
- forget bar lines,
- forget jazzy inflections,
- forget singing in a punctuated note-by-note manner,
- forget holding out long notes that build to dramatic cutoffs.
- Most of all: forget your singing personality and spin.

Chant is sung as a prayer that is spoken privately—with self surrender, deference, and humility. The one difference that it has from spoken prayer is that it uses music. If you can remember that, the rest will fall into place.

To prepare to chant, think of yourself praying in private, but audibly. Now add notes and move them up and down. Your style is always *legato*. The chant is the

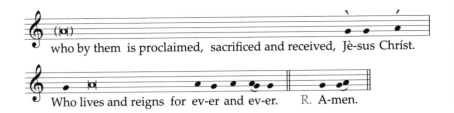

who by them is proclaimed, sacrificed and received, Jè-sus Chríst.

Who lives and reigns for ev-er and ev-er.   R. A-men.

same—always smooth and extended. If you break the *legato* in the middle of a phrase, the spell will be broken. This is especially important with moving notes on one syllable.

In the space of two short sentences, let me suggest the two most common notions of chant: 1) it is distinct from song and speech; 2) it is the equivalent of "intone," that is to say, that it is not tuneful.

Yet, the word "chant" also is used to describe Gregorian Plainsong that, though it includes passages that are "intoned," is arguably rife with flowing and even "tuneful" melodies. Where, then, is the line between chant and song, and what is chant's relationship to other musical terms, such as "intone"?

A second tone called "simple" also is provided. Curiously, the simple tone is more complex than the solemn tone but still not that difficult. As the solemn tone fluctuates around two tones (reciting tone and lower neighbor), the simple tone revolves around two tones that are a third apart. The underlying scheme for the tones is generally bipartite—the sentence is divided into two halves. In the first half, an intonation formula leads to a reciting tone that is followed by a cadence (mediant). If the first half of the phrase is sufficiently long, the line is inflected (flex) before proceeding to the mediant. The second half may begin with another intonation, return to a reciting tone, and end with a final cadence (full stop). On the mediant, one passes to the lower note through a passing tone, returning immediately to the reciting tone, thus cuing the hearer that more is to follow. At the end of the sentence, the melody descends a fifth, thus indicating aurally that the sentence is finished. Applying these principles to the same Collect (Epiphany), we see that **Church** is the flex point, whereas, the mediant is **frankincense or myrrh.** Note that the back slash is placed over the note where one begins to move—two syllables before the final accent.

The system of pointing is a brilliant way to sing grammar and punctuation and thus communicate meaning.

Simple Tone

The presidential prayers (Collects, Prayers over the Offerings, Prayers after Communion) may also be sung according to the simple tone, which follows.

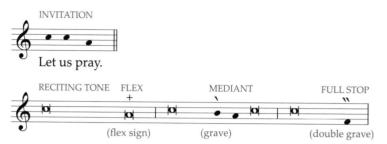

Let us pray.

For the Flex and Full Stop, the pointing depends upon where the accent falls. When the final syllable is accented, a flex (+) sign or double grave (⌶) is to be given to it. When the final syllable is not accented, this syllable is sung on the Reciting Tone and the flex sign or double grave is to be placed so as to indicate where one descends for the non-accented syllable(s). Examples:

...on the gifts of your   CHURCH,
...from among your BLESS - ings

...Jesus   CHRIST
...reDEMP - tion.

For the Mediant cadence, the grave (\) is placed two syllables before the final accent, without respect to the accentuation of these two syllables.

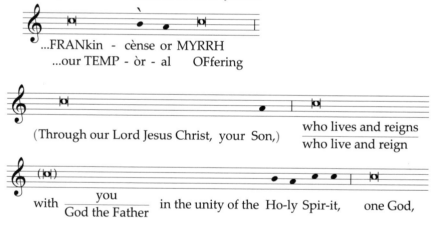

...FRANkin - cènse or MYRRH
...our TEMP - òr - al   OFfering

(Through our Lord Jesus Christ, your Son,)   who lives and reigns
who live and reign

with ____you____   in the unity of the Ho-ly Spir-it,   one God,
God the Father

It also must be understood that, in Plainsong, the notation is not and was never meant to indicate absolute pitch. Rather, the pitch is relative to the person singing. So the singer chooses a comfortable pitch within the singing range and builds the melody around this. It must, therefore, be well understood that the notes read on the stave (the five lines) are to be sung at the pitch that is within the compass of the singer(s), according to the size of the building and the special character of the piece. The instructions indicate the notes "G" and "A." It might be more beneficial to translate these into solfege terminology and call these "sol" and "la." Thus, one would simply choose a comfortable tone in the middle of the vocal range and sing up the scale, "do-re-mi-fa-sol-la." "La" is your reciting tone and "sol" is the start and return. Another way to approach this is to find a note in the middle of your range (not too low, otherwise, the chant will sound muddy) and make that tone the starting tone; then sing from "do" to "re" and "re" will be the reciting tone.

Finally, a word must be said about the vertical lines punctuating the music. In modern notation, these are called bar lines, and the notes fit within these lines to measure out the music. In Plain chant,

Note the two closing formulas. The first is Trinitarian with two variations. In the first variation, the Trinity is directed in the Second Person, whereas, in the second variation, God is spoken about in the Third Person. Therefore, the adjustment must be made with the verb **lives** and **live**. The second formula is **made through Christ our Lord** without reference to the other persons of the Trinity.

Applying the simple tone to the Collect on which the solemn tone was demonstrated (First Sunday in Advent), we note that the long first half of the sentence is broken with a flex. The flex is the aural equivalent of a comma. The second half of the praise marks the result that is hoped for (**so that**). The sentence ends on the word **kingdom** and the leap downward is a clear indication that the end has been reached. The Trinitarian conclusion is addressed directly to Christ (**You**) and the appropriate adjustment is made to the verb (**lives**). Just before the full stop, the melody moves on the words **Holy Spirit**, giving a clear indication that the end is coming, marked by the fifth leap downward, thus cuing the assembly for the **Amen**.

however, normal speech patterns govern the flow of the music. Therefore, the music is not fit between the bar lines.

Full and double bars mark the end of a significant phrase. They are treated as full stops and preceded by a slight *ritardando*. Half bars mark less significant sections; breaths may be taken, but the rhythm should not be significantly interrupted.

Quarter bars mark shorter musical phrases. The rhythm should not be interrupted, and breathing, if needed, should steal time from the note preceding the bar line.

Full bar lines also serve as musical rests. Following the bar line, time is added using rests that are equal in value to either a single or double pulse (where the note receives a single pulse, equivalent to an eighth note). The value of the rest depends on the rhythm of the phrase following the bar line. To review, a full vertical line in a double set of vertical lines means to pause and take a breath. This marks the completion of a sentence or a full thought. A half-bar usually divides a long line into smaller bite-size portions. A short breath can certainly be taken at the half-bar, provided that it does not hinder the intelligibility of

Let us look now at how an Offertory prayer is pointed. The sentence is divided into two parts with the conclusion added immediately after the full stop. Since the first phrase is sufficiently long, we add a flex on the word **us**, pausing with a breath before moving to the mediant. Since the mediant does not fall on a period, we simply lift (or breathe, if necessary) before moving to the second part, ending on the word **redemption**. The concluding formula is very simple, **Through Christ our Lord**, without any mention of the Trinity. Since this phrase is so brief, it can be moved directly into after the full stop.

Applying the simple tone to the Offertory prayer for Epiphany, we again note the bipartite division of the sentence. The flex marks the word **Church**, subdividing the first half into two halves. The second half moves directly without breath to the full stop. A full vertical line comes after the word **Christ**, thus a breath is taken.

the text. The text reigns supreme in importance. Finally, sometimes a short vertical line on the top line of the stave punctuates the music. These are called quarter-lines. Think of these as commas. A short lift or pause can help in making the text understandable without necessitating a breath.

Finally, we will discuss pointing a text. Musical notation does not need to be added in order to chant a text. The system that is offered in these pages uses forward and backward slashes that can be written above the words as a cue for when to move. Simple and solemn tones are provided that prescribe the intervals, or the distance, between the notes. A limited number of notes are involved, thus there will not be great consternation once you catch on to the formulas and the system of pointing a text. The flex is the intermediate pause in a long sentence. The backward slash points down—indicating the direction of the melody. The full stop uses a back slash followed by a forward slash, again pointing first down, then back up. The simple tone, in addition to the flex and full stop, provides a mediant stop. The intervals are a little different from the solemn but quite manageable.

Tones for the Readings
I. Old Testament and Acts of the Apostles

INTRODUCTION

A reading from the Book of the Prophet I - sai - ah.
A reading from the Book of the Prophet E - zek - i - el.
A reading from the first Book of   Kings.
                    second
A reading from the Book of   Prov - erbs.
A reading from the Book of   Ex - o - dus.
A reading from the Book of   Wis - dom.
A reading from the Acts of the   A - pos - tles.

RECITING TONE   FLEX   FULL STOP

*accent on   accent not on   accent on   accent not on
last syllable   last syllable   last syllable   last syllable*

QUESTION   2 1

CONCLUSION

*accent on   accent not on
last syllable   last syllable*

ACCLAMATION

The word of the Lord.   Thanks be to God.

The Old Testament and Acts of the Apostles have their own leitmotif, indicating their position in the Liturgy of the Word on Sundays and feasts as the First Reading. On weekdays, when there is only one reading in addition to the Gospel, the formula can signal the assembly whether the First Reading is from the Old Testament or is an Epistle.

The interval leap downward is a fifth. The lower note should fall on the syllable following the accented syllable. Thus, I-SAI-ah differs from E-ZEK-i-el, like PRO-verbs is accentuated differently from EX-o-dus.

The reciting tone is on the high "do," so choose a tone in the upper part of your vocal range. Try not to sing too low in your range, as the text will appear to have a muddy presentation. The flex can be used when it makes sense grammatically (usually indicated by a comma). The full stop marks the period at the end of a sentence. Any time there is a question, another formula is used that ends on a rising melodic line. This resembles spoken speech, in which our voices are raised at the end of a question.

The acclamation at the end also uses the descending fifth, just another cue that this is the Old Testament or the Acts of the Apostles. The assembly's "Amen" imitates the same interval.

Singing the scriptural texts in the Liturgy of the Word can be rewarding, fun, and challenging. Music serves in this context as a vehicle by which the text is delivered. Certain musical forms are derived and function as punctuation for the text. For example, as in spoken language, a question is indicated by raising the voice at the end of the sentence, so in chant, a question is indicated melodically by an ascending line. Furthermore, the Old and New Testaments are distinguished by the distance of the intervals. In this section, I will start with reflections about music that are prompted by the scriptures.

The Bible is replete with references to music. At the beginning of the Old Testament is an indication that Jubal was "the ancestor of all who play the lyre and the pipe" (Genesis 4:21). But professional musicians do not appear in the Bible before David's time. Even before professional musicians became the norm during David's reign, the concept of court musicians existed. The young David was called to soothe Saul with music (1 Samuel 16:16–23). In this sense, David was a minstrel (2 Kings 3:15)—a player of stringed instruments.

David introduced music into the sanctuary worship. His son and successor

The flex is used at the end of major clauses within a sentence. In short sentences it may be omitted, and in long sentences it may be used more than once. For the flex, one leaves the reciting tone either on the last syllable or an earlier syllable, as the accentuation demands. The flex should not be used to introduce a question. The full stop is used at the end of every sentence. The question formula is used for all questions, except when the question occurs at the end of a reading. In the question formula, one leaves the reciting tone two syllables before the last accent. In long questions, the ending is used only for the last clause of the question, with the reciting tone for the first clause.

Solomon later retained it after the Temple was built (2 Samuel 6:5; 1 Kings 10:12). Music must have been considered an important part of the service, since Hezekiah and Josiah, the two reform kings, saw to it that music was included in the reformation (2 Chronicles 29:25; 35:15).

Asaph, Heman, and Jeduthun (Ethan) helped David set up the sanctuary worship. Asaph headed a choir of singers and musicians who were stationed before the Ark of the Covenant in Jerusalem. Heman and Jeduthun had similar choirs at the old tabernacle at Gibeon (1 Chronicles 16:4-6, 39–42). These choirs had 4,000 members (1 Chronicles 23:5); 288 of these were trained musicians who directed the lesser-skilled musicians (1 Chronicles 25:7–8). All the musicians were divided into 24 courses, each containing 12 skilled musicians. An orchestra consisting of stringed instruments (harps and lyres) and cymbals accompanied the singers (1 Chronicles 15:19–21).

Our greatest clue to Hebraic music lies in the book of Psalms, the earliest existing hymnal. As hymns, these individual Psalms were suitable for chanting and singing in worship. The Bible gives a glimpse of musical terminology in the headings of the Psalms that appear in the Hebrew language, the language in which the Old Testament was written. The meaning of the terminology, however, is, to a large extent,

First Reading for the First Sunday of Advent, Year B (NAB)

Isaiah 63:16b-17, 19b; 64:2-7

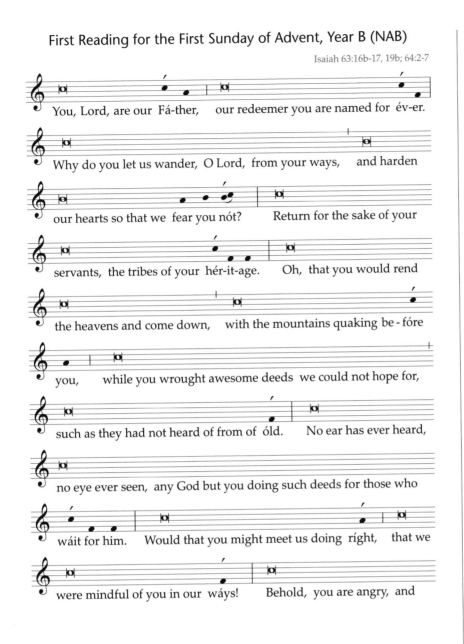

Applying the principle of pointing a text, let us look at the First Reading for the First Sunday of Advent, from Isaiah. The music is supplied below the text, so that you can follow how the pointing functions. A flex is placed after **Father**, to indicate direct address. Then a short breath or lift can be observed. At the end of the first sentence, a descent of an interval of a fifth is on the word **ever**. For visual clarity, the forward slash is placed over the syllable before the melodic move to remind us to move on the next syllable. The second sentence is a question. To prepare for this grammatical structure, move off the reciting tone about halfway through the sentence (where the flex would normally fall) only to descend and rise again at the end of the sentence, indicating the interrogatory character. The last syllable receives two notes. Back off the second note and lengthen it to come to a natural stop. The third sentence is so brief that no flex is needed. At the end, leap down a fifth. The forward slash is placed over the antepenultimate syllable, since this is the accented syllable. Sentence four is subdivided into two parts, with the usual flex and full stop, followed by a big breath. The fifth sentence does not have a flex, but it would be permissible and desirable to place lifts at commas (after **heard** and **seen**), for the sake of intelligibility. We anticipate the length of the sixth sentence and plan a flex after **right**.

The sentence beginning with **Behold** is a command and is a series of brief statements, thus two flexes are before the full stop.

obscure, since they apparently were lost as early as 250 BC, the approximate date of the Greek translation of the Old Testament. (See Nelson's *Illustrated Bible Dictionary*, Thomas Nelson Publishers, 1986.)

Thus, singing the Old Testament reading seems to be consistent with the way in which music was regarded. As with a Wagner opera, a leitmotif helps the hearer know immediately that the text being declaimed is from the Hebrew scriptures.

An open fifth is used to mark the full stops, conclusions, and acclamation after the reading. This is the distance from the upper "do," descending to "fa." It sounds very empty, since it does not have an intermediary tone that would establish it as major or minor, even though we are talking about modal music rather than tonal.

(A semicolon can be treated like a flex.)

we are sín-ful;   all of us have become like unclean people,   all our
good deeds are like polluted rágs;   we have all withered like leaves,
and our guilt carries us away like the wínd.   There is none who
calls upon your name,   who rouses himself to clíng to you;   for you
have hidden your face from us and have delivered us up to our gúilt.
Yet, O Lord, you are our fá-ther;   we are the clay and you the
potter: we are all the work of your hánds.

The sentence, beginning with **There is none**, is sufficiently long and thus subdivided into two parts with a flex marking the semi-colon.

The last sentence follows the same pattern of placing a flex after **father**, indicating the punctuation. Curiously, the colon received no attention other than a quarter bar, indicating a lift. This can be explained that **we are all the work**. Both express the same idea.

The principle behind pointing, however, is that one must decide how to render the punctuation and grammar.

On page 295 the rules for chanting the First Reading, whether it be from the Old Testament or from the Acts of the Apostles, are delineated. These are not extremely complicated. When a sentence can be divided into two parts, the intermediate stop is accented with a flex, which is the distance from upper "do" down a third to "la." At the end of the sentence is a final cadence of a fifth—from upper "do" down to "fa." When the word in either case is accented on the second to last syllable, adjustments are made so the movement reflects the natural language accent.

For questions, move down one note from the reciting tone to "ti," and at the end of the sentence, move down again to "la," only to travel back up the scale to the original reciting tone, lifting the melody much like raising the tone in spoken speech.

Tones for the Readings
II. The Epistle and the Book of Revelation

INTRODUCTION

A reading from the [first / second] Letter of the blessed A-pos-tle Paul

to the Co-rin-thi-ans.
to the Ga-la-tians.
to the Phi-lip-pi-ans.
to the E-phe-sians.
to the Thes-sa-lo-ni-ans.
to the Ro-mans.
to the He-brews.
to___ Ti-tus.
to___ Ti-mo-thy.

Or:

A reading from the Book of Re-ve-la-tion of the blessed
A reading [from the first / from the sec-ond] Let-ter of the blessed

A-pos-tle John.
A-pos-tle Pe-ter.
A-pos-tle James.

The tone for the Second Reading on Sundays and Feasts, indicating the letters or book of Revelation, is a little more florid. Both the name of the author and the community to whom the letter is addressed receives special treatment. In the case of the book of Revelation, the genre of the writing is accentuated musically as well as the Johannine authorship. To avoid confusion with Saint Paul, the letters of Saints Peter and James are dealt with a little differently than the Pauline corpus. The rule of thumb is that when the penultimate (just before the end) syllable is strong, it is to be moved on. If the antepen-ultimate (third to the end) syllable is strong, that is to be moved on and adjustments made to the penultimate syllable. In all these cases, however, it is simpler just to memorize the formu-las, so that they can be sung without much thought or any hesitation.

No evidence exists that the New Testament Church used any form of instrumental music during worship services. In fact, the first use of any kind of instrumental music in New Testament churches did not occur for several hundred years after the church was established in 29–33 AD. But plenty of citations support the fact that songs and hymns were sung.

If we understand the nature of worship, the question becomes clearer. Singing (and later, musical instruments) form an integral part of the worship. New Testament worship was characterized by a joy and thanksgiving because of God's gracious redemption in Christ. This early Christian worship focused on God's saving work in Jesus Christ. True worship was that which occurred under the inspiration of God's Spirit (John 4:23–24; Philippians 3:3). The Jewish Sabbath was quickly replaced by the first day of the week as the time for weekly public worship (Acts 20:7; 1 Corinthians 16:2). It was called the Lord's Day (Revelation 1:10) and was the occasion for celebration of the Resurrection, since Jesus arose on the first day of the week (Mark 16:2).

At first, worship services were conducted in private homes. Possibly for a time, the first Christians worshipped in the synagogues as well as private homes. Some scholars believe that Jewish Christians would go to the synagogues on Saturday and to their own meeting on Sunday. Many early Christians of Jewish background continued to follow the law and customs of

As with the tone for the First Reading, the tone for the Second Reading (the Epistles or book of Revelation) has its own leitmotif. The reciting tone is simple enough. The mediant is called the "flex" in the former case but clearly has the same function. The pattern is simple—"do-la-do-ti-la." In the case of weak syllables on the penultimate syllable, adaptations must to made to move on the antepenultimate syllable. The full stop, marking the end of a sentence, is more florid, in that it moves above and below the reciting tone. The pattern is "do-re-ti-la-ti."

The problem arises in knowing how many syllables to count back to begin the mediant and the full stop, so as to not run out of syllables or have too many syllables before the melody concludes.

The example here indicates the solution while dealing with strong and weak accents.

The same application of the full stop is indicated for varying speech patterns and accent patterns. Singing these will demonstrate that this is natural and should not be overthought.

Each sentence (or group of phrases) in the body of the reading takes the following three elements:

The mediant is used at the end of major clauses within a sentence. In short sentences it may be omitted, and in long sentences it may be used more than once. For the mediant, one always leaves the reciting tone three syllables before the last accent, and then completes the line as indicated for last accent on the final syllable or last accent not on the final syllable. The mediant should not be used to introduce a question. The full stop is used at the end of every sentence, with the formula applied as indicated for the various combinations and penultimate accent and last accent. The question formula is used for all questions, except when the question occurs at the end of a reading. In the question formula, one leaves the reciting tone two syllables before the last accent. In long questions, the ending is used only for the last clause of the question, with the reciting tone for the first clause. The conclusion with its two elements is used for the last two lines of the reading. For these two elements, one leaves the reciting tone one syllable before the last accent and then on the last accent.

The Mediant and the Full Stop are pointed according to the following accent patterns.

MEDIANT ACCENT PATTERNS

When the last accent is on the final syllable:

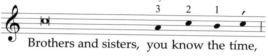

When the last accent does not fall on the final syllable:

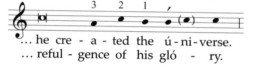

FULL STOP ACCENT PATTERNS   When the last accent is on the final syllable:

Penultimate accent followed by one unaccented syllable: … ab-sólved___   from sín.
Penultimate accent followed by two unaccented syllables: … the wón-ders   of Gód.
Penultimate accent followed by three unaccented syllables:… the wón-ders of his lóve.

their people. They observed the Sabbath and the Jewish holy days, such as the great annual festivals. However, the Apostle Paul held himself free from any obligation to these and never laid an obligation to observe them on his converts (Colossians 2:16). The New Testament contains no references to annual Christian festivals.

Although the New Testament does not instruct worshippers with a specific procedure to follow in their services, several elements appear regularly in the worship practices of the early Church. Prayer, apparently, had a leading place in Christian worship. The letters of Paul regularly open with references to prayer, instructing to "pray without ceasing" (1 Thessalonians 5:17). Praise, either by individuals or in hymns sung in common, reflects the frequent use of Psalms in the synagogue. Also, possible fragments of Christian hymns appear scattered through the New Testament (Acts 4:24–30; Ephesians 5:14; 1 Timothy 3:16; Revelation 4:8, 11; 5:9–10, 12–13).

Lessons from the Bible to be read and studied were another part of the worship of the New Testament Church. Emphasis was probably given to the messianic prophecies that had been fulfilled in Jesus Christ. His teachings also received a primary place.

Prophecy, inspired preaching by one filled with the Holy Spirit, helped build up the Church, the Body of Christ (Ephesians 12:6). Contributions were also collected on

When the last accent does not fall on the final syllable:

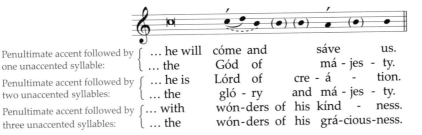

Penultimate accent followed by one unaccented syllable:	{ ... he will	cóme and	sáve	us.
	{ ... the	Gód of	má - jes - ty.	
Penultimate accent followed by two unaccented syllables:	{ ... he is	Lórd of	cre - á - tion.	
	{ ... the	gló - ry	and má - jes - ty.	
Penultimate accent followed by three unaccented syllables:	{ ... with	wón-ders of his kínd - ness.	
	{ ... the	wón-ders of his grá-cious-ness.	

QUESTIONS

Questions are pointed with two syllables before the final accent:

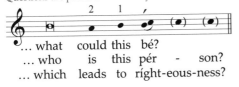

... what could this bé?
... who is this pér - son?
... which leads to right-eous-ness?

The question again is indicated by a rising melodic pattern, much like is done in spoken language.

CONCLUSION

The end of the reading is pointed with two elements as follows.

Leave the reciting tone one syllable before the last accent: Leave the reciting tone on the last accent:

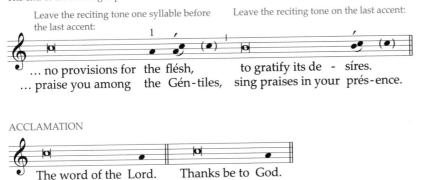

... no provisions for the flésh,   to gratify its de - síres.
... praise you among the Gén-tiles,   sing praises in your prés-ence.

The conclusion is a leap downward from the reciting tone of a third, returning to the reciting tone, then down a second only to return again to the reciting tone. The melodic pattern is "do-la-do-ti-do." If the last word or syllable is accented, then the two-note end falls on the ultimate syllable. If they are unaccented, then the two-note motive falls on the penultimate element.

ACCLAMATION

The word of the Lord.   Thanks be to God.

The acclamation is a downward move of a third—from "do" to "la."

the first day of each week (1 Corinthians 16:2). Other details about the worship procedures of the early Christians in the time of the New Testament are spotty, but these elements must have been included in the weekly worship service. (See Nelson's *Illustrated Bible Dictionary*, Thomas Nelson Publishers, 1986.)

When Jesus told the Samaritan woman at the well that a time would come when people would worship in spirit and truth and not in the temple (John 4:23–24), Jesus was contrasting worship under the Law of

Moses versus the worship in the Christian Dispensation. Temple worship was characterized by priests offering sacrifices for the people. In fact, worship in the Old Testament was performed by the priests on behalf of the people.

Under New Testament teachings, each person is to worship God in spirit and truth. To define the use of singing, how and what worship is must be understood.

Again, as with a Wagnerian opera, the leitmotif that helps us distinguish the Second Reading (Epistles or book of

Revelation) from the First Reading is the interval of a descending third. To sing this, find a note in the upper part of the vocal register. This note is "do." Now sing down "do-ti-la." Another characteristic of this formula is that in the full-stop pattern we sing both below and one note above the reciting tone. When a question is in the text, the formula is similar to the pattern for the First Reading.

This is an application of the system of text pointing of the Second Reading for the First Sunday of Advent. The music is supplied below the markings, called "text," so that melodic moves can be followed, but if the principles of pointing are understood, the music is superfluous. It can be proffered that the pointed text without the music flows better as sung speech.

Follow essentially the punctuation marks to know where and when to move melodically.

Once singing this text has been mastered, choose any text from the Lectionary and practice pointing it. Remember first to read the text aloud, noting the punctuation. Note also the ends of sentences and how the accent pattern presents itself. Also determine if any flexes will be used on long sentences. Proceed to point, making your decisions on the intelligibility of the text. There is no absolute right or wrong on this matter.

Second Reading for the First Sunday of Advent, Year A (NAB)

Romans 13:11-14

Brothers and sisters, you know the tíme;   it is the hour now for you to a-wáke from sléep.   For our salvation is nearer now than when we first be-líeved;   the night is advanced, the dáy is at hánd. Let us then throw off the works of dárk-ness   and put on the ár-mor of líght;   let us conduct ourselves properly as in the day, not in or-gies and drúnk-en-ness,   not in promiscui-ty and li-cén-tious-ness,   not in rí-val-ry and jéal-ous-y.   But put on the Lord Jesus Christ, and make no provision for the desires of the flésh.

Notice the formula "Brothers and sisters" can be added before any reading of an epistle. This takes into consideration that these texts were addressed to the early Christians as real letters. Adding the formula establishes the epistolary context of the reading. This custom is found in the Latin *editio typica* of the Lectionary. For example, it is typical to begin reading from the letters with the expression *Fratres* (brothers and sisters implied), *Carissimi* (My dearest), even when we are joining the letter not at the beginning but midway

through. Another formula in the Latin Lectionary for the Old Testament and Epistles is *In diebus illis* (In those days). Much in a similar fashion, the Gospel pericopes begin with *in illo tempore* (at that time). These last two formulas mark an undetermined time in the past. Whereas, "brothers and sisters" personalizes the reading and reminds the hearers that they are the ones being addressed in the letter.

To learn how to set a text for chanting, consider practicing with the above text that has the music underlay. In order to get

the hand of posing questions musically, look at the Old Testament reading on page 295. Aurally, you will easily detect how these musical tools can assist in making the readings intelligible and render them more solemn because they are chanted.

Tones for the Readings
III. The Gospel

The tone for the Gospel reading, as one might suspect, is a little more florid than the chant for the First Reading and somewhat similar to the chant for the Second Reading. Following the principle of progressive solemnity, this graduated complexity adds to the proclamation of the biblical readings and avoids having all of the text sound the same. The characteristic musical motive for the Gospel is the third (from "do" down to "la"). The rule of thumb is that when the penultimate (just before the end) syllable is strong, it is moved on. If the antepenultimate (third to the end) syllable is strong, it is moved on and adjustments made to the penultimate syllable. In all these cases, however, it is simpler just to memorize the formulas so that they can be sung without much thought or any hesitation.

Questions are again signaled by a rising melodic pattern, much like spoken language.

The mediant is used at the end of major clauses within a sentence. In short sentences it may be omitted, and in long sentences it may be used more than once. It should not be used to introduce a question. The full stop is used at the end of every sentence. The question formula is used for all questions, except when the question occurs at the end of a Gospel reading. In the question formula, one leaves the reciting tone two syllables before the last accent. In long questions, the ending is used only for the last clause of the question, with the reciting tone for the first clause. The conclusion with its two elements is used for the last two lines of the reading. For each of these two elements, one leaves the reciting tone on the last accent.

The question must be asked as to why sing the Sacred Scriptures when we are so accustomed to hearing them read. The simple answer might be that singing raises the level of speech. Singing is to speech what poetry is to prose. It has the power to heighten the level of communication and deepen the sensibility of what is being communicated. Singing without instruments holds a special pride of place, since such singing makes clear that the music is in service to the text being proclaimed.

A cappella music originally was, and still often is, used in religious music, especially in church. Gregorian chant is an example of a cappella singing, as is the majority of secular vocal music from the Renaissance. The madrigal, up until its development in the early Baroque period into an instrumentally accompanied form, is also usually in a cappella form. Jewish and Christian music were originally a cappella, and this tradition has existed continuously in both of these faiths as well as in Islam.

So why sing texts that can be recited? This comes under the notion of progressive solemnity. The notion that the assembly sings the liturgy rather than just sings at the liturgy—this is the essence of progressive solemnity. The parts of the liturgy itself are of a higher priority than any musical extras tacked on. And parts of the liturgy associated with the Gospel and Eucharistic Prayer are the most important of all.

The system of text pointing is applied to the Gospel Reading for Pentecost. The music is supplied below the markings, or "text," so that you can follow the melodic moves, but once the principles of pointing are understood, the music is superfluous. It can even be proffered that the pointed text without the music flows better as sung speech.

Follow essentially the punctuation marks to know where and when to move melodically. Note also how the forward and backward slashes cue the singer as to when to move melodically.

Once singing this text is mastered, choose any text from the Lectionary and practice pointing it. Remember first to read the text aloud, noting the punctuation. Note also the ends of sentences and how the accent pattern presents itself. Also determine if any flexes will be used on long sentences. Proceed to point it, making your decisions on the intelligibility of the text. There is no absolute right or wrong on this matter.

Gospel Reading for Pentecost (NAB)

John 20:19-23

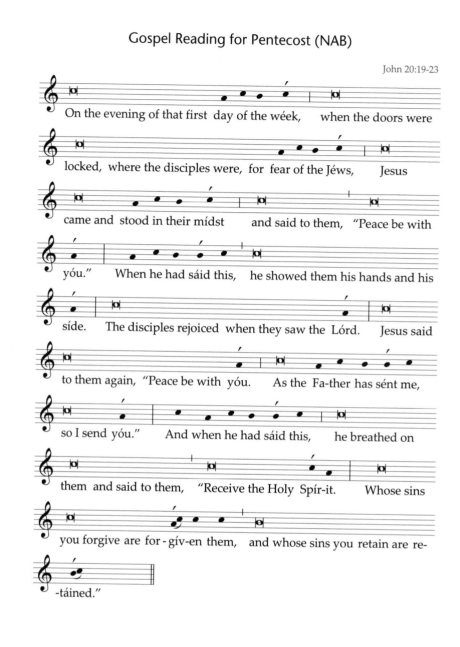

Singing by the gathered assembly and ministers is important at all celebrations. Not every part that can be sung should necessarily be sung at every celebration; rather "preference is to be given to those [parts] that are of greater importance" (GIRM, 40).

Special provision for music in singing the scriptures is also found in the *General Instruction of the Liturgy of the Hours* (GILH). The concession of #271 assumes that daily singing is the ideal: "It is particularly appro-

priate that there be singing at least on Sundays and holydays, so that the different degrees of solemnity will thus come to be recognized."

Musicians are given two priorities: "It is the same with the hours: all are not of equal importance; thus it is desirable that those that are the true hinges of the office, that is, morning prayer and evening prayer, should receive greater prominence through the use of singing" (272).

The principle of progressive solemnity is applied not only to liturgical items of greater or lesser importance but also to practical or pastoral considerations: "A celebration with singing throughout is commendable, provided it has artistic and spiritual excellence; but it may be useful on occasion to apply the principle of 'progressive solemnity.' There are practical reasons for this, as well as the fact that, in this way,

Tones for the Readings
III. The Gospel
(Solemn Tone)

In addition to the simple tone for the proclamation of the Gospel, there is also a solemn tone. It lies lower in the vocal register and the melodic patterns are slightly more complex.

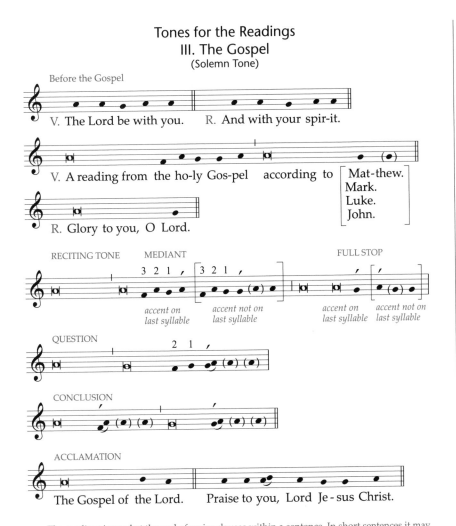

The mediant is used at the end of major clauses within a sentence. In short sentences it may be omitted, and in long sentences it may be used more than once. It should not be used to introduce a question. The full stop is used at the end of every sentence. The question formula is used for all questions, except when the question occurs at the end of a Gospel reading. In the question formula, one leaves the reciting tone two syllables before the last accent. In long questions, the ending is used only for the last clause of the question, with the reciting tone for the first clause. The conclusion with its two elements is used for the last two lines of the reading. For each of these two elements, one leaves the reciting tone on the last accent.

the various elements of liturgical celebration are not treated indiscriminately, but each can again be given its connatural meaning and genuine function. The Liturgy of the Hours is, then, not seen as a beautiful memorial of the past demanding intact preservation as an object of admiration; rather, it is seen as open to constantly new forms of life and growth and to being the unmistakable sign of a community's vibrant vitality" (273).

The principle of progressive solemnity, therefore, is one that recognizes several intermediate stages between singing the liturgy in full and just reciting all the parts. Its application offers the possibility of a rich and pleasing variety. The criteria are the particular day or hour being celebrated, the character of the individual elements comprising the office, the size and composition of the community, as well as the number of singers available in the circumstances.

With this increased range of variation, it is possible for the public praise of the

Church to be sung more frequently than formerly and to be adapted in a variety of ways to different circumstances. There is also great hope that new ways and expressions of public worship may be found for our age, as has clearly always occurred in the life of the Church.

The *General Instruction of the Liturgy of the Hours* covers a lot of ground, and its principles seem to fit the parish celebration of Mass. A full musical liturgy must have both "artistic and spiritual" quality. Though

The system of text pointing is applied to the Gospel Reading for Pentecost. The music is supplied below the markings, or "text," so that the melodic moves can be followed, but once the principles of pointing are understood, the music is superfluous. It can even be proffered that the pointed text without the music flows better as sung speech.

Follow essentially the punctuation marks to know where and when to move melodically.

Once you have mastered singing this text, choose any text from the Lectionary and practice pointing it. Remember first to read the text aloud, noting the punctuation. Note also the ends of sentences and how the accent pattern presents itself. Also determine if any flexes will be used on long sentences. Proceed to point the text, making your decisions on the intelligibility of the text. There is no absolute right or wrong on this matter.

Gospel Reading for Pentecost (NAB)

John 20:19-23

each quality builds on the other, one does not necessarily presume the other.

Just as do the tones for the First and Second Readings, the Gospel has a melody that is immediately recognizable and cues the assembly to what is being sung. Two sets of tones are provided, one for ordinary use and the other for more solemn occasions. In general, the chant for ordinary use hovers around the reciting tone of the high "do." Only three notes are used, namely "la-ti-do," but the patterns are more complex than what we have seen thus far. Again, a special pattern is established for indicating questions. Rules are provided for the mediant stop, but it would be far easier to listen to a recording than to describe the patterns verbally.

The solemn tone is interesting in that it is situated in the lower vocal range. (It is noteworthy that, in the Western music tradition, the higher registers, such as soprano or tenor voices, are employed for important roles; yet, in the sung Plainchant settings of the Passion, Jesus is the bass, while Judas is a tenor.) Again, only three notes are used throughout—"fa-sol-la," with "la" the reciting tone.

In both modes, a passage from the Gospel is included for each one to help demonstrate how the modes are applied to a text.

THE CREED
Credo III

I be-lieve in one God, the Fa-ther al-might-y, mak-er of heav-en and earth, of all things vis-i-ble and in-vis-i-ble.

I be-lieve in one Lord Je-sus Christ, the On-ly Be-got-ten Son of God, born of the Fa-ther be-fore all a-ges. God from God, Light from Light, true God from true God, be-got-ten, not made, con-sub-stan-tial with the Fa-ther; through him all things were made.

For us men and for our sal-va-tion he came down from heav-en,

At the words that follow, up to and including **and became man**, all bow.

and by the Ho-ly Spir-it was in-car-nate of the Vir-gin Mar-y,

and be-came man.

For our sake he was cru-ci-fied un-der Pon-tius Pi-late, he

The melody for the sung Creed is an adaptation of Credo III from the Latin version but with significant modifications to accommodate the English language. It is close enough to the Latin to be recognizable, but different enough to merit special attention. For the most part, it is a simple syllabic stepwise melodic construction. However, some of the important words are set with three notes on the accented syllable. For example, **one, all, in-VIS-ible, JE-sus, FA-ther**, etc., all receive three notes. Back off the second and third notes, lest the melody become too choppy.

One performance suggestion is to alternate sentences between choir and assembly led by a cantor, or possibly between a cantor and the assembly. The double vertical bars are the logical alternations.

Coordinate the bowing gesture with the text. The tempo might slow here to give a reverential accent.

The tempo resumes the original speed here.

Following the discussion about the suitability of singing the scripture readings at Mass, we must turn to another thorny question—that of singing the Creed. The original function of creeds and creedal statements was the establishment of orthodox faith. The standard definition of orthodoxy is "right teaching or right belief." However, a closer examination of the word indicates that this is a derived meaning. The word actually means "right praise." While it may appear that we have mistranslated or misunderstood the word, the reality is that right praise and right teaching and belief go together. They are joined and cannot be separated. The joining of right praise and right belief is best seen in the use of the creeds of the Church, specifically in the Apostles' and Nicene Creeds.

Both of these Creeds used in the Eucharistic Liturgy speak of the true scriptural faith that we believe and confess and the true praise of God in which we join. What we believe and confess cannot be separated from the true praise and thanksgiving of the Lord expressed in the Liturgy of the Word and the Liturgy of the Eucharist. They belong together and ought to be inseparably joined together.

It may seem strange to congregations to suggest that singing is the proper rendering of the Creeds in the liturgy. Sing the Creed? The didactic texts of the Creeds do not seem to lend themselves to singing. Yet, when the great composers of the past prepared music for the Eucharistic Liturgy,

Finally, a few words are in order about the current translation. The English language is rich in vocabulary, drawing ostensibly from two language sources: Latin, usually through the French, and Anglo Saxon, characterized by monosyllabic words. Consequently, choices always must be made in translating from Latin into English. The current translation is remarkably close to the Latin *editio typica*. Words such as "consubstantial" and "incarnate" are easily recognized as Latin cognates. These choices may give occasion to speak about the mystery of the hypostatic union and the Greek term *homoousious*, as well as the mystery of the Incarnation. The Council of Niceaea introduced the word *homoousious* or "consubstantial," meaning "of one substance" into the Creed.

they set the *Kyrie*, the *Gloria in excelsis*, the Creed, the *Sanctus* (Holy, Holy, Holy), and the *Angus Dei* to music. The music for the Creed was invariably provided and invariably sung.

If we examine the Eucharistic Liturgy, we discover that creed and praise of the Lord go together. The Mass is an exposition or expansion of the Creed, or put another way, the Creed summarizes what we have been singing and praying through the entire Eucharist. "In the name of the Father, and of the Son, and of the Holy Spirit"—the words of the baptismal formula begin the Mass. Those baptismal words are a shorthand form for the entire Apostles' Creed, the creed that summarizes the Christian faith in the Rite of Baptism. What is the faith, the belief, the teaching into which the candidate is being baptized? Here it is summarized in the Apostles' Creed. It is imposed and given in the words of Christ, "In the name of the Father, and of the Son, and of the Holy Spirit." With those creedal words, the liturgy begins.

The litany form of the *Kyrie* expresses several parts of the Creed in the language of praise. "For the peace from above and for our salvation, let us pray to the Lord." Those words take us to the middle of the

and I look for-ward to the res-ur-rec-tion of the dead   and the life

of the world to come.   A - - men.

At the **Amen** is a remarkable shift from syllabic chant with a few words treated neumatically (two or three notes per syllable) to melismatic chant. The melisma is a decorative phrase or passage in vocal music, especially one in which one syllable of a plainsong text is sung to a melodic sequence of several notes, highlights certain words that are so well-known that singing such a large number of notes does not jeopardize the intelligibility of the text. Choirs and congregations usually revel in such melodic constructions.

Nicene Creed, "For us men and for our salvation he came down from heaven." Here the work of redemption is expounded.

Just as the Eucharistic Liturgy begins with the baptismal formula summary of the Creeds, "In the name of the Father, and of the Son, and of the Holy Spirit," so also the Mass ends in a similar fashion as the blessing invokes the names of the Trinity. The blessing takes us back to the Old Testament, to the very words that the Lord gave to the first high priest Aaron, with

which he was to bless the people of Israel. We close with those same words of blessing, a triple-fold use of the Lord's name. "The LORD bless . . . the LORD let his face shine upon you . . . the LORD look upon you kindly and give you peace!" (Numbers 6: 24–26). At the end of the Creed, we shout the word "Amen." So be it! So we believe. So we worship. Orthodox-right praise that leads us to right belief and confession.

I am suggesting that singing the Creed will elevate the language of these commonly held texts and guard against a rote recitation of many words without giving heed to their meaning. I might also suggest that singing the Creed from time to time (following the principle of progressive solemnity) may also add a degree of special festivity. Note that a musical Plainchant version is found in the Missal.

The Prayer of the Faithful is in a call-response, or litanic, form. The petitions can be sung on a reciting tone and, according to the terminal notes, will elicit the correct response from the assembly. Four tones derived from the Latin modes are presented here, and other modern forms have also been devised that elicit the proper response from the assembly. In example "A," the cantor descends from "do" as the reciting tone to "la," then back to "do" (as with a flex), then terminates with "do-do-ti-re-mi." This cues the assembly for form A (resembling the Latin *Te rogamus audi nos*).

In example B, the reciting tone is lower on the "sol" and at the end of the petition, the cantor goes up a second and returns to the reciting tone resembling the flex. For the termination, the cantor sings "sol-sol sol-la-do-ti-la-sol." This cues the assembly to sing Form B, which is in imitation of the termination that was just heard.

In example C, the formula is also derived from a Latin tone and the ending gives a sure cue to the assembly, who imitate in singing "Lord, hear our prayer" or "Lord, have mercy." Some scholars opine that this was the original position of the *Kyrie, eleison*, thus example D, uses the *Kyrie* with the cantor intoning the petition, calling the assembly to prayer and then intoning the *Kyrie*, to which the assembly simply repeats in imitation.

PRAYER OF THE FAITHFUL

The text that follows the dagger (†) in the invocations given below can also be used to conclude intentions that are not sung; alternatively, the final words of the individual intentions can take its place.

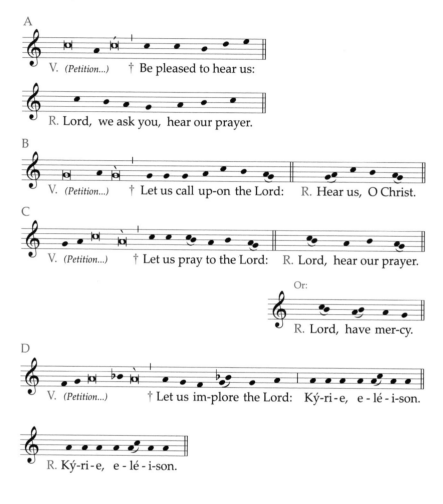

In the Universal Prayer, or Prayer of the Faithful, the people respond in some sense to the Word of God that they have received in faith and, exercising the office of their baptismal priesthood, offer prayers to God for the salvation of all. It is desirable that there usually be such a form of prayer in Masses celebrated with the people, so that petitions may be offered for holy Church, for those who govern with authority over us, for those weighed down by various needs, for all humanity, for the salvation of the whole world, and for the local community.

It is for the Priest Celebrant to regulate this prayer from the chair. He himself begins it with a brief introduction, by which he calls upon the faithful to pray, and, likewise, he concludes it with an oration. The intentions announced should be sober, be composed with a wise liberty and in few words, and should be expressive of the prayer of the entire community.

The intercessions are announced from the ambo or from another suitable place, by the Deacon, a cantor, a reader, or one of the faithful. The people, for their part, stand and give expression to their prayer by an invocation resembling a litany. Thus, music can bring out the litanic character of this series of petitions.

See Appendix V for a further reflection on the Universal Prayer or Prayer of the Faithful.

The Lord's Prayer
Tone B (Mozarabic)

After the chalice and paten have been set down, the Priest, with hands joined, sings:

At the Savior's com - mand   and formed by di - vine teach-ing,

we dare to say:

He extends his hands and, together with the people, continues:

Our Father, who art in heav-en,   hallowed be thy name;   thy king-

-dom come, thy will be done   on earth as it is in heav-en.   Give us

this day our dai-ly bread,   and forgive us our tres-pass-es,   as we

forgive those who tres-pass a-gainst us;   and lead us not in-to

temp-ta-tion,   but de-liver us from evil.

This chant is an adaptation from the Latin chant version. The chant in the Order of Mass is adapted by Robert Snow and better known in the United States. Care should be taken that one or the other is used consistently to avoid liturgical mishaps.

If the invitation is sung, it will cue the assembly which version will follow. The sung introduction also will establish the key and ensure that the prayer is seamless without unnecessary stops and starts. If the prayer is sung, it would be suggested to sing at least the doxology in the same mode, and if the presider is able, the embolism that separates the prayer proper from the doxology.

The structure of the Lord's Prayer at a Roman Rite Eucharist consists of four elements. The first is a call to the prayer chanted by the Priest. The second is the chanting or recitation of the body of the prayer along with the Priest, the third is an expansion, technically called an "embolism," on the final petition of the Lord's Prayer, said or chanted by the Priest. Fourth, or finally, the community along with the Priest, chants the doxology. It is important that those four elements be experienced as a unit. If the invitation is chanted, then the Priest's embolism also should be chanted. If the body of the prayer is chanted, the doxology of the prayer is chanted, too. The gestures also support the structure of the prayer. The first part is an invitation to prayer, thus the Priest joins his hands and addresses the assembly. In the body of the prayer, the Priest assumes the orans position, which he continues to maintain through the embolism, demonstrating that the embolism is simply an extension or an amplification of the line "Deliver us from evil." The doxology, "For the kingdom, the power and the glory," flow logically from the embolism to conclude the prayer on a high note of praise. Due to the liturgical insertion of the embolism, it is easy to think that the Lord's prayer ends with the words, "Deliver us from evil." But the doxological conclusion is the logical termination of such a prayer. In the same way, when we pray the Psalms at the Liturgy of the Hours, we automatically add a doxology at the end of each Psalm, ending on a positive note of Trinitarian praise.

The invitation serves as an introduction to the Lord's Prayer. Although the music resembles the prior composition of the Lord's Prayer, it differs, beginning at the notes for **teaching**. Those notes cue the assembly for this version.

The Lord's Prayer
Tone C (Solemn Anaphora Tone)

After the chalice and paten have been set down, the Priest, with hands joined, sings:

At the Savior's com - mand   and formed by di - vine teach-ing,

we dare to say:

He extends his hands and, together with the people, continues:

Our Fa-ther, who art in heav-en,   hal-lowed be thy name;   thy

king-dom come,   thy will be done   on earth as it is in heav-en.

Give us this day our dai-ly bread,   and for-give us our tres-pass-es,

as we forgive those who tres-pass a-gainst us;   and lead us not in-

-to temp - ta-tion,   but deliver us from e - vil.

This text that separates the prayer proper from the doxology is called an embolism. The word literally means a patch, as it patches the two elements together. The embolism picks up on the words "deliver us from evil" and amplifies their meaning, reorienting the prayer in an eschatological sense. The prayer concludes with "deliver us from evil" in Matthew, and with "lead us not into temptation" in Luke. The liturgical form is Matthean. Some Christians, particularly Protestants,

conclude the prayer with a doxology, an addendum appearing in some manuscripts of Matthew. The justification for this is seen in the parallel practice of Christians praying the Psalms in the Liturgy of the Hours, where at the end of each Psalm, or Psalm part, a doxology is interpolated in order to orientate the prayer in a Christian fashion. It is also argued that early Christians would have automatically added the doxology, since to end a prayer with the word "evil" or "temptation" would be unseemly.

Ideally, if the Our Father is sung, the Priest should sing the invitation and embolism. Singing the invitation will cue the assembly that the prayer itself is to be sung and will establish the musical key in which it will be sung. Singing the embolism will bridge the prayer to the doxology and impress upon those praying it that it is a single prayer unit. But if singing the prayer in its entirety is not possible, at least the doxology should be sung in a congruent manner to the prayer proper, lest the prayer appear fragmented.

At the Solemn Blessing

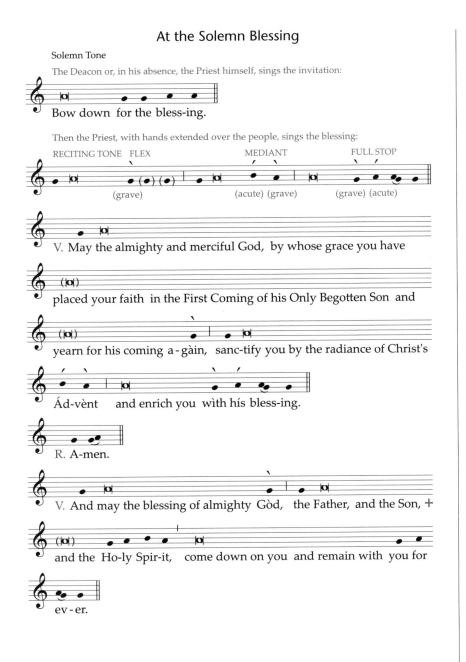

Solemn Tone

The Deacon or, in his absence, the Priest himself, sings the invitation:

Bow down for the bless-ing.

Then the Priest, with hands extended over the people, sings the blessing:

RECITING TONE FLEX   MEDIANT   FULL STOP

(grave)   (acute) (grave)   (grave) (acute)

V. May the almighty and merciful God, by whose grace you have

placed your faith in the First Coming of his Only Begotten Son and

yearn for his coming a-gàin, sanc-tify you by the radiance of Christ's

Ád-vènt   and enrich you wìth hís bless-ing.

R. A-men.

V. And may the blessing of almighty Gòd,   the Father, and the Son, ✠

and the Ho-ly Spir-it,   come down on you and remain with you for

ev - er.

It is highly advised to learn and teach the sung version of the Solemn Blessing because the music helps to cue the "Amens" at the end of each section. This has been one of the most problematic areas in the Mass since the Second Vatican Council, because people did not know when to respond.

The pointing method is used again here, so that any blessing can be sung. In long sentences, it can be divided into two parts and, if need be, a flex added to the first part to break the length. It is the terminus that is important for the cuing of the assembly's "Amens."

The gesture of blessing should coordinate with the text in such a way that the Priest's right hand reaches a vertical high point on the word "Father," a vertical low point on "Son," and the Priest's horizontal left "Holy" and the priest's horizontal right on "Spirit."

Solemn Blessing: As at other macro-units of the Eucharistic Liturgy, the interchange "The Lord be with you / And with your Spirit" that marks major units of the Eucharistic Liturgy, e.g., the Introductory Rites, the proclamation of the Gospel, the beginning of the Eucharistic Prayer, marks the beginning of the Concluding Rites. The coordination of the gesture and the text is the same as at the beginning of Mass, namely, that this is addressed to the assembly. The Priest Celebrant follows this with a Trinitarian blessing, which may be in a simple or more extended (a Prayer over the People or a Solemn Blessing) form.

Note that the Missal offers chants for both of these, suggesting that is the preferred form that these dialogues be executed. Since the Solemn Blessing evokes an "Amen" from the assembly, music helps cue the response.

Let me reflect briefly on the different ways we bless or ask for a blessing. In Judaism, rather than requesting a blessing, God is blessed. The most common form of Jewish liturgical blessings generally begins with the formula, *Baruch ata Adonai Eloheinu melech ha-olam.* The translation of this is "Blessed are You, Lord, our God, King of the universe." By and large, most Jewish blessing begins with this formula. It is noteworthy that God is blessed rather than asking God's blessing. Perhaps, the concept employed is that God knows what to do, so one approaches God with this confidence.

The gesture of blessing should coordinate with the text in such a way that the Priest's right hand reaches a vertical high point on the word "Father," a vertical low point on "Son," and the Priest's horizontal left on "Holy" and the Priest's horizontal right on "Spirit."

The simple tone provides an alternate melodic form. It is introduced by the Deacon (or the Priest, in the absence of a Deacon) to instruct the people to bow down for the blessing. The melody will help cue what follows. The system of pointing is employed here and can be used with any blessing text or Prayer over the People.

R. A-men.

Or, in some Ritual Masses:

V. And may almighty God bless all of you, who are gathered here, the Father, (✝) and the Son, and the for these sacred rites,

Ho-ly (✝) Spir-it.

R. A-men.

Simple Tone

The Deacon or, in his absence, the Priest himself, sings the invitation:

Bow down for the bless-ing.

Then the Priest, with hands extended over the people, sings the blessing:

RECITING TONE   FLEX   MEDIANT   FULL STOP
(flex sign)   (grave) (acute)   (double grave)

V. May the almighty and merciful God, by whose grace you have

placed your faith in the First Coming of his Only Begotten Son and

---

Christians, on the other hand, are influenced by the text: "Ask and it will be given to you; seek and you will find; knock and the door will be opened to you. For everyone who asks, receives; and the one who seeks, finds; and to the one who knocks, the door will be opened" (Matthew 7:78).

In Luke 11, we are told that one time when Jesus was praying, his disciples were standing nearby listening and they said to him, "Lord, teach us to pray, just as John taught his disciples." (v. 1) So Jesus taught them the prayer that we often refer to as the Lord's Prayer: "Father, hallowed be your name, / your kingdom come. / Give us each day our daily bread / and forgive us our sins / for we ourselves forgive everyone in debt to us, / and do not subject us to the final test" (v. 2–4).

Jesus continued, saying to the disciples, "Suppose one of you has a friend to whom he goes at midnight and says, 'Friend, lend me three loaves of bread, for a friend of mine has arrived at my house from a journey and I have nothing to offer him,' and he says in reply from within, 'Do not bother me; the door has already been locked and my children and I are already in bed. I cannot get up to give you anything'" (9–10).

Then he talked to the disciples about a father: "What father among you would hand his son a snake when he asks for a fish? Or hand him a scorpion when he asks for an egg? If you then, who are wicked

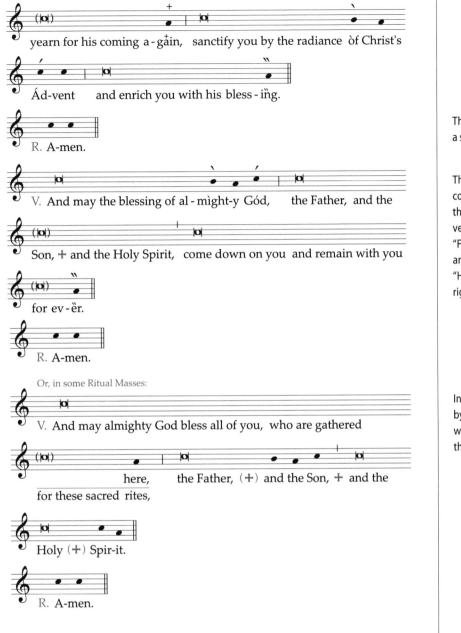

yearn for his coming a-gain,   sanctify you by the radiance òf Christ's

Ád-vent   and enrich you with his bless-ìng.

R. A-men.

V. And may the blessing of al-mìght-y Gód,   the Father, and the

Son, ✝ and the Holy Spirit, come down on you and remain with you

for ev-ẽr.

R. A-men.

Or, in some Ritual Masses:

V. And may almighty God bless all of you, who are gathered

_____ here,   the Father, (✝) and the Son, ✝ and the
for these sacred rites,

Holy (✝) Spir-it.

R. A-men.

The assembly response to this form is a simple recto-tono "Amen."

The gesture of blessing should coordinate with the text in such a way that the priest's right hand reaches a vertical high point on the word "Father," a vertical low point on "Son," and the Priest's horizontal left on "Holy" and the Priest's horizontal right on "Spirit."

In the Pontifical Mass presided over by the Bishop or a regular liturgy in which a Bishop may give the blessing, this example is sung.

know how to give good gifts to your children, how much more will the Father in heaven give the holy Spirit to those who ask him?" (11–13).

By contrast in James 4:3 we read, "You ask but do not receive, because you ask wrongly, to spend it on your passions." If we will pray according to God's will, he will give us what we ask. "You give me that good and perfect gift, that which is good and right for me, even though I might not know what that is. I am asking You to give that to me."

Our Solemn Blessings, in all 20 versions, are mindful that we ask God's blessing but according to God's will and not ours. With this in mind, examine the Solemn Blessings provided in the Missal and verify if this is true in our worship.

There are certain days throughout the year that have special announcements or texts. For example, at the Easter Vigil we hear the Exsultet text—the only occasion that we hear it during the liturgical year. There is the solemn announcement for the date of Easter, since the date shifts every year. Along with the date of Easter, the other dates associated with it must also be announced, such as Ash Wednesday, Ascension, Pentecost, and the Solemnity of the Body and Blood Christi. The date for the First Sunday of Advent is also anticipated.

If a Deacon is capable of singing this text, he should do so from the ambo. Due to the musical complexity, however, a cantor also may make this solemn announcement.

The music is generally syllabic but important words like **Savior** and **Jesus** are treated melismatically to give them special emphasis. Since this is a proclamation about time, the word "season" is also accented with a long melisma.

The Announcement of Easter and the Moveable Feasts

On the Epiphany of the Lord, after the singing of the Gospel, a Deacon or cantor, in keeping with an ancient practice of Holy Church, announces from the ambo the moveable feasts of the current year according to this formula:

The Easter solemnity, revised and restored by Pius XII in 1951, and then the Order of Holy Week in 1955, were favorably received by the Church of the Roman Rite. The Second Vatican Council, especially in the *Constitution on the Sacred Liturgy*, repeatedly drawing upon tradition called attention to Christ's Paschal Mystery and pointed out that it is the font from which all Sacraments and sacramentals draw their power. Just as the week has its beginning and climax in the celebration of Sunday, which always has a paschal character, so the summit of the whole liturgical year is in the sacred Easter Triduum of the Passion and Resurrection of the Lord, which is prepared for by the period of Lent and prolonged for 50 days.

Since the date for Easter shifts every year within the Gregorian Calendar, the solemn proclamation on Epiphany announces this date with great pomp. This Gregorian Calendar regulates the ceremonial cycle of the Roman Catholic Church and provides ecclesiastical rules that determine the date of Easter. This can be traced back to 325 at the First Council of Nicaea convened by the Roman Emperor Constantine. At that time, the Roman world used the Julian Calendar (put in place by Julius Caesar). The Council decided to keep Easter on a Sunday, the same Sunday throughout the world. To fix incontrovertibly the date for Easter, and to make it determinable indefinitely in advance, the Council constructed special tables to compute the date. These tables

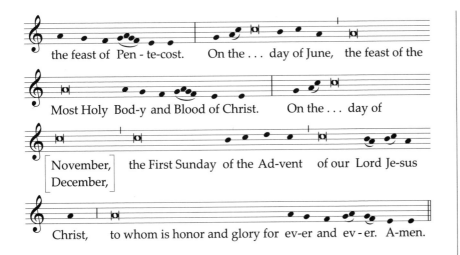

the feast of Pen - te-cost.   On the . . . day of June,   the feast of the

Most Holy Bod-y and Blood of Christ.   On the . . . day of

November,   the First Sunday of the Ad-vent   of our Lord Je-sus
December,

Christ,   to whom is honor and glory for ev-er and ev - er. A-men.

It is unclear that the assembly is supposed to sing the "Amen," but the formula "for ever and ever" with its musical notation would certainly elicit a response.

were revised in the following few centuries, resulting eventually in the tables constructed by the sixth-century Abbot of Scythia, Dionysis Exiguus. Nonetheless, different means of calculations continued in use throughout the Christian world.

In 1582, Gregory XIII completed a reconstruction of the Julian Calendar and produced new Easter tables. A major difference between the Julian and Gregorian Calendar is the "leap year rule." By the 1700s, though, most of western Europe

had adopted the Gregorian Calendar. The Eastern Christian churches still determine the Easter dates using the older Julian Calendar method.

The ecclesiastical rules are: Easter falls on the first Sunday following the first ecclesiastical full moon that occurs on or after the day of the vernal equinox; this particular ecclesiastical full moon is the 14th day of a tabular lunation (new moon); and the vernal equinox is fixed as March 21.

Because of this, Easter can never occur before March 22 or later than April 25. The Gregorian dates for the ecclesiastical full moon come from the Gregorian tables. The western (Roman Catholic and Protestant) Christian churches use the Gregorian tables; many Eastern (Orthodox) Christian churches use the older tables based on the Julian Calendar.

There are certain days throughout the year that have special announcements or texts. For example, at the Easter Vigil we hear the Exsultet text—the only occasion that we hear it during the liturgical year. So, too, there is the solemn announcement of the Nativity of the Lord taken from the Roman Martyrology. The announcement sees all time as having been consecrated by God and redeemed by Christ, so it begins with creation and bring us up to the present moment. It not only recounts salvation history, strictly speaking, but all of secular history as being a part of God's plan.

This text is not a part of the Christmas liturgy, per se, but can be used in anticipation of the Vigil Mass on December 24.

The entire first part of the announcement is marked by the open fifth interval, which is also associated with the chanting of the Old Testament.

Be sure to take breaths and pause after each full vertical line. This will help with the intelligibility of the text.

THE NATIVITY OF OUR LORD JESUS CHRIST
from the *Roman Martyrology*

The announcement of the Solemnity of the Nativity of the Lord from the *Roman Martyrology* draws upon Sacred Scripture to declare in a formal way the birth of Christ. It begins with creation and relates the birth of the Lord to the major events and personages of sacred and secular history. The particular events contained in the announcement help pastorally to situate the birth of Jesus in the context of salvation history.

This text, *The Nativity of our Lord Jesus Christ,* may be chanted or recited, most appropriately on December 24, during the celebration of the Liturgy of the Hours. It may also be chanted or recited before the beginning of Christmas Mass during the Night. It may not replace any part of the Mass.

The twenty-fifth day of De-cem-ber,   when ages beyond number

had run their course from the creation of the world,   when God in the

beginning created hea - ven and earth,   and formed man in his own

like-ness;   when century upon century had passed since the Al-

-mighty set his bow in the clouds after the Great Flood,   as a sign of

covenant and peace;   in the twenty-first century since Abraham,

our father in faith,   came out of the Ur of the Chal-dees;   in the

thirteenth century since the People of Israel were led by Moses in the

---

This Proclamation of the Birth of Christ comes from the Roman Martyrology, the official listing of the Saints celebrated by the Roman Rite of the Catholic Church. Traditionally, it has been read on Christmas Eve, before the celebration of Midnight Mass. It situates the Nativity of Christ within the context of salvation history, making reference not only to biblical events but also to the Greek and Roman worlds. The coming of Christ at Christmas, then, is seen as the summit of both sacred and secular

history. It begins with the creation of the world, mentions certain key events in the history of the people of Israel, and concludes with the birth of Jesus during the Roman Era.

In the 1980s, Pope John Paul II restored the Proclamation of the Birth of Christ to the papal celebration of Midnight Mass. Many parishes have followed the restored custom. A new translation "Approved for Use in the Dioceses of the United States of America by the United States Conference

of Catholic Bishops and Confirmed by the Apostolic See" was published in 1994 (repr. in Sacramentary Supplement, 2004). Our present translation of the proclamation is a revision. In several respects, the new translation is a significant improvement over the various older translations.

The main reason it is better might seem paradoxical; namely, that it is less precise than most older translations in referring to specific years for certain events in early biblical history. For example, while

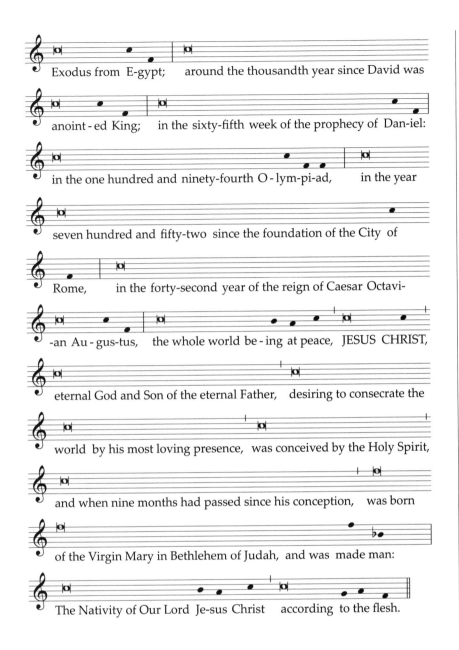

Exodus from E-gypt;   around the thousandth year since David was anoint-ed King;   in the sixty-fifth week of the prophecy of Dan-iel: in the one hundred and ninety-fourth O-lym-pi-ad,   in the year seven hundred and fifty-two since the foundation of the City of Rome,   in the forty-second year of the reign of Caesar Octavi--an Au-gus-tus,   the whole world be-ing at peace, JESUS CHRIST, eternal God and Son of the eternal Father,   desiring to consecrate the world by his most loving presence,   was conceived by the Holy Spirit, and when nine months had passed since his conception,   was born of the Virgin Mary in Bethlehem of Judah, and was made man: The Nativity of Our Lord Je-sus Christ   according to the flesh.

The music is generally syllabic throughout, thus the intelligibility of the text is never in jeopardy. The only words emphasized are **Jesus Christ** but this is not achieved through a melodic construction. Rather, the inflection of the voice is important.

Once the name of **Christ** is announced, the chant moves above the reciting tone, reminiscent of the tone used for the Gospel. Thus, musically the melodies move us through salvation history.

The last line is particularly important for the solemn character of the announcement.

the birth of Jesus is situated "in the year two-thousand nine-hundred and fifty-seven after the flood" (of Noah) in the older translations, the new translation states, "century upon century had passed / since the Almighty set his bow in the clouds after the Great Flood."

In this and similar cases, less precision is actually better, since it more closely reflects contemporary Church teaching and biblical scholarship. Proclaiming exact numbers of years inevitably gives most people the impression that we know exactly when these biblical events took place, thereby, unwittingly reinforcing a type of biblical fundamentalism or pseudo-historical literalism that does not conform to the principles of Catholic biblical interpretation. Considering how long ago these events are said to have taken place and how few historically reliable sources we have for events of the distant past (especially anything before the time of King David), it is better not to give the impression that dates are or can be known with great precision.

The word Christmas derives from the combination of Christ and Mass; it is the Solemnity of the Nativity of Our Lord and Savior Jesus Christ. Second in the liturgical calendar only to Easter, Christmas is celebrated by many as if it were the most important of Christian feasts.

Text without music:

The Twenty-fifth Day of December,
when ages beyond number had run their course
    from the creation of the world,
when God in the beginning created heaven and earth,
and formed man in his own likeness;
when century upon century had passed
since the Almighty set his bow in the clouds after the Great Flood,
as a sign of covenant and peace;
in the twenty-first century since Abraham, our father in faith,
came out of Ur of the Chaldees;
in the thirteenth century since the People of Israel were led
    by Moses in the Exodus from Egypt;
around the thousandth year since David was anointed King;
in the sixty-fifth week of the prophecy of Daniel;
in the one hundred and ninety-fourth Olympiad;
in the year seven hundred and fifty-two
    since the foundation of the City of Rome;
in the forty-second year of the reign of Caesar Octavian Augustus,
the whole world being at peace,

JESUS CHRIST, eternal God and Son of the eternal Father,
desiring to consecrate the world by his most loving presence,
was conceived by the Holy Spirit,
and when nine months had passed since his conception,
was born of the Virgin Mary in Bethlehem of Judah, and
    was made man:

The Nativity of Our Lord Jesus Christ according to the flesh.

Therefore, people are often surprised to find that Christmas was not celebrated by the earliest Christians. The custom was to celebrate a Saint's birth into eternal life—in other words, his death. Thus, Good Friday (Christ's death) and Easter Sunday (His Resurrection) took center stage.

It took a while, though, for the Church to develop the feast of Christmas. While it may have been celebrated in Egypt as early as the third century, it did not spread throughout the Christian world until the middle of the fourth century. It was first celebrated along with Epiphany, on January 6; but slowly Christmas was separated out into its own feast, on December 25. By the middle of the sixth century, Christians had begun to observe Advent, the time of preparation for Christmas, with fasting; and the 12 days of Christmas, from Christmas Day to Epiphany, had become established.

To this day, the Church celebrates only three birthdays: Christmas; the Nativity of the Blessed Virgin Mary; and the Birth of John the Baptist. The common thread in the celebrations is that these three persons were born without sin.

APPENDIX II

RITE FOR THE BLESSING AND SPRINKLING OF WATER

1. On Sundays, especially in Easter Time, the blessing and sprinkling of water as a memorial of Baptism may take place from time to time in all churches and chapels, even in Masses anticipated on Saturday evenings.

    If this rite is celebrated during Mass, it takes the place of the usual Penitential Act at the beginning of Mass.

2. After the greeting, the Priest stands at his chair and faces the people. With a vessel containing the water to be blessed before him, he calls upon the people to pray in these or similar words:

> **Dear brethren (brothers and sisters),**
> **let us humbly beseech the Lord our God**
> **to bless this water he has created,**
> **which will be sprinkled on us**
> **as a memorial of our Baptism.**
> **May he help us by his grace**
> **to remain faithful to the Spirit we have received.**

And after a brief pause for silence, he continues with hands joined:

> **Almighty ever-living God,**
> **who willed that through water,**
> **the fountain of life and the source of purification,**
> **even souls should be cleansed**
> **and receive the gift of eternal life;**
> **be pleased, we pray, to ✠ bless this water,**
> **by which we seek protection on this your day, O Lord.**
> **Renew the living spring of your grace within us**
> **and grant that by this water we may be defended**
> **from all ills of spirit and body,**
> **and so approach you with hearts made clean**
> **and worthily receive your salvation.**
> **Through Christ our Lord.**
> R. Amen.

Or:

The rubric states that the Priest may pray "in these or similar words." Although the blessing of water found in the Easter Vigil is probably too long, the prayer might allude to some of the events in scripture that mention water.

A musical setting of the blessing of water is found in the Mass for the Easter Vigil. The text beautifully elicits Old and New Testament references to water, particularly as it foreshadowed Baptism. The musical motif might be used to set the blessing text to the left, making the connection between holy water and baptismal water.

Asperges is the older name for the Rite for the Blessing and Sprinkling of Water, now an option at the beginning of Sunday Mass, replacing the Penitential Act. The rite has its origins at least as early as the ninth century with Pope Leo IV. In the Tridentine Mass, the form was: Celebrant sprinkles the altar, himself, and assisting ministers with holy water. He sprinkles the people, either from the sanctuary or passing through the aisles. During this, the chanting includes: the proper antiphon: *Asperges me, Domine* during the year, or *Vidi aquam* during the Paschaltide, Psalm 51:1 during the year, or Psalm 118:1 during Paschaltide or *Gloria Patri* (omitted during Passiontide). The antiphon is repeated. The Priest Celebrant sings versicles and prayer.

The object of the *Asperges* Rite is to prepare the congregation for the celebration of Mass by moving them to sentiments of penance and reverence suggested by the words of Psalm [51], or by impressing on them that they are about to assist at the sacrifice of our redemption, as suggested in the Psalm at Easter Time.

The rite takes on the character of a baptismal remembrance, as seen in the invitation that precedes any of the three options: "Dear brethren (brothers and sisters), / let us humbly beseech the Lord our God / to bless this water he has created, / which will be sprinkled on us as a memorial of our Baptism. / May he help us by his grace / to remain faithful to the Spirit we have received." After this invitation and a

Almighty Lord and God,
who are the source and origin of all life,
whether of body or soul,
we ask you to + bless this water,
which we use in confidence
to implore forgiveness for our sins
and to obtain the protection of your grace
against all illness and every snare of the enemy.
Grant, O Lord, in your mercy,
that living waters may always spring up for our salvation,
and so may we approach you with a pure heart
and avoid all danger to body and soul.
Through Christ our Lord.
R. Amen.

Or, during Easter Time:

Lord our God,
in your mercy be present to your people's prayers,
and, for us who recall the wondrous work of our creation
and the still greater work of our redemption,
graciously + bless this water.
For you created water to make the fields fruitful
and to refresh and cleanse our bodies.
You also made water the instrument of your mercy:
for through water you freed your people from slavery
and quenched their thirst in the desert;
through water the Prophets proclaimed the new covenant
you were to enter upon with the human race;
and last of all,
through water, which Christ made holy in the Jordan,
you have renewed our corrupted nature
in the bath of regeneration.
Therefore, may this water be for us
a memorial of the Baptism we have received,
and grant that we may share
in the gladness of our brothers and sisters
who at Easter have received their Baptism.
Through Christ our Lord.
R. Amen.

brief pause, the celebrant may chose any of three blessing prayers. They begin: 1. "Almighty ever-living God, who willed that through water, / the fountain of life and the source of purification." 2. "Almighty Lord and God, / who are the source and origin of all life, / whether of body or soul." 3. "Lord our God, / in your mercy be present to your people's prayers / and, for us who recall the wondrous works of creation / and the still greater work of our redemption.

The third prayer option is reserved for Easter Time, and recounts the events in our salvation history linked to water (for example, the crossing of the Red Sea, Moses calling forth water from the rock, the baptism of Christ in the Jordan). As an option, the celebrant may mix salt with the holy water, where this is customary. The prayer of blessing over the salt recalls the prophet Elisha throwing salt into a spring to purify it (2 Kings 2:19–22).

The rubric then states: "Taking the aspergillum, the Priest sprinkles himself and the ministers, then the clergy and people, moving through the church, if appropriate." Meanwhile, an antiphon or another appropriate chant is sung.

The "antiphon" mentioned may certainly be the traditional chants, *Asperges me or Vidi aquam* [which can be found in the *Liber Usualis*]. An adaptation of the chant may be used, such as "I Saw Water Flowing," which uses the melody for the

3.   Where the circumstances of the place or the custom of the people suggest that the mixing of salt be preserved in the blessing of water, the Priest may bless salt, saying:

We humbly ask you, almighty God:
be pleased in your faithful love to bless ✠ this salt
you have created,
for it was you who commanded the prophet Elisha
to cast salt into water,
that impure water might be purified.
Grant, O Lord, we pray,
that, wherever this mixture of salt and water is sprinkled,
every attack of the enemy may be repulsed
and your Holy Spirit may be present
to keep us safe at all times.
Through Christ our Lord.
R. Amen.

Then he pours the salt into the water, without saying anything.

4.   Afterward, taking the aspergillum, the Priest sprinkles himself and the ministers, then the clergy and people, moving through the church, if appropriate.

Meanwhile, one of the following chants, or another appropriate chant is sung.

Outside Easter Time

Antiphon 1   Ps 51 (50): 9

Sprinkle me with hyssop, O Lord, and I shall be cleansed;
wash me and I shall be whiter than snow.

Antiphon 2   Ez 36: 25–26

I will pour clean water upon you,
and you will be made clean of all your impurities,
and I shall give you a new spirit, says the Lord.

Hymn   Cf. 1 Pt 1: 3–5

Blessed be the God and Father of our Lord Jesus Christ,
who in his great mercy has given us new birth into a living hope
through the Resurrection of Jesus Christ from the dead,
into an inheritance that will not perish,
preserved for us in heaven
for the salvation to be revealed in the last time!

traditional *Vidi aquam* in an English version with congregational refrain. A baptismal hymn also may be sung, although it must be remembered that the Entrance Chant has occurred just before the Sprinkling Rite, and the Gloria (except in Advent and Lent) will immediately follow. After the sprinkling, the celebrant returns to the altar and says the final prayer of the rite:

"May almighty God cleanse us of our sins, / and through the celebration of this Eucharist / make us worthy to share at the table of his Kingdom."

The reference to "cleanse us of our sins" is very important, as this rite replaces the Penitential Act. Priests who omit this prayer, through ignorance or laziness, are depriving the congregation of this necessary reference.

While in the East the Priest uses a sort of brush for the sprinkling, and the Pope uses a large sprig of hyssop (referencing Psalm 51), the usual implement for the sprinkling is the aspergillum, whose name

comes from the Latin *aspergere* ("to sprinkle"). This has a long metal or wooden handle with a hollow metal sphere pierced with many holes. The aspergillum is dipped in the aspersorium, sometimes called aspersory, which is a metal bucket holding the holy water.

The Sprinkling Rite has particular significance at any Mass with baptismal themes and is certainly called for during the post-baptismal, mystogogical season of Easter, where it should be

During Easter Time

Antiphon 1

Cf. Ez 47: 1–2, 9

I saw water flowing from the Temple,
from its right-hand side, alleluia:
and all to whom this water came
were saved and shall say: Alleluia, alleluia.

Antiphon 2

Cf. Wis 3: 8; Ez 36: 25

On the day of my resurrection, says the Lord, alleluia,
I will gather the nations and assemble the kingdoms
and I will pour clean water upon you, alleluia.

Antiphon 3

Cf. Dn 3: 77, 79

You springs and all that moves in the waters,
sing a hymn to God, alleluia.

Antiphon 4

1 Pt 2: 9

O chosen race, royal priesthood, holy nation,
proclaim the mighty works of him
who called you out of darkness into his wonderful light, alleluia.

Antiphon 5

From your side, O Christ,
bursts forth a spring of water,
by which the squalor of the world is washed away
and life is made new again, alleluia.

5. When he returns to his chair and the singing is over, the Priest stands facing the people and, with hands joined, says:

**May almighty God cleanse us of our sins,
and through the celebration of this Eucharist
make us worthy to share at the table of his Kingdom.**
R. Amen.

6. Then, when it is prescribed, the hymn Gloria in excelsis (Glory to God in the highest) is sung or said.

used every Sunday. It is common to celebrate the Sprinkling Rite instead of the Penitential Act on the Sundays of Easter Time. However, sometimes a concern is raised that the Introductory Rites become too prominent—with Entrance Chant, singing during the sprinkling, and then the Gloria. Some have attempted to solve this dilemma by sprinkling during the Gloria, but such an approach distorts the structure of the Sprinkling Rite (the closing prayer often gets abandoned) and misunderstands the purpose of the Gloria—which is to give praise to God in response to the Penitential Act (or Sprinkling Rite).

In the United States Bishops' *Introduction to the Order of Mass* (#74) the following model is offered: the first part of the Introductory Rites (Sign of the Cross, Greeting, Prayer over the Water) are done at the entrance of the church. The sprinkling itself takes place as the ministers process to the sanctuary—so the Entrance Chant and the hymn accompanying the sprinkling rite become one and the same. The Priest closes the Sprinkling Rite (May almighty God cleanse us), and then the Gloria is sung.

APPENDIX III

RITE OF DEPUTING A MINISTER TO DISTRIBUTE HOLY COMMUNION ON A SINGLE OCCASION

1. The Diocesan Bishop has the faculty to permit individual Priests exercising sacred duties to depute a suitable member of the faithful to distribute Holy Communion with them on a single occasion, in cases of real necessity.

2. When one of the faithful is deputed to distribute Communion on a single occasion in such cases, it is fitting that a mandate to do so should be conferred according to the following rite.

3. After the Priest Celebrant himself has received the Sacrament in the usual way, the extraordinary minister comes to the altar and stands before the Celebrant, who blesses him or her with these words:

> **May the Lord ✠ bless you,**
> **so that at this Mass you may minister**
> **the Body and Blood of Christ**
> **to your brothers and sisters.**

And he or she replies:

> **Amen.**

4. If the extraordinary minister is to receive the Most Holy Eucharist, the Priest gives Communion to the minister. Then the Priest gives him or her the ciborium or vessel with the hosts or the chalice and together they go to administer Communion to the faithful.

In every celebration of the Eucharist, there should be a sufficient number of ministers of Communion so that the distribution will be reverent and orderly. Bishops, Priests, and Deacons distribute Holy Communion in virtue of their office as ordinary ministers of the Body and Blood of the Lord.

When the size of the congregation or the incapacity of the Bishop, Priest, or Deacon requires, the celebrant may be assisted by other Bishops, Priests, or Deacons. If such ordinary ministers of Holy Communion are not present, "the Priest may call upon extraordinary ministers to assist him, that is, duly instituted acolytes or even other faithful who have been duly deputed for this purpose. In case of necessity, the Priest may also depute suitable faithful for this single occasion" (GIRM, 162).

In the United States, lay persons have been granted permission to be extraordinary ministers of Holy Communion to assist when enough ordinary ministers are not available.

Extraordinary ministers of Holy Communion should receive sufficient spiritual, theological, and practical preparation to fulfill their role with knowledge and reverence. In all matters, they should follow the guidance of the diocesan Bishop (*Norms for the Distribution and Reception of Holy Communion under Both Kinds for the Dioceses of the United States of America*).

APPENDIX IV

RITE OF BLESSING A CHALICE AND A PATEN WITHIN MASS

1. Since the chalice and paten are used for the offering and consecration of the bread and wine and for communion, they are reserved exclusively and permanently for the celebration of the Eucharist, and so become "sacred vessels."

2. The intention of reserving these vessels exclusively for the celebration of the Eucharist is made manifest before the community of the faithful by a special blessing which is appropriate to impart during Mass.

3. Any Priest may bless a chalice and paten, provided these vessels have been made according to the norms indicated above in the *General Instruction of the Roman Missal*, nos. 327–332.

4. If only a chalice or only a paten is to be blessed, the texts should be suitably adapted.

5. After the reading of the word of God, a homily is given in which the Priest explains both the biblical readings and the meaning of the blessing of a chalice and paten that are used in the celebration of the Lord's Supper.

6. When the Universal Prayer is concluded, the ministers, or representatives of the community presenting the chalice and paten, place these latter on the altar. Then the Priest moves to the altar, while there is sung this antiphon:

Antiphon
**The chalice of salvation I will raise,
and I will call on the name of the Lord.**

Another appropriate chant may also be sung.

7. When the singing is over, the Priest says:
    Let us pray.

The GIRM, 327–332, is clear on the requisites for the sacred vessels. The vessels are held in special honor, especially the chalice and paten. The articles stress that the vessels are to be of precious metal, though they may be made of other materials considered "precious or noble." The preference is that the materials for these vessels do not break or deteriorate.

"Sacred vessels are to be made from precious metal. If they are made from metal that rusts or from a metal less precious than gold, then ordinarily they should be gilded on the inside.

"In the Dioceses of the United States of America, sacred vessels may also be made from other solid materials which in the common estimation in each region are considered precious or noble, for example, ebony or other harder woods, provided that such materials are suitable for sacred use. In this case, preference is always to be given to materials that do not break or deteriorate. This applies to all vessels that are intended to hold the hosts, such as the paten, the ciborium, the pyx, the monstrance, and others of this kind.

And all pray in silence for a while. Then the Priest continues:

With joy, Lord God,
we place on your altar this chalice and paten
for the celebration of the sacrifice of the new covenant:
may the Body and Blood of your Son,
offered and received by means of these vessels,
make them holy.
Grant, we pray, O Lord,
that, celebrating the unblemished sacrifice,
we may be renewed by your Sacraments on earth
and endowed with your Spirit,
until with the Saints we come to delight in your banquet
in the Kingdom of Heaven.
Glory and honor to you for ever.

All reply:

Blessed be God for ever.

8. The ministers then place the corporal on the altar. Some of the faithful carry forward bread, wine, and water for the celebration of the Lord's Sacrifice. The Priest puts the offerings on the newly blessed paten and in the newly blessed chalice and offers them in the usual way. Meanwhile, if appropriate, this antiphon with Psalm 115 is sung:

Antiphon

The chalice of salvation I will raise,
and I will offer a sacrifice of praise (E.T. **alleluia).**

Psalm 116 (115)

I trusted, even when I said,
"I am sorely afflicted,"
and when I said in my alarm,
"These people are all liars."

(The antiphon is repeated)

How can I repay the LORD
for all his goodness to me?
The cup of salvation I will raise;
I will call on the name of the LORD.

(The antiphon is repeated)

"As regards chalices and other vessels that are intended to serve as receptacles for the Blood of the Lord, they are to have a bowl material that does not absorb liquids. The base, on the other hand, may be made of other solid and worthy materials" (GIRM, 328–330).

"As regards the form of the sacred vessels, it is for the artist to fashion them in a manner that is more particularly in keeping with the customs of each region, provided the individual vessels are suitable for their intended liturgical use and are clearly distinguishable from vessels intended for everyday use" (GIRM, 332).

For the blessing of sacred vessels, the rites prescribed in the liturgical books are to be followed.

Psalm 116 is particularly appropriate for the blessing of sacred vessels, because it references the "cup of salvation" and makes allusions to cultic matters in the context of the temple in Jerusalem. Since this rite does not have a formal blessing

My vows to the LORD I will fulfill
before all his people.
How precious in the eyes of the LORD
is the death of his faithful.

(The antiphon is repeated)

Your servant, LORD, your servant am I,
the son of your handmaid;
you have loosened my bonds.
A thanksgiving sacrifice I make;
I will call on the name of the LORD.

(The antiphon is repeated)

My vows to the LORD I will fulfill
before all his people,
in the courts of the house of the LORD,
in your midst, O Jerusalem.

(The antiphon is repeated)

Another appropriate chant may also be sung.

9. After the prayer **With humble spirit**, it is appropriate for the Priest to incense the gifts and the altar.

10. According to the circumstances of the celebration, it is fitting that the faithful receive the Blood of Christ from the newly blessed chalice.

prayer, we might say that the form of blessing is by use. The paten and chalice are placed on the corporal on the altar and the Priest says the following prayer: "may the Body and Blood of your Son, / offered and received by means of these vessels, / make them holy. . . ." The gifts are then presented and placed on the newly blessed paten and in the chalice. Incense may be used, but it is unclear whether the intent is to incense the vessels or the gifts.

That chrism or holy water are not used in the rite also indicates that the vessels are blessed through use or by touching that which is precious.

A similar principle applies concerning contact relics. These were items which had been in contact with the bodies of the Saints such as cloths or dust. In the early Church, pilgrims going to Jerusalem would pour oil over relics, especially the Stone of the Anointing (the thirteenth Station of the Cross inside the Church of the Holy Sepulchre), believed to be the place where Jesus' body was prepared for burial. Then they would bring the oil home in glass ampoules around their necks for veneration.

APPENDIX V

EXAMPLES OF FORMULARIES FOR THE UNIVERSAL PRAYER

1. GENERAL FORMULA I

Priest's Introduction

**To God the Father almighty,
dear brothers and sisters,
may every prayer of our heart be directed,
for his will it is that all humanity should be saved
and come to the knowledge of the truth.**

Intentions

1. **For the holy Church of God,
that the Lord may graciously watch over her and care for her,
let us pray to the Lord.**
R. Grant this, almighty God.

2. **For the peoples of all the world,
that the Lord may graciously preserve harmony among them,
let us pray to the Lord.**
R. Grant this, almighty God.

3. **For all who are oppressed by any kind of need,
that the Lord may graciously grant them relief,
let us pray to the Lord.**
R. Grant this, almighty God.

4. **For ourselves and our own community,
that the Lord may graciously receive us
as a sacrifice acceptable to himself,
let us pray to the Lord.**
R. Grant this, almighty God.

Priest's Prayer

**O God, our refuge and our strength,
hear the prayers of your Church,
for you yourself are the source of all devotion,
and grant, we pray, that what we ask in faith
we may truly obtain.
Through Christ our Lord.**
R. Amen.

The Universal Prayer also may be chanted. See the four formularies on page 308. Additionally, other modern compositions may be used.

It is important that the petition cues the response from the assembly, so that the response flows smoothly and logically from what precedes it.

If the Priest is able, he could introduce with a sung invitation to prayer and conclude with a sung prayer. These parts, however, should be musically congruent with the petitions to avoid ritual fragmentation. If the invitation and concluding prayer cannot be sung in the same modality as the petitions, it may be better to simply recite them.

The Missal presents several examples that can serve as models for composing the Universal Prayer or Prayer of the Faithful. The form of the prayer is always the same. The Priest invites all the faithful to make prayers for the community and the world. The petitions are addressed to God or to Christ, followed by a closing prayer that is addressed to God through Christ.

The history of the Universal Prayer is a rich one, reaching back to our Jewish ancestors. Stephen S. Wilbricht, csc, an associate professor at Stonehill College, explored the roots of this intercessory prayer in the following article "The History, Theology, and Practice of the Prayer of the Faithful" condensed from the November 2010 *Pastoral Liturgy*.

The History, Theology and Practice of the Prayer of the Faithful

When Jesus returned to Capernaum after some days, it became known that he was at home. Many gathered together so that there was no longer room for them, not even around the door; and he preached the word to them. They came bringing to him a paralytic carried by four men. Unable to get near Jesus because of the crowd, they opened up the roof above him. After they had broken through, they let down the mat on which the paralytic lay. When Jesus saw their faith, he said to the paralytic, "Child, your sins are forgiven . . . I say to you, stand up, take your mat and go to your home." And he stood up, and immediately took the mat and went out before all of them; so that they were

In composing the Universal Prayers, notice the general order that is offered in the sample formularies. Note as well the general nature of these petitions. Nevertheless, the petitions should take into consideration what is occurring in the world, the Church, and locally.

2. GENERAL FORMULA II

Priest's Introduction

**Brothers and sisters,
as we now make our prayer
for our community and for the world,
let us all pray to Christ the Lord,
not only for ourselves and our own needs,
but for the entire people.**

Intentions

1a. **For the whole Christian people,
let us beseech the abundance of divine goodness.**
R. Christ, hear us. or Christ, graciously hear us.

1b. **For all who do not yet believe,
let us implore the giver of all spiritual gifts.**
R. Christ, hear us.

2a. **For those who hold public office,
let us call upon the power of the Lord.**
R. Christ, hear us.

2b. **For favorable weather and abundant fruits from the earth,
let us entreat the Lord, the ruler of the world.**
R. Christ, hear us.

3a. **For our brothers and sisters
who cannot be present at this sacred assembly,
let us beseech him who observes all things.**
R. Christ, hear us.

3b. **For the repose of the souls of the faithful departed,
let us call upon the judge of all humanity.**
R. Christ, hear us.

4a. **For all of us who pray in faith
and ask the mercy of the Lord,
let us entreat the compassion of our Savior.**
R. Christ, hear us.

amazed and glorified God, saying, "We have never seen anything like this." (Mark 2:1–5, 11–12)

The Lord's curing of the paralytic lowered through the roof by the ingenuity of several concerned bystanders is a story of intercession. Within the local community of Capernaum there is a perceived need. The pain and paralysis of the sick man is shared 'by the town. A decision is made to bring the man into Jesus' presence. The para-lyzed man asks for nothing; it is the persis-tence and energy of the intercessors—the ones who break open the roof and lower his mat—that move Jesus to heal and restore the man to full health.

The ritual practice of interceding for the needs of the Church and of the world is a serious business of displaying faith in the mercy and compassion of God. The Prayer of the Faithful is the movement of present-ing the world to God so that, in return, God's kingdom may be recognized on earth. The liturgical act of interceding for others is the way in which the Church, as Christ's body, responds to the proclaimed Word, so that all suffering and strife may be overcome in the communion it antici-pates. Through a renewed appreciation of the history, theology, and practice of the Prayer of the Faithful, the people of God might better embrace their vocation to offer prayers to God for the redemption of all creation.

4b. **For ourselves and those close to us**
who await the Lord's goodness,
let us call upon the mercy of Christ the Lord.
R. Christ, hear us.

Priest's Prayer

Incline your merciful ear to our prayers,
we ask, O Lord,
and listen in kindness to the supplications of those who call
on you.
Through Christ our Lord.
R. Amen.

3. ADVENT

Priest's Introduction

As we await with longing
the coming of our Lord Jesus Christ,
dear brothers and sisters,
let us with renewed devotion beseech his mercy,
that, as he came into the world
to bring the good news to the poor
and heal the contrite of heart,
so in our own time, also,
he may bring salvation to all in need.

Intentions

1a. **That Christ may visit his holy Church**
and keep watch over her always,
let us pray to the Lord.
R. Lord, have mercy. or Kyrie, eleison.

1b. **That Christ may fill the Pope,**
our Bishop, and the whole Order of Bishops
with spiritual gifts and graces,
let us pray to the Lord.
R. Lord, have mercy. or Kyrie, eleison.

The Universal Prayer also may be chanted. See the four formularies on page 308. Additionally, other modern compositions may be used.

It is important that the petition cues the response from the congregation, so that the response flows smoothly and logically from what precedes it.

If the Priest is able, he could introduce with a sung invitation to prayer and conclude with a sung prayer. These parts, however, should be musically congruent with the petitions to avoid ritual fragmentation. If the invitation and concluding prayer cannot be sung in the same modality as the petitions, it may be better to simply recite them.

History

While the renewal of the people's role in the act of intercession—a result of the liturgical reforms of the Second Vatican Council—retrieved a component of the Mass that had disappeared for almost fifteen hundred years, it must be recognized that intercessory prayer is deeply planted in the heritage of the Church. The early Church took its cues for intercessory prayer from the Jewish synagogue, especially its recitation of the psalms. The psalms not only offer words of praise and blessing to God, they plead for pressing needs of the community. "The continual refrain of blessing makes each petition a reason to praise and a sign of the expected grace of God" (Walter C. Huffman, *The Prayer of the Faithful: Understanding and Creatively Using the Prayer of the Church*, Minneapolis, Augsburg Publishing House, 1986, p. 24).

The first followers of Jesus Christ understood their prayer to be mediated from Christ himself. Saint Paul and his fellow heralds of the Gospel testify to the belief that the action of holding the needs of the world before God is a form of participating in the offering of Christ. The author of the first letter to Timothy writes: "First of all, then, I urge that supplications, prayers, intercessions, and thanksgivings be made for everyone, for kings and all who are in high positions" (2:1–2).

Thus, from its very start, the Christian Church understood itself as commissioned to participate in the work of salvation, not only through the Lord's command to memorialize his presence through the eating and drinking of his Body and Blood,

In composing the Universal Prayers, notice the general order that is offered in the sample formularies. Note, as well, the general nature of these petitions. Nevertheless, the petitions should take into consideration what is currently happening in the world, the Church, and locally.

2a. **That under the protection of Christ our times may be peaceful, let us pray to the Lord.**
R. Lord, have mercy. or Kyrie, eleison.

2b. **That Christ may guide the minds of those who govern us to promote the common good according to his will, let us pray to the Lord.**
R. Lord, have mercy. or Kyrie, eleison.

3a. **That Christ may banish disease, drive out hunger, and ward off every affliction, let us pray to the Lord.**
R. Lord, have mercy. or Kyrie, eleison.

3b. **That Christ in his mercy may free all who suffer persecution, let us pray to the Lord.**
R. Lord, have mercy. or Kyrie, eleison.

4a. **That as witnesses to Christ's love before all we may abide in the truth, let us pray to the Lord.**
R. Lord, have mercy. or Kyrie, eleison.

4b. **That Christ may find us watching when he comes, let us pray to the Lord.**
R. Lord, have mercy. or Kyrie, eleison.

Priest's Prayer

Almighty ever-living God, who bring salvation to all and desire that no one should perish, hear the prayers of your people and grant that the course of our world may be directed by your peaceful rule and your Church rejoice in tranquility and devotion. Through Christ our Lord.
R. Amen.

but also through articulating the desires of the world to God through his Son. It is for this very reason that universal intercessions are intertwined with the Eucharist.

The first concrete liturgical evidence for the Prayer of the Faithful can be found in the writings of the second century apologist Justin Martyr. Written around the year 150, Justin describes the Christian assembly at prayer, in which "the prayers" serve to link the celebration of Baptism with the Eucharist.

After we have thus baptized him who has believed and has given his assent, we take him to those who are called brethren where they are assembled, to make common prayers earnestly for ourselves and for him who has been enlightened and for all others everywhere. ("First Apology 65.1," taken from R.C.D. Jasper and G. J. Cuming, *Prayers of the Eucharist: Early and Reformed*, Collegeville, Liturgical Press, 1990, p. 28)

Intercessions were undoubtedly part of a faith response of the already baptized.

Naturally, those who were not fully part of the body of Christ could not partake in their utterance. Such is the testimony provided by Hippolytus of Rome, near the turn of the third century, who writes that the newly baptized "shall pray together with all the people. But they shall not previously pray with the faithful before they have undergone all these things" ("Apostolic Tradition, xxii," in *The Treatise on the Apostolic Tradition of St. Hippolytus of Rome*, eds. Gregory Dix and Henry Chadwick, London, The Alban Press, 1968, p. 39).

4. CHRISTMAS TIME

Priest's Introduction

On this day (on this night, in this time)
when the goodness and kindness of God our Savior have
    appeared,
let us, dear brothers and sisters,
humbly pour forth to him our prayers,
trusting not in our own good works, but in his mercy.

Intentions

1. For the Church of God,
    that in integrity of faith she may await
    and may welcome with joy
    him whom the immaculate Virgin conceived by a word
    and wondrously brought to birth,
    let us pray to the Lord.
    R. Lord, have mercy.

2. For the progress and peace of the whole world,
    that what is given in time may become a reward in eternity,
    let us pray to the Lord.
    R. Lord, have mercy.

3. For those oppressed by hunger, sickness or loneliness,
    that through the mystery of the Nativity (Epiphany) of Christ
    they may find relief in both mind and body,
    let us pray to the Lord.
    R. Lord, have mercy.

4. For the families of our congregation,
    that, receiving Christ,
    they may learn also to welcome him in the poor,
    let us pray to the Lord.
    R. Lord, have mercy.

Another piece of historical evidence for the ancient pattern of Christian intercessory prayer comes from Rome and the Good Friday service. In a style that seems elaborate for a sober liturgy, the Good Friday intercessions each have three parts: 1) an invitation to pray for a particular need, 2) silent prayer, and 3) a concluding collect voiced by the priest. The intentions that survive in our present Good Friday liturgy are: for the Church, for the Pope, for the clergy and laity of the Church, for those preparing for Baptism, for the unity of Christians, for the Jewish people, for those who do not believe in Christ, for those who do not believe in God, for all in public office, and for those in special need.

The threefold structure for each of these intentions "successfully combined the silent devotion of the individual and the vocal prayer of the congregation and in addition also helped the people to give themselves both in body and soul to the service of God" (Theodor Klauser, *A Short History of the Western Liturgy*, London, Oxford University Press, 1965, p. 49).

However, a practical drawback of this form of prayer is that it was quite tedious and time-consuming in relation to the rest of the liturgy. It was the liturgical reform of Pope Gelasius I (492–496) that instituted the Eastern custom of a call-and-response style of intercessory prayer, with the deacon announcing the petition and the assembly responding with *Domine, exaudi et miserere* ("Lord, hear and have mercy"). At Milan and other parts of the West, this response was abbreviated to the Greek *Kyrie eleison* (see Robert Cabié, *The Church*

The Universal Prayer also may be chanted. See the four formularies on page 308. Additionally, other modern compositions may be used.

It is important that the petition cues the response from the assembly, so that the response flows smoothly and logically from what precedes it.

If the Priest is able, he could introduce the intentions with a sung invitation to prayer and conclude with a sung prayer. These parts, however, should be musically congruent with the petitions to avoid ritual fragmentation. If the invitation and concluding prayer cannot be sung in the same modality as the petitions, it may be better to recite them.

Priest's Prayer

> **We pray, O Lord our God,**
> **that the Virgin Mary,**
> **who merited to bear God and man in her chaste womb,**
> **may commend the prayers of your faithful in your sight.**
> **Through Christ our Lord.**
> R. Amen.

5. LENT I

Priest's Introduction

> **We should pour forth prayers at all times,**
> **dear brothers and sisters,**
> **but, above all, in these days of Lent**
> **we ought to watch more intently with Christ**
> **and direct our petitions more fervently to God.**

Intentions

1. **For the whole Christian people,**
   that in this sacred time they may be more abundantly nourished
   by every word that comes from the mouth of God,
   let us pray to the Lord.

2. **For the whole world,**
   that in lasting tranquility and peace
   our days may truly become
   the acceptable time of grace and salvation,
   let us pray to the Lord.

3. **For sinners and the neglectful,**
   that in this time of reconciliation
   they may return to Christ,
   let us pray to the Lord.

4. **For ourselves,**
   that God may at last stir up in our hearts
   aversion for our sins,
   let us pray to the Lord.

at Prayer, Volume II: The Eucharist, edited by A. G. Martimort, Collegeville, Liturgical Press, 1986, p. 72).

Praying the intercessions in litany form (the typical practice of the Roman West today) coincides with another reform instituted by Gelasius, the moving of the intercessions from their position following the Word to the opening of Mass. In this placement, petitions serve not as a faith response to the Word of God but as a means of seeking God's mercy to celebrate well the subsequent liturgy. Pope Gregory the Great (590–604), seeking to streamline a liturgy that had grown to almost three hours, further modified the intercessions by reducing them to three and eliminating the deacon's invitation on non-festal days.

It is likely, however, that both Gelasius and Gregory based reforms not only on the length of the liturgy but on the fact that the Roman canon already contained many instances of intercessory prayer. As a result, the Prayer of the Faithful was virtually taken away from the people in the assembly and given exclusively to the priest at the altar. "To enshrine the major intercessory element of the liturgy in the eucharistic prayer severely diminished the corporate expression of this prayer" (Huffman, p. 27). Thus, from the late sixth century until the 1960s, what little intercessory prayer remained in the Roman liturgy was attached to the sacrificial offering of Christ rather than the proclamation of his Word.

Theology

Returning to the story of Jesus' healing of the paralytic, three aspects of the encoun-

Priest's Prayer

Grant, we pray, O Lord,
that your people may turn to you with all their heart,
so that whatever they dare to ask in fitting prayer
they may receive by your mercy.
Through Christ our Lord.
R. Amen.

6. LENT II

Priest's Introduction

As the Solemnity of Easter approaches, dear friends,
let our prayer to the Lord be all the more insistent,
that all of us, and the whole multitude of the baptized,
together with the entire world,
may come to share more abundantly in this sacred mystery.

Intentions

1. That God may be pleased to increase faith and understanding
   in the catechumens who are to be initiated by Holy Baptism
   in the coming Paschal Solemnity,
   let us pray to the Lord.

2. That peoples in need may find help
   and that peace and security may be firmly established everywhere,
   let us pray to the Lord.

3. That all who are afflicted or suffering temptation
   may be strengthened by his grace,
   let us pray to the Lord.

4. That all of us may learn to distribute the fruits of self-denial
   for the good of those in need,
   let us pray to the Lord.

Priest's Prayer

Have mercy, O Lord, on the prayers of your Church
and turn with compassion to the hearts that bow before you,
that those you make sharers in the divine mystery
may never be left without your assistance.
Through Christ our Lord.
R. Amen.

In composing the Universal Prayers, notice the general order that is offered in the sample formularies. Note, as well, the general nature of these petitions. Nevertheless, the petitions should take into consideration what is currently occurring in the world, the Church, and locally.

ter help to frame a theology for the Prayer of the Faithful within Mass. First, there is the face-to-face meeting among Jesus, the man in need, and those gathered at the house. Second, this assembly is made possible due to the perseverance and ingenuity of the ones who display faith. Finally, the healing bolsters the faith of the crowd and serves to glorify God. In the end, even Jesus and his miraculous powers fade into the background as the greatness of God is revealed.

The Prayer of the Faithful mirrors this movement. The community prays for the needs of the Church and the world, since the suffering of a part is the concern of the whole. An assembly is formed not only by strength and unity but by weakness and brokenness. The Prayer of the Faithful reinforces our oneness as the body of Christ and our dependence upon God's mercy; it is a faith response to the proclamation of God's Word that seeks to root out all pain and bestow compassion and love. Finally, in a liturgical context, these prayers not

only bind the community closer together in Christ, they magnify God's name through the realization of a world renewed in grace.

Ultimately, the Prayer of the Faithful requires of the Church an attitude of surrender, in which personal needs are transcended by attention to the needs of others. In a sense, they call for a contemplative spirit that detects in their words a yearning for the fullness of God's kingdom. "Unless prayer responds to the world of ambiguity," writes Don Saliers, "it cannot fully fathom the world of glory" (*Worship and*

The Universal Prayer may be chanted. See the four formularies on page 308. Additionally, other modern composition may be used.

It is important that the petition cues the response from the assembly, so that the response flows smoothly and logically from what precedes it.

If the Priest is able, he could introduce the intentions with a sung invitation to prayer and conclude with a sung prayer. These parts, however, should be musically congruent with the petitions to avoid ritual fragmentation. If the invitation and concluding prayer cannot be sung in the same modality as the petitions, it may be better to recite them.

7. WEEKDAYS OF HOLY WEEK

Priest's Introduction

**In this time of the Lord's Passion,
when Christ offered prayers and supplications to his Father
with loud cries and tears,
let us humbly beseech God,
that in answer to his Son's reverent submission
he may in mercy hear our prayers also.**

Intentions

1. **That the Church, the Bride of Christ,
   may be more fully cleansed by his Blood
   in this time of his Passion,
   let us pray to the Lord.**

2. **That through the Blood of Christ's Cross
   all things in the world
   may be brought to peace for the sake of salvation,
   let us pray to the Lord.**

3. **That God may grant fortitude and patience
   to all who through sickness or hardship
   have a share in Christ's Passion,
   let us pray to the Lord.**

4. **That we may all be led through the Lord's Passion and Cross
   to the glory of his Resurrection,
   let us pray to the Lord.**

Priest's Prayer

**Be present, O Lord, to your people at prayer,
so that what they do not have the confidence or presumption to ask
they may obtain by the merits of your Son's Passion.
Who lives and reigns for ever and ever.**
R. Amen.

Spirituality, Philadelphia, The Westminster Press, 1984, p. 96). To put it another way, the Prayer of the Faithful is one of the ways the liturgy rehearses our participation as Christ's disciples in a kingdom that is both temporal and other-worldly.

Thus, the intercessions are fundamentally the prayer of Christ; they are his yearning for the coming of God's kingdom. The liturgy is the celebration of our surrender to Christ in the power of the Holy Spirit so that we (and all the world) might be offered to the Father.

The Prayer of the Faithful serves to anticipate a world that is nothing less than a "perfect offering" in Christ.

The *General Instruction of the Roman Missal* (GIRM), 69, places substantial emphasis on these prayers as a duty of baptismal faith, stating that, in the Prayer of the Faithful, people respond to the word of God. These prayers reveal and renew our relational commitments. Mark Searle states: "Prayer is an expression of our responsibility for our brothers and sisters under God: it is not a shifting of

responsibility" (*Liturgy Made Simple*, Collegeville: Liturgical Press, 1981, p. 50). Clearly, prayer lifted up to God entails an accompanying commitment to action.

In the story of the paralytic, we can only assume that those who lowered the man before the Lord were forever changed because of this encounter. In the same way, offering intercessions requires an accompanying openness to conversion and a new world view. We intercede for

8. EASTER TIME

Priest's Introduction

Dear brothers and sisters,
filled with paschal joy,
let us pray more earnestly to God
that he, who graciously listened
to the prayers and supplications of his beloved Son,
may now be pleased to look upon us in our lowliness.

Intentions

1. For the shepherds of our souls,
   that they may have the strength to govern wisely
   the flock entrusted to them by the Good Shepherd,
   let us pray to the Lord.

2. For the whole world,
   that it may truly know the peace given by Christ,
   let us pray to the Lord.

3. For our brothers and sisters who suffer,
   that their sorrow may be turned to gladness
   which no one can take from them,
   let us pray to the Lord.

4. For our own community,
   that it may bear witness with great confidence
   to the Resurrection of Christ,
   let us pray to the Lord.

Priest's Prayer

O God, who know that our life in this present age
is subject to suffering and need,
hear the desires of those who cry to you
and receive the prayers of those who believe in you.
Through Christ our Lord.
R. Amen.

In composing the petitions for the Universal Prayer, notice the general order that is offered in the sample formularies. Note, as well, the general nature of these petitions. Nevertheless, the petitions should take into consideration what is occurring in the world, the Church and locally.

others, not to change God but to be changed ourselves by God's will:

While the encounter between the Lord and the paralyzed man produces a physical cure, it is possible that the major change, conversion, takes place in the assembly gathered in the house. So it is with our weekly liturgical intercession. We come together, learn to surrender ourselves as Christ's body, and yearn to be plunged deeper into the mystery of God's will, even in the pain, frustrations, and sorrows we know to be true.

Practice

Sacrosanctum Concilium (SC), 53, mandates that "the 'common prayer' or 'prayer of the faithful' is to be restored after the Gospel and homily, especially on Sundays and holy days of obligation." More than 40 years after the release of this document, we must assess the success of the restoration of the Prayer of the Faithful. Are these prayers understood as the bridge that links the Liturgy of the Word to the Liturgy of the Eucharist? Are they interpreted as the moment when the Church, formed by the

Word of God, truly sees itself in the Lord's presence and begs for his intercession? Do these prayers mistakenly lead people to a place in which private petitions outweigh a communal outlook? What can be done for ongoing reform?

First of all, there is great need to remind our assemblies of what intercession means in the act of liturgical prayer. The Prayer of the Faithful is the prayer of a particular assembly gathered in worship, a prayer that belongs to the Body of Christ. It is the prayer of a specific people's hearts,

The Universal Prayer may be chanted. See the four formularies on page 308. Additionally, other modern compositions may be used.

It is important that the petition cues the response from the assembly, so that the response flows smoothly and logically from what precedes it.

If the Priest is able, he could introduce the intentions with a sung invitation and conclude with a sung prayer. These parts, however, should be musically congruent with the petitions to avoid ritual fragmentation. If the invitation and concluding prayer cannot be sung
in the same modality as the petitions, it may be better to recite them.

9. ORDINARY TIME I

Priest's Introduction

Dear brothers and sisters,
gathered as one to celebrate the good things
we have received from our God,
let us ask him to prompt in us
prayers that are worthy of his hearing.

Intentions

1. **For N. our Pope and N. our Bishop**
   and all the clergy,
   with the people entrusted to their charge,
   let us pray to the Lord.

2. **For those who hold public office**
   and those who assist them in promoting the common good,
   let us pray to the Lord.

3. **For those who travel by sea, land or air,**
   for captives and all held in prison,
   let us pray to the Lord.

4. **For all of us gathered in this sacred place**
   by faith and devotion
   and by love and reverence for God,
   let us pray to the Lord.

Priest's Prayer

May the petitions of your Church
be pleasing in your sight, O Lord,
so that we may receive from your mercy
what we cannot ask out of confidence in our own merits
Through Christ our Lord.
R. Amen.

and for this reason, it must be applicable to real life. However, it is composed of "general" intercessions, meaning they must be universal and applicable to the entire Church. "This is a prayer of intercession, a supplication addressed to God. It is not a prayer of thanksgiving or anything else. The general intercessions provide a time and form of prayer for the whole Church, for the world, for those in need and for the faithful present in the particular congregation" (*Together We Pray*, ed. Robert Borg, Collegeville, Liturgical Press, 1993, p.

xi). Keeping the petitions universal and, at the same time, relevant to a local community is often a difficult task; the hope is that, in the "general," specific needs can be addressed.

One way to ensure that intercession functions properly is to enhance the roles involved in the project of making our prayer the prayer of Christ. Let us begin with the role of the priest celebrant. The GIRM instructs that the priest opens the Prayer of the Faithful "with a brief introduction, by which he invites the faithful to

pray, and likewise he concludes it with a prayer" (GIRM, 71). The presider sets both the tone and the tempo for this prayer by inviting the community to pray. What is called for here is for the presider to be in touch with Christ's presence and actively engaged with the community. A paucity of words and silence of spirit might best forge the way to contemplation of Christ's healing presence.

This leads to a second liturgical role, namely the person(s) proclaiming the community's intentions. This traditionally

10. ORDINARY TIME II

Priest's Introduction

**We have all gathered here,
dear brothers and sisters,
to celebrate the mysteries of our redemption;
let us therefore ask almighty God
that the whole world may be watered
from these springs of all blessing and life.**

Intentions

1. **For all who have vowed themselves to God,
that with his help they may faithfully keep to their resolve,
let us pray to the Lord.**

2. **For peace among nations,
that, delivered from all turmoil,
the peoples may serve God in freedom of heart,
let us pray to the Lord.**

3. **For the elderly who suffer from isolation or sickness,
that they may be strengthened
by our love of them as brothers and sisters,
let us pray to the Lord.**

4. **For ourselves gathered here,
that, as God does not cease to sustain us
with the things of this life,
we may know how to use them in such a way
that we may hold even now
to the things that endure for ever,
let us pray to the Lord.**

Priest's Prayer

**May your mercy, we beseech you, O Lord,
be with your people who cry to you,
so that what they seek at your prompting
they may obtain by your ready generosity.
Through Christ our Lord.**
    R. Amen.

The General Formulas printed above, nos. 1–2, may also be used in Ordinary Time.

In composing the petitions for the Universal Prayer, notice the general order that is offered in the sample formularies. Note, as well, the general nature of these petitions. Nevertheless, the petitions should take into consideration what is occurring in the world, the Church, and locally.

belongs to the deacon, who, since the early Church, functions as the primary minister of charity and is most capable of recognizing the needs of the local community. These intercessions should be modeled after the following pattern: for the needs of the Church; for public authorities and the salvation of the whole world; for those burdened by any kind of difficulty; and for the local community.

Perhaps it may be the case that the intercessions become more locally focused and personally specific as they move from the universal Church to the needs of the world to those of the local community. However, they are never to express private need. This is particularly true in the case of petitions that list the sick or the deceased of the parish; these are the prayers of the Church that await the coming of the kingdom.

A third role is that of the assembly. In describing the participation of the assembly in the Prayer of the Faithful, GIRM, 71, states that the people "give expression to their prayer" by an invocation or praying in silence. The words "give expression" are particularly important as they require a focused involvement in the action of intercession. Just as the friends of the paralytic actively seek the Lord's help, so a concentrated investment is demanded of the entire assembly. Saliers offers this recommendation: "Liturgical participation thus requires learning to 'pray with' Christ's ongoing intercession, and to be attentive to the Holy Spirit's 'sighing in us and through us' when we do not know how to pray for ourselves as we ought" ("Pastoral Liturgy

The Universal Prayer may be chanted. See the four formularies on page 308. Additionally, other modern compositions may be used.

It is important that the petition cues the response from the assembly, so that the response flows smoothly and logically from what precedes it.

If the Priest is able, he could introduce the intentions with a sung invitation and conclude with a sung prayer. These parts, however, should be musically congruent with the petitions to avoid ritual fragmentation. If the invitation and concluding prayer cannot be sung in the same modality as the petitions, it may be better to recite them.

11. IN MASSES FOR THE DEAD

Priest's Introduction

**Let us in faith call upon God the almighty Father,
who raised Christ his Son from the dead,
as we pray for the salvation of the living and the dead.**

Intentions

1. **That God may establish the Christian people in faith and unity,
let us pray to the Lord.**

2. **That he may rescue the entire world from all the evils of war,
let us pray to the Lord.**

3. **That he may be pleased to show himself a father
to our brothers and sisters
who lack work, food or housing,
let us pray to the Lord.**

4a. **That he may be pleased
to admit for ever to the company of the Saints
his deceased servant N.,
who once through Baptism received the seed of eternal life,
let us pray to the Lord.**

4b. **That on the last day he may raise up N.,
who fed on the Body of Christ,
the Bread of eternal life,
let us pray to the Lord.**

(Or for a Priest):

**That he may grant N. a share in the heavenly liturgy,
for he exercised the priestly office in the Church,
let us pray to the Lord.**

and Character Ethics: As We Worship So We Shall Be," *Source and Summit*, eds. Joanne M. Pierce and Michael Downey, Collegeville, Liturgical Press, 1999, p. 190).

The question must be raised: how does the assembly learn to "pray with" Christ and to be aware of the movement of the Holy Spirit in Christ's collective body? This is no easy task to be sure, but it is certainly necessary if the Prayer of the Faithful is to be understood as a substantial offering made in Christ for the glorification of God. At the core of this dilemma are the liturgical dynamics of rhythm, poetry, and silence. How might practicing these skills enhance our liturgical prayer?

Rhythm People are drawn into music by a repetitive cadence. The Prayer of the Faithful should be developed in such a way as to promote rhythm. Certainly, the ancient Roman form of intercession—invitation to prayer, silence, and collect—offers a definite rhythm. Perhaps, we could be more creative with using such a structure. A way to support rhythm is to incorporate music during the Prayer of the Faithful. A Taizé-like chant that floats beneath the surface of the spoken intercession may help a community to form one body in voicing its needs.

Poetry The Prayer of the Faithful is a means of training our ears to hear expressive ways of communicating hope in God's mercy and tender care. Those responsible for preparing the Prayer of the Faithful and those who act as intercessors are obliged to treat the prayers as an art form that leads people into mystery. The composition of the petitions should conjure

4c. **That he may grant to the souls
of our brothers and sisters, friends, and benefactors
the reward of their labors,
let us pray to the Lord.**

4d. **That he may welcome into the light of his face
all who have fallen asleep in the hope of the resurrection,
let us pray to the Lord.**

4e. **That he may graciously help and comfort
our brothers and sisters who are suffering affliction,
let us pray to the Lord.**

4f. **That he may be pleased to gather into his glorious Kingdom
all who have gathered here in faith and devotion,
let us pray to the Lord.**

Priest's Prayer

**May the prayer of those who cry to you
benefit the souls of your servants, O Lord:
free them, we pray, from all their sins
and make them sharers in your redemption.
Through Christ our Lord.**
R. Amen.

In composing the petitions for the Universal Prayer, notice the general order that is offered in the sample formularies. Note, as well, the general nature of these petitions. Nevertheless, the petitions should take into consideration what is currently occurring in the world, the Church, and locally.

connections and insights. The Prayer of the Faithful should be poetic enough to allow the community to understand itself immersed in the life struggles of the world.

Silence This third demand for the praying of the Prayer of the Faithful is challenging given that our culture is threatened by silence. The assembly needs the posture of silence for full participation in the prayers, precisely because silence provides space for the contemplation of Christ's presence. Yes, intercessions call for a response, but the Church must learn to respond out of the depths of silence.

Conclusion
After Jesus healed the paralytic, the man's newfound ability to walk amazed the crowd. Even the skeptics in the gathering were able to see the breakthrough of God's love, causing the house to become a place of worship, resounding with praise of God's name. In a sense, our liturgical practice of uttering corporate prayer for the needs of the Church and the world is no less radical and no less awesome. We hear the Word of God and respond in faith; our intercessions demonstrate our unswerving trust in God's providence. The prayers we voice help to make us Christ's body, not only in our liturgical gathering but in our world view and in our commitment to help usher in God's kingdom. The Prayer of the Faithful challenges us to believe that no sin, sorrow, or suffering in this fragile world can compare to the glory to be revealed by God, leaving us to echo the words of the skeptics: "We have never seen anything like this!"

APPENDIX VI

[In the Dioceses of the United States]
SAMPLE INVOCATIONS
FOR THE PENITENTIAL ACT

**Brethren (brothers and sisters), let us acknowledge our sins,
and so prepare ourselves to celebrate the sacred mysteries.**

A brief pause for silence follows.

The Priest, or a Deacon or another minister, then may use one of the following invocations
with Kyrie, eleison (Lord, have mercy):

I

The Priest:

**Lord Jesus, you came to gather the nations into the peace of God's
kingdom:
Lord, have mercy.**

The people reply:

Lord, have mercy.

The Priest:

**Lord Jesus, you come in word and sacrament to strengthen us in
holiness:
Christ, have mercy.**

The people:

Christ, have mercy.

The Priest:

**Lord Jesus, you will come in glory with salvation for your people:
Lord, have mercy.**

The people:

Lord, have mercy.

The absolution by the Priest follows:

**May almighty God have mercy on us,
forgive us our sins
and bring us to everlasting life.**

The people reply:

Amen.

The Penitential Act may also be chanted according to the plainchant form or sung in a more modern musical setting. For examples of how to chant it, see pages 283–284.

If the troped version is sung, the "Lord, have mercy" or *Kyrie eleison* should flow logically. If the Priest is able to sing, he can sing the absolution in the same modality as the tropes were sung. This will ensure ritual coherence and avoid musical fragmentation.

In the Penitential Act, the Priest calls upon the whole community to prepare to enter the celebration by first calling to mind our sinfulness. After the invitation, there is a brief call for silence. The Penitential Act is enacted by means of a formula for confession. It concludes with the Priest's absolution, which, however, lacks the efficacy of the Sacrament of Penance.

From time to time on Sundays, especially during Easter Time, instead of the customary Penitential Act, the blessing and sprinkling of water may take place as a reminder of Baptism. The Rite for the Blessing and Sprinkling of Water is in Appendix II.

The *Kyrie* is the other way to celebrate the Penitential Act. In this option, invocations are prefixed to the acclamation "Lord, have mercy / Christ, have mercy." This form can be executed by the Priest, Deacon, or another minister, most likely the cantor. The Missal shows a clear indication that the invocations, as well as the "Lord, have mercy / Christ, have mercy," be chanted.

Seven sample invocations are in this appendix, but we are not limited to these. These are intended as models for the construction of further invocations. These invocatory tropes might pick up on themes from the scriptures, especially the Gospel of the day. However, these invocations must be Christo-centric, insofar as they are titles or characteristics of Christ, as the sample invocations demonstrate. They are not to be mini-examinations of conscience in which the invocations focus on the

II

The Priest:

Lord Jesus, you are mighty God and Prince of peace:
Lord, have mercy.

The people reply:

Lord, have mercy.

The Priest:

Lord Jesus, you are the Son of God and Son of Mary:
Christ, have mercy.

The people:

Christ, have mercy.

The Priest:

Lord Jesus, you are Word made flesh and splendor of the Father:
Lord, have mercy.

The people:

Lord, have mercy.

The absolution by the Priest follows:

May almighty God have mercy on us,
forgive us our sins
and bring us to everlasting life.

The people reply:

Amen.

Since *Kyrie, eleison* is one of the few vestiges of when the early Christian liturgy was celebrated in Greek and since the expression has such beautiful overtones related to God's merciful love, it is appropriate to interchange *Kyrie, eleison* for the "Lord, have mercy," and *Christe, eleison* for the "Christ, have mercy."

The expression *Kyrie, eleison* may also be used as a response to the petitions for the Universal Prayer.

---

assembly's misdeeds. (An example of such an invocation would be "We have been unjust. Lord, have mercy"). Secondly, we are not to follow the pattern of the medieval tropes, in which the first invocation was addressed to God the Father, the second to God the Son, and the third to God the Holy Spirit.

The "Lord, have mercy," "Christ have mercy" have equal weight in the vernacular and in Greek, so communities may pray the invocation in either language. The liturgy of the early Church was in Greek

before converting to Latin as the vernacular of that age. Since the *Kyrie* is one of the few vestiges of the early Church, it is desirable to use it, from to time, and to preach on its theological meaning.

With the *Kyrie* we are proclaiming God's loving mercy in the person of Christ. Central to the tropes is the idea of God's *hesed*, the Hebrew word for "kindness." It is also commonly translated as "loving-kindness," "merciful love," or "loving mercy." When we ask for God to be merciful, we

also are proclaiming God's eternal and boundless love manifested in Christ.

It's interesting that two chant settings for the *Kyrie, eleison* appear in the Missal. One setting is for option three of the Penitential Act and the other setting is for when the *Kyrie* is sung on its own. The melodies for the "Lord, have mercy" should be musically related, whereas in the Kyrie litany, they can be freestanding.

The Penitential Act may also be chanted according to the plainchant form or sung in a more modern musical setting. For examples of how to chant the Penitential Act, see pages 283–284.

If the troped version is sung, the "Lord, have mercy" or *Kyrie, eleison* should flow logically. If the Priest is able, he can sing the absolution in the same modality as the tropes were sung. This will ensure ritual coherence and avoid musical fragmentation.

III

The Priest:

Lord Jesus, you came to reconcile us to one another and to the Father:
Lord, have mercy.

The people reply:

Lord, have mercy.

The Priest:

Lord Jesus, you heal the wounds of sin and division:
Christ, have mercy.

The people:

Christ, have mercy.

The Priest:

Lord Jesus, you intercede for us with your Father:
Lord, have mercy.

The people:

Lord, have mercy.

The absolution by the Priest follows:

May almighty God have mercy on us,
forgive us our sins
and bring us to everlasting life.

The people reply:

Amen.

The adaptation of the Gregorian Chant allows only a rote response when sung in English. But when sung in Greek, either the rote response or the historical ending is provided. In the chant tradition, there are at least 18 settings of the *Kyrie*. The one appearing in the Missal is the simplest one—Masses for ferias throughout the year. The vernacular version borrows the melody from the Latin, adapting it to the English. In time as congregations becomes more secure, more difficult versions may be attempted, but many of the Latin chants are so florid that the simple Penitential Act could easily take more time than merited.

Let us look at how the troped versions might be used, indicating the appropriateness for certain feasts and liturgical times.

Sample setting I would be perfect for liturgies dealing with Christian unity or when the Gospel is proclaiming the coming of the kingdom of God. The second trope references both Word and Sacrament and lends itself to discuss the passage in *Dei Verbum* that speaks to this as the two tables: "The church has always venerated the divine Scriptures as she venerated the Body of the Lord, in so far as she never ceases, particularly in the sacred liturgy, to partake of the bread of life and to offer it to the faithful from the one table of the Word of God and the Body of Christ" (*Dei Verbum*, 21).

IV

The Priest:

Lord Jesus, you raise the dead to life in the Spirit:
Lord, have mercy.

The people reply:

Lord, have mercy.

The Priest:

Lord Jesus, you bring pardon and peace to the sinner:
Christ, have mercy.

The people:

Christ, have mercy.

The Priest:

Lord Jesus, you bring light to those in darkness:
Lord, have mercy.

The people:

Lord, have mercy.

The absolution by the Priest follows:

May almighty God have mercy on us,
forgive us our sins
and bring us to everlasting life.

The people reply:

Amen.

Since *Kyrie, eleison* is one of the few vestiges of when the early Christian liturgy was celebrated in Greek, and since the expression has such beautiful overtones related to God's merciful love, it is appropriate to interchange *Kyrie, eleison* for "Lord, have mercy," and *Christe, eleison* for "Christ, have mercy."

The expression *Kyrie, eleison* may be used also as a response to the petitions for the Universal Prayer.

Although *Dei Verbum* speaks of the one table, the language of two tables has become increasingly more familiar since the Second Vatican Council. In addition to the table of the Lord's Supper, there is the table of the scriptures. In the GIRM, we read: "In the readings, the table of God's word is spread before the faithful, and the treasures of the Bible are opened to them" (GIRM 57, citing the *Constitution on the Sacred Liturgy*, 51). The two tables correspond to the distinction between the Liturgy of the Word and the Liturgy of the Eucharist.

Sample two references Christ as mighty God and Prince of peace, as well as Son of God and Son of Mary. Any feast that is celebrating the theanthropic nature of Christ as divine and human would benefit from this text. The third invocation talks about Christ as the "Word made flesh and the splendor of the Father," lending itself to feasts celebrating the Incarnation and those celebrating Mary as the *Theotokos* or God bearer.

Sample three addresses Christ as reconciler, healer, and intercessor. Any liturgies that focus on Jesus as the mediator between God and people, using this form would set the stage beautifully. This form would lend itself to be yoked with the Eucharistic Prayers for Reconciliation.

Sample four has several foci. Jesus is the one who raises us to life in the Spirit. He brings us pardon and peace. He also

The Penitential Act may be chanted according to the Plainchant form or sung in a more modern musical setting. For examples of how to chant it, see pages 283–284.

If the troped version is sung, the "Lord, have mercy" or *Kyrie, eleison* should flow logically. If the Priest is able, he can sing the absolution in the same modality as the tropes were sung. This will ensure ritual coherence and avoid musical fragmentation.

V

The Priest:

Lord Jesus, you raise us to new life:
Lord, have mercy.

The people reply:

Lord, have mercy.

The Priest:

Lord Jesus, you forgive us our sins:
Christ, have mercy.

The people:

Christ, have mercy.

The Priest:

Lord Jesus, you feed us with your body and blood:
Lord, have mercy.

The people:

Lord, have mercy.

The absolution by the Priest follows:

May almighty God have mercy on us,
forgive us our sins
and bring us to everlasting life.

The people reply:

Amen.

brings us out of darkness into the light. The first part could be used during Lent, particularly on the Fifth Sunday of Lent when the Year A reading is read, That reading, from John 11:1–45. is the account of Lazarus being raised from the dead. Easter Time also is an appropriate period for these invocations. Certainly, the theme of moving from darkness into the light suggests a Christmas use.

Setting five again speaks to Christ as the one who raises us to life, but the second trope addresses his role in forgiving our sins. This might suggest that death is really a result of sin and Resurrection is linked to forgiveness. The third invocation states that we are fed on his body and blood, suggesting any Eucharistic feast.

Sample six is derived from John's account of the Gospel. The first invocation evokes John 14:6: "I am the way and the truth and the life. No one comes to the Father but through Me." The third allusion is to Jesus as the good shepherd, and also a Johannine theme. "I am the Good Shepherd; I know mine and mine know me" (John 10). Combining the two images of shepherd and way, one can also speak to the passage in John in which Jesus refers to

VI

The Priest:

Lord Jesus, you have shown us the way to the Father:
Lord, have mercy.

The people reply:

Lord, have mercy.

The Priest:

Lord Jesus, you have given us the consolation of the truth:
Christ, have mercy.

The people:

Christ, have mercy.

The Priest:

Lord Jesus, you are the Good Shepherd, leading us into everlasting
    life:
Lord, have mercy.

The people:

Lord, have mercy.

The absolution by the Priest follows:

May almighty God have mercy on us,
forgive us our sins
and bring us to everlasting life.

The people reply:

Amen.

Since *Kyrie, eleison* is one of the few vestiges of when the early Christian liturgy was celebrated in Greek and since the expression has such beautiful overtones related to God's merciful love, it is appropriate to interchange *Kyrie, eleison* for the "Lord, have mercy," and *Christe, eleison* for the "Christ, have mercy."

The expression *Kyrie, eleison* may also be used as a response to the petitions for the Universal Prayer.

---

himself as the sheepgate. Any time reference is made to shepherds and shepherding, this form of the Penitential Act would be appropriate but it is especially fitting for the Fourth Sunday of Easter, often called Good Shepherd Sunday.

The Jewish people had longed used the Good Shepherd image for God. It goes all the way back to Genesis 49:24, which states that Joseph was saved "By the power of the Mighty One of Jacob, because

of the Shepherd, the Rock of Israel, the God of your father." Such imagery was used by Moses, Isaiah, Jeremiah, Ezekiel, Amos, Zechariah, and, of course, by David in his Psalms. Psalm 80 begins "Shepherd of Israel, listen, guide of the flock of Joseph! from your throne upon the cherubim, reveal yourself." And, of course, there is Psalm 23: "The Lord is my shepherd; there is nothing I lack."

In using the image of the Good Shepherd, Christ was building upon his rich Jewish heritage. This form of the Penitential Act is extremely rich.

The last sample set of tropes focus on Christ as healer and forgiver of sins. There is a rich tradition that images Jesus as a doctor. The *Christus medicus* image was used by Ignatius of Antioch in his Letter to the Ephesians 7.2: "One physician there is,

The Penitential Act may also be chanted according to the plainchant form or sung in a more modern musical setting. For examples of how to chant the Penitential Act, see pages 283–284.

If the troped version is sung, the "Lord, have mercy" or *Kyrie, eleison* should flow logically. If the Priest is able, he can sing the absolution in the same modality as the tropes were sung. This will ensure ritual coherence and avoid musical fragmentation.

VII

The Priest:
Lord Jesus, you healed the sick:
Lord, have mercy.

The people reply:
Lord, have mercy.

The Priest:
Lord Jesus, you forgave sinners:
Christ, have mercy.

The people:
Christ, have mercy.

The Priest:
Lord Jesus, you gave yourself to heal us and bring us strength:
Lord, have mercy.

The people:
Lord, have mercy.

The absolution by the Priest follows:
May almighty God have mercy on us,
forgive us our sins
and bring us to everlasting life.

The people reply:
Amen.

---

both fleshly and spiritual, begotten and unbegotten, God become flesh, true life in death, both from Mary and from God; first subject to suffering then not subject to suffering—Jesus Christ our Lord."

Origen of Alexandria was also fond of this image in speaking about healing from sin: "The Christian [. . .] calls [sinners] in order to bind up their 'wounds' with the Word and apply to [their] soul, festering in vices, drugs [taken] from the Word, analo-gous to wine and oil and emollients and the rest of the soul's medicinal remedies" (Contra Celsum, 3.61–62).

In the early Middle Ages, the image of Christ as doctor was applied, in particular, to the Sacrament of Reconciliation. Penance was the true medicine. Basil of Caesaria in his *Asceticon magnum* certainly under-stood it in this way: " The art of medicine [has been granted us] as a pattern for the healing of the soul, to guide us in the removal of excess and in the augmentation of what is deficient: it has been granted us by the God who directs our whole life."

PREPARATION FOR MASS

Prayer of Saint Ambrose

I draw near, loving Lord Jesus Christ,
to the table of your most delightful banquet
in fear and trembling,
a sinner, presuming not upon my own merits,
but trusting rather in your goodness and mercy.
I have a heart and body defiled by my many offenses,
a mind and tongue
over which I have kept no good watch.
Therefore, O loving God, O awesome Majesty,
I turn in my misery, caught in snares,
to you the fountain of mercy,
hastening to you for healing,
flying to you for protection;
and while I do not look forward to having you as Judge,
I long to have you as Savior.
To you, O Lord, I display my wounds,
to you I uncover my shame.
I am aware of my many and great sins,
for which I fear,
but I hope in your mercies,
which are without number.
Look upon me, then, with eyes of mercy,
Lord Jesus Christ, eternal King,
God and Man, crucified for mankind.
Listen to me, as I place my hope in you,
have pity on me, full of miseries and sins,
you, who will never cease
to let the fountain of compassion flow.
Hail, O Saving Victim,
offered for me and for the whole human race
on the wood of the Cross.
Hail, O noble and precious Blood,
flowing from the wounds
of Jesus Christ, my crucified Lord,
and washing away the sins of all the world.

Saint Ambrose, 340–397. Feast December 7th. Ambrose, the first Doctor of the Church, is called a Pastoral Doctor. Composed hymns as well as prayers. He placed the church first, with each member as his highest priority. He held that praying correctly would shape people's faith and help root out heresy, especially regarding Christ.

The prayers in this section are to enhance the spiritual life of priests. There is not a mandate to pray any of them. What is important is that Priests tend to their prayer lives with the understanding that ministry flows from their spiritual life. The following "Reflection on the Spirituality of the Priest," by Father Ron Lewinski, a priest of the Archdiocese of Chicago, was condensed from the March 2010 article in *Pastoral Liturgy*. In the article, he tells about how he has nourished his prayer life during his nearly 40 years as a Priest.

Reflections on the Spirituality of the Priest

My spirituality as a priest has taken shape over a lifetime of ministry. Configured to Christ through ordination, my spirituality has been formed by my pastoral experience, spiritual discipline, relationships, and the aging process. This commentary on the spirituality of priests flows from my experience. Although these reflections are that of one priest, themes will resonate with many priests, offering common ground for the spiritual life of all priests.

Reflecting on how my spirituality as a priest has been shaped, I can identify three principal sources of grace: the liturgy, pastoral care, and ongoing formation and personal spiritual discipline.

Remember, Lord, your creature,
whom you redeemed by your Blood.
I am repentant of my sins,
I desire to put right what I have done.
Take from me, therefore, most merciful Father,
all my iniquities and sins,
so that, purified in mind and body,
I may worthily taste the Holy of Holies.
And grant that this sacred foretaste
of your Body and Blood
which I, though unworthy, intend to receive,
may be the remission of my sins,
the perfect cleansing of my faults,
the banishment of shameful thoughts,
and the rebirth of right sentiments;
and may it encourage
a wholesome and effective performance
of deeds pleasing to you
and be a most firm defense of body and soul
against the snares of my enemies.
Amen.

The Liturgy

Preaching and presiding are central to a priest's life. As a minister of the word of God, I am constantly challenged. I realize that the Gospel I preach is not my own; I am a servant of the word. In my preparation for preaching, I find my greatest potential for spiritual growth. Before I begin to think about what I will preach, I hold myself accountable to the text. Until I can answer what the scriptures have to say to me, I am not ready to preach. I am aware that I am in need of the same saving word that I proclaim and preach. My spirituality has matured and been shaped by the preaching task. The words from the Rite of Ordination still have impact: "Meditate on the law of God, believe what you read, teach what you believe, and put into practice what you teach" (#14). Taking the time to prepare for Mass by reading and praying over the appointed scriptures has become the daily bread of my spiritual discipline. Some days the orations and snapshot story of a saint whose feast we are celebrating help me discover an insight into the word of God that inspires my preaching.

At times, no matter how long I have pondered the biblical texts, I have felt uninspired. how difficult it is, then, to feel confident about preaching an effective message. and yet, how often after preaching a message that I felt was empty and irrelevant, someone has said, "Father, thank you for your homily. It spoke directly to me today and moved me very deeply." I have learned how the Holy Spirit can deliver my feeble words and with grace into the depths of

Prayer of Saint Thomas Aquinas

Almighty eternal God,
behold, I come to the Sacrament
of your Only Begotten Son,
our Lord Jesus Christ,
as one sick to the physician of life,
as one unclean to the fountain of mercy,
as one blind to the light of eternal brightness,
as one poor and needy to the Lord of heaven and earth.
I ask, therefore, for the abundance of your immense generosity,
that you may graciously cure my sickness,
wash away my defilement,
give light to my blindness,
enrich my poverty,
clothe my nakedness,
so that I may receive the bread of Angels,
the King of kings and Lord of lords,
with such reverence and humility,
such contrition and devotion,
such purity and faith,
such purpose and intention
as are conducive to the salvation of my soul.
Grant, I pray, that I may receive
not only the Sacrament of the Lord's Body and Blood,
but also the reality and power of that Sacrament.
O most gentle God,
grant that I may so receive
the Body of your Only Begotten Son our Lord Jesus Christ,
which he took from the Virgin Mary,
that I may be made worthy to be incorporated into his Mystical Body
and to be counted among its members.
O most loving Father,
grant that I may at last gaze for ever
upon the unveiled face of your beloved Son,
whom I, a wayfarer,
propose to receive now veiled under these species:
Who lives and reigns with you for ever and ever.
Amen.

Thomas Aquinas, 1225–1274. Priest and Doctor of the Church. Feast January 28th. Considered the Church's greatest theologian and philosopher. Best-known works: *Summa Theologica* and the *Summa Contra Gentiles*. Much of modern philosophy was conceived as a reaction against, or as an agreement with his ideas, particularly in the areas of ethics, natural law, and political theory. Composed hymns *Pange Lingua* and *Verbum Supernum Prodiens*.

someone's soul. This humbling experience profoundly shapes a priest's spirituality. I've learned to rely less on my acquired knowledge and preaching skills and more on the power of the Holy Spirit.

I sense most clearly what it means to be a priest when I preside at the liturgy. The Church teaches us that the priest acts in *persona Christi capitis*. This means that Christ has chosen me to be a living instrument in the work of salvation. I am the sacrament of Christ's presence. I mediate the reconciliation, mercy, and saving grace of Christ cruci-

fied and risen. As a living icon of Christ, I cannot allow my personality to get in the way. And yet I must be a worthy icon of the whole Christ, allowing my humanness to be transparent. I strive to be genuine and loving as Christ the Shepherd. In learning to pattern my mind and heart on the mind and ministry of Jesus at work in the liturgy, my spirituality continues to take form.

Because of the multiple liturgies at which priests are expected to preside, there is a danger of losing the sense of awe and wonder in the mysteries we celebrate.

When I preside over liturgies with the unchurched or uncatechized, especially at weddings and funerals, there is a danger of becoming discouraged or disillusioned. I feel the temptation to fall into contempt of the congregation. In these situations, I have had to take a deep breath and remind myself that God is the one who saves us through the liturgy, not I. Nevertheless, it is hard to perceive the full impact of the liturgy when you are the only one singing. The need for a new evangelization speaks loudly.

O most blessed Virgin Mary,
Mother of tenderness and mercy,
I, a miserable and unworthy sinner,
fly to you with all the affection of my heart
and I beseech your motherly love,
that, as you stood by your most dear Son,
while he hung on the Cross,
so, in your kindness,
you may be pleased to stand by me, a poor sinner,
and all Priests who today are offering the Sacrifice
here and throughout the entire holy Church,
so that with your gracious help
we may offer a worthy and acceptable oblation
in the sight of the most high and undivided Trinity.
Amen.

Formula of Intent

My intention is to celebrate Mass
and to consecrate the Body and Blood of our Lord Jesus Christ
according to the Rite of Holy Roman Church,
to the praise of almighty God
and all the Church triumphant,
for my good
and that of all the Church militant,
for all who have commended themselves to my prayers
in general and in particular,
and for the welfare of Holy Roman Church.
Amen.

May the almighty and merciful Lord
grant us joy with peace,
amendment of life,
room for true repentance,
the grace and consolation of the Holy Spirit
and perseverance in good works.
Amen.

The formation of my spiritual life did not begin, of course, with ordination. The seminary provided the rich soil in which my spirituality as a priest would be cultivated. My appreciation for the sacraments of initiation started in the seminary. Studying the patristic accounts of Baptism, I was struck by how seriously the early Church took the sacraments of initiation and how beautifully and convincingly it taught what it means to die and rise with Christ in Baptism. My baptismal studies were truly a conversion experience that led to a profound appreciation of my Baptism. Each time I pour water over an infant's head or step into the font to baptize an adult, I continue to stand in awe before the mystery of regeneration. With each Baptism, I hear the voice of the early Church Fathers preaching eloquently about Baptism, and I feel the grace of the sacrament rekindled within me.

As a confessor in the sacrament of Penance, I am frequently challenged by the sincere confession of my sisters and brothers. I come face to face not only with the darkness of sin, but the power of conversion and grace. I have encountered saints in the confessional whose remorse for sin has challenged me to a holier life. I have listened to penitents confessing with tears, longing to return to the Church. Someone will ask, "Father, can God ever forgive me for what I've done in the past?" When I say with authority, "God forgives you. He wants you to accept the fullness of his mercy," I realize that I speak *in persona Christi*, and I sense that Christ is working through my human weakness. In the cele-

THANKSGIVING AFTER MASS

Prayer of Saint Thomas Aquinas

I give you thanks,
Lord, holy Father, almighty and eternal God,
who have been pleased to nourish me,
a sinner and your unworthy servant,
with the precious Body and Blood
of your Son, our Lord Jesus Christ:
this through no merits of mine,
but due solely to the graciousness of your mercy.

And I pray that this Holy Communion
may not be for me an offense to be punished,
but a saving plea for forgiveness.
May it be for me the armor of faith,
and the shield of good will.
May it cancel my faults,
destroy concupiscence and carnal passion,
increase charity and patience, humility and obedience
and all the virtues,
may it be a firm defense against the snares of all my enemies,
both visible and invisible,
the complete calming of my impulses,
both of the flesh and of the spirit,
a firm adherence to you, the one true God,
and the joyful completion of my life's course.

And I beseech you to lead me, a sinner,
to that banquet beyond all telling,
where with your Son and the Holy Spirit
you are the true light of your Saints,
fullness of satisfied desire, eternal gladness,
consummate delight and perfect happiness.
Through Christ our Lord.
Amen.

bration of the sacraments I feel blessed as a recipient of rebounding grace. Afterward, I've often had to find a place for private prayer to savor the experience and surrender myself to God in quiet contemplation. In anointing the sick I have confronted the cross of sickness and suffering. I see the pain. I sense the fear. And I wonder how well I accept the cross that I preach. Do I find meaning in my suffering? How will I react when I am faced with serious illness or death? In these pastoral encounters, I meet the living saints who peacefully accept the cross of suffering. I have been humbled by the simple faith and surrender to God that I have witnessed in young and old.

Pastoral Care

It is difficult to talk about pastoral care apart from the liturgy, for everything priests do leads to the celebration of the liturgy, most especially the Eucharist. The liturgy is the "source and summit" of the Church's life. And so it is for me as a priest. I draw from the liturgy the love and impetus to serve. I bring to the liturgy the fruit of my labor: a com-

munity prepared to offer praise and thanksgiving and to offer their lives together with Christ in sacrifice to the Father. In the Rite of Ordination, the newly ordained priest kneels before the bishop who presents the paten and chalice to the priest and says, "Accept from the holy people of God the gifts to be offered to him. / Know what you are doing and imitate the mystery you celebrate: / model your life on the mystery of the Lord's cross" (#26). What are the gifts priests are to offer to God? Are they not the gift of themselves? To accept from the people the gifts

Prayer to the Most Holy Redeemer

Soul of Christ, sanctify me.
Body of Christ, save me.
Blood of Christ, embolden me.
Water from the side of Christ, wash me.
Passion of Christ, strengthen me.
O good Jesus, hear me.
Within your wounds hide me.
Never permit me to be parted from you.
From the evil Enemy defend me.
At the hour of my death call me
and bid me come to you,
that with your Saints I may praise you
for age upon age.
Amen.

Prayer of Self-Offering

Receive, Lord, my entire freedom.
Accept the whole of my memory,
my intellect and my will.
Whatever I have or possess,
it was you who gave it to me;
I restore it to you in full,
and I surrender it completely
to the guidance of your will.
Give me only love of you
together with your grace,
and I am rich enough
and ask for nothing more.
Amen.

to be offered to God presumes that I have been leading God's people toward the altar. The gifts they bring are their joys and sorrows, their successes and losses, their hopes and their fears—their entire lives. My pastoral work is directed to the altar where I become aware of the personal stories and pastoral encounters of the week.

My pastoral care reaches a high point at the altar when I have encouraged God's people to bring their lives to the altar, to place themselves in the bread and in the cup. I offer God not just bread and wine but the lives of those I serve. To this, I add my life as a man and a priest. When I call on the Holy Spirit to sanctify and change these gifts on the altar, I am aware that I am asking God to change us, to make us a living sacrifice of praise.

At points in the liturgy the connection between pastoral care and the rites of the Church poignantly come together. The silence that precedes the Collect has always been particularly meaningful for me. In this instance, I pause after saying, "Let us pray, " to look at the congregation before me and to recognize, in the people before me, the joys and sorrows that I have met in the past week. With hands outstretched, I consciously try to collect in my arms all who have been entrusted to my pastoral care. I realize at that moment that this is the heart of my priesthood, "accepting from the people of God the gifts to be offered to him." When I do this, the generic prayers of the Missal suddenly come alive.

My ministry, *in persona Christi,* at the altar stretches outward into the community where I must incarnate in my person the love and mercy of God. That sometimes

Prayer to Our Lord Jesus Christ Crucified

Behold, O good and loving Jesus,
that I cast myself on my knees before you
and, with the greatest fervor of spirit,
I pray and beseech you to instill into my heart
ardent sentiments of faith, hope and charity,
with true repentance for my sins
and a most firm purpose of amendment.
With deep affection and sorrow
I ponder intimately
and contemplate in my mind your five wounds,
having before my eyes what the prophet David
had already put in your mouth about yourself, O good Jesus:
They have pierced my hands and my feet;
they have numbered all my bones (Ps 21: 17–18).

requires getting beyond my prejudices or attitudes.

As a man and as a Christian, I am one with the community of faith to which I am bound through ordination. The parish community is a rich source of blessings for me. While sharing critical and intimate moments of people's lives, I feel like I have entered into the holy of holies. I see the Lord at work in his people, and i believe the Lord uses them in making me the priest he wants me to be.

As a priest, I accept responsibility for forming the community of which I am a part.

A priest is not ordained to be a private chaplain but to father a community. I believe that most parish priests have a burning desire to form a parish that is strong in faith and witness and bound closely together in charity and peace.

Ongoing Formation
While my sacramental ministry and pastoral care of the community have an enormous influence on my spirituality, ongoing formation and personal spiritual discipline also play a significant role. In my private prayer

and meditation, and especially times of solitude, my pastoral and sacramental ministry come together in my conversation with Christ. Without this private time for prayer and meditation, I would soon begin to operate on empty. My most effective preaching, teaching, pastoral care, and community building flow from my encounter with Christ in prayer.

The nature of my prayer takes many forms, drawing from the enormous treasure house of Catholic prayer. Early morning has been a good time for me to pray. Once the

Pope Saint Clement XI, 1649–1721.
Acquired Christian manuscripts in Syriac and other places in the Middle East, greatly expanding the *Biblioteca Apostolica Vaticana*'s collection of Syriac works.

This long prayer (almost 400 words) is called "universal" because of its sweeping themes.

The prayer begins with *Credo*, the first word of the various creeds, but it quickly moves to the other theological virtues of hope and love and then continues with a more somber penitential tone throughout the prayer. The prayer could qualify for the genre of private sacerdotal dispositional prayers or apologia.

The Universal Prayer Attributed to Pope Clement XI

I believe, O Lord, but may I believe more firmly;
I hope, but may I hope more securely;
I love, but may I love more ardently;
I sorrow, but may I sorrow more deeply.

I adore you as my first beginning;
I long for you as my last end;
I praise you as my constant benefactor;
I invoke you as my gracious protector.

By your wisdom direct me,
by your righteousness restrain me,
by your indulgence console me,
by your power protect me.

I offer you, Lord, my thoughts to be directed to you,
my words, to be about you,
my deeds, to respect your will,
my trials, to be endured for you.

I will whatever you will,
I will it because you will it,
I will it in the way you will it,
I will it for as long as you will it.

Lord, enlighten my understanding, I pray:
arouse my will,
cleanse my heart,
sanctify my soul.

May I weep for past sins,
repel future temptations,
correct evil inclinations,
nurture appropriate virtues.

Give me, good God,
love for you, hatred for myself,
zeal for my neighbor,
contempt for the world.

May I strive to obey superiors,
to help those dependent on me,

day begins, it can be a struggle to step aside for even a few minutes of prayer. I find it fairly easy and always fruitful to pray before celebrating any rites of the Church. The busyness of a parish priest can become an excuse, however, for not spending quality time in prayer. Personal spiritual discipline is only a discipline if there is a plan and a commitment to keep it.

The Liturgy of the Hours is a stable anchor. Even when I am tired, the prayers that the Church provides move me along. I have learned to make the Liturgy of the

Hours my intentional and specific prayer for others, especially the community I pastor. Praying the Hours serves as an attitude adjustment for my ministry. The constant repetition of psalms of trust and praise moves me into pastoral ministry with praise on my lips to counteract any negative feelings or fears with which I might otherwise approach my daily ministry.

While daily prayer in small segments is often the best I can do, I try to set aside lengthier periods for prayer and meditation. It may be an hour in silence before the

Blessed Sacrament. It may be a long, prayerful walk in the woods. I've tried to make a monthly day-at-home retreat. My annual retreat to Gethsemani Abbey remains the powerhouse of my spiritual life. In the silence of the monastery, I have come to appreciate that there's a bit of a monk inside me. When I don't take the time to feed that part of my soul, things get out of focus, stress builds up, and discouragement settles in.

The sacrament of Reconciliation continues to be very important for me. It is when I am confessing my sins that I appreci-

to have care for my friends,
forgiveness for my enemies.

May I conquer sensuality by austerity,
avarice by generosity,
anger by gentleness,
lukewarmness by fervor.

Render me prudent in planning,
steadfast in dangers,
patient in adversity,
humble in prosperity.

Make me, O Lord, attentive at prayer,
moderate at meals,
diligent in work,
steadfast in intent.

May I be careful to maintain interior innocence,
outward modesty,
exemplary behavior,
a regular life.

May I be always watchful in subduing nature,
in nourishing grace,
in observing your law,
in winning salvation.

May I learn from you
how precarious are earthly things,
how great divine things,
how fleeting is time,
how lasting things eternal.

Grant that I may prepare for death,
fear judgment,
flee hell,
gain paradise.
Through Christ our Lord.
Amen.

ate what mercy and redemption has to do with me. Being a confessor has often motivated me to celebrate the sacrament for the sake of my soul.

If finding time for prayer is difficult, so too is finding time for ongoing formation. But I know that unless I avail myself of opportunities for continuing education, I will have little to offer others. Reading and studying have been important in developing a richer spiritual life. Spiritual reading gives me fresh inspiration, which, in turn, benefits my preaching and teaching. I like to think that in my library I am surrounded with spiritual friends to whom I can readily turn.

I have found writing and teaching to be a useful tool in strengthening my interior life. Writing and teaching force me to clarify my thinking and my beliefs and to go deeper into that which I would not otherwise. Writing, especially, allows me to reflect and hear myself in another way.

I learned a long time ago that progress in the spiritual life requires the help of others. We priests talk about spiritual matters all the time, so it's easy to forget our need for spiritual direction. Spiritual direction has held me accountable for my soul and enabled me to see myself as I might otherwise not notice.

In addition to one-on-one spiritual direction, many priests have formed priests' prayer groups or support groups. Whether it is a regularly scheduled spiritual fraternity or a frequent practice of connecting with spiritual friends, these relationships reinforce a priest's awareness that he is a member of a presbyterate. I have come to appreciate the value of the priestly fraternity

This prayer, in Latin, *O Maria, virgo et mater sanctissima*, is intended to be prayed after Mass in thanksgiving. The prayer is similar to *O Sanctissima*, a hymn in Latin to the Blessed Virgin Mary. It is claimed that the tune of the hymn is Sicilian. The tune is sometimes called Sicilian Mariners Hymn or Mariners Hymn.

Prayers to the Blessed Virgin Mary

O Mary, Virgin and Mother most holy,
behold, I have received your most dear Son,
whom you conceived in your immaculate womb,
brought forth, nursed and embraced most tenderly.
Behold him at whose sight
you used to rejoice and be filled with all delight;
him whom, humbly and lovingly,
once again I present
and offer him to you
to be clasped in your arms,
to be loved by your heart,
and to be offered up to the Most Holy Trinity
as the supreme worship of adoration,
for your own honor and glory
and for my needs and for those of the whole world.
I ask you therefore, most loving Mother:
entreat for me the forgiveness of all my sins
and, in abundant measure, the grace
of serving him in the future more faithfully,
and at the last, final grace,
so that with you I may praise him
for all the ages of ages.
Amen.

Hail, Mary, full of grace, the Lord is with you;
blessed are you among women,
and blessed is the fruit of your womb, Jesus.
Holy Mary, Mother of God,
pray for us sinners
now and at the hour of our death.
Amen.

more than ever as we struggle to meet the changes and challenges of contemporary ministry. In fraternity with others, I am reminded that I am not building my kingdom. There is a strength and special grace that grows out of a spiritual fraternity within a presbyterate that cannot be discovered on one's own.

I recognize that cultivating friends and maintaining close relationships has a significant bearing on my spiritual life. These relationships keep me human, hold me accountable, and accept me for who I am.

My friendships with fellow priests and understanding laity have given me the strength and confidence to carry on with my work even when it is most difficult.

Conclusion

Defining a priest's spirituality is no easy task. In addition to all the above that has influenced my spirituality is the element of aging. I am not the same man today that I was when I was ordained 37 years ago. I have gained much experience. I have had my share of crosses and failures. I get dis-

couraged when I realize that I don't have the physical ability to do all that I once did. I still would like to accomplish many things, yet I soberly recognize that I will not have enough time to achieve them before I die. There is a gradual attempt to let go of what does not matter and to trust more deeply what does. These kind of age-related sentiments have a significant bearing on my spirituality. For every priest, as for any individual, a healthy spiritual life is an ongoing work.

ADDITIONAL RESOURCE:
SOLEMN BLESSINGS
WITH POINTED TEXT

Solemn Tone

For the invitation, the Deacon (or in his absence, the Priest) sings "Bow down for the blessing." The two-note melodic motive of "la-sol-la" is the cue for the solemn tone. Each of the petitions may be delivered as one, two, or three parts, depending upon the length of the sentence. The usual subdivision is tripartite (indicated by A-B-C), requiring the text to be pointed using the flex, mediant, and full stop formulas. A shorter sentence will be divided into two parts (indicated by B-C). A short sentence will not be divided (indicated by C). The ending of each phrase indicates if it is flex, mediant, or full stop. See page 311 to learn the melodic shapes of the three formulas.

For the flex (A), move from the *sol* to *la* as the reciting tone and terminate with *sol* on the syllable marked in bold. If the sentence is of sufficient length, it will be broken with a mediant (B). Move from *sol* back to the reciting tone *la* and on the second to the last syllable, rise to *ti* on the italicized syllable, then back to *la* on the bold syllable. Whatever the length of the sentence, the full stop (C) indicates the its end. The stop functions as a period and elicits the sung "Amen" from the assembly. The formula is from the reciting tone. Move down a note to *sol* on the bold syllable, to *la* on the italicized syllable, then the double note *la-sol* on the second to last syllable, if it is strong. When the accent falls on the antepenultimate syllable, distribute the double note over two syllables.

(SOLEMN TONE)

BLESSINGS AT THE END OF MASS AND PRAYERS OVER THE PEOPLE

SOLEMN BLESSINGS

The following blessings may be used, at the discretion of the Priest, at the end of the celebration of Mass, or of a Liturgy of the Word, or of the Office, or of the Sacraments.

The Deacon or, in his absence, the Priest himself, says the invitation: **Bow down for the blessing**. Then the Priest, with hands extended over the people, says the blessing, with all responding: **Amen**.

I. For Celebrations in the Different Liturgical Times

1.   Advent

A   May the almighty and merciful God,
    by whose grace you have placed your faith
    in the First Coming of his Only Begotten Son
    and yearn for his coming a**gain**
B   sanctify you by the radiance of Christ's *Ad***vent**
C   and enrich you **with** *his* blessing.
    R. Amen.

A   As you run the race of this present **life**,
B   may he make you firm *in* **faith**,
C   joyful in hope and act**ive** *in* charity.
    R. Amen.

A   So that, rejoicing now with devotion
    at the Redeemer's coming in the **flesh**,
B   you may be endowed with the rich reward of eter*nal* **life**
C   when he comes a**gain** *in* majesty.
    R. Amen.

    And may the blessing of almighty God,
    the Father, and the Son, ✛ and the Holy Spirit,
    come down on you and remain with you for ever.
    R. Amen.

2.   The Nativity of the Lord

A   May the God of infinite goodness,
    who by the Incarnation of his Son has driven darkness from the world
    and by that glorious Birth has illumined this most holy **night (day)**,

(continued on page 360)

The Roman Missal provides two tones for the Solemn Blessings: a solemn tone and a simple tone.

The usual form is for the blessing is for the Deacon or Priest, after the liturgical greeting "The Lord be with you," to invite the assembly to bow their heads for the blessing. (The differing melodic tones in this invitation provides the musical cue to the assembly as to whether the solemn or simple tone will be used.) The Priest, with

outstretched hands, palms down, extended over the people, sings each part of the blessing according to the tone introduced in the invitation, to which the people respond, "Amen."

1. Advent: This Solemn Blessing addresses the many advents of Christ. The first part emphasizes the "first coming" fulfilling God's design and opening the way to eternal salvation. The third part emphasizes

the Second Coming, when all will be made manifest and we will inherit the promise. The middle part looks to the present, while we are running the "race," a reference drawn from Galatians 2:2 and 5:7. For Christians, the time of Advent serves as a reminder, both to the original waiting of the Jewish people for the birth of their Messiah and the waiting of Christians for Christ's return.

(SIMPLE TONE)

BLESSINGS AT THE END OF MASS AND PRAYERS OVER THE PEOPLE

SOLEMN BLESSINGS

The following blessings may be used, at the discretion of the Priest, at the end of the celebration of Mass, or of a Liturgy of the Word, or of the Office, or of the Sacraments.

The Deacon or, in his absence, the Priest himself, says the invitation: **Bow down for the blessing**. Then the Priest, with hands extended over the people, says the blessing, with all responding: **Amen**.

I. For Celebrations in the Different Liturgical Times

1. Advent

    A May the almighty and merciful God,
    by whose grace you have placed your faith
    in the First Coming of his Only Begotten Son
    and yearn for his coming a**gain**

    B sanctify you by the radiance **of** Christ's *Adv*ent

    C and enrich you with his bless*ing*.
    R. Amen.

    A As you run the race of this present **life**,

    B may he make you **firm** in *faith*,

    C joyful in hope and active in char*ity*.
    R. Amen.

    A So that, rejoicing now with devotion
    at the Redeemer's coming in the **flesh**,

    B you may be endowed with the rich reward of et*er*nal *life*

    C when he comes again in ma*jes*ty.
    R. Amen.

    And may the blessing of al**might**y *God*,
    the Father, and the Son, ✠ and the Holy Spirit,
    come down on you and remain with you for ev*er*.
    R. Amen.

2. The Nativity of the Lord

    A May the God of infinite goodness,
    who by the Incarnation of his Son has driven darkness from the world
    and by that glorious Birth has illumined this most holy **night** (**day**),

(continued on page 361)

Simple Tone

The invitation to bow heads gives the melodic cue (*do-la-do-ti-do*) that the simple tone will be used. See page 312 to learn the melodic formulas for the flex, mediant and full stop. For the Flex (A), the underlined bold syllable indicates to move down from the reciting tone *do* to *la*. For the mediant (B), move from the reciting tone *do* down to *ti* on the bold syllable, then to *la* on the next syllable and back to *do* on the italicized syllable. For the full stop (C), begin on the reciting tone *do* and drop down to *la* on the italicized syllable.

Trinitarian Blessing

The concluding blessing in the name of the Trinity varies from the Solemn to the Simple tone and should be memorized using the examples on pages 311 and 312. The alternate form that exists for some Ritual Masses is found on page 313.

---

2. The Nativity of the Lord: The blessing evokes three themes associated with Christmas: light dispersing the darkness, the announcement of good news to the shepherds, and the mystery of the Incarnation. The emphasis on light also reminds us that in the northern hemisphere we are in the darkest time of the year. The winter solstice, however, has just occurred, and gradually, almost impercep- tibly, the days get longer. The light has bro- ken the back of darkness. The new light (Christ) shines in the darkness to dispel it. The shepherds were the first to receive the Good News of the divine birth that we have received ourselves today. Mention of the mystery of the Incarnation draws us into the deeper meaning of the Incarnation—the Word made flesh. The theme of the Word becoming flesh, char- acteristic of the Prologue of the Gospel according to John, is interpreted theologi- cally for its deeper sense. Tertullian, for example, states that the flesh is the hinge of our salvation (*caro cardis salutis*).

Solemn Tone

For the invitation, the Deacon (or in his absence, the Priest) sings "Bow down for the blessing." The two-note melodic motive of "la-sol-la" is the cue for the solemn tone. Each of the petitions may be delivered as one, two, or three parts, depending upon the length of the sentence. The usual subdivision is tripartite (indicated by A-B-C), requiring the text to be pointed using the flex, mediant, and full stop formulas. A shorter sentence will be divided into two parts (indicated by B-C). A short sentence will not be divided (indicated by C). The ending of each phrase indicates if it is flex, mediant, or full stop. See page 311 to learn the melodic shapes of the three formulas.

For the flex (A), move from the *sol* to *la* as the reciting tone and terminate with *sol* on the syllable marked in bold. If the sentence is of sufficient length, it will be broken with a mediant (B). Move from *sol* back to the reciting tone *la* and on the second to the last syllable, rise to *ti* on the italicized syllable, then back to *la* on the bold syllable. Whatever the length of the sentence, the full stop (C) indicates the its end. The stop functions as a period and elicits the sung "Amen" from the assembly. The formula is from the reciting tone. Move down a note to *sol* on the bold syllable, to *la* on the italicized syllable, then the double note *la-sol* on the second to last syllable, if it is strong. When the accent falls on the antepenultimate syllable, distribute the double note over two syllables.

(SOLEMN TONE)

B drive far from you the darkness *of* **vice**
C and illumine your hearts with the **light** *of* virtue.
 R. Amen.
A May God, who willed that the great joy
 of his Son's saving Birth
 be announced to shepherds by the An**gel**,
B fill your minds with the gladness *he* **gives**
C and make you heralds *of his* Gospel.
 R. Amen.

A And may God, who by the Incarnation
 brought together the earthly and heavenly **realm**,
B fill you with the gift of his peace and *favor*
C and make you sharers with the **Church** *in* heaven.
 R. Amen.

 And may the blessing of almighty **God**,
 the Father, and the Son, ✛ and the Holy Spirit,
 come down on you and remain with you for ever.
 R. Amen.

3.   The Beginning of the Year
A May God, the source and origin of all bless**ing**,
B grant you grace,
 pour out his blessing in a**bund**ance,
C and keep you safe from harm through**out** *the* year.
 R. Amen.

A May he give you integrity in the **faith**,
B endurance in hope,
 and perseverance in *charity*
C with holy patience **to** *the* end.
 R. Amen.

A May he order your days and your deeds in his **peace**,
B grant your prayers in this and in eve*ry* **place**,
C and lead you happily **to** *eternal* life.
 R. Amen.

 And may the blessing of almighty **God**,
 the Father, and the Son, ✛ and the Holy Spirit,
 come down on you and remain with you for ever.
 R. Amen.

(continued on page 362)

3. The Beginning of the Year: In the first part we pray for grace in abundance; in the second, the three theological virtues are sought; and in the third, we pray that our days be ordered and our deeds be peaceful. It is typical in new year's greetings to wish people abundant blessings and prosperity, but this blessing need not be limited to January 1. To use the blessing at other times, omit the reference "through out this year." Reference to God as the source and origin may strike the ear as somewhat redundant, but this is a direct translation of *fons et origo*, and there is a certain poetic quality to the phrase. The second part of the blessing is particularly beautiful, as we pray for the integrity of faith, endurance of hope, and perseverance in charity, adding that we also be given the gift of patience to the end. This idea gets picked up again in the third part, during which we ask that our present deeds be peaceful and that our days terminate with eternal life.

(SIMPLE TONE)

B drive far from you the dark**ness** of *vice*
C and illumine your hearts with the light of vir*tue*.
R. Amen.

A May God, who willed that the great joy
of his Son's saving Birth
be announced to shepherds by the An**gel**,
B fill your minds with the glad**ness** he *gives*
C and make you heralds of his *Gos*pel.
R. Amen.

A And may God, who by the Incarnation
brought together the earthly and heavenly **realm**,
B fill you with the gift of his **peace** and *favor*
C and make you sharers with the Church in *hea*ven.
R. Amen.

And may the blessing of al**might**y *God*,
the Father, and the Son, ✝ and the Holy Spirit,
come down on you and remain with you for *ever*.
R. Amen.

3. The Beginning of the Year

A May God, the source and origin of all blessing,
grant you **grace**,
B pour out his blessing **in** a*bund*ance,
C and keep you safe from harm throughout the *year*.
R. Amen.

A May he give you integrity in the **faith**,
B endu**rance** in *hope*,
C and perseverance in charity
with holy patience to the *end*.
R. Amen.

A May he order your days and your deeds in his **peace**,
B grant your prayers in this and in **every** *place*,
C and lead you happily to eternal *life*.
R. Amen.

And may the blessing of al**might**y *God*,
the Father, and the Son, ✝ and the Holy Spirit,
come down on you and remain with you for ev*er*.
R. Amen.

Simple Tone

The invitation to bow heads gives the melodic cue (*do-la-do-ti-do*) that the simple tone will be used. See page 312 to learn the melodic formulae for the flex, mediant and full stop. For the Flex (A), the underlined bold syllable indicates to move down from the reciting tone *do* to *la*. For the mediant (B), move from the reciting tone *do* down to *ti* on the bold syllable, then to *la* on the next syllable and back to *do* on the italicized syllable. For the full stop (C), begin on the reciting tone *do* and drop down to *la* on the italicized syllable.

Trinitarian Blessing

The concluding blessing in the name of the Trinity varies from the Solemn to the Simple tone and should be memorized using the examples on pages 311 and 313. The alternate form that exists for some Ritual Masses is found on page 313.

(*continued on page 363*)

Solemn Tone

For the invitation, the Deacon (or in his absence, the Priest) sings "Bow down for the blessing." The two-note melodic motive of "la-sol-la" is the cue for the solemn tone. Each of the petitions may be delivered as one, two, or three parts, depending upon the length of the sentence. The usual subdivision is tripartite (indicated by A-B-C), requiring the text to be pointed using the flex, mediant, and full stop formulas. A shorter sentence will be divided into two parts (indicated by B-C). A short sentence will not be divided (indicated by C). The ending of each phrase indicates if it is flex, mediant, or full stop. See page 311 to learn the melodic shapes of the three formulas.

For the flex (A), move from the *sol* to *la* as the reciting tone and terminate with *sol* on the syllable marked in bold. If the sentence is of sufficient length, it will be broken with a mediant (B). Move from *sol* back to the reciting tone *la* and on the second to the last syllable, rise to *ti* on the italicized syllable, then back to *la* on the bold syllable. Whatever the length of the sentence, the full stop (C) indicates the its end. The stop functions as a period and elicits the sung "Amen" from the assembly. The formula is from the reciting tone. Move down a note to *sol* on the bold syllable, to *la* on the italicized syllable, then the double note *la-sol* on the second to last syllable, if it is strong. When the accent falls on the antepenultimate syllable, distribute the double note over two syllables.

4. The Epiphany of the Lord

   A May God, who has called you
       out of darkness into his wonderful **light**,
   B pour out in kindness his blessing upon you
       and make your *hearts* **firm**
   C in faith, **hope** *and* charity.
       R. Amen.

   A And since in all confidence you follow Christ,
       who today appeared in the world
       as a light shining in dark**ness**,
   B may God make *you*, **too**,
   C a light for your broth**ers** *and* sisters.
       R. Amen.

   A And so when your pilgrimage is end**ed**,
   B may you come to him
       whom the Magi sought as they followed the star
       and whom they found with great joy, the Light *from* **Light**,
   C who is **Christ** *the* Lord.
       R. Amen.

       And may the blessing of almighty **God**,
       the Father, and the Son, ✝ and the Holy Spirit,
       come down on you and remain with you for ever.
       R. Amen.

5. The Passion of the Lord

   A May God, the Father of mercies,
       who has given you an example of love
       in the Passion of his Only Begotten **Son**,
   B grant that, by serving God and your *neigh***bor**,
   C you may lay hold of the wondrous gift **of** *his* blessing.
       R. Amen.

   A So that you may receive the reward of everlasting life from **him**,
   B through whose earth*ly* **Death**
   C you believe that you escape eter*nal* death.
       R. Amen.

   B And by following the example of his self *abase***ment**,
   C may you possess a share in his **Res***ur*rection.
       R. Amen.

(continued on page 364)

4. The Epiphany of the Lord: What is unique to the Epiphany in the West is that Christ is the "light for the nations." That Christ is revealed to the Gentiles is meant that he is revealing himself to us. The light that was shining for the Jews is explicitly extended to the Gentiles, which means us. "Epiphany" means "manifestation" or "shining forth," and its significance is as real to us as it was to those who saw Jesus in the flesh. The epiphany of Christ takes place for us, not by a miraculous sight "out there" to be seen by those who happen to be present, but by a willingness to see. Epiphany, like insight, is a kind of seeing in a new way. Thus, our lives are, in fact, full of epiphanies. The "star" that points to Christ shines in the minds and hearts of those who refuse to take life for granted but who wonder and marvel and seek love and meaning, and are willing to journey afar to find it.

(SIMPLE TONE)

4.   The Epiphany of the Lord

> **A** May God, who has called you
> out of darkness into his wonderful **light**,
>
> **B** pour out in kindness his blessing upon you
> and make **your** hearts *firm*
>
> **C** in faith, hope and char*ity*.
> R. Amen.

> **A** And since in all confidence you follow Christ,
> who today appeared in the world
> as a light shining in dark**ness**,
>
> **B** may God **make** you, *too*,
>
> **C** a light for your brothers and sist*ers*.
> R. Amen.

> **A** And so when your pilgrimage is end**ed**,
>
> **B** may you come to him
> whom the Magi sought as they followed the star
> and whom they found with great joy, the **Light** from *Light*,
>
> **C** who is Christ the *Lord*.
> R. Amen.

> And may the blessing of al**might**y *God*,
> the Father, and the Son, ✚ and the Holy Spirit,
> come down on you and remain with you for ev*er*.
> R. Amen.

5.   The Passion of the Lord

> **A** May God, the Father of mercies,
> who has given you an example of love
> in the Passion of his Only Begotten **Son**,
>
> **B** grant that, by serving God **and** your *neigh*bor,
>
> **C** you may lay hold of the wondrous gift of his bless*ing*.
> R. Amen.

> **B** So that you may receive the reward of everlasting **life** from *him*,
>
> **C** through whose earthly Death
> you believe that you escape eternal *death*.
> R. Amen.

> **B** And by following the example of his **self** a*base*ment,
>
> **C** may you possess a share in his Resurrec*tion*.
> R. Amen.

(continued on page 365)

Simple Tone

The invitation to bow heads gives the melodic cue (*do-la-do-ti-do*) that the simple tone will be used. See page 312 to learn the melodic formulae for the flex, mediant and full stop. For the Flex (A), the underlined bold syllable indicates to move down from the reciting tone *do* to *la*. For the mediant (B), move from the reciting tone *do* down to *ti* on the bold syllable, then to *la* on the next syllable and back to *do* on the italicized syllable. For the full stop (C), begin on the reciting tone *do* and drop down to *la* on the italicized syllable.

Trinitarian Blessing

The concluding blessing in the name of the Trinity varies from the Solemn to the Simple tone and should be memorized using the examples on pages 311 and 312. The alternate form that exists for some Ritual Masses is found on page 313.

5. The Passion of the Lord: The Cross of Christ, rather than an instrument of torture, is depicted as a sign or an example of love that calls for Christians to live their lives in imitation of it. The Cross is translated into acts of service toward God and neighbor. Just as Christ lived a full human life in obedience to God "to death, even death on a cross" (Philippians 2:8), so, too, we are called to follow his example of self-abasement in order that we might share in his Resurrection. In the Paschal Mystery, the two are never separated, so that even on the feast of Christ's Passion, we anticipate already his Resurrection.

Solemn Tone

For the invitation, the Deacon (or in his absence, the Priest) sings "Bow down for the blessing." The two-note melodic motive of "la-sol-la" is the cue for the solemn tone. Each of the petitions may be delivered as one, two, or three parts, depending upon the length of the sentence. The usual subdivision is tripartite (indicated by A-B-C), requiring the text to be pointed using the flex, mediant, and full stop formulas. A shorter sentence will be divided into two parts (indicated by B-C). A short sentence will not be divided (indicated by C). The ending of each phrase indicates if it is flex, mediant, or full stop. See page 311 to learn the melodic shapes of the three formulas.

For the flex (A), move from the *sol* to *la* as the reciting tone and terminate with *sol* on the syllable marked in bold. If the sentence is of sufficient length, it will be broken with a mediant (B). Move from *sol* back to the reciting tone *la* and on the second to the last syllable, rise to *ti* on the italicized syllable, then back to *la* on the bold syllable. Whatever the length of the sentence, the full stop (C) indicates the its end. The stop functions as a period and elicits the sung "Amen" from the assembly. The formula is from the reciting tone. Move down a note to *sol* on the bold syllable, to *la* on the italicized syllable, then the double note *la-sol* on the second to last syllable, if it is strong. When the accent falls on the antepenultimate syllable, distribute the double note over two syllables.

(SOLEMN TONE)

And may the blessing of almighty **God**,
the Father, and the Son, ✝ and the Holy Spirit,
come down on you and remain with you for ever.
R. Amen.

6.   Easter Time

A May God, who by the Resurrection of his Only Begotten **Son**
B was pleased to confer on you
the gift of redemption and of a*dop***tion**,
C give you gladness **by** *his* blessing.
R. Amen.

B May he, by whose redeeming work
you have received the gift of everlasting *free***dom**,
C make you heirs to an eter**nal** *in*heritance.
R. Amen.

A And may you, who have already risen with Christ
in Baptism through **faith**,
B by living in a right manner on *this* **earth**,
C be united with him in the home**land** *of* heaven.
R. Amen.

And may the blessing of almighty **God**,
the Father, and the Son, ✝ and the Holy Spirit,
come down on you and remain with you for ever.
R. Amen.

7.   The Ascension of the Lord

A May almighty God **bless** you,
B for on this very day his Only Begotten Son
pierced the heights of *heaven*
C and unlocked for you the way
to ascend to **where** *he* is.
R. Amen.

B May he grant that,
as Christ after his Resurrection
was seen plainly by his dis*ci***ples**,
C so when he comes as Judge
he may show himself merciful to you for **all** *eternity*.
R. Amen.

A And may you, who believe he is seated
with the Father in his ma**jest**y,

(continued on page 366)

6. Easter Time: "O day of days! O joyous feast of Easter! Thou queen of all the days of seasons bring. Today we raise joyful Alleluias. Today we greet our risen Lord and king." (from "The Risen Lord," by Adele Clere Ogden). "Hallowed, chosen dawn of praise, Easter, queen of all our days" (from "Christ the Lord Is Risen Today"; text ascribed to Wipo of Burgundy, tune Gaudeamus Pariter). So we sing that Easter is queen of all the days of the Christian year. Given the centrality of this festive event, this Solemn Blessing would be appropriate throughout all 50 days of Easter Time, marking with progressive solemnity its absolute importance.

At the Easter Vigil, catechumens are baptized, confirmed, and brought to the Eucharistic table. They are made children by adoption. The first part of the blessing, then, references that all the baptized are endowed with the gift of redemption and adoption. The third part evokes the baptismal theme again. Christians are to live in this changing world with their eyes fixed

(SIMPLE TONE)

And may the blessing of al**might**y *God*,
the Father, and the Son, ✝ and the Holy Spirit,
come down on you and remain with you for ev*er*.
R. Amen.

6.   Easter Time

B   May God, who by the Resurrection of his Only Begotten Son
was pleased to confer on you
the gift of redemption and **of** a*dop*tion,
C   give you gladness by his bless*ing*.
R. Amen.

B   May he, by whose redeeming work
you have received the gift of ever**last**ing *free*dom,
C   make you heirs to an eternal inher*itance*.
R. Amen.

A   And may you, who have already risen with Christ
in Baptism through **<u>faith</u>**,
B   by living in a right manner **on** this *earth*,
C   be united with him in the homeland of heav*en*.
R. Amen.

And may the blessing of al**might**y *God*,
the Father, and the Son, ✝ and the Holy Spirit,
come down on you and remain with you for ev*er*.
R. Amen.

7.   The Ascension of the Lord

A   May almighty God bless **<u>you</u>**,
C   for on this very day his Only Begotten Son
pierced the heights of heaven
and unlocked for you the way
to ascend to where he *is*.
R. Amen.

B   May he grant that,
as Christ after his Resurrection
was seen plainly by **his** dis*ci*ples,
C   so when he comes as Judge
he may show himself merciful to you for all eter*nity*.
R. Amen.

B   And may you, who believe he is seated

(continued on page 367)

Simple Tone

The invitation to bow heads gives the melodic cue (*do-la-do-ti-do*) that the simple tone will be used. See page 312 to learn the melodic formulae for the flex, mediant and full stop. For the Flex (A), the underlined bold syllable indicates to move down from the reciting tone *do* to *la*. For the mediant (B), move from the reciting tone *do* down to *ti* on the bold syllable, then to *la* on the next syllable and back to *do* on the italicized syllable. For the full stop (C), begin on the reciting tone *do* and drop down to *la* on the italicized syllable.

Trinitarian Blessing

The concluding blessing in the name of the Trinity varies from the Solemn to the Simple tone and should be memorized using the examples on pages 311 and 313. The alternate form that exists for some Ritual Masses is found on page 313.

on a world that is unchangeable. Christians are "aliens" in this world. Thus, while we live on this earth, we are already praying to be united with God in our "homeland of heaven." The second part reiterates this idea of everlasting freedom and eternal inheritance, brought about by the redemption in Christ. The eternal effect of Christ's Death and Resurrection reminds all the baptized of the magnitude of God's love.

7. The Ascension of the Lord: This Solemn Blessing is grounded in the Lucan narrative in the Gospel account and the Acts of the Apostles. It alludes to the scene in Acts 1:6–11, in which the Apostles watched as Jesus "was lifted up, and a cloud took him from their sight." As the Apostles continued to look at the sky, two men dressed in white told them, "This Jesus who has been taken up from you into

heaven will return. . . ." In the Gospel account, Luke recounts, "They did him homage and then returned to Jerusalem with great joy" (24:52). The joy that was theirs should be ours today as we celebrate Christ's Ascension. Key to this blessing is that Christ ascends to unlock the heights of heaven for us and to sit in majesty with God as judge.

Solemn Tone

For the invitation, the Deacon (or in his absence, the Priest) sings "Bow down for the blessing." The two-note melodic motive of "la-sol-la" is the cue for the solemn tone. Each of the petitions may be delivered as one, two, or three parts, depending upon the length of the sentence. The usual subdivision is tripartite (indicated by A-B-C), requiring the text to be pointed using the flex, mediant, and full stop formulas. A shorter sentence will be divided into two parts (indicated by B-C). A short sentence will not be divided (indicated by C). The ending of each phrase indicates if it is flex, mediant, or full stop. See page 311 to learn the melodic shapes of the three formulas.

For the flex (A), move from the *sol* to *la* as the reciting tone and terminate with *sol* on the syllable marked in bold. If the sentence is of sufficient length, it will be broken with a mediant (B). Move from *sol* back to the reciting tone *la* and on the second to the last syllable, rise to *ti* on the italicized syllable, then back to *la* on the bold syllable. Whatever the length of the sentence, the full stop (C) indicates the its end. The stop functions as a period and elicits the sung "Amen" from the assembly. The formula is from the reciting tone. Move down a note to *sol* on the bold syllable, to *la* on the italicized syllable, then the double note *la-sol* on the second to last syllable, if it is strong. When the accent falls on the antepenultimate syllable, distribute the double note over two syllables.

(SOLEMN TONE)

B　know with joy the fulfillment of his *pro*mise
C　to stay with you until the **end** *of* time.
　　R. Amen.

And may the blessing of almighty **God**,
the Father, and the Son, ✝ and the Holy Spirit,
come down on you and remain with you for ever.
　　R. Amen.

8.　The Holy Spirit

A　May God, the Father of **lights**,
B　who was pleased to enlighten the disciples' minds
　　by the outpouring of the Spirit, the *Para*clete,
C　grant you gladness by his blessing
　　and make you always abound with the gifts of **the** *same* Spirit.
　　R. Amen.

A　May the wondrous flame that appeared above the dis**ciples**,
B　powerfully cleanse your hearts from every *e*vil
C　and pervade them with its puri*fy*ing light.
　　R. Amen.

A　And may God, who has been pleased to unite many tongues
　　in the profession of one **faith**,
B　give you perseverance in that *same* **faith**
C　and, by believing, may you journey from hope **to** *clear* vision.
　　R. Amen.

And may the blessing of almighty **God**,
the Father, and the Son, ✝ and the Holy Spirit,
come down on you and remain with you for ever.
　　R. Amen.

9.　Ordinary Time I

A　May the Lord bless you and **keep** you.
　　R. Amen.

B　May he let his face shine upon you
　　and show you his *mer*cy.
　　R. Amen.

C　May he turn his countenance towards you
　　and give **you** *his* peace.
　　R. Amen.

(continued on page 368)

8. The Holy Spirit: This Solemn Blessing is suitable for Pentecost, but the content of the blessing does not limit its use only to this solemnity. The Spirit is summoned to enlighten the minds and to bring gladness. The image of the flame or tongues of fire characterize the Pentecost account in Acts 2:3: "Then there appeared to them tongues as of fire, which parted and came to rest on each one of them." These same tongues led to the *glossolalia* event. We pray that we, too, may receive the flames that will enflame our hearts and that we may receive tongues, not so much to speak in foreign languages, but to profess our common faith that leads to our hope for a clear vision of God.

(SIMPLE TONE)

with the Father **in** his *ma*jesty,

C know with joy the fulfillment of his promise
to stay with you until the end of *time*.
R. Amen.

And may the blessing of al**might**y *God*,
the Father, and the Son, ✝ and the Holy Spirit,
come down on you and remain with you for ev*er*.
R. Amen.

8.   The Holy Spirit

A May God, the Father of <u>**lights**</u>,

B who was pleased to enlighten the disciples' minds
by the outpouring of the Spirit, the **Par**a*clete*,

C grant you gladness by his blessing
and make you always abound with the gifts of the same Spir*it*.
R. Amen.

B May the wondrous flame that appeared above **the** dis*ci*ples,

C powerfully cleanse your hearts from every evil
and pervade them with its purifying *light*.
R. Amen.

B And may God, who has been pleased to unite many tongues
in the profession **of** one *faith*,

C give you perseverance in that same faith
and, by believing, may you journey from hope to clear vis*ion*.
R. Amen.

And may the blessing of al**might**y *God*,
the Father, and the Son, ✝ and the Holy Spirit,
come down on you and remain with you for ev*er*.
R. Amen.

9.   Ordinary Time I

A May the Lord bless you and keep <u>**you**</u>.
R. Amen.

B May he let his face shine upon you
and show **you** his *mer*cy.
R. Amen.

C May he turn his countenance towards you
and give you his *peace*.
R. Amen.

(continued on page 369)

Simple Tone

The invitation to bow heads gives the melodic cue (*do-la-do-ti-do*) that the simple tone will be used. See page 312 to learn the melodic formulae for the flex, mediant and full stop. For the Flex (A), the underlined bold syllable indicates to move down from the reciting tone *do* to *la*. For the mediant (B), move from the reciting tone *do* down to *ti* on the bold syllable, then to *la* on the next syllable and back to *do* on the italicized syllable. For the full stop (C), begin on the reciting tone *do* and drop down to *la* on the italicized syllable.

Trinitarian Blessing

The concluding blessing in the name of the Trinity varies from the Solemn to the Simple tone and should be memorized using the examples on pages 311 and 313. The alternate form that exists for some Ritual Masses is found on page 313.

9. Ordinary Time I: This text is called the priestly blessing of Aaron (Numbers 6:24). The priests of the Old Testament were solemnly to bless the people in the name of the Lord. To be under the almighty protection of God our Savior; to enjoy his favor as the smile of a loving Father, or as the gleaming beams of the sun; while he mercifully forgives our sins, supplies our wants, consoles the heart, and prepares us by his grace for eternal glory— these things form the substance of this blessing and the sum total of all blessings. In so rich a list of mercies, worldly joys are not worthy to be mentioned. In the original, God's name is repeated three times.

Solemn Tone

For the invitation, the Deacon (or in his absence, the Priest) sings "Bow down for the blessing." The two-note melodic motive of "la-sol-la" is the cue for the solemn tone. Each of the petitions may be delivered as one, two, or three parts, depending upon the length of the sentence. The usual subdivision is tripartite (indicated by A-B-C), requiring the text to be pointed using the flex, mediant, and full stop formulas. A shorter sentence will be divided into two parts (indicated by B-C). A short sentence will not be divided (indicated by C). The ending of each phrase indicates if it is flex, mediant, or full stop. See page 311 to learn the melodic shapes of the three formulas.

For the flex (A), move from the *sol* to *la* as the reciting tone and terminate with *sol* on the syllable marked in bold. If the sentence is of sufficient length, it will be broken with a mediant (B). Move from *sol* back to the reciting tone *la* and on the second to the last syllable, rise to *ti* on the italicized syllable, then back to *la* on the bold syllable. Whatever the length of the sentence, the full stop (C) indicates the its end. The stop functions as a period and elicits the sung "Amen" from the assembly. The formula is from the reciting tone. Move down a note to *sol* on the bold syllable, to *la* on the italicized syllable, then the double note *la-sol* on the second to last syllable, if it is strong. When the accent falls on the antepenultimate syllable, distribute the double note over two syllables.

(SOLEMN TONE)

And may the blessing of almighty **God**,
the Father, and the Son, ✠ and the Holy Spirit,
come down on you and remain with you for ever.
R. Amen.

10. Ordinary Time II

   A May the peace of **God**,
   B which surpasses all under*stand***ing**,
   C keep your hearts and minds
      in the knowledge and love of God,
      and of his Son, our Lord **Je***sus* Christ.
      R. Amen.

And may the blessing of almighty **God**,
the Father, and the Son, ✠ and the Holy Spirit,
come down on you and remain with you for ever.
R. Amen.

11. Ordinary Time III

   A May almighty God bless you in his kindness
      and pour out saving wisdom **up***on* you.
      R. Amen.

   B May he nourish you always with the teachings of the faith
      and make you persevere in ho*ly* **deeds**.
      R. Amen.

   C May he turn your steps towards himself
      and show you the path of chari**ty** *and* peace.
      R. Amen.

And may the blessing of almighty **God**,
the Father, and the Son, ✠ and the Holy Spirit,
come down on you and remain with you for ever.
R. Amen.

12. Ordinary Time IV

   A May the God of all consolation order your days in his peace
      and grant you the gifts of his **bless**ing.
      R. Amen.

   B May he free you always from every *distress*
   C and confirm your hearts **in** *his* love.
      R. Amen.

(continued on page 370)

10. Ordinary Time II: This Solemn Blessing is unusual, in that the form is not tripartite, but rather a simple statement derived from Philippians 4:7: "Then the peace of God that surpasses all understanding will guard your hearts and minds in Christ Jesus." We find Old Testament parallel, such as Isaiah 26:3: "A nation of firm purpose you keep in peace; / in peace, for its trust in you." The epistles are replete with this kind of blessing. In Colossians 3:15, we read: "And let the peace of Christ control your hearts, the peace into which you were also called into one body. And be thankful." Also, the resurrected Christ greeted his disciples in the upper room with "Peace be with you" (John 20:19). We find a longer reflection on this theme of peace in John 14:27.

(SIMPLE TONE)

And may the blessing of al**might**y *God*,
the Father, and the Son, ✝ and the Holy Spirit,
come down on you and remain with you for ev*er*.
R. Amen.

10. Ordinary Time II

   A May the peace of God,
      which surpasses all understand**ing**,

   B keep your hearts and minds
      in the knowledge and **love** of *God*,

   C and of his Son, our Lord Jesus *Christ*.
      R. Amen.
      And may the blessing of al**might**y *God*,
      the Father, and the Son, ✝ and the Holy Spirit,
      come down on you and remain with you for ev*er*.
      R. Amen.

11. Ordinary Time III

   A May almighty God bless you in his kindness
      and pour out saving wisdom u**pon** you.
      R. Amen.

   B May he nourish you always with the teachings of the faith
      and make you persevere in **ho**ly *deeds*.
      R. Amen.

   C May he turn your steps towards himself
      and show you the path of charity and *peace*.
      R. Amen.

      And may the blessing of al**might**y *God*,
      the Father, and the Son, ✝ and the Holy Spirit,
      come down on you and remain with you for ev*er*.
      R. Amen.

12. Ordinary Time IV

   A May the God of all consolation order your days in his peace
      and grant you the gifts of his bless**ing**.
      R. Amen.

   B May he free you always from every distress
      and confirm your hearts **in** his *love*.
      R. Amen.

(continued on page 371)

Simple Tone

The invitation to bow heads gives the melodic cue (*do-la-do-ti-do*) that the simple tone will be used. See page 312 to learn the melodic formulas for the flex, mediant and full stop. For the Flex (A), the underlined bold syllable indicates to move down from the reciting tone *do* to *la*. For the mediant (B), move from the reciting tone *do* down to *ti* on the bold syllable, then to *la* on the next syllable and back to *do* on the italicized syllable. For the full stop (C), begin on the reciting tone *do* and drop down to *la* on the italicized syllable.

Trinitarian Blessing

The concluding blessing in the name of the Trinity varies from the Solemn to the Simple tone and should be memorized using the examples on pages 311 and 313. The alternate form that exists for some Ritual Masses is found on page 313.

11. Ordinary Time III: This Solemn Blessing turns on three sets of double requests: that God may bless with kindness and pour out wisdom, that God may nourish with faith and preserve our deeds, and that God may turn steps toward him and show us the path of charity and peace. Kindness here evokes the Hebrew word *hesed*, which means "love," "kindness," and "mercy." Wisdom can mean *sophia*, as is the term in the Septuagint for the Hebrew *chokhmah*. In Judaism, *chokhmah* appears alongside the *shekhinah*, "the Glory of God," as an expression of the feminine aspect of God.

12. Ordinary Time IV: This Solemn Blessing also turns on three sets of double wishes: may God order days toward peace and grant blessing; may God free us from distress and confirm our hearts in love; and may God effect good works and the three theological virtues and bring us to a happy end. The expression "God of all consolation" seems to reflect 2 Corinthians 1:3: "Blessed be the God and Father of our Lord Jesus Christ, the Father of compassion and God of all encouragement."

Solemn Tone

For the invitation, the Deacon (or in his absence, the Priest) sings "Bow down for the blessing." The two-note melodic motive of "la-sol-la" is the cue for the solemn tone. Each of the petitions may be delivered as one, two, or three parts, depending upon the length of the sentence. The usual subdivision is tripartite (indicated by A-B-C), requiring the text to be pointed using the flex, mediant, and full stop formulas. A shorter sentence will be divided into two parts (indicated by B-C). A short sentence will not be divided (indicated by C). The ending of each phrase indicates if it is flex, mediant, or full stop. See page 311 to learn the melodic shapes of the three formulas.

For the flex (A), move from the *sol* to *la* as the reciting tone and terminate with *sol* on the syllable marked in bold. If the sentence is of sufficient length, it will be broken with a mediant (B). Move from *sol* back to the reciting tone *la* and on the second to the last syllable, rise to *ti* on the italicized syllable, then back to *la* on the bold syllable. Whatever the length of the sentence, the full stop (C) indicates the its end. The stop functions as a period and elicits the sung "Amen" from the assembly. The formula is from the reciting tone. Move down a note to *sol* on the bold syllable, to *la* on the italicized syllable, then the double note *la-sol* on the second to last syllable, if it is strong. When the accent falls on the antepenultimate syllable, distribute the double note over two syllables.

(SOLEMN TONE)

A So that on this life's journey
you may be effective in good **works**,
B rich in the gifts of hope, faith and *char*ity,
C and may come happily **to** *e*ternal life.
R. Amen.

And may the blessing of almighty **God**,
the Father, and the Son, ✝ and the Holy Spirit,
come down on you and remain with you for ever.
R. Amen.

13. Ordinary Time V

A May almighty God always keep every adversity far from you
and in his kindness pour out upon you the gifts of his bless**ing**.
R. Amen.

B May God keep your hearts attentive to *his* **words**,
C that they may be filled with ever**last***ing* gladness.
R. Amen.

A And so, may you always understand what is good and **right**,
B and be found ever hastening along
in the path of God's *commands*,
C made coheirs with the citi**zens** *of* heaven.
R. Amen.

And may the blessing of almighty **God**,
the Father, and the Son, ✝ and the Holy Spirit,
come down on you and remain with you for ever.
R. Amen.

14. Ordinary Time VI

A May God bless you with every heavenly **bless**ing,
B make you always holy and pure in *his* **sight**,
C pour out in abundance upon you the riches of his glory,
and teach you with the **words** *of* truth;
B may he instruct you in the Gospel of sal*va***tion**,
C and ever endow you with frat**er***nal* charity.
C Through **Christ** *our* Lord.
R. Amen.

And may the blessing of almighty **God**,
the Father, and the Son, ✝ and the Holy Spirit,
come down on you and remain with you for ever.
R. Amen.

(continued on page 372)

13. Ordinary Time V: Again, this Solemn Blessing consists of three wishes, but only the first and the third are organized in paired sets. The second wish is unusual, in that it expresses a purpose or result in the subordinate clause—that our hearts may be filled with everlasting gladness. The second wish flows into the third, which has an eschatological hope—as we hasten to become coheirs with the citizens of heaven. This last line evokes Philippians 3:20: "But our citizenship is in heaven, and from it we also await a savior, the Lord Jesus Christ. He will change our lowly body to conform with his glorified body by the power that enables him also to bring all things into subjection to himself."

(SIMPLE TONE)

A So that on this life's journey
you may be effective in good **<u>works</u>**,

B rich in the gifts of hope, **faith** and *char*ity,

C and may come happily to eternal *life*.
R. Amen.

And may the blessing of al**might**y *God*,
the Father, and the Son, ✠ and the Holy Spirit,
come down on you and remain with you for ev*er*.
R. Amen.

13. Ordinary Time V

A May almighty God always keep every adversity far from you
and in his kindness pour out upon you the gifts of his bless**<u>ing</u>**.
R. Amen.

B May God keep your hearts attentive **to** his *words*,

C that they may be filled with everlasting glad*ness*.
R. Amen.

A And so, may you always understand what is good and **<u>right</u>**,

B and be found ever hastening along
in the path of **God's** com*mands*,

C made coheirs with the citizens of heav*en*.
R. Amen.

And may the blessing of al**might**y *God*,
the Father, and the Son, ✠ and the Holy Spirit,
come down on you and remain with you for ev*er*.
R. Amen.

14. Ordinary Time VI

A May God bless you with every heavenly blessing,
make you always holy and pure in his sight,
pour out in abundance upon you the riches of his glory,
and teach you with the words of **<u>truth</u>**;

B may he instruct you in the Gospel **of** sal*va*tion,

C and ever endow you with fraternal char*ity*.

C Through Christ our **Lord**.
R. Amen.

And may the blessing of al**might**y *God*,
the Father, and the Son, ✠ and the Holy Spirit,
come down on you and remain with you for ev*er*.
R. Amen.

(continued on page 373)

Simple Tone

The invitation to bow heads gives the melodic cue (*do-la-do-ti-do*) that the simple tone will be used. See page 312 to learn the melodic formulas for the flex, mediant and full stop.
For the Flex (A), the underlined bold syllable is when you move down from the reciting tone *do* to *la*. For the mediant (B), move from the reciting tone *do* down to *ti* on the bold syllable, then to *la* on the next syllable and back to *do* on the italicized syllable. For the full stop (C), begin on the reciting tone *do* and drop down to *la* on the italicized syllable.

Trinitarian Blessing

The concluding blessing in the name of the Trinity varies from the Solemn to the Simple tones and should simply be memorized using the examples on pages 311 and 313. An alternate form exists for some Ritual Masses, that is found on page 313.

14. Ordinary Time VI: This Solemn Blessing is unusual, in that we have six wishes, but they are not arranged in three sets of couplets. Rather, we pray as in a litany for a number of things: that God may bless, sanctify, enrich, teach, instruct, endow. Rather than pairing ideas, such as teaching and instructing, the blessing is organized more like a chain of wishes. Thus, blessing leads to sanctification, which in turn enriches us with the glory of God. Teaching the words of truth automatically leads to the instruction in the Gospel of salvation that is translated into fraternal charity.

Contrast may be made between earthly and heavenly blessing. For example, in Ephesians 1:3 we read: "Blessed be the God and Father of our Lord Jesus Christ, who has blessed us in Christ with every spiritual blessing in the heavens." Again, we find the distinction between human love and God's love in Psalm 103:11: "As the heavens tower over the earth, / so God's love towers over the faithful."

Solemn Tone

For the invitation, the Deacon (or in his absence, the Priest) sings "Bow down for the blessing." The two-note melodic motive of "la-sol-la" is the cue for the solemn tone. Each of the petitions may be delivered as one, two, or three parts, depending upon the length of the sentence. The usual subdivision is tripartite (indicated by A-B-C), requiring the text to be pointed using the flex, mediant, and full stop formulas. A shorter sentence will be divided into two parts (indicated by B-C). A short sentence will not be divided (indicated by C). The ending of each phrase indicates if it is flex, mediant, or full stop. See page 311 to learn the melodic shapes of the three formulas.

For the flex (A), move from the *sol* to *la* as the reciting tone and terminate with *sol* on the syllable marked in bold. If the sentence is of sufficient length, it will be broken with a mediant (B). Move from *sol* back to the reciting tone *la* and on the second to the last syllable, rise to *ti* on the italicized syllable, then back to *la* on the bold syllable. Whatever the length of the sentence, the full stop (C) indicates the its end. The stop functions as a period and elicits the sung "Amen" from the assembly. The formula is from the reciting tone. Move down a note to *sol* on the bold syllable, to *la* on the italicized syllable, then the double note *la-sol* on the second to last syllable, if it is strong. When the accent falls on the antepenultimate syllable, distribute the double note over two syllables.

(SOLEMN TONE)

II. For Celebrations of the Saints

15. The Blessed Virgin Mary

 A May God, who through the childbearing of the Blessed Virgin **Ma**ry
 B willed in his great kindness to redeem the hu*man* **race**,
 C be pleased to enrich you **with** *his* blessing.
 R. Amen.

 B May you know always and everywhere the protection *of* **her**,
 C through whom you have been found worthy to receive the au**thor** *of* life.
 R. Amen.

 B May you, who have devoutly gathered on *this* **day**,
 C carry away with you the gifts of spiritual joys and heaven**ly** *rewards*.
 R. Amen.

 And may the blessing of almighty **God**,
 the Father, and the Son, ✛ and the Holy Spirit,
 come down on you and remain with you for ever.
 R. Amen.

16. Saints Peter and Paul, Apostles

 A May almighty God bless **you**,
 B for he has made you steadfast in Saint Peter's saving con*fess***ion**
 C and through it has set you on the solid rock **of** *the* Church's faith.
 R. Amen.

 A And having instructed you
 by the tireless preaching of Saint **Paul**,
 B may God teach you constantly by his e*xam***ple**
 C to win brothers and sis**ters** *for* Christ.
 R. Amen.

 A So that by the keys of St Peter and the words of St **Paul**,
 B and by the support of their inter*cess***ion**,
 C God may bring us happily to that homeland
 that Peter attained on a cross
 and Paul by the blade **of** *a* sword.
 R. Amen.

 And may the blessing of almighty **God**,
 the Father, and the Son, ✛ and the Holy Spirit,
 come down on you and remain with you for ever.
 R. Amen.

(continued on page 374)

15. The Blessed Virgin Mary: The Solemn Blessing of the Blessed Virgin Mary, in the usual tripartite form, refers to Mary as the *Theotokos,* the protector, and the example of Christian life. It alludes to the account of the Annunciation in Luke 1:26–35. There we read, "The holy Spirit will come upon you, and the power of the Most High will overshadow you. Therefore, the child to be born will be called holy, the Son of God" (35). The first part of the bless-ing focuses on the motherhood of Mary, and as such, may be appropriate for the particular feasts of her birth (September 8, nine months after her Immaculate Conception on December 8) and especially the Solemnity of Mary, the Holy Mother of God (January 1). The blessing is also suit-able for optional memorials (votive Masses) on Saturdays in Ordinary Time when no obligatory memorial occurs in honor of the Blessed Virgin Mary.

(SIMPLE TONE)

II. For Celebrations of the Saints

15. The Blessed Virgin Mary

B May God, who through the childbearing of the Blessed Virgin Mary
willed in his great kindness to redeem the **hu**man *race*,

C be pleased to enrich you with his bless*ing*.
R. Amen.

B May you know always and everywhere the protec**tion** of *her*,

C through whom you have been found worthy to receive the author of *life*.
R. Amen.

B May you, who have devoutly gathered **on** this *day*,

C carry away with you the gifts of spiritual joys and heavenly rew*ards*.
R. Amen.

And may the blessing of al**might**y *God*,
the Father, and the Son, ✠ and the Holy Spirit,
come down on you and remain with you for ev*er*.
R. Amen.

16. Saints Peter and Paul, Apostles

A May almighty God bless **you**,

C for he has made you steadfast in Saint Peter's saving confession
and through it has set you on the solid rock of the Church's *faith*.
R. Amen.

B And having instructed you
by the tireless preaching **of** Saint *Paul*,

C may God teach you constantly by his example
to win brothers and sisters for *Christ*.
R. Amen.

A So that by the keys of St Peter and the words of St **Paul**,

B and by the support of their in**ter***cession*,

C God may bring us happily to that homeland
that Peter attained on a cross
and Paul by the blade of a *sword*.
R. Amen.

And may the blessing of al**might**y *God*,
the Father, and the Son, ✠ and the Holy Spirit,
come down on you and remain with you for ev*er*.
R. Amen.

(continued on page 375)

Simple Tone

The invitation to bow heads gives the melodic cue (*do-la-do-ti-do*) that the simple tone will be used. See page 312 to learn the melodic formulas for the flex, mediant and full stop.
For the Flex (A), the underlined bold syllable is when you move down from the reciting tone *do* to *la*. For the mediant (B), move from the reciting tone *do* down to *ti* on the bold syllable, then to *la* on the next syllable and back to *do* on the italicized syllable. For the full stop (C), begin on the reciting tone *do* and drop down to *la* on the italicized syllable.

Trinitarian Blessing

The concluding blessing in the name of the Trinity varies from the Solemn to the Simple tones and should simply be memorized using the examples on pages 311 and 312. An alternate form exists for some Ritual Masses, that is found on page 313.

16. Saints Peter and Paul, Apostles: In spite of the famous "incident at Antioch"—the early Christian dispute between the Apostles Paul and Peter that occurred in the city of Antioch around the middle of the first century regarding whether Christian converts had to observe the Mosaic Law (see Galatians 2:11–14), Peter and Paul were paired together as the two Apostles to Rome since they both died there. The hymn *Decora lux* captures the importance of these two Apostles among the others. "*O Roma felix quae duorum principum es consacrata glorioso sanguine*" ("O happy Rome! Who in thy martyr princes' blood, A twofold stream, art washed and doubly sanctified"). This hymn is sung to Peter and Paul, the two princes of Rome, on the Solemnity of Peter and Paul, Apostles, on June 29.

Solemn Tone

For the invitation, the Deacon (or in his absence, the Priest) sings "Bow down for the blessing." The two-note melodic motive of "la-sol-la" is the cue for the solemn tone. Each of the petitions may be delivered as one, two, or three parts, depending upon the length of the sentence. The usual subdivision is tripartite (indicated by A-B-C), requiring the text to be pointed using the flex, mediant, and full stop formulas. A shorter sentence will be divided into two parts (indicated by B-C). A short sentence will not be divided (indicated by C). The ending of each phrase indicates if it is flex, mediant, or full stop. See page 311 to learn the melodic shapes of the three formulas.

For the flex (A), move from the *sol* to *la* as the reciting tone and terminate with *sol* on the syllable marked in bold. If the sentence is of sufficient length, it will be broken with a mediant (B). Move from *sol* back to the reciting tone *la* and on the second to the last syllable, rise to *ti* on the italicized syllable, then back to *la* on the bold syllable. Whatever the length of the sentence, the full stop (C) indicates the its end. The stop functions as a period and elicits the sung "Amen" from the assembly. The formula is from the reciting tone. Move down a note to *sol* on the bold syllable, to *la* on the italicized syllable, then the double note *la-sol* on the second to last syllable, if it is strong. When the accent falls on the antepenultimate syllable, distribute the double note over two syllables.

(SOLEMN TONE)

17.   The Apostles

    A May God, who has granted you
        to stand firm on apostolic founda**tions**,
    B graciously bless you through the glorious *me***rits**
    C of the holy Apostles N. *and* N. (the holy A*pos*t*le* N.).
        R. Amen.

    A And may he who endowed you
        with the teaching and example of the Apos**tles**,
    B make you, under their pro*tec***tion**,
    C witnesses to the truth be*fore* all.
        R. Amen.

    A So that through the intercession of the Apos**tles**,
    B you may inherit the eternal *home***land**,
    C for by their teaching you possess firm**ness** *of* faith.
        R. Amen.

    And may the blessing of almighty **God**,
    the Father, and the Son, ✝ and the Holy Spirit,
    come down on you and remain with you for ever.
    R. Amen.

18.   All Saints

    A May God, the glory and joy of the **Saints**,
    B who has caused you to be strengthened
        by means of their outstand*ing* **prayers**,
    C bless you with un**end***ing* blessings
        R. Amen.

    A Freed through their intercession from present ills
        and formed by the example of their holy way of **life**,
    B may you be ever de*vo***ted**
    C to serving God **and** *your* neighbor.
        R. Amen.

    A So that, together with all,
        you may possess the joys of the home**land**,
    B where Holy Church rejoices
        that her children are admitted in perpetu*al* **peace**
    C to the company of the citi**zens** *of* heaven.
        R. Amen.

    And may the blessing of almighty **God**,
    the Father, and the Son, ✝ and the Holy Spirit,
    come down on you and remain with you for ever.
    R. Amen.

(*continued on page 376*)

17. The Apostles: The Solemn Blessing of the Apostles draws on the scriptural allusion in John 10:11 and 14. "I am the good shepherd. A good shepherd lays down his life for the sheep . . . I am the good shepherd, and I know mine, and mine know me." This Blessing underscores how the "Apostles," or "those you have appointed shepherds" carry out the work of Christ, continuing to govern and shepherd the flock. The blessing highlights three things that Apostles as pastors are to do for the Church; they are foundations, teachers, and intercessors.

(SIMPLE TONE)

17. The Apostles

    B May God, who has granted you
        to stand firm on apostol**ic** found*a*tions,
    C graciously bless you through the glorious merits
        of the holy Apostles *N.* and *N.* (the holy Apostle *N.*).
        R. Amen.

    A And may he who endowed you
        with the teaching and example of the Apos<u>**tles**</u>,
    B make you, under **their** pro*tec*tion,
    C witnesses to the truth before *all*.
        R. Amen.

    A So that through the intercession of the Apos<u>**tles**</u>,
    B you may inherit the eter**nal** *home*land,
    C for by their teaching you possess firmness of ***faith***.
        R. Amen.

    And may the blessing of al**might**y *God*,
    the Father, and the Son, ✝ and the Holy Spirit,
    come down on you and remain with you for ev*er*.
    R. Amen.

18. All Saints

    A May God, the glory and joy of the <u>**Saints**</u>,
    B who has caused you to be strengthened
        by means of their out**stand**ing *prayers*,
    C bless you with unending bless*ings*
        R. Amen.

    B Freed through their intercession from present ills
        and formed by the example of their holy **way** of *life*,
    C may you be ever devoted
        to serving God and your neigh*bor*.
        R. Amen.

    A So that, together with <u>**all**</u>,
    B you may possess the joys **of** the *home*land,
    C where Holy Church rejoices
        that her children are admitted in perpetual peace
        to the company of the citizens of heav*en*.
        R. Amen.

    And may the blessing of al**might**y *God*,
    the Father, and the Son, ✝ and the Holy Spirit,
    come down on you and remain with you for ev*er*.
    R. Amen. *(continued on page 377)*

Simple Tone

The invitation to bow heads gives the melodic cue (*do-la-do-ti-do*) that the simple tone will be used. See page 312 to learn the melodic formulas for the flex, mediant and full stop. For the Flex (A), the underlined bold syllable is when you move down from the reciting tone *do* to *la*. For the mediant (B), move from the reciting tone *do* down to *ti* on the bold syllable, then to *la* on the next syllable and back to *do* on the italicized syllable. For the full stop (C), begin on the reciting tone *do* and drop down to *la* on the italicized syllable.

Trinitarian Blessing

The concluding blessing in the name of the Trinity varies from the Solemn to the Simple tones and should simply be memorized using the examples on pages 311 and 312. An alternate form exists for some Ritual Masses, that is found on page 313.

---

18. All Saints: Taken together, the three parts of the Solemn Blessing for All Saints constitute a statement about how God relates to the Saints. All three petitions are made to God but grant blessing due to the prayers of the Saints. In the second part, God helps us follow the Saints' example, and in the third, we petition to enter into the Saints' company as citizens of heaven. The Saints model for us a way of life; they are comrades; and they intercede for us. They are not to be mistaken as mediators. Mediation is the role of Christ.

Solemn Tone

For the invitation, the Deacon (or in his absence, the Priest) sings "Bow down for the blessing." The two-note melodic motive of "la-sol-la" is the cue for the solemn tone. Each of the petitions may be delivered as one, two, or three parts, depending upon the length of the sentence. The usual subdivision is tripartite (indicated by A-B-C), requiring the text to be pointed using the flex, mediant, and full stop formulas. A shorter sentence will be divided into two parts (indicated by B-C). A short sentence will not be divided (indicated by C). The ending of each phrase indicates if it is flex, mediant, or full stop. See page 311 to learn the melodic shapes of the three formulas.

For the flex (A), move from the *sol* to *la* as the reciting tone and terminate with *sol* on the syllable marked in bold. If the sentence is of sufficient length, it will be broken with a mediant (B). Move from *sol* back to the reciting tone *la* and on the second to the last syllable, rise to *ti* on the italicized syllable, then back to *la* on the bold syllable. Whatever the length of the sentence, the full stop (C) indicates the its end. The stop functions as a period and elicits the sung "Amen" from the assembly. The formula is from the reciting tone. Move down a note to *sol* on the bold syllable, to *la* on the italicized syllable, then the double note *la-sol* on the second to last syllable, if it is strong. When the accent falls on the antepenultimate syllable, distribute the double note over two syllables.

(SOLEMN TONES)

III. Other Blessings

19. For the Dedication of a Church

    A May God, the Lord of heaven and **earth**,
    B who has gathered you today for the dedication of *this* **church**,
    C make you abound in **heav***en*ly blessings.
        R. Amen.

    A And may he who has willed that all his scattered children
         should be gathered together in his **Son**,
    B grant that you may become his *tem*ple
    C and the dwelling place of the **Ho***ly* Spirit.
        R. Amen.

    A And so, when you are thoroughly **cleansed**,
    B may God dwell within you
         and grant you to possess with all *the* **Saints**
    C the inheritance of e**ter***nal* happiness.
        R. Amen.

        And may the blessing of almighty **God**,
        the Father, ✝ and the Son, ✝ and the Holy ✝ Spirit,
        come down on you and remain with you for ever.
        R. Amen.

20. In Celebrations for the Dead

    A May the God of all consolation **bless** you,
    B for in his unfathomable goodness he created the hu*man* **race**,
    C and in the Resurrection of his Only Begotten Son
         he has given believers the hope of ris**ing** *again*.
        R. Amen.

    A To us who are alive, may God grant pardon for our **sins**,
    B and to all *the* **dead**, **C** a place of **light** *and* peace.
        R. Amen.

    B So may we all live happily for ever *with* **Christ**,
    C whom we believe truly rose **from** *the* dead.
        R. Amen.

        And may the blessing of almighty **God**,
        the Father, and the Son, ✝ and the Holy Spirit,
        come down on you and remain with you for ever.
        R. Amen.

19. For the Dedication of a Church: In the strict sense, the Rite of Dedication of a Church denotes the building, but in the more primary sense, the Church is the People of God who are the living stones. Just as the term "Church" refers to the living temple, God's People, the term "church" also has been used to describe the building in which the Christian community gathers to hear the word of God, to pray together, to receive the Sacraments, and celebrate the Eucharist. Dedication means setting the building apart for something special or to commit or devote that building to the work of God. The dedication of a church building takes place soon after the building has been completed. A special liturgy occurs during which prayers are said to request that God bless the building, and to pray for all those who will worship in that building in the future.

(SIMPLE TONE)

III. Other Blessings

19. For the Dedication of a Church

   A May God, the Lord of heaven and **earth**,

   B who has gathered you today for the dedication **of** this *church*,

   C make you abound in heavenly bless*ings*.
       R. Amen.

   B And may he who has willed that all his scattered children
      should be gathered together **in** his *Son*,

   C grant that you may become his temple
      and the dwelling place of the Holy Spir*it*.
       R. Amen.

   B And so, when you are thor**ough**ly *cleansed*,

   C may God dwell within you
      and grant you to possess with all the Saints
      the inheritance of eternal happ*iness*.
       R. Amen.

    And may the blessing of almighty *God*,
    the Father, ✝ and the Son, ✝ and the Holy ✝ Spirit,
    come down on you and remain with you for ev*er*.
       R. Amen.

20. In Celebrations for the Dead

   A May the God of all consolation bless **you**,

   B for in his unfathomable goodness he created the **hu**man *race*,

   C and in the Resurrection of his Only Begotten Son
      he has given believers the hope of rising a*gain*.
       R. Amen.

   A To us who are alive, may God grant pardon for our **sins**,

   C and to all the dead, a place of light and *peace*.
       R. Amen.

   B So may we all live happily for ev**er** with *Christ*,

   C whom we believe truly rose from the *dead*.
       R. Amen.

    And may the blessing of al**might**y *God*,
    the Father, and the Son, ✝ and the Holy Spirit,
    come down on you and remain with you for ev*er*.
       R. Amen.

Simple Tone

The invitation to bow heads gives the melodic cue (*do-la-do-ti-do*) that the simple tone will be used. See page 312 to learn the melodic formulas for the flex, mediant and full stop. For the Flex (A), the underlined bold syllable is when you move down from the reciting tone *do* to *la*. For the mediant (B), move from the reciting tone *do* down to *ti* on the bold syllable, then to *la* on the next syllable and back to *do* on the italicized syllable. For the full stop (C), begin on the reciting tone *do* and drop down to *la* on the italicized syllable.

Trinitarian Blessing

The concluding blessing in the name of the Trinity varies from the Solemn to the Simple tones and should simply be memorized using the examples on pages 311 and 312. An alternate form exists for some Ritual Masses, that is found on page 313.

---

20. For the Dead: The strongest biblical material underlying the theology of death is 1 Corinthians 15:55–56. Those verses provide a question and answer about death: "Where, O death, is your victory? / Where, O death, is your sting?" / The sting of death is sin, and the power of sin is the law." In this blessing, we first pray to the God of consolation to bless us with hope.

In the second part, we pray for the living (for forgiveness) and the dead (that they may find a place of light and peace). The third petition, for all, capitulates in the Christian belief in the Resurrection of Christ.